WOMEN, GENDER
AND WORK

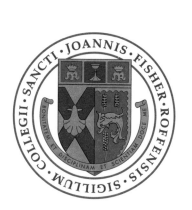

Lavery Library

St. John Fisher
College
Rochester, New York

WOMEN, GENDER AND WORK

What is equality and how do we get there?

Edited by

MARTHA FETHEROLF LOUTFI

INTERNATIONAL LABOUR OFFICE · GENEVA

Loutfi, Martha Fetherolf (ed.)
Women, gender and work: What is equality and how do we get there?
Geneva, International Labour Office, 2001

Woman worker, equal employment opportunity, equal treatment, affirmative action, comparison, developed country, developing country
14.04.2

ISBN 92-2-111386-8

ILO Cataloguing in Publication Data

Printed in Switzerland   PCL

PREFACE

For the ILO a gender perspective on the world of work is now an imperative. Until recent years there was little sensitivity — in any society or organization — to gender differences, and the range of women's interests was largely ignored. Early steps concerned protection more than rights. However, since its inception the ILO has confronted issues of importance to women workers, starting with the horrors of night work at the beginning of the twentieth century. One of many signs of the dramatic developments in the intervening years is that the former priority prohibition of night work for women has been denounced by many countries for its discrimination against women. In the early 1970s there was a concerted international effort to raise women's status and to enshrine equality of men and women as a right, and many subsequent advances can be traced to that effort. Institutions of the United Nations system, including the ILO, created structures and programmes for that purpose, and they provided forums for productive exchanges between people in all countries.

Over the years the ILO has published many reports and studies that deal with aspects of women workers' problems and priorities as well as analyses on discrimination and equality. The *International Labour Review* — the multilingual and multidisciplinary flagship journal of the ILO — has taken up many aspects of equality and women workers' rights over the years since it was created in 1921. In the past several years it has published the empirical and analytical findings of internationally known economists, philosophers, lawyers, sociologists and statisticians on this subject. But here, for the first time, a range of those studies are brought together.[1]

In this anthology you will find a selection of 22 articles that have been published in the *International Labour Review* between 1996 and 2000 on many dimensions of women, gender and work. The first of the selected articles sets the framework in terms of the value of work, rights, and goals. Articles then examine the meaning of equality between men and women, measurement and indicators of inequality and equal opportunity, occupational segregation and differences in earnings, part-time work and parental leave, the distribution of unpaid work and caring labour, social protection, affirmative action, the emergence of supranational law, managerial styles, sexual harassment, and the changing nature of the family. Taken together, and introduced by a substantial overview, this volume constitutes a valuable package of information and analysis — reference material of value to policy-makers, researchers, students, activists and, in general, men and women of good will across the globe who seek inspiration — and evidence.

Note

[1] The only other publication comprised of articles published in the *International Labour Review* is, to the knowledge of the editor of this anthology, the *Retrospective* issue of the *ILR* (1996/3-4). That special issue is a major reference containing 18 articles published between 1921 and 1996 — in celebration of the 75th anniversary of the *ILR*. Some influential personalities are represented, including Albert Thomas, John D. Rockefeller Jr., Ernest Mahaim, Bertil Ohlin, Abba Lerner, Alva Myrdal, Michal Kalecki, Colin Clark, Nicolas Valticos, Jan Tinbergen and Amartya Sen.

ACKNOWLEDGEMENTS

Special thanks are due to the 24 authors, in universities and institutes and in the International Labour Office, who kindly and voluntarily contributed this material to the *International Labour Review*. Appended you will find notes on the contributors. In addition, the titles and abstracts of each chapter are provided in French and Spanish.

The material they contributed was checked, carefully edited and revised by the staff of the *ILR* — Patrick Bollé, Monique Grimaud, Mark Lansky, Luis Lázaro Martínez, Marie-Christine Nallet, Kate Pfeiffenberger, and Christine L. Smith. And then it was turned into presentable and publishable form by staff in the document production, printing and distribution service, especially José Garcia and Prabha Sundaram.

The preparation and finalization of this volume owes a great deal to the ILO officials in the publications production and marketing units, especially May Ballerio-Hofman, Luisito Cabrera and Lauren Elsaesser. The support of the chief of the Publications Bureau, David Freedman, was indispensable to the publication of this volume.

CONTENTS

Part IV: Objectives, policy: What does it take?

Part V: The role of law: Where have we gotten?

PART I

INTRODUCTION

WOMEN, GENDER AND WORK — AN OVERVIEW

Martha Fetherolf LOUTFI*

1

Women have entered paid employment in enormous numbers since 1900 — in a century which saw many economies move from being dependent on agriculture to industry and then to a predominance of services. But the more important story concerns the dramatic change in women's status, notwithstanding the glaring inequalities that remain. That change has helped to provoke a wide-ranging debate on the appropriate roles of men and women, but also deep reflection on basic human values, including the place of work in life as a whole. Drawing together the results of analysis by philosophers, economists, lawyers and statisticians we can better understand the process under way and what is needed to achieve equality in practice — which is in the interest of us all.

By historical standards there have been enormous gains in the past 100 years. Developments in science, technology, knowledge, health, literacy, life expectancy and political participation are amongst those that often come first to mind. But perhaps none has been so dramatic and pervasive in its impact as women's gradual acquisition of human rights. Where a century ago women were often excluded from the full exercise of those civil rights which many men enjoyed,[1] and most women never attained the status of full legal adults, now equality is conceivable. Men across the globe have had to come to terms with women exercising their recently acquired rights in the workplace, in politics — and at home. Yet nowhere has actual equality been achieved. The respective roles of men and women are still undergoing profound change, in the process

---

* Martha Fetherolf Loutfi, an economist, is Editor-in-Chief of the *International Labour Review.*

transforming the nature of the family, society, culture and politics along with economics and the world of work.

This is a time when basic values are subject to questioning by many people, partly a result of those upheavals in the social order. So it behoves all of us, caught up as we are in this transformation, to understand as best we can the nature of the process and the values at stake. And to use that knowledge to ensure that the emerging order brings along those who are disenfranchised, excluded, forgotten. We may see a future world in which there is an end to heavy labour, where people are empowered and participate fully over their whole life cycle, and live in societies that are profoundly human. *Or*, we may see the gruesome alternative — a descent to unbreachable inequality, widespread violence and chaos. Which way society goes is highly dependent on public policy.[2]

Despite the impressive gains that women have made and the progress toward gender equality that must be noted, there are significant inequalities that must be addressed if one is to speak seriously of social justice. A neglected dimension is effective control of the use of property — public as well as private: "inequality in command over property is the single most important form of persisting economic inequality between women and men", in the words of Bina Agarwal.[3] She also points out that gender inequality assumes both material and ideological forms, the latter embedded in social norms and perceptions that are strongly influenced by the increasingly global mass media.

It is also time to take into account more of the various ways in which men and women may be different. Some, especially among those that are physical and biological, are irreducible; many are certainly remediable. All need to be examined. Many differences between men and women, such as those in income, life expectancy, educational attainment, can be seen and measured; and redressed. Laws and government policies can be examined to determine whether there is discrimination against men or women. But many other differences — and the causes of most — lie in what is covered under the term "gender". That term refers to the social constructs — the institutions — that greatly influence our behaviour and interactions. When one speaks of gender roles, those are roles linked to sex and sexual stereotypes that are largely determined by the culture and society in which each of us lives. "Gender" is not (and should not be used as) equivalent to "female" or a euphemism for "sex". It is quite appropriate to seek both equality between men and women *and* gender equality, with the latter implying roles that may well be different but are equal in status and social esteem. There will always be social and institutional constructs around what is male and female, but they need not be unequal in value. There is a focus on women in the pages that follow, but there is also an attempt to elucidate gender roles, to consider the ways in which they may also be unequal, and to discuss policy options for reducing that inequality. Such inequality is usually but not always to the detriment of women — which reinforces the argument for gender analysis alongside legitimate feminist enquiry. Once the serious analysis underway on masculinities and gender matures,[4] we can expect to discover ways of transcending the legacy of the "gender wars" and the natural limitations of purely feminist enquiry and male reactions to arrive at reintegration at a higher level.

As put clearly by Amartya Sen: "traditional inequalities, such as unequal treatment of women in sexist societies, often survive by making the respective identities, which may include subservient roles of the traditional underdog, matters for unquestioning acceptance, rather than reflective examination. But the unquestioned presumptions are merely unquestioned — not unquestionable."[5] What follows contributes to that essential examination.

CONCEPTS, VALUES

Important as work is for income, production and status, people are not defined solely by their work, nor is it possible to ignore the effects of factors outside the workplace on a person's status at work. To seek equality at work without seeking equality in the larger society — and at home — is illusory. Thus an examination of the issues surrounding women, gender and work must be holistic. This means considering the role of productive work in life as a whole and the distribution of unpaid work as well as the myriad questions relating to employment.

The value attached to work is the subject of *Dominique Méda's* philosophical investigation in "New perspectives on work as value" (Chapter 2). She sees work reflecting the recent historical developments that have made economic transactions central to social life. Her retrospective shows how work — a historically determined social construct — came to be regarded as an integral feature of the human condition. There is no inherent reason why work need be identified with the very essence of humankind, as a means of fulfilment in relation to the self, to others and to nature. Not being immutable nor, she would argue, desirable, the central role accorded work is an imperative object of examination. She argues both for a more specific concept of work, one that does not pretend to subsume all the range of human activity and interests, and for a reappraisal of the attention given to work as the central determinant of the social bond. This means asking the question — largely neglected by our contemporary civilization — what constitutes a good society? The answer, she posits, may lie in some sense of a fully active society comprised of fully active human beings, and wherein employment is only a part.[6]

Amartya Sen, in "Work and rights" (Chapter 3), argues for "an adequately broad approach to the conditions that govern our lives and work." To focus not just on the interests of some workers, such as the organized or those in the informal sector, or on youth, to the detriment of the aged. A truly inclusive, universal approach means confronting those ethical conflicts that are real, but not giving rein to "imagined conflicts" and "unexamined prejudices". Then there are certain basic and universal rights to be defended that transcend legislation. Yet if decent work is to be the goal — as the ILO is now arguing — work must also be placed in a broad economic, political and social framework. He stresses the critical role of democratic openness and freedoms. But he goes further still. Human beings need not be seen primarily as citizens of particular countries; we need not "accept that the interactions between citizens of different countries must be inevitably intermediated through the relations between distinct nations. Many global institutions, including those central to our working lives, have to go well beyond the limits of 'international' relations. ... The increasingly globalized world economy calls for a similarly globalized approach to basic ethics and political and social procedures." That is a daunting but worthy challenge, one that can also be seen as giving a context to the generic argument of Dominique Méda for a fully active society.

It follows of course that such a society values men and women equally. Assessment of progress and design of policy for achieving equality between men and women are made difficult by an inadequate formulation of the objective. There are many specific indicators available, in the economic and in other domains. There are competing measures of progress or deterioration in gender equity (such as equal pay for work of equal value), or of negatives to avoid (such as discrimination and sexual harassment). But it is difficult to find any useful formulation of gender equity as an end state to which society aspires. *Martha Nussbaum* takes up that challenge here in "Women and equality: The capabilities approach" (Chapter 4). She starts with human dignity and the idea it incorporates of equal worth — of rich and poor, rural and urban, female and male. The freedom and opportunity that equal worth implies is widely violated on grounds of sex, and many existing value systems deny liberty of choice, let alone access to the resources that would make choice possible. She sets out to define a cross-cultural norm that is relevant and appropriate for all persons. In view of the limitations of alternatives, such as those based on resource allocation or preferences alone, there is a powerful case for applying what, following Amartya Sen, has come to be known as a capabilities approach. Its great strength comes from the importance it gives to enabling a person to function to the full extent of her or his human capability. Each person is a bearer of value.

A list of the elements necessary for "truly human functioning" across cultures can be constructed. Nussbaum suggests it include life, bodily health and integrity, human senses, emotion, reason, affiliation, play ... She argues that "the basic intuition from which the capability approach begins, in the political arena, is that human abilities exert a moral claim that they be developed". Not to do so "gives us a sense of waste and tragedy". But it is essential to remember that "capability, not functioning, is the appropriate political goal". The liberties she advocates are not only instrumental; they are also of intrinsic value. While close to those of human rights they arguably offer additional clarity of definition, motivation and goals, and the language in which they are expressed is not derived from a particular cultural tradition. As she explains, we need fulfilment of both human rights and human capabilities. For women, "their unequal failure in capability is a problem of justice".

STATISTICS AND INFORMATION: WHAT DO WE KNOW?

By any measure there have been far-reaching developments in the world of work this century. An enormous increase in the labour force has resulted from the multiplication of the world's population and a doubling of life expectancy; a dramatic reduction in the material content of national product has freed the majority of workers, especially men, from heavy and dangerous physical labour; the general spread of democratic institutions has given a voice to people, including in the workplace; women have entered the regular labour market in astounding numbers. It is timely to take stock of what developments have occurred as the employment of women approaches that of men, and now there is a significant volume of data disaggregated by sex that can be drawn upon.

Few people realize how critical statistics are to the allocation of resources, policy formulation and legislation. Phenomena — and people — that are not counted or measured are quite easily ignored. Data on individual and group characteristics are preconditions for supportive policies. When plans for national censuses are set (usually every ten years) there sometimes is a debate on labels and categories — precisely because of their importance in the subsequent formulation of national policy — but then attention wanes and those not covered are forgotten. Since the collection of good national data is expensive, that which is not deemed a top priority is often counted poorly. Women and the work they do are frequently neglected — and are surely undercounted — despite decades of effort on the part of those who are concerned about the distortion that results. In "Gender issues in labour statistics" (Chapter 5), *Adriana Mata Greenwood* explains that "to serve users, labour statistics need to reflect reality as closely as possible". However, since statistical categories reflect what are perceived to be the "core" employment and unemployment situations, in which men dominate, and women are often found in "other" work situations, the neglect of women's work is pernicious. As she points out, the "systematic under-reporting and misrepresentation of women's contribution to the economy ... perpetuate a vicious circle of inequality between men and women".

Underlying the imbalance in statistics is a problem in the popular perception of what is work. Myths that serve to undervalue certain activities do untold damage: society as a whole loses out when only market valuation matters. There are a number of areas she suggests be better covered in labour statistics so they can reveal the real nature of an economy's productive work. Among these are intermittent and other forms of underemployment, informal-sector work, non-market work activities and unpaid work in general. One might add the distribution and control of the gains from work. As science continues to reveal ways far beyond the visible biological in which men and women differ, it becomes even more of an imperative to measure accurately their respective work activities so that sensible policies can be designed and destructive ones avoided. Mata Greenwood presents a clear and constructive overview of changes that deserve support.

The most glaring problem of under-valuation concerns unpaid productive work — most of which is, not incidentally, done by women. Attempts to improve its measurement and thereby its perceived value have been under way for decades, but little of the result has been incorporated into national labour statistics or the measurement of national product. There is purposive resistance, but also indifference and ignorance. *Lourdes Benería* (Chapter 6) explains what progress has been made and the contending arguments in "The enduring debate over unpaid labour".

Work in the subsistence and informal sectors, domestic and voluntary work are all seriously undercounted. But there are critics who argue that it would be a waste of resources to gather more accurate statistics, or that such work is too qualitatively different, or that the effort is theoretically misguided. The problem arises, of course, from the way in which "work" is generally defined. As Benería points out, underlying that is the fundamental question of what is *value* and *of value to society*. And she gives further impetus to those who believe in a fairer valuation of women's work — and men's.

There is at least one area where people are perhaps less confused than they ought to be: there are some surprising ways in which data do not convey what they seem to. In order to determine the pattern of changes in the labour force and to design policies to redress discrimination or other unacceptable inequities it is essential to obtain accurate and relevant data by sex, marital status, race, ethnic or linguistic group or other category. Yet data that appear to be factual and objective may rather be the result of highly distorted enquiries. Few people can mislead as to their sex, but replies to questions on race, ethnicity or caste may be quite another matter. And incentives to being included in one or another category are not unimportant factors in the production of "data". There can be substantial discretion, especially in those countries where data are obtained from respondents rather than from administrative records. People "can choose to downplay or emphasize the characteristics of their birth and upbringing, motivated by personal, cultural, financial or political factors" — in the words of *Carolyn Shaw Bell* (Chapter 7). The desirability of being identified with one or another category of the population may change, making time series even more problematic. As a result, social scientists may unwittingly collect flawed data which then constitute false premises for social policy. In "Data on race, ethnicity and gender: Caveats for the user" she sounds an alarm: be wary when collecting or using data. It may be tempting to leave out or ignore the small print and long annexes to data sets, but you do so at your peril.

One of the most intractable aspects of employment that must be confronted if economic efficiency and equity objectives are to be pursued seriously is the segregation of occupations by sex. It is, as *Richard Anker* argues (Chapter 8), one of the most important and enduring aspects of labour markets around the world — at all levels of development, under all political systems and in diverse religious, social and environmental settings. In "Theories of occupational segregation by sex: An overview" he reviews the explanations for the existence and persistence of occupational segregation of men and women. To explain employers' and women's "preferences" for segregation he takes up in turn neo-classical and human capital theories, institutional and labour market theories, and non-economic and feminist or gender theories. Drawing on the results of a vast empirical examination he has undertaken of occupational segregation by sex,[7] he comments on the relative explanatory power of the different theories. And he concludes that, while all are supported to some extent by the evidence, "gender theories provide the most compelling explanations for the sex segregation of occupations".

Derek Robinson applies his expertise in analysing pay structures to the key issue of unequal pay for men and women. In "Differences in occupational earnings by sex" (Chapter 9) he provides the results of a careful examination of earnings in narrowly-defined occupational categories. Using available disaggregated data (from the ILO's October Inquiry) that allow the comparison of like activities, he shows empirically the extent of inequality in earnings between men and women in the same occupation. Detailed results are given for two major occupational groupings — for medical personnel and for public service, banking and insurance. This is the kind of systematic analysis that is necessary in order to determine where unequal pay for substantially similar work occurs — a crucial step in identifying and redressing discrimination-based inequality in pay.

It is often assumed that as a result of their advanced social policies the Nordic countries are also the most equal in general; their early attention to equality for women is certainly noteworthy.[8] In "Occupational segregation by sex in Nordic countries: An empirical investigation" (Chapter 10) *Helinä Melkas and Richard Anker* examine the data for Finland, Norway and Sweden. They reach the somewhat surprising conclusion that occupational segregation by sex is relatively high in these countries, especially horizontal segregation (separation of occupations). Economic and social policies may ensure that this does not translate into exceptional gaps in wages and income, but, as they argue, "a gender-segregated labour market is not something which should be taken as natural and inevitable...". It entails inefficiencies and inequality which only a much higher degree of integration of men and women across occupations can correct.

"Part-time work: Solution or trap?" (Chapter 11) by *Patrick Bollé* covers an issue of importance for trade unions, for workers generally and for families. While there is a widespread tendency for an increasing proportion of the labour force to work part time, the explanations vary. For a good many workers, the chance to work part time is liberating, facilitating a desired combination of work, family responsibilities and civic and leisure activities. For others, it is the result of a lack of opportunities for full-time work. Some governments, faced with high unemployment, encourage part-time work beyond what would be voluntarily chosen in order to reduce unemployment rolls. Here, after first discussing questions of definition and methodology, a range of issues at both the individual and macro levels are taken up, and data are given on the extent of part-time work and its relationship to the labour force participation rates of women and to union density. Bollé provides a very useful overview of this complex and politically sensitive issue of social policy.

Taking up another point of gender conflict, in "Women in management: Closer to breaking through the glass ceiling?" (Chapter 12), *Linda Wirth* summarizes research she has undertaken on the question. She discusses women's substantial gains in management but also what still remains of the "glass ceiling" that hinders their rise to the very top of corporate hierarchies. Data comparing women's share in professional and managerial employment in 1986-88 and 1993-95 reveal significant gains in many countries, even in that short interval; in three of the countries for which data are available — Australia, Canada and the United States — women's share in administrative and managerial employment rose above 40 per cent. As she points out, women have availed themselves of the new educational and training opportunities in large numbers, and that has had a significant bearing on their rise in the hierarchy. Though traditional perceptions continue to influence women's education and career choices, those choices are expanding, and women are increasingly found in non-traditional occupations. Social values have begun to change. But women's share of posts at the very top in any country is still extremely small — a few percentage points at best. One result of that persistent glass ceiling is that more and more women move out and run their own small and medium-sized enterprises, "bringing their talent and experience to the development of more dynamic and flexible companies and leaving behind the rigid work arrangements and attitudes which hindered their rise to top management levels". In the process, they are beginning to redefine the world of business.

Sara Elder and Lawrence Jeffrey Johnson summarize what current international data reveal on gender differences in the labour market in "Sex-specific labour market indicators: What they show" (Chapter 13). They present highlights from research they have carried out for the ILO on indicators of labour force participation, employment (by status and by sector), working time, work in the informal sector, unemployment, and education for women and men. While the results confirm many of the patterns already described in other studies, their findings strengthen the statistical bases for those conclusions and are thus a welcome addition to the evidence of differences in the labour market experience of men and women.

OBJECTIVES, POLICY: WHAT DOES IT TAKE?

Good data, well used, are essential to good policy. Such use is well demonstrated by *Janneke Plantenga and Johan Hansen,* who examine the extent of equal opportunity in "Assessing equal opportunities in the European Union" (Chapter 14). In this remarkable empirical study, one finds a highly relevant operational definition of equal opportunity in employment. They first select a limited number of indicators of the gender gap (such as the relative employment rates and wages of men and women and the distribution of unpaid work); and of the absolute situation of women in the labour market (such as women's employment and unemployment rates and their representation in higher positions). Those indicators are then estimated for the 15 Member States of the European Union. The results may be surprising. There are too many industrialized countries where opportunities are now even less equal than they were a decade ago. But the authors do not end their study with the diagnosis: they go on to analyse overall country performance on equality in relation to the basic determinants of equal opportunity — economic growth, the structure of the tax system, attitudes to women's employment, working time arrangements, and the availability of childcare facilities and parental leave. In other words, they break the question of equal opportunity down into its constituent elements and then use available data to address the larger policy issues, all in an unusually integrated fashion. This preliminary study already indicates some clear policy priorities for those who are serious about achieving equal opportunity, and it should be an incitement to further examination of the empirical evidence and refinement of the method.

In "The family, flexible work and social cohesion at risk" (Chapter 15), *Martin Carnoy* points out that "globalization and the intensified economic competition it engenders are profoundly altering the way we live and relate to each other." The particular strains imposed on the family by that competition, and the flexibility it demands, are the focus of his analysis. The family — which is, along with the workplace, the principal means by which people are socially integrated — is called upon to play an even greater sustaining role than in the past because of the increased individualization and differentiation at work. Yet the family itself is undergoing changes, such as slower formation and shorter duration, that tend to undermine its ability to fulfil that role. This raises questions about the various options or models of flexible work on offer. Social cohesion is at risk, perhaps as never before. Carnoy thus puts the family at the centre of an integrated view of adjustment to an emerging world order.

One of the critical interactions between the family and work is centred around caregiving. It has a fundamental impact on people's well-being and thus transcends the specific value of other forms of productive, reproductive and volunteer work. If its value were to be fully attributed it would surely be costly, and the measured productivity of other activities might well be reduced. *Lee Badgett and Nancy Folbre* (Chapter 16) examine the relationship between caring labour, social expectations and economic factors in "Assigning care: Gender norms and economic outcomes". Care is given both freely and through the market. One could argue that care *services* are mediated by the market and that care*giving* is formally voluntary. But that would imply accepting the pre-eminence of those spheres and underplay the gender norms that assign all forms of care largely to women. In the view of Badgett and Folbre, the Marxist tradition and Weberian scholarship would assimilate caregiving to unalienated labour, located in the family and community and outside the modern market sphere whereas, in a capitalist system, both forms persist, and they fall largely to women.

The social norms which define women's greater responsibility for providing both remunerated and unpaid care are not, they argue, benign; nor can that responsibility be explained, as neoclassical economics might do, as simple altruism. Nor do biological determinism or culture offer acceptable answers. "Feminist theory emphasizes the coercive dimensions of social norms of masculinity and femininity, describing norms as important elements of gendered structures of constraint." The authors argue that "men as a group have much to gain by encouraging women's caring propensities" — in what amounts to socially imposed altruism. In their view it is time to challenge occupational stereotypes, difficult as that process is. The authors argue that resistance results from the cost: "Men are reluctant to assume responsibilities that will lower their market income, just as they are reluctant to enter caring occupations that pay less than most male jobs." Yet norms of masculinity and femininity are being contested, and alternative social contracts are possible — and worthy of serious debate.

In "Parental leave" (Chapter 17) *Patrick Bollé* deals with a key area of public policy that affects the feasible balance between familial, professional and civic activities for those responsible for young children. As he points out, parental leave may offer new opportunities that allow workers to arrange a preferred distribution between work and life outside work; as such, it can contribute to social progress by a variety of measures. But such arrangements are still in the category of the "atypical", and they are not always voluntary. Without access to childcare there may not be an alternative — other than to quit work altogether. Bollé outlines different forms (and definitions) and then the take-up rates, advantages and disadvantages. As he notes, "men show little enthusiasm for parental leave", so it has mainly served to offer women greater flexibility. Yet that may come at a price in terms of career, and as long as that risk is serious, the gender imbalance is likely to persist.

Julie Nelson, an economist, discusses some of the biases that inhibit analysts from taking a more comprehensive view of economic activity and of women's contributions in particular. In "Labour, gender and the economic/social divide" (Chapter 18) she points out the traditional ways in which academic specialities delimit subjects for analysis, often leaving out important but messy questions less amenable to a quantitative approach. Drawing on feminist literature she discusses a range of characteristics that are often linked to a presumed masculine/feminine divide, such as economic/social, rational/emotional, rigorous/intuitive. This is another way of demonstrating the damage done — in analysis as well as at the human level — by a focus on the market to the exclusion of all else of value. After offering a critique of narrow economic analysis and illustrating its pitfalls, Nelson suggests other paths worth exploring. She argues for a broader concept of economics, including one that takes account of the roles of women and men in provisioning.

A sense of feminine and masculine characteristics across cultures is posited by *Marie-Thérèse Claes* in "Women, men and management styles" (Chapter 19). To some extent, women are now sought as managers for their supposed advantages in communication and teamwork. What are perceived as feminine characteristics, such as cooperation and flexibility, seem to be well suited to a world of uncertainty and stress. She argues that "the masculine culture of large corporations cannot easily adapt to a context of uncertainty and constant evolution." She in effect reinforces the argument of Carnoy in respect of pressures from globalization. The vision she sets out is one in which "the masculine and feminine models co-exist and operate in synergy". We must incorporate both elements in order to manage businesses — and other organizations — in a way that satisfies both commercial and human needs. This gives a hint of what gender equality in this domain might look like.

Another way in which traditional perceptions of male and female roles lead to inferior outcomes for women is through the presumed relation of dependency that underlies social protection systems. In "Equal treatment, social protection and income security for women" (Chapter 20) *Linda Luckhaus* applies various definitions of equality to the question of discrimination in social protection. Her particular focus is on the level and regularity of income — the central concern of social protection. Apart from paid employment, the principal sources of income security are sexual relationships with partners of the opposite sex and social protection systems. Like other researchers on the subject of inequality, she finds that the asymmetric distribution of caring labour lies at the heart of inequality. "Unpaid caring work, not the sex of the unpaid worker, is the clue to understanding why social protection systems prove a fragile source of income for women", she argues. But it is the presumed financial dependency that undercuts many attempts at achieving equality. Social protection systems have tended on balance to reproduce the inequality found in other spheres.[9] The careful reflection required to develop genuinely equal systems has been absent. Reinforced by documentation on many judicial decisions that purport to advance equality but often do otherwise, this study provides a major reference on the subject.

THE ROLE OF LAW: WHERE HAVE WE GOTTEN?

One means of achieving justice is affirmative action, "an extension of the notion of equality of opportunity and non-discrimination", as *Jane Hodges Aeberhard* explains (Chapter 21). While there are continuing debates surrounding policies of affirmative action in some countries, democratically elected governments continue to adopt legislation supporting it as a means of countering discrimination in employment on the basis of race and sex. In "Affirmative action in employment: Recent court approaches to a difficult concept", she describes the differing outcomes that have emerged from courts even as they confront similar facts.

By reviewing recent court decisions in a number of countries, especially the United States, South Africa and Europe, Hodges demonstrates that the application of the law often lacks the coherence and effectiveness that is expected of such an important instrument for opposing discrimination. The resulting confusion in the jurisprudence is cause for concern — both for victims of discrimination and for policy-makers responsible for eliminating discrimination. She argues that consideration of a new normative initiative to provide greater clarity would be timely.

The law has the potential to be a major instrument for achieving and maintaining equality of opportunity and treatment. *Ingeborg Heide* examines the development of European law on that issue in "Supranational action against sex discrimination: Equal pay and equal treatment in the European Union" (Chapter 22). This timely review of European law is placed in its larger historical and social context. As such it constitutes an unusual reference work on the development of European institutions and the emergence of supranational law. She goes on to illustrate that development with highlights from the case law of the European Court of Justice in respect of equal pay and equal treatment, and shows how the concept of non-discrimination has evolved. This is a most useful source of information on equality legislation and current case law in the European Union. In addition, by showing the manner in which this supranational law is evolving it helps us understand the potential for genuinely global as distinct from international action.

At the workplace there is confusion as to what constitutes acceptable behaviour of men and women towards each other. Within the past decade many countries have adopted legislation specifically to address various behavioural abuses, and sexual harassment in particular. Others have started to apply non-discrimination or other general legislation to claims of sexual harassment such that a body of jurisprudence has been built up even where there is no specific legislation against it. The proportion of women in the labour force continues to rise, and it behoves all participants therein to understand the limits so that the workplace can be both human and respectful of human rights. Women and men, employers and workers, personnel managers, lawyers and judges all need to know what constitutes sexual harassment at work, what rules apply, what are the limits. In "Sexual harassment in employment: Recent judicial and arbitral trends" (Chapter 23) *Jane Hodges Aeberhard* describes current trends in court action against sexual harassment in employment, drawing on a wide literature. She points out the use of labour and other legislation on equal employment opportunities, human rights, health and safety, even tort and criminal law for countering sexual harassment. The questions of liability, remedies and sanctions are also taken up. This is an invaluable review of a difficult and controversial subject.

SOME CONCLUDING REMARKS

Though it is not yet time for general celebration, the gains made this century in gender equity have been enormous, and that in a period of unprecedented improvement for men and women together. The world's population has increased some four-fold this century, life expectancy has roughly doubled, and the present 6 billion people on earth do on average enjoy the highest standard of living of any time in history. That is notwithstanding the fact that there are more people than ever living in deep poverty and deprivation. But sexual stereotypes and mutual incomprehension persist, and they still constrain progress toward achieving gender equality, which is ultimately necessary for the progress of society overall.

One striking feature of the material covered in this anthology is that though only one author was asked to examine the changing family, most found it central to their examination of other aspects of *women, gender and work*. Perhaps that should not have been surprising, given that the historic sexual division of labour has well served the preservation of inequality generally. It is perhaps a sign of how far we have finally come in the debate on equality that it has become possible to examine, dispassionately, the distribution of unpaid work in general and especially household work and caregiving. The relative shares of men and women in household work are quite logically a key indicator of equality of opportunity in employment, as is shown in the study by Plantenga and Hansen. The highly unequal distribution of caring work, whether marketed or not, is, according to Badgett and Folbre, linked not just to inequality generally but also to marriageability. As Carnoy shows, the family is fraying under the pressures of labour market competition and uncertain gender roles just as the need for its sustaining force grows stronger as individuals confront enormous uncertainty and stress in the wake of globalization. Parental leave, discussed by Bollé, can help people achieve a fair balance between the familial, professional, civic and cultural activities that go into making up what Méda calls a fully active society.

It must of course be remembered that the nuclear family is not the only norm out there. But whatever form they take, families across the globe face new challenges that test their ability to provide both the sustaining bonds and the autonomy that are needed of them. This reinforces the importance of focusing attention on the changing roles of men and women if one is to define constructive policies for economic and social development and pursue their effective implementation. With increased labour force participation, women's life choices have expanded. Both law and public policy have helped narrow the inequalities between men and women, in the process unleashing untold human resources. That in turn expands life options for men as well as women. But there is still a very long way to go.

It is sometimes thought that the private sphere is somehow separate from government, but one must avoid falling into that trap. The optimism we all need in order to plan for the future, to invest in the next generations, depends importantly on achieving a good balance between personal responsibility and effective, just government. That is the principal reason for the strong policy focus in the material contained in the chapters that follow. It is necessary to probe some of the outstanding questions that affect the roles of both men and women and the nature of the family, to reflect on the use of legislation to advance gender equity, and to determine whether there is progress or regression. Whether analysing basic concepts, discussing statistical information, outlining objectives or considering the role of law, the point is not only to deepen our understanding but also to move forward; to signal what can be changed for the better while retaining that which ought to endure.

How governments structure the tax system, how social payments such as pensions and health benefits are calculated and funded, the maintenance of infrastructure, incentives to productive investment, trade liberalization — these and many other public choices have enormous effects on family structure and survival, on the allocation of time, on investment in the education of the coming generations, and even on the relative humaneness of our interactions with each other. It is necessary to remember that public policy matters. New communication and information technologies empower us. But they also make it easy to misuse what should be private data and to move unproductive capital around the globe with impunity. So they illustrate why there is an even greater need than in the past for the State to get the incentives right and to enforce common rules and laws. There is no one else out there to protect the public interest.

This anthology, substantial and wide-ranging as it is, cannot of course constitute the definitive statement on the subject of *women, gender and work*. There are many topics that have a bearing on the subject, and it has not been possible to cover all. Among those that await further examination from a gender perspective are agriculture and land rights, control of mass media, workers' organizations and labour standards, to which should be added the specific problems of men and work and men's stake in gender equality. This theme has been taken up to advance, not conclude the debate. It concerns after all a subject of continuing deep individual and social interest, touching as it does the range of our personal and professional, private and collective interests and capabilities. This anthology is a contribution to what must be a continuing attention to our world, in all its permutations and complexity, through the distinct eyes of men and women, so that we may better understand the whole; and ourselves.

Notes

[1] Though a number of countries provided for popular voting, only one country, New Zealand, allowed women the right to vote.

[2] Most economists — and most other human beings — know instinctively if not consciously that many factors over which no one has control influence our destiny, though much of people's struggles have been to influence the largest possible range, from weather to our genes. Geography may to a large extent be a nation's destiny (for a recent attempt to put this and other causes in perspective, see David S. Landes' thought-provoking analysis, *The wealth and poverty of nations: Why some are so rich and some so poor*, New York, W. W. Norton, 1998; and see also Jared Diamond: *Guns, germs and steel: The fates of human societies*, New York and London, W. W. Norton, 1977.). But it is the nature of the ILO — and the predilection of the present author — to focus on those problems that can be resolved. Thus the aspects of life indicated so far and to follow in this overview are those that are in fact amenable to change, especially by public policy but also by private action.

[3] Bina Agarwal: *Gender inequality — some critical neglected dimensions*, address to the ILO Symposium on Decent Work for Women, Geneva, 24 March 2000. (http://www.ilo.org/bureau/gender/beijing/agarwal.htm). It should be noted that much of the early research on women and development focused on access to resources including land and other property — an issue that, though unresolved, has slipped in priority on the international agenda. A key early contribution is that of Ester Boserup: *Women's role in economic development* (London, Allen and Unwin, 1970). For a review of some research a decade later see Martha F. Loutfi: *Rural women: Unequal partners in development* (Geneva, ILO, 1980).

[4] See, for example, Cecile Jackson: "Men's work, masculinities and gender divisions of labour", in *The Journal of Development Studies* (London), Vol. 36, No. 1, Oct. 1999, pp. 89-108; and Sylvia Chant: "From 'woman-blind' to 'man-kind': Should men have more space in gender and development?", in *IDS Bulletin* (Brighton), Vol. 31, No. 2, Feb. 2000.

[5] Amartya Sen: *Reason before Identity*, The Romanes Lecture for 1998, University of Oxford, 17 November 1998. Oxford University Press, 1999, p. 19.

[6] In a subsequent paper, she argues that women and feminist analysis may serve as a catalyst for changing the role of work in life as a whole, and sets out four principal kinds of activity — productive, familial, political and cultural — that together underlie individual and social well-being ("Les femmes peuvent-elles changer la place du travail dans la vie?" in *Droit Social* (Paris), No. 5, May 2000, pp. 463-470).

[7] Richard Anker: *Gender and jobs: Sex segregation of occupations in the world*. ILO, Geneva, 1998.

[8] See, for example, Alva Myrdal's 1939 article in the *International Labour Review*, "A programme for family security in Sweden", of which an abridged version was published in the *Retrospective* issue — Vol. 135 (1996), No. 3-4.

[9] This is also a conclusion of the ILO report — *World Labour Report: Income security and social protection in a changing world* (Geneva, 2000). One of its five principal policy conclusions concerns the link between social protection and gender. It finds that "social protection can actually reinforce the inequality from which women suffer in the labour market when, for example, particular groups of employees are excluded, such as domestic employees, part-time workers and homeworkers. Women are heavily represented in these groups" (p. 229). In addition, the push for equality has arguably led to a tendency to level down, as the less costly option. That report draws attention to the central role played by the unequal sharing of caring work in maintaining inequality between men and women; and it makes a number of suggestions for improving income security for women and making systems more equal in their impact while strengthening protection overall.

PART II

CONCEPTS, VALUES

NEW PERSPECTIVES ON WORK AS VALUE

Dominique MÉDA*

2

The concept of work and the all-important role it has acquired in western societies are historical constructs, not an expression of the essence of humanity. To charge work alone — under the ambiguous label of "activity" — with the creation and mainten- ance of the social bond is to submit to the exchange-based version of that bond promoted by economics. It passes over the primary concern of philosophers and citizens, namely the idea of the "good society", the proper goals of society, the nature of social wealth, and the distribution of basic goods (including work) most likely to promote social cohesion.

Developing "perspectives on work" calls for an understanding of how work came to play the all-important role it has in society today: what was the underlying historical process? what forces brought this situ- ation about? In other words, what needs to be done is to lay bare the rationale whereby work — a historically determined construct if ever there was one — has come to be regarded as an inherent feature of the human condition, as the only means of fulfilling all individual and social aspirations.

It is high time to put an end to the fruitless debates about whether work is or is not at the centre of modern life and to reveal the historical process whereby work has come to dominate the entirety of individual and social time and space. This is an urgent task — for unless it is under- taken there can be no understanding both why work is today the main vehicle for the formation of social relationships and for self-fulfilment, and that this has not always been the case or will be in the future. The

Originally published in *International Labour Review*, Vol. 135 (1996), No. 6.

* Philosopher. This chapter is a revised and updated version of an earlier article on the future of work ("La fin de la valeur travail?" in *Esprit* (Paris), No. 214 (Aug.-Sep.), 1995.

place taken by work in contemporary social organization is an outcome, a fact, not a structural feature of all human societies.

In other words, it is by accident and not on account of the immutable nature of things that work has become the essential mechanism for the achievement of social integration and self-fulfilment, and the origins of this fact lie not buried in the mists of time but in the response to a certain historically situated state of affairs from which the world may now be emerging, and from which it is certainly desirable to emerge. It is necessary to distinguish the question of the amount of work which will be available in the future from the question of the place that work rightfully occupies in personal and societal life.

The interesting question — and which should be of major concern to every politician and citizen — is this: what are the necessary conditions for the construction and preservation of the good society, that is, a society forming a well-integrated whole, providing a mooring and a source of identity for its citizens, able to deal with all manner of strains, both internal (xenophobia, violence, inequality ...) and external, a society unlikely to dissolve into atoms, i.e. into individuals, at the first threat? It is the question of the good constitution, of good government, which all previous societies have had to ask themselves, which has for centuries lain at the heart of political philosophy and practice, and which, alone, our own civilization has neglected to ask.

Work alone — in the sense of paid participation by individuals in the productive process — cannot weave together and sustain the system of social relationships which is central to a society's cohesion and its insertion in a particular historical period. This is especially evident when one sees how the notion of work prevailing today is a misshapen creature resulting from the numerous meanings conferred on the word over the past two hundred years.

THE INVENTION OF WORK

"Work" as a category passed through three broad stages before acquiring the meaning it has today. In the eighteenth century it appears both as a means of increasing wealth and as a mechanism for the emancipation of the individual — another category then emerging. That these two dimensions coincided was significant: if work is an individual service which can be the subject of exchange and of contractual arrangements, it is also the sum of all individual effort — of the efforts and industry of an entire nation — whereby the individual is integrated into society as a whole and social relationships are organized. But at the time work was neither positively valued nor glorified. In the nineteenth century a further crucial dimension was added. The nineteenth century's distinctive contribution was to transform, civilize and humanize the world, whilst also enabling individuals to develop their potential; this process was termed *Bildung* by contemporary German culture and eventually came to be known simply as work. Whether termed a movement of the Spirit, of God or of humanity, it was the leading factor in the humanization of the world.

A true ideology of work emerges during this period, contemporaneously with the proliferation of inhuman working conditions and with the debate on pauperism. Work is presented on the one hand as a truly creative freedom, a symbol of human endeavour whose full realization is fettered by the way in which production is organized and which will provide the basis for the eventual creation of a more just social order based on capacities, on the individual's contribution to production; and, on the other hand, as the facilitating factor of common endeavour.

Work thus becomes a synonym for creation (in the sense that as something of the producer's self goes into the object produced, it is a means of self-expression) and at the same time a collective creation (in the sense that by expressing self an image of self is produced for others). As Marx says, once work is no longer alienated and people can produce freely there will be no more need for money since the goods and services produced will reveal people to each other as they are revealed to themselves.

> Suppose we had produced things as human beings. ... Our productions would be so many mirrors reflecting our nature.[1]

This illustrates very well the type of future society imagined by the nineteenth century in general and by Marx in particular: in this vision, production and therefore work are the site of the alchemy of social relationships in a philosophy of mutual expressiveness and recognition. Marx succeeds in synthesizing English political economy and the German philosophy of expressiveness, placing himself in the tradition of a philosophy of humanization: humanity is seen as pursuing not only material affluence, but also the humanization and civilization of the world. From that moment on all utopian hopes and efforts concentrated on the productive sphere: production would not only improve material living conditions but would also create the conditions for the full realization of potential at both personal and social levels. In the same period, in Marx, Proudhon, Louis Blanc and in socialist (and also liberal) philosophy as a whole, work became synonymous with fully human endeavour: the activity proper to humankind is work, and the most fundamentally human activity is work itself.

However, Marx remains consistent, he is aware that work has yet to become a liberating creative activity — or at least that it is still only potentially so, not yet a reality. That basic need will be satisfied only when humanity comes to produce in conditions of absolute freedom, when wage labour is abolished and a world of abundance created. Then work will no longer be equated with drudgery, suffering or sacrifice, it will be pure self-fulfilment, pure expressive power; then and only then will the difference between work and leisure disappear.

Also relevant to our subject, the third stage (which was theorized in German social democracy) consists of a recovery of the socialist heritage — the belief in the inherently fulfilling nature of work and in the necessity of the pursuit of abundance — combined with a fundamental change in its doctrinal content. Instead of abolishing wage labour, in both its discourse and practice German social democracy made wages into the vehicle whereby wealth was to be distributed and a new social order — more just because based on labour and on capacities, and truly collective through the organization of the producers — gradually come into being. From then on the State was entrusted with the related tasks of guaranteeing continued economic growth and full employment, in other words of offering to all access to the riches which were pouring forth. But this stands in total contradiction with the thought of Marx, because in the original discourse of social democracy fulfilment was to come from work itself, whereas in this new version it is only thanks to increasing wages and consumption that this can be achieved. In the words of Habermas:

> For the burdens that continue to be connected with the cushioned status of dependent wage labour, the citizen is compensated in his role as client of the welfare state bureaucracies with legal claims, and in his role as consumer of mass-produced goods with buying power. The lever for the pacification of class antagonisms thus continues to be the neutralization of the conflict potential inherent in the status of the wage labourer.[2]

In other words social democracy, which in this sense remains the dominant view today, is based on a profound contradiction (from which contemporary left-wing parties have been unable to extricate themselves) in that it approaches work as the principal path to human fulfilment, both personal and collective, but without providing the means of producing a work of creation (since work is undertaken for a purpose extraneous to itself) let alone a collective work of creation achieved through authentic cooperation. Thus social democracy has confused two conceptions of work which socialist thought had traditionally taken care to distinguish: actually existing, alienated work which is the object of political action aimed at reducing the time it takes up, and freed work, which one day should become life's most basic need albeit fundamentally changing its meaning.

What do we learn from this historical summary? That work is a construct, that it has definitely not always been associated with the creation of value, with the transformation of the natural world, or with self-fulfilment; that it is multi-faceted because of its multiple meanings (as a factor of production, as creative freedom, as a mechanism for the distribution of income, status and security), but also because it is a mixture of elements, some objective and some made up largely of Utopia, fantasy and dream. From this two consequences follow: on the one hand we are the victims of a retrospective illusion, believing as we do that work has always existed — are we not told that it is already there in the Bible, that men have worked since time immemorial, even though it is centuries of reinterpretation which forced into one category activities which in their time were experienced in highly diverse ways?[3] On the other hand, contemporary discourse on work does not distinguish between its different dimensions. Does it mean work as a factor of production whose efficiency must constantly increase thus creating ever more wealth, whatever the consequences for the way in which work is undertaken? Does it mean work as the vision of an activity inherent to the human condition, enabling humanity to express itself, for humans to gain mutual recognition and to engage together in creative effort? Or does it simply refer, more prosaically, to employment and the system whereby income, status and security are distributed?

WORK AND THE SOCIAL BOND

This backward glance shows how for the last two centuries work has been the central social bond, the basis for the construction of the "social contract", the foundation of the hierarchy of positions and pay. It then follows — indeed to say so becomes a tautology — that to have work is today the primary condition for belonging to society, the central factor in the construction of a person's identity; that people who are without work lack everything; and that work is the only available collective endeavour, since the rest belongs to the private sphere. This must be the case, since work has become the central axis around which social relations as a whole have come to be organized, in societies which for the last two centuries have made the pursuit of affluence their sole concern. So we simply cannot imagine any other collective endeavour, any way of expressing ourselves or any basis for relating socially to one another save through work. Are we forever condemned to reinvent work, forever driven to place everything under man's yoke, in accordance with the theories of Bacon, Saint-Simon and Marx, and to do so exclusively in the form of work? As advanced societies succeed in satisfying their needs with an ever-decreasing expenditure of time, will they still feel impelled to seek out ever more opportunities for the creation of value, ever newer horizons to strive towards? When will we finally decide that we have attained this famous state of abundance, the dream after which we have hankered for so long? The answer, of course, is never. Abundance is a limitless concept, the path to it an asymptotic curve leading nowhere.

But perhaps today a point in history has been reached when this line of reasoning ceases to be tenable, when it can finally be realized, on the one hand, that work cannot fulfil all the functions heaped upon it over such a short period, and on the other, that it is precisely on account of our inability to extricate ourselves from traditional modes of thought that we cannot solve our problems. If work is not the only means whereby an individual can achieve self-fulfilment, if it is not necessarily the main vehicle for the tying of social bonds, if the use made of the world can be measured in non-monetary terms, maybe then the attempt to save the social bond by making all activities into work will be seen for the absurdity which it surely is. For, once again, the central problem in contemporary societies is not the growing scarcity of production but rather, first, the criteria of distribution of what is produced, and therefore the question of universal access to what remains the main vector of income distribution and of status allocation; and, second, the extreme fragility of the social bond. Has the time not come to employ some mechanism other than work as the basis for distributing the wealth of a nation and for cementing the social bond?

Returning to the utopian and contradictory expectations which humanity has of work, two points should be emphasized.

First, the idea that work, in the sense of paid participation in the production of goods and services, would be the most appropriate vehicle for personal fulfilment — as some would have it, a "positive passion".[4] This idea should be approached with extreme caution, because it contradicts the fact that work is primarily the means to an end, production, and is therefore subordinate to a force external to itself, namely the logic of ever-increasing efficiency. Also because access to fulfilling types of work is nowadays a realistic prospect for only a small part of the economically active population. And finally, because the small number of surveys of people's perceptions and aspirations show that once the issue of income is removed from the picture, individual aspirations shift to other, freely chosen activities, undertaken under different conditions, at different levels of intensity, and fulfilment ceases to depend exclusively on work. This idea needs developing: work is not the only way for individuals to find fulfilment, and if one could but recall that the reduction operated by Marx in relation to Hegel's thought consisted precisely in combining the many means of civilizing the world into the single category of work, it would become clear that what in German is called "culture" cannot and should not be reduced to work.

The time has come to restore to words their proper meaning and to stop confusing culture — the development of human capacities with all the suffering, creation, and joy that entails — with work alone, as if reading, learning, education, art, friendship, cuisine, and no doubt much else besides should all be subsumed under the heading of work. To believe that these are all merely work, to confound these highly varied activities and ways of living out one's humanity with a paid activity whose sole recompense is as a contribution to national product, is to confound action with production — yet, as Aristotle already explained, life is action not production. Stated in even clearer terms, the last two centuries have seen not the reduction of a timeless pseudo-concept of work to paid work, but rather the reduction of the entire range and variety of activities to work alone — and thus the invention of the concept of work itself.

And second, it is also time to undertake a thorough reappraisal of the idea that work is the only way to create and maintain the social bond — indeed, to question the very nature of a social bond which is shaped by work. To be sure, there will be some who say that over time work has been intimately related to economics and that economics itself creates a particular social bond in which all are needed for each individual's subsistence and in which participation in the functioning of society is linked to each person's ability to contribute to production and therefore to exchange. But is this type of social bond an adequate basis for society? As Louis Dumont and, more recently, Alain Supiot[5] and Robert Castel[6] have said, it is on account of the institution of contract and of the labour market that it became possible for a more "egalitarian" social order to emerge, for the dominance of ties of personal dependence to be overcome, and for individuals to be emancipated from traditional forms of authority. At the same time the chance to transform part of one's abilities into money, into unconstrained purchasing power, has contributed greatly to strengthening the basis of individual independence. This no one could deny, least of all women for whom this emancipation has recently progressed at an accelerated pace. But the problem is whether this is history's last word or whether, after the successive stages of communities founded on personal dependence *(Gemeinschaft)* and later on contract and personal autonomy, it is now possible, indeed indispensable, to move on to a third stage in which the advantages of the first two would be preserved and, above all, the disadvantages of contract-based societies overcome.

In other words, does the economic bond alone suffice to create a true sense of belonging, of belonging together, a true solidarity among the members of society? For that is the central issue in the debate on the social "fracture" and on social "cohesion" (two concepts which should also one day be subjected to a more critical gaze). That is undeniably the issue at stake, when the question is asked whether society can achieve a measure of cohesion and whether we have the means to implement policies to reduce the social polarization currently attracting so much attention. But before such policies can be evolved, society needs first to be represented as having a reality, a good of its own, its existence and cohesion must themselves be regarded as a good. And in that case, is there any use for the model of society and its underlying philosophy offered by the discipline of economics?

CRITIQUE OF ECONOMICS

It is reasonable to hold that contemporary economics, whose theoretical foundations are those developed by eighteenth-century economists despite the vast changes in the subject since then, continues to be based on a profoundly dated conception of humanity and society, in which society only ever appears as the external framework for autonomous individuals who conduct exchanges according to rules which, though social in nature, are still, like society, ultimately the creation of those individuals alone. Economics has kept to the individualist and contractualist assumptions of a period which never succeeded in imagining society as something more than the result of a contract between individuals who perforce lost something of themselves on their entry into that society. For the same reason, the eighteenth century was never able to imagine social riches as something more than the sum of individuals' enrichment through exchange, and had no concept of wealth as a heritage held in trust. In other words, economics sees no value in an individual's development towards a goal other than exchange, or in any form of "enrichment" of society which has a truly collective (as opposed to an aggregative) dimension or is measurable in terms other than those of "production".

For economics, then, no value can be placed either on the existence of healthy, peace-loving, happy, civically aware, tolerant, non-violent individuals, or on the establishment of a "good society", that is a just, peace-seeking, closely knit and cultivated society. Economics conceives of social wealth only in the form of increasing GNP because it continues to hold to a representation of society as a mere "collection of individuals". And it cannot develop a broader conception thereof because it continues to believe in the eighteenth-century assumptions that the expansion of wealth will suffice for individuals to become sufficiently employed and civilized so as to live together. Economists also continue to believe that increasing production is good in itself, since in that way all those vast unsatisfied needs can be met, even though for the most part this expansion does not meet the needs of the most deprived, because such issues are regarded as falling outside the subject's competence — as belonging rather to ethics. I would only recall the following from the critique of economics which I have developed at greater length elsewhere: [7] just as the invention of the contract signified an enormous step forward in the formalization of human relations in the eighteenth century and provided the basis for individual autonomy, so economics provided the extremely valuable tools which opened the way to the formalization and conceptualization of the increase in production which our countries needed, and thus underpinned a particular way of developing the world. In the process, however, economics concentrated all attention on one particular means of creating value, and concealed from view other dimensions, other means of translating human capabilities into value and developing them, in short, other ways of living in society.

Even if economists respond to this criticism by maintaining that they do not confuse growth indicators with welfare indicators, that confusion does exist, and all the more so because of the absence of the time, the space and the structures necessary to translate the world into value by means other than those measured in monetary terms. When Hegel said that civil society — the locus of political economy, needs and individual interest — should be circumscribed and integrated in a political community, he meant precisely that there are several ways of approaching the civilization of the world and of participating in the life of society: to be sure, contribution to the production of goods and services has its place, but so do political activities, religion, art, philosophy, science, and the elaboration of ever more sophisticated ways of living and cooperating, whether in the form of political institutions, rules of justice or whatever.

From the beginning of the nineteenth century a particular current of thought drew attention to the dangers arising from a purely economic approach to the development of the world, and also to the dual character of the economic bond: its emancipatory potential, but also its potential for bringing about the dissolution of established societies. Hegel and Tocqueville developed their theories at the same time and on the same theme: civil (or bourgeois) society represented the destruction of the old feudal order and the rise of a new one based on individual freedom and equality, but also contained the seeds of a new danger: the "atomization" of society, on account of its inability to preserve a minimum of solidarity and effective bonds. Hence these writers' obsessive concern to confine purely economic logic within certain limits and their desire to integrate it into a political community of rights and duties based on institutions and giving substance to the social bond. Thus it can be seen — as an entire German tradition from Hegel to Habermas, passing through Hannah Arendt, has insisted — that to make a society, and especially a good society, production alone is not enough, political institutions must also be built, loci where social bonds are forged in some other way than by mere juxtaposition in mechanical productive cooperation. It is also necessary to talk, discuss, debate, and participate, to provide not only for the sphere devoted to production, but also for the continuous existence of a public sphere set aside for debate, for specifically political activity.

Smith and Marx both believed that the social order could be founded on production, and also that these conflicts, agreements and disagreements, taken together, could be solved in the sphere of production alone. They denied the need for a specifically political sphere which could impose rules and limits on the productive sphere but also counterbalance it, raise issues and develop types of relationship having nothing to do with production of any kind. This belief seems to be shared by those who, today, disagree with the need to reduce the space occupied by work, production and economics so as to create a truly public, and therefore political, space. Such is the place taken by production that this is now thought to be virtually impossible: very little room is left between those who believe that individuals would use time freed up in this way not to take part in politics but rather to extend their leisure activities, and those who think that politics is far too serious a business to be left to the ignorant masses.

And yet, with a populist note entering the highly justified criticism of élites which has been going on, though barely audibly and quite ineffectively, perhaps the time has come to reflect on the relationship between economic and productive development on the one hand, and the "depoliticization of the masses", as Habermas calls it, on the other. The issue is not one of repoliticizing the masses, but rather of developing public spaces where choice and democracy can be effectively exercised, which means at the most local level, and in this way to redistribute not only work (and its fruits) but also political activity in the simplest, noblest and most straightforward sense of the word — namely the discussion of ends to pursue, of the means to be marshalled to attain them, and of the sharing-out of wealth and functions. In other words, the task ahead is to reduce the space occupied by work so as to make way for the activity which is essential to the long-term cohesion of societies and which has the best prospect of cementing the social bond, namely the activity of politics.

THE AMBIGUOUS NOTION OF A FULLY ACTIVE SOCIETY

This idea presupposes two simultaneous shifts: a reduction of the place taken by work in individual and social life (with the work to be done spread across the whole working population), and the development, in the time and space thus vacated by work, of new private and public activities — related on the one hand to friendship, family and emotional and cultural life, on the other to the public sphere and politics in particular — which are at least as essential to individual fulfilment and to democracy. This idea deserves the status of a normative ideal to guide action, and thus to ward off the worst of the fates now haunting society, namely polarization, fragmentation and atomization.

Other "solutions" have recently been proposed to these problems. The ideas of a universal social benefit (in recognition of the weakening link between work and income) or of the emergence of a third sector (of voluntary, "convivial" or solidarity-based activities to provide for those excluded from the formal productive sector)[8] both seem to contain the seeds of a process of polarization. Both are founded on the incapacity of an ever-increasing number of individuals to remain within the traditional productive system for whom a "softer" alternative is arranged, leading in all likelihood in the medium-to-long term to a second-rate existence compared with that led by the managers of the established productive system. A life with less security, fewer rights and lower status.

Other possible solutions remain stuck in the narrow and misguided framework of traditional indicators of wealth and continue to focus exclusively on the growth of commercial exchanges of goods and services, without any concern for the content of this growth or for its redistribution. These solutions do nothing to help solve the central issue of the quality of the individual elements constituting the social bond and offer no response to the "democratic deficit" which is as much a problem for society today as the employment deficit and the uneven distribution of work.

The normative ideal proposed here points towards what might well be called a fully active society, but only on condition that such full activity characterizes not only society as a whole but also each individual. A society in which it is acceptable that some can have good, secure and well-paid jobs, while others undertake socially useful jobs with less security and less pay, cannot avoid the risk of division.

A fully active society is one which ensures each individual access to the entire range of human activities or, more precisely, to the whole range of activities which the individual is capable of undertaking alone or as part of a group. This means that everyone should simultaneously have access to political, productive and cultural activities, as well as to the private activities involving friendship, family and emotional ties. Thus the idea of full activity goes far beyond the merely productive to encompass the entirety of human activities necessary for personal and social fulfilment in all its diversity and richness.

This does not mean replacing work with political or private activity. It means preventing productive activity from invading all the available individual and social time and space, thus permitting a new organization of the various uses individuals make of their time, and their coordination with the allocation of time by society as a whole.

With this ideal of multi-activity it will be possible to intervene legitimately in the time-space left to work: only once the value of speech, debate, education, and leisure time to our immediate surroundings and to the functioning of society itself has been demonstrated, will the formulation of consistent work and employment policies be possible.

For the time being, if these ideas appear utopian, that is because there is no scale by which to measure the benefits for society of healthy individuals, inclined to peaceful coexistence and mature discussion, untainted by racism and living in a less polluted atmosphere. And this is because of the limitations of eighteenth-century conceptions of wealth — which would be called medieval did they not date back merely two hundred years — and of the contractualist vision of society which was the cornerstone of the "science", especially the economics, of that time.

So long as the "wealth" of a society continues to be defined exclusively as the result of the commercial exchange of material goods and services — a definition roughly embodied in national accounts — one remains caught in this vicious circle. For this reason, if society aspires to the possibility one day of a careful redistribution of work among individuals, to a genuine practice of political activity in an appropriate public sphere (above all, the city) and to the articulation of different social time frames, then one must reconsider what is meant by the wealth of a society (in terms of flows but especially stock, comprising human as well as material qualities) and by the vision which underlies it.

It is possible to describe this solution as "full employment" (avoiding misleading debates on the disappearance or replacement of work, or the alarmist talk about people renouncing the goal of full employment). In this perspective, full employment would simply mean that everyone has access to employment on a fair and equitable basis, but that this employment occupies fewer hours, leaving everyone the space and time to devote to other private and collective activities.

If this is the desired form of full employment and if the real question is the best way to base the political community on solidarity and to breathe life into the social bond, then it must also be the case that the solution to the employment problem necessitates a vast public debate on the purpose of life in society, on the nature of society's riches, and on the distribution of basic goods (including work itself) which will do most to promote social cohesion.

Notes

[1] Karl Marx: "Excerpt-notes of 1844", in G. Hillman (ed.): *Texte zu Methode und Praxis*, Hamburg, 1966, pp. 180ff; translated in David McLellan: *Marx before Marxism*, London, Macmillan, 1970, p. 179. For an interpretation of Marx's concept of work, see Dominique Méda: *Le travail: une valeur en disparition*, Paris, Aubier, 1995, Ch. IV.

[2] Jürgen Habermas: "The new obscurity: The crisis of the Welfare State and the exhaustion of utopian energies", in *The new conservatism: Cultural criticism and the historian's debate*, Cambridge, Polity Press, 1989, p. 55.

[3] For further details on the way in which history is retrospectively represented, and on societies without work, see Dominique Méda, op. cit., Ch. II, "Des sociétés sans travail?".

[4] Daniel Mothé: "Le mythe du temps libéré", in *Esprit* (Paris), No. 204 (Aug.-Sep.), 1994.

[5] Alain Supiot: "Le travail, liberté partagée", in *Droit social* (Paris), No. 9/10 (Sep.), 1993, p. 715.

[6] Robert Castel: *Les métamorphoses de la question sociale: chronique du salariat*, Paris, Fayard, 1994.

[7] Dominique Méda, op. cit., Ch. VIII, "Critique de l'économie", and Ch. IX, "Réinventer la politique".

[8] As in, for example, Jeremy Rifkin: *The end of work*, New York, G. B. Putnam's Sons, 1995; or Jean-Marc Ferry: *L'allocation universelle*, Paris, Cerf, 1995.

WORK AND RIGHTS
Amartya SEN*

3

This examines four conceptual features of "decent work" which are essential to its achievement in a context of globalization. First is an inclusive approach, not just focusing on some groups of workers. Universality means facing difficult questions — some perceived conflicts of interest are real — but a comprehensive framework makes it possible to address them. The second feature is rights-based thinking which acknowledges basic rights that transcend legal recognition. The third is placing work within a broad economic, political and social context — one that includes democratic values. And fourth, the extension of thinking from international to the truly global.

This is a crucial moment in the history of working people across the world. The first flush of globalization is nearing its completion, and we can begin to take a scrutinized and integrated view of the challenges it poses as well as the opportunities it offers. The process of economic globalization is seen as a terrorizing prospect by many precariously placed individuals and communities, and yet it can be made efficacious and rewarding if we take an adequately broad approach to the conditions that govern our lives and work. There is need for well-deliberated action in support of social and political as well as economic changes that can transform a dreaded anticipation into a constructive reality.

This is also a historic moment for the ILO as custodian of workers' rights within the United Nations system. Its new Director-General — the first from outside the industrialized world — has chosen to lead the organization in a concerted effort to achieve decent work for all women

---

Originally published in *International Labour Review*, Vol. 139 (2000), No. 2.

* Master, Trinity College, Cambridge, and Lamont University Professor Emeritus, Harvard University. This chapter is based on his address to the 87th Session of the International Labour Conference, Geneva, 15 June 1999.

and men who seek it across the globe (see ILO, 1999). My own close association with the ILO goes back much more than a quarter of a century. In the seventies, I had the privilege of advising the ILO, and of doing some work for it (see, for example, Sen, 1975, 1981). But my first working association with the ILO was in 1963, when I was despatched to Cairo. Already in the 1970s I was trying to persuade the ILO to take a broad approach to the idea of working rights — though admittedly what I did then was rather crude and rough. I was trying to invoke ideas not only of rights but also of metarights. So I do particularly welcome this new initiative of the ILO to achieve decent work.

What, then, is the nature of this start, and where does all this fit into the contemporary intellectual discourse on economic arrangements, social values and political realities? I should like to identify four specific features of the approach which may be especially important to examine. I shall have the opportunity of scrutinizing only two of these issues in any detail, but I shall briefly comment on the other two distinctive features.

OBJECTIVES AND GOALS

The first important feature in the new ILO vision is the articulation of its goal: the promotion of "opportunities for women and men to obtain decent and productive work, in conditions of freedom, equity, security and human dignity" (ILO, 1999, p. 3). The reach of this objective is indeed momentously large: it includes *all* workers, wherever and in whatever sector they work; not just workers in the organized sector, nor only wage workers, but also unregulated wage workers, the self-employed, and the homeworkers. The ILO aims to respond to the terrible fact that "the world is full of overworked and unemployed people" (ILO, 1999, pp. 3, 4).

This universality of coverage, pervasiveness of concern and comprehensive conception of goals is a well-chosen alternative to acting only in the interest of *some* groups of workers, such as those in the organized sector, or those already in employment, or those already covered by explicit rules and regulations. Of course universality implies facing many difficult questions which need not arise if the domain of concern is restricted to narrower groups, such as workers in the organized sector (leaving out the unorganized sector), or even all wage workers (leaving out homeworkers), or even all people actively in work (leaving out the unemployed).

The case for choosing such a broad focus rests on the importance of a comprehensive approach. There are different parts of the working population whose fortunes do not always move together, and in furthering the interests and demands of one group, it is easy to neglect the interests and demands of others. Indeed, it has often been alleged that labour organizations sometimes confine their advocacy to very narrow groups, such as unionized workers, and that narrowness of the outlook can feed the neglect of legitimate concerns of other groups and also of the costs imposed on them (unorganized labourers, or family-based workers, or the long-term unemployed, for example). Similarly (on the other side), by focusing specifically on the interests of workers in the informal sector, it is also possible to neglect the hard-earned gains of people in organized industry, through an attempt — often recommended (if only implicitly) — to level them down to the predicament of unorganized and unprotected workers.

Working people fall into distinct groups with their own specific concerns and plights, and it behoves the ILO to pay attention simultaneously to the diverse concerns that are involved. Given the massive levels of unemployment that exist in many countries of the world today — indeed even in the rich economies of western Europe — it is right that policy attention be focused on expanding jobs and work opportunities. And yet the conditions of work are important too. It is a question of placing the diverse concerns within a comprehensive assessment, so that the curing of unemployment is not treated as a reason for doing away with reasonable conditions of work of those already employed, nor is the protection of the already-employed workers used as an excuse to keep the jobless in a state of social exclusion from the labour market and employment. The need for trade-offs is often exaggerated and is typically based on very rudimentary reasoning. Further, even when trade-offs have to be faced, they can be more reasonably — and more justly — addressed by taking an inclusive approach, which balances competing concern, than by simply giving full priority to just one group over another.

The aged and the unemployed

The need for a broad and inclusive approach can be well illustrated by referring to another issue — that of ageing and the dependency ratio — which is often juxtaposed, in an unexamined way, to the problem of unemployment and availability of work. There are two principles in some tension with each other that are frequently invoked simultaneously in dealing with these different issues in an intellectually autarchic way.

Addressing the growing proportion of the aged population, it is often lamented that since old people cannot work, they have to be supported by those who are young enough to work. This leads inescapably to a sharp increase in the so-called dependency ratio. As it happens, this fact itself demands more scrutiny. There is, in fact, considerable evidence that the increase in longevity that has resulted from medical achievements has also elongated the disability-free length of working lives over which a person can work (see, for example, Manton, Corder and Stallard,

1997). The possibility of elongating working lives is further reinforced by the nature of technical progress that makes less demand on physical strength.

This being the case, it is natural to suggest that one way of reducing the burden of dependency related to ageing is to raise the retirement age — or at least give people in good health the option to go on working. In resisting this proposal, it is frequently argued that if this were done, then the aged will replace the younger workers and there will be more unemployment among the young. But this argument is in real tension with the previous claim that the root of the problem lies in the fact that old people cannot work, and the young who can work have to support the old.

If health and working ability ultimately determine how much work can potentially be done (and certainly social and economic arrangements can be geared to make sure that to a great extent the potential is realized), then surely the trade-off with youthful unemployment is a real *non sequitur*. The absolute size of the working population does not, in itself, cause more unemployment; for example, it is not the case that countries with a larger working population typically have a larger proportion of unemployment (consider the United States compared to France or Italy or Spain or Belgium). There are many big issues to be faced in scrutinizing proposals for revising the retirement age, but linking unemployment to the absolute size of the working population does not enrich this discussion. Indeed, we see here a messy argument based on combining two mutually contrary gut reactions: (i) the gut reaction that the source of the problem related to an ageing population is that the old cannot work and the young must support them; and (ii) the gut reaction that the young must lose jobs if the older people do work. The combination of these unscrutinized feelings is to produce a hopeless impasse which rides just on unexamined possibilities, based on a simple presumption of conflict that may or may not actually exist.

The practice of being driven by imagined conflicts and being led by partisan solutions is as counterproductive in dealing with issues of ageing and employment as it is in addressing the problem of working conditions on one hand and the need for employment on the other. Conflicts cannot be made to *go away* by simply ignoring them on behalf of one group or another. Nor need conflicts invariably *arise* merely because some elementary textbook reasoning suggests that they might conceivably exist, under certain hypothesized conditions. There is a need for facing empirical possibilities with open-mindedness. There is also a need for openly addressing ethical issues involving conflict, when it does arise, through balancing the interests of groups with contrary interests, rather than giving total priority to the interests of one group against another.

Child labour and its prevention

Similar questions arise in dealing with the difficult problem of child labour. It is often claimed that the abolition of child labour will harm the interests of the children themselves since they may end up starving because of a lack of family income and also because of increased neglect. It is certainly right that the fact of family poverty must be considered in dealing with this issue. But it is not at all clear why it must be presumed that the abolition of child labour will lead only to a reduction of family income and further neglect of children, without any other economic or social or educational adjustment. In fact, that would be a particularly unlikely scenario for "the worst forms of child labour" (slavery, bondage, prostitution, trafficking) which are the focus of the recently adopted Convention concerning the prohibition and immediate action for the elimination of the worst forms of child labour (Convention No. 182 (1999)).

The case for a broader and more inclusive economic analysis and ethical examination is very strong in all these cases. One must not fall prey to unexamined prejudices or premature pessimism.

RIGHTS OF THE WORKING PEOPLE

The second conceptual feature that needs to be stressed is the idea of rights. Along with the formulation of overall objectives, the domain of practical reasoning extends beyond the aggregative objectives to the recognition of rights of workers.

What makes this rights-based formulation particularly significant is that the rights covered are not confined only to established labour legislation, nor only to the task — important as it is — of establishing new legal rights through fresh legislation. Rather, the evaluative framework begins with acknowledging certain basic rights, whether or not they are legislated, as being a part of a decent society.[1] The practical implications that emanate from this acknowledgement can go beyond new legislation to other types of social, political and economic actions.

The framework of rights-based thinking extends to ethical claims that transcend legal recognition. This is strongly in line with what is becoming increasingly the United Nations' general approach to practical policy through rights-based reasoning. The framework of rights-based thinking is thus extended from the pure domain of legality to the broader arena of social ethics. These rights can thus be seen as being *prior* (rather than posterior) to legal recognition. Indeed, social acknowledgement of these rights can be taken to be an invitation to the State to catch up with social ethics. But the invitation is not merely to produce fresh legislation — important as it is — since the realization of rights can also be helped by other developments, such as creation of new institutions, better working of existing ones and, last but not the least, by a general societal commitment to work for appropriate functioning of social, political and economic arrangements to facilitate widely recognized rights.[2]

There are really two contrasts here: one between legal rights and socially accepted principles of justice, and another between rights-based reasoning and goal-based formulations of social ethics. In scrutinizing the approach, we have to ask how well rights-based reasoning integrates with goal-based programming. These two basic precepts have sometimes been seen, especially by legal theorists, as providing alternative ethical outlooks that are in some tension with each other (see, for example, Dworkin, 1977). Are we to be guided, in case of a conflict, by the primacy of our social goals, or by the priority of individual rights? Can the two perspectives be simultaneously invoked without running into an internal contradiction? I believe that the two approaches are not really in tension with each other, provided they are appropriately formulated. However, the underlying methodological question has to be addressed, and I shall briefly examine the reasons for thinking that there is no deep conflict here.[3]

Rights and goals

The question that has to be faced is this: why cannot the fulfilment of rights be among the goals to be pursued? The presumption that there must be a conflict here has indeed been asserted, but the question is why we should accept this claim. There will quite possibly be a real impasse here if we want to make the fulfilment of each right a matter of absolute adherence (with no room for give and take and no possibility of acceptable trade-offs), as some libertarians do. But most rights-based reasoning in political debates, for example on human rights, need not — and indeed does not — take that form.

If the formulation is carefully done to allow trade-offs that have to be faced, then it is indeed possible to value the realization of rights as well as the fulfilment of other objectives and goals. The rights at work can be broadly integrated within the same overall framework which also demands opportunities for women and men to obtain decent and productive work, in conditions of freedom, equity, security and human dignity. To pay attention to any of these demands does not require us to ignore — or override — all other concerns. For example, the rights of those at work can be considered along with — and not instead of — the interests of the unemployed.

Rights and obligations

There is a different type of question that is sometimes raised, focusing on the relation between rights and duties. Some have taken the view that rights can be sensibly formulated only in combination with correlated duties. Those who insist on that binary linkage tend to be very critical, in general, of any discussion of rights (for example, invoking the rhetoric of "human rights") without specification of responsible agents and their duties to bring about the fulfilment of these rights. Demands for human rights are then seen just as loose talk. And similar scepticism is aimed at such statements as "all those who work have rights at work".

A basic concern that motivates some of this scepticism is: how can we be sure that rights are, in fact, realizable unless they are matched by corresponding duties? Indeed, some do not see any sense in a right unless it is balanced by what Immanuel Kant called a "perfect obligation" — a specific duty of a particular agent for the actual realization of that right (Kant, 1788).

This presumption can be the basis of rejection of rights-based thinking in many areas of practical reason. Indeed, aside from general scepticism that tends to come from many lawyers, there are also distinguished philosophers who have argued in favour of the binary linkage between rights and exact duties of specified individuals or agencies (see, for example, O'Neill, 1996).

We can, however, ask: why this insistence? Why demand the absolute necessity of a co-specified perfect obligation for a potential right to qualify as a real right? Certainly, a perfect obligation would help a great deal towards the realization of rights, but why cannot there be *unrealized* rights? We do not, in any obvious sense, contradict ourselves by saying: "These people had all these rights, but alas they were not realized, because they were not institutionally grounded." Something else has to be invoked to jump from pessimism about the *fulfilment* of rights, all the way to the *denial* of the rights themselves.

This distinction may appear to be partly a matter of language, and it might be thought that the rejection can be based on how the term "rights" functions in common discourse. But in public debates and discussion the term "rights" is used much more widely than would be permitted by the insistence on strict binary relations. Perhaps the perceived problem arises from an implicit attempt to see the use of rights in political or moral discourse through a close analogy with rights in a legal system, with its demand for specification of correlated duties. In contrast, in normative discussions rights are often championed as entitlements or powers or immunities which it would be good for people to have. Human rights are seen as rights shared by all — irrespective of citizenship — advantages that everyone *should* have. The claims are addressed generally (and as Kant might say, "imperfectly") to anyone who can help, even though no particular person or agency may be charged to bring about singlehandedly the fulfilment of the rights involved. Even if it is not feasible that everyone can have the fulfilment of their rights in this sense (if, for example, it is not yet possible to eliminate undernourishment altogether), credit can still be taken for the *extent* to which these alleged rights are fulfilled. The recognition of such claims as rights may not only be an ethically important statement, it can also help to focus attention on these matters, making their fulfilment that much more likely — or quicker.

This is indeed the form in which many major champions of rights-based thinking have tried to use the idea of rights, going back all the way to Tom Paine and Mary Wollstonecraft.[4] The invoking of the idea of rights is neither in tension with a broadly goal-based ethical framework, nor ruled out by some presumed necessity of perfect obligations allegedly needed to make sense of the idea of rights. The broad approach can be defended not just in terms of good commonsense appeal, but also in terms of capturing the variety of values and concerns that tend to arise in public discussions and demands.

SOCIAL AND POLITICAL BROADENING

Another distinguishing feature of the approach is that it situates conditions of work and employment within a broad economic, political and social framework. It addresses, for example, not merely the requirements of labour legislation and practice, but also the need for an open society and the promotion of social dialogue. The lives of working people are, of course, directly affected by the rules and conventions that govern their employment and work, but they are also influenced, ultimately, by their freedoms as citizens with a voice who can influence policies and even institutional choices.

In fact, it can be shown that "protection against vulnerability and contingency" is, to a great extent, conditional on the working of democratic participation and the operation of political incentives. I have argued elsewhere that it is a remarkable fact in the history of famines that famines do not occur in democracies. Indeed, no substantial famine has ever occurred in a democratic country — no matter how poor.[5] This is because famines are, in fact, extremely easy to prevent if the government tries to prevent them, and a government in a multi-party democracy with elections and a free media has strong political incentives to undertake famine prevention. This would indicate that political freedom in the form of democratic arrangements helps to safeguard economic freedom (especially from extreme starvation) and the freedom to survive (against famine mortality).

The security provided by democracy may not be sorely missed when a country is lucky enough to be facing no serious calamity, when everything is running along smoothly. But the danger of insecurity arising from changes in economic or other circumstances (or from uncorrected mistakes of policy) can lurk solidly behind what looks like a healthy state. This is an important connection to bear in mind in examining the political aspects of the recent "Asian economic crisis".

The problems of some of the east and south-east Asian economies bring out, among other things, the penalty of undemocratic governance. This is so in two striking respects, involving the neglect of two crucial instrumental freedoms, viz. "protective security" (what we have been just discussing) and "transparency guarantee" (an issue that is closely linked with the provision of adequate incentives to economic and political agents). Both relate directly or indirectly to safeguarding decent work and to promoting decent lives.[6]

Taking the latter issue first, the development of the financial crisis in some of these economies was closely linked with the lack of transparency in business, in particular the lack of public participation in reviewing financial and business arrangements. The absence of an effective democratic forum has been consequential in this failing. The opportunity that would have been provided by democratic processes to challenge the hold of selected families or groups — in several of these countries — could have made a big difference.

The discipline of financial reform that the International Monetary Fund tried to impose on the economies in default was, to a great extent, necessitated by the lack of openness and disclosure, and the involvement of unscrupulous business linkages, that were characteristic in parts of these economies. The point here is not to comment on whether the IMF's management of the crises was exactly right, or whether the insistence on immediate reforms could have been sensibly postponed until financial confidence had returned in these economies. No matter how these adjustments would have been best done, the contribution of the lack of transparency and freedom in predisposing these economies to economic crises cannot be easily doubted.

The pattern of risk and improper investments, especially by politically influential families, could have been placed under much greater scrutiny if democratic critics had demanded this in, say, Indonesia or South Korea. But of course neither of these countries then had the democratic system that would have encouraged such demands to come from outside the government. The unchallenged power of the rulers was easily translated into an unquestioned acceptance of the lack of accountability and openness, often reinforced by strong family links between the government and the financial bosses. In the emergence of the economic crises, the undemocratic nature of the governments played an important part.

Second, once the financial crisis led to a general economic recession, the protective power of democracy — not unlike that which prevents famines in democratic countries — was badly missed. The newly dispossessed did not have the hearing they needed. A fall of total gross national product of, say, even 10 per cent may not look like much, if it follows the experience of past economic growth of 5 or 10 per cent every year for some decades. And yet that decline can ruin lives and create misery for millions if the burden of contraction is not shared together but allowed to be heaped on those — the unemployed or those newly made economically redundant — who can least bear it. The vulnerable in Indonesia may not have missed democracy acutely when things went up and up, but that very lacuna kept their voice muffled and ineffective as the unequally shared crisis developed. The protective role of democracy is strongly missed when it is most needed.

The comprehensive view of society that informs the approach adopted in the ILO vision of decent work (ILO, 1999) provides a more promising understanding of the needs of institutions and policies in pursuit of the rights and interests of working people. It is not adequate to concentrate only on labour legislation since people do not live and work in a compartmentalized environment. The linkages between economic, political and social actions can be critical to the realization of rights and to the pursuit of the broad objectives of decent work and adequate living for working people.

INTERNATIONAL VERSUS GLOBAL

I turn now to the fourth and final distinctive feature of the approach under discussion. While an organization such as the ILO has to go beyond national policies (without overlooking the instrumental importance of actions by governments and societies within nations), there is a critical distinction between an "international" approach and a "global" one. An *international* approach is inescapably parasitic on the relation between nations, since it works through the intermediary of distinct countries and nations. In contrast, a truly *global* approach need not see human beings only as (or even primarily as) citizens of particular countries, nor accept that the interactions between citizens of different countries must be inevitably intermediated through the relations between distinct nations. Many global institutions, including those central to our working lives, have to go well beyond the limits of "international" relations.[7]

The beginnings of a truly global approach can be readily detected in the analysis underlying the new directions of the ILO. The increasingly globalized world economy calls for a similarly globalized approach to basic ethics and political and social procedures. The market economy itself is not merely an international system; its global connections extend well beyond the relation between nations. Capitalist ethics, with its strong as well as weak points, is a quintessentially global culture, not just an international construct. In dealing with conditions of working lives as well as the interests and rights of workers in general, there is a similar necessity to go beyond the narrow limits of international relations.

A global approach is, of course, a part of the heritage of labour movements in world history. This rich heritage — often neglected in official discussions — can indeed be fruitfully invoked in rising to the challenges of decent work in the contemporary world. A universalist understanding of work and working relations can be linked to a tradition of solidarity and commitment. The need for invoking such a global approach has never been stronger than it is now. The economically globalizing world, with all its opportunities as well as problems, calls for a similarly globalized understanding of the priority of decent work and of its manifold demands on economic, political and social arrangements. To recognize this pervasive need is itself a hopeful beginning.

Notes

[1] A key instrument that reflects this is the ILO Declaration on Fundamental Principles and Rights at Work. For the full text of that 1998 Declaration and for helpful discussion, see the special issue of the *International Labour Review* on "Labour Rights, Human Rights" (Vol. 137 (1998), No. 2, pp. 253-257 and pp. 223-227 respectively).

[2] This and related issues are discussed in Sen, 1999a.

[3] I have discussed these issues in Sen, 1982a, 1985 and forthcoming.

[4] Tom Paine's *Rights of man* and Mary Wollstonecraft's *A vindication of the rights of woman* were both published in 1792.

[5] I have discussed this in Sen, 1982b and 1984; and jointly with Jean Drèze in Drèze and Sen, 1989.

[6] I have investigated these connections in Sen, 1999a.

[7] I have discussed the distinctions involved in Sen, 1999b.

References

Drèze, Jean; Sen, Amartya. 1989. *Hunger and public action*. Oxford, Clarendon Press.

Dworkin, Ronald. 1977. *Taking rights seriously*. London, Duckworth.

ILO. 1999. *Decent work*. Report of the Director-General of the ILO to the 87th Session of the International Labour Conference. Geneva.

Kant, Immanuel. 1788. *Critique of practical reason*. Translated by L. W. Beck. New York, NY, Bobbs-Merrill, 1956.

Manton, Kenneth G.; Corder, Larry; Stallard, Eric. 1997. "Chronic Disability Trends in Elderly United States Populations: 1982-1994", in *Proceedings of the National Academy of Sciences*, No. 94 (March 1997).

O'Neill, Onora. 1996. *Towards justice and virtue*. Cambridge, Cambridge University Press.

Paine, Thomas. 1792. *Rights of man: Being an answer to Mr. Burke's attack on the French Revolution*. Boston, Faust.

Sen, Amartya. Forthcoming. "Consequential evaluation and practical reason", in *Journal of Philosophy* (New York).

—. 1999a. *Development as freedom*. New York, NY, Alfred A. Knopf, and Oxford, Oxford University Press.

—. 1999b. "Global justice: Beyond international equity", in Inge Kaul, Isabelle Grunberg and Marc A. stern (eds.): *Global public goods: International cooperation in the 21st century*. New York, Oxford University Press.

Women, gender and work

—. 1985. "Well-being, agency and freedom: Dewey Lectures 1984", in *Journal of Philosophy* (New York), Vol. 82.

—. 1984. *Resources, values and development*. Cambridge, MA, Harvard University Press.

—. 1982a. "Rights and agency", in *Philosophy and Public Affairs* (Princeton), Vol. 11.

—. 1982b. "Development: Which way now?", in *Economic Journal* (Oxford), Vol. 92, Dec.

—. 1981. *Poverty and famines: An essay on entitlement and deprivation*. A study prepared for the ILO within the framework of the World Employment Programme. Oxford, Clarendon Press.

—. 1975. *Employment, technology and development*. A study prepared for the ILO within the framework of the World Employment Programme. Oxford, Clarendon Press.

Wollstonecraft, Mary. 1792. *A vindication of the rights of woman: With strictures on political and moral subjects*. Boston, Thomas and Andrews. Text available online at: http://www.constitution.org/woll/row.txt [visited on 11 May 2000].

WOMEN AND EQUALITY: THE CAPABILITIES APPROACH

Martha NUSSBAUM*

4

Human dignity, involving the idea of equal worth, is the starting point in this cross-cultural application of the capabilities approach to the question of equality. As a formulation of the objective it transcends the conventional criteria of preference satisfaction and resource allocation. Focusing on what fully human beings are able to be and to do, a set of distinct human functional capabilities to guide political planning is suggested. While each component helps to define the quality of life, the capability for practical reason and affiliation suffuse the others, for they help to define what it is to be truly human.

I found myself beautiful as a free human mind.

> Mrinal, in Rabindranath Tagore's "Letter from a wife" (1990, p. 102)

It is obvious that the *human* eye gratifies itself in a way different from the crude, non-human eye; the human *ear* different from the crude ear, etc. ...The *sense* caught up in crude practical need has only a *restricted* sense. For the starving man, it is not the human form of food that exists, but only its abstract being as food; it could just as well be there in its crudest form, and it would be impossible to say wherein this feeding activity differs from that of *animals*.

> Marx, *Economic and Philosophical Manuscripts* (1844)

SEX AND SOCIAL JUSTICE

Human beings have a dignity that deserves respect from laws and social institutions. This idea has many origins in many traditions; by now it is at the core of modern democratic thought and practice all over the

---

Originally published in *International Labour Review*, Vol. 138 (1999), No. 3.

* Ernst Freund Professor of Law and Ethics, The Law School, The Divinity School, and the Departments of Philosophy and of Classics, The University of Chicago.

world. The idea of human dignity is usually taken to involve an idea of *equal* worth: rich and poor, rural and urban, female and male, all are equally deserving of respect, just in virtue of being human, and this respect should not be abridged on account of a characteristic that is distributed by the whims of fortune. Often, too, this idea of equal worth is connected to ideas of freedom and opportunity: to respect the equal worth of persons is, among other things, to promote their ability to fashion a life in accordance with their own view of what is deepest and most important.

But human dignity is frequently violated on grounds of sex. Many women all over the world find themselves treated unequally with respect to employment, bodily safety and integrity, basic nutrition and health care, education and political voice. In many cases these hardships are caused by their being women, and in many cases laws and institutions construct or perpetuate these inequalities. All over the world, women are resisting inequality and claiming the right to be treated with respect.

But how should we think about this struggle? What account shall we use of the goals to be sought and the evils to be avoided? We cannot avoid using some normative framework that crosses cultural boundaries when we think of concepts such as women's "quality of life" their "living standard" their "development" and their "basic entitlements". All of these are normative concepts, and require us to defend a particular normative position if we would use them in any fruitful way. In default of an alternative, development economics will supply some less than perfect accounts of norms and goals, such as increased GNP per capita, or preference satisfaction. (These approaches are criticized below.) This chapter first addresses the worries that arise when we attempt to use any cross-cultural framework in talking about improvements in women's lives. Next, the dominant economic approaches are examined. Finally, there is a defence of the "capabilities approach", an approach to the priorities of development that focuses not on preference satisfaction but on what people are actually able to do and to be. It is argued that this approach is the most fruitful for such purposes, that it has good answers to the problems that plague the other approaches.[1]

THE NEED FOR CROSS-CULTURAL OBJECTIVES

Before we can advance further defending a particular account of the objectives of development, we must face a challenge that has recently arisen, both in feminist circles and in discussions of international development policy. The question that must be confronted is whether we should be looking for a set of cross-cultural objectives in the first place, where women's opportunities are concerned. Obviously enough, women are already doing that in many areas. Women in the informal sector, for example, are increasingly organizing on an international level to set goals and priorities.[2] But this process is controversial, both intellectually and politically. Where do these normative categories come from? — it will be asked. And how can they be justified as appropriate for cultures that have traditionally used different normative categories? The challenge asks us to defend our entire procedure, showing that it is not merely an exercise of colonial power.

Now of course no critical social theory confines itself to the categories of each culture's daily life. If it did, it probably could not perform its special task as theory, which involves the systematization and critical scrutiny of intuitions that in daily life are often unexamined. Theory gives people a set of terms with which to criticize abuses that otherwise might lurk nameless in the background. Terms such as "sexual harassment" and "hostile work environment" are some obvious examples of this point. But even if one defends theory as in general valuable for practice, it may still be problematic to use concepts that originate in one culture to describe and assess realities in another — and all the more problematic if the culture described has been colonized and oppressed by the describer's culture. For such reasons, attempts by international feminists today to use a universal language of justice, human rights, or human functioning to assess the lives of women in developing countries is bound to encounter charges of Westernizing and colonizing — even when the universal categories are introduced by activists who live and work within the very countries in question. For, it is standardly said, such women are alienated from their culture, and are faddishly aping a Western political agenda.

Sometimes this objection is simply a political stratagem to discredit opponents who are pressing for change. The right reply to such strategies is to insist on the indigenous origins of the demand for change, and to unmask the interested motives of the objector. But sometimes, too, a similar objection is made in good faith by thinkers about culture. Three standard arguments are heard, all of which must be honestly confronted.

First, one hears what is called here the *argument from culture*. Traditional cultures, the argument goes, contain their own norms of what women's lives should be: frequently norms of female modesty, deference, obedience and self-sacrifice. Feminists should not assume without argument that those are bad norms, incapable of constructing good and flourishing lives for women. By contrast, the norms proposed by feminists seem to this opponent suspiciously "Western", because they involve an emphasis on choice and opportunity.

An answer to this argument will emerge from the proposal to be made here. It certainly does not preclude any woman's choice to lead a traditional life, so long as she does so with certain economic and political opportunities firmly in place. But we should begin by emphasizing that the notion of tradition used in the argument is far too simple. Cultures are scenes of debate and contestation. They contain dominant voices, and they also contain the voices of women, which have not always been heard. It would be implausible to suggest that the many groups working to improve the employment conditions of women in the informal sector, for example, are brainwashing women into striving for economic opportunities: clearly, they provide means to ends women already want, and a context of female solidarity within which to pursue those ends. Where they do alter existing preferences, they typically do so by giving women a richer sense of both their own possibilities and their equal worth, in a way that looks more like a self-realization (as Tagore's heroine vividly states) than like brainwashing. Indeed, what may possibly be "Western" is the arrogant supposition that choice and economic agency are solely Western values! In short, because cultures are scenes of debate, appealing to culture gives us questions rather than answers. It certainly does not show that cross-cultural norms are a bad answer to those questions.

Let us now consider the argument called here the *argument from the good of diversity*. This argument reminds us that our world is rich in part because we do not all agree on a single set of practices and norms. We think the world's different languages have worth and beauty, and that it would be a bad thing, diminishing the expressive resources of human life generally, if any language should cease to exist. So, too, cultural norms have their own distinctive beauty; the world risks becoming impoverished as it becomes more homogeneous.

Here we should distinguish two claims the objector might be making. She might be claiming that diversity is good as such; or she might simply be saying that there are problems with the values of economic efficiency and consumerism that are increasingly dominating our interlocking world. This second claim, of course, does not yet say anything against cross-cultural norms; it just suggests that their content should be critical of some dominant economic norms. So the real challenge to our enterprise lies in the first claim. To meet it we must ask how far cultural diversity really is like linguistic diversity. The trouble with the analogy is that languages do not harm people, whereas cultural practices frequently do. We could think that threatened languages such as Cornish and Breton should be preserved, without thinking the same about domestic violence: it is not worth preserving simply because it is there and very old. In the end, then, the objection doesn't undermine the search for cross-cultural norms, it requires it: for what it invites us to ask is whether the cultural values in question are among the ones worth preserving, and this entails at least a very general cross-cultural framework of assessment — one that will tell us when we are better off letting a practice die out.

Finally, we have the *argument from paternalism*. This argument says that when we use a set of cross-cultural norms as benchmarks for the world's varied societies, we show too little respect for people's freedom as agents (and, in a related way, their role as democratic citizens). People are the best judges of what is good for them, and if we say that their own choices are not good for them we treat them like children. This is an important point, and one that any viable cross-cultural proposal should bear firmly in mind. But it hardly seems incompatible with the endorsement of cross-cultural norms. Indeed, it appears to endorse explicitly at least some cross-cultural norms, such as the political liberties and other opportunities for choice. Thinking about paternalism gives us a strong reason to respect the variety of ways citizens actually choose to lead their lives in a pluralistic society, and therefore to seek a set of cross-cultural norms that protect freedom and choice of the most significant sorts. But this means that we will naturally value religious toleration, associative freedom, and the other major liberties. These liberties are themselves cross-cultural norms, and they are not compatible with the views that many real people and societies hold.

We can make a further claim: many existing value systems are themselves highly paternalistic, particularly toward women. They treat them as unequal under the law, as lacking full civil capacity, as not having the property rights, associative liberties and employment rights of males. If we encounter a system like this, it is in one sense paternalistic to say, sorry, that is unacceptable under the universal norms of equality and liberty that we would like to defend. In that way, any bill of rights is "paternalistic" vis à vis families, or groups, or practices, or even pieces of legislation, that treat people with insufficient or unequal respect. The Indian Constitution, for example, is in that sense paternalistic when it tells people that it is from now on illegal to use caste or sex as grounds of discrimination. But that is hardly a good argument against fundamental constitutional rights or, more generally, against opposing the attempts of some people to tyrannize others. We dislike paternalism because there is something else that we like, namely liberty of choice in fundamental matters. It is fully consistent to reject some forms of paternalism while supporting those that underwrite these basic values.

Nor does the protection of choice require only a formal defence of basic liberties. The various liberties of choice have material preconditions, in whose absence there is merely a simulacrum of choice. Many women who have in a sense the "choice" to go to school simply cannot do so: the economic circumstances of their lives make this impossible. Women who "can" have economic independence, in the sense that no law prevents them, may be prevented simply by lacking assets, or access to credit. In short, liberty is not just a matter of having rights on paper, it requires being in a material position to exercise those rights. And this requires resources. The State that is going to guarantee people rights effectively is going to have to recognize norms beyond the small menu of basic rights: it will have to take a stand about the redistribution of wealth and income, about employment, land rights, health, education. If we think that these norms are important cross-culturally, we will need to take an international position on pushing toward these goals. That requires yet more universalism and in a sense paternalism; but we could hardly say that the many women who live in abusive or repressive marriages and have no assets and no opportunity to seek employment outside the home are especially free to do as they wish.

The argument from paternalism indicates, then, that we should prefer a cross-cultural normative account that focuses on empowerment and opportunity, leaving people plenty of space to determine their course in life once those opportunities are secured to them. It does not give us any good reason to reject the whole idea of cross-cultural norms, and gives some strong reasons why we should seek such norms, including in our account not only the basic liberties, but also forms of economic empowerment that are crucial in making the liberties truly available to people. And the argument suggests one thing more: that the account we search for should seek empowerment and opportunity for each and every person, respecting each as an end, rather than simply as the agent or supporter of ends of others. Women are too often treated as members of an organic unit, such as the family or the community is supposed to be, and their interests subordinated to the larger goals of that unit, which means, typically, those of its male members. However, the impressive economic growth of a region means nothing to women whose husbands deprive them of control over household income. We need to consider not just the aggregate, whether in a region or in a family; we need to consider the distribution of resources and opportunities *to each person*, thinking of each as worthy of regard in her own right.

THE DEFECTS OF TRADITIONAL ECONOMIC APPROACHES

Another way of seeing why cross-cultural norms are badly needed in the international policy arena is to consider what the alternative has typically been. The most prevalent approach to measuring quality of life in a nation used to be simply to ask about GNP per capita. This approach tries to weasel out of making any cross-cultural claims about what has value — although, notice, it does assume the universal value of opulence. What it omits, however, is much more significant. We are not even told about the distribution of wealth and income, and countries with similar aggregate figures can exhibit great distributional variations. Circus girl Sissy Jupe, in Dickens's *Hard Times* (1854), already saw the problem with this absence of normative concern for distribution: she says that the economic approach doesn't tell her "who has got the money and whether any of it is mine". So, too, with women around the world: the fact that one nation or region is in general more prosperous than another is only a part of the story — it doesn't tell us what government has done for women in various social classes, or how they are doing. To know that, we would need to look at their lives; but then we need to specify, beyond distribution of wealth and income itself, what parts of lives we ought to look at — such as life expectancy, infant mortality, educational opportunities, health care, employment opportunities, land rights, political liberties. Seeing what is absent from the GNP account nudges us sharply in the direction of mapping out these and other basic goods in a universal way, so that we can use the list of basic goods to compare quality of life across societies.

A further problem with all resource-based approaches, even those that are sensitive to distribution, is that individuals vary in their ability to convert resources into functionings. Some of these differences are straightforwardly physical. Nutritional needs vary with age, occupation and sex. A pregnant or lactating woman needs more nutrients than a non-pregnant woman. A child needs more protein than an adult. A person whose limbs work well needs few resources to be mobile, whereas a person with paralysed limbs needs many more resources to achieve the same level of mobility. Many such variations can escape our notice if we live in a prosperous nation that can afford to bring all individuals to a high level of physical attainment; in the developing world we must be highly alert to these variations in need. Again, some of the pertinent variations are social, connected with traditional hierarchies. If we wish to bring all citizens of a nation to the same level of educational attainment, we will need to devote more resources to those who encounter obstacles from traditional hierarchy or prejudice: thus women's literacy will prove more expensive than men's literacy in many parts of the world. If we operate only with an index of resources, we will frequently reinforce inequalities that are highly relevant to well-being.

If we turn from resource-based approaches to preference-based approaches, we encounter another set of difficulties.[3] Preferences are not exogenous, given independently of economic and social conditions. They are at least in part constructed by those conditions. Women often have no preference for economic independence before they learn about avenues through which women like them might pursue this goal; nor do they think of themselves as citizens with rights that were being ignored, before they learn of their rights and are encouraged to believe in their equal worth. All of these ideas, and the preferences based on them, frequently take shape for women in programmes of education sponsored by women's organizations of various types. Men's preferences, too, are socially shaped and often misshaped. Men frequently have a strong preference that their wives should do all the childcare and all the housework — often in addition to working an eight-hour day. Such preferences, too, are not fixed in the nature of things: they are constructed by social traditions of privilege and subordination. Thus a preference-based approach typically will reinforce inequalities: especially those inequalities that are entrenched enough to have crept into people's very desires.

THE CAPABILITIES APPROACH

A reasonable answer to all these concerns — capable of giving good guidance to government establishing basic constitutional principles and to international agencies assessing the quality of life — is given by a version of the *capabilities approach* — an approach to quality of life assessment pioneered within economics by Amartya Sen,[4] and by now highly influential through the *Human Development Reports* of the UNDP (see UNDP, 1993, 1994, 1995, 1996, 1997, 1998, 1999).[5] The version of this approach argued here is in several ways different from Sen's; it is laid out as currently defended.

The central question asked by the capabilities approach is not, "How satisfied is this woman?" or even "How much in the way of resources is she able to command?" It is, instead, "What is she actually able to do and to be?" Taking a stand for political purposes on a working list of functions that would appear to be of central importance in human life, users of this approach ask: "Is the person capable of this, or not?" They ask not only about the person's satisfaction with what she does, but about what she does, and what she is in a position to do (what her opportunities and liberties are). They ask not just about the resources that are present, but about how those do or do not go to work, enabling the woman to function.

The intuitive idea behind the approach is twofold: first, that there are certain functions that are particularly central in human life, in the sense that their presence or absence is typically understood to be a mark of the presence or absence of human life. Second — and this is what Marx found in Aristotle — that there is something that it is to do these functions in a truly human way, not a merely animal way. We judge, frequently enough, that a life has been so impoverished that it is not worthy of the dignity of the human being, that it is a life in which one goes on living, but more or less like an animal, not being able to develop and exercise one's human powers. In Marx's example, a starving person cannot use food in a fully human way — by which he seems to mean a way infused by practical reasoning and sociability. He or she just grabs at the food in order to survive, and the many social and rational ingredients of human feeding cannot make their appearance. Similarly, the senses of a human being can operate at a merely animal level — if they are not cultivated by appropriate education, by leisure for play and self-expression, by valuable associations with others; and we should add to the list some items that Marx probably would not endorse, such as expressive and associational liberty, and the freedom of worship. The core idea is that of the human being as a dignified free being who shapes his or her own life, rather than being passively shaped or pushed around by the world in the manner of a flock or herd animal.

At one extreme, we may judge that the absence of capability for a central function is so acute that the person is not really a human being at all, or any longer — as in the case of certain very severe forms of mental disability, or senile dementia. But that boundary is of lesser interest (important though it is for medical ethics) than is a higher one, the level at which a person's capability is "truly human", that is, *worthy* of a human being. The idea thus contains a notion of human worth or dignity.

Notice that the approach makes each person a bearer of value, and an end. Marx, like his bourgeois forebears, holds that it is profoundly wrong to subordinate the ends of some individuals to those of others. That is at the core of what exploitation is, to treat a person as a mere object for the use of others. What this approach is after is a society in which individuals are treated as each worthy of regard, and in which each has been put in a position to live really humanly.

It is possible to produce an account of these necessary elements of truly human functioning that commands a broad cross-cultural consensus, a list that can be endorsed for political purposes by people who otherwise have very different views of what a complete good life for a human being would be. The list is supposed to provide a focus for quality of life assessment and for political planning, and it aims to select capabilities that are of central importance, whatever else the person pursues. They therefore have a special claim to be supported for political purposes in a pluralistic society.[6]

The list represents the result of years of cross-cultural discussion,[7] and comparisons between earlier and later versions will show that the input of other voices has shaped its content in many ways. It remains open-ended and humble; it can always be contested and remade. Nor does it deny that the items on the list are to some extent differently constructed by different societies. Indeed part of the idea of the list is that those items can be more concretely specified in accordance with local beliefs and circumstances. The box below sets out the current version of functional capabilities.

The list of capabilities is, emphatically, a list of separate components. We cannot satisfy the need for one of them by giving people a larger amount of another one. All are of central importance and all are distinct in quality. The irreducible plurality of the list limits the trade-offs that it will be reasonable to make, and thus limits the applicability of quantitative cost-benefit analysis. At the same time, the items on the list are related to one another in many complex ways. One of the most effective ways of promoting women's control over their environment, and their effective right of political participation, is to promote women's literacy. Women who can seek employment outside the home have more resources in protecting their bodily integrity from assaults within it. Such facts give us still more reason not to promote one capability at the expense of the others.

Among the capabilities, two, practical reason and affiliation, stand out as being of special importance, since they both organize and suffuse all the others, making their pursuit truly human. To use one's senses in a

Central human functional capabilities

1. **Life.** Being able to live to the end of a human life of normal length; not dying prematurely, or before one's life is so diminished as to be not worth living.

2. **Bodily health.** Being able to have good health, including reproductive health;* to be adequately nourished; to have adequate shelter.

3. **Bodily integrity.** Being able to move freely from place to place; to be secure against violent assault, including sexual assault and domestic violence; having opportunities for sexual satisfaction and for choice in matters of reproduction.

4. **Senses, imagination and thought.** Being able to use the senses, to imagine, think and reason — and to do these things in a "truly human" way, a way informed and cultivated by an adequate education, including, but by no means limited to, literacy and basic mathematical and scientific training. Being able to use imagination and thought in connection with experiencing and producing works and events of one's own choice, religious, literary, musical, and so forth. Being able to use one's mind in ways protected by guarantees of freedom of expression with respect to both political and artistic speech, and freedom of religious exercise. Being able to have pleasurable experiences, and to avoid non-necessary pain.

5. **Emotions.** Being able to have attachments to things and people outside ourselves; to love those who love and care for us, to grieve at their absence; in general, to love, to grieve, to experience longing, gratitude, and justified anger. Not having one's emotional development blighted by fear and anxiety. (Supporting this capability means supporting forms of human association that can be shown to be crucial in people's development.)

6. **Practical reason.** Being able to form a conception of the good and to engage in critical reflection about the planning of one's life (which entails protection for the liberty of conscience).

7. **Affiliation.**

A. Being able to live with and toward others, to recognize and show concern for other human beings, to engage in various forms of social interaction; to be able to imagine the situation of another and to have compassion for that situation; to have the capability for both justice and friendship. (Protecting this capability means protecting institutions that constitute and nourish such forms of affiliation, and also protecting the freedom of assembly and political speech.)

B. Having the social bases of self-respect and non-humiliation; being able to be treated as a dignified being whose worth is equal to that of others. This entails protections against discrimination on the basis of race, sex, sexual orientation, religion, caste, ethnicity, or national origin.

8. **Other species.** Being able to live with concern for and in relation to animals, plants and the world of nature.

9. **Play.** Being able to laugh, to play, to enjoy recreational activities.

10. **Control over one's environment.**

A. Political. Being able to participate effectively in political choices that govern one's life; having the right of political participation, protections of free speech and association.

B. Material. Being able to hold property (both land and movable goods); having the right to seek employment on an equal basis with others; having freedom from unwarranted search and seizure. In work, being able to work as a human being, exercising practical reason and entering into meaningful relationships of mutual recognition with other workers.

---

*The 1994 International Conference on Population and Development (ICPD) adopted a definition of reproductive health that fits well with the intuitive idea of truly human functioning that guides this list: "Reproductive health is a state of complete physical, mental and social well-being and not merely the absence of disease or infirmity, in all matters relating to the reproductive system and to its functions and processes. Reproductive health therefore implies that people are able to have a satisfying and safe sex life and that they have the capability to reproduce and the freedom to decide if, when and how often to do so" (United Nations, 1995, p. 40, para. 7.2). The definition goes on to say that it also implies information and access to family planning methods of their choice. A brief summary of the ICPD's recommendations, adopted by the Panel on Reproductive Health of the Committee on Population established by the National Research Council specifies three requirements of reproductive health: "1. Every sex act should be free of coercion and infection. 2. Every pregnancy should be intended. 3. Every birth should be healthy" (see Tsui, Wasserheit and Haaga, 1997, p. 14).

way not infused by the characteristically human use of thought and planning is to use them in an incompletely human manner. Tagore's heroine describes herself as "a free human mind" — and this idea of herself infuses all her other functions. At the same time, to reason for oneself without at all considering the circumstances and needs of others is, again, to behave in an incompletely human way.

The basic intuition from which the capability approach begins, in the political arena, is that human abilities exert a moral claim that they be developed. Human beings are creatures such that, provided with the right educational and material support, they can become fully capable of these human functions. That is, they are creatures with certain lower-level capabilities (called here "basic capabilities"[8]) to perform the functions in question. When these capabilities are deprived of the nourishment that would transform them into the high-level capabilities that figure on the list, they are fruitless, cut off, in some way but a shadow of themselves. If a turtle were given a life that afforded a merely animal level of functioning, we would have no indignation, no sense of waste and tragedy. When a human being is given a life that blights powers of human action and expression, that does give us a sense of waste and tragedy — the tragedy expressed, for example, in Tagore's heroine's statement to her husband, when she says, "I am not one to die easily." In her view, a life without dignity and choice, a life in which she can be no more than an appendage, was a type of death of her humanity.

We begin, then, with a sense of the worth and dignity of basic human powers, thinking of them as claims to a chance for functioning, claims that give rise to correlated social and political duties. And in fact there are three different types of capabilities that play a role in the analysis. First, there are *basic capabilities*: the innate equipment of individuals that is the necessary basis for developing the more advanced capability, and a ground of moral concern. Second, there are *internal capabilities*: that is, states of the person herself that are, so far as the person herself is concerned, sufficient conditions for the exercise of the requisite functions. A woman who has not suffered genital mutilation has the *internal capability* for sexual pleasure; most adult human beings everywhere have the *internal capability* for religious freedom and the freedom of speech. Finally, there are *combined capabilities*, which may be defined as internal capabilities *combined with* suitable external conditions for the exercise of the function. A woman who is not mutilated but who has been widowed as a child and is forbidden to remarry has the internal but not the combined capability for sexual expression — and, in most such cases, for employment, and political participation (see Chen, forthcoming and 1995). Citizens of repressive non-democratic regimes have the internal but not the combined capability to exercise thought and speech in accordance with their conscience. The above list, then, is a list of *combined capabilities*. To realize one of the items on the list entails not only promoting appropriate development of people's internal powers, but also preparing the environment so that it is favourable for the exercise of practical reason and the other major functions.

OBJECTIVES OF DEVELOPMENT: FUNCTIONING AND CAPABILITY

We have considered both functioning and capability. How are they related? Getting clear about this is crucial in defining the relation of the "capabilities approach" to our concerns about paternalism and pluralism. For if we were to take functioning itself as the goal of public policy, a liberal pluralist would rightly judge that we were precluding many choices that citizens may make in accordance with their own conceptions of the good. A deeply religious person may prefer not to be well-nourished, but to engage in strenuous fasting. Whether for religious or for other reasons, a person may prefer a celibate life to one containing sexual expression. A person may prefer to work with an intense dedication that precludes recreation and play. Does the declaration of the list mean that these are not fully human or flourishing lives? Does it mean to instruct government to nudge or push people into functioning of the requisite sort, no matter what they prefer?

It is important that the answer to these questions is no. Capability, not functioning, is the appropriate political goal. This is so because of the very great importance the approach attaches to practical reason, as a good that both suffuses all the other functions, making them fully human, and also figures, itself, as a central function on the list. The person with plenty of food may always choose to fast, but there is a great difference between fasting and starving, and it is this difference that we wish to capture. Again, the person who has normal opportunities for sexual satisfaction can always choose a life of celibacy, and the approach says nothing against this. What it does speak against (for example) is the practice of female genital mutilation, which deprives individuals of the opportunity to choose sexual functioning and, indeed, the opportunity to choose celibacy as well (see Nussbaum, 1999, chaps. 3-4). A person who has opportunities for play can always choose a workaholic life; again, there is a great difference between that chosen life and a life constrained by insufficient maximum-hour protections and/or the "double day" that makes women unable to play in many parts of the world.

Once again, we must stress in this context that the objective is to be understood in terms of *combined capabilities*. To secure a capability to a person it is not sufficient to produce good internal states of readiness to act. It is necessary, as well, to prepare the material and institutional environment so that people are actually able to function. Women burdened by the "double day" may be *internally* incapable of play — if, for example, they have been kept indoors and zealously guarded since infancy, married at age six, and forbidden to engage in the kind of imaginative exploration that male children standardly enjoy. Young girls in rural Rajasthan, for example, have great difficulty *learning* to play in an educational programme run by local activists — because their capacity for play has not been nourished early in childhood. On the other hand, there are also many women in the world who are perfectly capable of play in the internal sense, but unable to play because of the crushing demands of the "double day". Such a woman does not have the *combined capability* for play in the sense intended by the list. Capability is thus a demanding notion. In its focus on the environment of choice, it is highly attentive to the goal of functioning, and instructs governments to keep it always in view. On the other hand, it does not push people into functioning: once the stage is fully set, the choice is theirs.

CAPABILITIES AND THE HUMAN RIGHTS MOVEMENT

One might construct a view based on the idea of capabilities without giving a large place to the traditional political rights and liberties, which have historically been so central to the international human rights movement. Thus one might imagine a capabilities approach that diverged sharply from the international human rights approach. The version of the capabilities approach presented here, however, by making the idea of human choice and freedom central, entails a strong protection for these traditional rights and liberties. The political liberties have a central importance in making well-being human. A society that aims at well-being while overriding these has delivered to its members an incompletely human level of satisfaction. As Amartya Sen has recently written, "Political rights are important not only for the fulfilment of needs, they are crucial also for the formulation of needs. And this idea relates, in the end, to the respect that we owe each other as fellow human beings" (Sen, 1994, p. 38).[9] There are many reasons to think that political liberties have an instrumental role in preventing material disaster (in particular famine[10]), and in promoting economic well-being. But their role is not merely instrumental: they are valuable in their own right.

Thus capabilities have a very close relationship to human rights, as understood in contemporary international discussions. In effect they encompass the terrain covered by both the so-called first-generation rights (political and civil liberties) and the so-called second-generation rights (economic and social rights). Further, the list incorporates some sex-specific rights (in the area of bodily integrity, for example) that have been strongly defended by feminists in the human rights movement, and added, with some struggle, to international human rights instruments. The role played by capabilities is also very similar to that played by human rights:

they provide the philosophical underpinning for basic constitutional principles. Because the language of rights is well-established, the defender of capabilities needs to show what is added by this new language.[11]

The idea of human rights is by no means crystal clear. Rights have been understood in many different ways, and difficult theoretical questions are frequently obscured by the use of rights language, which can give the illusion of agreement where there is deep philosophical disagreement. People differ about what the *basis* of a rights claim is: rationality, sentience, and mere life have all had their defenders. They differ, too, about whether rights are prepolitical or artifacts of laws and institutions. (Kant held the latter view, although the dominant human rights tradition has held the former.) They differ about whether rights belong only to individual persons, or also to groups. They differ about whether rights are to be regarded as side-constraints on goal-promoting action (meaning that one may pursue one's other goals only within the constraints imposed by people's rights), or rather as one part of the social goal that is being promoted. (The latter approach permits trade-offs between rights and other goals, whereas the former makes rights sacrosanct.) They differ, again, about the relationship between rights and duties: if A has a right to S, then does this mean that there is always someone who has a duty to provide S, and how shall we decide who that someone is? They differ, finally, about what rights are to be understood as rights *to*. Are human rights primarily rights to be treated in certain ways? Rights to a certain level of achieved well-being? Rights to resources with which one may pursue one's life plan? Rights to certain opportunities and capacities with which one may make choices about one's life plan?

The account of central capabilities has the advantage of taking clear positions on these disputed issues, while stating clearly what the motivating concerns are and what the goal is. Bernard Williams put this point eloquently, commenting on Sen's 1987 Tanner Lectures:

> I am not very happy myself with taking rights as the starting point. The notion of a basic human right seems to me obscure enough, and I would rather come at it from the perspective of basic human capabilities. I would prefer capabilities to do the work, and if we are going to have a language or rhetoric of rights, to have it delivered from them, rather than the other way round (Williams, 1987, p. 100).

As Williams says, however, the relationship between the two concepts needs further scrutiny, given the dominance of rights language in the international development world.

In some areas, the best way of thinking about what rights are is to see them as capabilities. The right to political participation, the right to religious free exercise, the right of free speech — these and others are all best thought of as capacities to function. In other words, to secure a right to a citizen in these areas is to put them (both in terms of their internal powers and in terms of their material and institutional environment) in a position of capability to function in that area. (Of course there is another sense of "right" that is more like "basic capabilities": people have a right to religious freedom just in virtue of being human, even if the state they live in has not guaranteed them this freedom.) By defining rights in terms of capabilities, we make it clear that a people in country C don't really have the right to political participation just because this language exists on paper: they really have this right only if there are effective measures to make people truly capable of political exercise. Women in many nations have a nominal right of political participation without having this right in the sense of capability: for example, they may be threatened with violence should they leave the home. In short, thinking in terms of capability gives us a benchmark as we think about what it is really to secure a right to someone.

There is another set of rights, largely those in the area of property and economic advantage, which seem analytically different in their relationship to capabilities. Take, for example, the right to shelter and housing. These are rights that can be analysed in a number of distinct ways: in terms of resources, or utility (satisfaction), or capabilities. (Once again, we must distinguish the claim that "A has a right to shelter" — which frequently refers to A's moral claim in virtue of being human — from the statement that "country C gives its citizens the right to shelter". It is the second sentence whose analysis is being discussed here.) Here again, however, it seems valuable to understand these rights in terms of capabilities. If we think of the right to shelter as a right to a certain amount of resources, then we get into the very problem discussed above: giving resources to people does not always bring differently situated people up to the same level of capability to function. The utility-based analysis also encounters a problem: traditionally deprived people may be satisfied with a very low living standard, believing that this is all they have any hope of getting. A capabilities analysis, by contrast, looks at how people are actually enabled to live. Analysing economic and material rights in terms of capabilities thus enables us to set forth clearly a rationale we have for spending unequal amounts of money on the disadvantaged, or creating special programmes to assist their transition to full capability.

The language of capabilities has one further advantage over the language of rights: it is not strongly linked to one particular cultural and historical tradition, as the language of rights is believed to be. This belief is not very accurate: although the term "rights" is associated with the European Enlightenment, its component ideas have deep roots in many traditions.[12] Where India is concerned, for example, even apart from the recent validation of rights language in Indian legal and constitutional traditions, the salient component ideas have deep roots in far earlier areas of Indian thought — in ideas of religious toleration developed since the edicts of Ashoka in the third century BC, in the thought about Hindu/Muslim relations in the Mogul Empire, and, of course, in many progressive and humanist thinkers of the nineteenth and twentieth centuries, who certainly cannot be described simply as Westernizers, with no respect for their own traditions (see Sen, 1997a).[13] Tagore portrays the conception of freedom used by the young wife in his story as having ancient origins in Indian traditions, in the quest of Rajput queen Meerabai for joyful self-expression. (Meerabai left her privileged palace life to become an itinerant singer, joyfully pursuing both independence and art.) The idea of herself as "a free human mind" is represented as one that she derives, not from any external infusion, but from a combination of experience and history.

So "rights" are not exclusively Western, in the sense that matters most; they can be endorsed from a variety of perspectives. None the less, the language of capabilities enables us to bypass this troublesome debate. When we speak simply of what people are actually able to do and to be, we do not even give the appearance of privileging a Western idea. Ideas of activity and ability are everywhere, and there is no culture in which people do not ask themselves what they are able to do, what opportunities they have for functioning. Certainly in international discussions of women's work, ideas of control over the conditions of one's activity are absolutely central, and nobody would suggest that these ideas are exclusively Western. They arise when women get together to discuss what they want, and what their lives lack.

If we have the language of capabilities, do we also need the language of rights? The language of rights still plays four important roles in public discourse, despite its unsatisfactory features. First, when used in the first way, as in the sentence "A has a right to have the basic political liberties secured to her by her government", this language reminds us that people have justified and urgent claims to certain types of urgent treatment, no matter what the world around them has done about that. As suggested earlier, this role of rights language lies very close to "basic capabilities", in the sense that the *justification for* saying that people have such natural rights usually proceeds by pointing to some capability-like feature of persons (rationality, language) that they actually have at least on a rudimentary level. And without such a justification the appeal to rights is quite mysterious. However, there is no doubt that one might recognize the basic capabilities of people and yet still deny that this entails that they have rights in the sense of justified claims to certain types of treatment. We know that this inference has not been made through a great deal of the world's history. So appealing to rights communicates more than does the bare appeal to basic capabilities, without any further ethical argument of the sort supplied here. Rights language indicates that we do have such an argument and that we draw strong normative conclusions from the fact of the basic capabilities.

Second, even at the next level, when we are talking about rights guaranteed by the State, the language of rights places great emphasis on the importance and the basic role of the corresponding spheres of ability. To say, "Here's a list of things that people ought to be able to do and to be" has only a vague normative resonance. To say, "Here is a list of fundamental rights", is more rhetorically direct. It tells people right away that we are dealing with an especially urgent set of functions, backed up by a sense of the justified claim that all humans have to such things, in virtue of being human.

Third, rights language has value because of the emphasis it places on people's choice and autonomy. The language of capabilities was designed to leave room for choice, and to communicate the idea that there is a big difference between pushing people into functioning in ways you consider valuable and leaving the choice up to them. But there are approaches using an Aristotelian language of functioning and capability that do not emphasize liberty in the way that the approach presented in this article does: Marxist Aristotelianism and some forms of Catholic Thomist Aristotelianism are illiberal in this sense. If we have the language of rights in play as well, it helps us to lay extra emphasis on the important fact that the appropriate political goal is the ability of people to choose to function in certain ways, not simply their actual functionings.

Finally, in the areas where we disagree about the proper analysis of rights talk — where the claims of utility, resources, and capabilities are still being worked out — the language of rights preserves a sense of the terrain of agreement, while we continue to deliberate about the proper type of analysis at the more specific level.

CAPABILITIES AS OBJECTIVES FOR WOMEN'S DEVELOPMENT

Legitimate concerns for diversity, pluralism and personal freedom are not incompatible with the recognition of cross-cultural norms. Indeed, cross-cultural norms are actually required if we are to protect diversity, pluralism, and freedom, treating each human being as an agent and an end. The best way to hold all these concerns together is to formulate the objectives as a set of capabilities for fully human functioning, emphasizing the fact that capabilities protect, and do not close off, spheres of human freedom.

Used to evaluate the lives of women who are struggling for equality in many different countries, developing and developed, the capabilities framework does not look like an alien importation: it squares pretty well with demands women are already making in many global and national political contexts. It might therefore seem superfluous to put these items on a list: why not just let women decide what they will demand in each case? To answer that question, we should point out that the international development debate is already using a normative language. Where the capabilities approach has not caught on — as it has in the *Human Development Reports* of the UNDP — a much less adequate theoretical language still prevails, whether it is the language of preference-satisfaction or the language of economic growth. We need the capabilities approach as a humanly rich alternative to these inadequate theories of human development.

Women all over the world have lacked support for central human functions, and that lack of support is to some extent caused by their being women. But women, unlike rocks and trees, have the potential to become capable of these human functions, given sufficient nutrition, education and other support. That is why their unequal failure in capability is a problem of justice. It is up to all human beings to solve this problem. A cross-cultural conception of human capabilities gives us good guidance as we pursue this difficult task.

Notes

[1] More extensive versions of the arguments made here (and more case studies from development work in India) can be found in Nussbaum (forthcoming, chap. 1). For earlier articulations of the author's views on capabilities see Nussbaum (1988, 1990, 1992, 1993, 1995a, 1995b, 1997a, 1997b and 1999, chap. 1, pp. 29-54).

[2] See WIEGO (1999); the steering committee of WIEGO (Women in Informal Employment: Globalizing and Organizing) includes Ela Bhatt of SEWA, and Martha Chen, who has been a leading participant in discussions of the "capabilities approach" at the World Institute for Development Economics Research, in the "quality of life" project directed by Martha Nussbaum and Amartya Sen (see Chen, 1995).

[3] Nussbaum (forthcoming, chap. 2) gives an extensive account of economic preference-based approaches, arguing that they are defective without reliance on a substantive list of goals such as that provided by the capabilities approach.

[4] The initial statement is in Sen, 1980 (reprinted in Sen, 1982); see also various essays in Sen (1984, 1985a, 1985b, 1992, 1993 and 1995) and Drèze and Sen (1989 and 1995).

[5] For related approaches in economics, see Dasgupta (1993), Agarwal (1994), Alkire (1999), Anand and Harris (1994), Stewart (1996), Pattanaik (1998), Desai (1990), Chakraborty (1996). For discussion of the approach, see Aman (1991) and Basu, Pattanaik and Suzumura (1995).

[6] Obviously, this is a broader view of the political than is that of many theorists in the Western liberal tradition, for whom the nation state remains the basic unit. It envisages not only domestic deliberations but also cross-cultural quality of life assessments and other forms of international deliberation and planning.

[7] For some examples of the academic part of these discussions, see Verma (1995), Chen (1995), Nzegwu (1995), Valdes (1995), and Li (1995).

[8] See the fuller discussion in Nussbaum (forthcoming, chap. 1).

[9] Compare Rawls (1996, pp. 187-188), who connects freedom and need in a related way.

[10] Sen (1981) argues that free press and open political debate are crucial in preventing food shortage from becoming full-blown famine.

[11] The material of this section is further developed in Nussbaum (1997b).

[12] On India and China, see Sen (1997a); see also Taylor (1999).

[13] On Tagore, see Sen (1997b) and Bardhan (1990). For the language of rights in the Indian independence struggles, see Nehru, 1936, p. 612.

References

Agarwal, Bina. 1994. *A field of one's own: Gender and land rights in South Asia.* Cambridge, Cambridge University Press.

Alkire, Sabina. 1999. *Operationalizing Amartya Sen's capability approach to human development: A framework for identifying valuable capabilities.* Unpublished D. Phil. Dissertation. Oxford, Oxford University.

Aman, K. (ed.). 1991. *Ethical principles for development: Needs, capabilities or rights.* Montclair, N J, Montclair State University Press.

Anand, Sudhir; Harris, Christopher J. 1994. "Choosing a welfare indicator", in *American Economic Review* (Nashville, TN), Vol. 84, No. 2 (May), pp. 226-231.

Bardhan, Kalpana. 1990. "Introduction", in Kalpana Bardhan (ed.): *Of women, outcastes, peasants, and rebels: A selection of Bengali short stories.* Berkeley, CA, University of California Press, pp. 1-49.

Basu, Kanshik; Pattanaik, Prasanta; Suzumura, Kataro (eds.). 1995. *Choice, welfare, and development: A festschrift in honour of Amartya K. Sen.* Oxford, Clarendon Press.

Chakraborty, Achin. 1996. *The concept and measurement of the standard of living.* Unpublished Ph.D. Thesis. Riverside, CA, University of California at Riverside.

Chen, Martha A. Forthcoming. *Perpetual mourning: Widowhood in rural India.* Delhi, Oxford University Press/Philadelphia, PA, University of Pennsylvania Press.

—. 1995. "A matter of survival: Women's right to employment in India and Bangladesh", in Nussbaum and Glover, pp. 37-57.

Dasgupta, Partha. 1993. *An inquiry into well-being and destitution.* Oxford, Clarendon Press.

Desai, Meghnad. 1990. "Poverty and capability: Towards an empirically implementable measure". Suntory-Toyota International Centre Discussion Paper No. 27. London, London School of Economics, Development Economics Research Programme.

Dickens, Charles. 1854. *Hard times.* London, Bantam Classic, 1991.

Drèze, Jean; Sen, Amartya. 1995. *India: Economic development and social opportunity.* Delhi, Oxford University Press.

—; —. 1989. *Hunger and public action.* Oxford, Clarendon Press.

Li, Xiaorong. 1995. "Gender inequality in China and cultural relativism", in Nussbaum and Glover, pp. 407-425.

Marx, Karl. 1844. "Economic and philosophical manuscripts", in Penguin Classics (ed.): *Karl Marx: Early writings.* London, Penguin, 1992.

Nehru, Jawaharlal. 1936. *Autobiography.* The centenary edition. Delhi, Oxford University Press, 1986.

Nussbaum, Martha. Forthcoming. *Women and human development: The capabilities approach.* Cambridge, Cambridge University Press.

—. 1999. *Sex and social Justice.* New York, NY, Oxford University Press.

—. 1997a. "The good as discipline, the good as freedom", in David A. Crocker and Toby Linden (eds.): *Ethics of consumption: The good life, justice, and global stewardship.* Lanham, MD, Rowman and Littlefield, pp. 312-411.

—. 1997b. "Capabilities and human rights", in *Fordham Law Review* (New York , NY), Vol. 66, No. 2 (Nov.), pp. 273-300.

—. 1995a. "Aristotle on human nature and the foundations of ethics", in J. E. J. Altham and Ross Harrison (eds.): *World, mind and ethics: Essays on the ethical philosophy of Bernard Williams.* Cambridge, Cambridge University Press, pp. 86-131.

—. 1995b. "Human capabilities, female human beings", in Nussbaum and Glover, pp. 61-104.

—. 1993. "Non-relative virtues: An Aristotelian approach", in Martha Nussbaum and Amartya Sen (eds.): *The quality of life*. Oxford, Clarendon Press, pp. 242-276.

—. 1992. "Human functioning and social justice: In defence of Aristotelian essentialism" in *Political Theory* (Thousand Oaks, CA), Vol. 20, No. 2, pp. 202-246.

—. 1990. "Aristotelian social democracy", in R. Bruce Douglass, Gerald Mara and Henry Richardson (eds.): *Liberalism and the good*. New York, NY, Routledge, pp. 203-252.

—. 1988. "Nature, function, and capability: Aristotle on political distribution", in *Oxford Studies in Ancient Philosophy* (Oxford), Supplementary Vol. 1, pp. 145-184.

—; Glover, Jonathan (eds.). 1995. *Women, culture, and development: A study of human capabilities*. A study prepared for the World Institute for Development Economics Research (WIDER) of the United Nations University. Oxford, Clarendon Press.

Nzegwu, Nkiru. 1995. "Recovering Igbo traditions: A case for indigenous women's organizations in development", in Nussbaum and Glover, pp. 444-465.

Pattanaik, Prasanta. 1998. "Cultural indicators of well-being: Some conceptual issues", in UNESCO (ed.): *World Culture Report: Culture, creativity, and markets*. Paris, UNESCO, pp. 333-339.

Rawls, John. 1996. *Political liberalism*. New York, NY, Columbia University Press.

Sen, Amartya. 1997a. "Human rights and Asian values", in *The New Republic* (Washington, DC), 14-21 July, pp. 33-41.

—. 1997b. "Tagore and his India", in *New York Review of Books* (New York, NY), 26 June, pp. 55-63.

—. 1995. "Gender inequality and theories of justice", in Nussbaum and Glover, pp. 153-198.

—. 1994. "Freedoms and needs", in *The New Republic* (Washington, DC), 10-17 Jan., pp. 31-38.

—. 1993. "Capability and well-being", in Martha Nussbaum and Amartya Sen (eds.): *The quality of life*. Oxford, Clarendon Press, pp. 30-53.

—. 1992. *Inequality reexamined*. Oxford, Clarendon Press/Cambridge, MA, Harvard University Press.

—. 1985a. *Commodities and capabilities*. Amsterdam, North-Holland.

—. 1985b. "Well-being, agency, and freedom: The Dewey Lectures", in *Journal of Philosophy* (New York, NY), Vol. 82, No. 4 (Apr.), pp. 169-220.

—. 1984. *Resources, values, and development*. Oxford, Basil Blackwell/Cambridge, MA, MIT Press.

—. 1982. *Choice, welfare, and measurement*. Oxford, Basil Blackwell/Cambridge, MA, MIT Press.

—. 1981. *Poverty and famines: An essay on entitlement and deprivation*. Oxford, Clarendon Press.

—. 1980. "Equality of what?", in S. McMurrin (ed.): *The Tanner Lectures on Human Values — Volume 1*. Cambridge, Cambridge University Press.

Stewart, Frances. 1996. "Basic needs, capabilities, and human development", in Avner Offer (ed.): *In pursuit of the quality of Life*. Oxford, Oxford University Press.

Tagore, Rabindranath. 1990. "Letter from a wife", in Bardhan, pp. 96-109.

Taylor, Charles. 1999. "Conditions of an unforced consensus on human rights", in Joanne R. Bauer and Daniel A. Bell (eds.): *The East Asian challenge for human rights*. Cambridge, Cambridge University Press, pp. 124-146.

Tsui, Amy O.; Wasserheit, Judith N.; Haaga, John G. (eds.). 1997. *Reproductive health in developing countries*. Washington, DC, National Academy Press.

UNDP. Various years. *Human Development Report 1993-1999*. New York, NY, United Nations Development Programme.

United Nations. 1995. *Report of the International Conference on Population and Development — Cairo, 5-13 September 1994*. Document A/CONF.171/13/Rev.1. New York, NY.

Valdés, Margarita M. 1995. "Inequality in capabilities between men and women in Mexico", in Nussbaum and Glover, pp. 426-432.

Verma, Roop Rekha. 1995. "Femininity, equality, and personhood", in Nussbaum and Glover, pp. 433-443.

WIEGO. 1999. *Report on the proceedings of the Annual Meeting and Public Seminar, 12-14 April*. Ottawa.

Williams, Bernard. 1987. "The standard of living: Interests and capabilities", in Amartya Sen and Geoffrey Hawthorn (eds.): *The standard of living*. Cambridge, Cambridge University Press, pp. 94-102.

PART III

STATISTICS AND INFORMATION:
WHAT DO WE KNOW?

GENDER ISSUES IN LABOUR STATISTICS

Adriana MATA GREENWOOD*

5

The process of producing labour statistics inevitably simplifies reality, highlighting certain aspects and ignoring others, depending on the priorities and objectives involved and the data collection methods available. The main features needed for labour statistics to reflect fully and in all their diversity the respective situations of women and men in the labour market are presented. And the topics needing to be covered and the detail required for significant distinctions to emerge are identified, and how the choice of measurement method and the manner of data presentation can influence the final result is explained.

Labour statistics describe the numbers, structure, characteristics and contributions of the participants in the labour market and how these change over time. Conventionally, they cover many topics concerning the size and structure of the labour force and the characteristics of workers and employers. From an economic perspective, these statistics are necessary for analysing, evaluating and monitoring the way the economy is performing and the effectiveness of current and longer-term economic policies. From a social perspective, they are also necessary for designing policies and programmes for job creation, training and retraining schemes, and for assisting vulnerable groups, including the young, the old, women, etc., in finding and securing employment. To serve users, labour statistics need to reflect reality as closely as possible. This means that they should comprehensively cover all persons who actually participate in the labour market, and should describe their various work situations in equal detail and depth.

Originally published in *International Labour Review*, Vol. 138 (1999), No. 3.

* ILO Bureau of Statistics, Geneva. This article is adapted from an ILO Bureau of Statistics working paper, *Incorporating gender issues in labour statistics* (forthcoming).

However, the production of statistics requires that reality be simplified — codified — into synthetic categories which highlight certain aspects of this reality while ignoring others. Whether these aspects are highlighted or ignored depends mainly on the *available methods of data collection* and on the *priorities and objectives* of the data collection process. The various methods of data collection all have their limitations, and measurement priorities depend to a large extent on the perceptions society has of how the labour market functions — perceptions which are not immutable. As a result, national labour statistics have generally been successful at identifying and characterizing "core" employment and unemployment situations, which reflect the conventional view of what "work" and "joblessness" are all about: i.e. workers in full-time regular employment in formal sector enterprises and persons who are looking for such jobs. They have been less successful at identifying and describing other work situations.

Women are often to be found in these other work situations, which may go unnoticed or be inadequately described in labour statistics (United Nations, 1991). The validity of labour statistics would therefore be enhanced by a better understanding of what women do and how they behave in the labour market. Attempts to reflect as fully as possible women's work as compared with men's would reveal the statistics' strengths and shortcomings and would provide indications of how and where they can be improved. There are other reasons justifying such an endeavour. First, it would provide more complete information to users of the statistics, such as market analysts and policy decision-makers, which is important because men and women often do very different types of work and labour market changes tend to affect them differently. Second, it would enable users to understand and analyse female workers' particular position and constraints as compared with those of male workers, and would provide a more solid basis for promoting equality between the sexes in the labour market. For the systematic under-reporting and misrepresentation of women's contribution to the economy help maintain a distorted perception of the nature of a country's economy and its human resources, and thus perpetuate a vicious circle of inequality between men and women, and inappropriate policies and programmes.

So, it is important to establish the characteristics labour statistics need to acquire before they can fully reflect the similarities and differences in the respective situations of men and women in the labour market. This chapter seeks to establish the most important of these characteristics.

GENDER ISSUES IN LABOUR STATISTICS

It is generally accepted that inequality between men and women stems from attitudes, prejudices and assumptions concerning the different roles assigned to men and women in society (Overholt et al., 1984). These roles, which are learned, e.g., those of parent, housekeeper, provider of basic needs, etc., largely determine the type of work men and women do. For example, given their traditional role as homemakers, more female than male workers tend to combine economic activities with household (non-economic) activities, to work intermittently over the year and to work closer to home, often even at home for pay or in a family enterprise for family profit. Furthermore, because of their assigned role as dependent members of the household, women tend to be relatively more active than men in non-market activities and in the informal sector; to be considered by others and even by themselves as economically inactive; to receive less education, and thus to be more confined in occupations requiring lower skills and paying less well; to be considered as secondary workers in their family enterprise even when they have equal responsibility; and, in times of economic downturn or structural adjustment, to be amongst the first dismissed from their paid jobs. In addition, women find it hard to break through the "glass ceiling", which blocks their access to managerial or decision-making positions. Given structural constraints due to family responsibilities, women who are available and willing to work tend actively to seek work much less than men in the same situation, and employers tend to be reluctant to employ women outside typically female occupations.

Another area of gender differentiation is the allocation of resources and benefits among the members of a household. It has been observed, for example, that women who are self-employed have more limited access to production resources than men, which lowers their income (Dixon-Mueller and Anker, 1990). Furthermore, women do not necessarily have control over their use of the resources available to them, nor do they necessarily reap the full benefits accruing from their efforts. Women's and men's gender roles also determine their different needs and constraints. For example, the degree to which women actually participate in and contribute to the production process is highly dependent on their marital status, on whether they have small children, and on whether they have to care for other persons in their households. Men's participation in and contribution to the production process are also affected by these factors, but not in a constraining way.

In order to improve the description of the labour market and to provide a solid basis for promoting equality between women and men, gender differences such as those described above need to be considered when labour statistics are produced. Consequently, when determining which topics to include and how to define, measure and present them, one must consider how to reflect the distinct contributions, constraints and needs of women and of men in the resulting statistics.

TOPICS TO COVER

Statistics are needed on the numbers of men and women producing the goods and services in a country (the employed population) and on the numbers of men and women exerting pressure on the labour market for jobs (the unemployed population). Various subgroups of the employed population are especially important for such an analysis:

— persons who, though working, are in jobs with insufficient hours of work (the population in time-related, or visible, underemployment);

— persons whose jobs are ill suited to them for other, labour-market related reasons (the population in inadequate employment situations);

— persons who work in small, unregistered economic units (those employed in the informal sector); and

— children who are in inappropriate work situations (child labour).

These population groups need to be further subdivided into more homogeneous categories, according to other work-related characteristics, for instance:

— occupation, given that men and women generally do very different jobs;

— employment status, in view of the steady decline of regular wage employment and the increase in other employment situations, such as casual and temporary/seasonal employment and self-employment, where men and women are present in different degrees;

— income from employment, given the pervasive difference between men's and women's income levels in all countries even after correcting for hours worked and level of education;

— working time, in order to provide a more accurate measure of their participation in the labour market;[1]

— participation in industrial disputes, as women are said to be more passive and less unionized than men, and may tend to be indirectly rather than directly implicated in industrial action and to work in industries less prone to industrial disputes;

— statistics of occupational injuries, given that men and women do very different jobs and thus face very different hazards.

All these topics are conventionally covered in national labour statistical programmes, as established by the ILO's Labour Statistics Convention, 1985 (No. 160), and therefore international guidelines on their measurement exist.[2]

However, it is clear that the topics likely to increase understanding of men's and women's position and interrelation in the labour market go well beyond those covered by conventional labour statistics. For example, information is needed on:

— the numbers of persons who "work" in the wider sense of the term, i.e. including workers producing goods and services for own consumption, given women's significant participation in these types of activity;

— workers' working-time arrangements, to indicate the degree to which men and women work in what is known as "regular full-time" working schedules or in more irregular schedules, such as intermittent or part-time employment, annualized working hours and other variable time schedules;

— overtime work, to evaluate whether establishments' responses to changing market demand affect men and women in different ways;

— absence from work, to indicate any differences in the types of absence taken by men and women, in particular in view of family responsibilities;

— occupational diseases, given men's tendency to be more exposed to injuries and women's tendency to be more exposed to diseases (Messing, 1998).

More information is also required on home-based work; contingent (or non-permanent) employment; levels of poverty; union participation; the duration of employment, unemployment and underemployment; access to productive resources; and the allocation of benefits among household members, etc. It may also be useful to calculate composite indexes or measures to reflect the respective occupational segregation, wage differentials, annual hours of work, etc., of men and women.

DEFINING THE TOPICS

The crucial role played by definitions and classifications[3] in the production of relevant statistics is often underestimated. Definitions and classifications determine what is to be covered and in how much detail, and are the basis for the whole data production process. Thus, the quality of the resulting figures depends on how well these definitions and classifications mirror the actual situation of the different participants in the labour market. A change in definition can cause a change in the resulting statistics which may not reflect any change in reality. Therefore, when analysing time series or cross-country data, it is important to assess first whether observed changes are actually due to difference in definition.

In order to be useful in making gender distinctions, definitions should recognize that women and men do not necessarily perform the same tasks, that they do not always behave in the same way, and that they are not subject to the same constraints. In this connection, coverage and detail are essential. Definitions need both to cover all qualifying work situations, regardless of whether they are performed by a man or a woman; and to describe the different work situations in sufficient detail to bring out any gender distinctions.

Coverage

The range of activities constituting what is understood as "work" affects the scope of all topics in labour statistics. Employment, unemployment and income statistics are concerned only with persons carrying out or seeking to carry out "work". Occupational injury statistics include persons experiencing an injury only if it was sustained while performing such activities. And so on.

But, to be useful in making gender distinctions, "work" needs to cover *all* the activities carried out to produce the goods and services in society, regardless of whether they are remunerated, declared to the tax authorities, carried out intermittently, casually, simultaneously or seasonally, etc.; and regardless of whether the goods or services produced are intended for sale, for barter or for own household consumption. At present, however, the definition of "work" is limited to "economic" activities, i.e., those which contribute to the production of goods and services[4] according to a country's System of National Accounts (SNA). Such activities include those carried out to produce goods or render services for sale or barter in the market; and activities to produce goods for own consumption if they represent a significant proportion of those goods produced in the country. Domestic or personal services provided by unpaid household members[5] are excluded. In practice, few countries include the production of goods for own consumption within the scope of measured employment and none includes services for own consumption. Most work excluded from the scope of "economic" activities is done by women (UNDP, 1995), and this is an important cause of the underestimation of women's participation in production and of their contribution to the well-being of society. Thus, from the outset, labour statistics reflect at best a partial reality.

Child labour is one area in which such restricted coverage of "economic" activities dramatically affects the capacity of labour statistics to reflect reality. Statistics on child labour commonly show that more boys than girls work. This, however, conceals the fact that there are many children engaged in unpaid household activities who are prevented from going to school, just as if they were working for pay. As is to be expected, when these unpaid activities are included under child labour, it then emerges that more girls than boys work (Ashagrie, 1998). In view of the impact of such exclusions on policy decisions, the ILO systematically recommends that all countries include all (or a subset of) unpaid household activities in their national statistics on child labour.

Coverage of workers and work situations may also be affected by the criteria used to define a topic, and these often exclude particular groups of workers. Because the sex composition of these groups is generally uneven, the usefulness of resulting statistics for reflecting gender differences is hampered. Most of the time such exclusions affect more women than men, but not always. For example, some national definitions of employment exclude contributing (unpaid) family workers who work fewer than a fixed number of hours. The effect is probably greater on the number of women identified as employed, since unpaid family work is more prevalent among women than among men. Conversely, many countries exclude the armed forces from employment statistics, which affects more men than women. In many countries (e.g. in Scandinavia), a large proportion of paid workers are entitled to take relatively extended leave without losing their jobs, and national estimates of employment show a larger proportion of workers on extended forms of leave than those of other countries. Because of the likely family-related nature of such leave, e.g. for maternity reasons, most of these workers are women. The high levels of female employment reported in such countries may therefore partly reflect a definitional effect of generous leave entitlement, as in other countries an important proportion of these workers would not be classified as employed.

National definitions of employment in the informal sector may exclude persons whose main job is in the public service or agriculture, for example, but who have a second job in the informal sector; most of them are men. The definitions may also exclude certain activities in which women predominate, regardless of whether these activities otherwise satisfy the criteria for inclusion in the informal sector. Examples include: agricultural activities, activities by enterprises exclusively engaged in the production for own final use, activities of paid domestic workers and of outworkers.

Conversely, national definitions of time-related (or visible) underemployment, in line with international guidelines, generally exclude employed persons who work for more hours than a certain fixed threshold, which is considered to represent the level of "full-time employment" in legislation, collective agreements or usual practice in establishments. Those working at or above this threshold are considered to be fully employed even if they are willing and available to work additional hours. Unfortunately, in many countries the chosen threshold does not truly reflect "full" employment, because many workers are in fact compelled to work beyond those hours in order just to make a decent living. Most such workers are men.

National definitions of unemployment generally include unemployed persons who are "actively seeking work". But not everyone who wants to work actively seeks it, nor does everyone consider that their attempts to find it constitute "actively seeking work". Consequently, they do not report themselves as doing so. Thus, in countries where "formal" ways of finding work, e.g., through labour exchanges, are limited to the cities, or where more "informal" channels are commonly used, national definitions may exclude persons who are in fact looking for self-employment or for paid employment but who do not consider that their activities amount to "actively seeking work". Furthermore, in line with the standard international definition of unemployment, most national definitions exclude persons who want to work but do not "seek" work at all, either because work opportunities are so limited that they know there are none in practice, or because they have restricted labour mobility, or because they face discrimination or structural, social and cultural barriers in their search for work. Many of these workers, most of whom are women, tend to react positively to an actual chance of employment.

Statistics on income from employment also tend to be partial, for several reasons. They usually exclude wage and non-wage benefits such as social security benefits, profit-related pay and irregular payments, which may be significant in many cases and where differences between men and women may be important. Most important of all, national statistics usually exclude the remuneration of the self-employed where, again, there may be considerable differences between men and women.

Coverage may also be affected by the use of short reference periods. Definitions which aim at complete coverage of work situations should cover seasonal and occasional activities. However, international and national definitions of employment and unemployment generally provide an image of the labour force situation during a particular reference week. Statistics based on these definitions are useful for monitoring changes over time when the dominant form of employment is regular, full-time, non-agricultural, paid employment, but are less useful for monitoring other forms of employment. Since more women than men tend to work in seasonal and casual activities and/or on an intermittent basis throughout the year alternating household non-market activities with economic activities, measures of employment and unemployment based on a short reference period can only partially reflect this more complex reality. In order to capture this fully, it is necessary to identify persons who experienced employment or unemployment at any time within a longer period, for example, 12 months. Statistics on the experience of employment or unemployment within a 12-month period exist in a number of countries, but they tend to identify the predominant activity over that period, in line with international guidelines. However, this measure conceals seasonal patterns of work and excludes persons who, though working part of the year, are inactive for most of it. Many of these workers are women.

Detail

For definitions to be useful for gender concerns they need to ensure that men's and women's characteristics are described in sufficient detail to allow significant distinctions to emerge. The classification of occupations, for example, needs to be refined at a detailed level (Anker, 1998). If only broad occupational groups are used, the occupational segregation between men and women remains hidden: an analysis of the managerial group as a whole, for example, will not reveal that women managers tend to be concentrated in small enterprises, while managers in larger companies are men.

Similarly, to detect gender differences in workers' employment status, it is not enough merely to distinguish between "employees", "employers" and "own account workers", as most countries do. These are very heterogeneous categories, each comprising a diversity of employment situations. For example, the category "employees" includes not only regular employees but also outworkers (home-based workers), casual employees, work-gang members, etc. Women tend to predominate in the latter situations. In addition to employers and core own-account workers, the category of "self-employed workers" includes subsistence workers, share croppers, members of producer cooperatives, etc., amongst whom women are particularly numerous.

In income statistics, the various components of income must be identified separately, as they may not accrue to women and men to the same degree. For example, in systems where income statistics include social security benefits received by virtue of workers' employment status (as recommended in international guidelines), a worker's income includes all such benefits relating to his or her dependants. Similarly, the income of self-employed workers includes the income generated by the economic activities of the worker's contributing (unpaid) family members, as well as dependants' social security benefits. As men tend to be the primary earners in households, these income components can be expected to be more important for them than for women. Therefore, income statistics that include such components probably show a greater disparity between men and women in employment than statistics which do not include them. Estimates of the value of unpaid work are also important for gender distinctions. If such estimates attribute an economic value to unpaid work (most of it by women), this tends to reduce the differences between the measured contributions of men and women to the economy or their households.

Similarly, to enable valid gender comparisons as regards working time, it is important to separate out its various components (e.g. overtime, absence from work, work at home, travelling time, etc.), as they may affect women and men to different degrees.

Another relevant issue here is the need for female and male workers' characteristics to be described equally in substance and in detail. For example, all occupational groups at each level of a national classification of occupations should be identified separately to the same extent according to specified criteria. Thus, it is important to evaluate whether the distinctions made in occupational groups in which women predominate (e.g. clerical, agricultural and elementary occupations) are as detailed as those made in occupational groups where men predominate (e.g. in crafts and machine operators). Most national classifications tend to bulk in a few occupational groups the jobs in which women predominate, whereas jobs where men are numerous tend to be distinguished in greater detail.

In practice, women's situation may not be described equally as regards employment status. According to international guidelines, women who work in association, and on an equal footing, with their husbands in a family enterprise, are in partnership with them and should therefore be classified in the same employment status category as they are, i.e. as "core own-account workers" or "employers". However, there is a tendency in national statistics to classify women in such situations as contributing (or unpaid) family workers.

Many of the shortcomings found in national statistics regarding coverage and detail are due to measurement limitations. As will be seen below, measurement methodologies often limit the type and range of information that can be produced. However, in other cases, some of the responsibility lies with the international guidelines which serve as models for national definitions. International guidelines seldom explicitly address the implications for gender of using one set of criteria as opposed to another. Though it may not always be possible or practical to revise these guidelines, it may be useful for the ILO to recommend that those groups of workers who tend to be excluded from the various labour topics be identified and described separately.

MEASUREMENT METHODS

The choice of measurement method can also affect the extent to which the resulting statistics reveal possible gender differences. Labour statistics are collected through household-based surveys, establishment-based surveys and administrative records. Each methodology has distinct features regarding the workers and work situations covered, and the control over the type and range of data collected. To understand the strengths and limitations of data gathered by each method and to interpret the resulting statistics correctly, it is important to be aware of these differences.

Administrative records, for example, contain information registered as a result of the administrative functions of an agency, e.g. an employment exchange office, insurance company, social security institution, tax authority or labour inspectorate. These records can provide information about each unit in the population covered by the agency's operations, so statistics can be produced for small geographical areas and population groups. Establishment-based surveys generally require the respondents to search for the requested information in records kept by employers about individual workers or about groups of workers in the establishments. These records may be able to provide information that is accurate and consistent over time on employment, earnings and hours of work over a specified period of time, depending on the record-keeping needs and practices of the establishment. Household-based surveys obtain information from the workers themselves through replies to a standard questionnaire, and can enumerate the whole population (population censuses) or a sample of it (household sample surveys). They are able to cover a much larger range of subjects than the other types of sources, because the subjects that can be covered are limited only by the capacity of household members to provide the information from their own knowledge; but when they are based on samples, the detail the resulting statistics can provide is limited.

Coverage of topics

Statistics obtained from records kept by establishments and by other agencies are limited by the type and range of information available. Establishment records are designed to monitor payment and attendance, and the records kept by other agencies are designed to support administrative procedures; in neither case is information recorded to provide the basis for statistics. The definitions used by these records do not therefore necessarily correspond to statistical definitions and in many cases little can be done to adjust the resulting data (ILO/EASMAT, 1997). For example, establishments record paid overtime and authorized leave, which are not equivalent to total overtime and actual leave: the implication for gender distinctions depends on whether men and women experience recorded overtime and authorized leave to the same extent as they do total overtime and actual leave. Employers include in their wage records all regular cash payments to employees, but may exclude payments in kind, one-off payments, such as profit-related bonuses, 13th month payments, etc. (ILO, 1998); the implication for gender differences will be important if the excluded components accrue predominantly to one or other sex. Conversely, records kept by insurance companies on occupational injuries typically concern compensated injuries only and records kept by employment offices on unemployment and underemployment relate only to persons who register there to find work. Moreover, the administrative procedure may discriminate against women or men, thus under-reporting their actual numbers: for instance, persons in precarious employment situations may be disqualified from claiming compensation when they are injured — a situation that may affect more women than men (Messing, 1998).

Furthermore, records kept by establishments or administrative agencies may not include information about characteristics which are useful for understanding gender issues properly. For example, they may not register information on the age of workers, their level of education or other descriptive characteristics. Sometimes, the records do not even include information whereby it is possible to differentiate between men and women workers!

By contrast with information stemming from registers, household-based surveys permit far more control over the type and range of data collected, the underlying concepts, data item definitions and classifications. This measurement method can be rendered largely independent of respondents' perceptions or understanding of the concepts used for statistics. The classification of a person in a particular category can be determined on the basis of combined replies to a sequence of questions rather than on the reply to a direct question which requires respondents to classify themselves on the basis of their own understanding of their work situation. For example, persons can be classified as unemployed on the basis of whether they actively sought work and were available for work (the defining criteria), rather than on their own understanding of what it means to be unemployed. Similarly, quantitative information, for example on hours of work or on income, can be determined on the basis of replies to the elements that compose the measure, instead of on direct questions of the type: "How many hours did you work last week?" or "How much did you earn last month?". The challenge is to formulate questions that ensure accurate application of the defining criteria. The more independent the measure is of workers' perceptions of their situation, the higher the chance that women will receive equal statistical treatment.

Unfortunately, in practice this approach is not widely used in household-based surveys, given the need to limit the size of questionnaires and the length of interviews. In addition, respondents may not understand or may misinterpret the questions being asked and they may forget certain activities or purposely provide incorrect information, especially on sensitive subjects, such as income. When a household member gives information about other members of the households, she or he may not be fully aware of those persons' activities, in particular if these occur irregularly.

Coverage of workers

Records kept by establishments or administrative agencies rarely cover the whole population, and the excluded groups are generally those in which women predominate, which reduces the usefulness of these sources for making gender distinctions. Establishment-based surveys tend to cover only regular employees who work in medium-sized and large establishments. They may exclude managerial staff as well as peripheral workers, such as outworkers, part-time workers, casual employees and workers contracted from agencies. Similarly, administrative records cover only persons concerned by the work of the agencies which keep them. In many countries, this coverage is very low relative to the total employed population, being limited to regular full-time employees in the formal sector and excluding self-employed workers, casual and seasonal employees, outworkers and sometimes also part-time workers. As women tend to predominate in the excluded groups of workers, administrative records cannot be expected fully to reflect their characteristics and contribution in the economy. For example, employment statistics based on insurance records obviously include only insured workers. Unemployment insurance records provide information only on persons entitled to benefits when not working or on employed persons entitled to benefits when working fewer hours than their contractual hours. And statistics on industrial disputes largely concern legal strikes involving a large number of workers and lasting several days, tend to record only workers directly involved, and to exclude workers indirectly affected, of whom many are women.

Unlike establishment-based surveys and administrative records, household-based surveys can cover all workers, including the self-employed, casual workers, unpaid family workers, outworkers and paid workers in small production units. Given that these are groups in which women predominate, it is thus the best source for statistics properly reflecting gender-based differences.

PRESENTATION OF DATA

The way statistics are presented is central to the reflection of gender concerns. Tables and figures should portray differences in men's and women's contributions, conditions and constraints. This implies disaggregation by variables which describe the demographic, economic, social and family context of workers. All statistics on the numbers of employed and unemployed persons and their characteristics should make it possible to compare women with men. This means that, as a minimum, establishments' records and other administrative records should include information on persons' sex and that the statistical system should always publish statistics disaggregated by sex.

But statistics on the characteristics of workers should also be disaggregated by other variables which help describe the differences or similarities between men and women. For example, statistics on income should distinguish workers' hours of work and level of education, two factors which affect the level of total income earned. Similarly, for a more comprehensive picture of men's and women's occupational injuries, statistics should be presented for hours of work and seniority, and be shown by occupational groups.

Most important of all, statistics on the structure and characteristics of the labour force should be disaggregated by variables which reflect workers' personal and family situation, in order to provide a more complete picture of women's labour force participation and behaviour compared to men's. Such variables include age, level of education, whether the household includes children needing care, or other adults requiring assistance (e.g. handicapped persons, older family members), etc. All these factors variously constrain the time and energy which women and men can devote to their "economic" work. In many societies, a person's marital status also strongly affects participation in the labour force, and in polygamous societies an important variable is rank within marriage (ACOPAM, 1996). Another relevant descriptive variable is the type of household (e.g. single parent, female headed, etc.).

Though these variables are essential to the description of gender-based differences and similarities in the labour market, few countries actually present their statistics in this way. One reason may be that only household-based surveys are sufficiently flexible to produce such statistics, but the fact that international guidelines have never addressed the importance of linking labour market topics with workers' family context is certainly also important.

CONCLUSION

This chapter presents a number of features which labour statistics should display if they are usefully to address gender concerns. First of all, they need to cover topics which are relevant to revealing gender distinctions and similarities in the world of work.

Second, these topics must be defined and measured in such a way as to achieve complete coverage of workers and work situations, and to describe their characteristics in sufficient detail to make these distinctions apparent. At present, the coverage of workers and work situations remains incomplete mainly because the defined scope of labour statistics excludes unpaid services for own household consumption and, consequently, the contribution to the economy of a vast number of workers, most of whom are women. Furthermore, certain groups of workers tend to be excluded from the scope of the various topics because of the criteria used in the definitions, or because of coverage limitations of the data collection method used. Because the sex composition of these groups is not generally even, the usefulness of the resulting statistics for reflecting gender issues is reduced. To improve this situation, it may be useful to develop international guidelines on how to identify and describe better the groups of workers who tend to be excluded from statistics.

Finally, in order adequately to pinpoint the factors that cause differences between men and women at work, a minium requirement is sex disaggregation of information. But that alone is not sufficient. Data on the persons' work situation must be presented in the context of their personal and family situation, particularly as regards the presence of young children and/or other members requiring care in the household — a practice currently adopted by only a few countries.

Notes

[1] The "number of persons employed" counts persons who work full time equally with those who work only a few hours during the week. Women work on average fewer hours than men (on economic activities) and as a consequence a measure of volume of employment based on the hours worked will reduce their relative participation in the labour market as compared to a measure based on head counts. Still, much of women's work remains unrecognized given that it excludes many unpaid activities carried out for the benefit of their households. If these activities were included in the scope of employment, and the hours spent in them were included in the measure of hours of work, then women's share of working hours would typically be greater than men's.

[2] Current international guidelines can be consulted at http://www.ilo.org/stat/public/english/ 120stat/res/index.htm.

[3] A classification groups together units of a "similar" kind — "similarity" being determined in relation to specific criteria related to a characteristic of the units — often hierarchically, in order to describe the characteristic in a systematic and simplified way. In labour statistics, the three major classifications concern occupations, industries and employment status.

[4] Activities of this type may include: growing or gathering field crops, cutting firewood, carrying water, weaving baskets and mats, making clay pots and plates, weaving textiles, and other handicrafts.

[5] Activities of this type include: cleaning dwelling and household goods; preparing and serving meals; caring for, training and instructing children; caring for the sick, invalid or old people; transporting household members or their goods, etc.

References

ACOPAM (Appui associatif et cooperatif aux initiatives de développement à la base). 1996. *Genre et développement: Analyse de la place des femmes. Une experience au Sahel.* Geneva, ILO.

Anker, Richard. 1998. *Gender and jobs: Sex segregation of occupations in the world.* Geneva, ILO.

Ashagrie, Kebebew. 1998. *Statistics on working children and hazardous labour in brief.* Mimeo. Geneva, ILO. April.

Dixon-Mueller, Ruth; Anker, Richard. 1990. *Assessing women's economic contributions to development.* Training in Population, Human Resources and Development Planning Paper No. 6. Geneva, ILO.

ILO. 1998. *Measurement of income from employment.* Sixteenth International Conference of Labour Statisticians, Geneva, 6-15 Oct., Report II (ICLS/16/1998/II). Geneva.

—/EASMAT (East Asia Multidisciplinary Advisory Team). 1997. *Labour statistics based on administrative records: Guidelines on compilation and presentation.* Bangkok.

Mata Greenwood, Adriana. Forthcoming. *Incorporating gender issues in labour statistics.* Working Paper No. 99-1. Geneva, ILO.

Messing, Karen. 1998. *One-eyed science: Occupational health and women workers.* Philadelphia, PA, Temple University Press.

Overholt, Catherine, et al. 1984. "Women in development: A framework for project analysis", in Catherine Overholt, Mary B. Anderson, Kathleen Cloud, and James E. Austin (eds.): *Gender roles in development projects: A case book.* West Hartford, CT, Kumarian Press, pp. 3-15.

United Nations. 1991. *The world's women 1970-1990: Trends and statistics.* Social Statistics and Indicators, Series K, No. 8. New York, NY.

UNDP. 1995. *Human Development Report 1995.* New York, NY.

THE ENDURING DEBATE OVER UNPAID LABOUR

6

Lourdes BENERÍA*

Debate over the measurement of unpaid work — and hence over the underestimation of women's work in labour force and national accounting statistics — is not new. The main theoretical and practical issues addressed over many years are summarized, and the progress made on conceptual, theoretical and methodological aspects of the question, as well as new issues described. And there is a response to three types of continuing critique: that the efforts make no useful impact; that unpaid work is qualitatively different from market work and should not be treated in the same way; and that the efforts are theoretically misguided.

Conceptual and theoretical norms are at the root of statistical biases leading to the underestimation of women's work in labour force and national accounting statistics. Initially viewed as a way of making women's work more visible, the effort to account for women's work has gradually evolved to include all unpaid work by whomever it is performed (men, women, children). The evolution of this effort illustrates how the questions raised by feminists have a relevance transcending feminism and challenging basic tenets in conventional economic thinking.

Ester Boserup, in her classic 1970 book, *Woman's role in economic development*, pointed out that "the subsistence activities usually omitted in the statistics of production and income are largely women's work" (Boserup, 1970, p. 163). She was a pioneer in emphasizing the time-consuming character of these activities which, in rural economies, include physically demanding tasks such as fetching wood and carrying water as well as food production and the "crude processing of basic foods".

Originally published in *International Labour Review*, Vol. 138 (1999), No. 3.

* Professor of City and Regional Planning and Women's Studies, Cornell University.

Even earlier, Margaret Reid, in her 1934 book, *Economics of household production*, expressed concern about the exclusion of domestic production from national income accounts and designed a method to estimate the value of home-based work. Then, from the late 1960s, the international women's movement prepared the ground for a new look at the estimation of women's economic activities. The issue was then seen as symbolizing society's undervaluation of women and of their contribution to social well-being. The four world conferences on women held under the auspices of the United Nations since 1975 have been instrumental in getting the topic incorporated into the United Nations agendas and subsequent plans of action. At a different level, Marylin Waring's 1988 book, *If women counted*, contributed to making the issue better known to a large audience. Over the past 20 years, national governments and individual researchers and activist groups have contributed significantly to this effort.

An important body of mainstream literature has developed on time allocation data, including unpaid work. The first systematic collection of these data occurred in the USSR in 1924, the objective then being to collect information about specific topics such as leisure time and community-oriented work (Juster and Stafford, 1991). Since the 1960s, national and comparative studies of time use have been carried out for a variety of purposes, such as the expansion of national accounting statistics and the analysis of household behaviour. This work has taken place in both industrialized and developing countries (for a summary of the literature and definitions, see Goldschmidt-Clermont, 1982; Juster and Stafford, 1991). Such studies, although useful and often with objectives parallel to those of the effort to account for unpaid work, do not usually include a specifically feminist concern regarding their implications for women.

This chapter seeks to summarize some of the theoretical and practical issues in the effort made during the past 20 years to account for women's unpaid work and assesses the current status.[1]

ACCOUNTING FOR UNPAID WORK

Unpaid work is still substantially underestimated in national and international statistics on the labour force, GNP, and national income. Labour force statistics and national income accounts were designed primarily to gather information about the level of remunerated economic activity and changes over time, and to provide a basis for economic policy and planning. Given that the market is generally considered to be the core focus of economic activity, the statistical concept of being "at work" is (and has been historically) defined as a subset of "employment", in terms of engagement in work "for pay or profit" (see ILO, 1955, p. 43). Likewise, the inclusion of subsistence production in national income accounts is in terms of its connection to the market. The story of the decrease in GNP when a man marries his housekeeper is well known to readers of introductory economics textbooks. The decrease occurs because, although the household activities of the housekeeper-turned-wife are unchanged — or possibly increased — the wife is not paid a wage and so, as her work is not for the market, it is not considered economically significant.

Thus, the problem stems from the way "work" has been defined, both in theory and in conventional statistics, as a paid economic activity linked to the market. Until the Second World War, statistics on the economically active population were gathered by population censuses, but the unemployment problems arising from the Great Depression of the 1930s had already begun to generate increased interest in the collection of reliable labour statistics. In 1938, the Committee of Statistical Experts of the League of Nations recommended a definition of the concept "gainfully occupied", and drew up proposals to standardize census data in order to facilitate international comparisons (League of Nations, 1938; ILO, 1976, pp. 27-28). As a result, many countries expanded the collection of statistics on what would thenceforth be called "the labour force" (ILO, 1976, p. 25). In 1966, the United Nations Statistical Commission updated the earlier definitions, in order to provide a measure not only of the unemployed but also of labour availability. The adopted definition of "economically active population" referred to "all persons of either sex who furnish the supply of labour for the production of economic goods and services" (see ILO, 1976, p. 32). The objective of this definition was to facilitate estimates not only of employment and unemployment but of underemployment as well (for a more detailed account, see Benería, 1982).

Another aspect of this definition was the assumed link between the labour force and national product — active labour being defined as that which contributes to the national product plus the unemployed. This definition led to questionable measurements of work. Family members working part time can be classified as employed or underemployed when working in agriculture but not when engaged in household production, which means the exclusion of a large proportion of unpaid work from national product and income accounting as well as from labour force statistics. However, the problem of underestimation of unpaid work and the reasons underlying it differ for each of the four sectors in which unpaid work predominates, namely, subsistence production, the household economy, the informal sector, and volunteer work.

The subsistence sector

Despite considerable efforts made from 1938 onwards to improve labour force and national accounting statistics, the basic concepts remained essentially untouched until the late 1970s. One important exception was the effort to include estimates of subsistence production in GNP accounts. Methods to estimate the value of subsistence production and the proportion of the population engaged in it were recommended in the United Nations system of national accounts (SNA) from the 1950s, particularly for countries where this sector was relatively important. Thus, countries such as Nepal, Papua New Guinea, Tanzania and others developed methods of estimating the contributions of subsistence production to GNP. In 1960 a working party of African statisticians recommended that estimates of rural household activities, such as the backyard cultivation of vegetables, could and should be added to those of subsistence production in agriculture, forestry and fishing (Waring, 1988). Systematic implementation was another matter.

The effort to estimate subsistence production was advanced in 1982 when the Thirteenth International Conference of Labour Statisticians adopted a resolution incorporating the United Nations' 1966 definition of "economically active population", i.e. "all persons of either sex who furnish the supply of economic goods and services" (ILO, 1983, p. I/2). Whether or not this supply was furnished through the market was irrelevant. Although it was not entirely clear what constituted "economic goods and services", the new definition introduced an exception to the market criterion, justified by the notion that subsistence production represents "marketable goods". Consequently, it seemed logical to view the workers engaged in that sector as part of the labour force, including "family labour". Thus, despite the practical difficulties in estimating the market value of subsistence production, it became accepted practice without important theoretical or conceptual objections. The objective was to arrive at more accurate estimates of GNP and of economic growth or, as Ester Boserup had put it:

> [T]he present system of under-reporting subsistence activities not only makes the underdeveloped countries seem poorer than they really are in comparison with the more developed countries, but it also makes their rate of economic growth appear in a more favorable light than the facts warrant, since economic development entails a gradual replacement of the omitted subsistence activities by the creation of income in the non-subsistence sector which is recorded more correctly (Boserup, 1970, p. 163).

In practice, however, the participation of women in subsistence production is still not fully accounted for, partly because the boundaries between agricultural and domestic work can be difficult to trace, particularly for women. To the extent that women's unpaid agricultural labour is highly integrated with domestic activities — e.g. food cultivation, the fetching of wood, care of animals, and many others — the distinction between the conventional classifications of family labour (in agriculture) and domestic work is very thin and a clear-cut line is difficult to draw. In practice, there is a tendency to underestimate women's work in subsistence production whenever it is classified as domestic work.

The same problem appears when censuses classify workers according to their "main occupation". In such cases, the tendency to under-report female family workers in agriculture or any other type of non-domestic production is quite prevalent. Historically, such under-reporting has been observed in all regions and countries, and it was already pointed out by the ILO in 1977, referring in particular to north Africa and south-west Asia where "female unpaid family workers were, to a very large extent, not recorded" (ILO, 1977, p. 11). Since then, there has been an effort to include this category of workers in the labour force statistics of many countries. Even so, there is still reason to believe that under-reporting continues to occur for many reasons ranging from the relative irregularity of women's work in agriculture — for example, when it is mostly seasonal or marginal — to the deeply ingrained view, which assumes multiple cultural and historical forms, that "women's place is in the home". As a result national statistics regarding women's work are unreliable or non-existent and it is very difficult to make meaningful international comparisons (for further details, see Benería, 1982).

The informal sector

The sparse statistical information on the informal sector presents a different type of problem. This sector comprises a wide array of activities ranging from the clandestine production of (legal) goods and services to officially sanctioned micro-enterprises in all sorts of industries. In this case, the measurement problem is not one of conceptualization, given that the informal sector largely involves paid activities which fall within conventional definitions of work; the problem is posed by the difficulties of obtaining reliable statistics.

The absence of appropriate and systematic data collection in this case is a significant problem because the sector covers a large (and often growing) proportion of the workforce in many countries.[2] For women, the informal sector often provides a primary, if precarious, source of income. Their informal activities range from home work (industrial piece-work, for example) to preparing and selling foods on the streets, to self-employment and work in micro-enterprises. Contrary to earlier expectations, informal sector activities have not been gradually replaced by formal sector work; in fact, in many countries they have tended to absorb the large numbers of people who remained marginal to the "modern economy" or were expelled from it when unemployment rose (Portes and Castells, 1989). To be sure, many case studies and efforts at data collection of informal activities have been made, but the difficulties of systematic gathering of information are enormous as they mostly derive from the invisible and even clandestine character of significant portions of this sector — often involving activities that are bordering on the illegal — and from its unstable, precarious and unregulated nature.

However, periodic and systematic country surveys can provide estimates of the sector's weight in labour force and GNP estimates. For example, the United Nations prepared conceptual and methodological guidelines for the measurement of women's work in the informal sector — including industry and services — and carried out useful pilot studies, as in Burkina Faso, the Congo, the Gambia, and Zambia (UN Statistical Office/ECA/INSTRAW, 1991a and 1991b; INSTRAW, 1991). In each case, microeconomic survey data have been combined with macroeconomic information, according to data availability in each country. The objective of this information-gathering effort is to facilitate policy design and action to improve the working conditions of informal sector workers and to strengthen their bargaining power.

Domestic work

Domestic production and related activities pose problems less of underestimation than of total exclusion, because such activities have been perceived as simply falling outside the conventional definition of work. Historically, even authors who were open to the idea of defining domestic work as "production" did not accord it much priority. As stated by Blades, for example, "the production boundary should encompass non-monetary activities which are likely to be replaced by monetary activities as an economy becomes more specialized," but he concluded that "because of the practical difficulties of measurement the case for including housewives' general services is considerably weaker" (Blades, 1975, p. 7).

As mentioned earlier, apart from a few exceptions such as Margaret Reid, this exclusion was not much questioned until the late 1970s. Boserup argued strongly for the inclusion in national accounts "of food items obtained by collecting and hunting, of output of home crafts such as clothing, footwear, sleeping and sitting mats, baskets, clay pots, calabashes, fuel collected by women, funeral services, hair cuts, entertainment, and traditional administrative and medical services," together with "pounding, husking and grinding of foodstuffs and the slaughtering of animals" (Boserup, 1970, pp. 162-163). However, she saw these activities as mostly subsistence production, i.e. as "marketable goods," not as domestic work. Although she mentioned the omission of "domestic services of housewives" from national accounts, she was more vociferous about the exclusion of subsistence production. Yet she did also mention the need to include production for own consumption which is larger in the less industrialized and agricultural countries than in the more industrialized regions.

A reversal has been observed in the trend for domestic work to shift to the market as countries develop. As labour costs have increased over the years in the high-income countries, there has been a significant increase in self-help activities such as home construction, carpentry and repairs, which are often performed by men. These activities are then added to the bulk of unpaid work at the household level, a trend reinforced by a decreasing tendency to hire domestic workers in these countries (Langfeldt, 1987; Chadeau, 1989; UNDP, 1995). There is a debate about the extent to which the average number of market hours worked have decreased in the United States, for example, and some authors have estimated that the time allocated to unpaid work by men and women tended to converge between the 1960s and 1980s, a tendency also observed in other industrialized countries. However, these estimates do not take into consideration the extent to which many tasks are performed simultaneously. Floro, for example, has argued there is "growing evidence that the performance of overlapping activities over prolonged periods especially by women is not an isolated phenomenon" (Floro, 1995, p. 1920). As women's participation in market work has increased, work intensification resulting from overlapping activities requires a revision of the convergence thesis.

To sum up, production tends to shift out of the household during the development process, though at least part of it may return later, whether it is performed by women or men. If household production is not accounted for, growth rates are likely to be overestimated when this production shifts to the market; but they are likely to be underestimated when (normally) paid activities are taken up by (unpaid) household members. Given the dominant division of labour and women's role in the domestic sphere, the exclusion affects mostly but not exclusively women's work.

Volunteer work

As in domestic work, the wide range of tasks carried out in the charitable sector and the fact that these tasks are not directly linked to the market create both conceptual and methodological problems for their measurement. Volunteer work means work whose beneficiaries are not members of the immediate family and for which there cannot be any direct payment; furthermore, the work must be part of an organized programme. Volunteer work is thus clearly different from domestic work, though there are close connections between the two — as when volunteer work is carried out in a neighbourhood or community context — which can make the boundaries difficult to draw. In addition, while it is easy to define some charitable tasks as productive work, for instance, those done by unpaid job training and home-building organizations, others are more difficult to classify, for instance, some of the activities associated with a church. Yet even in the latter case, it is important to account for these tasks in some way, particularly if they provide free substitutes for what otherwise would have to be paid for in the market. Moreover, volunteer work is often of a professional nature, as in the case of the relatively high number of voluntary workers in the health sector (Gora and Nemerowicz, 1991).

Many factors influence the extent to which people engage in volunteer work, and the abundant gender asymmetries in this type of work show that gender is one them. In the United States women are more likely than men to engage in it, particularly married and relatively well-educated women with children aged under 18. There are many aspects to these gendered disparities, amongst them the fact that while cash contributions to charity (mostly by men) are tax-deductible, contributions in time (mostly by women) are not. In New Zealand, women mobilized around this issue in the mid-1980s, with the result that a question about time dedicated to volunteer work was included in the 1986 census of population (Waring, 1988).

Similarly, volunteer work also varies according to social characteristics. In the United States, a survey conducted in 1996 showed that it was correlated with income: the highest proportion (62 per cent) was among people with an annual income over US$75,000 and the lowest among those with an annual income below US$20,000 (AARP, 1997). However, these differences may be misleading since much remains to be done to document volunteer work worldwide. Amongst the poor, it can represent very significant individual and collective actions in times of crisis. One well-known example is the collective soup kitchens in the Andean countries during the 1980s and 1990s. Organized and run mostly by women, they functioned as means of survival in face of the drastic deterioration of living standards that resulted from structural adjustment policies and increasing urban poverty. It has been estimated that, in Lima, they involved 40,000 low-income women who jointly organized a federation of self-managed communal kitchens, located in 2,000 sites in Lima's poor neighbourhoods, pooling their resources to feed about 200,000 people as frequently as five times a week (Barrig, 1996; Lind, 1990). Managing such an impressive endeavour requires a wide range of skills — from contacting food providers to handling money and dealing with charitable institutions and other funding sources — some of which were acquired by the women as they engaged in survival strategies for their families and neighbours.

In fact, collective food kitchens raise questions about the conventional definition of volunteer work provided above, since the beneficiaries often include both members of the immediate family *and* of the community or neighbourhood, hence they straddle the boundaries between domestic and volunteer work. They also raise questions about the extent to which participation in volunteer work 'is freely chosen, since in the case of soup kitchens, it stems from urgent survival needs and from the inability of each individual household to meet these alone. Clearly, collective soup kitchens are not exclusive to the Andean region. They take different forms and are also to be found in high-income countries. In the

United States for example, soup kitchens serving the poor, unemployed and often homeless are often run by women.[3]

To sum up, accounting for women's work thus involved efforts on two fronts from the start. First, it required the refinement of categories and the improvement of data collection in those areas of paid work that were, in theory at least, included in conventional statistics. Second, it was the result of the need to rethink and redefine the concept of work and to develop ways of measuring unpaid work mostly involving domestic and volunteer work. The focus below will be on domestic work.

THE PROGRESS OF TWO DECADES

Although questions and objections still remain about the extent to which unpaid work should be measured, much progress has been made on practical issues over the past 20 years. This progress has occurred mainly on three fronts: conceptual, theoretical and methodological.

Progress on the conceptual front

As a result of a recommendation by the First World Conference on Women held in Nairobi in 1985, the United Nations International Research and Training Institute for the Advancement of Women (INSTRAW) and the Statistical Office of the United Nations Secretariat took the lead in reviewing and promoting the revision of national accounts and other statistical information on women's work. Most recommendations have suggested the development of separate or supplementary accounts that would permit the generation of "augmented" estimates of GNP (United Nations, 1989).[4]

The purpose of such "satellite accounts" is to measure the unpaid production of goods and services by households and to provide indicators of their contribution to welfare. This can be done either by using time as a unit of measurement — as in time-use surveys — or by imputing a monetary value to time inputs or to the goods and services produced. Given the numerous and varied tasks being performed in the home, the question of which tasks to include has been at the centre of discussion. The most accepted operational criterion is Margaret Reid's third-party principle, according to which domestic production refers to unpaid activities that can be performed by a third person for pay. Clearly, this criterion includes tasks such as shopping, cleaning, food preparation and childcare; it does not include leisure or personal activities such as watching television or getting dressed. This still leaves some ambiguities (the very rich or the ill may employ someone to help them dress), but on the whole it represents an important step in setting a standard of definition that can allow comparisons between countries.

The third-party principle has been criticized for assuming the market as the model of economic activity and therefore precluding "the existence of economic activity unique to the household, since anything that does not, or does not yet, have a commodity equivalent cannot be considered economic" (Wood, 1997, p. 50). But, although the principle assumes market production as the point of reference, it does not follow that a domestic activity without a market equivalent cannot be included; it can, as long as a third party can perform it. Wood goes further in criticizing the principle for its exclusion of personal activities such as "emotional caretaking, sex and childbirth from definitions of economic activity" (Wood, 1997, p. 52). This argument, however, brings the discussion of what should be considered "work" to a level at which it is very difficult to differentiate it from leisure and personal enjoyment. In any case, what needs to be emphasized is that, overall, a significant shift has taken place in the conceptualization of economic activity towards the inclusion of tasks that contribute to social reproduction and the maintenance of the labour force and which are not directly connected with the market.

Progress on the theoretical front

At the theoretical level, significant changes preceded or occurred in parallel with the conceptual and practical work on this issue over the past two decades, particularly as regards achieving greater understanding of the nature of domestic production. Since the 1950s, and especially the 1960s, economic analysis has focused increasingly on the household, within the framework of various theoretical paradigms and objectives. The neoclassical literature, particularly the New Household Economics, has analysed household production as a way to understand the gender division of labour and the participation of men and women in the paid labour force (Lloyd, 1975; Becker, 1991). Feminist versions of this analysis have pointed out some of its shortcomings and have placed greater emphasis on the social construction of gender roles and the extent to which it results in gender discrimination (Blau and Ferber, 1986). On the other hand, within the Marxian paradigm, the domestic labour debate of the 1970s emphasized the importance of domestic work for the daily maintenance and reproduction of the labour force. The emphasis here was on understanding the nature of domestic work, its links to the market, and the economic and social power relations established between paid and unpaid domestic work and between men and women (Gardiner, 1975; Molyneux, 1979; Deere, 1990). Questions about the application of the notion of exploitation to domestic work were also raised in the 1980s (Folbre, 1982).

From a feminist perspective, neither of these two approaches paid enough attention to gender and power relations within the household. However, they were useful in enhancing understanding of the economic significance of domestic work and the need to develop methods to evaluate its contribution to production and welfare. The more strictly feminist analyses further contributed to the elaboration of the theoretical dimensions of domestic work, and their political implications (Hartmann, 1987; Folbre, 1994; Bergmann, 1995).[5]

A different debate has occurred around one of the main obstacles to measuring household production and voluntary work, namely, the difficulty of comparing them with market production in view of the very different motives underlying such activities and the very different conditions under which they are carried out. In particular, as domestic work is not subject to the competitive pressures of the market, productivity levels in the two domains may differ considerably. Likewise, the quality of outputs can differ substantially, as in the case of childcare, the provision of meals, nurturing services and many other activities. Similar arguments can be applied to volunteer work. Is the problem then one of comparing like with unlike? This issue will be examined in greater detail below.

Of course, the effort to measure and document unpaid work has a number of purposes. One important objective is to bring the issue to light and render it socially appreciated. A second objective is to establish indicators of the contribution of unpaid work to social well-being and the reproduction of human resources, and to provide the basis for revising GNP and labour force statistics to that end. Third, the measurement of unpaid work is crucial to analyse the extent to which total work (paid and unpaid) is shared equally at household and society levels. Fourth, at both micro and macro levels, it can provide information on how time is allocated to paid and unpaid work and to leisure. Fifth, it is crucial to the attempt to give a gender dimension to budgets in order to make explicit that they are not neutral tools of resource allocation (Bakker and Elson, 1998). Sixth, the measurement of unpaid domestic work has associated practical uses, such as in litigation and in estimating monetary compensation in divorce cases (Cassels, 1993; Collins, 1993). Seventh, even if productivity levels are not comparable, time-use indicators can be used to analyse tendencies and trends in the share of paid/unpaid work over time. Finally, all of these can help governments and other institutions to design policy and action more effectively.

Progress on methodology

At the methodological level, substantial progress has been made on two fronts. One is the revision of data-gathering methods to capture with greater accuracy the contributions to GNP made by the various types of unpaid work (see below). The other is dealing with the complex task of designing methods to measure the value of unpaid work. The focus here is largely on domestic work, differentiating between input- and output-related methods and showing the difficulties and advantages of each.

Time-budget studies and surveys carried out in many countries have provided the empirical base for such a task, often with large sample sizes. Empirical studies have also been useful to analyse the actual content and complexities of domestic work and household dynamics. Two main approaches to measuring the value of domestic work have been introduced: one based on the imputation of value to labour time (an input-related method) and another based on the imputation of market prices to goods and services produced in the domestic sphere (an output-related method).

Different estimation methods have been used for each approach. For the input-related method, the problem is the value to impute to labour time. Three main methods have been identified:[6]
— The *global substitute* method uses the cost of a hired domestic worker, paid to carry out all types of household tasks;
— The *specialized substitute* method uses the average wage of a specialist with the appropriate skills for each specific household task;
— The *opportunity cost* method is based on the wage that the person performing domestic work can receive in the market.[7]

Each of these methods has advantages and disadvantages. The global substitute method tends to give very low estimates, given that domestic workers are at the lower end of the wage hierarchy. Moreover, a domestic worker is not likely to do all the work of the household; unless the full contribution of all household members is included, this will further reinforce the tendency toward low estimates. The specialized substitute method tends to generate high estimates, even though it is more indicative of the market value of household production. One practical problem associated with this method is the need to disaggregate each task, with the corresponding problems — mentioned earlier — of comparing unpaid and paid work. The opportunity cost method gives the widest range of estimates, depending on the skills and opportunity wage of the individual involved. This can result in rather absurd estimates since, for example, a meal prepared by a doctor will be imputed a higher value than an identical meal prepared by an unskilled worker, even if the latter is a better cook. Another problem in this case has been pointed out repeatedly: the fact that, if the cook is a full-time housewife, her opportunity costs (i.e. the income she would get in the paid labour force) are themselves correlated to her condition as a full-time housewife.

As for output-related estimates, they require some method for imputing value to domestic production and deducting the cost of inputs from it. Again the problem is determining which market goods and services are equivalent to those produced at home, and the price to impute to inputs such as labour and raw materials not purchased in the market (e.g. wood gathered by family members, or home-made utensils). Yet another problem is disparities in the quality of goods and services produced, which cannot be captured by an imputed "price". At the empirical level, this involves a tedious method requiring time-budget data, hourly wages, and a relatively high number of input and output prices (Goldschmidt-Clermont, 1987). While some of those data can be obtained from existing censuses, most have to be generated through surveys; this is precisely the type of information that satellite accounts could provide periodically. How often they should be elaborated depends on available resources and projected needs. Lutzel (1989), for example, suggested that they could be obtained every few years instead of annually.

Input vs. output methods raise other issues regarding their usefulness. For example, if the time needed to fetch water increases, input-related accounting will show an increase in time input while there is no corresponding increase in output. This suggests that, in terms of well-being, an output-related method is superior since it shows changes in well-being more accurately. Yet, from the perspective of documenting the time needed for domestic work, the input-related method is more explicit. Furthermore, the institutional and social dimensions of time complicate this issue. As Floro (1997) has argued, the notion of time and its uses varies from one country and culture to another, and, in some cases, activities that Westerners might see as recreational — such as traditional festivities and gift exchange — can represent unpaid work in other societies.

Emergence of new issues

The attempt to account for unpaid work continues to be important, as current labour market trends raise new questions about the links between paid and unpaid work and about their distribution and boundaries. A transition is currently taking place in the ways in which this distribution is affecting individuals, households and communities across countries.

First, the increasing participation of women in the paid labour force has reinforced the importance of the distribution of paid and unpaid work within the family. This is therefore an important gender equality issue.

Second, in the industrialized world the unemployed and marginalized from mainstream economic life have to negotiate survival strategies that involve an increasing reliance on unpaid work and even some forms of labour exchange not included in conventional statistics.[8] The same can be said for developing countries applying structural adjustment policies, which have resulted in the intensification of unpaid work in the household and in the community.

Third, the high incidence of underemployment and of part-time work in both high-income countries and the developing world results in cyclical or fluid combinations of paid and unpaid work which affect women and men in different ways. As will be argued below, measures of these changes are important to the assessment of variations in living standards and in contributions to social well-being. Similarly the current debate about the 35-hour week taking place particularly in western Europe has many gender implications for the distribution of paid and unpaid work. These discussions are conducted on the assumption that a reduction in working time will help to deal with unemployment. But, as Figart and Mutari have argued, the underlying assumption is that full-time, year-round employment is a social norm constructed around gendered assumptions, for instance that a full-time worker, presumably male, faces limited demands from unpaid work and family life (Figart and Mutari, 1998). A further assumption, they argue, is that the concentration of women in part-time work will continue, regardless of women's preferences. In the same way, households with more than one earner need to address the question of the distribution of working time if they are concerned about gender equality and about ensuring that caring work is fairly shared among household members.

Finally, given that unpaid work represents roughly between a quarter and a half of economic activity, depending on the country, its exclusion from national accounts is difficult to justify. There is some evidence that domestic work is increasing faster than market production. Australian data, for example, indicate that, between 1974 and 1992, household work grew at a rate of 2.4 per cent per year while the corresponding rate for market production was 1.2 per cent (Ironmonger, 1996). This can be attributed to a variety of causes ranging from the rapid increase in the number of small households (resulting in a loss in economies of scale), to the growing proportion of older people in the population, and to growing affluence. Ironmonger (1996) notes that this has happened despite an increase in female labour force participation rates and despite the diffusion of labour-saving household technologies.

All this explains why there has been increasing awareness of the importance of the sex distribution of paid and unpaid work in connection with achieving gender equality. The opening lines of the *Human Development Report 1995* underline this point: "One of the defining movements of the 20th century has been the relentless struggle for gender equality ... When this struggle finally succeeds — as it must — it will mark a great milestone in human progress. And along the way it will change most of today's premises for social, economic and political life" (UNDP, 1995, p. 1).

This forceful statement in defence of gender equality precedes the figures on the distribution of paid/unpaid work across countries, which were included for the first time in this edition of the report. The 1996 report of the Independent Commission on Population and Quality of Life (ICPQL), *Caring for the future*, also includes a call for the redefinition of work and for equality in the distribution of its output: "The Commission proposes ... to redefine work in a broad sense that encompasses both employment and unpaid activities ... benefiting society as a whole, families as well as individuals, and ensuring equitable distribution of the wealth generated" (ICPQL, 1996, p. 147).

Clearly, the effort to redefine work and measure unpaid work has gained much support. However, there is also opposition to it, as is to be expected given the complexity of the issue. The following section examines the various arguments casting doubt on this effort.

THE CONTINUING CRITIQUES

At least three types of objection have emerged against this effort to account for unpaid work. Two of them come from feminist circles; the third springs from the core of orthodox economics.

Useless effort

The first objection, which may be termed "the waste-of-time argument", results from the fear that the energy and resources required to generate statistics on unpaid work will have no impact on those engaged in it, particularly women. To what extent, for example, can such information serve to decrease the burden borne by poor women who have to toil many hours every day? Can it serve to increase their bargaining power at some level? This argument maintains that, in fact, greater social recognition of the importance of domestic work may rigidify further a division of labour which already relegates women to activities providing no financial autonomy and little control over the resources they need. Clearly such a result would not contribute to gender equality; on the contrary, it would perpetuate women's dependence on men. This argument reflects the doubts felt by some after the World Conference to Review and Appraise the Achievements of the United Nations Decade for Women, held in Nairobi in 1985. The report of that conference, setting out the *Nairobi Forward-looking Strategies for the Advancement of Women*, strongly recommended that appropriate efforts be made to measure the contribution of women's paid and unpaid work "to all aspects and sectors of development" — a first at the time (United Nations, 1985, p. 32, para. 120). The report thus significantly moved the action forward yet, in so doing, it also raised doubts about whether setting this agenda would make a qualitative difference to women's lives (see United Nations, 1985).

A similar version of this argument has been put forward by Barbara Bergmann who, though not objecting to the effort to account for unpaid work, considers that too much energy is spent on it. In her view, feminists should stress the need for women to engage in paid work in order to reduce their dependence on men and to increase their bargaining power in and outside the home. Thus, they should first focus their efforts on designing and implementing policies that facilitate the integration of women into the paid labour force, for example, childcare provision and maternity leave. Second, they should develop policies and action to enforce gender equality in the labour market, such as pay equity, affirmative action and comparable worth programmes. Bergmann is very sceptical that improved information on unpaid work can help women or that the inclusion in the calculation of GNP of food produced in the subsistence sector makes any difference to farmers.[9] She also fears that statistics on housework are likely to be used by those wishing "to glorify the housewife," for example certain right-wing groups in the United States, which can argue that housework is irreplaceable because it performs crucial services to society. Hence, she concludes that there is an anti-feminist motive in valorizing housework.

This type of objection ignores the fact that action as well as policy design and implementation need to have available as much systematically collected information as possible in order to make optimal estimates of the wide variety of tasks involved in unpaid work. The weight and distribution of unpaid work can be important in different ways. For example, having reliable estimates of the great amount of time spent by women fetching water in any country may prevent authorities from placing a low priority on the installation of running water on the grounds that fetching water does not take up much of women's time.

Again, too little is known about the extent to which an economic slowdown that increases unemployment and reduces income in a proportion of the population results in unpaid labour picking up the slack through the intensification of domestic work. It is known that the implementation of structural adjustment policies, such as those adopted by Third World countries in the 1980s and 1990s, led to coping strategies that required the intensification of unpaid work, of which a disproportionate burden fell on women. In such cases, a decrease in real income may not result in a corresponding decrease in well-being: it depends on the extent to which unpaid work makes up for the reduced ability to purchase goods from the market. An evaluation of these shifts cannot be made without systematic statistical information on unpaid work (Benería, 1996). As Floro has argued, more precise information on people's daily activities would help to assess the quality of their lives more accurately, and to develop indicators of work intensity, simultaneous performance of several tasks, stress, individual health, and even child neglect. This is because various aspects of work, such as its intensity and the length of the working day, have been shown to have an impact on the stress levels and health of workers and their families (Floro, 1996).

The effort to account for unpaid work must be viewed not as an end in itself but as a means to understand who contributes to human welfare and development and to what extent, and what action is required to distribute equally the pains and pleasures of work. The fear that some political groups might use the information for their own purposes must be set against the certainty that such information also serves to achieve a variety of positive outcomes, including the more accurate design of social policies and the organization of social safety nets.

The importance of "difference"

A second objection, which mostly concerns domestic and unpaid caring work, is perhaps more difficult to respond to since it springs from the notion that certain personal and relational aspects of this activity render it qualitatively very different from market work. As Himmelweit has argued, although recognizing such activity as "work" is important in making it visible and in validating women's contributions in the home, something is lost in the process. She questions "whether the best way for women's contribution to be appreciated [is] to force it into a pre-existing category of 'work' borrowed from an economics which inherently failed to value most of what made women's domestic contribution distinctive" (Himmelweit, 1995, p. 2).

She argues, for example, that "caring" is an ambiguous concept ranging from physical to emotional care; while the first "might to some extent be independent of the relation between the carer and the person cared for," the second requires that "the person doing the caring is inseparable from the care given" (Himmelweit, 1995, p. 8). She also points out a second characteristic of caring work, namely, that it is fulfilling for the carer. Hence her reluctance to view as conventional "work" the time spent on activities to give emotional care and support, which both provide the carer with a sense of fulfilment and, furthermore, are very difficult to quantify.

Himmelweit concludes that not everything needs to be seen as either "work" or "non-work", particularly since to do so may lead to the social undervaluation of activities that do not fit into the category of work: "by insisting that domestic activities gain recognition by conforming to an unchallenged category of work, the significance of caring and self-fulfilling activities remains unrecognized" (1995, p. 14). But this argument is problematic for various reasons.

First, greater visibility and documentation for these activities are likely to increase the recognition of their significance for human well-being, particularly if their nature is well understood and emphasized. As recent history demonstrates, this is exactly what the theoretical, methodological and practical efforts of the past three decades have accomplished.

Second, many unpaid activities are not caring or fulfilling, while some paid activities are. The shift of a significant proportion of caring work from the unpaid reproductive sphere to the market has not always involved the loss of some of its basic characteristics. For example, work motives associated with solidarity, altruism and caring can be found in the market as well as in unpaid work. So it is difficult to argue that there are no personal and relational aspects to some of the paid services offered through the market, despite the fact that the service is provided in exchange for pay. To be sure, some market-oriented caring services are unlikely to provide the same quality of care and emotional support as that offered by a loving family member — whether or not the caring work is based on love and affection, a sense of responsibility, respect, intrinsic enjoyment, altruism or informal *quid pro quo* expectations.[10] However, it is not difficult to find exceptions to both cases, i.e. market-based care providing selfless emotional support beyond the exchange contract, and family care based on selfish expectations or on some form of coercion.

Third, there is a dialectical relationship between market and non-market work such that, to some extent, the skills required in one sphere can be used in the other, and vice versa. It is therefore difficult to draw a clear dividing line between the two. Thus, a paid nanny or nurse may provide a high quality of personal care with skills learned at home; and managerial skills learned in the labour market may be used as a way to reduce unpaid working time in the household.

Fourth, in addition to caring labour, unpaid work includes other types of activity only indirectly related to caring, such as gathering wood, cleaning the house, and participating in community activities. The extent of these tasks may vary by country, cultural factors, and the social background of those performing them. In this sense, Himmelweit's argument has a built-in bias resulting from her focus on an urban nuclear family, and so does not include all forms of unpaid work.

Overall, however, Himmelweit makes important arguments which question the extent to which the selfless, caring work conventionally attributed to domestic labour can be projected on to other activities outside the household, including market activity, a subject which is discussed below.

Theoretically misguided

The third objection to the project of measuring unpaid work relates to theoretical and methodological questions springing from conventional economics. Though criticisms have been voiced by conventional economists, very few have been expressed in writing.[11] The discussion that follows focuses on a paper by Sujai Shivakumar, *Valuing women's work: Theoretical constraints in determining the worth of household and other non-market activity* (Shivakumar, 1997), which is a pioneering effort and captures many of the unwritten criticisms referred to above.

One of Shivakumar's objectives is to show that the monetary imputation of unpaid work "is not consistent with present conceptions of the theory of value in economics" and that this imputation is merely a "rhetorical effort" without theoretical foundation or a "dubious game of statistical football" (Shivakumar, 1997, p. 374). In order to elaborate this argument, he includes a historical account of the development of value theory in economics and formulates three main criticisms. First, he claims this attempt is inspired by socialist-feminism in terms of its rhetoric, forms of analysis and policy prescriptions, using gender as the central "tool of analysis", presenting alternative visions of economic processes and focusing economics on the notion of "provisioning of human life". Second, he argues that the attempt is based on Ricardian-Marxian notions of value based on the labour theory of value instead of the "modern" orthodox value theory based on subjective preferences and as indicated through market prices. For this reason, he views the attempt as theoretically unsound: "Modern economic theory does not support time-use analysis as a basis for imputing the monetary value of work ... The labour theory of value on which this type of analysis is based has roots in Ricardian-Marxian theory of value that is no longer recognized in economics" (Shivakumar, 1997, p. 333). In this sense, Shivakumar considers that the money value estimates, such as those included in the *Human Development Report 1995*, are meaningless because they are based on time-use data.

Third, Shivakumar criticizes the different methods used to estimate the value of unpaid work. In doing so, he repeats many of the methodological objections previously addressed by different authors. However, rather than pointing out the ways in which methodologies might be improved, he sees no redeeming value in the attempt to do it. Comparing the feminist efforts on unpaid work with those of the environmentalists who want environmental costs to be taken into consideration in national accounting statistics, he writes: "With no theoretical guideline on how to choose among alternative ways of conducting the valuation, the selection among alternative ways of imputation in environmental accounting then comes to reflect on the relative strengths of competing political interests" (Shivakumar, 1997, p. 405).

The estimates in the *Human Development Report 1995* did present many problems, but many of them derived from poor and insufficient data; a more constructive approach would view the data as the result of a pioneering but nevertheless important effort in need of improvement. Shivakumar also points out the problem of comparability between market and non-market time, but fails to mention that most advocates of the inclusion of unpaid work in national income accounts recognize this problem (hence the use of satellite accounts to avoid comparing like with unlike).

Shivakumar's critique is more fundamental in its insistence on the view that any monetary evaluation displays an ignorance of the concept of value as something realized through the exchange process. That is, the exchange process is viewed as the only source of value despite the fact that the value of non-market goods in subsistence production has been estimated for many years, and that many economists make use of "shadow prices" in their work. Moreover, a good proportion of domestic work is marketable, particularly as increasing portions of it are taken up by paid work. This includes wage work such as cleaning services and childcare provided by firms of different sizes (Meagher, 1997). However, Shivakumar does not make any reference to these facts. Within neoclassical economics, the imputing of market prices to household production is standard practice. Shivakumar does not make any reference to the fact that, in many ways, the New Household Economics pioneered the application of "modern" human capital theory to household production and decision-making and that other economists have also taken the task of analysing household production seriously (e.g. Fraumeni, 1998). It would be ironic to categorize the work of human capital theorists such as Jacob Mincer, Gary Becker and many other neoclassical economists as socialist-feminist and based on the labour theory of value.

In associating the effort to measure unpaid work with Ricardo and Marx, Shivakumar ignores the fact that orthodox Marxist theory would agree with his insistence on seeing value as originating only in the exchange process. In addition, it is far from clear that Marxian value theory is based on labour inputs without regard to the weight of demand to determine market value. Though he is right in affirming that gender as an analytical category and "the provisioning of human life" are central to feminist economics, that holds true for feminist approaches to other disciplines. He ignores the fact that the work on measuring unpaid labour has been carried out by a large number of professional men and women, some of them feminists, supporting diverse theoretical paradigms and practical politics.

Beyond these basic points, some of Shivakumar's criticisms are not well informed, for example, his statement that feminists "have not spelled out any particular policy prescription other than to seek to better inform policy makers" (1997, p. 394). Feminists have called for and suggested gender-aware policies in areas such as labour market policy, public services, structural adjustment packages, and agricultural policy (Sen and Grown, 1987; Palmer, 1991; Elson, 1995; UNDP, 1995), and many of these policies would benefit from more systematic statistical information and documentation regarding unpaid work. In sum, Shivakumar's paper reveals a strong irritation about the spoiling of a neatly-defined, presumably "objective" orthodox economic model by what he regards as the normative prescriptions of feminism. Although, to his credit, he does present some recommendations "to satisfy the Beijing mandate", his alternatives fall short of the task to be accomplished and do not solve some of the problems analysed.

CONCLUDING COMMENTS

The questions underlying this article are what is *value* and what is *of value to society*. The basic problem remains how to measure and evaluate human well-being and how to identify those who contribute to it. The point made has been that though current GNP statistics include what is bad for our health — such as carcinogenic chemicals in foods — or for the environment — such as the pollution produced by factories — still there is resistance to the measuring of work and production of goods and services that sustain and enhance human well-being. Yet, in Nancy Folbre's terms, societies and individuals ultimately need to know "who pays for the kids" (Folbre, 1994).

It is necessary to know, for example, who contributes to the survival strategies of the poor so that the best policies to overcome poverty can be designed. Unpaid work is not evenly distributed across class and social groups. Affluent households can employ (mostly) women for domestic work, and can also purchase goods and services that poorer households have to produce at home, without outside help. When lower-income women participate in the paid labour market, either their workload increases or standards of home-produced goods and childcare are lowered (Gimenez, 1990). There is also a significant difference in the total number of hours dedicated to domestic work by women with different levels of income. An empirical study carried out in Barcelona showed that the absolute value of domestic work was higher for middle-income households, followed by the lower-income and higher-income categories. However, domestic work in lower-income households represented a higher percentage of total household income (which included social income or the perceived value of public services) (Carrasco, 1992).

But there is more to the challenge of measuring unpaid work since, in Elizabeth Minninch's terms, it requires "transforming knowledge" or moving beyond the boundaries of conventional paradigms. This includes rethinking "mystified concepts" or "ideas, notions, categories and the like, that are so deeply familiar they are rarely questioned" and which result in "partial knowledge" (see Minninch, 1990, chap. 4). The challenge is to question current methods to measure well-being and who contributes to it in the community and society as a whole. Which leads one in turn to question the assumptions underlying received knowledge, in this case those linking "work" to paid labour time and the market.

This article has shown how discussion about the difference between paid and unpaid work leads one to question how far the economic rationality attached to market-related behaviour is the norm and the extent to which models of human behaviour are based on motives most commonly associated with unpaid work, such as altruism, empathy, collective responsibility and solidarity. Feminist economists have emphasized the need to construct models other than those based on the market-oriented motives of rational economic man. In Paula England's terms, conventional economic theory is based on a "separate-self model" of male behaviour which is different from the "relational model" more commonly associated with female behaviour (England, 1993). This raises questions about whether, as women's participation in the paid labour force increases around the world, we may witness two changes: a "masculinization" of women's values and behaviour and a "feminization" of market-oriented behaviour.

Notes

[1] This chapter draws on material developed more extensively in a forthcoming book by the same author on gender and the global economy.

[2] To illustrate, according to estimates presented at the 1998 annual meeting of the Inter-American Development Bank, four out of every five new jobs in Latin America are created in the informal sector, which accounts for 57 per cent of the region's workforce (*The Economist*, 1998).

[3] A soup kitchen visited by the author in an East Los Angeles church in 1992 was run entirely by Spanish-speaking women, who served dinner to about 100 men a day.

[4] For more details, see Benería (1992).

[5] For more details, see Benería (1995).

[6] For more details see, for example, Goldschmidt-Clermont (1982 and 1987), Benería (1992) and Fraumeni (1998).

[7] A variation of the opportunity cost method is the *lifetime income approach* (see Fraumeni, 1998).

[8] These strategies may consist of a form of paid work outside the mainstream monetary system, as when the creation of a local currency facilitates exchanges. One such case has been developed in Ithaca, NY, where "Ithaca money" is issued locally and used to exchange labour services as well as to purchase from the local stores that accept it. Even though these cases have little weight for the economy as a whole, they can be important at the local level and provide interesting examples of survival strategies.

[9] Author's conversation with Barbara Bergmann on 14 March 1998.

[10] For an analysis of caring motives, see Folbre and Weisskopf (1998).

[11] For example, some World Bank economists have been very critical of UNDP's efforts to include estimates of unpaid work in its *Human Development Report 1995*. However, to the author's knowledge, the objections have mostly been voiced in discussions and meetings, rather than in writing.

References

AARP (American Association of Retired Persons). 1997. *The AARP survey of civic involvement.* Washington, DC.

Bakker, Isabella; Elson, Diane. 1998. *Towards engendering budgets.* Alternative Federal Budget Papers Series, 1998. Ottawa, Canadian Center for Policy Alternatives.

Barrig, Maruja. 1996. "Nos habíamos amado tanto: Crisis del estado y organización femenina", in John Friedmann, Rebecca Abers and Lilian Autler (eds.): *Emergences: Women's struggles for livelihood in Latin America.* Los Angeles, CA, UCLA.

Becker, Gary. 1991. *A treatise on the family.* Enlarged edition. Cambridge, MA, Harvard University Press.

Benería, Lourdes. 1996. "Thou shalt not live by statistics alone but it might help", in *Feminist Economics* (London), Vol. 2, No. 3, pp. 139-142.

—. 1995. "Toward a greater integration of gender in economics", in *World Development* (Oxford), Vol. 23, No. 11 (Nov.), pp. 1839-1850.

—. 1992. "Accounting for women's work: The progress of two decades", in *World Development* (Oxford), Vol. 20, No.11 (Nov.), pp. 1547-1560.

—. 1982. "Accounting for women's work", in Lourdes Benería (ed.): *Women and development: The sexual division of labor in rural societies.* A study prepared for the International Labour Office within the framework of the World Employment Programme. New York, NY, Praeger, pp. 119-147.

Bergmann, Barbara. 1995. "Becker's theory of the family: Preposterous conclusions", in *Feminist Economics* (London), Vol. 1, No. 1, pp. 141-150.

Blades, Derek W. 1975. *Non-monetary (subsistence) activities in the national accounts of developing countries*. Paris, OECD.

Blau, Francine; Ferber, Marianne. 1986. *The economics of women, men and work*. Englewood Cliffs, NJ, Prentice-Hall.

Boserup, Ester. 1970. *Woman's role in economic development*. New York, NY, St. Martin's Press.

Carrasco, Cristina. 1992. *El trabajo doméstico y la reproducción social*. Madrid, Instituto de la Mujer.

Cassels, Jamie. 1993. "User requirements and data needs", in Statistics Canada/Status of Women Canada (eds.): *Summary of Proceedings of the International Conference on the Valuation and Measurement of Unpaid Work, Ottawa, 18-30 April*. Ottawa.

Chadeau, Ann. 1989. *Measuring household production: Conceptual issues and results for France*. Paper presented at the Second ECE/INSTRAW Joint Meeting on Statistics on Women, Geneva, 13-16 Nov.

Collins, Mary. 1993. "Opening remarks", in Statistics Canada/Status of Women Canada (eds.): *Summary of Proceedings of the International Conference on the Valuation and Measurement of Unpaid Work, Ottawa, 18-30 April*. Ottawa.

Deere, Carmen Diana. 1990. *Household and class relations: Peasants and landlords in Northern Peru*. Berkeley, CA, University of California Press.

The Economist (London). 1998. "Great reforms, nice growth, but where are the jobs?", in Vol. 346, No. 8060 (21-27 Mar.), pp. 67-68.

Elson, Diane. 1995. "Gender awareness in modeling structural adjustment", in *World Development* (Oxford), Vol. 23, No.11 (Nov.), pp. 1851-1868.

England, Paula. 1993. "The separative self: Androcentric bias in neoclassical assumptions", in Marianne A. Ferber and Julie A. Nelson (eds.): *Beyond economic man: Feminist theory and economics*. Chicago, IL, University of Chicago Press, pp. 37-53.

Figart, Deborah M.; Mutari, Ellen. 1998. "Degendering work time in comparative perspective: Alternative policy frameworks", in *Review of Social Economy* (London), Vol. 56, No. 4 (Winter), pp. 460-480.

Floro, Maria Sagrario. 1997. *Time as a numeraire: The institutional and social dimensions of time use*. Paper presented at the Rescheduling Time Symposium, University of Manchester, 6-7 Nov.

—. 1996. "We need new economic indicators to gauge work and well-being", in *The Chronicle of Higher Education* (Washington, DC), Vol. 43, No.15 (Dec.), pp. B4-B5.

—. 1995. "Economic restructuring, gender and the allocation of time", in *World Development* (Oxford), Vol. 23, No.11 (Nov.), pp. 1913-1929.

Folbre, Nancy. 1994. *Who pays for the kids? Gender and the structures of constraint*. New York, NY, Routledge.

—. 1982. "Exploitation comes home: A critique of the Marxian theory of family labour", in *Cambridge Journal of Economics* (London), Vol. 6, No. 4 (Dec.), pp. 317-329.

—; Weisskopf, Thomas. 1998. "Did father know best? Families, markets and the supply of caring labor", in Avner Ben-Ner and Louis Putterman (eds.): *Economics, values and organization*. Cambridge, Cambridge University Press, pp. 171-205.

Fraumeni, Barbara. 1998. *Expanding economic accounts for productivity analysis: A nonmarket and human capital perspective*. Paper presented at the Conference on Income and Wealth, organized by the National Bureau for Economic Research, 20-21 Mar.

Gardiner, Jean. 1975. "Women's domestic labour", in *New Left Review* (London), No. 89 (Jan.-Feb.), pp. 47-58.

Gimenez, Martha E. 1990. "The dialectics of waged and unwaged work: Waged work, domestic labor and household survival in the United States", in Jane L. Collins and Martha Gimenez (eds.): *Work without wages: Comparative studies of domestic labor and self-employment.* Albany, NY, State University of New York Press, pp. 25-45.

Goldschmidt-Clermont, Luisella. 1987. *Economic evaluations of unpaid household work: Africa, Asia, Latin America and Oceania.* Women, Work and Development Series, No. 14. Geneva, ILO.

—. 1982. *Unpaid work in the household: A review of economic evaluation methods.* Women, Work and Development Series, No. 1. Geneva, ILO.

Gora, Ann; Nemerowicz, Gloria. 1991. "Volunteers: Initial and sustaining motivations in service to the community", in *Research in the Sociology of Health Care* (Greenwich, CT), Vol. 9, pp. 233-246.

Hartmann, Heidi I. 1987. "The family as the locus of gender, class, and political struggle: The example of housework", in Sandra Harding (ed.): *Feminism and methodology.* Bloomington, IN, Indiana University Press, pp. 109-134.

Himmelweit, Susan. 1995. "The discovery of unpaid work: The social consequences of the expansion of work", in *Feminist Economics* (London), Vol. 1, No. 2 (Summer), pp. 1-19.

ICPQL. 1996. *Caring for the future: Making the next decades provide a life worth living.* Report of the Independent Commission on Population and Quality of Life. Oxford, Oxford University Press.

ILO. 1983. *Thirteenth International Conference of Labour Statisticians, 1982: Report of the Conference.* ICLS/13/D.11. Geneva.

—. 1977. *Labour force estimates and projections, 1950-2000 — Volume VI: Methodological supplement.* Second edition. Geneva.

—. 1976. *International recommendations on labour statistics.* Geneva.

—. 1955. *The Eighth International Conference of Labour Statisticians, 1954.* Report of the proceedings of the Eighth International Conference of Labour Statisticians. Geneva.

INSTRAW (United Nations International Research and Training Institute for the Advancement of Women). 1991. *Methods of collecting and analysing statistics on women in the informal sector and their contributions to national product: Results of regional workshops.* INSTRAW/BT/CRP.1. Santo Domingo, United Nations.

Ironmonger, Duncan. 1996. "Counting outputs, capital inputs and caring labor: Estimating Gross Household Product", in *Feminist Economics* (London), Vol. 2, No. 3, pp. 37-64.

Juster, F. Thomas; Stafford, Frank P. 1991. "The allocation of time: Empirical findings, behavioral models, and problems of measurement", in *Journal of Economic Literature* (Nashville, TN), Vol. 29, No. 2 (June), pp. 471-522.

Langfeldt, Enno. 1987. "Trabajo no remunerado en el contexto familiar", in *Revista de Estudios Económicos* (Santo Domingo), No. 1, pp. 131-146.

League of Nations. 1938. *Statistics of the gainfully occupied population: Definitions and classifications recommended by the Committee of Statistical Experts.* 1938, II.A.12, Studies and Reports on Statistical Methods, No.1. Geneva.

Lind, Amy. 1990. "Gender, power and development: Popular women's organizations and the politics of needs in Ecuador", in Arturo Escobar and Sonia Alvárez (eds.): *The making of social movements in Latin America.* Boulder, CO, Westview Press, pp. 134-149.

Lloyd, Cynthia B. (ed.). 1975. *Sex, discrimination, and the division of labor.* Columbia Studies in Economics, No. 8. New York, NY, Columbia University Press.

Lutzel, Heinrich. 1989. *Household production and national accounts*. Paper presented at the Second ECE/INSTRAW Joint Meeting on Statistics on Women, held in Geneva. 13-16 Nov.

Meagher, Gabrielle. 1997. "Recreating domestic service: Institutional cultures and the evolution of paid household work", in *Feminist Economics* (London), Vol. 3, No. 2 (Summer), pp. 1-28.

Minninch, Elizabeth Kamarck. 1990. *Transforming knowledge*. Philadelphia, PA, Temple University Press.

Molyneux, Maxine. 1979. "Beyond the domestic labour debate", in *New Left Review* (London), No.116 (July-Aug.), pp. 3-28.

Palmer, Ingrid. 1991. *Gender and population in the adjustment of African economies: Planning for change*. Women, Work and Development Series, No. 19. Geneva, ILO.

Portes, Alejandro; Castells, Manuel. 1989. *The informal economy*. Baltimore, MD, The Johns Hopkins University Press.

Reid, Margaret. 1934. *Economics of household production*. New York, NY, John Wiley.

Sen, Gita; Grown, Caren. 1987. *Development, crises and alternative visions: Third World women's perspectives*. New York, NY, Monthly Review Press.

Shivakumar, Sujai, 1997. *Valuing women's work: Theoretical constraints in determining the worth of household and other non-market activity*. Paper presented at the Workshop on Integrating Paid and Unpaid Work into National Policies, organized by UNDP, United Nations Statistical Division, UNIFEM, the Ministry of Foreign Affairs of the Republic of Korea, and the Women's Development Institute, and held in Seoul, 28-30 May.

United Nations. 1989. *1989 world survey on the role of women in development*. Centre for Social Development and Humanitarian Affairs, United Nations Office at Vienna, Document ST/CSDHA/6. New York, NY.

—. 1985. *Report of the World Conference to Review and Appraise the Achievements of the United Nations Decade for Women: Equality, Development and Peace*. Document A/CONF.116/28, 15 Sep. [see also A/CONF.116/28/Rev. 1 (85.IV.10), 1986]. New York, NY.

UNDP (United Nations Development Programme). 1995. *Human Development Report 1995*. New York, NY, Oxford University Press.

United Nations Statistical Office/ECA/INSTRAW. 1991a. *Handbook on compilation of statistics on women in the informal sector in industry, trade and services in Africa*. New York, NY, United Nations.

—. 1991b. *Synthesis of pilot studies on compilation of statistics on women in the informal sector in industry, trade, and services in African countries*. New York, NY, United Nations.

Waring, Marylin. 1988. *If women counted: A new feminist economics*. San Francisco, CA, Harper and Row.

Wood, Cynthia. 1997. "The FirstWorld/Third Party criterion: A feminist critique of production boundaries in economics", in *Feminist Economics* (London), Vol. 3, No. 3, pp. 47-68.

DATA ON RACE, ETHNICITY AND GENDER: CAVEATS FOR THE USER

7

Carolyn Shaw BELL*

> *Many familiar terms that indicate categories for data collection, such as those for race, ethnicity and gender on a census form, convey both more and less than is apparent. Inevitable changes in definition and in socio-demographic variables demand attention to the fine print, long footnotes and distant annexes that accompany good data sets. Otherwise, what seem to be objective details may be ambiguous or downright misleading. Only with due care to the explanations can the data be used effectively by social scientists for sound analysis and by policy-makers to design successful programmes.*

What are commonly known as "demographic characteristics" include a person's sex, ethnic or racial heritage, family ties, and so on. Some of these, like marital status, can reflect a person's choices or efforts; others, like age and sex, cannot. On the face of it ethnic background or race seem totally exogenous to the individual: how can a person change the colour of a parent's skin or the original culture of a grandparent? But in fact, in countries where information on these factors is obtained by questioning a respondent, some individuals can freely choose the way these characteristics enter into official data. In the United States, for example, people can define themselves as white, black, Hispanic, Asian, and so forth ; and they can choose to downplay or emphasize the characteristics of their birth and upbringing, motivated by personal, cultural, financial or political factors.

Except when collecting original data, most scholars in the social sciences use data which have already been arranged into groupings such as age, sex, ethnic background, and so on. This chapter aims to forewarn

Originally published in *International Labour Review*, Vol. 135 (1996), No. 5.

* Katharine Coman Professor of Economics, Emeritus, Wellesley College, United States.

such users as well as policy-makers of the deficiencies of many familiar data sets, while recognizing, of course, that such sets are indispensable to social analysis and to the design of policies to aid particular groups. The hazards should not go unnoticed — even less so when they can be corrected. The text begins with issues associated with classification by ethnicity or race because the pitfalls of such data, especially in the United States, arise from fairly simple well-known circumstances — which does not mean that these pitfalls themselves are well known, quite the contrary. The discussion of how classification by sex affects economic data then occupies the bulk of the chapter.

RACE AND ETHNICITY VARIABLES

Countries which include people of different ethnic or national heritage typically establish policies based on distinguishing between or discriminating among different groups. Any rule defining who is a "foreigner," or a "gypsy" or "Asian" or "German" will be difficult to apply over time if people marry outside the group and have children. Identifying second- or third-generation heritages can become impossible for orphans or children of single mothers unsure about the father's definition. Rarely, however, do published or accepted data sets indicate such potential shortcomings, and unwary users compare numbers of "native" and "alien" peoples thinking they are working with accurate statistics. Even where the data are based on apparently more definitive sources, such as birth certificates and other official documents, rather than on respondents' replies to census and other data collectors, one must investigate the details of the particular classification system used in order to be certain of the reliability of such data. Thus the way in which South Africa, under apartheid, defined those in the various categories of black, coloured, Afrikaner, and so on would not help anyone trying to understand the regulations governing the establishment of German nationality. It also means that international comparisons of ethnic diversity are particularly hazardous.

Because the United States decennial Census of Population began in 1790, and because the United States population has included people of colour since that time, the country's experience with "racial" classifications offers a useful example. Yet even in the United States it is quite impossible in 1996 to compare the number of black physicians or even of black people in the labour force with the number before 1970 because in earlier data the term "black" was not used to classify people. Earlier tabulations frequently show "white" and "non-white" as exclusive categories; "Negro" usually appeared as a subset of non-white. For many decades in both the nineteenth and twentieth centuries, the term "black" was simply not used in polite speech: "coloured people" was deemed more respectful on an informal basis, "Negro" being a more formal term.[1]

Until 1960 Census enumerators visited households to collect data; following specific instructions, they determined race by direct observation. For example, in 1890 they were cautioned to write "whether white, black, mulatto, quadroon, octoroon, Chinese, Japanese, or Indian ... The word 'black' shall be used to describe those persons who have 3/4 or more black blood; 'mulatto', those persons who have from 3/8 to 5/8 black blood; 'quadroon' those persons who have one-fourth black blood; and 'octoroon' those persons who have one-eighth or any trace of black blood." [2] Beginning in 1920 the term "Negro" appeared instead of "black", and "A person of mixed White and Negro blood was to be returned as Negro no matter how small the percentage of Negro blood; any mixture of white and other is reported as Other".[3]

By 1970, self-identification accounted for most of the Census data entries, although many people, especially in the older population, preferred "Negro" or "coloured people" to the new term "black", as they already had pride in themselves. When the Census, hoping for more accurate classifications, asked people to identify themselves as white, black, or other, some unknown number opted for "other" because many regarded the choice "black or Negro" as unacceptable. On the other hand, enumerators were instructed to classify as white anyone using the terms "Chicano, LaRaza, Mexican-American, Moslem or Brown".[4] By 1990, self-identification required each person to select one among 15 racial types listed, including white, black, Eskimo, Samoan and so forth. If the person replied "other", a following question asked to which group the person considered him/herself to belong.[5] It should be noted that the Census began using the terms "racial" or "race" to replace the old category of "colour" and that no scientific definition has ever been used.

Analysts who compare different groups implicitly or explicitly assume them to be distinct and mutually exclusive, but this is not necessarily so when the term "other" occurs. (The alternative is to list every possible choice.) [6] Overlap is particularly likely with data on people of "Hispanic" origin. The 1980 Census listed specific categories and a residual "Other Spanish/Hispanic" category; ten years later a respondent could write in a specific entry. None of these categories are racial, and analysts using such data should be careful to make this clear.

Decisions on the design and execution of the decennial Census reflect pressure from a variety of sources, including ethnic groups wishing to be recognized and Congressional representatives wanting to reduce costs. Other surveys picking up racial or ethnic data have to meet various considerations.

Currently, the decennial Census relies on self-identification for both racial and ethnic heritage and accepts categories based on national origin of self or ancestors or on sociocultural groups. But other surveys follow different formats. The Current Population Survey, conducted by the Bureau of the Census to pick up data on employment, household earnings, family composition, income, etc., uses four racial groups (and only "Black", not "Black or Negro") and 21 ethnic origin categories, including "Afro-American (Black, Negro)" and "Central or South American (Spanish countries)" along with the less ambiguous "German", "Italian", and so forth. The Survey of Income and Program Participation uses "White", "Black", and "other races," which includes American Indians, Japanese, Chinese, Filipinos, Pacific Islanders and "any other race except White and Black".[7]

The Center for Disease Control, charged with monitoring trends in diseases and with identifying groups at risk, uses a very simplified system of "White non-Hispanic", "Black non-Hispanic", "Hispanic", "Native American", "Asian and Pacific Islander", and "unspecified".[8]

At the time of writing the Office of Management and Budget is receiving comments on a proposed new directive on statistical standards for race and ethnicity, with an optimistic target date of January 1997. Congressional hearings, held in 1993, and a National Academy of Science report from the Committee on National Statistics have prompted many suggestions, e.g. adding "Middle Easterner" to the ethnic categories, changing "Black" to "African American," adding a "multi-racial" category for self-identification, and changing the term "Hispanic" to refer to a racial rather than an ethnic category.

As can be seen from the examples, racial and ethnic identification poses complex issues. So far, there has been general agreement on three principles, applicable to whatever finally emerges as the new standard. First, none of the racial or ethnic categories denote scientific or anthropological identification. Second, the entire process of determining racial or ethnic classifications must be guided by respect for the individual and for individual dignity: self-identification will be used as far as possible. And finally, whatever the final identifications selected they will not in any way determine eligibility for any federal programme.

In fact, of course, data on race and ethnicity have been used to monitor the impact of the Voting Rights Act, and for mapping new Congressional districts, monitoring the behaviour of banks under the Home Mortgage Disclosure Act and the Equal Credit Opportunity Act, and implementing federal affirmative action programmes. These issues far transcend the problems of analysts wishing to tabulate events using racial or ethnic categories as variables. But they should be warned: the data may well not be what they seem.

As for policies, the quandaries aroused in the United States by various proposals to differentiate between immigrants and others, and between legal and illegal immigrants, again provide useful examples. Citizenship exists for those who are born in the United States, and to most who are born elsewhere to United States citizens; naturalization applies to non-citizens who immigrate into the country. If an immigrant (legal or illegal) who is not a citizen has a child born in the country, that child holds United States citizenship. (Some of the proposals during the 1996 election campaign include the repeal of this provision.) Another alternative entails different rules depending on the immigrant's country of origin. None of the proposals deal with issues of compliance and enforcement, which obviously require identification of individuals according to their status.

A quite different complication has been introduced by people who wish to define themselves as "mixed", or in some cases as "mixed Cuban/native American", or "mixed white/Asian" — the permutations and combinations can of course be multitudinous. This proposal will not matter unless Congress uses such a category of mixed parentage in some legislation, including that authorizing the Census or any other statistical survey. What the proposal should suggest to the social scientist or policymaker is the possibility of abandoning ethnic or racial or national classifications altogether, especially in a country like the United States where obviously very few individuals can point to only one such identification back for more than a couple of generations.

GENDER AS AN ECONOMIC VARIABLE

Classifying people by sex at least poses no problem of overlapping groups. Self-identification with one of two choices, male or female, is the common practice.[9] Other terminological options, however, reflect cultural and language changes. The set of ideas or stereotypes associated with the terms "girl", "woman", "female", has so changed that today no certainty exists about any implied characteristics aside from purely biological features.

For economists, as for other social scientists, the construct "gender" contains much more meaning than that of sex. Once gender is recognized as encompassing important relationships between men and women, constructed by society or culture and therefore collective and imposed rather than chosen, its use in economic analysis should affect many of the standard explanations of education, occupation and, especially in poor countries, nutrition and childbearing.[10] Consequently this article reviews existing data sources in terms of their usefulness for gender-related analysis, particularly with respect to economics. Again, the examples come largely from the United States, partly because of the limitations of the author's expertise, and partly because that country has very rich data systems of considerable age.

The Current Population Survey (CPS), the source of data used in many economic research efforts, collects data monthly from some 60,000 households, a probability sample of the entire population. Most industrialized countries and many developing countries have established similar surveys to provide current data, and to allow cross-country comparisons, after careful attention to definitions and methodology to ensure that comparability is, in fact, possible. The Luxembourg Income Study is probably the best of such cross-national analyses, and its database contains all the necessary warnings. That study does not deal with the question of minorities but notes that, for most countries, the total number of people involved is small. Whether the omission is significant will, of course, depend on the country and on the particular question being studied: policies for guest workers in a number of European countries will obviously need such data, whether or not they are reliable.

In most such studies, the primary data usually come from one person reporting for the entire household. The initial contact, an interview visit, records background information; later questions may be asked over the telephone. The major longitudinal survey, the Survey of Income and Program Participation (SIPP), also has counterparts in other countries; the United States collects data on individuals from over 22,000 households three times yearly for two and a half years. SIPP also combines an initial interview with later telephoned inquiries.

First, the person reporting may not know everything necessary to provide information for every member of the household. That black male youths are undercounted by the Census of Population is partly attributable to this: it is not always clear to what household, if any, a teenager belongs and so he may go altogether unreported. Which is more likely: that a woman is ignorant about the details of her husband's or son's job or that a man is ignorant about the details of his wife's or daughter's job? The amount of error in the basic interview data has not been estimated, but many difficulties in the collection of data can be traced to assumptions about gender roles or behaviour.

A second problem was partly solved when the CPS questionnaire was revised in January 1994. For many years, the first question asked was "What were you doing during most of last week: working, keeping house, going to school, or something else?" This question was repeated for each member of the household. Aside from the choices offered, the interviewer could record other activities *if they were volunteered by the respondent*. Additional distinctions thus tabulated included: with a job but not at work, looking for work, unable to work, retired, or other. If the answer to the first question was not "working" there followed a series of questions beginning "Did you do any work at all last week?" This query could pick up someone with a brief work stint who did not identify the *major* activity as "working." For those who did work, the interviewer then asked about hours, wages, occupational and job history details. The entire approach left the definition of "work" itself open to a variety of interpretations. The word as used in common speech covers a complex of activities — study, therapy, exercise, practice of a skill — all of which require work, as do school homework and housework.

Other problems exist. Anyone working a 40-hour week who sleeps eight hours a night cannot, truthfully, select working as the major activity. But few answers involve this precision: most people answer in terms of a "workweek" of five or six days, not seven. *Because* of that latitude, the option "keeping house" was particularly troublesome.

Measuring accurately and honestly over seven days, many employed woman answered "keeping house" rather than "working." Although some employed men could also select this alternative, "keeping house" is associated with women and not men. Evidence that this option affected the validity of the data emerged years ago when analysts could not find the increasing number of women in the labour force reflected in an increasing number of retired women workers. For their major activity, most retired women workers selected "keeping house" rather than "retirement".

The new CPS questionnaire begins: "Last week did you do any work for pay?", and the Department of Labor boasted that the revision would count women's employment more accurately. For example, a new pool of discouraged workers has turned up among women who cite child care or family responsibilities as reasons for not working but who in fact want a job, are available for work, and have looked for work during the previous year. Evidently anyone working in the field of labour market analysis needs to be thoroughly familiar with both the present survey and its predecessors.

Many introductory courses in the social sciences can benefit from including this entire topic of employment data, survey methods, and how people answer questions. It usually interests students and can provide a highly useful learning experience. For example, role-playing in class, with a Census interviewer and two loquacious respondents, or entertaining a speaker from the local Census office, or arguing about the meaning of part-time and full-time work all serve to illustrate the importance of good data.

ECONOMIC TOPICS WHERE GENDER MATTERS

Consumption spending

Despite their interest in the consumption function or in the index of consumer sentiment at the macroeconomic level, economists have mostly ignored consumer spending, not least because it comes close to marketing, business activity, and other issues which they usually avoid. Yet spending patterns have been analysed for two-earner families, for single-mother families, and so on. Such work relies on periodic surveys of income and spending which, in the United States, date back to 1895. But they have occurred at irregular intervals, reflecting varying Congressional interest and understanding of what the statistics show. The Bureau of Labor Statistics (BLS) achieved some degree of insulation from such pressures by establishing the ongoing Consumer Expenditure Survey (CEX), now used to revise the Consumer Price Index (CPI).

Colin Campbell (1994) argues that consumption is denigrated, first, because economists focus on production and, second, because the Puritan work ethic has coloured the field. But he also points out that consumption (shopping, cooking, housekeeping, etc.) is seen as women's work and hence trivial, that satisfying genuine needs is permissible but that gratifying wants or desires is not essential as well as being worth less because it is performed by women. He chides economists for overlooking the most remarkable thing about technological change — not that innovation occurs but that consumers continually change what they crave. "No modern consumer, no matter how privileged or wealthy, can honestly say that there is nothing that he or she wants. It is this capacity to continuously 'discover' new wants that requires explaining" (Campbell, 1994, p. 507).

CEX data provide a link between micro- and macroeconomic analysis, and the December 1994 *Monthly Labor Review* contains an excellent introductory article, explaining the tie-in of CEX data to national income and product estimates from the Bureau of Economic Analysis in the Census (Branch, 1994).

Poverty measures and data

Data on income and wealth imply significant differences in the economic welfare of men and women. Many indicators suggest strongly that more women than men are poor although, because survey data use the household or family as the analytical unit, only headcounts, not tabulations by sex, provide most of the quantitative measures of income and wealth. Measuring poverty today is neither art nor science, as most serious analysts recognize. Yet reducing poverty has been set as a primary goal for economic development. The World Bank devoted its *World Development Report* in 1990 to the issue of poverty, and its ongoing Living Standards Measurement Study has produced a number of useful monographs warning of various conceptual and methodological pitfalls in the measurement of poverty.

The United States experience with a single poverty measure can be instructive. Mollie Orshansky,[11] who more than three decades ago developed the measure of poverty now in use, spent years urging that it be revised. The objective measure she created was so modified and adjusted as to lose all resemblance to the rigorous original.

Orshansky based her measure on two studies by the US Department of Agriculture (USDA). In 1955 it carried out a monumental study of food consumption (USDA 1955 Food Survey, published in several different publications over several years) which included both expenditure and nutritional data. Analysis showed that spending on food used roughly

33 per cent of income for families of two or more, whether farm or nonfarm. Orshansky derived a ratio of 27 per cent for two-person families and slightly below one-third for families of three or more from the same study.

The second USDA study was one in a long series of "Family Food Plans and Food Costs". These had struggled with nomenclature, using low-cost, economy, moderate, thrifty and other terms — left undefined. More recently the series adopted "lower", "moderate", and "higher" to emphasize the relativity of these plans. They developed the nutritional guidelines of the National Research Council into menus and shopping lists of food items and quantities, found by the Food Consumption Survey to be familiar to most US families. The study checked prices of all these items and calculated the total sum as food costs. Shortly before Orshansky published her article on measuring poverty, the USDA announced a new "economy" food plan, which cost 75-80 per cent of its existing low-cost plan and did not provide adequate nutrition over time. In her research Orshansky used the low-cost plan, although she reported that actual food allowances then granted to people receiving public assistance frequently fell below these amounts. She was also careful to warn readers of the assumptions common to all such food plans: the family followed the plan strictly, all members ate all of their meals at home, and family members possessed the requisite skills for shopping and food preparation.

Multiplying the food costs by the appropriate food/income ratio gave, for the first time, an objective measure using data on actual food spending. By deriving adjustments for family size, sex and age of its members, and rural and nonfarm habitation, Orshansky set out 246 cut-off points and then collapsed them into 124. She warned that the dollar figures based on food/income ratios might be questionable as a measure of poverty but that her findings could probably be used "as an interim guide to equivalent levels of living among families in different situations" (Orshansky, 1965, p. 12). In the event, her findings were adopted in 1965 by the Council of Economic Advisors to the President and have been used since then, with the dollar figures adjusted for price change as measured by the Consumer Price Index.

Questions about the poverty index have been raised by many, including Orshansky herself who deplored the widespread use for decades of a measure developed in 1955, despite the need for revision in terms of the food/income ratios, prices and, especially, the findings of new research on poverty. In 1992 Congress asked the National Academy of Sciences to investigate, and a number of Cabinet Departments added specific requests. The Standing Committee on National Statistics of the Commission on Behavioral and Social Sciences and Education of the National Research Council (the research arm of the Academy), created a special Panel whose report, *Measuring poverty*, was published in 1995.

The Panel's findings touch on most microeconomic issues of concern today, including the distribution of income, medical and health services, employment, and income maintenance programmes. Whether it is adopted by the Congress or not, the report will evoke considerable debate.

Since 1995, poverty measures have consisted of a set of US dollar values, called "thresholds", which can be compared with a family's income to determine its poverty status. Holding that a redefinition of poverty cannot, and probably should not, yield total figures differing substantially from these thresholds, the Panel calculated a poverty measure accordingly (one that would produce roughly the same number of poor people) while the numbers in subgroups vary. But the recommended method differs sharply from that in current use, especially in its treatment of several issues with special significance for women.

First, "resources available" to the family or individual are defined as after-tax money income *plus* the value of "near-money" benefits — e.g. food stamps but not Medicaid (the federally funded medical care programme for the poor) — and *minus* expenses needed to earn income — e.g. childcare costs, other work-related expenses, and out-of-pocket medical care costs including health insurance premiums. Second, the poverty threshold, for a base family of two adults and two children, is determined as a percentage of median annual expenditures (as shown in the CEX) on food, clothing and shelter. The report calculated poverty thresholds for different types of families with an equivalence scale reflecting the fact that children typically consume less than adults and that economies of scale exist in household management (Citro and Michael, 1995, pp. 4-6).

The report of the Panel deserves careful reading and analysis, but in any case, some implications are obvious for policies relating to race and gender. Those who criticize welfare, and the women who receive it, frequently argue that the poverty measure is unrealistic. Those who attack the current poverty measure itself frequently focus on the racial or gender characteristics of the poor. Apart from such criticisms, there is honest dispute about how to treat benefits, locational differences in the cost of living, and home ownership.

First, the reference household chosen by the panel is the traditional, familiar four-person, two-adult/two-child model. (Note that only children 0-18 years of age are included, even if older dependent ones are in the household.) The Panel argued that, although this third-ranking model (following, in order, two-adult/no child households and one-adult/two-child households) accounts for just 13 per cent of households, as a proportion of *the total population* members of such households represent 20 per cent, more than the 17 per cent living in married couple/no children households (a subset of two-adult households), and more than the 10 per cent in one-adult households (Citro and Michael, 1995, pp. 101, 102). The choice of this reference family type therefore implies a judgement that poverty should be measured in terms of the *whole* population.

Of the families below the poverty level as of 1993, over half reported a female "householder" and no spouse present. They accounted for 37 per cent of all poor people; those in married-couple households accounted for 35 per cent, and single individuals the remainder. Among the poor there were more children in single-women-headed households (8 million) than in married-couple families (5 million). Of poor families headed by single women, 90 per cent received some form of means-tested assistance; 72 per cent of married couple families did.[12]

In contrast to the total population, the population living below the poverty line is mostly female. Changes over time have reinforced this. The number and percentage of families below the poverty level have dropped steadily since 1959, while the number of families headed by women has more than doubled.[13] In such circumstances it is difficult to defend creating a poverty measure based on the experience of married couples with children, such families being mostly non-poor.

Poverty thresholds are adjusted for families of different sizes by weighting a child at 0.70 of an adult and allowing for economies of scale by raising the total number of resulting adult equivalents to a power between 0.65 and 0.75. The panel condemns the existing measure for its implicit recognition of economies of scale for the first child but significant diseconomies for the second, with scale economies appearing for the third to fifth child. The proposed new measure states clearly that all equivalence scales are arbitrary and justifies its choice with reference to the existing literature (Citro and Michael, 1995, pp. 159-182).

Very often women faced with a choice between welfare and work have to make similar calculations. Working through such a choice can be a useful exercise for students investigating the supply of labour and even more useful to policy-makers who write legislation without a clear understanding of the effects the new laws will have on poor people, the incentives they will confront, their behaviour and their outlook. For example, little direct notice has been taken of the NAS report, although the basic income maintenance law for poor women with children was totally revised after it appeared. In any case, the NAS report should be attended to, so that the new poverty measure is properly appreciated.

Sloppy language has created both stereotypes and dangerous thinking: one example is the so-called "feminization of poverty". This phrase suggests either that more women are now poor, or that poverty affects women and girls more now than it did previously. Such a conclusion is nonsensical, given that women outlive men. In the United States, before Social Security payments were indexed in 1972, almost one in three older people was poor, and most of them were women. The percentage of older adults living in poverty has dropped to about 12 per cent, while female-headed households (including many elderly women) now account for most of the poor. In other industrialized countries it is equally doubtful that any shift in the incidence of poverty from men to women has occurred. The same cannot be said for low-income developing countries, however. The process of development itself has brought new burdens for women, especially in neglected rural areas as urbanization and migration proceed and costs rise. Some income sources, traditionally reserved to women, have also disappeared as small-scale agriculture has declined and newer agricultural technologies are reserved for men. And only in a few developing countries do women have the political voice of their sisters in most industrialized societies.

Older adults in the population

The industrialized world as a whole faces a major demographic change as life expectancies and years of good health both increase steadily. In most developed countries the percentage of the population over 65 is growing rapidly, posing all sorts of new issues. There are shifts in the supply of labour and in aggregate demand, as well as problems of health and home care, retirement age, and so on. Since this expansion of the elderly population has taken place rapidly, it is not surprising that extensive data are lacking. One easy way to date a society's recognition of the problem is to look at data for age distribution, and note the year in which the top age group changed from "60 and over" to "70 to 79, 80 and over" or later to "80 to 89, 90 and over", for example.

Another stereotype with dangerous policy implications is that the elderly live on fixed incomes. In the United States, people still cling to that outmoded notion. By definition, almost everyone in the country over 65 years of age receives Social Security payments or Supplemental Security Income, and since 1972 these payments have been adjusted yearly for upward movements of the Consumer Price Index. The category of people over 65 contains, like any other population group, some who are well off, some who just get along, and some who are poor. But practically none of them lives on a fixed income.

The rapid increase in the number of elderly people, most of whom are women, has been well publicized but it is not readily understood, primarily because of inadequate data and insufficient analysis. For example, the rising numbers of grandparents who are caring for children, typically with neither parent present, are ignored in welfare policy debates.[14] Neither the programme Aid to Families with Dependent Children (AFDC) as presently constituted[15] nor any of the major attempts to reform welfare recognize grandparents as caregivers. Should grandparents be forced to take a job or register for training? Should they be denied benefits if another grandchild is added to the family? Women far outnumber men in this caregiver role (Mullen, 1995; Public Policy Institute, American Association of Retired Persons, 1995).

Where provisions for pensions or social security income require some kind of earnings history a rich source of data exists, including information on payments to the elderly. But because men outnumbered women in the workforce of most countries by a large percentage until a few decades ago, most of the compiled data or tabulations refer to men, with women included only as dependants or beneficiaries.

The major source of information on older adults in the United States, the Social Security Administration, has much more data on men than on women. A 10-year study of 11,000 Americans aged 58-63 in 1969 is still being extensively used to analyse retirement decisions and behaviour. The database covers men and single women: married women are included only as their husbands' dependants. Very little research on the retirement behaviour of women exists, yet findings concerning men do not necessarily apply to women.

Most age distributions top out with an open-ended class "65 and over"; the appearance of the class interval "65 to 74" became necessary when the size of this open-ended class grew unwieldy. People over 75 years of age (or over 85) are just beginning to receive attention: recent data show that the fastest growing segment, those over 85, do not threaten Medicare (the federal medical programme for older persons) since they typically remain healthy and die quickly. Women, of course, outnumber men in this group. In 1992 the 13 million men over 65 years of age included 4.7 million over 75 years. The 18 million women over 65 years included 10 million over 75.[16] The excess of females over males is greater at successively older ages.

A significant proportion of these *older* older women have incomes below the poverty line, but there are major gaps in data, especially on the composition of these households. The phenomenon of a 70-year-old woman caring for her 95-year-old mother and her 93-year-old aunt receives little attention beyond the anecdotal evidence provided by social workers and outreach agencies serving the elderly. Yet the situation where an adult member of the household supports a related adult is becoming much more common, at least in the United States.

This is the kind of policy issue that can be made alive to students and researchers, who can use their analytical skills and the interpretations of legislation or administrative rules to calculate income transfers and to assess the relative needs of these families.

INDIVIDUALS AND GENDER: MORE THAN A DATA PROBLEM

Most surveys gather data on families, households or consumer units. Sampling begins at the household level; economics and sociology distinguish individuals from families; hence the appearance in most basic sources of these three units of the family, the household, and the individual. In the United States this is the case for the decennial Census, Current Population Survey, Survey of Incomes and Program Participation (SIPP), Consumer Expenditure Survey, the National Longitudinal Surveys on Employment, the Michigan Panel Survey of Income Dynamics, and surveys of health, financial status, crime, and so forth. Collecting data and analysing economic events and conditions by families or by households is well entrenched.

After the Bureau of the Census abandoned the practice of defining the head of the family or household as the husband, it substituted a reference person, usually called a "householder". This person is the one in the household who owns, is buying or rents the living quarters. If no such identification is possible, the householder is any adult member of the household. No matter how the householder is defined, using a reference person to collect information does not provide comparable (or sometimes any) information about anyone else in the household, and many tabulations are therefore suspect. "Family income by level of education" is a good example: the householder's educational level may or may not indicate the level attained by other adults in the household.

Because data are collected on the family or household, most analyses of labour force participation and/or the income earned by working ignore the individual's participation. Except for the occasional circus act, families as such do not hold jobs and earn wages, it is the individual who does both (Bell, 1974; Bell, 1981). The existing data on families and households do not allow any analysis of the distinct contributions of men and of women to family income, or of the spending and saving decisions of men and of women from income, or of the employment decisions of individuals. The Luxembourg Income Study is a notable exception. This database, which makes cross-country comparisons and analysis safe, presents information on households and families, but also provides data on individuals.[17]

Women are particularly apt to be shortchanged by a household or family frame of reference because of the persistence of stereotypical thinking. Take the statement: "Both wife and husband are employed in 59 per cent of the families".[18] Most people (including economists and sociologists) calculate that if both spouses work in 60 per cent of the families, then 40 per cent are supported by a man. But the statement does not mean that at all. In fact, the total group of married-couple families will include some millions in which *neither* a wife nor husband is at work. Most are retired, but younger student couples account for a fair number. Furthermore, a significant number of married-couple families report that the husband is not employed but the wife is.[19]

The economic contribution of both men and women gets underestimated when the shared household or family income consists of more than money receipts. The more people in a household, the more unrecorded income there can be. Two kinds of error exist. One is the omission of all kinds of household production — the do-it-yourself assembling, repairing, modifying, cooking, freezing, and filing that accompany expenditures and enable consumption or use of purchased products. Home-based services proliferate not only among the poor to substitute for high-priced market goods, but also among people with higher incomes. Home production uses household capital — appliances, computers and automobiles, e.g. to produce goods and services for use within the household.

Gross Domestic Product is understated by more than just household production, since *all* volunteer effort goes unrecorded — not only that taking the form of coaching local sports teams, lobbying, religious activities and the like but also personal counselling and business consulting. Much of the private investment in building human capital is also omitted; think of the people learning a language, or a new skill in home refurbishing or cooking new dishes, from television, from local classes or from home study.

The second common error when analysing economic events using household or family data is to ignore the distribution of income *within* the household or to other households. Any figure for per capita income is likely to bear little resemblance to the actual real income of each family member. This would need to be derived from consumption expenditure and capital accumulation data collected on an individual basis. Private transfer income in both money and real terms also exists, but again, the corresponding data do not. SIPP provides some clues about real income transfers: 44 per cent of the men and 56 per cent of the women help some household member with personal care, getting around outside the home, preparing meals, keeping track of bills or money and doing housework. In 1986 some 6 million people provided some such care to a household member but 15 million people helped someone outside the household.[20]

CHILDCARE AND HUMAN CAPITAL INVESTMENT

Data on childcare nearly always assume that caring for children is a concern primarily of women. In labour market analysis, women's employment is taken to be a function of, among other things, the presence of children or of young children. Industrial relations experts have discovered the need to hire and keep skilled women workers and firms have built day care centres, invented programmes to care for sick children, welcomed family leave legislation, and so on. They have also discovered the beneficial effects of these programmes on absenteeism among men, leading a few farsighted policy-makers to herald the advent of "family policy" in place of "women's issues".

In the United States, the new poverty measure allows payments for childcare by employed family members to be subtracted from family resources: the amount, equal to actual expenditures taken from the CEX, is capped at the wages of the lowest paid adult family member. Survey data on childcare have always shown that much is provided directly by family members or relatives. With varying financial arrangements, the data suggest that many grandmothers care for children so that their mothers can earn income to buy food and clothing and shelter. That is the rationale for subtracting childcare expenses from resources.

But neither the NAS report nor any other analyst has provided estimates of the contribution of the grandmother — or the father or mother or big sister who supplied the childcare — to the value of home production and income. Childcare also needs analysis in terms of human capital formation. It may not be the case that GDP increases all that much when a very young child goes to pre-school rather than staying with Grandma.

The value of the mother — the person most likely to provide most childcare — was recognized by Alfred Marshall: "The most valuable of all capital is that invested in human beings; and of that capital the most precious part is the result of the care and influence of the mother, so long as she retains her tender and unselfish instincts, and has not been hardened by the strain and stress of unfeminine work" (Marshall, 1920, p. 564). It goes without saying that Marshall would have disapproved of the existence of millions of single-parent families, supported chiefly by women. He would also have taken issue with those who insist that women work in order to be eligible for welfare.

And he would clearly have supported the claim that the calculation of basic needs or a poverty level income for single mothers and their families must have a dimension additional to that for a family with two adults. Clair Brown's first brilliant analysis of the time-poor (1977) demonstrated that a single mother, lacking another person to help, cannot allocate time flexibly or efficiently.

The Luxembourg Income Study recognizes that poverty defined in terms of money income does not adequately describe the inadequate resources available to a single mother. The new *Measuring poverty* report devotes an entire appendix to this issue, noting that childcare services provided to the single mother as a condition of employment are no solution. Being time-poor implies more than just needing childcare during the workday; it implies giving up the command over time entailed in being the sole support of a dependent child.

The poverty threshold for a single mother with two children (a three-person family) should, in fact, be higher than that for a married couple with one child (also a three-person family). It is impossible to substitute money for time, but a larger income would certainly help. More importantly, single mothers with children could be perceived as being extra poor, rather than as undeserving.

CONCLUDING COMMENT

The analysis of gender, racial and ethnic issues in existing data must begin with examining the small print and then questioning the most basic definitions of racial and ethnic categories, and of families and individuals. It is all too easy for the analyst of contemporary events to overlook misidentification and unknown characteristics when working with socio-demographic variables. Familiarity with these issues should at least reduce the extent to which social scientists collect flawed data, and discourage policy-makers from going on to formulate programmes and legislation on false premises.

Notes

[1] See Henry Louis Gates' enchanting memoir, *Colored people* (Gates, 1994). I grew up in a New England town where I learned never to refer to coloured people or Negroes as "black", since this would have been as insulting as the term "nigger". It was not until I reached college age that I read poetry and novels using the term "black" with approval – and the slogan "Black is Beautiful" came into being some three decades later.

[2] United States Bureau of the Census: *200 years of U.S. Census taking; Population and housing questions, 1790-1990*, Washington, DC, US Government Printing Office, 1989, p. 36.

[3] ibid., p. 60.

[4] ibid., p. 83.

[5] ibid., p. 100.

[6] For an excellent discussion of the race-ethnicity problem see Jorge H. del Pina, 1992.

[7] Ross (1996) indicates a range of distinctions applied in this and other surveys.

[8] See the citation by del Pina (1992, p. 1) of James W. Buehler et al.: "The reporting of race and ethnicity in the National Notifiable Diseases Surveillance System", in *Public Health Reports* (Rockville, MD), Vol. 105 (1990), No. 1 (Jan.-Feb.), pp. 102-103.

[9] The increase in gay and lesbian households, especially those containing children, has not brought any hard data on their number, let alone on other aspects of their existence. Although it seems obvious that self-identification could, within the existing survey framework, provide useful data, it seems equally obvious that such a procedure is politically impossible.

[10] See the contributions to "Gender, adjustment and macroeconomics", a special issue of *World Development* (Tarrytown, NY), Vol. 23 (1995), No. 11 (Nov.), and particularly the report by Diane Elson (University of Manchester, United Kingdom) on the work of the project "Gender, Development and Macroeconomics". A conference held at the Kennedy School of Government (Harvard University) on 2 March 1996 drew largely on the papers published in this special volume.

[11] Her name is practically unknown, and yet economics students should be as familiar with it as they are with those who defined the Phillips curve, Okun's misery index, and Engel's law.

[12] United States Bureau of the Census: *Poverty in the United States: 1992 consumer income*, Current Population Reports, Series P-60, No. 185, Washington, DC, US Government Printing Office, 1993, p. xviii.

[13] Over half the poor families are headed by a woman, and two-thirds of the individuals counted as poor are white (ibid., pp. 6-7).

[14] As of March 1993, adults over 65 were responsible for one million families with children under 18.

[15] This programme, commonly called "welfare", is directly affected by the welfare legislation passed in 1996. Adults in families to date receiving such welfare benefits will be encouraged, even required, to work. And the federally funded and regulated programme has been replaced by block grants to the states to design and carry out their own income-maintenance programmes.

[16] United States Bureau of the Census: *Household and family characteristics, March, 1993*, Current Population Reports, Series P-27, No. 477, Washington, DC, US Government Printing Office, 1994.

[17] An excellent introduction to these data is in Smeeding, O'Higgins and Rainwater, 1990.

[18] United States Bureau of the Census: *Money income of household and persons in the United States: 1992*, Current Population Reports, Series, P-60, No. 184, Washington, DC, US Government Printing Office, 1993, pp. 77-78.

[19] ibid., pp. 77-83.

[20] United States Bureau of the Census: *The need for personal assistance with everyday activities: Recipients and caregivers*, Current Population Reports, Series P-70, No. 19, Washington, DC, US Government Printing Office, 1990.

References

Bell, Carolyn Shaw. 1981. "Demand, supply, and labor market analysis", in *Journal of Economic Issues* (East Lansing, MI), Vol. 15, No. 2 (June), pp. 423-434.

——. 1974. "Economics, sex, and gender", in *Social Science Quarterly* (Austin, TX), Winter.

Branch, E. Raphael. 1994. "The Consumer Expenditure Survey: A comparative analysis", in *Monthly Labor Review* (Washington, DC), Vol. 117, No. 12 (Dec.), pp. 47-55.

Brown, Clair (writing as Clair Vickery). 1977. "The time-poor: A new look at poverty", in *Journal of Human Resources, Education, Manpower, and Welfare Policies* (Madison, WI), Vol. 12, No. 1 (Winter), pp. 27-48.

Campbell, Colin. 1994. "Consuming goods and the good of consuming", in *Critical Review* (San Francisco, CA), Vol. 8, No. 4, pp. 503-520.

Citro, Constance F.; Michael, Robert T. (eds.). 1995. *Measuring poverty: A new approach.* Washington, DC, National Academy Press.

del Pina, Jorge H. 1992. *Exploring alternative race-ethnic comparisons in the current population surveys.* Series P-23, No. 182. Washington, DC, United States Department of Commerce, Economics and Statistics Administration, Bureau of the Census.

Gates, Henry Louis. 1994. *Colored people.* New York, Alfred Knopf.

Marshall, Alfred. *Principles of economics.* 8th edition, Book Six, Ch. 4, No. 3. New York, The MacMillan Company.

Mullen, Faith. 1995. *A tangled web: Public benefits, grandparents, and grandchildren.* Washington, DC, Public Policy Institute, American Association of Retired Persons.

Orshansky, Mollie. 1965. "Counting the poor: Another look at the poverty profile", in *Social Security Bulletin* (Washington, DC), Vol. 28, No. 1 (Jan.), pp. 3-29.

Public Policy Institute, American Association of Retired Persons. 1995. *Grandparents as caregivers.* Summary of a Working Meeting held at AARP. Washington, DC.

Ross, John M. 1996. *Employment/unemployment and earnings statistics: A guide to locating data in U.S. documents.* Lanham, MD, The Sparrow Press.

Smeeding, Timothy M.; O'Higgins, Michael; Rainwater, Lee (eds.). 1990. *Poverty, inequality and income distribution in comparative perspective: The Luxembourg Income Study (LIS).* New York, NY, Harvester Wheatsheaf.

THEORIES OF OCCUPATIONAL SEGREGATION BY SEX: AN OVERVIEW

8

Richard ANKER*

Occupational segregation by sex occurs everywhere, causing labour market rigidity and economic inefficiency, wasting human resources, preventing change, disadvantaging women and perpetuating gender inequalities. The principal theoretical explanations for its existence and persistence are reviewed: neo-classical and human capital; institutional and labour market segmentation; and gender discrimination. Its complex relationship with female-male pay differentials is also explored. Though all prove pertinent, the most compelling explanations of occupational segregation by sex are gender theories, given the enormous overlap in abilities and preferences of individual men and women.

Occupational segregation by sex is extensive in every region, at all economic development levels, under all political systems, and in diverse religious, social and cultural environments. It is one of the most important and enduring aspects of labour markets around the world.

There are several reasons to be concerned with occupational segregation. It is a major source of labour market rigidity and economic inefficiency. Excluding a majority of workers from a majority of occupations, as at present, is wasteful of human resources, increases labour market inflexibility, and reduces an economy's ability to adjust to change. With the globalization of production and intensified international competition, these factors have assumed greater importance.

Furthermore, occupational segregation by sex is detrimental to women. It has an important negative effect on how men view women

Originally published in *International Labour Review*, Vol. 136 (1997), No. 3.

* ILO, Geneva.

and on how women view themselves. This in turn negatively affects women's status and income and, consequently, many social variables such as mortality and morbidity, poverty and income inequality. The persistence of gender stereotypes also has negative effects on education and training and thus causes gender-based inequalities to be perpetuated into future generations.

The segmentation of occupations on the basis of workers' sex is thus an important labour market phenomenon deserving greater attention from policy-makers and lay persons concerned about equality, efficiency and social justice. This is demonstrated in the major new study undertaken by the present author (Anker, forthcoming) — with international comparisons and experiences providing especially valuable insights. The purpose of this chapter, which is drawn from that study, is to review the principal explanations for the existence and persistence of occupational segregation by sex. That is a necessary first step towards understanding the phenomenon in order then to deal with it. This chapter concludes with some observations on the relative value of the various theories in explaining occupational segregation.

THEORIES AND EXPLANATIONS

Researchers usually distinguish between labour supply and labour demand factors when explaining occupational segregation by sex. Factors related to labour supply generally focus on why women "prefer" certain types of occupation — for example, women may "prefer" those with flexible hours in order to allow time for childcare, and may also "prefer" occupations which are relatively easy to interrupt for a period of time to bear or rear children. Explanations related to labour demand focus on why employers generally "prefer" to hire women or men for particular occupations and why women and men have different opportunities for promotion and career development within firms.

The word "prefer" was put within quotation marks because, even when an individual chooses to accept work in a particular occupation or an employer chooses to employ either mainly men or mainly women, these decisions are influenced by learned cultural and social values that often discriminate against women (and sometimes against men) and stereotype occupations as "male" or "female". In other words, this "preference" is largely determined by learned, gender-related factors.

Theories explaining the existence of occupational segregation by sex can be classified into three broad categories: neo-classical and human capital theories; institutional and labour market segmentation theories; and non-economic and feminist or gender theories. Although these sets of theories overlap, this classification none the less provides a useful basis for discussion.

Before proceeding, it is important to point out that most of the research literature dealing with occupational segregation by sex is *not* concerned with occupational segregation *per se*, but with the effect it has on female-male pay differentials. For this reason, many theories and explanations treat the determinants of occupational segregation by sex and of male-female pay inequality as if these phenomena were the same. This is unfortunate, since female-male pay differentials have many sources and occupational segregation by sex is only one of them. Furthermore, sex segregation of occupations is an important topic in its own right.

The neo-classical, human capital model

Neo-classical economics assumes that workers and employers are rational and that labour markets function efficiently. According to this theory, workers seek out the best-paying jobs after taking into consideration their own personal endowments (e.g. education and experience), constraints (e.g. young child to take care of), and preferences (e.g. a pleasant work environment). Employers try to maximize profits by maximizing productivity and minimizing costs to the extent possible, but because of competition and efficient labour markets, employers pay workers their marginal product.

Labour supply

On the labour supply side, neo-classical/human capital theories stress the lower levels of female human capital in terms both of what women bring to the labour market (e.g. less education and less relevant fields of study), as well as what they acquire after joining the labour market (e.g. less experience than men owing to intermittent or truncated labour market participation because of marriage and/or household/childcare responsibilities).[1] In short, according to these theories, women rightfully receive lower pay than men because of their lower productivity.

The productivity-related variables of education and labour market experience are believed also to affect women's choice of occupation. The effect of education on choice of occupation hardly needs comment. However, two observations are worth making here. First, in low-income countries with small formal/modern labour markets, there are often many more educated, qualified persons of both sexes than there are formal sector jobs (therefore much sought after). This implies, all else being equal, that women should be reasonably well represented in a wide range of occupations in the formal sector (and at least in proportion to female-male educational levels). When this is not the case, it probably implies the presence of discrimination. Second, the relationship between a woman's education and experience and her occupation is bi-directional in nature. While women may not choose or be offered work in particular occupations because they do not have the appropriate education or experience, it is also true that many parents decide to give their daughters less education (and in subjects less relevant to the labour market) than they give their sons, and that women accumulate less labour market experience than men partly because they do not have the same labour market opportunities as men. These are very important factors helping to determine occupational segregation in the labour market. This phenomenon of reinforcement is not generally considered by neo-classical theory, which typically represents a static rather than a dynamic, longitudinal perspective.

Neo-classical theories also stress the fact that women are almost exclusively responsible for housework and childcare around the world (e.g. UNDP, 1995; United Nations, 1991).[2] These family responsibilities cause many women to gain less work experience than men owing either to early and permanent withdrawal from the labour force (e.g. because of marriage), or to temporary withdrawal from the labour force in order to care for young children. According to the theory, this implies that women would rationally choose occupations with relatively high starting pay, relatively low returns to experience, and relatively low penalties for temporary withdrawal from the labour force — including occupations which are flexible in terms of entry and working hours.

However, several problems arise if this theory is adopted as the only explanation for occupational segregation by sex. First, women's labour force commitment has increased greatly in recent decades, as indicated by the disappearance of the double-humped (or m-shaped) age-specific labour force participation curve. Second, the amount of household and family-based work which needs to be done has fallen in many countries in recent years owing to increasing age at marriage and falling fertility almost everywhere, as well as to the use of household aids (washers, cookers, vacuum cleaners, etc.) in higher-income countries. Third, the increasing incidence of female-headed households all over the world (Buvinic, 1995) implies that ever more women need to work continuously simply to earn a living. These various changes imply that women are gaining greater labour market experience which, according to neo-classical theory, should lead to major changes in the types of occupation women prefer and are offered. Despite all these changes, however, occupational segregation by sex remains very high all over the world (although it is true that in many countries it has fallen over the past two decades (see Anker, forthcoming)).

Fourth, amongst the most important occupations, many male-dominated ones (e.g. transport driver and auto mechanic) do not require more experience or continuity of employment than many female-dominated ones (e.g. secretary and other clerical worker). If anything, the opposite is true. Job evaluations based on comparable worth (see the section on pay differentials below) indicate that, for example, being a secretary (one of the most important "female" occupations in the world) requires considerably more knowledge and skills and makes more mental demands than being a delivery-truck driver (one of the most important "male" ones); yet secretaries receive lower pay.

Labour demand

According to neo-classical/human capital theory, many of the factors influencing women's and men's preferences for particular occupations also influence employers' preferences for male or female workers. Thus, jobs requiring a relatively high level of education are more likely to be offered to men than to women (although the relevance of this argument is somewhat questionable in the numerous countries where men and women have now achieved similar levels of education), as are jobs where experience and on-the-job training are relatively important (although, again, the relevance of this argument is decreasing in importance in many countries as women's labour force commitment increases).

In addition, women are often considered to be higher-cost workers (even when the same wage rate applies) because of a number of supposedly higher, indirect labour costs associated with women workers. According to the theory, this should affect the types of job employers offer women, depending on the relative importance of each of these factors for each occupation. For example, women are often said to have higher rates of absenteeism (probably in part because of family responsibilities which cause women to miss work in order to care for family members). Women are often said to be late to work more frequently (again probably in part because of family responsibilities). Women are also often said to have higher labour turnover rates, which can be an important indirect cost for employers, who have to find and train new workers. This higher turnover rate is said to occur because many women leave jobs in order to take care of young children (and, in some countries, because of marriage). Women workers may require separate toilet facilities at the workplace for themselves[3] and crèches for their children, since they do not wish to leave the children at home unattended.[4] Women are sometimes said to be less flexible than men as regards being able to stay late or to work on official leave days.

It is important to question assumptions that higher direct and indirect labour costs are associated with female workers than with male workers, especially in view of the relative paucity of empirical evidence either way. In this regard, a series of empirical studies in Third World countries are informative (Anker and Hein, 1985 and 1986). A total of 423 employers, 2,517 women workers and 803 men workers were interviewed, in five developing countries (Cyprus, Ghana, India, Mauritius and Sri Lanka), by means of structured survey questionnaires. Results from these studies call into question a number of the assumptions described above. For example, while individual women were found to have higher absenteeism rates, and many employers stressed the importance of this factor, on average the difference between male and female absenteeism rates proved to be small. Study results also indicated similar labour turnover rates for women and men. This unexpected result was due to the greater likelihood of men leaving for another job, and of women leaving their jobs for family reasons.

Labour laws and regulations sometimes directly affect the demand for women workers. Protective legislation sometimes prohibits women from working in certain occupations and/or under certain conditions. For example, women may be prohibited from night work (see the provisions of the ILO's Night Work (Women) Convention, 1919 (No. 4)); from working underground in mines (see the Underground Work (Women) Convention, 1935 (No. 45)); or from carrying heavy loads (see the Maximum Weight Convention, 1967 (No. 127)). Although protective laws and Conventions were drawn up with the best of intentions to protect women, many observers now believe that these laws are no longer relevant and should be changed (see, for example, Lim, 1996). Indeed, many ILO Conventions dealing with protective legislation are currently under review.

Labour laws and regulations can also increase the comparative cost of employing female workers. For example, paid maternity leave increases the cost of women workers relative to men and so can become an indirect form of sex discrimination if employers have to bear this cost.[5] Partly for this reason, and partly because the reproduction of subsequent generations is a concern for society as a whole, ILO Conventions on maternity leave recommend that maternity leave costs be borne by the State and not by employers. Another example sometimes mentioned in this connection is legislation requiring separate toilet facilities for men and women where the existing workforce and facilities are single sex.

Faced by the fact that the sex segregation of occupations and female-male pay differences persist and cannot be fully explained by different characteristics of men and women, neo-classical economists have developed complementary theories to explain the persistence of occupational segregation by sex, without abandoning their basic assumptions of rationality and efficient labour markets. Two of these theories (employers' taste for discrimination, and compensating differentials) are briefly described below. For the most part, these complementary theories focus on the demand side and on employers' motivation and behaviour. There are other complementary economic theories relating to labour market segmentation (such as dual labour markets, occupational overcrowding, statistical discrimination, and efficiency wages), the first three of which are described in the next section.

According to a model of employer behaviour developed by Becker (1971), employers — in common with many other citizens — are prejudiced against certain groups of workers. Usually, but not always, this prejudice — *a preference for discrimination* — is directed against persons who are different, because of visible characteristics such as race, disability, age or sex (Anker, 1995). Because of their prejudice, employers are said to sustain disutility (i.e. a cost) when they hire someone from the group discriminated against. Therefore, according to this theory, employers behave rationally when they hire fewer people from that group, since they can thus avoid such a "cost".

There are two main problems with Becker's model. First, it is unclear how this system can be sustained in a competitive economy. One would expect less prejudiced employers to hire more people from the group discriminated against in order to decrease costs and increase profits; this implies that over time the behaviour of unprejudiced employers would prevail because of competitive forces in the capitalist system. Second, even if one assumes that some employers are predisposed to discriminate, the great overlap in the skills, preferences, etc., of individual men and women should make it likely that both the sexes would be substantially represented in every occupation — but this is not the case. On the other hand, these problems could be explained by the existence of strongly held social values and stereotypes (see discussion below on feminist/gender theories) and by statistical discrimination theory (see discussion below on institutional and labour market segmentation theories).

The *compensating differentials model* is another neo-classically based economic theory sometimes mentioned as casting light on women's preference for certain occupations as well as on the lower pay in typical female occupations. According to this model, women prefer occupations with good working conditions as they wish to avoid unpleasant and dangerous working conditions and/or to have jobs with good fringe benefits, e.g. health insurance and crèches; the avoidance of unpleasant and dangerous conditions could be especially significant in cases where men are the chief breadwinners and women are secondary earners. In these circumstances, the lower monetary rewards in typical "female" occupations are said to be partly explained by some "pay" being taken in non-wage forms. While there may be some truth in this argument in countries where cultural values restrict the types of job women can do, it is much more difficult to accept in countries where a substantial percentage of women work and/or when women are the principal earners in the family. In any case, the explanation for the low pay in many typical "female" occupations (e.g. maids, salespersons and sewers) is unlikely to be the prevalence of pleasant working conditions.

In short, neo-classical economics and human capital theory make valuable contributions to understanding occupational segregation by sex and the typically lower pay of women workers. This theory highlights the important role played by systematic differences in the human capital accumulated by men and women.

All these factors negatively affect women's productivity and pay, and limit the occupations for which they qualify. For these reasons, neoclassical/human capital theories stress the need for policies to address non-labour market factors so as to reduce occupational segregation by sex. This implies that policy-makers should be concerned with non-labour-market variables such as education, family policy, family planning, and a more equal sharing between the sexes of child care and household work. As to labour market policies, these theories imply that policy-makers should seek to increase women's human capital, especially education and training in non-traditional occupations; to help women combine work and childcare/housework, possibly through the provision of crèches, or the reorganization of worktime, or the removal of parental leave provisions that indirectly discriminate against female workers; and to eliminate labour law provisions that prohibit the employment of women in certain occupations.

Institutional and labour market segmentation theories

Institutional and labour market segmentation theories also rely on well-established economic thought and neo-classical logic. Their starting-point is the assumption that institutions, such as unions and large enterprises, play an important role in determining who is hired, fired and promoted, and how much they are paid. Institutional theories also begin with the assumption that labour markets are segmented in certain ways. And while each labour market segment may function according to neo-classical theory, it is difficult for workers to pass from one segment to another.

The best-known is *dual labour market theory* which distinguishes between a "primary" and a "secondary" sector (Doeringer and Piore, 1971). Other labour market segmentation theories divide the labour market into "static" and "progressive" jobs (Standing, 1989) and "formal" and "informal" sectors (ILO, 1972). Jobs in the primary sector are relatively good in terms of pay, security, opportunities for advancement and working conditions. Secondary sector jobs tend to be relatively poor as regards pay, chances for promotion and working conditions, and to provide little protection or job security. These two labour markets are perceived as functioning independently of each other to a substantial degree, largely because firms in the primary sector have some market power which insulates them somewhat from competition, whereas those in the secondary sector face fierce competition. Although the distinction between primary and secondary sectors has become less marked in recent years in both industrialized and developing countries (because of increased subcontracting and the globalization of trade), it still retains a significant degree of relevance.

It is a relatively short step to adapt the concept of dual labour markets to occupational segregation by sex, with one labour market segment comprised of "female" occupations and another of "male" occupations.

This segmentation implies relatively low wage rates in "female" occupations because many women workers are "overcrowded" into a small number of "female" occupations (Bergmann, 1974; Edgeworth, 1922). "Male" occupations, on the other hand, benefit from reduced competition within a wider set of occupations and, consequently, tend to enjoy relatively high wage rates.

The nature of the jobs available in the primary sector would lead one to expect an under-representation of women and, since such jobs are more secure, firms in this sector can be expected to accord a relatively high value to firm-specific experience and low labour turnover. Consequently, given their generally more continuous labour market experience, male workers should tend to be favoured by primary sector employers. Furthermore, since primary sector firms can pay higher wages, they are in a position to cream off the best-qualified workers; this again implies that primary sector firms should tend to prefer men, who tend to be better educated and more experienced than women.

Another economic theory related to labour market segmentation is *statistical discrimination theory*. This is based on the assumption that there are differences, on average, in the productivity, skills, experience, etc., of distinct groups of workers (such as men and women), and high search and information costs associated with recruitment and promotion decisions. In such circumstances, it is argued, it is rational for employers to discriminate against groups of workers (such as women) when differences, on average, between the abilities of persons from different groups (e.g. women and men) cost less to sustain than the decision-making costs associated with identifying suitable individual workers of either sex. Statistical discrimination theory thus provides an explanation for how some occupations are almost entirely male even though many individual women have greater ability, more education, etc. than many individual men.[6]

One aspect ignored by statistical discrimination theory is the role played by occupational segregation by sex in perpetuating labour market discrimination into the next generation. Because women are generally discriminated against, they are likely to obtain less education than men and to pursue careers that reinforce the current segregation. A second problem with statistical discrimination theory is that it may be less relevant for explaining discrimination in promotion (as opposed to recruitment), since in many enterprises the information costs involved in the former may be less than those involved in the latter.

In summary, labour market segmentation theories are very useful for understanding sex inequality in the labour market, since they stress the existence of segregated labour markets and occupations. However, they do not explain *why* occupations are segmented by sex; after all, the same occupations are found in both primary and secondary labour markets. And, labour market segmentation theory is better at explaining vertical occupational segregation by sex (why men are more likely than women to have better-quality jobs in the same occupation), which is a major source of female-male wage differentials.

Despite the valuable contributions of neo-classical/human capital theory and institutional and labour market segmentation theories to the understanding of sex inequality in the labour market, they are less helpful in understanding occupational segregation by sex. In particular, they fail to consider adequately a number of critical, non-economic and non-labour market variables and forms of behaviour, mainly because these lie outside the competence (and often interest) of economists. Examples of such variables are: why women come to the labour market with lower levels of education and in less relevant subjects; why housework and childcare are almost always the sole responsibility of women; why important labour market segregation based on sex persists despite a wide overlap in the abilities of individual men and women; why the sex stereotyping of women in society generally is reflected so consistently in stereotypically "female" occupations; and why occupational segregation by sex has persisted so strongly despite recent major increases in the education and labour force commitment of women. Yet explaining these types of non-economic issues is critical to understanding occupational segregation by sex. Feminist or gender theories address many of these issues.

Feminist/gender theories and related explanations

Feminist or gender theories[7] are mainly concerned with non-labour market variables which economists take as given. A basic premise of gender theories is that women's disadvantaged position in the labour market is caused by, and is a reflection of, patriarchy and women's subordinate position in society and the family. In all societies, household work and child care are seen as women's chief responsibility, while being the breadwinner is perceived as men's main responsibility. The fact that these societal norms and perceptions bear little relation to the daily lives of many women, men and families does not detract from their influence on people's behaviour and their contribution to gender-based discrimination against women.

This division of responsibilities and the patriarchal ordering of society are instrumental in determining why women usually accumulate less human capital compared with men before entering the labour market — that is, why girls receive less education than boys, and are less likely to pursue fields of study, such as sciences and crafts, of greater relevance to the labour market. Overall, women are perceived as having a lesser need for labour market skills. These same influences are also instrumental[8] in explaining why women acquire less labour market experience, on average, because many of them withdraw from the labour force early, and many others withdraw from the labour force temporarily.

Gender theory makes a valuable contribution to explaining occupational segregation by sex by showing how closely the characteristics of "female" occupations mirror the common stereotypes of women and their supposed abilities. To illustrate this, table 1 lists 13 characteristics commonly attributed to women which may have an effect on occupational segregation by sex. These are divided into three groups of stereotypes (positive, negative and other). This list is much more complete than the common observation that "female" occupations are merely an extension of household activities.

The five "positive" stereotypes presented are: a caring nature; skill and experience in household-related work; greater manual dexterity; greater honesty; and attractive physical appearance. It seems logical to hypothesize that these characteristics, if true, would help "qualify" women for the following ISCO occupations: nurse, doctor, social worker, teacher, maid, housekeeper, cleaner, cook, waiter, launderer, hairdresser, spinner, weaver, knitter, tailor/dressmaker, midwife, sewer, typist, cashier/bookkeeper, salesperson, accountant, receptionist, street vendor and shop assistant.

The five "negative" stereotypes presented are: disinclination to supervise others; lesser physical strength; lesser ability in science and mathematics; lesser willingness to travel; and lesser willingness to face physical danger and to use physical force. These characteristics negatively affect women's acceptability in various occupations — which consequently helps ensure that they become typical "male" occupations. These stereotypes, if true, would help "disqualify" women for the following types of ISCO occupation: manager, supervisor, government executive officer/administrator, legislative official, construction worker, miner/quarrier, well driller, physical scientist, architect, engineer, mathematician, statistician, aircraft officer and worker, ship officer and worker, transport equipment driver/operator, fire-fighter, police officer and security guard.

Finally, three other stereotypes are presented: greater willingness to take orders, greater docility and lesser inclination to complain about work or working conditions, lesser inclination to join trade unions, greater tolerance of monotonous/repetitive work; greater willingness to accept lower wages and less need for income; and greater interest in working at home. These stereotypes have a greater influence on the general characteristics typifying "female" occupations (such as low pay, high flexibility, low status, less decision-making authority) than on qualifying or disqualifying women for particular occupations.

The influence of such sex stereotyping on occupational segregation by sex was brought out very clearly in a series of enterprise surveys sponsored by the ILO in transition economies (Bulgaria, the Czech Republic, Hungary and Slovakia) and developing countries (India, Cyprus, Sri Lanka and Ghana). Employers were asked directly whether they

Women, gender and work

Table 1. Stereotyped characteristics of women and their expected effect on occupational segregation by sex

Common stereotyped characteristics of woman[1]	Effect on occupational segregation	Examples of typical occupations affected[2]	Comments
Positive			
1. Caring nature	Helps qualify woman for occupations involving care for others, e.g. children, the sick, older people	Nurse Doctor Ayah Social worker Teacher Midwife	A characteristic often felt to be biologically determined, because women are mainly responsible for childcare in all societies. This is, however, a learned, gender-based characteristic. Note that occupations which involve caring but also require greater authority (e.g. medical doctor), are often male-dominated.
2. Skill (and experience) in household-related work	Helps qualify women for occupations that are frequently home-based (and almost always carried out by women), often as unpaid household work	Maid Housekeeper Cleaner Cook Waiter Launderer Hairdresser Spinner Sewer Weaver Knitter Tailor/dressmaker	Skill easily acquired (therefore, women's greater experience of these skills before entering the labour market should not be very important).
3. Greater manual dexterity	Helps qualify women for occupations where finger dexterity is important.	Sewer Knitter Spinner Weaver Tailor/dressmaker Typist	Belief is based partly on biological difference (sex); and partly on experience difference (gender) acquired in the home before joining the labour market (see also stereotype 2). Skill easily acquired. Occupations often similar to those noted under household-related work activities (see stereotype 2).
4. Greater honesty	Helps qualify women for occupations where money is handled and/or trust is important.	Cashier/book-keeper Salesperson Accountant	Higher-paid and higher-status occupations (e.g. accountant which is a professional occupation) are often male-dominated.
5. Attractive physical appearance	Helps qualify women for occupations where physical appearance helps attract and/or please customers.	Receptionist Salesperson Shop assistant	This advantage is often thought to accompany a more pleasant and accommodating personality suited to, e.g., reception or sales work. In other situations, sex appeal is used to attract male customers (e.g. barmaid or prostitute).

Theories of occ

Table 1. (cont.)

Women, gender

Table 1. (co

10. Lesse
wil
f

Negative

6. Disinclination to supervise others	Helps disqualify women for all types of supervisory and managerial occupations.	Manager (general; production; trade, catering and lodging) Supervisor (clerical; sales; production) Government executive and administrator Legislative official	This is in many ways a parallel to willingness to take orders (see stereotype 11). This often affects vertical occupational segregation (with lower-level jobs for women).
7. Lesser physical (muscular) strength	Helps disqualify women for occupations requiring heavy lifting and/or other physical effort.	Construction worker Miner/quarrier Well driller	There is considerable overlap in the physical strength of individual women and men, which means that many women are physically capable of doing such work. Becoming less and less important in today's economy.
8. Lesser ability in science and mathematics	Helps disqualify women for occupations where high levels of scientific and mathematical knowledge are required.	Physical scientist (chemist/physicist) Architect Engineer Mathematician Statistician	In this case, gender discrimination begins at school where girls are discouraged from specializing in mathematics or science. Some believe that this difference is biologically determined. If so, it is a small average difference with a large overlap in the abilities of individual men and women.
9. Lesser willingness to travel	Helps disqualify women for occupations where considerable travel is required.	Aircraft officer and worker Ship officer worker Transport equipment driver/ operator	Many women are willing to travel, e.g. airline stewardesses (who were originally selected for their physical appearance – see stereotype 5). Many drivers do not travel overnight.

...t.)

| | Helps disqualify women for occupations where physical danger is relatively great. | Fire-fighter Police officer Security guard Miner/quarrier | This is a learned, gender difference. |
| ...ingness to ...ce physical danger and use physical force | | | Many women are willing to be employed in these occupations. |

Other

11. Greater willingness to take orders Greater docility and lesser inclination to complain about work or working conditions Lesser inclination to join trade unions Greater willingness to do monotonous/ repetitive work	General characteristics which help qualify women for occupations and sectors of the economy where working conditions are poor, labour laws are not applied (e.g. the informal sector) and work is routinized.	Note: These general characteristic (11, 12, 13) qualify women for many jobs which are low paid, unskilled, unprotected and repetitious in nature.	These stereotypes have been combined because of their similar implication of a subservient nature. These are archetypes of learned (gender) characteristics.
12. Greater interest to accept lower wages Lesser need for income	General characteristics which help qualify women for low-paid occupations and sectors of the economy		Often related to (and justified by) the belief that women are secondary earners (i.e. not the main breadwinner). This is despite the increased incidence of female-headed households; and many families' need for more than one income. Often associated with occupations in highly competitive industries, where cost considerations are very important, notably those producing exports such as textiles.
13. Greater interest in working at home	Helps qualify women for occupations and sectors of the economy where work is organized in a home-based, "putting out" type of production system.		Usally poorly paid home-based work; often involves piecework. Home-based work is easy to combine with household/ childcare. "Putting out" production system is often set up specifically to make use of the available cheap female labour. Home-based work is increasing in importance.[3]

[1] Many of these stereotypes overlap in their effects. While some stereotypes help reinforce sex segregation of particular occupations (e.g. greater manual dexterity and skill at household-type work for sewer), the effects of other stereotypes counteract each other (e.g. physical appearance and disinclination to supervise others for sales supervisor).
[2] Almost all examples of occupations are taken from two- and three-digit ISCO-68 occupational classifications.
[3] *Bidi* making (local Indian cigarette), which is the largest non-agricultural occupation for women in India according to 1981 census data, is almost exclusively a home-based industry.

Source: Author's impressions; Anker and Hein, 1985 and 1986.

preferred to employ men or women for certain occupations and types of work. Given the directness and bluntness of the questions, it seems reasonable to assume that responses admitting sex bias represent only the tip of the iceberg. Despite the nature of the questions, however, many employers indicated that a person's sex is an important consideration affecting hiring and promotion decisions. In surveys in 1992/1993 conducted in the Czech Republic, Hungary and Slovakia, roughly 90 per cent of the employers interviewed indicated that they preferred to employ men to do repair and maintenance work, whereas virtually none preferred women; 35 to 55 per cent preferred to employ men in professional occupations, in general production and skilled operative occupations, compared with only about 10 per cent who preferred to employ women in these occupations (Paukert, 1995). In other enterprise surveys conducted in Hungary and Bulgaria in 1991/1992, 55 to 65 per cent of the employers interviewed preferred men in production occupations compared with 15 to 25 per cent who preferred women (Sziraczki and Windell, 1992). In Cyprus (1981), when asked a general question about whether certain types of job are considered more suitable for women or for men, 85 per cent of employers indicated a preference for employing men in certain jobs and 89 per cent indicated a preference for women in certain (other) jobs (House, 1986). In Lucknow, India (1982), roughly 60 per cent of the employers interviewed reported that women were unsuitable or less suitable than men for sales, production, service and executive/supervisory occupations (Papola, 1986). In Accra, Ghana (1982), 21 per cent of the employers interviewed indicated that they sometimes refused to hire women for fear they would become pregnant (Date-Bah, 1986).

Masculine stereotypes also play a role in determining the occupations which become typically "male" (such as engineer, truck driver, police officer, construction worker). In order to break down the sex segregation of occupations, therefore, it is important to change both male and female stereotypes and to integrate men into "female" occupations as well as women into "male" occupations. However, integrating men into typical "female" occupations is a controversial issue, since most labour market discrimination is directed against women, not men; moreover, such measures would contribute to eliminating one of the few labour market advantages women have. Yet breaking down the sex segregation of occupations is critical to improving women's labour market situation, and this goal cannot be accomplished without breaking down the sex stereotyping of men, women and occupations.

Why are "female" occupations flexible?

It seems clear that women's responsibility for housework and child care affects the types of job many women prefer, since job flexibility in terms of hours (or part-time jobs) and relatively easy entry/exit/re-entry enable women to combine work and family responsibilities more easily. On this, gender theories and neo-classical theories agree.

However, there are two possible reasons why "female" occupations tend to be flexible in terms of hours and labour turnover. It could be that women gravitate towards occupations with these characteristics (either because of women's preferences and characteristics and/or because employers prefer to employ women in these occupations), as explained by economic theory (see earlier discussion). Or it could be that occupations become "female", because of the sort of sex stereotyping just described — with flexible working conditions emerging as a consequence of the fact that these are "female" occupations.

Although neo-classical economic/human capital theory holds that the preferences of women and employers are responsible for the concentration of women in flexible occupations, feminist theory does not support such an unequivocal conclusion, since both the possibilities noted above are consistent with it. While family responsibilities can be expected to increase women's preferences for flexible occupations, the stereotyping of certain work as suitable for women can be expected to affect the types of occupation open to them.

The empirical analysis in Anker (forthcoming, Part III) provides some evidence indicating a high degree of consistency between the sex stereotyping of an occupation and the "feminine" stereotypes listed in table 1. It supports the conclusion that the flexibility and low pay associated with many typical "female" occupations are due, to a large extent, to the fact that these are "female" occupations. There is no reason to consider *any* occupation (regardless of sex stereotyping) as inherently either more or less flexible.[9]

Cultural restrictions on women's freedom

Gender theories also point out how cultural restrictions contribute to the establishment of what is acceptable work for women and how, in some countries, they effectively bar women from certain occupations. This is an extreme form of sex stereotyping. For example, in many Muslim countries, *purdah* effectively forbids women from interacting with unknown men in public. As a result, many Muslim women are strongly discouraged from taking sales jobs except in shops where the customers are all women; women are excluded from factory jobs except when the entire factory workforce is female.[10] Many other examples could be given. Cultural restrictions on women's freedom of movement are enforced through strong social sanctions, which often include sexual harassment or rude behaviour by men.

FEMALE-MALE PAY DIFFERENTIALS AND OCCUPATIONAL SEGREGATION BY SEX

Women's earnings are lower than men's throughout the world. As indicated by the ILO data in table 2, this is true in all regions of the world, whether one is comparing pay computed on a daily, weekly or monthly basis, or whether one is comparing non-agricultural workers as a whole or only manufacturing workers. Average female-male pay ratios in the world are roughly 60-70 per cent, based on a monthly reference period; 70-75 per cent, based on daily and weekly reference periods; and 75-80 per cent, based on an hourly reference period; the averages for OECD and developing countries are reasonably similar. Ratios appear to be especially low in east and south-east Asian countries as well as in some European countries (with Japan, the Republic of Korea, Malaysia, Singapore, Luxembourg and Cyprus the only countries having a ratio below 0.60). Ratios appear to be relatively high in Scandinavian countries, as well as in some other OECD and Third World countries (with Denmark, Iceland, Norway, Sweden, Australia, Sri Lanka, Turkey and Swaziland the only countries with a ratio clearly above 0.80).

Gunderson (1994) identifies five sources of male-female pay differentials: (i) differences in human capital endowments such as education and experience (caused mainly by non-labour market factors); (ii) differences in pay within the same occupation (caused by direct discrimination and dual labour markets); (iii) differences in pay for work of "equal value" (caused by the relationship between pay level in an occupation and the degree to which it is feminized); (iv) differences in jobs desired; and (v) differences in the jobs available. Occupational segregation by sex plays an important direct role in determining the last three sources of female-male pay differentials.

Comparable worth exercises provide good illustrations of how wage rates tend to be lower in "female" than "male" occupations. In these exercises, jobs are objectively evaluated and point scores established for factors such as responsibility, skill, education, physical effort, working conditions. The summation of these factor scores indicates in some objective sense the value of a job, and therefore its comparable worth. The greater the number of total points, the greater a job's worth or value. Figure 1 and table 3 provide examples drawn from the Washington State Government (United States) and the Toronto municipal government (Canada), respectively. In the case of jobs with similar worth (point scores), male-dominated occupations have substantially higher pay rates compared with female-dominated occupations. On the basis of these evaluations, pay rates are increased for the "female" jobs in order to help equalize pay in the "male" and "female" jobs which showed similar point scores.

Empirical studies analysing the determinants of male-female pay differences typically rely on regression analysis to separate out the

145

Women, gender and work

Table 2. Female-male wage ratios in the world, around 1990 [1]

Region/country/area	Reference period [2,3]	Female-male wage ratio	
		All non-agricultural	Manufacturing
OECD countries [4]			
Australia	Hourly	88.2	82.5
Belgium	Hourly	75.1	74.5
Denmark	Hourly	82.6	84.6
Finland	Hourly		77.3
France	Hourly	80.8	78.9
Germany (Fed. Rep. of)	Hourly	73.2	72.7
Greece	Hourly		78.4
Iceland	Hourly	87.0	
Ireland	Hourly		69.2
Luxembourg	Hourly	67.8	62.2
Netherlands	Hourly	77.5	75.0
New Zealand	Hourly	80.6	74.9
Norway	Hourly		86.4
Portugal	Hourly	69.1	69.0
Sweden	Hourly		88.9
Switzerland	Hourly	67.6	68.0
United Kingdom	Hourly	70.5	68.4
Average (unweighted)		**76.7**	**75.7**
Cyprus	Daily/weekly	59.0	58.0
Turkey	Daily/weekly	84.5	81.0
Average (unweighted)		**71.8**	**69.5**
Developing countries or areas [4]			
Sri Lanka	Hourly	91.2	
Average (unweighted)		**91.2**	
Egypt	Daily/weekly	80.7	68.0
Hong Kong, China	Daily/weekly	69.5	69.0
Sri Lanka	Daily/weekly	89.8	88.0
Average (unweighted)		**80.0**	**75.0**
Costa Rica	Monthly	66.0	74.0
Japan	Monthly	49.6	41.0
Kenya	Monthly	78.3	73.0
Korea (Rep. of)	Monthly	53.5	50.0
Malaysia	Monthly		50.1
Paraguay	Monthly	76.0	66.0
Singapore	Monthly	71.1	55.0
Swaziland	Monthly	106.6	88.0
Average (unweighted)		**71.6**	**62.1**
World averages (unweighted)			
	Hourly	**77.8**	**75.7**
	Daily/weekly	**76.7**	**71.2**
	Monthly	**71.6**	**62.1**

[1] Data year is 1990. [2] Countries are grouped according to reference period over which wages are estimated, because the female-male wage ratio decreases as the reference period increases (since women work fewer hours than men on average). For purposes of exposition, estimates for daily and weekly reference periods are combined. [3] Preference is given to estimate for shorter reference period if data are available for two or more reference periods. [4] Japan is included with other Asian countries (which are developing countries). Sri Lanka appears twice because of different reference periods.

Sources: ILO: *Yearbook of Labour Statistics* (Geneva), various issues.

Figure 1. Relationship between monthly salary and job worth points for men and women in the Washington State public service, 1974

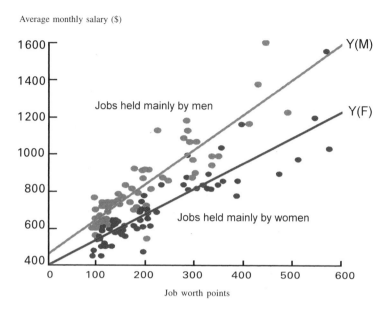

proportion attributable to differences in productivity-related variables (including human capital)[11] and other factors which affect wage rates[12] and differences in the returns men and women receive for their endowments. The first set of variables is felt to measure justifiable differences in wage rates, whereas the second set deals mainly with the functioning of the labour market and is seen as measuring discrimination (Oaxaca, 1973).

There have been scores of empirical studies of the female-male pay differential. A review of United States studies concludes that around one-third of the female-male differential is due to occupational segregation by sex (Treiman and Hartmann, 1981; World Bank, 1994), as do reviews of different national studies (Terrell, 1992; Gonzalez, 1991).[13]

Studies relating occupational segregation by sex to female-male pay differentials are also greatly affected by the level of disaggregation of the occupational data analysed. When very aggregated data (such as the usual seven major ISCO occupations) are used, occupational segregation's effect is underestimated, mainly because most occupational segregation by sex remains unobserved. As occupational data become more disaggregated, the observed level of sex segregation increases, and the portion of the female-male pay differential explained by occupational segregation tends to increase. A study from the United States (Treiman and Hartmann, 1981) illustrates this: the percentage of the female-male

Table 3. Pay equity[1] job evaluations for selected male and female job classes[2], Toronto municipal government

Selected female job classes			Selected male job classes		
Total points [3]	Pay rate [4]	Description	Total points [3]	Pay rate [4]	Description
1 559	17.22	Early childhood educator, grade 1	1 563	20.94	Automotive mechanic foreman
1 399	15.44	Early childhood educator, grade 2	1 179	16.36	Junior micro-computer technician
1 155	12.49	Nursing attendant	1 179	16.36	Junior micro-computer technician
1 034	13.02	Day-care housekeeper	1 034	14.28	Cook, grade 1
839	11.68	Housekeeping attendant	879	15.22	Security guard
652	11.42	Cleaner, light duties	694	14.21	Cleaner, heavy duties

[1] The phrases "pay equity" and "comparable worth" are equivalent; the former is used in Canada and the latter in the United States. [2] Job classes selected for this table are based in part on the job classes chosen as the main male comparators in the pay equity evaluations and in part on what are typical female jobs around the world. [3] Total points are obtained from a comparable worth review on 4 September 1992. Total points for job evaluation are based on the summation of points for the following factors using the following weights shown in brackets: skill (45%); responsibility (33%); effort (14%); and working conditions (8%). [4] Pay rates are hourly pay rates in Canadian dollars as at 1 January 1990.

Source: Canadian Union of Public Employees, mimeo, 1992.

earnings gap explained by occupational segregation by sex rose from about 10 per cent when 12 occupational categories were used, to 10 to 20 per cent when 222 occupations were used, and to at least 30 per cent when 479 occupations were used. Similarly, a study by Kidd and Shannon (1996) found that the percentage of the female-male wage gap explained rose from 12 to 18 and 27 per cent as the number of occupations classified increased from 9, to 17 and 36 using the same Oaxaca (1973) approach used by Treiman and Hartmann (1981); though no change was observed in this percentage when the Brown et al. (1980) approach was used, which estimates a separate equation for each occupation. OECD (1988) reports that average female earnings would have been 93.2 per cent of average male earnings in 1986, if men and women had been paid the same median earnings for each occupation based on 18 broad occupational groups; in contrast, this would have been 84.1 per cent on the basis of a much more disaggregated classification with 238 occupations.

After a fairly high level of detail in the occupational classification is reached, however, further disaggregation of the occupational data probably reduces the proportion of the female-male pay differential observed to be attributable to occupational segregation by sex. At the extreme of detailed job descriptions within establishments, there is usually very little difference in pay for men and women, since anti-discrimination laws make it illegal to pay different wages for the identical job within an enterprise.

The research literature on wage differentials provides a useful context in which to understand occupational segregation by sex, since it indicates that female-male pay differentials are due to many factors other than occupational segregation and differences in the human capital of men and women. It is only when these other factors are also taken into consideration that a coherent explanation can be found for both the level of female-male pay differentials and occupational segregation by sex in countries around the world. Indeed, several previous cross-national studies based on aggregated occupational data have noted that the simple correlation between the female-male pay ratio and occupational segregation by sex is not statistically significant and that sometimes this relationship is even positive (Rosenfeld and Kalleberg, 1991; Jacobs and Lim, 1992; Barbezat, 1993).

For example, Anker (forthcoming) finds that occupational segregation by sex is lower in Asia than in Europe and, within Europe, highest in Scandinavia. These results are unexpected and counter-intuitive if one is thinking only about female-male pay ratios since, as shown in table 2 and elsewhere (for example, Anker and Hein, 1986; Standing, 1989; Terrell, 1992), European countries tend to have higher female-male pay ratios compared with Asian countries. And among European countries, female-male pay ratios are highest in Scandinavia.

There are several possible explanations for these unexpected values. First, a major determinant of female-male pay differences across countries is the general level of pay differentials in a country (Blau and Khan, 1992; Gunderson, 1989). Second, in a related point, female-male pay differentials tend to be lower in countries with centralized wage setting (Gunderson, 1994; Rosenfeld and Kalleberg, 1991). Both of these factors undoubtedly help explain the relatively high female-male pay ratios in Scandinavia.

A third major source of pay differentials within countries is enterprise size. Large enterprises pay higher wage rates than do small enterprises to workers in apparently similar occupations (Gunderson, 1989 and 1994). Various explanations have been offered for this. One theory (that of compensating differentials) postulates that large enterprises pay a higher, so-called efficiency wage in order to attract the best talent. This has important implications for the average female-male wage ratio in a country, because men are more likely than women to be employed in large enterprises. This factor could be especially important in a country like Japan where about one-third of the labour force works in large enterprises, in which seniority is an especially important determinant of pay. That women have been largely excluded from these large firms undoubtedly helps to explain the low female-male wage ratio in Japan (despite its relatively low level of occupational segregation by sex).

Fourth, the research literature distinguishes between two different forms of occupational segregation by sex. Horizontal segregation refers to the distribution of men and women across occupations — for example, women may work as maids and secretaries and men as truck drivers and doctors. Vertical segregation refers to the distribution of men and women in the same occupation but with one sex more likely to be at a higher grade or level — for example, men are more likely to be production supervisors and women production workers, men more likely to be senior managers and women junior managers. Some authors stress the point that vertical segregation is more important (Hakim, 1992) or at least as important (Barbezat, 1993) a determinant of the female-male pay ratio as horizontal segregation. Of course, depending on the detail of the occupational classification, the same phenomenon could be observed as horizontal or vertical segregation. For example, when men work as doctors and women as nurses, this would be horizontal segregation in a three-digit ISCO classification where these two occupations are classified separately; but this same phenomenon would be vertical segregation in a two-digit ISCO classification where medical, dental and veterinary workers are combined into one occupational group. Irrespective of this measurement problem, it is clear that vertical segregation is a very important determinant of female-male pay differentials, because even a relatively detailed occupational classification of 250 or so occupations is rather crude for a modern economy. Referring again to the situation in Japan, it seems likely that vertical segregation is an especially important determinant of Japan's low female-male pay ratio. For example, Japanese women are more or less excluded from the managerial career path in large corporations, so that even when they get a job in a large company, they rarely get into a career track position (Lam, 1992).[14]

CONCLUDING REMARKS

This chapter is concerned with the sex segregation of occupations and labour market inequalities between men and women and explanations of why it occurs. This brief concluding section provides some general conclusions about the relevance and usefulness of the theories described for explaining this phenomenon; in so doing, it draws on results from a large empirical study of occupational segregation by sex by the author (Anker, forthcoming) where detailed occupational data for 41 countries and territories around the world are analysed.

The data analysed therein indicate that the majority of men and women in the world work in what can only be described as "male" or "female" occupations, given the high proportion which is either male or female. The data also indicate that there is considerable similarity all over the world in the types of occupation which are gender-stereotyped — determining and reinforcing the gender stereotypes shown in table 1.

These empirical results provide support for all three of the general theories described in this article. Neo-classical/human capital theories correctly point out how women are less well qualified than men for certain occupations because of differences in their education and years of experience. So, for example, all over the world men, not women, are engineers because very few women train to be engineers; on the other hand women, not men, are nurses because very few men train to be nurses. Labour market segmentation theories are correct in their basic premise that labour markets are indeed segmented, and this segmentation undoubtedly helps reduce wages in "female" occupations through the "overcrowding" effect.

However, data from the forthcoming study also indicate that gender theories provide the most compelling explanations for the sex segregation of occupations, given that they emphasize enormous overlap in the abilities and preferences of individual men and women. They also address the underlying reasons for segregation inside as well as outside the labour market. They help explain why the most important occupations in which women are employed around the world reinforce typical "female" stereotypes such as the caring, docile or home-based woman worker. They help explain why women acquire less experience than men, because women are overwhelmingly responsible for childcare at home. They help explain why women in certain countries are virtually excluded from occupations which involve public contact between men and women. They help explain how the restricted and inferior labour market opportunities for women associated with occupational segregation are perpetuated into the next generation, because such limited prospects cause many families — and many women — to underinvest in women's education, training and experience. They help explain why the part-time work and/ or flexible hours associated with so many "female" occupations are as much a reaction to the fact that these are "female" occupations as they are to the need for "flexibility" in these occupations. They help explain why, despite high unemployment rates, relatively few men in industrialized countries have so far been willing to enter typical "female" occupations.

With increasing competition across the globe, it is increasingly important for countries to make efficient use of their resources. What could be a more important source of labour market inefficiency than the extensive segmentation of male and female workers? With the impact of the women's liberation movement, and an increasing participation of women in the labour force and in public life, what could be more important than equal labour market opportunities for men and women? In both these respects, the sex segregation of occupations has an important influence. The stereotyping of men and women around the world has important implications for development and competitiveness.

Policy-makers need to address more seriously the inequality of labour market opportunities and its effect on both men and women. A wide variety of policies and programmes is needed — for example, facilitating policies to reduce the burden on women of family responsibilities; consciousness-raising programmes to remove gender stereotypes and prejudices; educational policies to bring about greater gender equality in schooling and training, especially with respect to opening access to non-traditional occupations for both men and women; and equal opportunity and affirmative action policies, especially those opening up new opportunities for men and women. Action is required on all these fronts to reduce occupational segregation between men and women with benefits not only for the present workforce and economy, but also for the future.

Notes

[1] A number of researchers have commented on the fact that female-male wage differentials are very small for single persons and that married persons account for almost all of the observed female-male wage differential (see for example, Blau and Khan, 1992, and World Bank, 1994, for general conclusions; Hakim, 1992, for the United Kingdom; Ogawa and Clark, 1995, for Japan).

[2] Even in Scandinavia, women continue to be mainly responsible for work and childcare according to time use data (UNDP, 1995; United Nations, 1991).

[3] Papola (1986) reports that this was one of the most common reasons for not hiring women given by employers interviewed in his enterprise survey in Lucknow, India.

[4] In Bangladesh, for example, some women need to bring their children, even their older daughters, to work. Garment manufacturers there report that women workers are unwilling to leave their 11-13 year old daughters alone at home, because this would negatively affect the girls' reputations and, consequently, marriage prospects (Myers, personal communication).

[5] It is possible, of course, to design maternity and childcare leave programmes as parental leave programmes. However, experience from countries which give new parents the choice of maternity or paternity leave indicates that relatively few fathers actually take paternity leave. An interesting policy to encourage men to take paternity leave is found in Norway where at least four weeks of a possible total of 52 weeks of parental leave must be taken by the father; if the father does not take up these four weeks of paternity leave, they are lost (Melkas and Anker, forthcoming).

[6] Two interesting institutional aspects of Scandinavian labour markets arise from a strong public commitment to: (i) gender equity; and (ii) full employment for all citizens. Public commitment to these goals directly affects the sex segregation of occupations. It leads to the creation of many public sector jobs in order to help women combine their family and work responsibilities. For example, Melkas and Anker (forthcoming) estimate that in 1990 approximately 10 per cent of women non-agricultural workers in Finland and Norway and 19 per cent of women non-agricultural workers in Sweden were in one of the following, generally public sector, occupations: child day-care centre worker, social worker, municipal home-help, and assistant nurse/attendant. Since these occupations are highly feminized (96, 75, 96, 92 per cent female, respectively, in Sweden, for example), this substantially increases occupational segregation by sex in Scandinavia and in part explains why such segregation is higher than in other European countries.

[7] This division of theories into three separate categories is done for heuristic purposes, as there is substantial overlap between them. For example, while the perpetuation of sex segregation in an occupation through sexual harassment by male workers is usually an issue only addressed by feminist theory, it could easily be incorporated into a neo-classical model of the labour market as an added expense for employers (since introduction of female workers in such a situation might disrupt the workplace and affect labour productivity).

[8] This point is illustrated by an experience of the author's during field work several years ago in Egypt. In response to a typical question on labour force participation ("What was your main activity in the past week?"), a female schoolteacher reported that she was a housewife. Upon being asked why she gave this answer when, in fact, she was a teacher, she responded by saying that teaching involved 20-30 hours of work per week, but that housework involved many more hours — and that the question had inquired about her "main activity" in terms of time.

[9] A similar conclusion was reached in a recent European Union report on the organization of teaching (Rubery and Fagan, 1993): "these characteristics of the profession [emphasis on caring role, convenient working hours, relatively low pay] may be a reflection of, and not a cause of, the dominance of women" (p. xv).

[10] A solution to this problem used by some garment factories in Bangladesh is to have single-sex shop-floors. In this way, factories have both male and female workers, but there is no interaction between men and women at the worksite.

[11] Variables typically used to measure a worker's human capital and productivity include the following: education, field of study, training, experience in the enterprise, experience in the labour market, age, size of firm, hours of work and health.

[12] Factors typically used to measure macro, meso and establishment level aspects that might affect a worker's wage rate include the following: size of establishment, sector of establishment, whether public or private, region, city size, whether unionized. Also sometimes included is the percentage of women in the occupation, although this variable is sometimes interpreted as measuring sex discrimination.

[13] Scott (1986) discusses the interesting case of Peru where female education levels increased over several decades to a point where they exceeded male levels — yet the average female-male pay ratio showed little change.

[14] Even in Nikko Securities, a large Japanese corporation which is considered a leader in promoting women's employment, very few women enter the career promotion track. According to a recent report (Manpower, 1994), Nikko Securities recruited a relatively high percentage of women for its managerial positions (148 men and 75 women), but not into the career track (148 men and only 3 women).

References

Anker, Richard. Forthcoming [1998]. *Gender and jobs: Sex segregation of occupations in the world*. Geneva, ILO.

—. 1995. "Labour market policies, vulnerable groups and poverty", in José B. Figueiredo and Zafar Shaheed (eds.): *Reducing poverty through labour market policies: New approaches to poverty analysis and policy — II*. Geneva, ILO International Institute for Labour Studies.

—; Hein, Catherine (eds.). 1986. *Sex inequalities in urban employment in the Third World*. London, Macmillan.

—; —. 1985. "Why Third World urban employers usually prefer men", in *International Labour Review* (Geneva), Vol. 124, No. 1, pp. 73-90.

Barbezat, Debra. 1993. *Occupational segmentation by sex in the world*. Interdepartmental Project on Women in Employment, Working Paper No. 13, IDP Women/WP-13. Geneva, ILO.

Becker, Gary S. 1971. *The economics of discrimination*. Second edition. Chicago, University of Chicago Press.

Bergmann, Barbara. 1974. "Occupational segregation, wages and profits when employers discriminate by wage or sex", in *Eastern Economic Journal* (Storrs, CT), Vol. 1, Nos. 2-3.

Blau, Francine D.; Khan, Lawrence M. 1992. "The gender earnings gap: Learning from international comparisons", in *American Economic Review* (Nashville, TN), Vol. 82, No. 2 (May), pp. 533-538.

Brown, Randall S.; Moon, Marilyn; Zoloth, Barbara S. 1980. "Incorporating occupational attainment in studies of male/female earnings differentials", in *Journal of Human Resources* (Madison, WI), Vol. 15, No. 1 (Winter), pp. 3-28.

Women, gender and work

Buvinic, Mayra. 1995. "The feminization of poverty? Research and policy needs", in José B. Figueiredo and Zafar Shaheed (eds.): *Reducing poverty through labour market policies: New approaches to poverty analysis and policy — II*. Geneva, ILO International Institute for Labour Studies.

Canadian Union of Public Employees. 1992. *Toronto Pay Equity Plan facts*. Mimeo. Toronto.

Date-Bah, Eugenia. 1986. "Sex segregation and discrimination in Accra-Tema: Causes and consequences", in Anker and Hein, pp. 235-276.

Doeringer, Peter; Piore, Michael. 1971. *Internal labor markets and manpower analysis*. Lexington, MA, D.C. Heath and Co.

Edgeworth, F. Y. 1922. "Equal pay to men and women for equal work", in *Economic Journal* (London), Vol. 32, No. 4 (Dec.), pp. 431-457.

Gonzalez, Pablo. 1991. *Indicators of the relative performance of women in the labour market*. Mimeo. Geneva, ILO.

Gunderson, Morley. 1994. *Comparable worth and gender discrimination: An international perspective*. Geneva, ILO.

—. 1989. "Male-female wage differentials and policy responses", in *Journal of Economic Literature* (Nashville, TN), Vol. 27, No. 1 (Mar.), pp. 46-72.

Hakim, Catherine. 1992. "Explaining trends in occupational segregation: The measurement, causes and consequences of the sexual division of labour", in *European Sociological Review* (Oxford), Vol. 8, No. 2, pp. 127-152.

House, William J. 1986. "The status and pay of women in the Cyprus labour market", in Anker and Hein, pp. 117-169.

ILO. 1990. *International Standard Classification of Occupations-88*. Geneva.

—. 1972. *Employment, incomes and inequality: A strategy for increasing productive employment in Kenya*. Geneva.

—. 1968. *International Standard Classification of Occupations-68*. Geneva.

—. Various years. *Yearbook of Labour Statistics*. Geneva.

Jacobs, Jerry A.; Lim, Suet T. 1992. "Trends in occupational and industrial sex segregation in 56 countries, 1960-80", in *Work and Occupations* (Newbury Park, CA), Vol. 19, No. 4 (Nov.), pp. 450-486.

Kidd, Michael P.; Shannon, Michael. 1996. "Does the level of occupational segregation affect estimates of the gender wage gap?", in *Industrial and Labor Relations Review* (Ithaca, NY), Vol. 49, No. 2 (Jan.), pp. 317-329.

Lam, Alice C. L. 1992. *Women and Japanese management: Discrimination and reform*. London, Routledge.

Lim, Lin Lean. 1996. *More and better jobs for women: An action guide*. Geneva, ILO.

Manpower. 1994. "Women on slow track to the top in Japan", in *Manpower Digest* (Milwaukee, WI), Sep.

Melkas, Helinä; Anker, Richard. Forthcoming. *Occupational segregation in the Nordic countries*. Geneva, ILO.

Oaxaca, Ronald. 1973. "Male-female wage differentials in urban labour markets", in *International Economic Review* (Philadelphia, PA), Vol. 14, No. 3 (Oct.), pp. 693-709.

OECD. 1988. "Women's activity, employment and earnings: A review of recent developments", in *OECD Employment Outlook* (Paris), Sep., pp. 129-172.

Ogawa, Naohiro; Clark, Robert L. 1995. "Earning patterns of Japanese women: 1976-1988", in *Economic Development and Cultural Change* (Chicago, IL), Vol. 43, No. 2 (Jan.), pp. 293-313.

Papola, T. S. 1986. "Women workers in the formal sector of Lucknow, India", in Anker and Hein, pp. 171-212.

Paukert, Liba. 1995. *Economic transition and women's employment in four Central European countries, 1989-1994.* Labour Market Paper No. 7. Geneva, ILO.

Rosenfeld, R.; Kalleberg, A. 1991. "Gender inequality in the labour market: A cross-national perspective", in *Acta Sociologica* (Oslo), Vol. 34, No. 1, pp. 207-225.

Rubery, Jill; Fagan, Collette. 1993. "Occupational segregation of women and men in the European Community", in *Social Europe* (Luxembourg), Supplement No. 3.

Scott, Alison MacEwen. 1986. "Economic development and urban women's work: The case of Lima, Peru", in Anker and Hein, pp. 313-365.

Standing, Guy. 1989. *Global feminization through flexible labour.* World Employment Programme Research, Working Paper No. 31, WEP 2-43/WP.31. Geneva, ILO.

Sziraczki, György; Windell, James. 1992. "Impact of employment restructuring on disadvantaged groups in Hungary and Bulgaria", in *International Labour Review* (Geneva), Vol. 131, No. 4-5, pp. 471-496.

Terrell, Katherine. 1992. "Female-male earnings differentials and occupational structure", in *International Labour Review* (Geneva), Vol. 131, No. 4-5, pp. 387-404.

Treiman, Donald J.; Hartmann, Heidi I. (eds.). 1981. *Women, work, and wages: Equal pay for jobs of equal value.* Washington, DC, National Academy Press.

United Nations. 1991. *The world's women 1970-1990: Trends and statistics.* New York.

UNDP. 1995. *Human Development Report.* New York, NY, Oxford University Press.

World Bank. 1994. *Enhancing women's participation in economic development.* Mimeo. Washington, DC.

DIFFERENCES IN OCCUPATIONAL EARNINGS BY SEX

9

Derek ROBINSON*

Does gender bias cause differences in pay? The reply necessitates precise measures of pay based on specification of education, experience and occupation. Original analyses of the female/male occupational wage gap in the diverse countries for which adequate data are available in the ILO's 1996 October Earnings Inquiry are presented. Empirical findings cover occupational groups in medicine and in public service, banking and insurance. In addition, some national trends and international differences are indicated. Also presented are major research findings on the female/male wage gap and methodological issues, with advice on the pitfalls to avoid.

The question of whether gender bias is a cause of differences in pay is important, persistent and still unresolved.[1] A critical element in examining that question is the precise measurement of pay differentials, which in turn requires specification of components determined by differences in education, experience and occupation, inter alia. This chapter reviews some of the major research findings concerning the female/male wage gap, looking first at questions addressed in attempting to measure wage gaps and some methodological issues. It then introduces some analyses of the female/male occupational wage gap based on data from the ILO's 1996 October Earnings Inquiry (OEI).[2] In order to approach an understanding of possible discrimination the categories are first discussed, then empirical findings given for two major groupings of occupations — in medicine and in public service, banking and insurance. Some suggestions as to national trends and international differences are offered, and a final section concludes.

Originally published in *International Labour Review*, Vol. 137 (1998), No. 1.

* Institute of Economics and Statistics, University of Oxford.

CONSIDERATIONS IN MEASURING GAPS IN EARNINGS

Some common questions are taken up in examinations of differential earnings by sex. One is whether there are differences in the average pay of men and women, and if so to what extent. All studies show that though in some situations women may earn more than men in certain narrowly-defined occupations, overall there is a general gap between the average pay of men and women in broad occupational or multi-occupational groupings, with women earning on average less than men. Evidence of the existence of such an overall average gap does not of course indicate whether or not gender-based discrimination underlies that difference. It is possible that men and women in each occupation are paid exactly the same wage but, as pay differs according to occupation, if the distribution of men and women across occupations varies there will be a difference in the overall average pay of men and women. It is well established that as a result of variations in the occupational distribution of men and women, there is an "overcrowding" of women in certain occupations and under-representation of women in others.[3]

The next questions then are the extent of the difference, its causes and the degree to which it is constant or changing. Various definitional problems immediately arise in this connection. Is the comparison between men and women doing exactly the same work in the same place or, at the other extreme, between all male and all female workers across the whole economy?

The simplest question to address is whether men and women performing the same work in the same place or establishment are paid the same or not. Yet in practice, even this is difficult to answer comprehensively, as to do so really requires detailed information on every worker in every establishment. And, though equal pay legislation largely prevents this obvious form of discrimination, such legislation does not require every woman in an establishment to be paid exactly the same as every man doing the same work in that establishment. Salary scales stipulating a range of pay for a job can satisfy legal requirements regarding equal pay despite differences in the pay actually received by men and women, provided that the reasons for these differences are not gender related. For example, equal pay legislation is not infringed by salary scales which have automatic increments based on length of service, although these may result in differences in the pay of men and women doing the same job in the same establishment.

Pay systems

Certain practices or elements in a payment system may have a wage-differentiating effect for men and women. For example, performance-related elements in pay may permit gender discrimination in their award or size. However, some studies have shown that women do better under incentive schemes based on results rather than on subjective evaluation (e.g. Gunderson, 1975) — a possible indicator of discrimination in pay systems without them.

Some allowances may automatically be paid to men, inflating their measured earnings: for example, in the case of both spouses employed by the civil service, payment of a child allowance may be made only to the man. Or the payment basis may lead to differences in earnings: if men work longer hours on average than women, men's average *weekly* or *monthly* earnings will be higher even if they are paid the same hourly rate. Men's average *hourly* earnings are also usually higher than women's, but to a lesser extent, as any overtime premium is spread over all the hours worked. Men may also have higher average hourly wages because of the greater proportion of women working part time — work which is typically paid at lower hourly rates.

Methodological questions – main approaches

Currently there is little evidence of significant differences in wages for men and women in the same narrowly-defined occupations in the same establishment. Because of difficulties involved in analysing men's and women's pay for performing the same tasks, most studies compare the average pay of a group of men and a group of women. Two very different methods of analysis are used in practice.

The first method consists simply of comparing the average or the median earnings of male and female full-time employees. There are obvious weaknesses in this relatively crude aggregate approach. It ignores any differences in productivity as it does not seek to compare the pay of men and women doing the same or similar work. Because this approach generally compares earnings of all workers in specified labour markets (national, sectoral, etc.) it may well not compare the earnings of men and women in the same broad occupations. Since the proportions of the male and female labour forces obviously vary from one occupational group to another, as already mentioned, then even where men and women are paid exactly the same wage within each occupation there will be differences between the average wage of men and women and, most probably, in their median wages, too.

The second method seeks to explain the differences by adjusting the data to take account of features which might explain differing productivity or marginal product of men and women by including in regression analysis measurable work-related characteristics which can be tested to see whether the returns to them are different for men and for women. This does not change the measured wage gap but can provide explanations for the size of the gap or for changes in it over time. Thus, years of education can be expected to affect productivity and, so, value of marginal product (Mincer and Polachek, 1974; Mincer and Ofek, 1982; Hill and O'Neill, 1992); so can years of work experience (Mincer and Polachek, 1974; Lofstrom and Gustafsson, 1991).

Other analyses test whether men and women with the same presumed productivity-influencing characteristics receive the same pay. One such characteristic is education measured by years of schooling. Others may be years of experience (both within a given establishment and in employment generally) and marital status. Some studies consider these variables to be indicators of relative productivity. But this is not necessarily the case: they may be indicators of possible or potential productivity, and it does not follow that all individuals use their potential productivity to the same extent. Some studies show that women may choose not to use their full productive potential, because of placing greater importance on other aspects of employment, such as convenient hours, or a need to change jobs when their spouses have to move.

Researchers in this area who seek to include the personal characteristics of male and female employees in their analysis adopt a different approach from that of researchers seeking merely to examine the relative wage disadvantage of women without differentiation of productivity-influencing characteristics. Because of differences in men's and women's average pay resulting from the varying rate of reward for the possession of measurable productivity-influencing characteristics, the overall male/female wage gap will be influenced by the general level of wage differentials or the wage structure in an individual country (Blau and Kahn, 1996). The prevailing level of wage inequality within occupations involving different skills is very important in explaining the overall female wage gap.

Occupational pay differentials by sex are present in every economy, although their size and on occasion their direction, for pairs of occupations, change. Comparing groups of men and women of different occupational compositions will therefore reveal differences in average earnings which are caused by differences in the structure of employment and the size of occupational differentials, and not only by differences in pay for men and women in the same occupation.

Structural changes in the economy can also affect the wages of both men and women, leading to changes in the measured male/female wage gap (Borooah and Lee, 1988). Changes in technology and production methods can variously affect demand for skills, thus modifying occupational pay differentials. Changes in world trade can affect some industries adversely and occupations in those industries may suffer a relative wage decline compared with the same occupations which are expanding elsewhere. While those changes are only a relatively minor contributing factor, blue-collar workers in traditional heavy industries and in consumer-goods industries in a number of industrialized market economies have experienced declining demand for their labour with a consequential reduction in their pay relative to blue-collar workers in other occupations or in the same occupations in other industries.

EQUAL PAY FOR WORK OF EQUAL VALUE

In a number of countries legislation now requires equal pay for women performing work of equal value or of comparable worth to that performed by men in the same establishment. The aim is to prevent management, or trade unions and management acting together in collective bargaining, from discriminating against women in female-dominated jobs by fixing lower relative wage levels for them, whether or not some form of job evaluation exercise has already been carried out. In effect, comparable worth analyses are checks against gender bias in the determination of the internal wage structure, even though these internal wage structures may themselves have been based on some form of job analysis and evaluation.

The comparisons are confined to the same establishment, as establishments may have different pay levels for every occupation for any of a number of legitimate reasons, perhaps because they are in a different product market with greater opportunities for excessive or supra-normal profits and so can afford to pay higher wages, sharing the rents from market imperfections with the labour force. It would therefore be inappropriate to compel a company in one product market to pay women wages which include the rent-sharing of men in a company in another product market. Similarly, wage levels may differ from one local labour market to another because of variations in labour supply and demand. Again, it would be inappropriate to compel an establishment to pay higher wages to women in jobs similar to those of men in different localities if the reason for the wage difference was the location in another labour market, for in those circumstances men in the two localities would probably also be paid different wage levels.

It is necessarily a matter of judgement whether two jobs are of comparable worth or require the same skills and abilities. An element of subjective or value judgement will always be involved and on occasion the application of comparable worth analysis means imposing one set of values for the components of different jobs dissimilar to the values adopted by the persons who set the original pay levels. Nevertheless, it has been known for some time that techniques of comparability can be devised which minimize the subjective elements of comparability and produce results which command wide acceptance (see, e.g., Aldrich and Buchele, 1986; Blau, 1977; Ehrenberg and Smith, 1987). Yet, legislative provisions generally seek to cover only cases of possible discrimination against one sex in pay levels in relation to the content and requirements of their jobs compared with those of the other sex rather than establishing internal pay equalities for jobs of comparable worth *per se*. This may be because of the belief that if there is no gender-based discrimination or (in some cases) no discrimination based on race, religion or ethnic origin, the State should not seek to become involved in relative pay determination.

Economic theory would conclude that in the absence of any market imperfections or demand-side discrimination, the pay gap between men and women with the same value of marginal product in the same location would be zero. Even in this highly restrictive case, however, a comparison of male and female pay may not be sufficient to establish the existence of discrimination. There can be real differences in the value of marginal products of men and women doing the same work: this has long been recognized as typically true for jobs which require physical strength. The presence of an occupational wage gap can therefore only be regarded as a first indication that wage discrimination may be being practised against women.

Effects of job segregation on pay

It has been established that female-dominated jobs or occupations pay relatively lower wages than male-dominated ones, so that both men and women in an occupation are paid less the greater the proportion of women employed in that occupation. This crowding effect is more marked for men than for women (Bergmann, 1974; O'Neill, 1985; Blau and Beller, 1988; Sorensen, 1990; Killingsworth, 1990; Groschen, 1991). Some of the effects of job segregation which can influence women's average pay relative to men's should not be present in a study of the average pay of men and women in a narrowly-defined occupation, unless there are distributional differences between men and women in the various product or local labour markets. Average pay for both men and women in one occupation might be lower relative to average pay in occupations with a larger proportion of male workers, but within each occupation the crowding hypothesis should have no impact on the relative pay of men and women within that occupation. Discrimination theory seeks to explain whether, and if so why, employers choose *not* to employ women in certain jobs where they could have the same value of marginal product as men and presumably at wages lower than those men are currently paid, despite the probable concomitant increase in effective or acceptable labour supply and reduction in wages of both men and women.

If there is discrimination in hiring into certain occupations, the determination of a wage gap will depend on the coverage chosen for the comparison of male and female pay. If a narrow occupational basis is selected, there may be no apparent wage gap. If there is occupational crowding, the choice of a broader group coverage might well identify a wage gap but, the result of crowding into certain occupations resulting in lower wages there for both men and women, that would reflect discrimination in hiring rather than wage discrimination as such.

Such a discussion is not just an academic exercise. If appropriate remedial policies are to be developed, it clearly matters whether the discrimination is practised in the wages paid to people doing the same work in the same tightly-defined occupations, or whether it is practised at the point of entry into certain occupations or jobs. The existence of a wage gap when a broader coverage of occupations is used might therefore indicate that either wage or hiring discrimination exists, or both.

Legislation to ensure equal opportunity may lead to reductions in the wage gap if it enables more women to be admitted into occupations previously dominated by men and thus, typically, paying higher wages. This tendency is strengthened if legislation requires affirmative action or positive discrimination in favour of women.

Value of narrow occupational categories for detecting gender bias

It is clear that the larger the occupational coverage of the group of workers, the greater the possibility that the measured relationship will be misleading given the greater variety included. Even if men and women in the same establishment are paid exactly the same wage, differences in their average pay will emerge if the two sets of workers are employed in different proportions in different establishments. The narrower the occupational coverage of the comparison, the more likely it is that any genuine underlying difference in the pay of men and women will be displayed and the smaller the possibility that distortions will appear as a result of including workers who, despite their identical occupational title, have different jobs, levels of productivity or human capital endowments (e.g. labourer, salesperson). Of course, it is quite possible that men and women with different levels of human capital, ability and/or education are influenced by the presence of discrimination, or by some other factor entirely, in their choice of or entry into that narrowly-defined occupation. However, there is some evidence that differences in the occupational distribution of men and women are a more important cause of the pay gap when narrower rather than broader occupational groupings are used (Treiman and Hartmann, 1985). The effects of women being crowded into lower-paid jobs can be diluted if broader groupings are used for the purposes of comparison since women in higher-paying jobs will thus be included. Much also depends on the particular occupations that are grouped together and the female percentage wage gap in each of them. Female percentages, or wage gaps of broader groupings, are in effect no more than weighted averages of the female percentages of all the narrower occupational groupings included in the larger aggregate, so there will be some occupations with larger and some with smaller female percentages than that for the overall average.

There are difficulties in matching job requirements with occupational titles and job classifications. Classical economic theory removes these difficulties, or ignores them, by assuming homogeneous labour for a given occupational title. In reality — a reality recognized by more recent economic reasoning as embodied in the efficiency wage hypothesis — labour is not homogeneous but heterogeneous, even as regards each individual worker and the effort-inputs supplied by an individual worker at different times and in different circumstances, in response notably to the relative wage paid compared with that which he/she believes might be paid in another job. It is also possible that the same nominal occupation has different job requirements with different effort-inputs depending on the industry or sub-sector of economic activity. Thus the breadth of industrial coverage of the classification for wage surveys can affect the average pay of men and women even when the analysis appears to be confined to narrowly-defined occupations.[4]

This difficulty is also raised by Gunderson (1989) in a literature survey. He found, inter alia, that factors originating outside the labour market, such as differences in household responsibilities, type of education or career interruptions, are important component causes of the overall wage gap. Differences in occupational distribution account for a substantial part of that gap. Pay differences within narrower occupations, however, at least in some establishments do not lead to large differences in average male and female wages. Differences between establishments account for a substantial part of the female wage gap. The productivity-adjusted wage gap is smaller in the public than in the private sector, and is smaller in the private sector the more competitive the product market. The longer the length of employment of women within an establishment, the smaller the wage gap.

APPROACHES TO MEASURING OCCUPATIONAL EARNINGS BY SEX

The occupational definitions used in the ILO's October Earnings Inquiry (OEI)[5] make it possible to study the specific questions of whether there is a wage gap between men and women in the same occupation, the direction and size of the gap, and whether it is changing. That is what is addressed here.

Three main measurements of pay

Pay scales or job rates

Basically, this approach measures the amount of pay that males and females in a given job or post are entitled to receive, rather than the average amount of pay actually received by groups of male and female workers. In many types of employment, particularly in the public sector or in non-manual occupations, individual workers are classified in a job grade to which a pay scale is applied. The scale usually consists of a basic pay range which may be supplemented by various types of allowances or additions based on specified factors such as location of work, type of work, changes in the cost of living, qualifications, number of dependent children, age or years of service. The last two factors are often transcribed into specified incremental steps so that progression from the minimum to the maximum rate on the scale occurs automatically according to predetermined conditions; however, there has recently been a tendency to introduce a discretionary element into the award of such predetermined increments, based perhaps on some form of personal or merit assessment.

It is now rare for gender-based differences to appear in the pay scales applicable to men and women in the same job, post or grade in either the public or the private sector. Although the OEI provides details of some scale minima and maxima, particularly for public service occupations, these have not been used in this study as they are always the same for both sexes.

However, if the basis for the analysis changes from posts, jobs or grades to individuals in those posts, jobs or grades, gender-based differences may emerge. For example, if all members of a specified grade are paid on the same pay scale consisting of a given minimum salary with annual increments based on length of service up to a specified maximum salary applicable to all, it is possible for female workers in that grade to have a lower (or higher) average salary than the male workers in that grade. In the conditions specified, this would mean that on average women had fewer (or more) years of service in that grade than men did.

Differences in the average pay of men and women should not necessarily be regarded as gender-based pay discrimination, as each individual remaining in that grade will receive the same rate of pay irrespective of sex. The extent of the difference in average pay for men and women could be attributable to the distribution of men and women across the various incremental steps in the scale and to the difference in pay between each step. But payment system rules may include conditions which in practice militate against women reaching the higher levels within that single scale. This could happen if on average women have a lower retirement age than men and if all workers entered the grade and salary scale at an age which, combined with the total possible number of increments, meant that women reached their normal retirement age before they attained the maximum on the salary scale. Alternatively, women may have had fewer opportunities to progress up a pay scale with a large number of increments because of breaks in their working careers as a result of family responsibilities. If no such discriminatory conditions apply, differences in average female and male pay from a single salary scale with increments based only on seniority within the grade would be determined by seniority distributional differences between men and women.

Variations in average male/female pay arising from seniority distributional differences could still suggest the presence of gender-based discrimination in the grade. However, they might be due to the fact that more women than men had recently been recruited, which would be consistent with positive hiring practices in favour of women. It could also be consistent with positive discrimination favouring women's promotion to the next highest grade, if the grade in question is one from which members of the higher grade are recruited. If the grade is one to which members are recruited from lower grades within the same establishment, a higher proportion of women with lower seniority than men could be consistent with positive discrimination favouring women's promotion from the lower grade.

If, however, the salary scale or job rate contains discretionary elements, such as merit pay or performance awards, or elements which may themselves be gender based or gender influenced, e.g. payment of rent or housing allowances according to rules differentiating between men and women, then differences in average payment could indicate gender-based discrimination. If there were differences in the distribution of men and women by seniority in the grade and elements of gender-based difference in payments, it would be necessary to obtain detailed information both about the distribution of men and women by seniority and location in the incremental salary scale as well as the distribution and size of gender-based pay elements.

Average wage or salary rates

The OEI defines average wage or salary rates as the rates paid for normal time of work, comprising: basic wages and salaries, cost-of-living allowances and other guaranteed and regularly paid allowances. The following should be excluded: overtime payments, bonuses and gratuities, family allowances, other social security payments made by the employer directly to employees and *ex gratia* payments in kind supplementary to normal wage and salary rates (ILO, 1996).

This definition is similar to that just discussed if the average salary scale payment considered is based on actual pay received rather than on entitlements. Similar differences in average pay thus defined can then emerge if no pay is received for time not worked because of lateness, absenteeism or sickness and if there are differences between men and women in the average time not worked for these reasons.

However, in many countries employment conditions, especially in the public service, may allow full pay during sickness; or there is little (if any) absenteeism and lateness is overlooked; or, because of severe worsening of real pay, pay system controls and the enforcement of rules regarding attendance and timekeeping degenerates so far that no sanctions are taken or even official records kept. In those cases, even where there are differences in time lost by men and women there is no difference in the average salary or wages they actually receive other than for reasons of occupational distribution.[6] Private sector employment conditions may be different, with less advantageous sick pay provisions and a more rigorous enforcement of timekeeping, so that differences may emerge in average wages and salaries for men and women even when there are no seniority distributional effects.

The OEI gives details of normal hours of work, which are defined as those set out in regulations, laws or collective agreements (see also ILO, 1997). These are the number of hours that should be worked by full-time workers before overtime premium is paid. Where there is a significant number of part-time workers (disproportionately female), converting average weekly or monthly wages into hourly wages by dividing by the number of normal hours will understate average female hourly wages and thus overstate the female disadvantage. Similar types of distortion may occur when average weekly or monthly wages of men and women are compared, as those for women may reflect a lower number of average normal hours worked. The data provided by the OEI do not allow the necessary adjustments to be made. However, some countries (e.g. Costa Rica, Estonia, Finland, Lithuania, Republic of Moldova and the United Kingdom) report the average number of normal (non-overtime premium) hours actually worked, not the number of normal hours set out in collective agreements. In such cases, there are no problems in converting average weekly wages into average hourly wages, even if there are proportionately more part-time women workers. And a few countries report average or prevailing hourly wages for some, if not all, occupations. Average actual hourly wages are obviously the best measure of wages as they take into account any differences in hours worked and can be used to estimate equivalent weekly or monthly wages by using normal hours as set out in collective agreements.

Average earnings

The OEI defines earnings as the remuneration in cash and kind paid to employees, as a rule at regular intervals, for time worked or work done, together with remuneration for time not worked, such as for annual vacation, other paid leave or holidays, and including those elements of earnings which are usually received regularly, before any deductions are made by the employer in respect of taxes, contributions of employees to social security and pension schemes, life insurance premiums, union dues and any other obligations of employees (ILO, 1996, p. 3). Excluded are employers' contributions to social security and pension schemes and any benefits received by employees from these schemes. Also excluded are severance and termination pay, irregular bonuses such as year-end and other one-time bonuses which accrue over a period longer than a pay period.

It is clear that overtime payments, comprising elements of average wages or salary as well as the premium itself, should be included, as these are payments for time worked or work done. Differences in average earnings for males and females on the same salary scale can arise from differences in average hours worked and possibly from differences in the average overtime premium per hour worked.

AVERAGE FEMALE PAY AS A PERCENTAGE OF AVERAGE MALE PAY

The OEI provides details of average male and female pay for some occupations in some countries. This enables one to calculate the *female percentage* — average female pay as a percentage of average male pay for the same occupation. In this section, comparisons of male and female pay are analysed for two important and contrasting occupational groupings – medical occupations, and public service, banking and finance.

Medical occupations

The results of comparing male and female pay in six medical occupations in a number of countries based on details from the 1996 October Earnings Inquiry are summarized in table 1. Four different measures of pay are shown; changes in the female percentages among them arise from differences in the countries covered as well as smallish differences due to modifications in the measurement of pay. Some countries provide appropriate information for certain occupations only. Column (3) shows the number of countries included, column (4) the lowest or minimum female percentage, column (5) the highest, and column (6) the unweighted average of the female percentages for the countries covered.

The table also shows in column (7) the range of the female percentages, which is the maximum country percentage as a ratio of the lowest female percentage for that occupation. The coefficient of variation (CV) in column (8) is a measure of the differences in the female percentages in all the countries included in the analysis.[7] The larger the CV the more the various national female percentages for that occupation differ. For example, comparing average hourly wages for general physicians and dentists, the CV for physicians (20.89) is lower than that for dentists (28.86), showing that the female percentages for physicians are grouped more closely together and there is relatively less difference between them than between those for dentists. The range for physicians is also smaller than for dentists, showing that the difference between the two extreme female percentages for dentists is greater than that for physicians. The occupation with the largest range need not necessarily have the largest CV, as the range compares only the two extreme female percentages while the CV takes them all into account. For example, the range for average

Table 1. Women's average wages and earnings as a percentage of men's in selected medical occupations

OEI number	Occupation	Number of countries	Minimum	Maximum	Average[1]	Range[2]	CV[3]	>100%[4]
(1)	(2)	(3)	(4)	(5)	(6)	(7)	(8)	(9)
Average hourly wages								
152	General physician	10	49.1	130.5	92.7	2.659	20.89	3
153	Dentist	8	57.8	169.3	106.6	2.930	28.86	3
154	Professional nurse	10	92.9	105.3	98.6	1.134	4.12	4
155	Auxiliary nurse	10	84.6	114.3	98.9	1.350	7.57	4
156	Physiotherapist	6	74.5	128.6	97.7	1.726	18.79	3
157	X-ray technician	9	80.3	145.7	103.5	1.814	19.05	3

Countries examined: Bahrain, Bolivia, Cyprus, El Salvador, Estonia, Finland, Ghana, Honduras, Republic of Moldova, Nigeria, Romania, Tajikistan, United Kingdom.

Average monthly wages								
152	General physician	12	57.3	120.8	93.6	2.110	15.30	3
153	Dentist	8	57.8	169.3	105.8	2.930	27.96	4
154	Professional nurse	11	86.3	114.1	99.8	1.323	7.24	5
155	Auxiliary nurse	11	75.1	114.3	99.5	1.521	9.25	5
156	Physiotherapist	7	74.5	128.6	100.3	1.726	18.54	4
157	X-ray technician	9	80.3	145.7	101.4	1.814	19.34	3

Countries examined: Bahrain, Bolivia, China, Cyprus, El Salvador, Estonia, Finland, Ghana, Honduras, Republic of Moldova, Nigeria, Romania, Singapore, Tajikistan, United Kingdom.

Average hourly earnings								
152	General physician	9	48.6	128.5	92.4	2.643	21.97	3
153	Dentist	5	67.5	136.6	95.7	2.023	26.51	3
154	Professional nurse	11	67.1	105.1	96.9	1.567	10.32	6
155	Auxiliary nurse	9	91.8	124.2	101.2	1.353	8.99	4
157	X-ray technician	6	82.6	139.5	98.8	1.689	19.08	2

Countries examined: Australia, Costa Rica, El Salvador, Estonia, Finland, Ghana, Republic of Moldova, Nigeria, Norway, Romania, Sri Lanka, Tajikistan, United Kingdom.

Average monthly earnings								
152	General physician	10	55.6	170.1	92.0	3.062	31.87	2
153	Dentist	5	60.6	129.4	90.6	2.136	27.57	1
154	Professional nurse	12	61.2	107.8	91.4	1.761	15.79	3
155	Auxiliary nurse	10	83.1	114.4	98.9	1.377	7.90	4
157	X-ray technician	6	82.6	104.2	93.2	1.262	6.95	1

Countries examined: Australia, Costa Rica, El Salvador, Estonia, Finland, Ghana, Republic of Moldova, Nigeria, Norway, Romania, Tajikistan, United Kingdom, United States.

[1] Average is the unweighted arithmetic mean of the percentages for the number of countries shown in column (3). [2] Range is the maximum in column (5) divided by the minimum in column (4). [3] CV is the standard deviation as a percentage of the average (coefficient of variation). [4] The number of countries where average female pay was higher than average male pay.

monthly wages of X-ray technicians is 1.814 and that of general physicians 2.110, yet X-ray technicians have a larger CV (19.34) than physicians (15.30).

Finally, column (9) shows the number of countries where the female percentage is larger than 100, i.e. where average female wages are higher than average male wages.

Results from applying the different measures

Overall, as regards *average hourly wages*, although the unweighted female average as a percentage of male average hourly wages for physicians for the ten countries concerned is 93 per cent, there is a wide range of average percentages for average hourly wages. There are three countries where the average hourly wages of female physicians are higher than those of male physicians, yet female physicians in Nigeria receive less than half the average hourly wages of male physicians. In Bolivia, women's average hourly wages are 30 per cent higher than men's. There is very little difference in the female percentage for professional nurses in the ten countries, and the range and CV are quite small, as they are for auxiliary nurses. For both of these occupations, women have higher average wages than men in four of the ten countries, and the range of female percentages is so small that it is clear men and women are on the same salary scale in each country.

The two occupations where the unweighted average is larger than 100 are dentists (107 per cent), for whom only three out of eight countries have female percentages greater than 100, and X-ray technicians (104 per cent), for whom three out of nine countries have female percentages greater than 100.

There is perhaps slightly greater diversity in the female percentages for *average monthly wages*. Physicians and dentists are the exception where both the range and the CV are lower, with the CV very slightly lower for physiotherapists. With physicians the lowest figure, again for Nigeria, is higher than for hourly wages, as the fact that women physicians have longer normal hours of work (56) compared with men (48) has no effect in reducing women's percentage for monthly wages but does for hourly wages. Similarly, the women's percentage excess over average male monthly wages in Bolivia is reduced to 21 per cent, as the effect of men's average normal hours of work (just over 44) compared with women's (41) is removed. The unweighted average for dentists and X-ray technicians continues to be larger than 100 although slightly lower than for average hourly wages, and that for physiotherapists rises to just over 100.

For both professional and auxiliary nurses the ranges and CV for average monthly wages are slightly larger than for average hourly wages and in five out of eleven countries women have higher average monthly wages.

With physiotherapists and X-ray technicians the range is the same for both hourly and monthly wages, with the CV falling very slightly for physiotherapists in monthly wages and rising a little for X-ray technicians.

There are rather more female percentages in excess of 100 if average monthly as opposed to hourly wages are used, but some of these changes may be due to differences between the countries included.

The variation between countries is much the same for *average hourly earnings*, with the spread of female percentages being a little greater for average hourly earnings for professional and auxiliary nurses. There is a noticeable increase in the CV for professional nurses and the number of countries with female percentages greater than 100 rises to six out of eleven, compared with four out of ten for hourly wages. The only instance of a female percentage exceeding 100 for either measure of earnings is for auxiliary nurses' average hourly earnings.

With *average monthly earnings* the spread for physicians is much larger than for monthly wages, with the CV doubling. In Costa Rica the very high female percentage for average monthly earnings (170 per cent) is due in part to the fact that women physicians work an average of 60 hours a week compared with a male average of only 45 hours. The excess for average hourly earnings was only 29 per cent. For dentists, however, though the range is considerably reduced, the CV falls only a little, indicating that while there has been a marked reduction in the highest female percentage and a small rise in the minimum, the others have widened; in only one country is the female percentage for monthly earnings larger than 100.

The female percentages for average monthly earnings are more varied than for average hourly earnings for physicians, dentists and professional nurses. They are a little less dispersed for auxiliary nurses and considerably less differentiated for X-ray technicians, where the CV is less than half that for hourly earnings. The unweighted average female percentage is, however, less than 100 for both average hourly and monthly earnings and, on the whole, women do less well than men in average monthly earnings. This may well be because men work longer hours and so presumably receive more overtime pay which has a greater effect on monthly than on hourly earnings.

In general, the results for medical occupations are not surprising. While the overall female percentage for the two nursing occupations for wages and the associated occupations of physiotherapists and X-ray technicians are slightly below 100, the overall difference is very small and totally compatible with men and women being on a common salary scale with the difference attributable to seniority differences. The size of the minimum and maximum female percentage is also compatible with a not excessively broad common salary scale.

With physicians, the overall average female percentage is consistent with common salary scales but the low minimum percentages in Nigeria raise some question as to whether male and female physicians there are even on the same salary scale. Even so, in three countries average female wages are higher than average male wages. With dentists, the overall female average percentage of both hourly and monthly wages is greater than 100.

Women dentists, professional nurses and X-ray technicians do less well when hourly earnings are measured and even less well with monthly earnings. For all occupations there are fewer countries with female percentages greater than 100 for monthly earnings.

Inter-country variation

With both physicians and dentists the wide range and CVs indicate that there is considerable variation between the different countries and that the use of a single overall average female percentage of male pay would be misleading. Using slightly different data, for example, the United Kingdom data for 1996 rather than for 1995, similar results are found by using the *standard error of the mean (sem)* as a percentage of the mean or overall average female percentage.[8] The *sem* is a measure of how far the overall average female percentage obtained from a sample is a good estimate of the overall average female percentage of the whole population of all countries. It estimates the reliability of the sample overall average female percentage by taking into account the variation of the different countries' female percentages and the number of countries included, i.e. the size of the sample. Expressing the *sem* as a percentage of the overall average female percentage obtained from the different countries covered by the OEI data gives another measure of how far the female percentage varies from country to country for a given occupation and for different measures of pay. The smaller the *sem* percentage, the more closely the countries' individual female percentages bunch together.

To avoid complications and possibly misleading results from very small samples, most analysis was limited to occupations and pay measures for which there were at least ten countries. Three medical occupations satisfied this criterion: general physicians, professional nurses and auxiliary nurses. General physicians have relatively large *sem* percentages, compared with both professional and auxiliary nurses. The smallest of all is for average hourly wages for professional nurses, with a *sem* percentage of 1.372. With the exception of monthly wages and earnings for auxiliary nurses, the *sem* percentages for average earnings are always larger than the corresponding figures for average wages. Auxiliary nurses have the lowest *sem* percentages for both hourly and monthly earnings of any of the three medical occupations.

For the two nursing occupations there is much less variation between countries, with the exception of average monthly earnings for professional nurses. The situation is similar for auxiliary nurses. There is relatively small variation between countries, the average of the female percentages is close to 100 and is 101.2 per cent for average hourly earnings. Somewhat unusually, average monthly earnings are less dispersed than average hourly earnings.

Average hourly wages for female physiotherapists are higher than for males in three of the six countries examined although the unweighted average of all the percentages is only 98 per cent. For monthly wages, the female percentages in four of the seven countries are higher than 100 and the average is 100.3 per cent. Even so, the female percentages range from three-quarters of male wages to more than a quarter as high again.

Female X-ray technicians have higher average wages than male for both hourly and monthly wages, although in only three of the nine countries do women have higher average wages than men. Fewer countries provide information about average earnings but women tend to do a little worse on earnings than on wages.

It is clear that differences in the occupational pay of men and women vary according to the measure of pay adopted. In some cases it may be reasonable to conclude that differences in average monthly wages of men and women in the same occupation reflect differences in the average seniority or place on an incremental salary scale of men and women. Comparisons of the pay of men and women using average monthly earnings reveal the largest dispersion among countries but cover up significant differences in hours worked. Where women work fewer hours than men involuntarily, and fewer hours explain the gap in earnings, one may infer that women are particularly disadvantaged, and it suggests greater gender-based discrimination than do the other measures.

Public service, banking and insurance

Similar information for certain occupations in public services (e.g. postal services or public administration (PA)) and in insurance and banking is shown in table 2.

The variation for both PA office clerks and bank tellers is usually quite small for both range and CV. The obvious interpretation is that in most, if not all, countries there is a single incremental salary scale for these occupations and differences in men's and women's pay reflect seniority and possibly some location payments. The average monthly wage of female PA office clerks in Ghana is 87 per cent that of males. If a single salary scale applies for Ghanaian male and female office clerks and the scale maximum is more than 15 per cent higher than the minimum, it is possible but not necessarily established that all this difference is due to seniority. The largest difference in favour of women is in Finland where female office clerks earn average hourly and monthly wages 5 per cent higher than those of men. If the pay arrangements for this occupation include all salary increments, it is possible that this difference in favour of women simply reflects higher average seniority of female PA office clerks.

173

Table 2. Women's average wages and earnings as a percentage of men's in selected occupations in the public service, banking and insurance

OEI number	Occupation	Number of countries	Minimum	Maximum	Average	Range	CV	>100%
(1)	(2)	(3)	(4)	(5)	(6)	(7)	(8)	(9)
Average hourly wages								
127	Postman	6	92.6	127.9	103.6	1.382	10.94	2
129	Bank accountant	7	80.7	104.6	90.7	1.296	11.17	2
131	Bank teller	10	78.4	105.9	92.9	1.352	8.72	2
136	Insurance agent	6	58.5	228.8	103.7	3.909	55.78	1
139a	Executive official: central gov't	6	71.1	97.2	82.8	1.367	12.65	0
139c	Executive official: local gov't	4	69.1	92.7	81.9	1.340	12.51	0
142	Office clerk: PA[1]	6	86.8	104.7	96.9	1.205	6.52	4

Countries examined: Antigua and Barbuda, Bahrain, Bolivia, Cyprus, El Salvador, Estonia, Finland, Ghana, Honduras, Romania, Tajikistan, United Kingdom.

OEI number	Occupation	Number of countries	Minimum	Maximum	Average	Range	CV	>100%
Average monthly wages								
126	PO[2] counter clerk	5	74.6	138.6	100.4	1.858	21.34	2
127	Postman	6	92.6	127.9	103.3	1.382	11.13	2
128	PO[2] switchboard operator	5	84.6	122.6	95.2	1.450	14.95	1
129	Bank accountant	9	80.7	107.3	89.1	1.329	11.39	2
131	Bank teller	12	78.4	105.9	92.1	1.352	8.13	2
132	Bank machine operator	5	78.5	116.2	93.2	1.480	14.29	1
133	Computer programmer: insurance	5	65.9	102.9	89.2	1.561	14.04	1
136	Insurance agent	8	58.5	228.8	101.7	3.909	49.56	2
139a	Executive official: central gov't	6	71.1	97.2	82.7	1.367	12.64	0
139c	Executive official: local gov't	5	69.3	92.7	79.9	1.337	12.42	0
142	Office clerk: PA[1]	6	86.8	104.7	96.5	1.205	6.59	2

Countries examined: Antigua and Barbuda, Bahrain, Bolivia, Cyprus, El Salvador, Estonia, Finland, Ghana, Honduras, Macau, Romania, Singapore, Tajikistan, United Kingdom.

OEI number	Occupation	Number of countries	Minimum	Maximum	Average	Range	CV	>100%
Average hourly earnings								
126	PO[2] counter clerk	5	87.5	127.2	101.4	1.454	13.50	2
127	Postman	6	89.0	126.6	101.0	1.423	12.09	3
129	Bank accountant	8	82.9	126.0	102.4	1.520	16.61	3
131	Bank teller	8	83.8	102.9	94.2	1.227	7.08	2
136	Insurance agent	5	55.6	228.8	105.5	4.115	59.66	1
141	Punch machine operator: PA[1]	5	74.7	103.8	89.8	1.389	11.09	1
142	Office clerk: PA[1]	5	86.6	98.9	93.3	1.142	5.85	0

Countries examined: Antigua and Barbuda, Australia, Costa Rica, El Salvador, Estonia, Ghana, Kyrgyzstan, Nigeria, Norway, Romania, Tajikistan, United Kingdom.

Table 2. (cont.)

OEI number	Occupation	Number of countries	Minimum	Maximum	Average	Range	CV	>100%
(1)	(2)	(3)	(4)	(5)	(6)	(7)	(8)	(9)
Average monthly earnings								
126	PO[2] counter clerk	7	87.5	127.2	100.5	1.454	11.63	2
127	Postman	8	88.6	126.6	97.7	1.429	12.01	2
128	PO[2] switchboard operator	4	68.3	100.1	84.3	1.466	13.39	1
129	Bank accountant	10	73.4	123.8	96.3	1.688	17.11	3
131	Bank teller	9	81.6	102.9	93.0	1.261	6.66	1
132	Bank machine operator	4	87.8	115.4	104.0	1.314	10.90	2
133	Computer programmer: insurance	5	75.5	102.9	90.1	1.363	10.88	1
135	Punch machine operator: insurance	7	81.0	122.4	96.6	1.511	15.79	2
136	Insurance agent	5	54.5	228.8	98.8	4.201	56.19	2
139a	Executive official: central gov't	5	71.9	97.8	89.3	1.360	10.55	0
139c	Executive official: local gov't	5	69.4	98.0	84.1	1.412	13.55	0
141	Punch machine operator: PA[1]	6	71.5	108.6	90.3	1.518	13.52	2
142	Office clerk: PA[1]	7	86.9	107.5	96.1	1.237	6.91	2

Countries examined: Antigua and Barbuda, Australia, Costa Rica, El Salvador, Estonia, Ghana, Kyrgyzstan, Macau, Norway, Romania, Sweden, Tajikistan, United Kingdom, United States.

[1] Public administration. [2] Post office.

While the overall female percentages for both hourly and monthly wages are less than 100 for bank tellers and in only two countries is the female percentage larger than 100, the range of the individual female percentages is quite consistent with common salary scales that at the extreme have a spread of 28 per cent between scale minimum and maximum. Both the range and CV are small for bank tellers on all measurements of pay. Though different banks may have a common salary scale for tellers in some countries, this is not the case everywhere. Interestingly, the overall female percentage for average earnings for bank tellers is a little higher than for average wages, and the CVs are lower. This is also the case with the *sem* percentage for average monthly earnings which is lower than that for both average hourly and monthly wages and although only nine countries provide details of average monthly earnings for tellers, the figure has been used for comparative purposes and ought to be reasonably acceptable. Bank teller is not an obviously "female" occupation, yet women do better on average earnings than on average wages. The variation of the female percentages for both average hourly and monthly earnings for bank accountants is somewhat higher than for tellers; this could be because a different salary scale applies in each bank in each country for this occupation, or because different categories of accountants with varying levels of qualifications and/or experience are subsumed under a single occupational heading. The *sem* percentage for bank accountants' average monthly earnings is more than twice as large as that for tellers.

The variation for postmen[9] and central government executive officials tends to be a little higher, but again could be within the range of the occupation's salary scale, as could the differences for post office counter clerks and telephone switchboard operators. Overall, postwomen have higher average hourly and monthly wages and higher hourly earnings than postmen, and female post office counter clerks have higher overall pay than men on all three measures of pay available, but in only two countries.

Somewhat surprisingly, perhaps, in no country do women executive officials in either central or local government have higher average pay than men. Men and women working for central government should be on the same salary scale and, in a number of countries, those working for local government, too.

The largest differences concern insurance agents, for which two obvious explanations are possible. First, that this occupation is paid substantial proportions of total remuneration on a commission or piecework basis. Second, that different insurance companies have their own payment scales and systems so there is no common salary scale. For both hourly and monthly wages, female insurance agents have a higher average overall percentage than males, even though in only one country for hourly wages and in two for monthly wages do women actually earn higher average wages than men. The overall average is pulled up by the very high figure for female insurance agents in Tajikistan, where they are paid 229 per cent of men's wages.

For most of these occupations, especially in the public service, the differences in average male and female pay could result from differences in seniority within a common salary scale. If this is the explanation, the question then arises of why in so many cases women have lower average pay than men, as one would expect to find rather similar numbers of female percentages above and below 100. Short of examining all individuals in each country, a possible answer is that women often have lower average seniority in a given occupation/grade because they have, on average, shorter periods of continuous employment at any particular date as a result of career breaks for child-bearing or child-rearing. But it may not be a result of a difference in seniority. In the banking and insurance occupations, it is also possible that different employers apply different salary scales and that the male/female pay differential reflects structural differences in the composition of employment. However, it is also possible that, despite a common salary scale in public service employment, pay includes certain other elements which favour men over women.

SUGGESTIONS OF RELATIVE PAY GAPS ACROSS AND WITHIN COUNTRIES

International comparisons

Studies of the overall female wage gap have established that differences between countries are often a function of the general wage structure. For example, if occupational differentials in the United States had been the same as in other countries, the overall female wage gap there would have been reduced to the same size as existed in Sweden and Australia, countries with small wage gaps (Blau and Kahn, 1996). In fact, the constancy of the male/female wage gap in the United States from the end of the Second World War up to 1975 was largely due to the failure of women to increase their skills relative to men's. The rise in women's labour force participation led to more women with comparatively low levels of education and work experience entering the labour market, thus diluting the women's average skill levels compared with men's (O'Neill, 1985; Smith and Ward, 1989; Goldin, 1989; O'Neill and Polachek, 1993). From 1976 the gap declined by an average of 1 per cent a year. About a third of the convergence is explained by measurable work-related characteristics (education and work experience) and the remainder by a relative increase in women's returns to experience, by declining wages in blue-collar work and by other factors.

Complications arising from the overall wage structure and wage inequalities are avoided if a narrowly-defined occupation is examined, as the question of whether it involves high or low skills should not affect the relative pay of men and women. In a number of countries, some female-dominated occupations show very similar female percentages. Thus, both professional and auxiliary nurses have small *sem* percentages compared with the overall female percentages; other measures of dispersion such as range and CV are also small for the female percentages in the various countries covered. However, the main reason for this is probably a common salary scale for men and women in each country.

There are some marked differences in the distribution of female percentages of pay in different countries. In El Salvador the female percentages for both average hourly and monthly earnings range from 28 per cent for salespersons (wholesale grocery trade) to 208 per cent for journalists, with a CV of 38.63 for average hourly earnings in 20 occupations. Nigeria has a smaller range for both average hourly and monthly earnings percentages but a larger CV. Again in Nigeria, four occupations have female percentages of less than 50 per cent while two are in excess of 150 per cent for average monthly earnings, and sewing machine operators have a female percentage for average hourly earnings of 239 per cent. The CVs for 24 occupations in Nigeria are large for all four measures of pay, ranging from 43.33 for average monthly wages to 49.14 for average hourly wages. At the other end of the spectrum, Finland has a CV for 53 occupations of 8.42 for average hourly wages and of 8.35 for average monthly wages, with a range of only 1.492. Norway with only 20 occupations has a CV of 3.48 for average monthly earnings and a range of only 1.178; 17 of those 20 occupations have a female percentage of between 90 and 100 per cent. Australia with 74 occupations has low CVs for average hourly and weekly earnings but only a few occupations with a female percentage greater than 100.

Broadly, the industrialized market economies have a narrower spread of female percentages and relatively smaller CVs, although the overall average female percentage is usually less than 100. Both Australia and the United States have some low female percentages and neither the United Kingdom nor the United States has an occupation with a female percentage equal to 100. Former centrally planned economies tend to have larger CVs and ranges, with some countries (e.g. Estonia and Romania) having a number of occupations where the female percentage is quite low, below 80 per cent. The exception is the Republic of Moldova which has an overall female percentage greater than 100 for three of the pay measures, but quite large CVs and ranges.

Of the two African countries, Ghana has relatively low CVs and ranges that are about the same as those of Australia and the United States, while Nigeria has large CVs and ranges and seven or eight out of 24 occupations with female percentages less than 60 per cent and one or two greater than 150 per cent.

Three Latin American countries have quite large CVs and ranges, with some very low female percentages. The spread for El Salvador is exceptionally wide, whereas Honduras has a variation somewhere between those of industrialized market economies and former centrally planned economies.

The Asian countries vary. Tajikistan has CVs and ranges as wide as the three Latin American countries and somewhat larger than the former centrally planned economies in Europe. Cyprus and Singapore have CVs which are similar to those of Estonia and Romania, but smaller ranges. China has a wide range and a largish CV.

The higher female percentage for sewing machine operators may result from piecework payment systems with women being more skilled in this occupation. Those for both teachers and office clerks are almost certainly the result of longer seniority of women in these occupations.

Time trends

For a few countries details are available on a consistent basis and over a number of years, so that it is possible to detect changes over time in female pay as a percentage of male pay (see table 3).

Details of average hourly and weekly earnings for occupations in Australia were given for 1990 and 1994. The unweighted average of the female percentages increased only a little, from 85 to 88 per cent for average weekly earnings, and from 88 to 90 per cent for average hourly earnings. There was a tendency for average female earnings to move slightly closer to those of men; in some of the occupations showing the lowest female percentages in 1990 these had moved up by 1994. There was also an increase in the number of occupations where women's average earnings were higher than men's.

Some occupations showed large changes in the female/male wage gap. Female wooden furniture finishers experienced a fall in the female pay ratio for average weekly earnings from 164 per cent in 1990 to 98 per cent in 1994, which was almost entirely due to a reduction in the large amount of overtime worked in 1990. The female ratio for average hourly wages fell by 27 percentage points, from 121 to 94 per cent. The female pay ratio percentage for average weekly earnings of thread and yarn spinners fell from 86 per cent in 1990 to 54 per cent in 1994, mainly because in 1994 men worked an average of 54 hours compared with only 40 hours for women. The ratio for average hourly earnings fell only 16 percentage points from 89 to 73 per cent. The hourly wage percentage also fell.

The female ratio for average hourly wages for automobile mechanics rose from 62 per cent in 1990 to 108 per cent in 1994 and for plumbers from 66 to 96 per cent while the female ratio for average weekly earnings for plumbers rose from 61 to 102 per cent. The ratio for air

Table 3. Changes in the female wage ratio over time[1]

Change in wage gap	Australia 1990-94 AWE[2]	Australia 1990-94 AHE[3]	Cyprus 1985-94 AME[4]	Cyprus 1985-94 AHW[5]	Cyprus 1985-94 AMW[6]	Finland 1985-94 AHW[5]	Hong Kong, China 1990-94 AHE[3]	Norway 1990-94 AME[4]	Singapore 1990-94 AMW[6]	UK 1990-95 AWE[2]	UK 1990-95 AHE[3]	USA 1986-95 MedWE[7]
− 69.9 -	1	0	0	0	0	0	0	0	0	0	0	0
− 60.0 -												
− 59.9 -												
− 50.0 -	0	0	0	0	0	0	0	0	0	0	0	0
− 49.9 -												
− 40.0 -	0	0	0	0	0	0	0	0	0	0	0	0
− 39.9 -												
− 30.0 -	1	0	1	2	2	0	0	0	0	0	0	0
− 29.9 -												
− 20.0 -	0	1	4	2	2	0	0	0	0	0	0	0
− 19.9 -												
− 10.0 -	5	3	7	5	5	4	1	0	5	0	0	1
− 9.9 -												
0.0	13	17	8	13	12	26	3	4	16	3	3	5
0.1 - 10.0	35	38	11	13	12	11	7	11	16	11	11	16
10.1 - 20.0	8	4	10	6	8	2	0	1	9	1	1	1
20.1 - 30.0	1	1	1	1	1	0	0	0	2	0	0	2
30.1 - 40.0	1	2	0	0	0	0	0	0	1	0	0	0
40.1 - 50.0	2	1	1	1	1	0	0	0	0	0	0	0
50.1 - 60.0	0	0	0	0	0	0	0	0	2	0	0	0
Total no. of occupations	67	67	43	43	43	43	11	16	51	15	15	25

[1] Change is female pay ratio in last year minus female pay ratio in first year, e.g. in Australia in 1990 female wooden furniture finishers earned $620 for 54 hours and men earned $377.40 for 39.9 hours, a female ratio of 164 per cent. In 1994 females earned $455.1 and men $466.7, a female ratio of 98 per cent. The difference is – 66 per cent; [2] AWE = average weekly earnings; [3] AHE = average hourly earnings. [4] AME = average monthly earnings. [5] AHW = average hourly wages. [6] AMW = average monthly wages. [7] MedWE = median weekly earnings.

traffic controllers increased from 83 to 111 per cent for average weekly earnings and from 81 to 114 per cent for average hourly earnings. Australia is somewhat unusual in that women have higher average earnings than men in a number of occupations.

In *Cyprus*, over the period 1985-94 there was a decrease in the female percentage in about half of the 43 occupations examined, so that average female pay as a proportion of male pay fell; there was an increase in about half the occupations examined. The female ratio for both hourly and monthly wages of telephone operators fell from 131 per cent in 1985 to 94 per cent in 1994 and for average monthly earnings from 115 to 94 per cent. The female percentage for hourly and monthly wages of office clerks in electric light and power fell from 86 per cent in 1985 to 54 per cent in 1994 and for average monthly earnings. Such a low female wage percentage as obtained in 1994 is seldom consistent with men and women being in the same occupational grade and on the same uniform salary scale. So either two grades are being combined and there are more men in the higher grade, or there are discretionary elements in wages which are more favourable to men. The female percentage for both hourly and monthly wages of auxiliary nurses rose from 72 per cent in 1985 to 114 per cent in 1994, a significant improvement for women on a common salary scale with men.

In *Finland*, 30 of the 43 occupations examined showed a decrease in the female percentage for average hourly wages between 1985 and 1994. But the changes were relatively small — only four of the decreases were larger than ten percentage points; only two of the 13 increases were larger than ten percentage points. The female percentage for bank tellers fell from 105 per cent in 1985 to 92 per cent in 1994, which is compatible with shifts in the seniority composition on a common salary scale or with some shifts in employment between banks if there are differences in salary scales between banks. The female ratio for insurance agents declined from 94 to 81 per cent, which is also compatible with a longish salary scale.

In *Singapore*, rather more than half of the 51 occupations showed an increase in the female percentage. The largest gains were for secondary-level teachers in mathematics where the female ratio for average monthly wages rose from 92 per cent in 1990 to 151 per cent in 1994. This seems a rather large change but, although no details of average hours worked are given, it seems unlikely that changes in hours could explain much of the increase. The wage gap was also reversed for waiters when the female percentage rose from 87 per cent in 1990 to 120 per cent in 1994. It is probable that some of this is due to a shift in the distribution of men and women working for employers applying different wage rates. Large changes in female percentages for private sector occupations can be explained more easily in terms of shifts in the distribution of men and women between higher- and lower-paying establishments.

There were only small changes in *Hong Kong, China,* even though seven of the eleven occupations showed an increase. The largest was only from 87 per cent in 1990 to 91 per cent in 1994 in the average earnings of office clerks in printing, publishing and allied industries. The largest decrease was from 81 to 70 per cent for electronic equipment assemblers.

In *Norway,* 12 of the 16 occupations examined showed an increase in the female percentage, but the changes were all relatively small. The largest improvement was for average monthly earnings of secondary-level technical teachers where the ratio rose from 87 per cent in 1990 to 97 per cent in 1994. None of the other occupations showed changes of more than three percentage points.

In the *United Kingdom,* three of the 15 occupations showed a widening of the female/male wage gap. The largest was a fall in average hourly earnings of executive officials in local authorities from 77 per cent in 1990 to 69 per cent in 1995; this could be due as much to shifts in occupational/grade employment as to shifts in the seniority composition of men and women. There is room for some discretion in the pay levels and grading and salary scales applied by local authorities in the United Kingdom, and men may be on higher scales than women for reasons of geographical location, size of local authority, or because grades and salary scales favour men. The largest improvement was for the average hourly earnings of general physicians, where the female ratio rose from 71 per cent in 1990 to 88 per cent in 1995, with a smaller improvement of 12 percentage points for average monthly earnings.

In the *United States,* 19 of the 25 broad non-industry-differentiating occupations showed an increase in the female ratio and six showed decreases. The largest decrease in median weekly earnings was for insurance agents where the ratio fell from 70 per cent in 1986 to 58 per cent in 1995; it could well have been due to differences in earnings from commission as well as to shifts in employment between employers applying different levels of pay. For both office clerks and salespersons, the female ratio rose by 21 percentage points but this could have arisen from changes in sex distribution among office clerks in different sectors or industries.

Overall, on the basis of the few countries for which usable data are available, there was some tendency for average female pay to improve relative to male pay in that the female percentages often increased, but this still left women earning lower average pay than men in the same occupation. Even with this general trend, there were some occupations in each of the eight countries examined where the female percentage fell and women's average pay came to represent a lower proportion of their male counterparts' average pay.

CONCLUSIONS

There can be no definitive, generally applicable conclusions even as to the extent of differences in pay between men and women, let alone whether those differences are a result of discrimination. But what has been shown is that even when pay by occupation is precisely defined, to compare comparable jobs, there tend to remain some significant differentials.

The use of occupational pay rather than averages for broad groups of occupations allows a more detailed examination of differences in male and female pay for similar work, as it avoids complications arising from occupational distributions and the associated issues of segregation, overcrowding and discrimination in hiring or promotion. Differences in the average pay of men and women in the same occupation can arise from a number of causes. Some may result from the use of different measures of pay. Women typically work fewer hours than men and are less likely to receive shift premia as they usually do less shift-work than men. Average monthly or weekly earnings may therefore differ because men work more or different hours than women; average hourly earnings will also be affected, though to a lesser extent, as premia are then spread over both normal and overtime hours. Average hourly wages for hours actually worked is the measure least likely to be affected by the number of hours worked or by shift premia. However, it may still indicate some gender bias if pay includes allowances related to family circumstances, as these may be paid only to men if both spouses are employed. If average hourly wages include components based on payment by results, there may be differences between men's and women's average wages if they have different average productivities.

Even if the same hourly wage is paid to men and women in the same occupation in the same establishment, differences may emerge in their average hourly wages because of variations in the wage rates applied by different establishments and if the distribution of men and women varies from one establishment to another. The emergence of a female wage gap on a narrowly-defined occupational basis may therefore reflect features other than gender-based wage differentiation in an establishment.

Women earn lower average wages and average earnings than men in most occupations in most countries for which the OEI provides details. In some cases it is reasonable to infer that women's lower average pay is because they have, on average, lower seniority in the occupation/grade than men. This is most obviously the case where there is a single salary scale applicable to both men and women with increments received solely on the basis of seniority, as is likely in the public service in many countries. In a number of cases the lower average female wage seems to be within the range covered by the salary scale so that seniority could be the explanation for the differences.

Comparison of *sem* percentages provides two indicators of the female wage gap. First, where there are enough examples to provide a satisfactory test, the data on occupations show that generally there is more similarity in female percentages for wages than for earnings, with exceptions for certain occupations. Second, the evidence is consistent with the conclusion that female percentages are more likely to be closely bunched together if men and women are paid on a common salary scale, as in public service employment. Though some of the occupations displaying greater similarity in female percentages are "female-dominated", e.g. nursing, the single salary scale effect is probably a more important explanation.

Even in public sector occupations with common salary scales there are still many examples of a female wage gap in the same narrowly-defined occupation. Unless a common salary scale includes supplementary elements which favour men, the only explanation for the female/male wage gap is the recent recruitment of far more women than men which has lowered their average seniority compared with men in those occupations. If not, then there should be more instances of female percentages greater than 100. Such an explanation seems less likely in other cases, especially in occupations where a common salary scale does not apparently apply. There may be gender-based reasons why women achieve lower seniority in the grade but these raise issues that are distinct from gender-based differentiation in pay.

In other cases it is not clear from the pay data why women have lower average wages than men. It could be that there is straightforward gender discrimination in the same establishment, but there is little evidence from other sources to suggest that this is currently a significant factor except where some form of payment by results is in operation. Equal pay legislation usually ensures that men and women in the same grade or occupation receive the same wages. If workers are paid according to piecework or output-based payment systems, differences in average wages may reflect differences in average productivity.

Another possible explanation is the different proportions of men and women employed in higher- and lower-paying establishments. Establishments often pay different wage levels to members of the same occupational classification. This may reflect variations in average skill levels within the same nominal occupation or may illustrate some version of efficiency wage theory. There may also be geographical differences in nominal wages depending on the proportions of men and women employed in different locations. This can lead to differences in average wages even if men and women in the same establishment are paid exactly the same wage; it is more likely to occur in the private than in the public sector.

Some differences in average wages and earnings are so large as to suggest either some form of gender discrimination in pay levels, or that occupational classification covers such a wide range of skills and abilities that dissimilar or unequal jobs and skill requirements are classified as being in the same occupation.

There are marked inter-country differences in female percentages. In some countries, the tendency is for women to be paid less than men almost irrespective of occupation, e.g. Nigeria, Ghana, Cyprus, Estonia, Finland, the United Kingdom and United States, where relatively few, or no, occupations have female percentages greater than 100.

While the number of countries and examples do not permit a more rigorous testing, the industrialized market economies apparently have a narrower spread of female percentages. Former centrally planned economies tend to show a greater variation in female percentages. Of the two African countries with a number of occupations with appropriate data, Ghana is similar to some industrialized market economies while Nigeria shows much greater variation in female percentages. In Latin America some of the percentages are quite low. Cyprus and Singapore have quite varied female percentages; Tajikistan and China are probably more varied.

There is some evidence to suggest an increase in female percentages and a reduction in women's comparative disadvantage, but in most countries there are still large and significant differences in men's and women's average pay in certain occupations.

The size of occupational differentials and the female percentage ratios obviously vary from country to country. The United States has wider occupational differentials than most industrialized market economies (especially for men), and female differentials for the same occupations are lower than those of men in both the United States and Australia. However, both these countries group occupations together making no distinction for sector of industry, so that the female percentages and the occupational differentials are for broad occupational coverage and, for the United States at least, the wider differentials may reflect internal differences in pay rather than differentials between narrowly-defined occupations.

Average hourly wages provide the best measure of relative female pay but these data are available in a few countries only, and only in Cyprus and Finland over any reasonable period. In Finland a majority of occupations (30 out of 43) had a fall in the female percentage over the period 1985-94, as did a slight majority in Cyprus (22 out of 43). In many cases, taking the occupations as a whole, there are not, in fact, major differences in the female percentages according to different measures of pay, but the percentages for an individual occupation can vary according to the measure used.

The recent continuation or enlargement of female wage gaps in public service employment in some countries may arise from the spread of personal assessment as the basis for granting annual wage increases, since women tend to do less well under this sort of payment system. The continuation of female wage gaps in occupations which are seen as entry grades into strong public service internal labour markets (e.g. office clerks) should give cause for some concern, if the lower average female seniority within the grade is caused by women's greater propensity to leave. If, however, it is caused by women's greater propensity to be promoted, this might be indicative of attempts to redress a past imbalance between men's and women's promotion opportunities.

What this chapter has shown is that there still are significant pay differences between men and women workers even when considering very comparable categories. Women still tend to receive lower average pay than men in the same occupation.

Notes

[1] Some relevant studies are Blau and Beller (1988); Cain (1986); England (1992); Fields and Wolff (1991); Groshen (1991); Macpherson and Hirsch (1995); Moulton (1986); O'Neill (1985); Sorenson (1989), (1990).

[2] See ILO: *Statistics on occupational wages and hours of work and food prices: October Inquiry results, 1994 and 1995*. Special supplement to the *Bulletin of Labour Statistics*, Geneva, 1996. This publication lists 159 occupations, but occupation 139 (government executive official) provides data for (a) central government, (b) regional or provincial government, and (c) local government, making a total of 161 occupations. Some of the occupations are differentiated by sector or sub-sector of industry.

[3] For a good introduction to some problems of measurement of women's wage disadvantage see Gonzalez and Watts (1995). A recent analysis of crowding of women in certain occupations and the effects of this on their pay is Grimshaw and Rubery (1998). Anker (1997) provides a recent survey of occupational segregation.

[4] This can be inferred from the analyses by Malkiel and Malkiel (1973), who used publications as a measure of productivity for a study on one (unnamed) profession.

[5] The occupational classification helps to separate occupations in different sectors of industry. While there may well be some differences in the actual definitions of occupation applied in various countries, each individual country uses the same occupational definitions for men and women. For that reason international comparisons are difficult. Because the OEI provides no details of the number of men and women employed in each occupation, it is not possible to recalculate weighted average pay for different groupings; nor is there any information about discrimination at the point of entry.

[6] There are various studies of declining managerial performance in public service employment in developing countries where public service pay has suffered severe reduction in real terms and where even the drastically reduced real pay has not been paid for several months. A good recent collection of studies is in Colclough (1997).

[7] The coefficient of variation is the standard deviation as a percentage of the unweighted mean of the observations. So CV = 100(SD)/mean. It is therefore a measure of the variation in the average female percentage of the different countries included.

[8] The standard error of the mean is calculated as a one-sample t-test which is then expressed as a percentage of the unweighted mean of the different countries' female percentages.

[9] The occupation is still listed as "postman" although women are employed in some countries.

References

Aldrich, Mark; Buchele, Robert. 1986. *The economics of comparable worth.* Cambridge, MA, Ballinger Pub. Co.

Anker, Richard. 1997. "Theories of occupational segregation by sex", in *International Labour Review* (Geneva), Vol. 136, No. 3, pp. 315-339.

Bergmann, B. 1974. "Occupational segregation, wages and profits when employers discriminate by race or sex", in *Eastern Economic Journal* (Smithfield, RI), Vol. 1, pp. 103-110.

Blau, Francine D. 1977. *Equal pay in the office.* Lexington, MA, Heath.

—.; Beller, Andrea H. 1988. "Trends in earnings differentials by gender: 1971-1981", in *Industrial and Labor Relations Review* (Ithaca, NY), Vol. 41, No. 4, pp. 513-529.

—.; Kahn, Lawrence M. 1996. "Wage structure and gender earning differentials: An international comparison", in *Economica* (Oxford), Vol. 63, No. 250 (supplement), pp. S29-S62.

Borooah, V. K.; Lee, K. C. 1988. "The effects of changes in Britain's industrial structure on female relative pay and employment", in *Economic Journal* (Oxford), 98, pp. 818-832.

Cain, Glen G. 1986. "The economic analysis of labor market discrimination: A survey", in Orley Ashenfelter and Richard Layard (eds.): *Handbook of labor economics.* Vol. 1, Amsterdam, North Holland.

Colclough, Christopher (ed.). 1997. *Public-sector pay and adjustment: Lessons from five countries.* London, Routledge.

Ehrenberg, Ronald G.; Smith, Robert S. 1987. "Comparable worth in the public sector", in David Wise (ed.): *Public sector payrolls.* Chicago, IL, University of Chicago Press.

England, Paula. 1992. *Comparable worth: Theories and evidence.* New York, Aldine de Gruyter.

Fields, Judith; Wolff, Edward N. 1991. "The decline of sex segregation and the wage gap, 1970-80", in *Journal of Human Resources* (Madison, WI), Vol. 26, No. 4, pp. 608-622.

Goldin, Claudia. 1989. "Life-cycle labour force participation of married women: Historical evidence and implications", in *Journal of Labor Economics* (Chicago, IL), Vol. 7, No. 1, pp. 20-47.

Gonzalez, Pablo; Watts, Martin J. 1995. *Measuring gender wage differentials and job segregation.* IDP Women Working Paper No. 24. Geneva, ILO.

Grimshaw, Damian; Rubery, Jill. 1998. *The concentration of women's employment and relative occupational pay: A statistical framework for comparative analysis.* Labour Market and Social Policy Occasional Papers No. 26, OECD/GD(97)186. Paris, OECD.

Groshen, Erica L. 1991. "The structure of the female/male wage differential: Is it who you are, what you do, or where you work?", in *Journal of Human Resources* (Madison, WI), Vol. 26, Summer, pp. 457-472.

Gunderson, Morley. 1989. "Male-female wage differentials and policy response", in *Journal of Economic Literature* (Nashville, TN), Vol. 27 (March), pp. 46-72.

—. 1975. "Male-female wage differentials and the impact of equal pay legislation", in *Review of Economics and Statistics* (Cambridge, MA), Vol. 57, No. 4, pp. 462-469.

Hill, M. Anne; O'Neill, June E. 1992. "Intercohort change in women's labor market status", in R. G. Ehrenberg (ed.): *Research in labor economics*, Vol. 13. Greenwich, CT, Jai Pr.

ILO. 1997. "Part-time work: Solution or trap?", in *International Labour Review* (Geneva), Vol. 136, No. 4, pp. 559-581.

—. 1996. *Statistics on occupational wages and hours of work and on food prices: October Inquiry results, 1994 and 1995.* Special supplement to the *Bulletin of Labour Statistics.* Geneva.

Killingsworth, Mark R. 1990. *The economics of comparable worth.* Kalamazoo, MI, W. E. Upjohn Institute for Employment Research.

Lofstrom, Asa; Gustafsson, Siv. 1991. "Policy changes and women's wages in Sweden", in *International Review of Comparative Public Policy* (Greenwich, CT), Vol. 3, pp. 313-330.

Macpherson, David A.; Hirsch, Barry T. 1995. "Wages and gender composition: Why do women's jobs pay less?", in *Journal of Labor Economics* (Chicago, IL), Vol. 13, No. 3, pp. 426-471.

Malkiel, Burton G.; Malkiel, Judith A. 1973. "Male-female pay differentials in professional employment", in *American Economic Review* (Nashville, TN), Vol. 63, No. 4, pp. 693-705.

Mincer, Jacob; Ofek, Haim. 1982. "Interrupted work careers: Depreciation and restoration of human capital", in *Journal of Human Resources* (Madison, WI), Vol. 17, No. 1, pp. 3-24.

—.; Polachek, Solomon. 1974. "Family investments in human capital: Earnings of women", in *Journal of Political Economy* (Chicago, IL), Vol. 82, No. 2, Part II, pp. S76-S108.

Moulton, Brent R. 1986. "Human capital accumulation and trends in male-female wage gap in the United States, 1956-83", in *Eastern Economic Journal* (Smithfield, RI), Vol. 12, No. 3, pp. 265-271.

O'Neill, June. 1985. "The trend in the male-female wage gap in the United States", in *Journal of Labor Economics* (Chicago, IL), Vol. 3, No. 1, Part 2, pp. S91-S116.

—.; Polachek, Solomon. 1993. "Why the gender gap in wages narrowed in the 1980s", in *Journal of Labor Economics* (Chicago, IL), Vol. 11, No. 1, Part 1, pp. 205-228.

Smith, James P.; Ward, Michael P. 1989. "Women in the labor market and in the family", in *Journal of Economic Perspectives* (Nashville, TN), Vol. 3, No. 1, pp. 9-23.

Sorensen, Elaine. 1990. "The crowding hypothesis and comparable worth issue", in *Journal of Human Resources* (Madison, WI), Vol. 25, No. 1, pp. 55-89.

—. 1989. "Measuring the pay disparity between typically female occupations and other jobs: A bivariate selectivity approach", in *Industrial and Labor Relations Review* (Ithaca, NY), Vol. 42, No. 4, pp. 624-639.

Treiman, Donald; Hartmann, Heidi (eds.). 1981. *Women, work and wages: Equal pay for jobs of equal value.* Washington, DC, National Academy Press.

OCCUPATIONAL SEGREGATION BY SEX IN NORDIC COUNTRIES: AN EMPIRICAL INVESTIGATION

10

Helinä MELKAS* and Richard ANKER**

The Nordic countries are commonly associated with strong political commitment to gender equality. But the reality is more complex. An examination of data for some 200 occupations over the period 1970-90 shows that one-third of all workers in Finland, Norway and Sweden would have to change occupation to eliminate occupational segregation by sex, which is substantially higher than that found in many other OECD countries. Often working in female-dominated occupations or atypical employment arrangements, women are under-represented in senior positions and typically earn less than men. The underlying segregation impairs not only gender equality but also overall economic efficiency.

The Nordic countries are widely known for their commitment to gender equity and their policies for women's integration into nearly all spheres of public life. It is therefore hardly surprising that the United Nations Development Programme (UNDP) has ranked them at the very top in its recent measure of women's status, the gender-related development index (GDI) (UNDP, 1995). Women in those countries have indeed entered the labour market in strength in recent decades, so that there are now roughly equal numbers of men and women workers in the labour force. Furthermore, the gap between male and female earnings in the Nordic countries is smaller than in other countries, and laws have been adopted on equal pay for equal work.

Originally published in *International Labour Review*, Vol. 136 (1997), No. 3.

* At the time of writing, researcher at the ILO; presently Ministry of Labour, Finland.
** ILO, Geneva. This article is drawn from a larger study of occupational segregation and labour market differentials in the Nordic countries of Finland, Norway and Sweden by the same authors.

However, there remains considerable gender inequality in the Nordic labour markets. Women are under-represented at higher levels, especially in the private sector. In the three Nordic countries examined here (Finland, Norway and Sweden), women work part-time much more than do men, partly because women still perform about two-thirds of all unpaid work at home. Although relatively high, women's earnings are significantly lower than men's; and in any given type of occupation, women usually have lower positions than men. Women are also more likely than are men to work in the public sector, where wages tend to be lower than in the private sector.

Finland, Norway and Sweden provide a unique opportunity to study occupational segregation by sex and labour market inequality between men and women in the Nordic countries.[1] First, they have detailed census data over time for over 200 occupations. This is important because the observed level of occupational segregation by sex is known to be sensitive to the level of disaggregation in the occupational data on which it is based (Anker, forthcoming). Second, the occupational classifications and coding used in these three countries are sufficiently similar to permit the construction of a reasonably comparative classification for all three countries. Indeed, they have an ongoing programme of meetings and consultations to harmonize their national labour statistics. Third, the Nordic region is in many ways exceptionally progressive as far as gender equity policy is concerned. Fourth, these three Nordic countries are sufficiently different to allow meaningful comparisons between them.

This chapter focuses on the extent of divergence between the general perception of equality and the reality of inequality in the Nordic labour market in terms of gender-based occupational segregation and equity. It describes women's present status in the Nordic labour markets as well as changes in labour market inequalities and occupational segregation by sex over the period 1970-90. The article addresses three overriding concerns. The first is how these three countries differ from other industrialized countries. The second is how these three Nordic countries differ from each other. The third is what could be the reasons for any differing patterns between Nordic and other countries as well as between these three Nordic countries.

The chapter is divided into three parts. The first part describes the phenomenon of labour market differences by sex, including a brief discussion of labour market characteristics in the three countries. The second part presents a statistical analysis of occupational segregation in these countries. Nordic labour market patterns in 1990 and changes since 1970 are described using statistics on female-dominated and male-dominated occupations and indices of inequality. The feminization of similar occupations where there is a clear difference in status is then considered. The third part summarizes findings and provides concluding comments.

OCCUPATIONAL SEGREGATION AND LABOUR MARKET DIFFERENTIALS BY SEX

Significance of occupational segregation

Gender-based occupational segregation is one of the most important factors contributing to inequality between men and women in labour markets around the world. It concerns both the tendency for men and women to be employed in different occupations (horizontal segregation), and the tendency for women and men to be employed in different positions within the same occupation or occupational group (vertical segregation). In a situation where there is an extremely detailed occupational classification, these two aspects of occupational segregation become equivalent.

Occupational segregation by sex negatively affects the efficiency of the labour market. Segregation causes labour market inflexibility because it restrains mobility between male and female occupations. For instance, when an enterprise needs a large group of new workers for an industry that is clearly male- or female-dominated, it may not find a sufficient number of qualified candidates for the posts.

Occupational segregation based on a worker's sex also has a negative impact on women, their career opportunities and pay, the quality of their working life and the valuation of their work (Anttalainen, 1986; Gunderson, 1994). The gender gap in pay is a consequence of both horizontal and vertical segregation. And, even where women enter traditionally male-dominated occupations — as has recently happened to a certain extent in many countries (Anker, forthcoming) — they are more likely than men to be found in lower-status and lower-paid positions (see, for example, Barbezat, 1993; Kandolin, 1993; Nordic Council of Ministers, 1994). The polarization of the labour market by gender also leads to qualitative differences between women's and men's work. Research has indeed shown that typical women's work generally involves less decision-making and independent planning than does typical men's work; it is also more restricted in space and time, and more monotonous (Kauppinen, Haavio-Mannila and Kandolin, 1989). This polarization affects educational decisions early in life (e.g. choice of a field of study) as well as later decisions about which parent will disrupt his/her career to look after young children, thereby reinforcing objective reasons for gender inequality in the labour market and perpetuating inequality across generations. All of this leads to unequal opportunities, undermining one of the cornerstones of overall equality in society.

However, sex-based occupational segregation also has a positive side for women as it protects some of women's employment from male competition (Kandolin, 1993), and maintains demand for female labour (Lehto, 1991). For example, it has been suggested that the recent expansion of the service sector of the economy has helped women (Rubery and Smith, 1996).

The Nordic labour markets

The "Nordic model"

One cannot describe the labour markets of the Nordic countries without first describing the structure of the Welfare State in these societies, in particular in comparison with other industrialized countries. The history and comprehensiveness of the Welfare State tell much about the underlying attitudes which govern — enable or restrict — women's activities in different spheres of life, including in the world of work.

It has been suggested that the Welfare State (in the widest sense of the concept) has become the established avenue of modernization, but different countries have committed themselves to its principles to differing extents (Julkunen, 1992). This can be clearly seen when comparing the Nordic countries with other western industrialized countries. According to Julkunen (1992), the western European and North American Welfare States can be divided into four groups: countries with a "conservative" social structure (Germany, France, Belgium, Holland, Luxembourg, northern Italy, Austria, Switzerland); the "Mediterranean belt" (Greece, Spain, Portugal, Southern Italy, Ireland); modern Nordic welfare-state countries (Denmark, Iceland, Finland, Norway, Sweden); and countries with a "liberal" social structure (United Kingdom, United States, Canada).

A similar division has been proposed by Lewis (1992), based on societal perceptions of the male breadwinner role and the extent to which women are viewed as dependents. She classifies the Nordic countries as "weak male breadwinner States". However, Lewis' distinction is not necessarily sufficient, since taxation systems and social benefit policies are also very relevant (Rubery and Smith, 1996). Generally speaking, the western and southern European Welfare States are based on men being breadwinners and on women being homemakers. The Nordic Welfare State, by contrast, is based on the normalization of women's participation in gainful employment and a weak male breadwinner role, with women's integration into the labour market and political decision-making being encouraged. Extensive social services have developed to support this model, and this has resulted in the monetization of previously unpaid household work (Nätti, 1994; Julkunen, 1992). In western and southern Europe, unpaid household work has been monetized to a much smaller extent.

One aim of the Nordic Welfare State has been a general redistribution of income and welfare. The State has been used as an instrument of equal rights. Unlike other European countries, the Nordic countries direct social security to all their citizens. Their employment policy has emphasized active rather than passive labour market policies with the aim of having all adults gainfully employed (Nätti, 1994). These countries have shown a stronger dedication to the policy goal of full employment than has the rest of Europe, or the United States.

Women's engagement in gainful employment has become not only an expectation, but also a necessity in the Nordic countries. The Nordic model's success in reducing pay differentials in general — including between women and men — has considerably undermined the possibility of men being the sole supporters of their families. Social services facilitating the combination of motherhood and gainful employment have become quite developed and have attained a high quality in the Nordic countries (Kauppinen-Toropainen, 1993; Julkunen, 1992; Nordic Council of Ministers, 1994).[2] Moreover, the gender neutrality of those services is unusual. For example, laws refer not only to maternity leave or maternity allowances but also to *parental* leave and *parental* allowances.

Thus, the Nordic societies are not built on the assumption that mothers are homemakers. The child day-care system, for example, has not been constructed only from an educational point of view but also, very importantly, to enable and encourage women's participation in the labour force. Also, school lunches have an important role to play in ensuring opportunities for mothers to engage in gainful employment. Furthermore, women's rights are not based on their marital status but on their citizenship or employment in the Nordic societies. Social security and services for married women doing unpaid household work do not depend on their husbands' employment status; women are treated as individuals, not as spouses (Nätti, 1994).

The public sector, "women's ally", has been a very important employer for women in the Nordic countries, especially in Sweden. The sphere of public sector services is large: education, health care, child day care and social services are virtually monopolized by the State. In 1992, the public sector accounted for 46, 44 and 58 per cent of total female employment in Finland, Norway and Sweden, respectively.

Statistical comparisons of women's status

Women's strong labour force participation in the Nordic countries is reflected in the fact that they comprise roughly half of the non-agricultural workforce — 49.8 per cent in Finland, 47.1 per cent in Norway and 49.5 per cent in Sweden in 1990. This numerical equality was reached at different times in the three countries. In Finland, the integration of women into the labour market was more or less completed by 1970 when women already comprised 45 per cent of all non-agricultural workers. In Norway, by contrast, women accounted for only 35 per cent of the non-agricultural labour force in 1970, with the percentage growing to 44 per cent in 1980 and 47 per cent in 1990. Sweden's experience is between those of Finland and Norway. By 1990, the labour markets of all three countries were thus supplied with roughly equal numbers of female and male workers. This compares to approximately 45 per cent in North America and 39 per cent in other European countries in the early 1990s.

There have been differences between the three Nordic countries in the evolution of the Welfare State and in women's labour force participation. In Finland, the integration of women into the labour market largely occurred before the development of the Welfare State. The other two countries went through a more distinct "housewife" or full-time home-maker phase between agrarian society and the integration of women into paid employment (Nätti, 1994; Kauppinen-Toropainen, 1993; Kauppinen-Toropainen, Kandolin and Haavio-Mannila, 1986). In Norway this occurred later than in Sweden, and the contribution of the public sector as an employer was somewhat smaller (Anttalainen, 1986). In Sweden, public service employment came to play an even more important role than it did in either Finland or Norway. Also in contrast to the experiences of Finland and Norway, the development of Sweden's child day-care system coincided with the increase in paid employment of mothers (Borchorst, 1990).

Whereas women's unemployment rate is higher than men's in almost all continental European countries (with an average ratio of 1.33 for other OECD countries in 1992-94 based on ILO and United Nations data), the opposite is true in Finland, Norway and Sweden, where women's unemployment rate is lower than men's (average ratio of 0.72). Indeed, Finland, Norway and Sweden have the lowest ratios of female-male unemployment in the OECD.

As noted above, labour market segregation has at least one favourable aspect for women in the Nordic countries, as they are more likely than are men to be employed in the public sector and in the service sector. In 1992, approximately half of all female employment was in the public sector in Finland, Norway and Sweden, as against about one-quarter of male employment. The public sector has been characterized by more secure employment than has the private sector (Nätti, 1994), and the service sector has been expanding. In the early 1970s, the public sector accounted for about one-quarter of all employment in the Nordic countries (somewhat more in Sweden). By the early 1990s, the proportion had risen to one-third or more (Nordic Council of Ministers, 1994). However, this pattern of a secure and expanding public sector has been changing, so prospects for women workers may become less rosy unless more attention is paid to their situation. Construction and other public works-type unemployment measures, for example, tend to favour men.

Pay differentials
Data on the hourly earnings of full-time female workers in manufacturing as a percentage of full-time male workers' earnings show smaller pay differentials in Finland, Norway and Sweden (at 78-89 per cent) than in the major industrialized countries (72-79 per cent). However, these

data tell only part of the story because manufacturing, which is relatively well paid, is itself male-dominated. Overall pay differentials also depend on other factors, such as differences in working hours (e.g. full-time or part-time work), in addition to occupation and position. Besides, it must be remembered that one of the main determinants of international differentials in female-male pay ratios is the overall level of wage inequality in each country (Blau and Khan, 1992), and Nordic countries are known to have small overall wage differentials. The bottom line, however, is that women in those countries still receive substantially less pay than do men. Moreover, gaps in overall income distribution have recently widened in the Nordic countries (Kandolin, 1993), and more and more women are finding themselves in part-time jobs or precarious forms of employment. Unless special measures to counteract these trends are enhanced, the earnings gap between men and women is therefore likely to widen.

In the Nordic countries, as elsewhere, part-time workers are more typically women than men. In 1993, over 40 per cent of the women workers in Norway and Sweden were engaged in part-time work. The corresponding figure for men was less than 10 per cent. In Finland, however, only 11 per cent of women worked part time in 1993, but this still comprises about 65 per cent of all part-timers, since Finland has an unusually small number of part-time workers.

The population of the Nordic countries enjoys a high level of education, with small male-female differences in the number of years of school completed. Women's high level of education has naturally contributed to the increase in female labour force participation. However, men and women pursue different fields of study in secondary school and later on. Indeed, it is striking how stereotyped the typical male and female fields of study are. Medical and health-related sciences, educational science, teacher training and the humanities are typical female-dominated fields, whereas engineering, and agricultural, mathematical and computer sciences are typical male-dominated fields. These persistent differences in education maintain gender segregation in the labour market (United Nations Economic Commission for Europe, 1995; Anttalainen, 1986), as they preserve and reinforce the gender stereotyping.

STATISTICAL ANALYSIS OF OCCUPATIONAL SEGREGATION BY SEX IN NORDIC LABOUR MARKETS

Description of data and comparability

The statistical analysis in this section is based on census data for 1970, 1980 and 1990 compiled by the Central Statistical Offices of Finland, Norway and Sweden. The original national data for 1990 included 296 occupations for Finland, 292 occupations for Norway, and 261 occupations for Sweden. In order to increase the comparability of country experiences, a common classification into 187 occupations was created for all three countries by comparing national occupational titles. This was relatively easy to do as all three countries have very similar coding systems. For the most part, it implied aggregating similar occupational categories.

This common occupational classification is used as the basis for most of the following empirical analysis. The analysis excludes agricultural occupations, inter alia because their classification has been inconsistent over time.[3] By comparison with the original national classifications, the common classification has both advantages (especially greater comparability) and disadvantages (especially loss of detail). However, the loss of detail is felt to be much less important than the gain from having comparable occupational data for the three countries. First, a major objective of this article is to draw conclusions about differences and similarities between Finland, Norway and Sweden, and a common occupational classification is critical for this. Second, the loss of detail may not be very important, since the level of detail in the common classification remains relatively high at 187 occupations. In any case, the more detailed original national data are still used to investigate specific topics like the percentage of women in higher- and lower-status occupations.

Patterns in the Nordic labour markets in 1990

Indices of inequality

A number of inequality indices are used in the research literature to measure occupational segregation. One of the reasons for the proliferation of inequality indices is that they all have disadvantages. For simplicity of exposition, however, only the index of dissimilarity (ID) is used here. This index is the most widely used in the research literature (see Anker, forthcoming, for a review); ID values range from 0 (no segregation, with equal percentages of women and men in each and every occupation) to 1 (complete segregation, with female workers in occupations where there are no male workers). Thus, the higher the ID value, the greater the segregation. In addition to this index, other measures of occupational segregation and concentration are used in subsequent sections. In this way, it is possible to build up a fairly complete picture of occupational segregation and gender inequality in Nordic labour markets.

Previous cross-national studies of occupational segregation by sex have generally found relatively high levels of segregation in the Nordic countries. This includes studies using crude, one-digit occupational data usually with seven broad occupational groups (e.g. professional/technical, clerical, services, agriculture, administrative/managerial, sales, production) as well as a recent study based on more detailed two- and three-digit occupational data (Anker, forthcoming).

Table 1. Female share of non-agricultural employment and index of dissimilarity (ID), 1970, 1980 and 1990[b]

Country	Year	Female share of non-agricultural employment (%)	ID[c]
Finland[a]	1970	44.6	.725
	1980	47.8	.709
	1990	49.8	.663
Norway[a]	1970	34.8	.736
	1980	43.9	.710
	1990	47.1	.635
Sweden[a]	1970	40.5	.731
	1980	46.3	.688
	1990	49.5	.641

[a] Based on a common occupational classification with 187 non-agricultural occupations. [b] For comparison, the ID values for 14 other OECD countries (adjusted to an occupational classification with 187 non-agricultural occupations) averaged .660 in 1970, .636 in 1980, and .610 in 1990. [c] For a definition of ID (index of dissimilarity) and other indices of inequality see Anker, forthcoming.

The results presented in table 1 and figure 1 confirm the findings of previous cross-national studies, with relatively high levels of occupational segregation by sex. Approximately 32 per cent of male and female workers in Finland, Norway and Sweden would need to change their occupations to eliminate the gender segregation of occupations. This level of segregation is substantially higher than that found in the other OECD countries. In 1990, whereas ID averaged .65 in these three Nordic countries based on data for 187 non-agricultural occupations, it was .55 in the United States based on 461 non-agricultural occupations, and .60 in France based on 433 non-agricultural occupations. Based on a classification with 75 non-agricultural occupations, ID is approximately .55 for 14 non-Nordic OECD countries, as compared to about .60 for the three Nordic countries (Anker, forthcoming).

Overall levels of occupational segregation by sex are very similar in Finland, Norway and Sweden. Furthermore, ID values declined more or less in tandem in all three countries over the period 1970-90. This means that the high level of occupational segregation by sex in Nordic countries is not a new phenomenon. Indeed, in 1970 the sex segregation of occupations was so strikingly high that ID values for that year are probably similar to those obtaining in many non-Asian developing countries today (Anker, forthcoming).

Changes in ID values over time can be decomposed and attributed to: (i) changes in the sex composition of occupations, (ii) changes in the size distribution of occupations and (iii) a residual. This can be done using typical standardization methods (as explained in Blau and Hendricks, 1979, for example). Identifying the relative importance of factors caus-

Figure 1. Changes in occupational segregation by sex, as measured by index of dissimilarity (ID), 1970-90

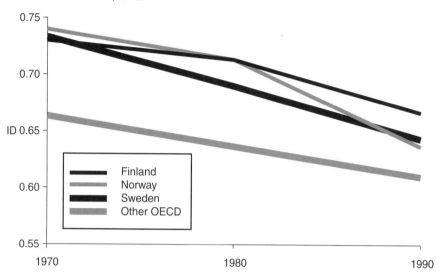

ing ID changes in this way is quite useful, since analysts and policy-makers are especially interested in the greater integration of men and women within occupations, i.e. (i) above. Table 2 indicates that progress in reducing occupational segregation by sex in the three countries has indeed been due almost exclusively to the increased integration of men and women within occupations (SEX) and not at all to shifts in the structure of employment (OCC). It is worth noting that the increased integration of men and women within occupations after 1970 was somewhat faster in Sweden than it was in Finland and Norway.

The foregoing analysis thus shows clear evidence that the Nordic countries have: (i) high rates of female labour force participation, and (ii) high levels of occupational segregation by sex, but (iii) decreasing occupational segregation over the period 1970-90.

Gender-biased occupations

It is also informative to analyse the extent to which the labour force is divided into gender-biased occupations, i.e. occupations in which the percentage of workers of either sex is so high that they could be called "male" or "female" occupations. Of course, there is no such thing as a "correct" definition of a male or female occupation. Thus, in analysing data for this purpose it must be borne in mind that the choice of a fixed numeric cut-off point can significantly influence the changes observed within a country over time or across countries at one point in time, espe-

Table 2. Changes in the index of dissimilarity (ID) attributable to (i) changes in the sex composition of occupations (SEX); (ii) changes in the size distribution of occupations (OCC); and (iii) residual (RES),[a,b] 1970s and 1980s

Country	1970-80[c]			1980-90[c]		
	SEX	OCC	RES	SEX	OCC	RES
Finland	−.022	−.004	.006	−.037	−.003	−.001
Norway	−.009	−.028	.001	−.049	.019	−.005
Sweden	−.079	.018	.017	−.036	−.004	−.008
Average	*−.037*	*−.005*	*.008*	*−.041*	*.004*	*−.005*

[a] See Blau and Hendricks (1979) and Anker (forthcoming) for a description of the standardization methodology used to decompose observed change in ID into components attributable to (i) integration of men and women within occupations (SEX); (ii) occupational structure of employment (OCC); and (iii) a residual (RES). [b] Based on classifications with 264, 291 and 261 non-agricultural occupations in Finland, Norway and Sweden, respectively. [c] Based on data for 10 and 9 other OECD countries for the 1970s and 1980s respectively, SEX changed by −.012 on average in the 1970s and −.010 in the 1980s; OCC changed by −.020 and −.017 on average over the same periods.

Source: Anker, forthcoming.

cially when one or more large occupations have a percentage of female or male workers very close to the cut-off point (e.g. 80.1 or 79.9 for a cut-off point of 80 per cent). It is for this reason that three definitions (70, 80 and 90 per cent of either sex) are used here.

Table 3 and figures 2 and 3 present the results for female workers in 1970, 1980 and 1990. Table 3 shows both the percentage of the female non-agricultural labour force working in female-dominated occupations and the number of occupations fitting each of the three definitions, i.e. occupations where at least 70, 80 or 90 per cent of workers are female. For purposes of comparison, average change for other OECD countries using the 80 per cent definition is also provided, based on classifications with approximately 75 non-agricultural occupations (see Anker, forthcoming).

In all three countries, a very high percentage of the female non-agricultural labour force worked in "female" occupations in 1990 — roughly 65 per cent were in occupations where at least 70 per cent of the workers were women, 55 per cent were in occupations where at least 80 per cent of the workers were women, and 40 per cent were in occupations where at least 90 per cent of the workers were women. These rates are not only high in absolute terms — as they indicate that a majority of non-agricultural women workers in Nordic countries work in a "female" occupation — but they are also high in a relative sense as they are much higher than in other industrialized countries. Based on a classification with 75 non-agricultural occupations, approximately 22 per cent of women workers in 14 other OECD countries work in an occupation where women comprise at least 80 per cent of the workforce. Based on a similar number of non-agricultural occupations, this percentage is more than twice as

Table 3. Proportion of female non-agricultural employment in female-dominated occupations, 1970, 1980 and 1990

Definition of female-dominated occupations / Country/year	≥70 per cent female	(No. of occupations)	≥80 per cent female[a]	(No. of occupations)	≥90 per cent female	(No. of occupations)
Finland						
1970	76.3	(49)	56.7	(35)	37.7	(22)
1980	75.2	(49)	61.0	(37)	54.2	(26)
1990	72.2	(49)	60.0	(35)	45.3	(21)
Norway						
1970	57.1	(24)	39.7	(19)	28.0	(9)
1980	72.1	(32)	55.6	(21)	35.9	(14)
1990	56.6	(33)	49.7	(20)	32.2	(12)
Sweden						
1970	72.9	(32)	40.9	(16)	37.5	(13)
1980	72.2	(34)	59.0	(23)	29.8	(13)
1990	69.2	(36)	58.2	(27)	42.2	(13)

Based on the common classification of 187 non-agricultural occupations for all three Nordic countries. [a] Average OECD value for 1990 using the 80 per cent definition is 22.4 (Anker, forthcoming), based on a classification with only 75 non-agricultural occupations (not 187 non-agricultural occupations as for Finland, Norway and Sweden). Based on a similar occupational classification of 75 non-agricultural occupations, a comparable percentage for the three Nordic countries for 1990 is 48.1. The average change for other OECD countries was –1.7 percentage points for the 1970s and –4.9 percentage points for the 1980s, based on data for nine and eleven other OECD countries, respectively (Anker, forthcoming).

high in the three Nordic countries, at 48 per cent (see Anker, forthcoming). Though similarly high in all three countries, the proportion of the female workforce employed in female-dominated occupations is somewhat lower in Norway than it is in Sweden and Finland (by roughly 10 percentage points in 1990).

As regards changes over the period 1970-90, all three Nordic countries are found to have had roughly the same experiences. Based on the 80 and 90 per cent definitions, the percentage of the female workforce in female-dominated occupations rose, whereas based on the 70 per cent definition it remained more or less unchanged. Over the same period, the number of female-dominated occupations generally remained unchanged. These observations are interesting in that they indicate that a disproportionate share of female labour force growth was absorbed into existing "female" occupations, which expanded, rather than into newly created female-dominated occupations. Women have also been entering male-dominated occupations.

Table 4 shows the male-dominated non-agricultural occupations (to the extent of at least 70, 80 and 90 per cent male). Just as for female-dominated occupations, there is strong similarity between the three Nordic countries. On average, based on the 70, 80 and 90 per cent definitions, respectively 69, 57 and 39 per cent of all male workers were work-

Figure 2. Percentage of female non-agricultural employment in female-dominated occupations, 1990

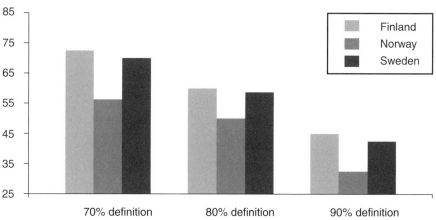

ing in a male-dominated occupation in 1990. These percentages come close to those given in table 3 for women (66, 56 and 40 per cent). They are also similar to those found for men in other OECD countries. In 1990, based on the 80 per cent definition, the proportion averaged 56 per cent for 14 other OECD countries using a classification of 75 non-agricultural occupations. Thus the extent to which men in Nordic countries work in male-dominated occupations is typical for OECD countries.

Figure 3. Percentage point change in percentage of total female non-agricultural employment in female-dominated occupations based on 80 per cent definition, 1970s and 1980s

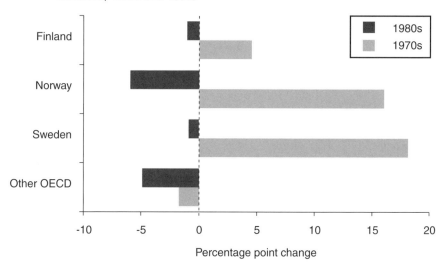

Table 4. Proportion of male non-agricultural employment in male-dominated occupations, 1970, 1980 and 1990

Definition of female-dominated occupations Country/year	≥70 per cent female	(No. of occupations)	≥80 per cent female[a]	(No. of occupations)	≥90 per cent female	(No. of occupations)
Finland						
1970	80.2	(91)	71.2	(67)	60.9	(51)
1980	74.9	(79)	68.1	(64)	43.1	(39)
1990	71.3	(71)	58.0	(58)	38.1	(36)
Norway						
1970	82.3	(118)	76.7	(98)	68.2	(74)
1980	78.7	(107)	71.8	(89)	55.7	(62)
1990	69.0	(94)	54.3	(69)	38.8	(44)
Sweden						
1970	84.2	(111)	76.8	(90)	59.7	(58)
1980	76.2	(99)	71.1	(79)	40.9	(45)
1990	66.1	(81)	58.1	(64)	39.8	(41)

Based on the common classification of 187 non-agricultural occupations for all three Nordic countries. [a] Average OECD value for 1990 using the 80 per cent definition is 56.2 (Anker, forthcoming), based on a classification with 75 non-agricultural occupations (not 187 non-agricultural occupations as for Finland, Norway and Sweden). Based on a similar occupational classification of 75 non-agricultural occupations, a comparable percentage for the three Nordic countries for 1990 is 56.2 per cent. The average change for other OECD countries was –4.4 percentage points for the 1970s and –6.7 percentage points for the 1980s, based on data for nine and eleven other OECD countries, respectively (Anker, forthcoming).

The Nordic countries display an interesting and unique pattern in the world with regard to gender-biased occupations (Anker, forthcoming). They have not only a high percentage of men working in male-dominated occupations (typical of many other OECD countries) but also a high percentage of women working in female-dominated occupations (not typical). This pattern helps to explain the relatively high level of occupational segregation by sex found in the Nordic countries as compared to other industrialized countries — it is mainly attributable to the large size of the female-dominated occupations. Thus, it could be argued that the relatively high level of sex segregation of occupations found in the Nordic countries may not be as bad for women in those countries as it is elsewhere.

The 1970s and 1980s witnessed a tremendous decrease in the number of male-dominated occupations, as well as in the percentage of the total male workforce working in such occupations (see figures 4 and 5). Furthermore, the more "masculinized" the male-dominated occupations were to begin with, the greater the decrease. Thus, on average, while the percentage of the total male workforce working in male-dominated occupations fell by 16.3 per cent (13.4 percentage points, from 82.2 to 68.8 per cent) for occupations where at least 70 per cent of workers were men, it fell by 24.2 per cent (18.1 percentage points, from 74.9 to 56.8 per cent)

Figure 4. Percentage of male non-agricultural employment in male-dominated occupations, 1990

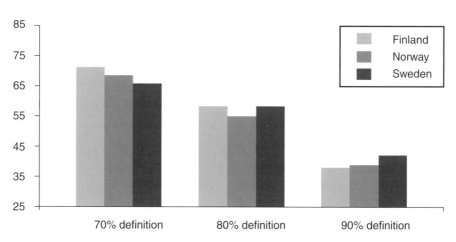

for occupations where at least 80 per cent of workers were men, and by 38.2 per cent (24.0 percentage points, from 62.9 to 38.9 per cent) for occupations where at least 90 per cent of workers were men. These are quite astounding falls over what is really a fairly short period of time, and they are putting men under increasing competitive pressure from women. In the Nordic countries, as elsewhere, men are very clearly losing their privileged position of having so many "male" occupations.

Figure 5. Percentage point change in percentage of total male non-agricultural employment in male-dominated occupations based on 80 per cent definition, 1970s and 1980s

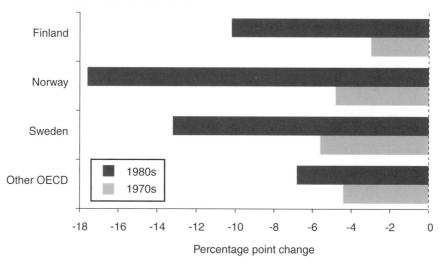

Table 5. The ten most feminized occupations in Finland, Norway and Sweden (based on percentage female in occupation) in 1990

Occupation	Finland		Norway		Sweden	
Housekeepers in private service, childcare in families and at home	99.9	(1)	97.7	(2)	96.5	(3)
Home helps (municipal)	99.1	(2)	96.5	(4)	96.0	(4)
Industrial sewers; other cutting, sewing, etc., occupations	97.7	(3)	93.0	(10)	81.6	(26)
Bath attendants, etc.	97.6	(4)	70.9	(33)	55.4	(57)
Milliners and hatmakers	97.4	(5)	57.7	(47)	94.4	(6)
Nurses	97.1	(6)	93.3	(9)	93.8	(7)
Secretaries, typists and stenographers	96.8	(7)	95.8	(5)	92.3	(10)
Hairdressers, barbers and beauticians, etc.	96.8	(8)	90.4	(11)	88.0	(16)
Kitchen assistants	95.8	(9)	89.4	(16)	86.4	(17)
Directors and nursing staff at child day-care centres and nursery schools	95.7	(10)	96.5	(3)	95.6	(5)
Assistant nurses and attendants	94.4	(12)	98.4	(1)	92.4	(9)
Telephone switchboard operators, etc.	89.1	(25)	95.8	(6)	97.8	(2)
Technical nursing assistants	92.6	(19)	95.2	(7)	90.8	(13)
Hotel and restaurant matrons	93.1	(15)	94.0	(8)	88.3	(15)
Dental assistants and other health workers	85.9	(27)	89.8	(14)	99.7	(1)
Tailors, salon seamstresses, etc.	85.1	(29)	53.6	(54)	93.3	(8)

Based on the common classification of 187 non-agricultural occupations for all three countries. The first number is the rate of feminization of the occupation. Number in parentheses is rank order in each country among 187 occupations classified (based on percentage female). Where an occupation was noted as being in the top ten for one of the countries, the results were also filled in for the other two countries.

Most "feminized" occupations

The ten occupations in which the proportions of female workers were the highest in each of the three countries in 1990 are shown in table 5 (for further details, see Melkas and Anker, forthcoming). If an occupation was noted as being in the top ten for any one country, the results were also filled in for the other two countries based on the common occupational classification discussed above.

There is great similarity between Finland, Norway and Sweden regarding which occupations are the most highly feminized. Five occupations are among the ten most feminized occupations in each of the three countries (housekeeper in private service, childcare in the home; home helps (municipal); nurse; secretary, typist and stenographer; directors and nursing staff at child day-care centres and nursery schools). And only

16 occupations are required to represent the ten most feminized occupations in all three countries. Furthermore, only three of the ten most feminized occupations in one country (Finland) are less than 80 per cent female in either or both of the other countries. Yet, even in these few cases — bath attendants, etc., in Norway and Sweden; milliners and hatmakers in Norway; tailors, salon seamstresses, etc., in Norway — the rate of feminization exceeds 50 per cent.

These "female" occupations clearly reflect a very high degree of gender-stereotyping in the Nordic countries. This stereotyping in the labour market is consistent with gender stereotypes in society at large and with the types of abilities and characteristics that are typically attributed to women. Thus, table 5 includes only occupations associated with (i) caring (e.g. nurse; housekeeper and childcare; teacher; home helps; health worker), (ii) manual dexterity (e.g. sewer, tailor; hatmaker; secretary; dental assistant), and (iii) typical household-related work (sewer; kitchen helper; hotel and restaurant matron; hairdresser; housekeeper and childcare; bath attendant). The only "exception" is telephone switchboard operator, which has been a "female" occupation from its inception.

Occupational status

Nordic countries are proud of their social and labour market policies on gender equality which are reflected inter alia in relatively high percentages of female parliamentarians and relatively low male-female wage differentials as compared to other countries. Yet this situation is not consistent with the high levels of occupational segregation by sex which exist in those countries as indicated above.

A possible explanation for this apparent inconsistency could be that "female" and "male" occupations are separate but equal, i.e. having similar pay and status. One way of testing whether this is the case would be to identify pairs or groups of occupations in which workers: (i) either perform similar activities or (ii) work side-by-side in occupations which have different social statuses (and almost always different pay levels to match). Accordingly, this section looks at the feminization of sets of matching occupations which have relatively high or relatively low status in terms of education, earnings and relative authority. Table 6 presents comparisons based on the common occupational classification.[4]

There is a wide gap in feminization between matching high- and low-status occupations in the Nordic countries. Women are much more likely to be concentrated in the low-status occupation of any matching pair or group. Based on the common occupational classification, the average gap for six sizeable occupations in 1990 ranged from approximately 35 per cent in Finland to approximately 50 per cent in both Sweden and Norway. Furthermore, only one of the nine matching pairs/groups shows a higher rate of feminization in the higher-status occupation (judges

205

as compared to barristers/solicitors). However, the period 1970-90 shows a clear tendency towards a narrowing of the gap in feminization between low- and high-status occupations — by between seven and ten percentage points on average — in the three Nordic countries.

Technical occupations

Engineering is definitely a "male" occupation in the Nordic countries. Roughly 90 per cent of engineers in Finland and Norway were men in 1990 (suitable data are not available for Sweden). Interestingly, there is very little difference in feminization between high- and low-status engineering occupations; rather, both are similarly masculinized. Furthermore, what little change occurred over the 1970s and 1980s in the feminization of engineering occupations tended to increase the feminization gap between high- and low-status engineering occupations. Clearly, engineering is an area of the Nordic labour market from which women are still largely excluded; and this applies to high- and low-status engineering occupations alike.

Another set of technical occupations covered is chemists and physicists as compared to laboratory assistants (see table 6). The latter lower-status occupation has a much higher rate of feminization as compared with the higher-paid and higher-status occupations of chemists and physicists in all three Nordic countries. In 1990, this feminization gap ranged from 32 per cent in Finland to 50 per cent in Sweden. It is interesting to note that Finland's experience over the period 1970-90 differs from that of the other two Nordic countries. Whereas the gap widened substantially in Norway and Sweden, it narrowed slightly in Finland — largely because the rate of feminization among Finland's laboratory assistants was already high in 1970.

Technical occupations are thus an area of the Nordic labour market where there is a great deal of sex segregation, both horizontal and vertical — not only do men predominate, but men are also more likely to occupy the higher-status and better paid occupations as compared to women.

Medical occupations

Nursing is an important occupation for women around the world (Anker, forthcoming). It is very much a "female" occupation in all three Nordic countries. This applies both to high-status registered nurses and to low-status assistant nurses, although the period 1970-90 shows a tendency for men to have entered slightly faster into the former, higher-status occupation than into the latter.

Comparatively, women are less likely than are men to be doctors. Only 24 per cent (Norway) to 45 per cent (Finland) of doctors are women. However, it is noteworthy that the feminization gap between high- and low-status medical occupations narrowed fairly rapidly over the two

Table 6. Comparing feminization of related occupations with differing status[a] in Finland, Norway and Sweden, 1970 and 1990 (basis: common classification)[b]

Pair/ group number	Lower and higher status occupation(s)	Per cent female in 1970			Per cent female in 1990			Feminization gap, low-high status occupations						Change in low-high gap 1970-1990		
								1970			1990					
		Finland	Norway	Sweden	Finland	Norway	Sweden	Finland	Norway	Sweden	Finland	Norway	Sweden	Finland	Norway	Sweden
1.	Laboratory assistants	65.9	47.0	54.3	73.8	74.2	83.3	37.8	19.5	31.8	32.4	38.9	50.1	-5.4	19.4	18.3
	Chemists and physicists	28.1	27.5	22.5	41.4	35.3	33.2									
2.	Assistant nurses, etc.	98.9	99.1	97.0	94.4	98.4	92.4	71.5	86.1	79.0	49.4	74.3	58.5	-22.1	-11.8	-20.5
	Nurses (registered)	99.3	97.6	99.3	97.1	93.3	93.8									
	Physicians	27.4	13.0	18.0	45.0	24.1	33.9									
3.	Dental assistants	*	99.6	100.0	99.5	99.9	99.7	*	78.1	72.1	32.2	70.6	58.5	*	-7.5	-13.6
	Dentists	*	21.5	27.9	67.3	29.3	41.2									
4.	Pre-primary school teachers	99.8	98.6	99.5	95.7	96.5	95.6	78.5	85.4	78.9	61.8	67.6	63.8	-16.7	-17.8	-15.1
	Primary school and specialized teachers	58.8	56.7	66.8	69.2	61.5	68.9									
	School principals and secondary school teachers	58.3	22.5	41.8	60.4	34.4	53.7									
	University teaching staff	21.3	13.2	20.6	33.9	28.9	31.8									
5.	Barristers and solicitors[c]	24.6	3.0	5.6	33.3	10.7	15.6	12.6	-5.5	-6.4	-12.8	-11.7	-22.1	-25.4	-6.2	-15.7
	Judges[c]	12.0	8.5	12.0	46.1	22.4	37.7									
6.	Kitchen assistants	96.1	90.0	96.9	95.8	89.4	86.4	9.2	45.2	23.3	13.2	32.3	28.2	4.0	-12.9	4.9
	Cooks	93.8	61.8	78.6	82.6	59.8	69.0									
	Kitchen managers, etc.	86.9	44.8	73.6	86.2	57.1	58.2									
7.	Photographic laboratory assistants[c]	81.2	66.5	63.6	77.2	77.3	61.2	50.2	49.2	46.2	54.0	44.6	41.6	3.8	-4.6	-4.6
	Photographers, etc.	31.0	17.3	17.4	23.0	32.7	19.6									
8.	Shop assistants	*	75.3	81.3	71.9	75.4	75.2	*	57.4	51.8	18.0	39.3	35.4	*	-18.1	-16.4
	Shop managers	*	17.9	29.5	53.9	36.1	39.8									
9.	Commercial gardening workers	62.8	39.3	28.7	52.8	45.9	24.6	40.8	30.1	25.5	16.9	15.1	11.2	-23.9	-15.0	-1.6
	Commercial gardening supervisors[c]	22.0	9.2	3.2	35.9	30.8	13.4									
	Total (unweighted) average:															
	All occupational groups							37.6	45.6	40.2	26.5	37.1	32.5	-10.7	-7.4	-6.6
	Substantial size occupational groups[c]							49.2	61.9	56.2	34.5	53.8	49.1	-10.1	-8.1	-7.1

If more than 2 occupations in the comparison, values for highest- and lowest-status occupations are used for calculation of low-high gap. *Occupation exists separately only in 1990 classification. [a]Occupations represented in this table are pairs, or groups, of related occupations with clearly different statuses in which workers either: (i) perform similar activities, or (ii) work side-by-side in different occupations. [b]Common classification has 187 non-agricultural occupations. [c]Indicates an occupation with less than 0.1 per cent of all non-agricultural workers in 1990 in at least two of the three Nordic countries. Substantial occupations have more than 0.1 per cent.

decades under study. This was due to women's entry into the "physicians" occupation, combined with the fact that relatively few men entered into nursing occupations.

Thus, while medical occupations are an important source of employment for women, they still show considerable sex segregation, with women much more likely than men to be in lower-status occupations (e.g. nurses and dental assistants as opposed to doctors and dentists). However, this gap narrowed over the period 1970-90 due to the increasing feminization of the occupation of physicians.

Teaching

Teaching is another very important occupation for women around the world, but also one in which there is considerable sex segregation (Anker, forthcoming). This applies to the Nordic countries as well. In 1990, approximately 96 per cent of pre-primary teachers in the Nordic countries were women, but as the school level increases the rate of feminization declines — to about 65 per cent for primary school teachers, 35-60 per cent for secondary school teachers and about 30 per cent for university teachers. As a result, the average gap in feminization between the highest- and lowest-status teaching occupations was approximately 65 per cent in the Nordic countries in 1990. By then, however, the gap had already narrowed by about 15 percentage points since 1970 in all three Nordic countries due to the increasing entry of women into university teaching jobs.

Administrative and legal occupations

According to data from Norway (corroborated by some data from Finland), there are large differences in feminization between related higher- and lower-status administrative occupations, with much lower feminization rates in higher-status administrative occupations than in lower-status administrative occupations (by approximately 30 per cent in 1990). Surprisingly, the gap widened by about 15 per cent on average over the two decades studied here. This should be a matter of concern for policy-makers in the Nordic countries.

The feminization of the related legal occupations of barristers and solicitors as compared to judges represents a very unusual case in that the rate of feminization is actually higher in the higher-status occupation of judges, as compared to the lower-status occupations of barristers and solicitors. In addition, the feminization gap between the higher- and lower-status occupations widened in favour of women over the period 1970-90. There are a number of possible explanations for these findings. First, the higher-status occupation of judges is less well paid — for similar skills and experience — than are the lower-status occupations of barristers and solicitors. Second, hours of work tend to be more regular for judges and therefore easier to combine with family responsibilities.

Service occupations

In the Nordic countries — as in the industrialized countries in general — service occupations are an area of the labour market in which women are over-represented relative to their share of total employment (Anker, forthcoming). Yet even here in the three Nordic countries there is an average gap of around 25 per cent in feminization between related higher- and lower-status occupations. This gap, however, narrowed by about 10 per cent on average over the period 1970-90. The case of shop personnel/assistants as compared to shop managers/supervisors provides a good example. Whereas women accounted for approximately 75 per cent of shop personnel in the three countries in 1990, they comprised only about 40 per cent of shop managers in Norway and Sweden and 50 per cent of them in Finland. An example of an especially wide gap between related higher- and lower-status service occupations is provided by the case of clerks and their supervisors in Finland's banking and insurance sector. Whereas in 1990, approximately 90 per cent of such clerks were women, only about 45 per cent of their supervisors were women. Postal and telecommunication service workers in Finland and postal workers in Norway provide an interesting exception: in these cases the rate of feminization was actually higher in the higher-status occupations in 1990. In Norway at least, this unusual pattern is due to an exceptional increase in the rate of feminization among postmasters and other postal supervisors, from 13 per cent in 1970 to 67 per cent in 1990.

CONCLUSION

Summary of findings

The foregoing analysis of occupational segregation by sex in the Nordic labour markets of Finland, Norway and Sweden shows that the level of gender-based occupational segregation has been, and continues to be, high in the Nordic countries — both in an absolute sense and relative to the levels found in other industrialized countries. Some changes are taking place, however, as sex segregation levels decreased quite substantially over the period 1970-90. Women have been considerably more eager to cross gender barriers between occupations than men who have generally preferred to stay in traditional "male" occupations.

Indeed, the period 1970-90 witnessed an especially rapid decline in the number of male-dominated occupations and in the percentage of the total employed non-agricultural male workforce working in male-dominated occupations in the Nordic countries. There are now far fewer "male" occupations than there were in the early 1970s.

What causes the Nordic countries to have a relatively high level of occupational segregation by sex is the extent to which women work in "female" occupations. The rates at which they do so are not only high in an absolute sense, but they are also much higher than in other industrialized countries. Thus, while approximately half of the employed non-agricultural female workforce of the Nordic countries is in "female" occupations, the corresponding proportion in other industrialized countries averages about one-quarter.

Finland, Norway and Sweden are also very similar as regards those occupations which are the most feminized and the largest employers of women. These occupations are highly sex-stereotyped, involving, for example, "caring" and household-related activities. These findings highlight the important link between the gender-stereotyping of the labour market, on the one hand, and gender stereotypes in Nordic society and the types of abilities and characteristics that are typically attributed to women, on the other. Indeed, the cross-country similarity, which is observed on a number of inequality statistics, implies that cultural and social values play a major role in determining and affecting the sex segregation of occupations, since one would expect greater differences across these countries in light of their differing economic experiences in recent decades. For example, whereas part-time workers comprise approximately 25 per cent of the employed labour force in Sweden and Norway, the proportion is only around 10 per cent in Finland.

An analysis of the extent of vertical segregation, as reflected in the feminization of closely related occupations with different statuses, shows quite clearly that women in the Nordic countries are concentrated in lower-status and lower-paid occupations. Again, the levels and (small downward) trends observed in this respect are very similar in all three Nordic countries studied here.

Concluding comments

Even though the Nordic countries are in many ways models as far as gender equality policies are concerned, women have considerably lower status in Nordic labour markets than do men, and occupational segregation by sex remains high. Also, recent trends such as the increase in atypical employment and the contraction of the public sector, which have been referred to only briefly in this article, are cause for new concern. It may well be that men will increasingly be regarded as "core workers" who obtain permanent contracts, while women — in particular younger women — have to content themselves with precarious statuses. Yet, in a world of increasing international communication and collaboration, women would gain new opportunities if their skills and abilities were recognized.

A fairly recent publication of the Nordic Council of Ministers states: "In all the Nordic countries, political unity prevails in the awareness that society can progress in a more democratic direction only when both women's and men's competence, knowledge, experiences, and values are recognized and allowed to influence and enrich development in all spheres of society" (Nordic Council of Ministers, 1994, p. 10). Gender-based occupational segregation is one of the most important factors contributing to women's lower status in the labour market. This segregation also negatively affects the efficiency of the labour market as a whole. In addition, gender-based occupational segregation hinders equal opportunities for women and men, which is one of the cornerstones of overall equality in society. Thus, the "political unity" that is said to prevail in the Nordic countries needs to be more effectively translated into practical action in the labour market. Attitudes change slowly, but awareness-raising can play a role in that process.

One could argue that the high degree of occupational segregation found in the Nordic countries — particularly horizontal segregation — is not in itself necessarily bad for women, as long as "male" and "female" occupations are reasonably similar in terms of pay, status, promotion opportunities, independence and authority. Indeed, such segregation could be seen as providing women with a relatively large (and growing) segment of the labour market in which they are protected from male workers. It could also be argued that an intermediate stage on women's way to labour force participation and then to gender equality in the labour market requires women to enter female-dominated occupations first, when the process of increasing labour force participation begins. This may correspond to women's preferences and make the transition considerably easier for society as a whole to accept.

Yet a gender-segregated labour market is not something which should be taken as inevitable or natural, especially in the long run. Nor should it be taken as natural and inevitable that men's parental role is totally subordinate: more equally-shared household and childcare responsibilities should be an important policy goal if women's labour market status is to be improved. In the Nordic countries, it is time to strive vigorously for ways of moving on to the next stage on the way to equal opportunities by achieving much greater integration of men and women across occupations. The separate male and female labour markets found in the Nordic countries are indeed far from equal, with occupational segregation typically translating into lower pay and fewer career opportunities for women workers.

Notes

[1] The remaining Nordic countries, Denmark and Iceland, are not included in this analysis, but should be considered in future research. Since the Nordic societies are relatively homogenous, one may argue that differences between the statuses of women and men can be more clearly distinguished than in other western societies with sharp contrasts between social classes (Taylor-Gooby, 1991).

[2] It has been argued that the Nordic Welfare State has been able to guarantee a high quality of public services because they are services for the entire population, not only for poor people (Julkunen, 1992).

[3] In any case, in 1990, agricultural occupations accounted for only approximately 8.5, 6.2 and 3.3 per cent of total employment (and 7.5, 3.7 and 1.5 per cent of female employment) in Finland, Norway and Sweden, respectively.

[4] The pairs and groups of occupations in table 6 have been identified for the purposes of this analysis only and are in no way intended to indicate higher or lower value in terms of economic contribution. A complete set of comparisons (21, 11 and 23 pairs or groups for Norway, Sweden and Finland respectively) based on national occupational classifications is available from the authors. This is not presented here for lack of space.

References

Anker, Richard. Forthcoming. *Gender and jobs: Sex segregation of occupations in the world.* Geneva, ILO.

Anttalainen, Marja-Liisa. 1986. *Sukupuolen mukaan kahtiajakautuneet työmarkkinat Pohjoismaissa* [Gender-based labour market segmentation in the Nordic countries]. Naistutkimusmonisteita 1:1986. Helsinki, Tasa-arvoasiain neuvottelukunta [Council for Equality between Men and Women].

Barbezat, Debra. 1993. *Occupational segmentation by sex in the world.* Interdepartmental Project on Equality for Women in Employment, Working Paper No. 13, IDP Women/WP-13. Geneva, ILO. Dec.

Blau, Francine D.; Hendricks, Wallace E. 1979. "Occupational segregation by sex: Trends and prospects", in *Journal of Human Resources* (Madison, WI), Vol. 14, No. 2 (Spring), pp. 197-210.

Blau, Francine; Khan, L. 1992. *The gender earnings gap: Some international evidence.* NBER Working Paper No. 4224. Cambridge, MA, National Bureau of Economic Research. Dec.

Borchorst, Anette. 1990. "Political motherhood and child care policies: A comparative approach to Britain and Scandinavia", in Clare Ungerson (ed.): *Gender and caring: Work and welfare in Britain and Scandinavia.* New York, Harvester Wheatsheaf, pp. 160-178.

Gunderson, Morley. 1994. *Comparable worth and gender discrimination: An international perspective.* Geneva, ILO.

Julkunen, Raija. 1992. *Hyvinvointivaltio käännekohdassa* [The Welfare State at a turning point]. Tampere, Vastapaino.

Kandolin, Irja. 1993. "Women's labor force participation and sex segregation in working life", in Kaisa Kauppinen-Toropainen (ed.): *OECD Panel Group on Women, Work and Health — National report: Finland.* Helsinki, Ministry of Social Affairs and Health/Institute of Occupational Health.

Kauppinen, Kaisa; Haavio-Mannila, Elina; Kandolin, Irja. 1989. "Who benefits from working in non-traditional workroles: Interaction patterns and quality of worklife", in *Acta Sociologica* (Oslo), Vol. 32, No. 4, pp. 389-403.

Kauppinen-Toropainen, Kaisa. 1993. "Introduction", in Kaisa Kauppinen-Toropainen (ed.): *OECD Panel Group on Women, Work and Health — National report: Finland.* Helsinki, Ministry of Social Affairs and Health/Institute of Occupational Health.

Kauppinen-Toropainen, Kaisa; Kandolin, Irja; Haavio-Mannila, Elina. 1986. "Töiden jakautuminen sukupuolen mukaan ja naisten työn laatu" [Occupational segregation by sex and the quality of women's work], in *Työterveyslaitoksen tutkimuksia* (Helsinki), Vol. 4, No. 3, pp. 209-222.

Lehto, Anna-Maija. 1991. *Työelämän laatu ja tasa-arvo: Naisten ja miesten työolojen muutoksia 1977-1990* [Quality of working life and equality: Changes in working conditions of women and men in 1977-1990]. Työolokomitean mietinnön 1991:39 liiteselvitys; Tilastokeskus, Tutkimuksia 189. Helsinki, Ministry of Labour/Statistics Finland.

Lewis, Jane. 1992. "Gender and the development of welfare régimes", in *Journal of European Social Policy* (Harlow), Vol. 2, No. 3, pp. 159-173.

Melkas, Helinä; Anker, Richard. Forthcoming. *Occupational segregation and labour market differentials by sex in the Nordic countries of Finland, Norway and Sweden.* Geneva, ILO.

Nätti, Jouko. 1994. *A Nordic model of women's employment.* Paper presented at the 16th Conference of the International Working Party on Labour Market Segmentation, Strasbourg, 15-19 July.

Nordic Council of Ministers. 1994. *Women and men in the Nordic countries: Facts and figures 1994.* Nord 1994:3. Copenhagen, Nordic Council of Ministers.

Rubery, Jill; Smith, Mark. 1996. *Factors influencing the integration of women into the economy.* Paper presented at the ILO/European Commission Seminar on Women and Work in Europe, held in Turin, 18-19 April.

Taylor-Gooby, Peter. 1991. "Welfare State regimes and welfare citizenship", in *Journal of European Social Policy* (Harlow), Vol. 1, No. 2, pp. 93-106.

UNDP. 1995. *Human development report 1995.* New York, Oxford University Press.

United Nations Economic Commission for Europe. 1995. *Women in the ECE region: A call for action.* Geneva, United Nations.

Uusitalo, Hannu. 1989. *Income distribution in Finland: The effects of the Welfare State and the structural changes in society on income distribution in Finland in 1966-1985.* Central Statistical Office Studies No. 148. Helsinki, Statistics Finland.

PART-TIME WORK: SOLUTION OR TRAP?
Patrick BOLLÉ*

11

Part-time work can facilitate the entry into — or exit from — the labour market. It can help workers reconcile employment with family, social and civic responsibilities. But it can also prove a trap, especially for women, by relegating those workers to the periphery of the labour market. This chapter reviews various issues concerning part-time work — first of all, its definition, estimation and international comparison; then the protection of part-time workers; and the trends, especially in relation to women's labour force participation. The danger in relying excessively on part-time work to counter unemployment is stressed.

Over the past 20 years there has been a trend increase in part-time relative to full-time employment, especially in many developed countries. In some cases this is the result of a political decision to promote part-time work, particularly in countries suffering from high unemployment. Indeed, there has been much public praise of its supposed merits as a means of reducing unemployment as well as of its benefits for workers and employers alike.

For workers it may offer the chance of a better balance between working life and family responsibilities, training, leisure or civic activities. It can also make it easier for workers progressively to enter the labour market or retire from employment. For employers it can permit not only greater flexibility in responding to market requirements — e.g. by increasing capacity utilization or extending opening hours — but also productivity gains. For policy-makers confronting high unemployment, the growth of part-time work may reduce the number of jobseekers or, at

Originally published as a "perspective" in *International Labour Review*, Vol. 136 (1997), No. 4.

* French language editor of the *International Labour Review*.

least, the number of people registered as such. In other words, it can lower politically-sensitive unemployment rates without requiring an increase in the total number of hours worked.

Of course, part-time work also has its drawbacks. Part-time workers are very often at a disadvantage in comparison with colleagues who do equivalent work full time. Typically, their hourly wages are lower; they are ineligible for certain social benefits; and their career prospects are more limited. Besides, unless working part time is voluntary, it may leave them only marginally better off than if they were unemployed. For employers, in addition to organizational difficulties, there are some fixed costs per worker — e.g. recruitment, training or social security contributions subject to wage ceilings — which may increase overall labour costs if the proportion of work done by part-timers is increased. Involuntary part-time work (by people who would prefer to be working full time) amounts to underemployment in macroeconomic and macrosocial terms. Beyond a certain threshold, it can weaken demand, with possible negative effects on growth and therefore on employment.

Many governments have adopted measures to facilitate part-time employment, even encouraging employers to hire part-timers in countries where unemployment is high. Such measures may target discrimination faced by part-time workers and reduce the fixed costs associated with part-time employment, in some cases even to the point of making it more attractive to employers than full-time work. But where these policies fall down is in generalizing from measures that help individual workers and employers to a national employment policy to increase the number of part-time jobs as a solution to unemployment; in a sense, this just amounts to a redistribution of work.

At the international level, two developments reflect the greater attention paid recently to the increase in part-time employment and the difficulties associated with it. The first was the adoption by the International Labour Conference in 1994 of the Part-Time Work Convention (No. 175) and Recommendation (No. 182). The second was the signing in 1997 of a framework agreement on the matter between the social partners of the European Union (EU), namely, the European Trade Union Confederation (ETUC), the Union of Industrial and Employers' Confederations of Europe (UNICE) and the European Centre of Enterprises with Public Participation (CEEP). This agreement was upgraded into a directive following its adoption by the EU Council of Ministers, in line with the provisions of the social protocol annexed to the Maastricht Treaty.

The purpose of the following pages is to present some of the benefits and drawbacks of part-time work and describe measures taken to make the most of the former and to counteract the latter, taking care to distinguish the individual and national levels. Micro-level considerations include the various forms of discrimination to which part-time workers are liable, the legal protection available to them and the role that part-time work can play in the labour force participation of women, young people and older workers — beneficial or a trap. The discussion of national policies covers trends in part-time employment and their main determinants; the employment consequences of measures to encourage part-time work; and the issue of reducing labour supply or increasing demand. But before taking up these two levels of consideration — in the second and third sections, respectively — it is first necessary to address the initial difficulty encountered in any discussion of part-time work: to define it. So the first section below discusses definitions and methodology, the difficulties involved in making international comparisons, and the relationship between part-time work and underemployment.

DEFINITION AND METHODOLOGY

Legal definitions, statistical definitions

Convention No. 175 offers the following definition: "the term 'part-time worker' means an employed person whose normal hours of work are less than those of comparable full-time workers". The reason that the concept of a "comparable" worker is mentioned is that "[t]he number of hours per week or per month that are regarded as being normal for full-time employees vary considerably according to the profession or activity concerned" (ILO, 1992, p. 5). For example, the number of hours spent by a teacher in the classroom, disregarding hours spent in preparation, fall well short of the number of hours considered normal for a manufacturing worker. As for hours of work, Convention No. 175 states that these may be calculated weekly or on average over a given period of employment. The definition contained in the European Framework Agreement is very similar to that of the Convention: "The term 'part-time worker' refers to an employee whose normal hours of work, calculated on a weekly basis or on average over a period of employment of up to one year, are less than the normal hours of work of a comparable full-time worker" (European Communities, 1998, p. 13). But these are legal definitions that serve to identify a particular category of workers enjoying certain rights — particularly the right not to be discriminated against in relation to workers in other categories — and/or to determine whether a given worker or group of workers is covered by the legislation governing part-time work. While such definitions may be useful at the individual level, they are not helpful as a basis for measuring the economy-wide incidence of part-time work.

Statisticians have three possible ways of establishing whether a household survey respondent is a part-time worker: they can rely on the respondent's judgement and ask directly whether he or she works part time; they can ask how many hours a week the person works, setting a threshold — e.g. 30 hours — below which the work is classified as part time; or they can combine the first two. The results achieved by the first method are likely to come close to those that would be obtained by using the legal definition of part-time work, but they may be affected by the subjective perceptions of respondents (especially where one person responds for all members of the household). Besides, this method might not work in the absence of an established standard for "normal" hours of work. The second method takes no account of the differences between occupations or activities; a full-time teacher with 28 hours of classroom work will fall into the part-time category. Combining the two methods allows corrections to be made.

In addition, there are several possible definitions of "hours of work", as "normal", "actual" or "usual" (see box 1).

Difficulty of international comparison

The situation becomes far more complicated when one seeks to compare the incidence of part-time work internationally. The phrase, "whose normal hours of work are less than those of comparable full-time workers", which appears in the ILO Convention, is interpreted differently, according to each country's national law. Thus in France a person working up to four-fifths of normal hours of work is considered part time, whereas in Spain a part-time worker is one who works up to two-thirds of the hours specified by collective agreement or of the hours normally worked in the enterprise. In Ireland and the United Kingdom, meanwhile, a person has to work less than 30 hours a week to be considered part time (van Bastelaer, Lemaître and Marianna, 1997, p. 7).

The same applies to statistical definitions. Some countries draw the line between part-time and full-time work by reference to usual weekly hours of work: 30 hours in Finland, Canada and New Zealand, 35 in Australia, Austria, Iceland, Japan, Sweden and the United States, 36 in Hungary and Turkey, 37 in Norway. Eurostat publishes data on 14 European Union countries (excluding Sweden) and on Iceland on the basis of self-assessment by the people concerned rather than a threshold. Lastly, some countries, including Germany, Spain, the Netherlands and the United Kingdom, combine the two methods. In Spain, for example, people who say they are part time but usually work more than 35 hours a week are counted as full time; conversely, those who say they are full time but work less than 30 hours are classified as part time (van Bastelaer, Lemaître and Marianna, 1997, p. 7). These national variations in definition naturally have an effect on the measured incidence of part-time work. For instance, if Canada's 30-hour threshold were applied in Sweden, the proportion of part-time to total employment would drop from 27 to 18 per cent, which is in fact the proportion currently obtaining in Canada. In Italy, half of those working less than 30 hours a week claim to work full

Box 1. Current international statistical standards on working time

Normal hours of work

(1) Normal hours of work are the hours of work fixed by or in pursuance of laws or regulations, collective agreements or arbitral awards.

(2) Where not fixed by or in pursuance of laws or regulations, collective agreements or arbitral awards, normal hours of work should be taken as meaning the number of hours per day or week in excess of which any time worked is remunerated at overtime rates or forms an exception to the rules or custom of the establishment to the classes of workers concerned.

Hours actually worked

(1) Statistics on hours actually worked should include —

    (a) hours actually worked during normal periods of work;

    (b) time worked in addition to hours worked during normal periods of work, and generally paid at higher than normal rates (overtime);

    (c) time spent at the place of work on work such as preparation of the workplace, repairs and maintenance, preparation and cleaning of tools and the preparation of receipts, time sheets and reports;

    (d) time spent at the place of work waiting or standing by for such reasons as a temporary lack of work, breakdown of machinery, or accidents, or time spent at the place of work during which no work is done but for which payment is made under a guaranteed employment contract;

    (e) time corresponding to short rest periods at the workplace, including tea and coffee breaks.

(2) Statistics on hours actually worked should exclude —

    (a) hours paid for but not worked, such as paid annual leave, paid public holidays and paid sick leave;

    (b) meal breaks;

    (c) time spent on travel from home to work and vice versa.

Usual hours of work

The concept of usual hours of work differs from that of hours actually worked, in that usual hours of work refers to a typical period rather than to a specified reference period, as in the case of hours actually worked. Usual hours of work per week or per day for a given activity may be defined as the hours worked during a typical week or day in that activity. The concept of usual hours of work applies both to persons at work and to persons temporarily absent from work.

Of the above definitions the first two appear in current international statistical standards on hours of work, as determined by the Resolution concerning statistics of hours of work adopted by the tenth International Conference of Labour Statisticians in 1962 (see ILO, 1997a, p. 46). The third, less homogeneous because it depends on the reference period chosen, is from Hussmanns, Mehran and Verma (1990). This definition is widely used for household surveys.

time, the other half claiming to work part time. If a threshold were applied, the proportion of part-time work would rise from 6 to 11 per cent (ibid., p. 6). Lastly, the 35-hour threshold applied in many countries could turn out to be equal to France's full-time working week if the bill introduced by the present Government becomes law.

The study for the OECD by van Bastelaer, Lemaître and Marianna on the definition of part-time work for the purpose of international comparison presents other notable findings:

(a) In countries where part-time work (national definitions) is common, [many] jobs of more than 30 usual hours per week are classified as part-time . . . These countries tend to use a definition based on a 35 usual hours threshold.

(b) In countries where part-time work (national definitions) is relatively less common, the incidence of jobs of less than 35 usual hours per week that are classified as full-time is high. Part-time jobs are generally identified on the basis of self-assessment in these countries.

(c) There is less variability among countries in the incidence of part-time work when the latter is defined by a threshold (whether 30 or 35 usual hours) than when national definitions are used. However, the application of a uniform threshold across countries does not substantially change the relative position of countries regarding the frequency of part-time work (1997, p. 12).

Although the study suggests adopting a 30-hour threshold for defining part-time work, the rest of this chapter uses data based on national definitions, which offer longer time series. While this limits direct international comparison, it enables an examination of national trends — which can be compared (see table 1).

Part-time work and underemployment

There is a fundamental distinction to be made between voluntary and involuntary part-time employment: whether people deliberately choose to work part time or accept reduced hours of work simply because they cannot find full-time employment. In the latter case, part-time work becomes a form of underemployment. Labour statisticians are keen to isolate this phenomenon, to define it as accurately as possible and to measure it with all possible precision, because this knowledge is indispensable for the formulation of effective employment policies. The issue is due to be examined by the sixteenth International Conference of Labour Statisticians in October 1998; the international statistical standards currently in force are those adopted at their thirteenth Conference (ILO, 1988, pp. 52-53).

There are two forms of underemployment: invisible and visible. Invisible underemployment "is primarily an analytical concept reflecting a misallocation of labour resources or a fundamental imbalance as between

Table 1. Proportion of part-time to total employment (according to national definitions)

Country	1973	1979	1983	1984	1985	1990	1992	1993	1994	1995	1996
Australia	11.9	15.9	17.5	17.7	18.1	21.3	24.5	23.9	24.4	24.8	25.0
Austria	6.4	7.6	8.4	—	—	8.9	9.0	10.1	12.1	13.9	14.9
Belgium	3.8	6.0	8.0	—	—	10.9	12.4	12.8	12.8	13.6	14.0
Canada	9.7	12.5	16.8	15.3	15.5	17.0	16.7	17.2	18.8	18.6	18.9
Czech Republic	—	—	—	—	—	—	—	—	6.4	6.2	5.9
Denmark	—	22.7	23.3	—	—	23.3	22.5	23.3	21.2	21.6	21.5
Finland	—	6.7	7.7	8.3	8.3	7.2	7.9	8.6	8.6	8.2	8.0
France	5.9	8.1	9.6	11.5	11.5	11.9	12.5	13.7	14.9	15.6	16.0
Germany	10.1	11.4	12.6	11.9	12.4	15.2	14.4	15.1	15.8	16.3	—
Greece	—	—	6.5	—	—	4.1	4.8	4.3	4.8	4.8	—
Hungary	—	—	—	—	—	—	—	—	—	4.9	4.9
Iceland[1]	—	—	—	—	—	26.8	27.8	27.3	27.7	28.3	27.9
Ireland	—	5.1	6.7	—	—	8.1	9.1	10.8	11.3	12.1	11.6
Italy	6.4	5.3	4.6	5.0	4.9	4.9	5.8	5.4	6.2	6.4	6.6
Japan	13.9	15.4	15.8	16.5	16.7	18.8	20.5	21.1	21.0	19.8	21.4
Luxembourg	5.8	5.8	6.8	—	—	6.9	6.9	7.3	8.0	7.9	7.6
Mexico[1]	—	—	—	—	—	24.2	24.0	24.9	25.3	25.3	23.8
Netherlands	—	16.6	21.0	—	—	31.6	32.5	33.4	36.4	37.4	36.5
New Zealand	11.2	13.9	15.3	—	—	20.0	21.6	21.2	21.6	21.5	22.4
Norway	23.0	27.3	29.6	—	—	26.3	26.9	27.1	26.4	26.5	26.5
Poland	—	—	—	—	—	—	11.0	—	10.6	10.6	10.6
Portugal	—	—	—	—	—	5.9	—	—	8.0	7.5	8.7
Spain	—	—	—	—	—	4.9	5.8	6.6	6.9	7.5	8.0
Sweden	—	23.6	24.8	24.6	24.0	23.3	24.3	24.9	24.9	24.3	23.6
Switzerland[1]	—	—	—	—	—	25.4	27.8	28.1	27.4	27.3	27.4
Turkey	—	—	—	—	—	20.6	19.3	24.8	23.6	20.3	23.9
United Kingdom	16.0	16.4	18.9	20.0	20.4	21.3	22.8	23.3	23.8	24.0	22.1
United States	15.6	16.4	18.4	17.6	17.4	16.9	17.5	17.5	18.9	18.6	18.3

— Nil or negligible.

[1] 1991 instead of 1990.

Sources: CES, 1997, pp. 49-50; OECD, 1997, table E, p. 177.

labour and other factors of production. Characteristic symptoms might be low income, underutilization of skill, low productivity" (ibid., p. 53, para. 15 (2)). Visible underemployment is directly linked with involuntary part-time employment and affects people "involuntarily working less than the normal duration of work determined for the activity, who [are] seeking or available for additional work" (ibid., p. 53, para. 18 (1)). It also includes those partially unemployed — that is, those affected by a temporary, collective reduction in their normal hours of work for economic, technical or structural reasons — who are excluded from the definition of part-time worker in Convention No. 175. These various concepts can be sketched as follows:

◀◀ .... Part-time work .... ▶▶

Voluntary	Involuntary	Partial unemployment	Invisible underemployment

◀◀ .... Visible underemployment .... ▶▶

◀◀ .... Underemployment .... ▶▶

A few observations are in order here. First, visible and invisible underemployment can overlap. When the labour market is depressed, skilled workers may accept not only unskilled but also part-time jobs. Secondly, the very notion of voluntary vs. involuntary part-time work is open to question: "Persons who report that they worked less than normal because of family responsibilities may have opted for these activities because they were unable to find more work in the first place. They may also be persons who although originally working short hours for personal reasons now desire more working hours but continue to declare the original (voluntary) reason for working short hours. Conversely, persons may report economic reasons for working short hours even if at present they are not willing to work additional hours" (ILO, 1997a, p. 13, para. 36). It should be added that some people may work part time for family reasons and be unavailable for more work and are therefore classed as "voluntary" whereas if childcare were available, for example, they would prefer to work more. All these issues are being actively discussed by labour statisticians, who seek to define these various phenomena with maximum precision (see ILO, 1997a and 1997b). And their interest is not only statistical; knowing whether part-time work is voluntary or, rather, represents underemployment has an effect on appropriate economic and social policy.

INDIVIDUAL ASPECTS OF PART-TIME WORK

"Individual aspects" refers here to everything relating to the benefits and drawbacks of part-time work for workers or employers. First one should consider the drawbacks — even discrimination — that may be suffered by a person who chooses to work shorter hours. Secondly, one should establish whether part-time work facilitates access to the labour market or whether it traps the worker in underemployment.

Legal protection of part-time workers against discrimination

In preparation for the International Labour Conference that adopted the Part-Time Work Convention and Recommendation, the ILO brought out a preliminary report that examines the conditions of employment of part-time workers (ILO, 1992, pp. 31-53).[1] The report also contained a questionnaire sent to member countries; their replies appeared in a later report (ILO, 1994). Together, the two documents provide an overview of part-time work and related legislation worldwide.

Part-time workers are on average paid lower hourly rates than full-time workers. Such differentiation can sometimes be observed even for equivalent work performed within the same establishment, but this is not generally the case. In fact, the differential becomes more apparent when one considers groups of workers. This is due to a number of factors: part-time workers "tend to work in sectors, and indeed in branches of sectors where the hourly rates of pay are low in comparison with the national average. They also tend to be employed in low-graded jobs and to be excluded from supervisory posts" (ILO, 1992, p. 34). Part-timers are more likely to be excluded from supplementary payments such as bonuses, holiday and sickness pay, training allowances, seniority payments, etc. A very important related question is that of the minimum number of hours of work required to qualify for certain entitlements, as in the case of redundancy pay or other benefits. Legislation already exists in this respect in some countries (see ILO, 1992, pp. 31-33), and judicial decisions have been reached on these questions; an earlier "perspective" focused on such judicial decisions taken in Europe (*International Labour Review*, 1994).[2]

The disparity in remuneration can also be attributed to the growing proportion of women and 15-25-year-olds in part-time employment, the former as a result of discriminatory practices, and the latter because of their recent arrival on the labour market. In the case of women, this can also be seen as a two-way process of cause and effect: they are paid less on average because greater numbers of them are in part-time work. Recalling that the Equal Remuneration Convention (No. 100), 1951, had been ratified by 111 member States by January 1992, the ILO pointed out in that year that: "Because of the prevalence of women in part-time employment the issue of equal pay for work of equal value is an important factor in relation to the pay and allowances of part-time workers" (ILO, 1992, p. 35).

Part-time workers are also at a disadvantage on account of their hours of work. This may well be obvious, but premium payments for overtime are often not made until a part-time employee has worked the equivalent of normal full-time hours. Overtime can thus be used as a means of achieving flexibility by maintaining part-time workers on relatively short basic hours and requesting them to work substantial overtime during peak periods. Under some laws or collective agreements, overtime rates apply once the normal part-time working hours are exceeded, though their provisions generally specify a maximum number of overtime hours so as to avoid too great a distortion between part-time and full-time labour costs.

Certain part-timers work "on call", without any guaranteed minimum weekly or monthly number of hours (the "zero hours" system) and are thus in a particularly vulnerable situation. Apart from the fact that they cannot rely on a minimum income, they are often excluded from certain rights and benefits, entitlement to which is subject to a minimum number of hours worked, calculated on a weekly, monthly or other basis. Here, too, some countries have adopted legislative provisions to give such workers a minimum of security in respect of the hours they work (see ILO, 1992, pp. 36-37).

Thus the ILO report notes that part-time workers are frequently at a disadvantage, individually or as a group, in respect of direct or indirect remuneration, social security benefits, training (including training in occupational health and safety), and participation in trade union activity or staff representation. These disadvantages are compounded by a type of discrimination, referred to as invisible (as it is scarcely quantifiable), which affects their advancement and promotion prospects. Here again, there is a striking similarity to the situation of working women generally, and this is no coincidence. Furthermore, deterioration in the employment conditions of part-time workers can lead, through a "levelling-down" process, to a deterioration in the situation of their full-time fellow workers. Convention No. 175 therefore establishes minimum standards for part-time employment, based on the two principles of proportionality and non-discrimination (see box 2). Since this is a very recent Convention, few ratification procedures have yet been completed, though the number of ratifications was sufficient for it to come into effect on 28 February 1998.

Part-time work: Not all that it seems

One of the supposed virtues of part-time work is that it facilitates the gradual entry of young persons into the labour market and enables older workers gradually to withdraw from wage employment. Another is that it makes it easier to reconcile family responsibilities with employment, with the added advantage of maintaining a link with working life and thus avoiding a total break — as in the case of parental leave — which can create problems as regards subsequent skills upgrading. In fact, it is within these three worker categories — youth, older workers and those with family responsibilities — that part-time work is most prevalent. According to a report of the European Commission on employment in Europe: "Over the Union as a whole, only around 3% of men of prime working age [24-49] who were employed were in part-time jobs in 1995. This contrasts with figures of 25% for young men aged 15 to 19 and 40% for the over 65s" (European Commission, 1996, p. 55). France's Economic

---

Box 2. Extract from the Convention concerning part-time work (No. 175)

Article 4

Measures shall be taken to ensure that part-time workers receive the same protection as that accorded to comparable full-time workers in respect of:
(a) the right to organize, the right to bargain collectively and the right to act as workers' representatives;
(b) occupational safety and health;
(c) discrimination in employment and occupation.

Article 5

Measures appropriate to national law and practice shall be taken to ensure that part-time workers do not, solely because they work part time, receive a basic wage which, calculated proportionately on a hourly, performance-related, or piece-rate basis, is lower than the basic wage of comparable full-time workers, calculated according to the same method.

Article 6

Statutory social security schemes which are based on occupational activity shall be adapted so that part-time workers enjoy conditions equivalent to those of comparable full-time workers; these conditions may be determined in proportion to hours of work, contributions or earnings, or through other methods consistent with national law and practice.

Article 7

Measures shall be taken to ensure that part-time workers receive conditions equivalent to those of comparable full-time workers in the fields of:
(a) maternity protection;
(b) termination of employment;
(c) paid annual leave and paid public holidays; and
(d) sick leave,

it being understood that pecuniary entitlements may be determined in proportion to hours of work or earnings.

---

and Social Council (CES) arrives at similar figures (see table 2), reporting that: "Contrary to widespread belief, the highest levels of part-time employment are not registered among women in the 25-49 age group, but among younger women and those over the age of 60. Part-time work, therefore, is not solely a stratagem for reconciling work or occupation with family responsibilities, but often corresponds to a period of gradual induction into or withdrawal from economic activity" (CES, 1997, p. 79). The CES report also states that the opposite situation obtained in the early 1980s, but that over the past 15 years part-time work has become more prevalent among young women "with the development of subsidized training courses and work experience contracts, which are generally offered on a part-time basis" (ibid., p. 79). Another hypothesis,

Table 2. Part-time employment in France according to age (percentage of workers in each age group), 1995

Age group	Men	Women
15-24	14.7	38.0
25-39	4.2	27.9
40-49	6.5	27.4
50-59	4.9	29.2
60 and over	20.7	38.6
Total	5.0	28.9

Source: CES, 1997, p. 79.

in no respect contradictory to that proposed by the CES, may help to explain this phenomenon: the improved labour market position of relatively qualified women — and especially their higher remuneration — has encouraged increasing numbers of them to work full time during their prime active years provided they can afford childcare and/or childcare facilities are available.

As regards the proportion of part-time work in older age groups, various early retirement schemes have been developed — often in response to high unemployment or to avoid redundancies during restructuring — with financial assistance from government or unemployment insurance funds. At enterprise level, however, such arrangements can have the disadvantage of causing an abrupt loss of skills and experience. For this reason, a number of countries — e.g. Belgium, France, Portugal and Spain — are promoting gradual retirement by offering older workers part-time work while encouraging employers to hire young persons, also on a part-time basis, so that the experienced workers can pass on their skills to the beginners.[3]

From the worker's point of view, part-time employment can fulfil two main functions: that of a "bridge" between employment and inactivity, and that of reconciling paid work and family responsibilities. This second function is evidenced by the fact that the vast majority of part-time workers are women (see table 3), who still assume the greater portion of family responsibilities — though this is still changing. There are, of course, other factors behind the disproportionate numbers of women in part-time work: inequalities in qualifications and pay, which means that in a married couple, the less well paid of the two is the one likely to work part time, or the fact that part-time employment is particularly widespread in the services sector, where women are relatively more numerous compared to manufacturing. The question that arises, therefore, is whether part-time work is not a trap, especially for women.

Table 3. Proportion of women in part-time employment, various years

Country	1973	1979	1983	1990	1992	1993	1994	1995	1996
Australia	79.4	78.7	78.0	78.1	75.0	75.3	74.2	74.4	73.4
Austria	85.8	87.8	88.4	89.7	89.6	89.7	85.3	83.8	84.2
Belgium	82.4	88.9	84.0	88.6	89.7	89.3	88.1	87.5	87.4
Canada	68.4	72.1	69.8	70.1	69.7	68.9	68.8	68.8	69.1
Czech Republic	—	—	—	—	—	—	70.0	73.3	71.9
Denmark	—	86.9	84.7	75.7	75.8	74.9	74.4	73.3	72.2
Finland	—	74.7	70.1	67.4	64.3	63.1	63.2	64.7	64.3
France	82.3	82.1	84.3	83.8	83.7	83.3	82.7	82.0	81.7
Germany	89.0	91.6	91.9	89.7	89.3	88.6	88.1	87.4	—
Greece	—	—	61.2	64.9	61.3	61.6	58.9	62.7	—
Hungary	—	—	—	—	—	—	—	70.5	72.3
Iceland[1]	—	—	—	82.1	82.1	80.4	79.3	78.4	78.8
Ireland	—	71.2	71.6	72.2	72.5	71.7	71.5	72.0	73.3
Italy	58.3	61.4	64.8	67.3	68.8	70.5	71.1	70.6	69.4
Japan	70.0	70.1	72.9	70.7	69.3	67.7	67.5	70.1	68.0
Luxembourg	87.5	87.5	86.7	82.2	91.2	—	89.5	91.0	88.0
Mexico[1]	—	—	—	45.6	46.3	46.1	47.8	50.0	51.9
Netherlands	—	76.4	78.4	70.8	75.2	75.7	73.8	73.6	73.8
New Zealand	72.3	77.7	79.8	76.4	73.3	74.2	75.0	74.0	74.3
Norway	76.4	77.0	77.2	81.6	80.1	80.5	80.8	80.5	79.3
Poland	—	—	—	53.6	—	—	56.6	56.9	57.2
Portugal	—	80.4	—	66.5	68.2	66.3	67.1	69.1	67.2
Spain	—	—	—	78.0	77.0	75.6	74.9	76.3	74.5
Sweden	—	87.5	86.6	83.5	82.3	81.3	80.1	80.1	79.5
Switzerland[1]	—	—	—	82.3	83.1	82.5	82.8	82.9	82.8
Turkey	—	—	—	54.4	59.3	50.2	51.7	50.9	48.3
United Kingdom	90.9	92.8	89.6	86.2	84.9	84.5	83.6	82.3	86.0
United States	66.0	68.0	66.8	67.2	66.4	66.2	67.3	68.0	67.9

— Nil or negligible.

[1] 1991 instead of 1990.

Sources: CES, 1997, pp. 52-53; OECD, 1997, table E, p. 177.

One way of tackling this question would be via the theory of labour market segmentation into primary markets (i.e. stable, well paid jobs with possibilities of advancement) and secondary markets (precarious, poorly paid jobs with no prospects of promotion), and to examine whether part-time jobs predominate in the secondary markets. One study has done so in the United Kingdom (Tam, 1997). Like the above-mentioned ILO report (1992), this study demonstrates that part-time jobs are worse than full-time jobs in several respects, including skill levels, wage rates, promotion prospects and relations with management. However, the argument that part-time jobs are secondary jobs is not borne out in the light of three criteria: job security, degree of supervision and irregularity of working hours. Irregular hours of course exist but do not appear to be the general rule. As for job security, there seems to be no appreciable difference between part-timers and full-timers in respect of duration of contract or protection against dismissal. However, the boundary between the two markets divides the part-time working population, in as much as the shorter the hours worked, the worse off the part-timer will be. Especially in the case of women, part-time work thus appears to be a factor that aggravates initial handicaps, such as low skill levels, and thereby weakens the worker's position on the labour market (Tam, 1997, pp. 240-243). The study concludes that:

> Part-time work experience carries cumulative disadvantages and has a negative effect on employment prospects.
> Moreover, because of the low-skill nature of part-time work, it has a channelling effect on women's lifetime employment prospects. This study shows that while part-time work is not associated with job insecurity and unemployment, it constitutes a trap which lowers women's lifetime employment prospects and earnings (Tam, 1997, p. 243).

Thus, where part-time work is accompanied by adequate legal protection — in accordance with the principles of proportionality and non-discrimination — and provided it is freely chosen by workers who are in a relatively strong position on the labour market, it can be an excellent means of dividing one's time between economic activity, family responsibilities and other pursuits. However, where it is imposed on or endured by workers in secondary jobs, it merely increases their difficulties and compromises their employment prospects. This being the case, the next question that needs to be examined is that of the effects of growth in part-time employment and, in particular, the effects of measures designed to promote it as a means of combating unemployment.

PART-TIME WORK AND THE JOB MARKET

As pointed out above, variations in definitions call for great caution when making international comparisons concerning part-time work. However, comparisons over time in one country do not present the same problem. There has been a notable increase in the proportion of part-time jobs in the industrialized countries over the past 20 years (see table 1). This seems to have coincided with the rise in women's labour market participation (see figures 1 and 2) and growth in service sector employment (ILO, 1992, p. 1).

Moreover, many of these countries are suffering from very high levels of unemployment. The promotion of part-time work was often seen as a means of reducing unemployment, as a form of "work-sharing" or redistribution of employment. It is indeed one of the policy options for reducing labour supply, as opposed to those aimed at increasing demand by boosting economic growth or its employment intensity. Yet the effectiveness of promoting part-time work as a means of combating unemployment depends on a number of factors: whether the causes of unemployment are structural or cyclical, the prospects for long-term growth in part-time employment, and the consequences of such growth.

The development of part-time work

The increase in the proportion of part-time employment can be expected to continue, because its main driving forces — service sector expansion, women's increased labour market participation, and employers' desire for flexibility — look set to persist. In fact, the service sector is proving to be the industrialized countries' main source of new jobs. As for women's participation rates, estimates and projections made by the ILO Bureau of Statistics indicate that they should continue to rise at least until 2010 (ILO, 1997c and 1986).

On closer examination of the available data, however, the development of part-time work does not seem to have followed a consistent pattern. Thus, while the OECD data for 1980 showed some relationship between part-time work and women's labour force participation (figure 1), the situation was less clear by 1995 (figure 2). Some of the former communist countries (Hungary, the Czech Republic and Poland) combine a high rate of female participation with a low incidence of part-time work — possibly a reflection of the employment structure under the former system coupled with the slow development of the services sector. Finland and the Netherlands were already exceptions in 1980, with two contrary configurations: a high level of female participation and little part-time work in Finland and the reverse in the Netherlands. In Mexico, where female participation rates are low, part-time work could be considered akin to underemployment. In other countries, while the relationship may be more apparent, it remains strongly subject to national income levels, cultural factors such as religion or attitudes towards women's role in society and, of course, regulatory frameworks. The above-mentioned CES study classified countries according to their ratios of part-time to total employment in 1993: under 10 per cent were Greece, Italy, Spain, Portugal, Luxemburg, Finland and Austria; between 10 and 20 per cent were the United States, Canada, Germany, France and Belgium; and over 20 per cent were Japan, the United Kingdom, Denmark, Australia, Sweden, Norway and the Netherlands. It also observed the following developments over the past two decades:

- the increase has occurred everywhere except in Greece;

- in the countries of the first group, especially in southern Europe, the growth of part-time work has been slow in countries where its proportion was low to start with;

- regarding the countries of the second group, growth has been more rapid in France and Belgium than in Canada and the United States where it levelled off between 1983 and 1992;

229

Figure 1. Part-time work and women's labour force participation, 1980 (Countries are classified in ascending order of rate of part-time employment)

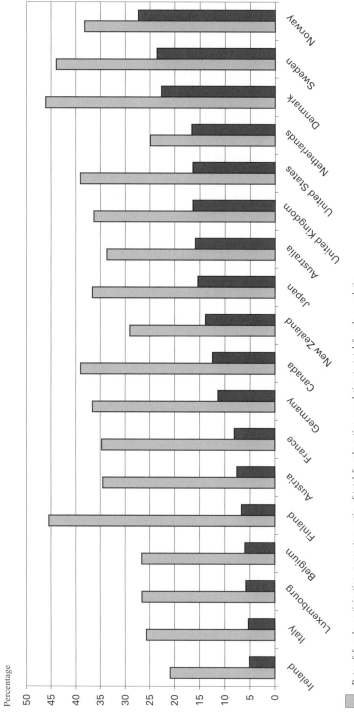

Percentage

☐ Rate of female participation, percentage ratio of total female active population to total female population.

■ Part-time employment as percentage of total employment, according to national definitions.

Sources: CES, 1997, pp. 49-50; OECD, 1997, table E, p. 177; ILO, 1997c, table 1, pp. 1-12.

Figure 2. Part-time work and women's labour force participation, 1995 (Countries are classified in ascending order of rate of part-time employment)

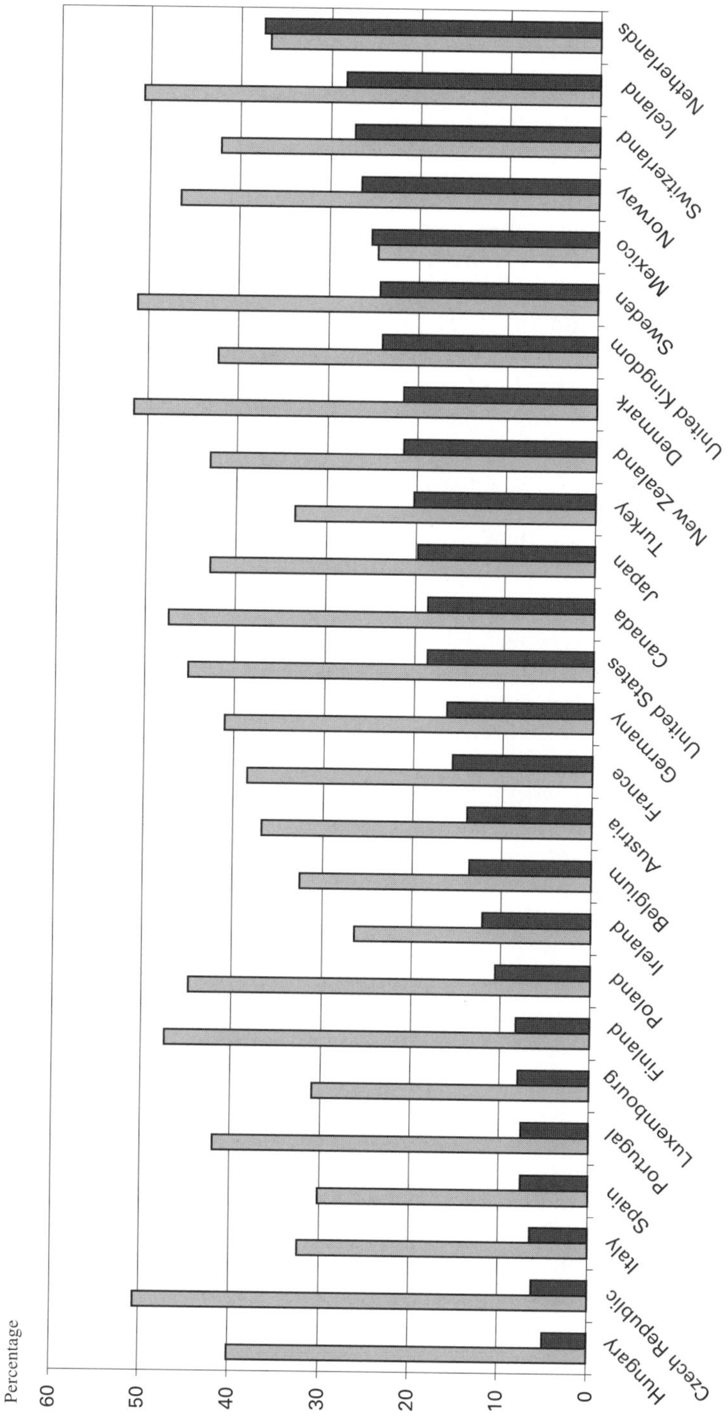

Percentage

Hungary
Czech Republic
Italy
Spain
Portugal
Luxembourg
Finland
Poland
Ireland
Belgium
Austria
France
Germany
United States
Canada
Japan
Turkey
New Zealand
Denmark
United Kingdom
Sweden
Mexico
Norway
Switzerland
Iceland
Netherlands

☐ Rate of female participation, percentage ratio of total female active population to total female population.

■ Part-time employment as percentage of total employment, according to national definitions.

Sources: CES, 1997, OECD, table E, p. 177; ILO, 1997c, table 1, pp. 1-12.

- in the third group of countries, the same levelling off occurred and, above all, "countries with a high proportion of part-time workers in relation to the total number of employed (between 17 and 25 per cent) seem to have settled at a level of about 25 per cent" (CES, 1997, pp. 49-51).

However, the proportion of women in part-time employment has tended to stabilize (see table 3 and CES, 1997, pp. 52-56).

Another finding is that "part-time jobs of more than 30 usual hours [are] common precisely in those countries where the incidence of part-time jobs is high, and full-time jobs of less than 35 hours common in countries where part-time work is rare" (van Bastelaer, Lemaître and Marianna, 1997, p. 10). In other words, it would appear (logically) that demand for part-time work is lower where normal working hours are relatively short; and part-time working hours remain relatively long where it is more usual, implying convergence between the reduction of normal working hours and part-time work.

In this connection the question arises of a possible relationship between the incidence of part-time work and trade union strength. It could indeed be hypothesized that strong unions are in a position to negotiate a reduction of normal working hours, and could thus reduce demand for part-time work. However, figure 3, which gives levels of part-time work and union density in 1995, shows no obvious relation between the two. In fact, trade union strength can operate in opposite directions. On the one hand, it can discourage part-time work if unions manage to obtain a reduction in normal working hours or the establishment of satisfactory childcare facilities for working parents, or if — as has long been the case in a number of countries — unions quite simply oppose this form of employment, which they tend to consider precarious. On the other hand, action by trade unions can encourage part-time work if they manage to obtain guarantees on wages or social benefits for part-time workers. This is probably the case in the Scandinavian countries, where both union density and part-time employment levels are high.

These observations imply that there are limits to the apparently linear, perhaps even inexorable, progression of part-time work as countries become more affluent, as women's labour force participation increases and as the service sector expands. Indeed, in the countries where it is most widespread, part-time work seems vulnerable to cyclical downturns (1983-92) and has tended to stabilize at a ceiling of about 25 per cent (except in the Netherlands). Besides, while part of the overall growth in part-time employment can be attributed to workers' preference for such work, some of it is the result of involuntary part-time work, i.e. underemployment.

Figure 3. Part-time work and union density, 1995 (Countries are classified in ascending order of rate of part-time employment)

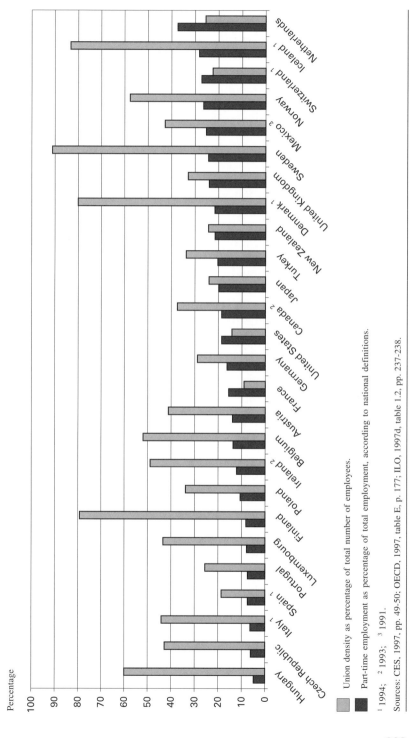

Percentage

Union density as percentage of total number of employees.

Part-time employment as percentage of total employment, according to national definitions.

[1] 1994; [2] 1993; [3] 1991.

Sources: CES, 1997, pp. 49-50; OECD, 1997, table E, p. 177; ILO, 1997d, table 1.2, pp. 237-238.

Facilitating part-time work or promoting underemployment?

The ILO report on part-time work lists the various measures introduced by member States to facilitate or encourage part-time work (see ILO, 1992). From the employers' point of view, part-time work long presented more drawbacks than advantages: it increases costs — e.g. fixed recruitment and training costs per employee and social security contributions subject to wage ceilings — and complicates work organization, e.g. coordination among part-time employees. But, economic change and the need for greater flexibility have also conferred advantages on part-time work when it comes to coping with extra workloads not requiring full-time workers or adjusting working and opening hours in the retail trade, for example. From the workers' point of view, the disadvantages of part-time employment have already been mentioned. Promotional measures therefore seek to overcome its disadvantages from both points of view by attenuating administrative barriers and targeting income tax issues, social security systems, unemployment benefits, job-sharing, career prospects and vocational training, as well as specific categories of workers, e.g. those with family responsibilities or older workers (for a detailed review, see ILO, 1992, pp. 54-71).

One set of promotional measures directly addresses the cost of part-time work, either generally or as a means of providing labour market access to new entrants (ILO, 1992, pp. 60-61). In general, such measures involve subsidizing part-time employment through tax relief or reduced social security contributions, as has been done in Germany, Belgium, France and the United Kingdom. The problem, however, is that such measures can overcompensate for the extra costs of part-time work to the point where it becomes more attractive for employers to recruit part-timers rather than full-time employees — especially since data from a number of countries suggest that the hourly productivity of part-time workers is often higher. In the United States, for example, the productivity of a half-time employee has been estimated at 64 per cent of that of a full-time worker. The figures for those working 60 and 70 per cent of normal working hours are 77 and 87 per cent, respectively (CES, 1997, p. 93). The explanations offered are that part-time employees work more intensively, with less absenteeism and job tedium, and that "part-time workers, especially when they formerly worked full time, may be expected to carry out a set of activities that normally would be carried out by a full-time worker" (ILO, 1992, p. 40).

Thus, as a result of promotional measures and higher productivity, there is a danger that involuntary part-time work will increase in countries where part-time employment is being encouraged as a means of combating unemployment. According to the CES report, this is what appears to have happened in France: "The accelerating growth of part-time employment during the first half of the 1990s is due, at least in part, to the financial incentives offered to enterprises by the public authorities

Table 4. Involuntary part-time workers as a percentage of the economically active population, 1983 and 1993[1]

Country	1983	1993
Australia	3.9	6.9
Belgium	2.4	3.8
Canada[2]	3.9	5.5
Denmark[3]	3.4	4.8
Finland	2.0	2.9
France	—	4.8
Germany[4]	0.9	1.5
Greece	3.7	3.1
Ireland[5]	2.3	3.3
Italy[6]	2.0	2.3
Japan[4]	2.1	1.9
Mexico	—	5.2
Netherlands[7]	5.7	5.6
New Zealand[8]	2.7	6.3
Portugal[8]	1.8	1.8
Spain[9]	2.0	1.0
Sweden[10, 11]	4.7	6.2
United Kingdom	1.9	3.2
United States	5.7	5.0

— Nil or negligible.

[1] The data refer to persons between the ages of 16 and 64, except in Australia, Finland, Japan, Mexico, New Zealand and Norway, where they concern persons between the ages of 15 and 64. In Canada, the data concern persons over the age of 15. [2] Involuntary part-time work includes only persons who have not found full-time work. [3] 1984 and 1993. [4] 1985 and 1993. [5] 1983 and 1992. [6] 1983 and 1991. [7] 1987 and 1991. [8] 1986 and 1993. [9] 1987 and 1993. [10] 1987 and 1992. [11] Involuntary part-time work includes only those working fewer hours for economic reasons.

Source: OECD, 1995, table 2.18, pp. 76-77.

since the end of 1992" (CES, 1997, p. 45). Indeed, between 1983 and 1992 France saw little change in its part-time employment levels: 1983 marked the beginning of wage restraint, and 1992 the subsidization of part-time work in response to rising unem-ployment, whereupon

> the proportion of part-time employees in the private sector declaring themselves willing to work longer hours — either while remaining part time or by going to full time — increased from 31.4 per cent in 1992 to 38.8 per cent in 1995. The increase was even more striking among men (40.6 to 50.8 per cent) and workers under the age of 25 (44.8 to 54.5 per cent). These figures are related to the increased numbers of subsidized work experience contracts offered to jobseekers and young people, most of them on a part-time basis. In 1995, 76.5 per cent of trainees and beneficiaries of subsidized contracts were working part time (CES, 1997, p. 99).

The OECD, for its part, has studied measures of labour market slack, focusing on discouraged workers and involuntary part-time workers (OECD, 1995). With regard to the latter, it notes that outside Japan and the United States their numbers were relatively stable over the 1980s, "although they did pick up in the recent downturn and only time will tell if they decline in the subsequent recovery" (ibid., p. 43; see also table 4). The OECD study finds no clear correlation between levels of unemployment and the incidence of involuntary part-time employment, but points to a relative correlation (with some exceptions) between part-time work and other indicators of economic recession. These findings suggest there might be some substitution effect as between unemployment and part-time work, partly because of institutional arrangements like subsidized gradual retirement.

As a supply-side policy measure designed to reduce unemployment, the promotion of part-time work thus appears to come up against two constraints. The first is that growth in the proportion of part-time to total employment may be subject to natural limits. The second is the risk of increasing underemployment. While this might well be the lesser of two evils, the underlying macroeconomic assumptions of such a policy must be considered too.

Reducing the labour supply v. increasing demand

Employment policy measures like the reduction of working time or the promotion of job-sharing or part-time work more or less explicitly assume that the volume of work available is now limited by advances in labour-saving technology, hence the theory of jobless growth or even "the end of work" (Rifkin, 1995). Another underlying assumption, albeit implicit, is that work is a homogeneous "commodity" to be shared out among workers. Yet the ILO's report *World Employment 1996/97* shows that the employment intensity of economic growth has not diminished but actually increased (ILO, 1996, p. 21). This would make slow economic growth the primary cause of the problem.

France is pursuing a policy of reducing normal working hours to combat unemployment, which stood at 12.3 per cent in December 1997; and the same is being envisaged in Italy (with 12.1 per cent unemployment in October 1997). France's Observatory of Economic Cycles (OFCE) has conducted a macroeconomic simulation which suggests this policy could create 500,000 jobs over five years, provided that reduced working time is accompanied by wage restraint (OFCE, 1998). Yet it now looks like western Europe's increased unemployment and recession of the early 1990s may have been caused by the steep rise in real interest rates that came with stringent monetary policies and by budgetary and wage restraint — largely associated with the requirements of the European monetary union and employment policies geared to cutting labour costs — all of which inhibited economic growth (see ILO, 1996, p. 82; Fitoussi, 1997a and 1997b). Indeed, any measures that might restrict domestic consumption or curb its incipient recovery of recent months seem likely to go against growth and employment. Involuntary part-time employment may well have just that effect: instead of being an exchange of wage restraint for leisure time as is the case with reduced working hours, it amounts to sharing out a given quantity of employment and income between more workers, thereby depressing their purchasing power with particularly adverse consequences for low-skill/low-income groups.

CONCLUSION

If it is freely chosen and protected by law, part-time employment no doubt offers workers a good way of striking a balance between the time they must spend earning a living and the time they wish to devote to other activities. It also gives employers greater flexibility in adjusting working hours to business requirements while achieving higher productivity. In this respect, the option of part-time employment seems well worth encouraging. Another reason for doing so is that workers — especially women — should not be forced to choose between full-time work and unemployment as the only alternatives on offer. However, those wishing to work full time should not be left facing a choice between unemployment and underemployment either. Policies designed to promote part-time work by lowering its cost below that of full-time employment are likely to have the perverse effect of increasing the proportion of involuntary part-time workers, i.e. underemployment, with adverse consequences both social — especially for women and other workers already at a disadvantage on the labour market — and economic, depressing demand, growth and employment.

Notes

[1] This is, of course, not the only aspect of part-time work covered in the report, which also deals with the definition, extent and characteristics of part-time work, measures to promote it and the position adopted by employers' and workers' organizations and by the ILO itself.

[2] That "perspective" also considered the questions of dismissal following an employee's refusal to change hours of work, of complementary pension schemes, and of overtime rates for part-time workers.

[3] On this subject see Lei Delsen and Geneviève Reday-Mulvey (eds.): *Gradual retirement in the OECD countries*, 1996, Aldershot, Dartmouth Publishing Co. Ltd.

References

Bastelaer, Alois van; Lemaître, Georges; Marianna, Pascal. 1997. *The definition of part-time work for the purpose of international comparisons*. Labour Market and Social Policy Occasional Papers, No. 22. OECD/GD(97)121. Paris, OECD.

CES (Conseil économique et social). 1997. "Avis et rapports du Conseil économique et social: Le travail à temps partiel", in *Journal officiel de la République française* (Paris), No. 1, 20 Feb.

European Commission. 1996. *Employment in Europe, 1996.* COM(96) 485. Luxembourg, Office for Official Publications of the European Communities.

European Communities. 1998. "Council Directive 97/81/EC of 15 December 1997 concerning the Framework Agreement on part-time work concluded by UNICE, CEEP and the ETUC", in *Official Journal of the European Communities* (Luxembourg), Vol. 41, No. L14, 20 Jan., pp. 9-14.

Fitoussi, Jean-Paul. 1997a. "Europe: la fin d'une histoire", in *Le Monde* (Paris), 28 Aug. 1997.

—. 1997b. "Europe: le commencement d'une aventure", in *Le Monde* (Paris), 29 Aug. 1997.

Hussmanns, Ralf; Mehran, Farhad; Verma, Vijay. 1990. *Surveys of economically active population, employment, unemployment and underemployment: An ILO manual on concepts and methods.* Geneva, ILO.

ILO. 1997a. *Underemployment: Concept and measurement.* Report I (MELS/1997/1), Meeting of Experts on Labour Statistics, Geneva, 14-23 Oct. 1997. Geneva.

—. 1997b. *Draft report of the discussion.* MELS/1997/R. 1 (Rev. 1), Meeting of Experts on Labour Statistics, Geneva, 14-23 Oct. 1997. Geneva.

—. 1997c. *Economically active population: 1950-2010. Volume 4: Northern America-Europe-Oceania.* STAT Working Paper No. 96-4. Geneva, ILO Bureau of Statistics.

—. 1997d. *World Labour Report 1997-98: Industrial relations, democracy and social stability.* Geneva.

—. 1996. *World Employment 1996/97: National policies in a global context.* Geneva.

—. 1994. *Part-time work.* Report IV (2 A), International Labour Conference, 80th Session, 1993. Geneva.

—. 1992. *Part-time work.* Report V (1), International Labour Conference, 80th Session, 1993. Geneva.

—. 1988. *Current international recommendations on labour statistics.* Geneva.

—. 1986. *Economically active population — Estimates and projections, 1950-2025. Volume 5: World Summary.* Geneva.

International Labour Review (Geneva). 1994. "Judicial decisions: Part-time work poses issues for European courts", in Vol. 133, No. 2, pp. 280-286.

OECD. 1997. *Employment Outlook.* Paris. July.

—. 1995. *Employment Outlook.* Paris. July.

OFCE (Observatoire français des conjonctures économiques). 1998. *La lettre de l'OFCE, Observations et diagnostics économiques* (Paris), No. 171, 21 Jan.

Rifkin, Jeremy. 1995. *The end of work: The decline of the global labor force and the dawn of the post-market era.* New York, NY, Putnam.

Tam, May. 1997. *Part-time employment: A bridge or a trap?* Aldershot, Avebury.

WOMEN IN MANAGEMENT: CLOSER TO BREAKING THROUGH THE GLASS CEILING?

12

Linda WIRTH*

Women have made enormous progress in many countries in obtaining a greater share of professional and management jobs. The data show the significant role played by education and the growing diversification of women's careers. Nevertheless, research findings demonstrate how unbreakable the glass ceiling is. Women's overall share of management jobs rarely exceeds 20 per cent in most countries, yet they represent more than 40 per cent of the world's labour force. The higher the position the more glaring the gap between men and women. It is suggested that some career-building strategies and enterprise policies can help to speed up women's advancement to the top jobs.

Today, individual women are creating "historical firsts" as they break through the "glass ceiling" — the invisible artificial barriers created by attitudinal and organizational prejudices that bar women from top executive jobs. For example, over the past year: the first woman to be prime minister was appointed in New Zealand; in Finland, for the first time a woman became President of the Central Bank; the United Nations had its first woman Commissioner for Human Rights, who was the former President of Ireland; and the World Health Organization had as its first woman Director-General, a former prime minister of Norway. These women may be exceptional cases, reflecting strong individual motivation and ability combined with lucky circumstances which allowed them to rise to top positions. Statistical evidence suggests, however, that they represent a distinct trend. An increasing number of women are in line to be selected

Originally published as a "perspective" in *International Labour Review*, Vol. 137 (1998), No. 1.

* ILO, Geneva. She prepared the ILO report *Breaking through the glass ceiling: Women in management* (Sectoral Activities Programme, Geneva, 1997).

for high-level positions in private companies, government and politics in the coming decade as a consequence of the swelling ranks of women in lower and middle management.

WOMEN MOVING INTO PROFESSIONAL AND MANAGERIAL JOBS

Data gathered and analysed by the ILO graphically illustrate the enormous progress made by women in a large number of countries in obtaining an ever-increasing share of professional and overall management positions. Internationally comparable ILO data[1] indicate women's major share of professional, technical and related work — over 40 per cent in many countries and as much as 60 per cent in some (see figure 1). Comparable data on the proportion of women in administrative and managerial jobs also reflect an increase in their share, although the level is lower and there is considerable variation between countries (see figure 2). Women occupy over 40 per cent of administrative and managerial jobs in a few countries, e.g. Australia, Canada and the United States, and around 20-30 per cent in Austria, Chile, Colombia, Costa Rica, Finland, Republic of Korea, Mexico, Norway, the Philippines, Singapore, Switzerland, United Kingdom, Uruguay and Venezuela (ILO, 1996, based on Major Group 2 of the International Standard Classification of Occupations (ISCO-68)). Data collected by the ILO under the 1988 International Standard Classification of Occupations (ISCO-88) show that in 1995, the proportion of women among legislators, senior officials and managers was 20-30 per cent in the Czech Republic, Denmark, El Salvador, Honduras, Hong Kong (China), Greece, Iceland, Ireland, Netherlands, Peru, Slovenia, Slovakia and Spain (ibid., based on Major Group 1 of the International Standard Classification of Occupations (ISCO-88)).

National studies and statistics, even when not internationally comparable, tend to confirm the rising trend of women in management roles as highlighted by ILO data. For example, in Thailand the proportion of women managers grew from 8 per cent in 1974 to 19 per cent in 1990 (Siengthai, 1996). A survey of over 1 million enterprises in Brazil indicated that women's share of management jobs had risen to 17 per cent by the end of the 1980s (de Avelar, 1994). In Hungary women increased their share of enterprise and organization managers from 16 to 25 per cent between 1980 and 1990 (ILO SEGREGAT database).

The movement of women into managerial jobs is by no means even across different economic sectors. Women have tended to fare better in areas traditionally dominated by women — so-called women's jobs. These include education and health services, finance and banking, and administrative, communications, personnel, support and other services. In the United States, women accounted for just over 50 per cent of all financial

Figure 1. Women's share of professional, technical and related work; 1986-88 and 1993-95

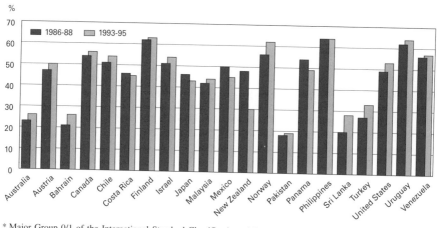

* Major Group 0/1 of the International Standard Classification of Occupations (ISCO-68).
Source: ILO, 1996, Table 2C, pp. 151-198.

Figure 2. Women's share of administrative and managerial work, 1985-87 and 1993-95

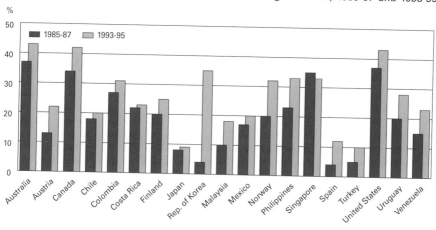

Source: ILO, 1996, Table 2C, pp. 151-198.

managers in 1996 (US Department of Labor, 1996). Traditionally, in many instances women have been able to obtain higher level positions in the public service because of governmental equal opportunity policies. For example, in the Philippines women increased their share of government executive career positions from 26 per cent in 1980 to 29 per cent in

1990 (CEDAW, 1996a). The growth of the tertiary sector in industrial-ized and industrializing countries has been of benefit to many women employed in services in terms of job opportunities and promotion. On the other hand, women have been less able to penetrate the ranks of management in manufacturing and construction, sectors which tend to employ more men. Just the same, even in sectors where the majority of employees are women and they have succeeded in obtaining higher-level jobs, men still generally hold significantly more of the managerial positions.

EDUCATION AND TRAINING: CRITICAL FACTORS FOR WOMEN TO REACH TOP JOBS

A major factor contributing to women's growing participation in professional and managerial work is the fact that they have availed them-selves of the educational and training opportunities opened up to them in most countries in recent years. Overall enrolment figures worldwide for 1994 show how the number of women reaching higher levels of educa-tion is approaching that of men. Standardized assessment tests in a number of countries indicate that girls perform as well as or even better than do boys on average. Recognition of that ability is being reflected further along in the soaring number of graduate and postgraduate university degrees being awarded to young women. Though girls and young women have impressively proved their capacity and interest in education, the key issue that remains is the application of gender criteria in the choice by girls and boys of subjects and courses. This usually begins at an early age with socialization in the home and at school as to what are suitable roles and occupations for men and women. Those regarded as appropri-ate for women are usually related to reproductive activities such as rear-ing children and caring for households. Thus, when women work in paid employment outside the home, their jobs have often been an extension of this type of activity in areas such as welfare, education, health, cater-ing, services and administrative support functions.[2] The majority of jobs for women are still to be found in these sectors and they tend to be lower skilled and less well paid. In many countries, they are often available on a part-time basis as it is usually women who are expected to juggle work and family care.

While social attitudes affect greatly the type of qualifications women seek to obtain, their choices are gradually changing, with increasing num-bers of young women now enrolling in business, law, mathematics, sci-entific and technological courses in many countries. Data for 11 of the 19 countries for which UNESCO statistics were available for the years 1994-95 indicate that women obtained 20 per cent or more of postgradu-ate degrees in mathematics and computer science. In several countries (e.g. Italy, Poland and Slovenia) they were awarded 50 per cent or more of such degrees (UNESCO, 1997, table 3.12). In the United States in the early 1990s women earned 47 per cent of bachelors' degrees, 34 per cent of masters' degrees and 24 per cent of doctorate degrees in the fields of business and management (Fagenson and Jackson, 1994). Even areas strongly resistant to change such as engineering and high technology demonstrate some progress. For example, in the Republic of Korea the percentage of women among engineering students rose from 3 per cent in 1985 to 7 per cent by the mid-1990s, in Australia from 5 to 9 per cent, in Tunisia from 10 to 15 per cent and in Spain from 11 to 21 per cent during the same period (UNESCO, 1997, table 3.11).

Such developments are a result of evolving social values, spearheaded by the women's movement and expressed in the promotion of gender equality in government policies and programmes, with particular attention to removing sex stereotyping from school curricula. Fundamental changes in the family structure in many countries increasingly reflect the importance of women's earnings in household income. An ever-growing number of the world's families are headed by women and, increasingly, men are no longer the main breadwinners. Roles of men are also changing in certain countries, as they either choose or are obliged to be at home to care for children or the elderly while their wife or partner goes out to work (see ILO, 1997).

One can conclude from the above that women will continue to move into and increase their share of professional and managerial jobs. They will have the qualifications and experience as well as the motivation and need to aspire to jobs with higher levels of responsibility and pay. The question that remains, of course, is the extent to which they will be able to break through the glass ceiling to attain the top executive jobs in companies and organizations.

WOMEN AT THE TOP

Research findings around the world underline just how unbreakable is the glass ceiling which prevents more women from reaching top management jobs in organizations and firms. With few exceptions, women's overall share of management jobs rarely exceeds 20 per cent in most countries, yet they represent more than 40 per cent of the world's labour force. The higher the position, the more glaring the gender gap. In the largest and most powerful organizations, the proportion of top positions held by women is generally 2 to 3 per cent. In the United States, where women are relatively well qualified and constitute 46 per cent of the workforce, a survey of the 500 largest companies (the "Fortune 500") showed that in 1996 they only held 2.4 per cent of the highest-level management jobs and accounted for a tiny 1.9 per cent of the highest-paid officers and directors (Catalyst, 1997). In Brazil, a 1991 survey of major corporations revealed that only about 3 per cent of top executives were women (de Avelar, 1994). A 1995 survey of the 70,000 largest German companies found that only 1 to 3 per cent of top executives and board members were women (Verlag Hoppenstedt GmbH, 1995).

Just how difficult it is for women to reach top positions is illustrated by studies showing that women are often better educated and qualified than men in the same job. Having to work harder and perform better than their male counterparts in order to move ahead are also characteristics frequently cited in surveys of women managers. An enterprise survey in Jamaica found that women had more years of schooling before joining the labour force than men, and they advanced more quickly than men at middle-management level, but it took significantly longer for women to reach top-level management positions (Gershenberg, 1994, p. 321). Another example, illustrating the progress of women in overall managerial jobs but at the same time being stuck at middle management level is that of the Turkish civil service: in 1996 women occupied 32 per cent of middle management positions, 12 per cent of general directorships and just over 2 per cent of under-secretary positions (CEDAW, 1996b, p. 66).

A real and practical constraint for women to achieve high-level positions is the disproportionate responsibility they still have for raising children and performing household tasks. An important feature of professional and especially managerial work is the long hours required to gain recognition and eventual promotion. Often career progression policies and structures are designed to emphasize the period between the ages of 30 and 40 as the most important for career development, the most intensive years for child rearing. Thus, women who wish to have both a family and a career must juggle heavy responsibilities in both domains. A more subtle constraint affecting women without family responsibilities is that they are nevertheless seen as potential mothers, with the result that investment in their training and career opportunities is often given less attention than that of their male counterparts, curtailing their chances of obtaining top jobs further down the road.

Surveys indicate that women in certain developing countries seem to experience fewer difficulties in obtaining management jobs. This could be explained by the fact that a smaller proportion of the population has attained higher education and so the skills and knowledge of qualified women are in demand. In addition, the extended family system and inexpensive domestic help provide crucial support for childcare and household maintenance, enabling women to devote more time to their careers.

TACKLING THE OBSTACLES

One of the main obstacles perceived by women is that of sex stereotyping regarding their ability and willingness to accept positions of responsibility, especially if long hours, travel and relocation are involved. This type of attitude assumes that all women have similar interests, ambitions and constraints when in fact they do not form a homogeneous group — just as men do not. The consequences for many women include being placed in less strategic areas of activity, not being given varied and challenging assignments and not being exposed to the full range of operations and activities of an enterprise or organization — crucial factors for climbing the ladder to top management jobs. This situation is obviously a vicious circle, as surveys of chief executive officers of companies reveal their view that few women possess appropriate business experience and that they have not been long enough in a variety of management positions to be selected for top executive jobs.

Diverse and complementary measures have been tried out by enterprises around the globe to recruit, retain and promote more women. An important step is the adoption by enterprises of an equal opportunity policy. Positive or affirmative action approaches often form part of an overall equality policy and are generally viewed as a conscious effort to level the playing field so that everyone has an equal chance.

Training in management skills, assertiveness training and on-the-job training in different areas to gain broader experience and knowledge of an organization's structure and functions are key instruments in providing women with the self-confidence, techniques, knowledge and contacts to move ahead in an organization.

Enterprise-based programmes for workers with family responsibilities reduce stress on employees and raise their productivity. Features of such programmes usually include maternity leave and parental or family-care leave, child and elder care facilities or services, and flexible work arrangements, such as part-time work, flexitime, compressed work weeks and telework. While these measures often aim to attract and retain women, it has also been found important that male employees be encouraged to take up such options. If only women make use of these options, they can be disadvantaged, as they may be regarded as less committed to their jobs. Men also have family responsibilities and need to find a healthy balance between work and personal life.

Enterprise commitment to policies and programmes to combat sexual harassment are fundamental in preventing acts of unwelcome sexual behaviour at the workplace for both men and women. They are particularly important for women moving into management, usually a predominantly male occupation, and one in which women managers may be resented by male subordinates, peers and higher-level managers.

Specific career-building strategies which have been found to help women advance include networking, career tracking and mentoring. Women's involvement in informal networks in enterprises are essential for obtaining invaluable information, visibility, contacts and support for performing effectively and obtaining higher-level jobs. As part of their human resource and equal opportunity policies, companies can consciously encourage and invite women to be part of such networks for their personal and professional life. Career tracking involves identifying women with high potential, and helping them gain visibility and experience through challenging and high-profile assignments. Special training may be provided, as well as coaching by high-level managers. Such career tracking is more readily available to men, since the job of manager has usually been considered a male occupation. Mentoring is a process in which older, experienced managers provide coaching, support and advice to younger potential managers. It has typically been practised by the pairing of older and younger men in an enterprise on an informal basis. As a strategy to promote women, enterprises in some countries are introducing formal mentoring programmes so that women with high potential can benefit from the advice and visibility provided by experienced executives. Mentoring also helps male managers understand better the differences between male and female approaches to management and the importance of including both approaches in the life of an enterprise.

Whichever strategies are developed in an enterprise or organization, the main factor in the successful recruitment and retaining of women is a firm commitment to gender equality by top management and the adoption of a comprehensive approach to ensure that gender equality is an issue at all levels and that all managers are held accountable on this matter. Apart from legal requirements and changing social views on women's roles, probably the most motivating factor for companies to promote women in management is the realization that it is good for business. Utilizing the full potential of trained and qualified women is not only a means of adding value within the enterprise, it is also a way of improving company image and eventually customer satisfaction with services and products that are more "women friendly". Women's visibility as managers reinforces this, especially in relation to women consumers.

An example of a group of over 300 organizations (including private and public enterprises) agreeing to increase the number of women in key business areas through voluntary positive action is Opportunity 2000 in the United Kingdom. Launched with a campaign in 1991, measures introduced include help with balancing work and home commitments, increasing women's self-confidence and encouraging women to consider non-traditional fields of work. Many of the organizations are attempting to bring about cultural change, for example in the "long hours culture" in which many employees fear being seen as uncommitted if they choose flexible work options. In these participating organizations, between 1994 and 1995 the proportion of women managers rose from 25 to 31 per cent, of senior managers from 12 to 17 per cent, and of directors from 8 to 16 per cent (Income Data Services, 1996, pp. 1-2).

Recent human resource policy development has involved experimenting with concepts such as *diversity management* and *total e-quality*. Diversity management recognizes that not all employees are the same and that their very differences and potential may entail a variety of benefits and improvements in productivity. Not only is gender a consideration (as in gender equality policies) but age, background, race, disability, personality and work style are also important factors in human resource management. Ensuring that employee composition better reflects the diversity of the population is regarded as essential for business and marketing. *Total e-quality* is an extension of the practice of total quality management, which strives to improve quality through emphasis on clients, work organization and processes and, above all, regarding employees as collaborators. Thus total e-quality implies encouraging a greater contribution from women and a better recognition, use and development of their aptitudes, recognizing that they may differ from those of men. The evolution of such approaches will no doubt be interesting to follow in terms of their impact on gender equality and the promotion of women to higher levels of management.

ILO DISCUSSES THE ISSUE

In December 1997, more than 100 participants attended a tripartite meeting on breaking through the glass ceiling, held at ILO headquarters in Geneva. Twenty countries were invited by the ILO's Governing Body to be represented by a tripartite national delegation. There were also observers from additional governments, as well as representatives from intergovernmental and non-governmental international organizations.

The discussion ranged widely, although there was a remarkable consensus on obstacles to women's career development. The dilemma of dividing time between work and family, on a daily basis as well as over a lifetime, was identified as a key gender issue, because the pressure to make difficult choices between career and family is often much greater on women than on men. Social attitudes and cultural biases were identified as major factors discriminating against women and holding them back from attaining higher-level jobs.

Such prejudices were often reflected in a subjective application of recruitment and promotion procedures and so there was a need to develop positive measures to break down the often invisible barriers blocking women's careers. The meeting identified many complementary strategies to promote women in management, covering areas such as training, networking, mentoring, review of recruitment and promotion systems, family-friendly policies, awareness raising, positive action, evolving enterprise culture, tripartite concertation, recognition of women's increasing economic role and contribution, promotion of women entrepreneurs and improved data collection. Supportive work environments and role models were considered crucial for women to enter, remain and advance in non-traditional jobs and to build a critical mass of women at higher levels in enterprises. Less stressful work schedules, along with the availability and acceptability of flexible working time arrangements and part-time work at managerial levels, were important in enabling both women and men to advance in their careers and meet their family responsibilities.

Finally, the meeting discussed the role of governments, employers' and workers' organizations and women's organizations in promoting gender equality and women in management. Participants stressed the importance of a tripartite approach and the strategic importance of ensuring more women in decision-making positions in the structure of organizations. Collective bargaining was considered a powerful mechanism to promote women into strategic positions in public and private enterprises.

Follow-up activities requested of the ILO include the preparation of a manual of best practice in promoting women in management, improved data collection and further research and monitoring of the situation of men and women in senior decision-making positions in both public and private sectors.

A number of key issues emerge from both the ILO research and the meeting itself. Firstly, central to the promotion of gender equality is equal access by women to education, whether it be basic literacy or advanced studies in technical areas traditionally dominated by men. Secondly, in the labour market, the breakdown of occupational segregation and the broadening of job options are fundamental in removing hindrances to women's promotion to higher-level responsibilities. Thirdly, breaking or dismantling the glass ceiling implies significant transformation of the workplace itself. Management approaches, work organization and structure, selection and promotion procedures need to evolve to ensure the full participation and contribution of both men and women. A major question in this regard is whether or not a standard 60-hour or longer work week for managers is detrimental to business, health, families and gender equality. Finally, setting up their own businesses is proving an area of potentially unlimited opportunities for women. This trend is very much in evidence in a number of countries where women successfully own and run a significant proportion of small and medium-sized businesses. Many of these women have in fact left large corporations, bringing their talent and experience to the development of more dynamic and flexible companies and leaving behind the rigid work arrangements and attitudes which hindered their rise to top management levels.

Notes

[1] ILO data collected on the basis of the International Standard Classification of Occupations (ISCO-68) constitute the most complete data set available allowing for broad international comparisons. ISCO-68 classifies different categories of managers, but data are only collected on a broad category which groups administrative and managerial workers together (Major Group 2). In 1988 a new International Standard Classification of Occupations (ISCO-88) was adopted in which managers are no longer in the same category as administrative workers, although data are collected according to a broad category entitled "legislators, senior officials and managers" (Major Group 1).

[2] This is true even in the Nordic countries where gender equality policies are firmly in place, accompanied by generous child care arrangements; see the list of the most feminized occupations in Melkas and Anker, 1997, p. 354, table 5.

References

de Avelar, Sonia. 1994. *Women in economic decision-making in Brazil: A glass-ceiling report.* United Nations Division for the Advancement of Women, EDM/1994/WP.8, 2 Nov. 1994. Paper prepared for the Expert Group Meeting on Women and Economic Decision-Making, held in New York, 7-11 Nov. New York, NY, United Nations.

Catalyst. 1997. "Women in business: A snapshot", in *INFO Brief* (New York, NY).

CEDAW (United Nations Committee on the Elimination of Discrimination against Women). 1996a. *Fourth periodic reports of States parties: The Philippines.* CEDAW/C/PHI/4, 25 July 1996. New York, NY, United Nations.

—. 1996b. *Second and third periodic reports of States parties: Turkey.* CEDAW/C/TUR/2-3, 6 Sep. 1996. New York, NY, United Nations.

Fagenson, Ellen A.; Jackson, Janice J. 1994. "The status of women managers in the United States", in Nancy J. Adler and Dafna N. Izraeli (eds.): *Competitive frontiers: Women managers in a global economy.* Cambridge, MA, Blackwell, pp. 388-404.

Gershenberg, Irving. 1994. "Gender, training, and the creation of a managerial elite: Multinationals and other firms in Jamaica", in *Journal of Developing Areas* (Macomb, IL), Vol. 28, No. 3 (Apr.), pp. 313-324.

ILO. 1997. "Perspectives: Parental leave", in *International Labour Review* (Geneva), Vol. 136, No. 1, pp. 109-128.

—. 1996. *Yearbook of labour statistics, 1996.* Geneva.

Income Data Services. 1996. *Opportunity 2000.* IDS Study 597. London. Mar.

Melkas, Helinä; Anker, Richard. 1997. "Occupational segregation by sex in Nordic countries: An empirical investigation", in *International Labour Review* (Geneva), Vol. 136, No. 3, pp. 341-363.

Siengthai, Sununta. 1996. *Women and economic decision-making in international financial institutions and transnational corporations in Thailand.* United Nations Division for the Advancement of Women, EDM/IFI-TNC/1996/WP.3, 1 Nov. 1996. Paper prepared for the Expert Group Meeting on Women and Economic Decision-Making in International Financial Institutions and Transnational Corporations, held in Boston, MA, 11-15 Nov. New York, NY, United Nations.

UNESCO. 1997. *Statistical Yearbook, 1996.* Paris, UNESCO/Lanham, MD, Bernan Press.

United States Department of Labor (Women's Bureau). 1996. *Facts on working women: Women in management.* http://gatekeeper.dol.gov/dol/wb/public/wb_pubs/wmgt.htm (Nov.) [visited 8 May 1998].

Verlag Hoppenstedt GmbH. 1995. Various press releases. Darmstadt. Dec.

SEX-SPECIFIC LABOUR MARKET INDICATORS: WHAT THEY SHOW

13

Sara ELDER* and Lawrence Jeffrey JOHNSON*

This describes worldwide trends in gender issues that emerge from an ILO project (KILM) to develop key labour market indicators to monitor new employment trends. Indicators were selected on criteria of conceptual relevance, data availability, and comparability across countries and regions. Assembled from several existing compilations, the data suggest that, worldwide, women's experience of the labour market is substantially different from men's: women work in different sectors, for fewer hours of paid work, have lower rates of schooling and literacy, are less likely to be self-employed and more likely to be unemployed, underemployed or outside the labour force.

After decades of work aimed at achieving equality between men and women, after the adoption of numerous international resolutions and instruments and after the passage of national legislation seeking to attain this goal, can improvement be declared — and quantified? Certainly, on the basis of information from many sources, it seems that there has been progress toward the elimination of sex discrimination in employment. In general, women's working conditions have improved, as has the legal environment for creating greater equality; job mobility has increased, wage gaps have narrowed, access to education has become easier and work schedules are more flexible. All these factors have contributed to a lessening of the constraints affecting female jobseekers and workers. Questions remain, however, as to the evidence of improvement.

Originally published in *International Labour Review*, Vol. 138 (1999), No. 4.

* Employment Strategy Department, ILO, Geneva. For a detailed exposition of the indicators and information on contributors to the overall study on labour market indicators from which this is drawn, see ILO (1999).

Box 1. Key indicators of the labour market

1.	Labour force participation rate	10.	Long-term unemployment
2.	Employment-to-population ratio	11.	Unemployment by educational attainment
3.	Status in employment	12.	Time-related underemployment
4.	Employment by sector	13.	Inactivity rate
5.	Part-time workers	14.	Educational attainment and illiteracy
6.	Hours of work	15.	Real manufacturing wage indices
7.	Urban informal sector employment	16.	Hourly compensation costs
8.	Unemployment	17.	Labour productivity and unit labour cost
9.	Youth unemployment	18.	Poverty and income distribution

Realistic and timely information is needed on the economic role of women and men for national and local policy-makers to assess the situation and design more effective labour market policies and programmes (see Mata Greenwood (1999); Bell (1996)). Unfortunately, such information is often lacking.

In order to address the need for better labour market information, the ILO undertook a project known as Key Indicators of the Labour Market (KILM), whose objectives have been to develop a set of labour market indicators for as many countries as possible, and to widen the availability of the indicators for monitoring new employment trends. Eighteen labour market indicators were selected, based on criteria of conceptual relevance, availability of data,[1] and their comparability across countries and regions; see box 1.

These key labour market indicators were constructed for as many countries, areas and territories as possible, for 1980, 1990 and annually thereafter. A special effort was made to highlight the gender issues associated with each indicator. The data generally allow for comparisons between and within countries and regions concerning women's access to paid work and schooling, and provide insights into differences in the quality of work carried out by women compared to men. The set of indicators also provides an international perspective on changes over time in women's labour market activities and in the status of women workers.

The overall picture given by the information available supports the view that, worldwide, women's experience of the labour market is substantially different from that of men. Women typically work in different sectors and for fewer hours of paid work, have lower rates of schooling and literacy, and are more likely to be unemployed, underemployed or outside the labour force altogether.

Many of the indicators show greater inter-country variation for women than for men. This suggests that culture, societal norms, traditions and government policies may all play a greater role in determining women's economic activities than men's. Significantly, many of the male/

female differences in the data point to the fact that market work represents only a portion of women's overall responsibilities: most of the
world's women must devote a large portion of their time to unpaid household responsibilities, childcare and subsistence labour. However, in
order to further knowledge of gender-based differences in the world of
work, more information than that available in this analysis would be
needed, for example, on activities "not in the labour force" or in the
informal sector, on occupational segregation, and on sex-based wage
differentials. This article focuses on the trends which can be revealed
through an analysis of KILM data.

LABOUR FORCE PARTICIPATION

The labour force participation rate is an indicator of the overall level
of labour market activity, and its breakdown by sex and age group provides a profile of the distribution of the economically active population
within a country. It is calculated by expressing the number of persons in
the labour force as a percentage of the working-age population.[2]

In every country for which information is available, women are less
likely than men to participate in the labour force.[3] This reflects the fact
that demographic, social, legal and cultural trends and norms determine
whether or not women's activities are regarded as economic, with the
result that women experience greater difficulty obtaining entry to the
labour market than do men. Furthermore, in addition to overcoming the
numerous educational, institutional and cultural barriers which may prevent them from gaining access to the labour market, most women must
also deal with the competing demands of housework and childcare.

Unlike men's labour force participation rates, which are high in all
countries, there is great cross-country variation in women's rates. The
countries with the lowest female labour force participation rates are in
Latin America and the Caribbean, the Middle East and north Africa. The
countries with the highest rates are in Scandinavia, amongst the transition economies and in sub-Saharan Africa. In 1997, a year for which data
are available for 52 countries, the lowest rate is found in Turkey (27.8 per
cent) and the highest rate in Iceland (68.4 per cent). Data for 1995 (available for 178 countries) are more revealing: of 15 countries with female
participation rates of under 30 per cent, 12 are located in the Middle
East; however, male labour force participation rates in those countries
are not below 60 per cent. Of the 23 countries in which female labour
force participation rates exceed 70 per cent, 14 are in sub-Saharan Africa
and eight are in Asia and the Pacific.

In many countries, women's low labour force participation rates can
be attributed to cultural factors. In the Middle East and north Africa, for
example, the education of young women and women's work outside the

253

home are often discouraged, owing to strict sex segregation for reasons of religion and marriageability. Cultural practices and high fertility rates also play a large role in limiting women's economic opportunities. Among the industrialized countries, Scandinavian countries have high female participation rates reflecting high levels of education, as well as government policies and subsidies for childcare that reduce discrimination and enable women to combine market work and family responsibilities. In several sub-Saharan countries, it is women's large share in agricultural work that accounts for their high labour force participation. In several of the transition economies, women's high labour force participation reflects a history of policies aimed at mobilizing the working-age population for employment dating back to the period of centrally controlled economies.

For the overwhelming majority of countries, the gap between women's and men's labour force participation rates narrowed between 1980 and 1997. This stemmed both from declining male rates and from rising female rates. In the industrialized countries, men's rates may have declined partly because of statutory pension schemes encouraging early retirement. In other economies, decreasing employment in the male-dominated industrial sector may have led to a reduction in the labour force activity of older men. The increase in women's labour force participation reflects, among other things, their rising educational levels; the growth of the service sector, which includes industries in such areas as retailing, health care and education where women have a particularly high representation;[4] and changing norms and laws concerning women's economic roles. Significantly, while economic development often brings about an increase in women's labour force participation, the question of whether women stake a claim to their country's growing wealth ultimately depends on that country's commitment to women's economic equality with men. This commitment is reflected in anti-discrimination policies with respect to work, property and contracts, policies to assist families in meeting their responsibilities, and policies to ensure a minimum living wage and decent working conditions.

The profiles of male and female labour force participation rates by age group also show specific patterns (see figures 1 and 2). The male profile generally has an inverted-U shape, in which labour force participation starts at low values for younger persons, increases as they leave school and enter the labour market, reaches a high plateau in the prime ages (25 to 54 years), and then decreases at the older ages as retirement from economic activity occurs.

For women, labour force participation is generally lower than for men in each age category. At prime ages, the female rates are not only lower than the corresponding male values but often exhibit a somewhat different pattern. During this period of their life-cycle, women tend to retreat from the labour force to give birth to and rear children, returning

Figure 1. Examples of male labour force participation across age groups (percentages)

Male labour force participation rate

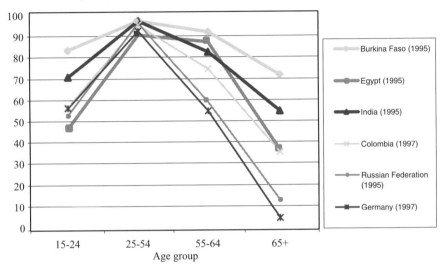

Figure 2. Examples of female labour force participation across age groups (percentages)

Female labour force participation rate

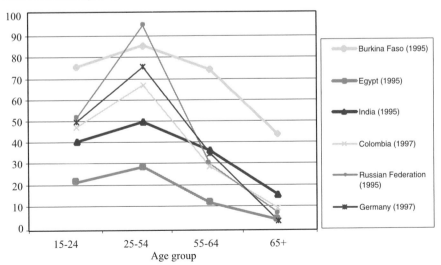

— but at a lower rate — to economically active life as the children grow up. In industrialized countries, however, women's participation rates are increasingly similar in profile to those of men and are markedly approaching male levels as well.

EMPLOYMENT

Employment-to-population ratio

As an indicator of the employment situation in a country, the employment-to-population ratio ranks in importance with the unemployment rate and, for some countries, it may be considered the most important indicator of the extent to which the population is engaged in productive labour market activities. Unemployment statistics conceal such problems as a vast informal sector and poor — or non-existent — social protection. Thus, one must also look to statistics on employment for evidence of positive or negative labour market situations.

Virtually every country in the world that collects statistics on labour market status has, either potentially or in fact, data on employment-to-population ratios. All that is required are data on the population of working age and, for the same time periods, figures on total employment. Employment-to-population ratios are of particular interest when compared by sex, as the relative closeness or disparity of the percentages for men and women may reveal overall disparities in male and female labour market activities.

In the 45 countries with fairly continuous statistics since 1990, nearly all had decreasing employment-to-population ratios for men, while many, but by no means all, had rising ratios for women. It would appear that men's changing work patterns have had a pronounced impact on overall work percentages in many countries. Clues as to the reasons for this change may be found in the KILM data for male labour force participation rates, which show that men aged 55 to 64 years and 65 years and over, and also those aged 25 to 54 years, had declining participation rates in many countries. An important reason for this has been a tendency towards earlier retirement. The movement of women into the labour market has been a counteracting development.

As explained above, women's employment may be rising for a wide variety of reasons, including increases in the occupations in which women are typically employed, women's gains in education and training and, in some countries, the progress of female employment in areas traditionally considered "men's work" in certain occupations or industries. Furthermore, in some countries, government programmes and part-time work options have made it easier for women to enter employment and to integrate labour market and family work.

Even with declining male employment-to-population ratios and rising female ratios, sizeable differences remain. As is to be expected, the lowest sex differentials are to be found among the industrialized countries, in Scandinavia in particular, where cultural and legal norms result in greater employment equality. In 1997, the male-to-female gap in Sweden was only 5.5 percentage points (employment-to-population ratios of 65.6 per cent for males and 60.1 per cent for females). By contrast, the gap in numerous countries in Latin America and the Caribbean remains quite high — between 20 and 40 percentage points — as these are countries with a tradition of women staying at home.

As with the measurement of labour force participation, one possible factor influencing the difference between the employment-to-population ratios of women and men is the potential for undercounting female employment. The employed population covers all types of employment situations, including those in which the people concerned do not perceive themselves as persons who "work", or are not perceived by others as "working". As more women than men are found in such situations, it is to be expected that unless special measures are taken, there will be a greater tendency to underestimate the numbers of women in employment than the numbers of men in employment.

Another measurement issue which may principally affect women concerns employed persons who did not work at all during the reference period for which data were collected (they are often described as "with a job but not at work"). Countries with legislation allowing workers to take relatively extended leaves of absence while maintaining their jobs will have a higher proportion of workers absent from work for long periods. Many of these workers are women on extended maternity leave. These countries will also tend to have higher employment-to-population ratios for women than other countries. This is typically the case in Scandinavia, where it is not uncommon for workers to take unpaid leave for several years, after which they have the guarantee of returning to their former employment; such arrangements also occur in some of the transition economies.

Employment status

Indicators of status in employment distinguish between three categories of the employed, namely: (a) wage and salaried workers, or employees; (b) self-employed workers, or employers, persons working on their own account and members of cooperatives; and (c) contributing family workers (also termed unpaid family workers). These three groups of workers are presented as percentages of the total employed for both sexes and for females and males separately.

Men are more likely than women to be self-employed in all regions of the world. While in most countries for which data are available the gap between the share of self-employment in men's total employment and the corresponding share of women is comparatively small (less than 10 percentage points), in some countries it reaches over 20 percentage points, for example, in Bangladesh, Ethiopia, Greece, Indonesia, Pakistan, the Syrian Arab Republic, Thailand and Turkey.

Given that the proportion of men in self-employment is higher in practically all countries, women are more likely than men to enter wage and salaried work or to carry out unpaid family work; indeed, in all countries, women dominate unpaid family work. The data show that non-salaried men tend to be self-employed, while non-salaried women tend to be unpaid family workers. There are several possible reasons for this. First, women may have less access to credit, capital, land and materials, any or all of which may be necessary to start and maintain a business. Also, in some countries, cultural norms may prevent women from working on their own, interacting with the public or supervising other workers. Alternatively, women may lack the training and education to work on their own or they may face time constraints because of their traditional family responsibilities.

Another very important reason arises from the limitations of measurement. Many countries have difficulty in gathering accurate employment data by status in employment and by sex. Because of biased reporting or misclassification, substantial numbers of women may be reported as unpaid family workers even when they work in association and on an equal footing with their partners in the family enterprise or farm (United Nations, 1997, p. 220). Also, as stated above, female employment tends to be underestimated, especially when women are engaged in subsistence agriculture or manufacturing, because these activities are often considered an extension of their domestic responsibilities.

The data show that, in most countries in the world, paid employment is predominant, for both women and men. However, it is probable that women and men differ in the specific type of paid employment situation. The wide range covered by this category can mask certain issues concerning the comparative *quality* of female and of male employment. Indeed, paid employment as a home-worker, casual employee or work-gang member, all of which are forms of employment in which women tend to predominate, differs so vastly from employment, say, as a stock-broker as to be almost incomparable.

It is also highly probable, and supported by the available data, that women who are self-employed are more likely to be own-account workers and members of producers' cooperatives than to be employers, whereas the opposite is the case for men. Even among own-account workers, women and men will tend to differ, women being more numerous among, say, subsistence workers and men more numerous among sharecroppers. The more disaggregated the data, the more differences between men and women will be revealed.

Employment by sector

Employment by sector is a measure of the persons employed in a particular economic sector (agriculture, industry and the service sector) expressed as a percentage of total employment. The agricultural sector comprises activities in agriculture, hunting, forestry and fishing; the industrial sector comprises mining and quarrying, manufacturing, construction and public utilities (electricity, gas and water); and the service sector consists of wholesale and retail trade, restaurants and hotels, transport, storage and communications, finance, insurance, real estate and business services, and community, social and personal services.[5]

In all regions of the world, men account for a higher proportion of total employment in the industrial sector. By contrast, women's share of employment in the service sector is more likely to exceed men's. Generally speaking, industrialized countries and transition economies have higher proportions of men than women in agricultural production. In Asia and the Pacific and in sub-Saharan Africa, women's share of agricultural production is typically greater than men's. In fact, in countries in these regions, where rates of female labour force participation are among the highest in the world, the majority of female workers can be assumed to be engaged in agricultural pursuits. Women's contribution to the agricultural sector may not be so apparent in other regions of the world, perhaps because the statistics for some of these countries cover only urban areas (particularly in Latin America) or paid employment in the formal sector. Because of this limited coverage, the contribution of women (and men) in agriculture and small enterprises will tend to be underestimated. Moreover, the activities of workers engaged in subsistence and other unpaid work, in which women are more numerous than men, may also be under-reported. The contrast between women's and men's participation in industry, services and agriculture may therefore be less pronounced than it seems.

Since wage rates in the service sector are on average below those in the industrial sector, the greater concentration of women in the service sector and of men in the industrial sector is probably a factor in persisting higher male wages. Women may be drawn into lower-paid service activities because of barriers raised by employers or trade unions, or by cultural attitudes which make it more difficult for them to enter industrial employment. Women may also have more restricted access to the education and training required for industrial jobs. Furthermore, because work in the service sector often reflects the type of work women traditionally do in the home, such as childcare, nursing and cleaning, women are seen as particularly well suited for this type of work. In situations where childcare is not available, women may choose to work in specific types of service that offer greater flexibility allowing them to combine family responsibilities with employment.

Analysis of data beyond the three broad sectors, each comprising a heterogeneous set of economic activities, would very likely yield a wealth of possible leads for further studies in this area. For example, the service sector ranges from sophisticated services such as banking, insurance, real estate activities and medical and education services to very elementary ones, such as domestic service, with those relating to the retail trade falling somewhere in between. Though there is a higher proportion of female employment in the service sector overall, it is to be expected that women will tend to be concentrated in just a few services, for example, in the retail trade and, in developing countries, in domestic service. Similarly, though men dominate the industrial sector as a whole, women may predominate in particular activities such as textiles and food manufacturing, where the work more closely resembles the type of work women do in the home.

Part-time work

Part-time work is that carried out by individuals with jobs whose working hours amount to less than "full time"; it is expressed as a proportion of total employment. "Less than full time", however, is not consistently quantified throughout the world, partly because there is no international agreement on the minimum number of hours in a week that constitute full-time work. The dividing line is determined either on a country-by-country basis or through the use of special estimations. The indicator in question includes data on total part-time employment as a percentage of total employment. Another useful measure is the total number of women employed part time expressed as a percentage of total part-time employment.

The reason there is no official ILO definition on the point at which full-time work begins is largely because there are such wide inter-country variations on this point. Accordingly, to date, international statisticians have agreed on a definition of the part-time worker as "an employed person whose normal hours of work are less than those of comparable full-time workers" (ILO, 1994, p. 7). Many individual countries have established their own demarcation lines between full- and part-time work, however, and the typical dividing line runs somewhere between 30 and 40 hours a week. Some countries have established dividing lines based on respondents' interpretations of their personal work situations, rather than a specific standard expressed in hours.

In almost all countries, a much larger proportion of women than men work part time. Women thus account for well over half of all part-time workers in the 43 countries for which statistics are available. In the 1990s, participation in part-time work by both women and men has tended to rise in most countries.

Part-time work is a practical means for women to earn some income while maintaining a share of family responsibilities. In order to analyse more precisely the labour market participation of women and men in relation to their family situation, it would be useful to contrast the incidence of part-time work of women and men who have young children with that of those who do not.

From the point of view of employers seeking to minimize costs, use of part-time staff can make it easier to cope with cyclical demand for the products or services offered. Part-time workers are often not protected by various forms of labour legislation and so, for example, are not covered by social security or other benefits. Because women are more likely than men to accept part-time work, it follows that female workers are likely to be more vulnerable to job insecurity, and to lack of job benefits and basic workers' rights.

Informal sector employment

Urban informal sector employment is expressed as a percentage of total urban employment, i.e. it is the ratio of the number of persons employed in the informal sector in urban areas to the total number of employed persons in the same areas. In many countries, especially in Latin America and Africa, country-wide data on the informal sector simply do not exist; they are available for urban areas only. Equally significant is the fact that some countries include small-scale or unregistered agricultural activities in their definition of the informal sector, while others do not. However, since the vast majority of agricultural activities in most countries are undertaken in rural areas, a restriction to urban areas appeared likely to enhance considerably the international comparability of the informal sector employment indicator.[6]

In practically all Asian and African countries for which data disaggregated by sex are available, the share of informal sector employment in total employment is greater for women than for men. In many countries, the differences are substantial. Even the absolute number of women employed in the informal sector exceeds that of men in some countries.

Statistics on employment in the informal sector can help significantly in gaining recognition for the contribution of all workers, particularly women, to the economy. Indeed, the informal sector has been considered as

> the fallback position for women who are excluded from paid employment. ...
> The dominant aspect of the informal sector is self-employment. It is an important source of livelihood for women in the developing world, especially in those areas where cultural norms bar them from work outside the home or where, because of conflict with household responsibilities, they cannot undertake regular employee working hours (United Nations, 1997, p. 232).

Of course, the reasons for women engaging in informal sector employment vary greatly from country to country. Some women may consider it a positive means of supplementing household income while balancing household responsibilities. Unfortunately, comparable international data to quantify informal sector employment remain very difficult to accumulate.

Two measurement issues may have an impact on the number of women and men identified as belonging to the informal sector. The first relates to the activities explicitly excluded from the scope of the informal sector in the international definition. These include (a) activities carried out by enterprises exclusively engaged in production for own final use (that is, all persons who produce goods for the consumption of their own households); (b) paid domestic activities performed by maids, watchmen, drivers and gardeners in private households; and (c) activities of homeworkers with paid employment jobs, when their employer belongs to the formal sector, as is usually the case. These activities occupy a sort of grey area between informal and formal employment and since women are more likely than men to be engaged in one of the three forms of employment outlined above, their exclusion would tend to decrease the number of women identified as belonging to the informal sector.

National measures of employment in the informal sector vary significantly with respect to the international definition of employment. Still, this definition may have a significant influence over whether countries decide to include or exclude such activities (for example, domestic workers are excluded in practically all countries covered by this indicator). Unfortunately, when these activities are not included in the informal sector in national measurements, they may not be separately identified at all.

The second issue relates to the manner in which data are collected. Because informal sector units often operate on the margin of legality, a certain amount of under-reporting is inevitable, even in purely statistical surveys which promise confidentiality. There is also a risk of under-enumerating informal sector work because people surveyed tend to discount their economic contribution when it occurs in "invisible" or small-scale economic units. Special data collection strategies would therefore be required to identify female informal sector workers properly, but in practice there is a tendency to disregard the need to do so.

Wages

The data illustrate trends in average real wages in manufacturing, as wage statistics for manufacturing employees are more widely available than those for other industries and sectors. Information on wage levels is essential in evaluating the living standards and conditions of work and life of workers in both industrialized and developing countries. The availability of data disaggregated by sex offers a means of assessing the extent of progress toward equal pay.

Throughout the world women typically receive less pay than men. This is partly because women more often hold low-level, low-paid jobs in female-dominated occupations. In addition, men are more likely to have regular full-time work and enjoy greater seniority and benefits (United Nations, 1997, p. 230). Despite considerable progress in the movement of women into all occupations, women are still disproportionately represented in the relatively low-paid range of service jobs — clerk, teacher, health care provider, etc.[7] However, as this indicator is limited to the manufacturing industry, sex-based segregation by industry does not apply as an explanatory factor.

Whereas there continue to be wage disparities for women and men, the trends in real manufacturing wages show that, for some countries, wages are rising more rapidly for women than for men. This has been particularly evident in several industrialized countries. In Ireland, for example, manufacturing wage growth for women during the 1990s outstripped that for men. The wage index for women in the Republic of Korea rose from 45 in 1980 to 158 in 1997, compared with an increase from 50 to 142 for men over the same period, and in Singapore, the real wage index for women outpaced the male gain in the 1990s to an even greater extent.

UNEMPLOYMENT, UNDEREMPLOYMENT AND INACTIVITY

Unemployment

The unemployment rate is defined as the total unemployed (for a country or a specific group of workers) divided by the relevant labour force, which itself is the sum of the employed and the unemployed.[8]

Rates of unemployment are almost always higher for women than for men. Four possible reasons are proposed here. First, women are more likely to leave and then re-enter the labour force for personal reasons. Because of their higher entry and exit rates at any one time, proportionally more women will be looking for a job. Second, because women are likely to have a narrower range of career options than men, there may be greater competition for the jobs that are available to women, entailing longer periods of job-seeking for women. Third, women in many countries are more likely to lack the level and range of education and training required for employment (see the section on education below). Finally, women are likely to be the first affected by the lay-offs that often accompany restructuring.

A measurement issue that may affect the extent to which women and men are included in unemployment measures concerns the stipulation that workers be available for work during the reference period. Such a short availability period excludes persons who, before starting work, need to make personal arrangements regarding, for example, childcare or housing. It will also exclude those who are not available for work during the short reference period but will be soon afterwards. It is reasonable to assume that more women than men would fall into this category. Various countries have acknowledged this coverage problem and have extended the "availability" period to the two weeks following and including the reference period. Still, women are more likely than men to be excluded from unemployment, probably because this period is not sufficiently long to consider constraints more likely to affect women (Eurostat, 1998).

Labour economists and statisticians recognize that a conventional unemployment rate is not ideally suited to all types of analysis or need. Focusing exclusively on the unemployment rate is insufficient if one seeks to understand the shortcomings of the labour market. In addition to showing overall unemployment, therefore, the KILM data include three specific indicators aimed at quantifying the composition of the unemployed: youth unemployment, long-term unemployment, and unemployment by educational attainment.

Unemployment by educational attainment

Data on unemployment by educational attainment can illustrate the interdependence of gender-based differences in unemployment and in education. The data[9] show that men with only primary education are more likely to be unemployed than women with the same level of education. By contrast, amongst persons with a post-secondary education, men are less likely than women to be unemployed. This result may occur because women with only primary or secondary education are more likely to leave the labour force — or fail to enter it in the first place — than women with more extensive education.

Women with higher education generally have more employment opportunities than women with less education; it is also more costly for them to withdraw from the labour force. By comparison, women with only primary or secondary schooling may have more limited opportunities, so that leaving the labour force either to care for their families or to enter unpaid family work (as "employed") would not be as costly in terms of opportunities forgone. The same is less likely to hold for men, since their returns from education are smaller than women's (ILO, 1998a, p. 146).

Time-related underemployment

Time-related underemployment, previously known as visible underemployment, exists "when the hours of work of an employed person are insufficient in relation to an alternative employment situation in which the person is willing and available to engage".[10] This contrasts with the definition of unemployment, which includes workers only if they report having actively sought work. There is evidence that the number of time-related underemployed persons would decrease significantly if only those who report having sought to work additional hours were included and that the decrease would be greater for women than for men. This situation seems to illustrate the fact that women tend not to look for additional work even if they actually want it, perhaps because the time required for job-seeking may compete with the time needed for activities related to the role assigned to them by society — caring for their households and family members.

Time-related underemployment affects women to a somewhat greater extent than men in most countries where data are available. Indeed, whether this form of underemployment increases or decreases over time, women's rates tend to be several percentage points higher than men's. In most countries, time-related underemployment is a growing phenomenon. Those few countries where it has decreased in recent years are countries where this form of underemployment is not widespread, suggesting that labour market inadequacies there may manifest themselves in other ways.

Inactivity

The inactivity rate represents the proportion of the working-age population not in the labour force. In KILM this indicator is limited to prime-age workers, i.e. those aged 25 to 54 years, who are the workers considered most likely to be active labour force participants, since most of them have completed their education and have not yet reached retirement age.

For all the countries covered in the indicator, women's inactivity rates exceed men's. The gap between men's and women's rates ranges from between 10 and 20 percentage points to over 80 points (in Pakistan and the Gaza Strip). Country variation in this respect stems directly, from inter-country variation in women's inactivity rates. Worldwide, men's inactivity rates are likely to be less than 10 per cent and, indeed, for many countries are around 5 per cent or less, while women's inactivity rates vary dramatically by region and by country within regions.

Despite women's higher inactivity rates, most countries have experienced a decrease in the gap between men's and women's rates over time, which is due almost entirely to reduced inactivity among women. In some instances, this has been accompanied by small increases in male inactivity, as women take jobs that might have been filled by their male counterparts; but this is by no means a usual occurrence.

The simultaneous inter-country similarity in men's inactivity rates and variation in women's inactivity rates illustrate the differing impact that economic and social factors have on women's and men's economic activities. Regardless of country differences in economic, cultural, religious and political factors, men's inactivity rates have remained at very low levels. Women's rates, however, have changed dramatically in response to these factors and perhaps to others. In the industrialized countries, the decline in women's inactivity rates over the years results from a wide variety of reasons, including women's rising educational levels, anti-discrimination policies, policies that enable parents to combine market work and family care, and changes in family consumption patterns.

EDUCATION

The major educational attainment levels used are primary, secondary and tertiary education.[11] Primary education aims at providing the basic elements of education (for example, at elementary or primary school and middle school; literacy programmes for adults are also classified under primary education). Secondary education is provided at high schools, teacher-training schools at this level, and schools of a vocational or technical nature. Tertiary education is provided at universities, teacher-training colleges, higher vocational schools and, sometimes, institutions for distance-learning.

In almost all regions of the world, women and men with only primary education tend to be less active in the labour force, while those with tertiary levels of education have comparatively high rates of labour force participation. The data show that this trend is stronger for women. Thus, whereas men in the total population are more likely than women to be educated at tertiary level, in the total labour force it is women who are more likely to be educated at tertiary level. Conversely, women outpace men in the attainment of primary-level education if measured against the population, and men outpace women if measured against the labour force. This outcome is probably due to the relatively lower returns to primary education and the relatively higher returns to tertiary education that women display in comparison to men.

Compared to women who lack a tertiary education, women with higher levels of education may have greater and more remunerative labour market opportunities and suffer higher costs from dropping out of the labour force. By contrast, less educated women may have fewer financial incentives to stay in the labour force. The same may not apply to men since, by comparison with men educated at tertiary level, men with just primary education still have relatively good labour market opportunities.

Women often face higher opportunity costs as regards education, which may ultimately restrict their access to jobs. In many countries, this problem begins at the tertiary level. In Asia and the Pacific, however, where the household and labour market work of young women may be crucial for family subsistence, sex-based differences in costs can arise at an early age, thus discouraging girls' attendance at primary and secondary school. Many families with limited resources choose to educate sons rather than daughters if the sons are expected to be future family wage earners. Economics aside, cultural, social and political norms of sex-based segregation and discrimination tend to hinder women's access to schooling further.

Women's relatively limited access to educational opportunities is reflected in higher female illiteracy rates worldwide. In almost all the countries for which data on illiteracy are available, women are more likely than men to be illiterate. The illiteracy gap is particularly acute in south-central Asia, sub-Saharan Africa, the Middle East and north Africa. However, even where the gaps between men and women are greatest in this respect, the trend over the past decade or more is towards a diminishing gap, mainly because of increased literacy among women.

CONCLUDING REMARKS

In sum, the evidence from diverse sources, now consolidated in key indicators, shows the following main differences between women's and men's experience of the labour market.

In general, women participate in the labour market to a lesser degree than men, but there is considerable variation in female labour force participation rates around the world. Yet the gap between male and female labour force participation has lessened in almost all countries in the past two decades.

In most countries, the female employment-to-population ratio has increased while the corresponding male ratio has decreased. Nevertheless the gap between male and female employment-to-population ratios remains high, ranging from approximately 10 percentage points in the industrialized countries to 40 percentage points in some countries in Latin America.

In all regions of the world, men are more likely than women to be self-employed. In family-based enterprises, the contributing family workers are predominantly female.

Also, in all regions of the world, higher proportions of men than of women are employed in the industrial sector. Women's share of employment in the service sector is likely to be greater than men's. For Asia and the Pacific and sub-Saharan Africa, the proportion of women employed in agricultural production is typically greater than that of men.

In most countries, for the past ten years there has been a growing trend towards part-time work. On average, a larger proportion of women than of men work part time.

In most Asian and African countries for which sex-disaggregated data are available the share of the informal sector in women's total employment is greater than in men's total employment. However, in Latin America and the Caribbean, the shares of men and of women in informal sector employment are roughly equal.

Women generally receive less pay than men, but manufacturing wages are rising more quickly for women than for men.

With the exception of countries in sub-Saharan Africa, female unemployment rates are higher than male unemployment rates. In general, youth unemployment rates for females exceed the rates for males. In most countries with available data, more women than men would like to, and are available to, work more hours than their current jobs allow. Women with a post-secondary level of education are more likely to be unemployed than their male counterparts.

In almost all regions of the world, women and men with only primary education tend to be less economically active, whereas those with tertiary education (and especially women among them) have comparatively high levels of labour force participation.

Notes

[1] The data were assembled directly from existing data compilations held by various international organizations. In addition to the ILO (headquarters and regional offices), these sources included the Organisation of Economic Co-operation and Development (OECD), the United Nations Industrial Development Organization (UNIDO), the United Nations Statistics Division, the World Bank, the Statistical Office of the European Union (EUROSTAT), the United Nations Educational, Scientific and Cultural Organization (UNESCO), and the United States Bureau of Labor Statistics.

[2] To some degree, the way in which the labour force is measured can have an effect on differences in the extent to which women and men are included in the counts. The labour force is the sum of the employed and the unemployed populations. Unless specific probes are part of the data collection instrument, certain groups of workers could be subject to underestimation, for example, employed persons who (a) work only for a few hours, especially if they do not do so regularly; (b) are in unpaid employment situations; or (c) work near or in their home, thus mixing work and personal activities during the day. The activities of women as unpaid family workers in agriculture, for example, might easily be overlooked. Since women are engaged in these economic activities more often than men, it is to be expected that there will be a greater tendency to underestimate the number of women in employment than the number of men in employment.

[3] Table 1 in ILO (1999) sets out latest available data on the labour force participation rates in all countries for which it is possible — at present 179. It is the basic source for much of what follows.

[4] The growth of the service sector is supported by data in the indicator on employment by sector. Of nearly 200 countries with available data, an increase in the number of persons employed in the service sector from earliest to latest year of data availability occurred in 176 countries, 91 per cent of the countries with available data.

[5] The three sectors are defined by the International Standard Industrial Classification (ISIC) System (Revisions 2 and 3); see United Nations (1990).

[6] The definitions for the informal sector are based, as closely as possible, on the Resolution concerning statistics of employment in the informal sector, adopted by the 15th International Conference of Labour Statisticians, Geneva, 1993 (ILO, 1993, pp. 51-64).

[7] For a useful discussion of occupational segregation of the sexes, see Anker (1998).

[8] Unemployed persons are defined as those individuals without work, seeking work in a recent past period, and currently available for work, according to the Resolution concerning statistics of the economically active population, employment, unemployment and underemployment, adopted by the 13th International Conference of Labour Statisticians, Geneva, 1982 (ILO, 1988, p. 51).

[9] The data on educational attainment are based on the following categories of schooling: less than one year; less than primary level; primary level; secondary level; and tertiary level.

[10] ILO: Resolution concerning the measurement of underemployment and inadequate employment situations, adopted by the 16th International Conference of Labour Statisticians, Geneva, 1998 (ILO, 1998b, p. 50).

[11] These are drawn from the International Standard Classification of Education (ISCED) designed by the United Nations Educational, Scientific and Cultural Organization; see UNESCO (1998).

References

Anker, Richard. 1998. *Gender and jobs: Sex segregation of occupations in the world.* Geneva, ILO.

Bell, Carolyn Shaw. 1996. "Data on race, ethnicity and gender: Caveats for the user", in *International Labour Review* (Geneva), Vol. 135, No. 5, pp. 535-551.

Eurostat. 1998. "Services in Europe: Key figures", in *Statistics in focus* (Luxembourg), No. 5.

ILO. 1999. *Key Indicators of the Labour Market, 1999.* Printed form: ISBN 92-2-110833-1. CD-ROM form: ISBN 92-2-110834-1. KILM website: http://www.ilo.org/public/english/60empfor/polemp/kilm/kilm.htm.

—. 1998a. *World Employment Report 1998-99. Employability in the global economy: How training matters.* Geneva.

—. 1998b. *Report of the Conference.* Sixteenth International Conference of Labour Statisticians, Geneva, 6-15 October 1998. Text of Resolution also available on the ILO's website at: http://www.ilo.org/public/english/120stat/res/underemp.htm.

—. 1994. *Part-time work.* Report IV (2B), International Labour Conference, 81st Session, 1994. Geneva.

—. 1993. *Report of the Conference.* Fifteenth International Conference of Labour Statisticians, Geneva, 19-28 January 1993. Text of Resolution also available on the ILO's website at: http://www.ilo.org/public/english/120stat/res/infsec.htm.

—. 1988. *Current international recommendations on labour statistics: 1988 edition.* Geneva. Text of Resolution also available on the ILO's website at: http://www.ilo.org/public/english/120stat/res/ecacpop.htm.

Mata Greenwood, Adriana. 1999. "Gender issues in labour statistics", in *International Labour Review* (Geneva), Vol. 138 , No. 3, pp. 273-286.

UNESCO. 1998. *International Standard Classification of Education/ISCED 1997.* Paris. Also available on website at: http://unescostat.unesco.org/documents/isced.asp.

United Nations. 1997. *Handbook for producing national statistical reports on women and men.* Social statistics indicators. Series K, No. 14. UN Sales No. E.97.XVII.10. New York, NY.

—. 1990. *International Standard Industrial Classification for all Economic Activities.* Series M, No. 4, Rev. 3. UN Sales No. E.90.XVII.11. New York, NY. Also available on United Nations' website at: http://www.un.org/Depts/unsd/class/isicmain.htm.

PART IV

OBJECTIVES, POLICY:
WHAT DOES IT TAKE?

ASSESSING EQUAL OPPORTUNITIES IN THE EUROPEAN UNION

14

Janneke PLANTENGA* and Johan HANSEN**

To evaluate usefully the extent of equal opportunity demands innovative methodology. Indicators of the relative opportunities of men and women (the "gender gap") are selected, including differences in employment, wages and the sharing of unpaid work; and also indicators of women's absolute situation in the labour market. These indicators are then estimated empirically for 15 Member States, with highly revealing results. To close the circle, the main determinants of equal opportunity are posited, including the rate of economic growth, tax systems, working-time regimes, childcare facilities and parental leave arrangements. Seeing country performance in that light produces compelling lessons for policy.

Reinforcing equal opportunities is one of the four pillars of the European Union's new strategy on employment policy. Within Europe, it is generally acknowledged that the position of women on the labour market merits particular attention, as a higher participation rate of women will contribute in a decisive manner to the employment growth that is needed to maintain the prosperity of the Union's Member States. In more practical terms, this means that Member States should tackle "gender gaps", take appropriate action to allow women and men to reconcile work and family life, and facilitate the integration of women and men in the labour market.

Originally published in *International Labour Review*, Vol. 138 (1999), No. 4.

* Lecturer, Institute of Economics, Utrecht University; ** Ph.D. candidate, Department of Sociology and Interuniversity Centre for Social Science Theory and Methodology (ICS), Utrecht University. This article draws on and extends the coverage of an earlier report prepared by the same authors, as coordinators for the European Commission Group of Experts "Gender and Employment", and funded by the Community Action Programme for Equal Opportunities (1996-2000) (Plantenga and Hansen, 1999).

Effective monitoring of the measures taken depends on the development of a common set of indicators, which could be used as benchmarks against which to assess actual performance. Performance indicators play a vital role in signalling the strong or weak aspects of a national situation and in monitoring progress. Until now, however, it has been unclear which indicators are the most appropriate for evaluating national practices with regard to equal opportunities. As a result, verification of progress at national level is difficult, and cross-country comparison is severely hampered.

This chapter presents a set of comparable indicators to facilitate the process of evaluation and assessment. In doing so, it strives to achieve a dual goal. First, it aims to contribute to the methodology on assessing equal opportunities. In this sense, it is primarily concerned with the question of which indicators are important. Second, it undertakes an empirical exploration aimed at identifying countries that have achieved relative success in promoting equal opportunities and the reasons for performance gaps. At the same time, however, its underlying ambitions have to remain modest. "Equal opportunities" is a term with a variety of meanings and this article is but an initial exploration. It is concerned more with formulating the right questions than with generating definitive answers, though it does aim to advance the process of assessment. While its empirical exploration focuses on the countries of the European Union, it can be hoped that the methodology will have wider application.

SELECTING PERFORMANCE INDICATORS AND BENCHMARKING

Benchmarking was first introduced in the private sector as a means of enhancing efficiency by measuring the performance of one organization against a standard (Tronti, 1998). In essence, this means improving performance by looking at and analysing the achievements of others. This process has been described as "the practice of being humble enough to admit that someone else is better at something, and being wise enough to learn how to match and even surpass them at it" (Rolstadås, 1995, p. 212).

Over the past decade, benchmarking has also become common in the public sphere. Here its primary aim has been to improve the efficiency and effectiveness of government policy and/or the performance of public-sector organizations. Using this instrument in policy-making is not without difficulties, however. Socio-economic policy, for example, cannot be easily defined in terms of input and output, and performance may be affected by national particularities as well as international trends. This highly complicates the selection of a benchmark. For example: "Can the UK be designated the best performer because it attracts so many direct investments? Or should it be the Netherlands, as a country that still offers generous social security benefits? Both countries are winners in the fight against unemployment (at least if the unemployment rate is taken as the benchmark)" (Tronti, 1998, p. 34). Besides, a simple transfer of best practices might be impossible, due to different national structures, institutional environments and societal preferences. Obviously, such problems are particularly prone to arise with regard to gender relations, which differ greatly between the Member States of the European Union. The validity of policy recommendations in this field tends to be highly sensitive to context — e.g. what is relevant for Ireland could be completely unimportant in Denmark, and vice versa. Policy benchmarking in the field of equal opportunities should therefore always proceed with care, taking account of national contexts and the political feasibility of alternative policy options (Tronti, 1998, p. 41; see also Rubery, 1999, p. 9).

Strictly speaking, "equal opportunities" refers to a formal equality concept centring on "equal starting points" for women and men. Often, however, it is used more broadly to indicate the achievement of equal results. The ultimate goal of equal opportunities is then material equality, e.g. an equal distribution of work, care tasks and income. In the context of the European Union's social policy, equal opportunity is indeed often synonymous with such material equality, implying a broad definition of the term. The promotion of equal opportunities can then be defined as a process aimed at eliminating inequalities and promoting equality between women and men. From the very outset, this means that the concept of equal opportunities does not refer to women alone. Rather, it implies a change in the lives of both women and men through the promotion of greater equality in the distribution of paid and unpaid work between them (Rubery, 1999, p. 7). The question then is how to operationalize such a broad definition of equal opportunities. In other words: What are the relevant indicators?

In general, indicators should allow easy monitoring of current trends and facilitate inter-country comparison in terms of overall performance targets. The indicators selected must therefore be practical; they should be easy to read, meaningful and consistent. It would also appear sensible to limit their number; a large collection of indicators could obscure the most salient developments. A further important consideration here is that the indicators must be derived from Eurostat-material: after all, international comparisons require harmonized statistics (European Commission, 1998a).

At the same time, it should be borne in mind that equal opportunities is a term with diverse dimensions and many layers of meaning. Thus, the selection of indicators cannot be dictated by practical considerations alone if it is to do justice to the complexity of the concept. Accordingly, it is proposed to assess equal opportunities in national situations by taking two different approaches. The first focuses on an equal division of paid and unpaid work, and the second, on the position of women in the labour market.

The distribution of paid and unpaid work

The point of departure here is that equal opportunities policy should focus on the distribution of paid and unpaid work with the ultimate objective of eliminating differences between women and men in this respect. This operationalization conforms closely to the European Council's 1999 Employment Guidelines, which state that

> Member States will attempt to reduce the gap in unemployment rates between women and men by actively supporting the increased employment of women and will take action to bring about a balanced representation of women and men in all sectors and occupations. They will initiate positive steps to promote equal pay for equal work or work of equal value and to diminish differentials in incomes between women and men. In order to reduce gender gaps, Member States will also consider an increased use of measures for the advancement of women (European Council, 1999, p. 8).

If tackling "gender gaps" is the central focus, then the benchmark for country A is country U (Utopia) where an equal division of paid and unpaid work has already been achieved. Country A's final score will offer an indication of the existing inequalities between the positions of women and men and, as such, can be compared with the score of country B. To operationalize this approach, the following six indicators have been selected:

(1) employment rate of women compared to men's (head count);

(2) employment rate of mothers with young children (aged seven or less) compared to that of fathers (full-time equivalents);

(3) relative concentration of women in higher positions compared to men;

(4) male-female wage gap;

(5) proportion of women earning less than 50 per cent of national median income (on a yearly basis) compared to the corresponding proportion of men;

(6) male-female gap in unpaid time spent on caring for children and other persons.

Indicators (1) and (2) offer insight into the accessibility of the labour market for women and men. It is open to debate whether employment rates should be corrected for the number of hours worked, that is whether employment rates should be calculated from a simple head count or in full-time equivalents. In this article, indicator (1) is calculated on the basis of a simple head count and thus refers to the number of women (or men) "in touch" with the labour market, without any correction for the number of hours worked. Indicator (2), however, is expressed in full-time equivalents as the number of hours worked is especially important in the case of young parents. This indicator therefore provides information about the way young mothers and fathers are "addressed" by the various Member States, showing whether there is equal labour-market participation or, rather, a more specialized division of roles.

Whereas indicators (1) and (2) refer mainly to the quantitative aspects of the labour-market position of women (and men), indicators (3) and (4) offer information on their qualitative situation. Indicator (3) shows the extent of vertical segregation, by calculating the proportion of women (and men) employed in higher positions. The indicator reaches the value of "1" if the proportion of women in higher occupational categories is equal to their share of total employment, that is if women are not under-represented in higher positions. Indicator (4) focuses on the pay differential between women and men; this indicator reflects many of the differences between women and men, such as education, job choice, duration of employment contract, etc.

Indicator (5) provides information on the annual income generated by women and men. Given that women typically work fewer hours in paid employment, and that their hourly earnings tend to be lower, indicator (5) gives information on the economic power of women and men. Indicator (6), finally, refers to the unequal distribution of unpaid care work. This is a significant indicator of gender equity, not only because an equal distribution of unpaid work must be seen as a major precondition for an equal distribution of paid work, but also because an equal distribution of unpaid work should be perceived as an important emancipatory goal in itself. The assumption is that in a truly emancipated society, every citizen can participate in a balanced manner in all spheres of life — work, care and leisure.

The advantage of this set of indicators lies in its broad approach to paid and unpaid work and its explicit comparison between women and men. But it also has disadvantages. Specifically, if equality between women and men is defined as the absence of gender gaps, then insight into absolute levels is lost. For example, from a gender perspective, unemployment in Ireland looks better than it does in Austria because unemployment in Ireland in 1997 was 15.1 per cent among men and 16 per cent among women; whereas the corresponding figures for Austria were 3.5 and 5.3 per cent. Moreover, movements over time are difficult to evaluate because the gender gap in unemployment can be reduced either by a rise in the employment rate of women or by a rise in the unemployment rate of men. In short, some variables do not lend themselves to analyses based on reducing gender gaps and — however important they may be — must be left out of the equation.

In order to address these problems, national practices relating to equal opportunities are also charted in another way, namely, using a set of indictors that focus on the position of women on the labour market.

Women's position on the labour market

The emphasis here is on the absolute levels of employment and unemployment by age group. In this approach, the benchmark is not Utopia, but the mean of the three European countries with the highest (most positive or least negative) score on the given indicator. Country A's ultimate score thus indicates the degree to which its national situation deviates from that of the highest achieving Member States. This approach features the following indicators:

(1) female employment rate (head count);

(2) employment rate of mothers with children aged seven or less (full-time equivalents);

(3) employment rate of women aged 50-64 (full-time equivalents);

(4) proportion of women in higher positions;

(5) female unemployment rate;

(6) female youth unemployment rate.

The selection criteria for the first two indicators are similar to those mentioned in connection with the first set of indicators above; the assumption is that they offer a reasonable picture of the employment position of women. Indicator (3) focuses on a vulnerable group in the labour market — older women. The employment rate in this category provides information on the (im)possibility of combining paid work and care throughout the life cycle and/or the (im)possibility of re-entering the labour market. Indicator (4) again refers to the extent of vertical segregation. In contrast to the first set of indicators, here the proportion of women in higher occupational categories is calculated "absolutely" by dividing the number of women in such positions by the total number of persons employed in higher positions. The last two indicators refer to unemployment levels. Indicator (5) gives an overall picture; indicator (6) shows the rates for another vulnerable group: young women.

The advantage of this set of indicators is its focus on paid work, which fits in well with the general spirit of the European Council's 1999 Employment Guidelines and the underlying research (see European Commission, 1999a). However, the focus on paid work also has a disadvantage in that it implicitly takes paid work as an ideal worth striving for without taking any account of unpaid work. This highlights the fact that benchmarking based exclusively on quantitative scores can be misleading; a correct evaluation of specific developments requires insight into their full context.

BENCHMARKING EQUAL OPPORTUNITIES
IN THE EUROPEAN UNION

The results of the benchmarking procedure are charted in figures 1 to 4. The method adopted here is the radar-chart approach, one of a number of tools developed to identify best performances (Tronti, 1998). A radar chart consists of several axes radiating from a centre, each of which represents a separate indicator. And each indicator is scaled in such a way that the highest score — i.e. the best performance — is equal to "1". By comparing a country's actual score with this benchmark score it is possible to calculate its relative score (or relative performance). The actual values on the axes are then used to delineate a calculable area: the larger the area — i.e. the closer a country's actual values are to the ideal benchmarks — the more favourable the situation of the country concerned. The total surface of the diagram can then be calculated in a so-called SMOP index (Surface Measure of Overall Performance) summarizing each country's overall situation for comparison (see Speckesser, Schütz and Schmid, 1998, pp. 76 et seq.).

Equal opportunities, referring to an equal distribution of paid and unpaid work

In the first instance equal opportunities are defined by reference to an equal distribution of paid and unpaid work. The cross-national comparison based on the corresponding SMOP index is charted in figure 1. Immediately striking are the low values of the SMOP index; on a scale of 0 to 1, all countries score less than 0.5. Comparatively, the Scandinavian countries do best, while the Netherlands comes in last with a value of 0.18.

Further analysis of the relevant data on the basis of the radar charts shows that differences between women and men on the first indicator (employment rate) are relatively moderate (see figure 2). The Union-wide average is just above 0.7. In this respect, only Spain, Greece and Italy score considerably lower, while Denmark and Sweden score considerably higher. Inter-country differences increase significantly when the employment rates of fathers and mothers with young children are compared — indicating that in some countries the employment rate of women is still strongly influenced by family status. At 0.75, Sweden has the most equitable score on the relative employment of mothers with a child under seven, followed by Denmark and Finland. The Netherlands clearly loses ground on this indicator with a score of only 0.29.

The score on indicator (3) — the relative concentration of women in higher positions — is striking. Spain scores high on this indicator, as does Luxembourg. Sweden, by contrast, is disappointing; in spite of its high rate of female employment, women are clearly underrepresented in

Figure 1. Comparing equal opportunities by reference to an equal distribution of paid and unpaid work, SMOP-index 1997 (standardized to value "1")

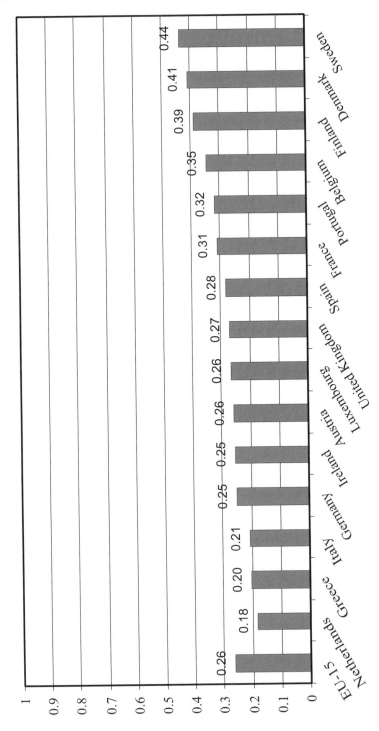

Figure 2. Distribution of paid and unpaid work: Radar charts for six European countries, 1997

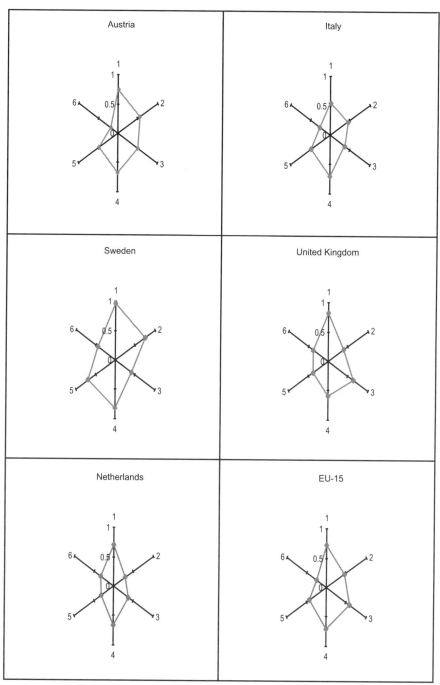

the higher occupational categories. This result confirms earlier research which showed there was no logical link between the extent of (vertical) segregation and the level of labour-market participation; there is indeed no evidence that higher rates of female participation in the labour force and/or higher levels of economic development reduce the level of vertical segregation (Rubery and Fagan, 1995).

Indicator (4) — the male-female wage gap — is based on unpublished data from the "Structure of Earnings Survey" and refers to the gross hourly wages of women as a percentage of the gross hourly wages of men (overtime excluded). Scores here range from 0.59 in the United Kingdom to 0.82 in Sweden, with the Union-wide average at 0.70. If the difference in hours worked is also taken into account in addition to the hourly pay differential, then the disparity between women and men clearly becomes much greater, as shown by the scores on indicator (5). Denmark and Sweden still score relatively high at 0.67; but Luxembourg and Ireland show values of 0.27. This means that in these two countries almost four times as many women as men earn less than 50 per cent of the national median income. Finally, all countries score badly on indicator (6) — male-female gap in unpaid time. Here national performance is measured from unpublished data of the "European Community Household Panel", which gives information on the time women and men spend looking after children and other persons. The average score is around 0.24. This means that women spend about four times as much time as men on caring tasks. The division is somewhat more equitable only in Denmark and Sweden, which score 0.55 and 0.44 respectively. The division is most unequal in Greece and Portugal, which both score 0.15.

Equal opportunities, referring to the position of women on the labour market

In this second approach, equal opportunities are not defined in terms of gender equity, but by reference to the position of women on the labour market. The results for 1997 are presented in figures 3 and 4. Variation between countries turns out to be much greater with this second set of indicators than it was when the first set was used. Here Austria, Denmark, Portugal, Sweden and Luxembourg display the highest overall performance, whereas Italy and Spain perform especially poorly.

A more detailed analysis on the basis of the radar charts indicates that the high scores of Austria and Sweden are the results of somewhat different labour market patterns. Sweden performs well on the right-hand side of the chart, i.e. on the employment indicators, with less favourable scores on the unemployment indicators. Austria, by contrast, performs well on the left-hand side of the chart, i.e. on the unemployment indicators. But its scores on employment indicators are less favourable than Sweden's. Italy's low score appears to be largely due to high unemploy-

Figure 3. Comparing equal opportunities by reference to the position of women on the labour market, SMOP-index 1997 (standardized to value "1")

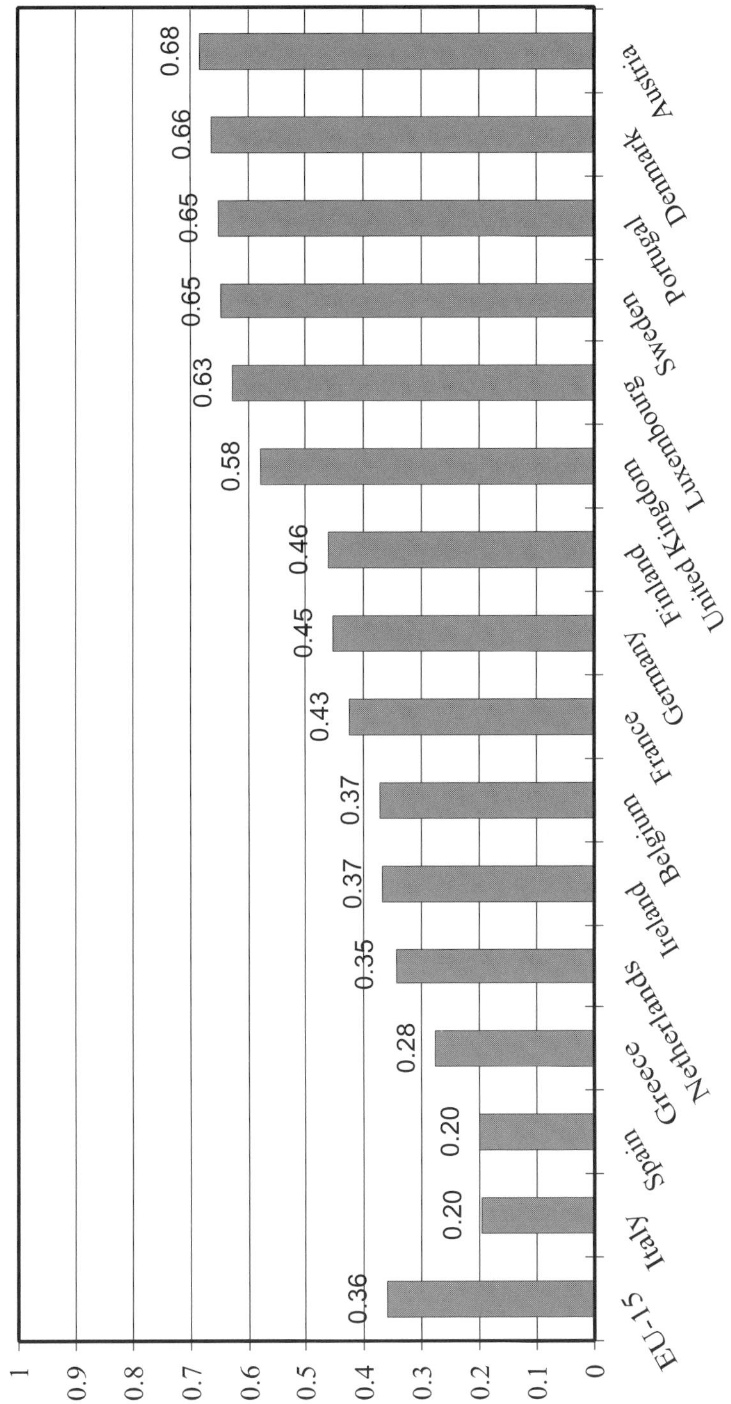

Women, gender and work

Figure 4. Position of women on the labour market: Radar charts of six European
countries, 1997

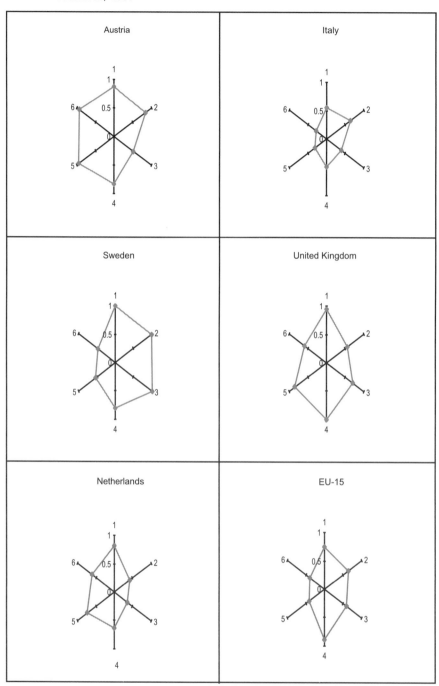

ment among women. In 1997, its female unemployment rate was 16.6 per cent with female youth unemployment at 13.5 per cent. However, at 36.7 per cent, its female employment rate is also below average. Italy only scores reasonably well on indicator (2): the employment rate of women with children under seven.

Equal opportunities in the European Union: Overall performance

The results of both of the foregoing analyses can now be summarized in a single composite index for 1997, as shown in figure 5. From this presentation, it appears that the countries can be broadly grouped into four clusters. The first consists of those scoring below the Union-wide average, i.e. Italy, Greece, Spain and the Netherlands. The second comprises countries whose overall performance matches or slightly exceeds that average, i.e. Ireland, Germany, Belgium and France. The third cluster consists of countries that perform above average, i.e. the United Kingdom, Finland, Luxembourg, Austria, and Portugal. Finally, two countries stand out for their particularly good score: Sweden and Denmark.

A word of caution seems in order, however. The results obtained through the radar chart approach, as well as the index measuring overall performance, reflect both the choice of indicators and an assumption of equal weighting across all indicators. In particular, the choice of indicators is conditioned by the availability of comparable data, with the result that indicators of income and time are relatively underdeveloped. In addition, high participation rates are valued positively, regardless of wage levels and social infrastructure (e.g. availability of childcare, shop opening hours, etc.). None the less, the indicators seem "solid" enough to help identify the strengths and weaknesses of national situations and monitor progress in the field of equal opportunities.

KEY DETERMINANTS

Benchmarking equal opportunities has so far been a rather mechanical process, amounting to little more than a simple comparison of scores without any real focus on context, causes, etc. The very value of benchmarking lies in this basic comparison, stripped of any explanation or direct reference to factors which influence outcomes. The analysis of relative scores comes as a second stage which questions the background to apparent differences in performance. For example, why does the Netherlands score less than Austria, and why does Ireland come in behind Denmark?

The starting point of this chapter was that the current status of equal opportunities, as documented above, should be interpreted as the result

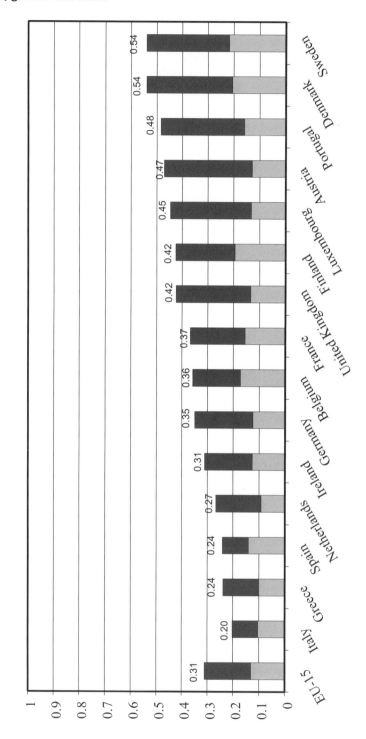

Figure 5. Performance summary: Distribution of paid and unpaid work and position of women on the labour market in the 15 Member States, 1997

of a highly complex process in which economic, sociological, political and cultural factors all play a part. The economic situation, for example, plays an important role in determining demand for labour and levels and trends in unemployment. Equal opportunities, however, are not only a matter of supply and demand. Attitudes also play a part, as do the ways in which those attitudes are anchored into social organization. This relates, inter alia, to income and employment policies, the division between public and private care, and the extent to which care activities are remunerated.

Against this backdrop (and given the need to keep the workload within the limits of this chapter) it has been decided to chart differences between countries using a total of six factors, namely:

- economic growth and employment;
- attitudes towards women's employment;
- tax system;
- working-time regime;
- childcare facilities;
- leave arrangements.

The first two factors refer to fundamental determinants of labour market performance, such as economic growth and the supply of female labour. In a complex interplay between the employment regime and socio-economic policy, these factors contribute substantially to shaping the ultimate equal opportunities environment. The next two factors reflect the employment regime, defined here as the set of interlocking social and economic arrangements. A tax system, for example, might act as an incentive or as a disincentive to the employment of women; a working-time regime may also be more or less favourable to dual career patterns. The last two factors refer explicitly to socio-economic policy and, more particularly, to those areas of policy which are considered important from an equal opportunities perspective.

Of course, within the context of this chapter, only the main features of the various determining factors can be discussed. On the basis of harmonized data, the aim is to relate the performance level to a limited number of social and economic indicators. Relating input to output — though a highly complicated procedure — should in principle give some information about the efficiency of different socio-economic settings from an equal opportunities point of view.

Economic growth and employment

Generally speaking, the first half of the 1990s was characterized in Europe by recession, little net job creation and rising unemployment. Economic recovery, which began in 1994, gathered momentum in the

Table 1. Annual growth rates of GDP and employment, 1992-97

	Real GDP growth			Total employment growth		
	1996	1997	Average growth 1992-97	1996	1997	Average growth 1992-97
Austria	1.6	2.5	1.8	−1.30	0.25	0.95
Belgium	1.5	2.7	1.4	−0.05	1.24	0.36
Denmark	2.5	2.9	2.6	1.34	2.56	0.71
Finland	3.6	5.9	3.6	1.36	3.98	0.06
France	1.6	2.3	1.5	0.01	0.09	−0.03
Germany	1.3	2.2	1.4	−1.14	−1.56	−1.09
Greece	2.6	3.5	1.6	1.23	−0.39	0.92
Ireland	8.6	10.0	8.2	3.65	4.97	3.63
Italy	0.7	1.5	1.2	0.48	0.03	−1.36
Luxembourg	2.6	4.1	3.6	2.58	...	1.86
Netherlands	3.3	3.4	2.6	2.13	2.79	1.47
Portugal	3.0	3.7	2.1	0.68	1.92	0.00
Spain	2.3	3.4	1.9	2.94	2.98	0.64
Sweden	1.3	1.8	1.6	−0.58	−1.04	−1.40
United Kingdom	2.2	3.5	3.0	0.93	1.66	0.65
EU-15	..	2.6	..	..	0.53	..

... Data not available. .. Data not applicable.

Source: Compiled from European Commission, 1999b, Part II.

second half of the decade due to improved competitiveness in international markets and strong growth in domestic demand. Higher economic growth also resulted in (modest) employment growth in the European Union. Total employment now stands at 149 million, but remains below the peak level reached in 1991 at the start of the recession (European Commission, 1998b, p. 7 and 1999b, p. 17).

There are considerable variations in growth rates across the different countries (see table 1). Ireland, in particular, has recorded high growth rates in both GDP and employment. Overall, the Irish economy grew by 45 per cent over the period 1992-97, achieving large and continuous employment gains in the process. Luxembourg, the Netherlands, Austria and Greece also performed relatively well in terms of job creation, although Greece — despite good economic performance — sustained a slight decline in its employment growth rate in 1997 after a steady average annual increase over the period 1992-97 (European Commission, 1999b, p. 69). In Italy, Germany and Sweden, by contrast, the situation has been less favourable. Italy experienced only moderate GDP growth in the period 1992-97. In the same period, employment decreased sharply with a marginal rise in 1996 and 1997, largely due to female employ-

Table 2. Views by women and men about employment, 1996

	"I tend to agree that it is just as important for a woman to have a job as it is for a man"		"I tend to agree with the following statement: When jobs are scarce, men should have priority over women"	
	Men	Women	Men	Women
Austria	68	79	43	29
Belgium	81	86	54	44
Denmark	92	91	8	11
Finland	94	96	13	13
France	84	93	33	26
Germany	80	87	37	26
– West Germany	76	84	39	29
– East Germany	94	98	32	17
Greece	84	91	58	42
Ireland	78	84	39	29
Italy	87	89	48	38
Luxembourg	77	83	33	32
Netherlands	83	86	27	26
Portugal	91	95	47	35
Spain	86	92	32	29
Sweden	97	97	8	8
United Kingdom	79	83	30	32
EU-15	83	89	36	29

Source: Compiled from European Commission, 1998c.

ment. In general, the Italian labour market is characterized by low employment and high unemployment and a severe imbalance between the North and the South (European Commission, 1999b, pp. 85-86). In Germany, the working population was 7 per cent smaller in 1997 than it was before the start of the recession in 1991 — a loss of over 2.5 million jobs. A large share of job losses occurred in the new Länder (former East Germany), where employment declined by some 17 per cent over this same period (European Commission, 1998b, p. 10). Employment also declined in Sweden due to a structural shock in the mid-1990s which led to cuts in government spending and public-sector employment (European Commission, 1999b, p. 109).

Attitudes towards women's employment

As well as involving personal choice and being subject to economic constraints, the question of women going out to work is also imbedded in a cultural belief system. In general, younger generations tend to be more in favour of working women, so the long-term trend is positive. In fact, in 1996, 86 per cent of Europeans considered that it was just as

Table 3. Types of family taxation in the European Union

	Joint taxation	Allowances and credits		Single parent
		Child	Couple	
Group A: Independent tax, few family tax instruments				
Denmark	N	N	N	N
Finland	N	N	N	N
Sweden	N	N	N	N
United Kingdom	N	N	N	Y
Group B: Independent tax: many family tax instruments				
Austria	N	Y	N	Y
Greece	N	Y	Y	N
Italy	N	Y	Y	N
Netherlands	N	N	Y	Y
Group C: Optional joint taxation				
Belgium	Y	Y	Y	Y
Germany	Y	Y	Y	Y
Ireland	Y	N	N	Y
Spain	Y	Y	Y	N
Group D: Mandatory joint taxation				
France	Y	N	Y	N
Luxembourg	Y	N	N	Y
Portugal	Y	N	Y	N

Source: O'Donoghue and Sutherland, 1998, p. 21.

important for a woman to have a job as it was for a man. In all age groups, this view was more prevalent among women than it was among men (89 per cent of women compared to 83 per cent of men). The virtual unanimity among young women corresponds closely to the long-term trend: 96 per cent of the women aged 15-24 tended to agree that it was as important for a woman to have a job as it was for a man (European Commission, 1998c, p. 26). Comparing attitudes by country, it appears that the classification is headed by Swedish men, 97 per cent of whom consider work to be just as important for women as it is for men (see table 2). They are followed by the men of the former German Democratic Republic and by Finnish, Danish and Portuguese men, with percentages ranging from 91 to 94. Surprisingly, Austrian men score rather low, with only 68 per cent holding the opinion that paid work is as important for women as it is for men. While there seems to be a certain consensus on this issue between women and men in Sweden, the differences between them are quite marked in Austria, France and the former West Germany.

Opinions vary more widely when paid jobs become scarce. In this case, 32 per cent of the European population believe that men should be given priority access to employment. Support for this view is higher among men (36 per cent) than among women (29 per cent). Outcomes by country suggest a sharp contrast between Sweden, Finland and Denmark — whose emphasis on gender equity results in a low percentage of women and men favouring male priority — and Belgium and Greece, where more than 40 per cent of the women and a considerable majority of the men tend to agree with such priority. Also in Italy, Portugal and Austria a substantial percentage of both women and men seem to favour male priority when jobs are scarce, while Germany, France and Spain are close to the European Union average.

Fiscal regime

Tax systems are often complex in their structure and consequences. Taxes are primarily an instrument for raising revenues, but the fiscal system can also be a policy tool in other areas, and a reflection of underlying notions about society. In many countries the question of whether the income tax regime should be geared to individuals or households has been an important issue, and it is this distinction which is especially important for female employment. Under a system of joint taxation, a secondary earner faces the marginal rate of the primary earner from the first unit of earnings. In a progressive system, this tax rate will be higher than if the couple were taxed as two separate individuals. Joint taxation therefore provides a disincentive for secondary workers (mostly women) relative to individual taxation (OECD, 1997, p. 57; Rubery, Smith, Fagan and Grimshaw, 1998, pp. 210-213). "Modified" individual systems follow the principle of individual taxation, but provide additional tax relief to individuals with household dependents, for example by permitting a transference of the basic tax relief. Transferable allowances provide a reinforcement of the breadwinner role and may discourage labour market (re-)entry for women, although the disincentive will probably be less than that faced under joint taxation. Table 3 summarizes the different tax systems in the participating countries. The focus is on whether each country has an individual- or household-based system, and on any exceptions to the general rule (see Meulders, 1999).

The first group of countries consists of Denmark, Finland, Sweden and the United Kingdom. The system in these countries is based on independent taxation of individuals; they do not have major tax-based redistributive mechanisms for couples and/or children. The second group consists of countries using independent taxation, but which have instruments accounting for both couples and children. The Dutch tax system, for example, is characterized by a so-called progressive graded system based on income brackets with a basic allowance. In principle, the system treats women and men as individuals; each faces the same structure of tax rates. However, in case of marriage (or cohabitation) the unpaid partner is allowed to transfer the basic allowance to the breadwinner (Grift, 1998). The Austrian tax system follows the principle of individual taxation and regards the incomes of married partners as the incomes of two single persons. There is, however, a tax credit for couples on a single income, weakening the system of individualization (Pastner, 1999, p. 20).

The third and fourth groups use a system of joint taxation, be it optional or mandatory. In Belgium, for example, married couples are taxed as two separate individuals, but if one of the spouses does not have an income or if the earned income is very low, a family quotient is applied. The spouse with an income can transfer up to 30 per cent of the joint income to the spouse with no or very low income. The transferred income is viewed as a fictional salary for working at home (Meulders and Hecq, 1999, p. 7). Income splitting is even stronger in Germany where 50 per cent of the earnings of the primary earner can be assigned to the non-employed spouse (Maier and Rapp, 1999, p. 12). Unless both spouses have the same earnings, income splitting increases the tax on the lower income while reducing that on the higher income compared to what it would be if taxed on an individual basis. In general, joint taxation provides a clear benefit for families living on a high single (or, at least, unequally distributed) income.

In principle non-individual systems all imply a disadvantage from an equal opportunities perspective, but it nevertheless remains difficult to draw specific conclusions on the effects of the various fiscal regimes. Not only are differences hard to chart, but research into the effects of marginal tax rates on labour supply also fails to generate unequivocal results. Indeed, the actual size of the labour response to marginal tax rates "is still the subject of debate among empirical economists after more than 20 years of analysis" (OECD, 1994, p. 58). It would thus appear that the actual fiscal regime sends out a signal on what is considered the most desirable division of labour, rather than exerting strong influence on the actual behaviour of women.

Working-time regime

A country's working-time regime can — like its fiscal regime — either promote or diminish gender equality. Differences in working time between men and women arise primarily from the unequal division of unpaid work, but the extent and form that those differences take in the labour market are moderated or mediated by national working-time regimes, defined as "the national set of legal, voluntary and customary regulations which influence working time practice" (Rubery, Smith and Fagan, 1998, p. 72). Working-time regimes can promote or diminish gen-

Table 4. Working-time regimes in the 15 Member States, 1997

	Average full-time hours, employees	Full-time hours worked by women as a percentage of full-time hours worked by men	Share of employees on long working hours (46 or more per week)	Share of female employees in part-time jobs with long hours (25 or more per week)	Share of employees in part-time jobs with short hours (10 or less per week)
Austria	40.0	99.0	3.3	11.7	2.4
Belgium	38.3	95.6	3.2	10.4	2.1
Denmark	38.6	95.7	5.5	17.6	7.5
Finland	39.1	96.0	4.2	6.8	2.6
France	39.7	95.3	6.8	13.0	3.2
Germany	40.1	97.5	6.2	9.0	6.8
Greece	40.5	94.0	17.6	1.6	0.0
Ireland	40.1	91.1	10.5	3.5	4.1
Italy	38.5	91.2	9.1	3.8	0.0
Luxembourg	39.5	93.8	3.8	0.0	0.0
Netherlands	39.2	98.7	1.0	18.5	17.3
Portugal	40.9	92.4	10.0	2.5	2.2
Spain	40.6	96.4	7.8	2.9	3.7
Sweden	40.1	99.8	2.2	24.1	3.7
United Kingdom	44.0	89.1	24.0	10.6	9.4
European Union	40.4	94.4	9.9	9.9	5.9

Source: Eurostat, 1998.

der equality by limiting or extending full-time working hours, by promoting or discouraging part-time work, and by influencing the terms and conditions under which overtime, unsocial hours or atypical employment contracts are undertaken. More specifically, seven characteristics of working-time regimes have been identified as being relatively favourable for gender equality, namely:

- relatively short full-time hours;
- a small male-female gap in average full-time hours;
- small proportions of both women and men on very long hours;
- opportunities for women to work long part-time/short full-time hours;
- a small proportion of women in jobs involving short hours of work;
- a low rate of unsocial hours worked by both women and men;
- relatively equal employment of women and men on unsocial hours and no particular tendency to use female part-time work to cover unsocial hours (Rubery, Smith and Fagan, 1998, pp. 79-80).

These characteristics are based on the twin principles of a better balance of time allocation as between women and men and a better balance in the allocation of time between paid and unpaid work. Table 4 gives some information on these issues, although a straightforward comparison between countries is difficult, due to lack of data and the fact that the interpretation of available data is not always self-evident.

Table 4 shows fairly wide differences between countries which cannot be easily combined within one coherent framework. Nevertheless, it seems fair to say that the Swedish working-time regime is not unfavourable for gender equality: Sweden displays virtually no male-female gap in respect of full-time working hours, a low share of employees on long working hours, and a very favourable ratio between employees in part-time jobs with long hours and those in part-time jobs with short hours. Belgium, Denmark, France and Austria also appear to offer a rather favourable working-time regime. In comparison, the situation in Greece, Ireland, Luxembourg, Portugal and the United Kingdom seems less favourable; here, the share of employees on long working hours is relatively high, while the share of female employees in part-time jobs with long hours is relatively low. The United Kingdom, in particular, is quite extreme with 24 per cent of employees on long working hours. The situation in the Netherlands is also rather exceptional in the sense that the share of employees on long working hours is very low. The most striking point, however, is its large share of part-time workers, especially the proportion of those on short hours which is far above the European Union average. This is (partly) the result of an explicit policy of encouraging individualized working-time arrangements because of the flexibility they offer both the employer and the employee. The outcomes are controversial, however. Because of the high percentage of women working part time, women in the Netherlands work only 66 per cent on average of the weekly hours worked by men, compared to an average of 80 per cent for the European Union as a whole (Plantenga, Schippers and Siegers, 1999, p. 101).

Childcare facilities

Personal services are extremely important in the lives of working parents. This applies in particular to childcare services, as care responsibilities constitute a major obstacle to (full) employment. The importance of measures in this area has also been recognized at the highest level within the European Union. In March 1992, the European Council passed a recommendation on childcare to the effect that Member States "should take and/or progressively encourage initiatives to enable women and men to reconcile their occupational, family and upbringing responsibilities arising from the care of children" (European Council, 1992, p. 17). But this recommendation is an example of soft law; there are no sanctions for non-compliance and its interpretation by Member States is discretionary (Roelofs, 1995, p. 129). In practice, the level and nature of childcare differs considerably between countries (see table 5).

Table 5. Provision of publicly funded childcare services

Country (year)	Children attending/places available in publicly funded services for children aged 0-6 (percentage of number of children in corresponding age group)	
	0-3 years	3-6 years
Austria (1994)	3	75
Belgium (1993)	30	95
Denmark (1994)	48	82
Finland (1994)	21	53
France (1993)	23	99
Germany (1996)		
– West	2.2	85.2
– East	41.3	116.8
Greece (1993)	3	70
Ireland (1993)	2	55
Italy (1991)	6	91
Netherlands (1993)	8	71
Norway (1995)	31*	72
Portugal (1993)	12	48
Spain (1993)	2	84
Sweden (1994)	33	72
United Kingdom (1993)	2	60

*Age group 1-2 years.

Source: Deven et al., 1997, table 1.1.

The organization of childcare is closely related to general cultural attitudes towards the family. Some countries pursue a highly reserved policy on this issue because children are seen above all as the private responsibility of parents. Parents may then be supported financially through child allowance and/or fiscal arrangements covering care for their children; but the actual care remains within the family. This family-based system applies, for example, to Germany and Austria. Regulations in both countries are based on the assumption of a full-time female care-taker in what Maier and Rapp describe as a "three-phase-model" of mothers' employment. Such a system, they argue, "follows a track of (at least partial) withdrawal from employment during care periods ... by offering time (i.e. leave periods) and money (i.e. child allowance and parental leave allowances)" (Maier and Rapp, 1999, p. 15). As a result, in Germany and Austria there is a dearth of publicly provided and publicly subsidized private childcare for children under the age of three. Other countries with elements of a family-based system and with a low level of childcare provision are Greece, Ireland, Italy, the Netherlands, Spain and the United Kingdom.

Figure 6. Consecutive weeks of maternity plus parental leave available to the family

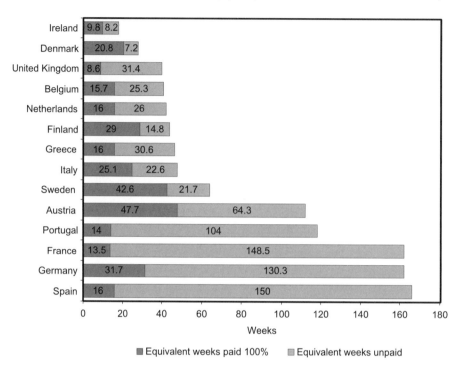

Source: Bettio and Prectal, 1998, p. 19.

Only five countries have a relatively well developed childcare system for young children: Belgium, Denmark, Finland, France and Sweden. These same countries also provide medium to high volumes of facilities for older children. In Germany there is a striking imbalance in the availability of such services between the eastern and western parts of the country. Recently, in order to streamline social policy, some efforts have been made to increase overall supply. Children older than three are now legally entitled to a place in a public care centre, but the legal entitlement actually guarantees a place in a relatively costly part-time care centre, offering only five hours a day and no lunch (Bettio and Prechal, 1998, p. 27).

Leave arrangements

Parental leave is another important instrument in facilitating a combination of employment and family responsibilities. Since June 1996, national policy in this field has been underpinned by a directive of the

Table 6. Overall performance in relation to determining factors

	Overall performance	Economic growth and employment	Attitudes	Fiscal regime	Working-time regime	Child-care facilities	Leave arrange-ments
Italy	Low	−	−	+/−	+/−	+/−	+/−
Greece	Low	+	−	+/−	−	−	+/−
Spain	Low	+/−	+/−	+/−	+/−	−	+/−
Netherlands	Low	+	+	+/−	(+)	−	+/−
Ireland	Medium	++	+/−	+/−	−	−	−
Germany	Medium	−	+/−	+/−	+/−	−	++
Belgium	Medium	+/−	−	+/−	+	+	+
France	Medium	+/−	+/−	+/−	+	+	+/−
United Kingdom	Medium/high	+/−	+/−	+	−−	−	−
Finland	Medium/high	+/−	++	+	+/−	+	++
Luxembourg	Medium/high	+	+/−	+/−	−	...	...
Austria	Medium/high	+	−	+/−	+	−	++
Portugal	Medium/high	+/−	+/−	+/−	−	+/−	+/−
Denmark	High	+/−	++	+	+	+	+
Sweden	High	−	++	+	++	+	++

European Council which obliges Member States (in principle by June 1998) to introduce legislation on parental leave that will enable parents to care full-time for their child over a period of three months (see European Council, 1996). In principle, this refers to an individual, non-transferable entitlement.

This directive ensures that a certain minimum standard is guaranteed within the Member States. Over and above this, however, there is a broad range of national regulations, with countries differing as to payments, duration, flexibility and statutory entitlement. For example, Austria has legislated paid parental leave for up to two years which can also be taken on a part-time basis, whereas in the Netherlands, parental leave is unpaid, lasts only six months and should, in principle, be taken on a part-time basis. Differences between countries are hard to chart, because the distinctions between parental, maternity and paternity leave are blurred. In the Nordic countries in particular, the available data cover both people taking parental leave and those taking what would, in other countries, be called maternity or paternity leave (Bruning and Plantenga, 1999).

In order fully to reflect the extent of institutional variations, figure 6 gives an overview of the maximum combined duration of maternity and parental leaves. Differences between countries are considerable in this respect, from between 166 and 162 weeks in Spain, Germany and France, down to 18 weeks in Ireland. The ranking of countries changes significantly, however, if only the duration of paid leave is taken into account. On the basis of this indicator, Sweden and Austria are the most generous countries, with an equivalent of 42.6 and 47.7 weeks on full earnings, respectively (Bettio and Prechal, 1998, p. 20).

Obviously, formal regulations say little about the actual impact of such measures on equal opportunities. This calls for information on the popularity of the measures, i.e. take-up rates and actual duration of leave taken. Although (comparable) data on these points are scarce, the information available suggests that parental leave only plays a significant role in Austria, Germany, Sweden and Finland. Belgium and Denmark have a relatively popular programme for career interruption which is often used for the purpose of childcare. Ireland only legislated parental leave in June 1998; the United Kingdom is expected to follow in 1999 (Bruning and Plantenga, 1999).

ASSESSING EQUAL OPPORTUNITIES: AN OVERVIEW

The question now is whether overall performance can be understood from scores on determining factors. Obviously, this is a potential minefield. Given the nature of this research, only the main aspects of the various factors have been discussed without much attention to mutual interrelations and socio-economic context. Causalities may be less unequivocal than suggested in this article and context may explain everything. Yet if all of these complicating factors are put aside and an attempt at evaluation were undertaken none the less, then the result would be as shown in table 6.

Sweden and Denmark

Based on table 6, the high scores of Sweden and Denmark on equal opportunities are comprehensible in the light of the determining factors considered. In both countries, the fiscal and working-time regimes comprise few disincentives against an equitable labour market for women and men; both countries pursue an active policy on childcare, and gender equity in paid employment is hardly an issue of contention. The only "minuses" are to be found in the field of economic growth and structural change. More generally, any remaining gender inequality in these two countries appears to stem primarily from the vestiges of an unequal division of unpaid work. The organization of the employment regime is strongly oriented towards gender equality; and the same applies to social policy. The fact that women still spend (more than) twice as much time on care activities as men, however, implies that women continue to work under different conditions.

Italy, Greece, Spain and the Netherlands

A striking common feature of the lowest scoring countries is their lack of a consistent care policy. None of these countries pursues an explicit policy on childcare or parental leave. Moreover, the employment regime in these countries comprises few positive incentives, whereas cultural attitudes, especially in Italy and Greece, seem to favour men's employment over women's.

The most striking factor in the situation of the Netherlands is its working-time regime (to indicate its complex and rather contested nature the "plus" sign is put between parentheses). In this case, the lack of an explicit care policy appears to be compensated by a working-time policy geared to individualized arrangements. Employees can adjust their working times to suit their individual requirements without being disproportionately punished through loss of income, social security and (up to a point) career prospects (Plantenga, Schippers and Siegers, 1999). The result of this strategy in terms of equal opportunities, however, seems dubious. Apparently, a policy focusing on working time without a complementary policy on care is insufficient to achieve a certain level of gender equity in terms of work, income and care.

Ireland, Belgium, Germany and France

These four countries make up the middle category. As in the countries of southern Europe and the Netherlands, Ireland's employment regime offers few positive incentives. Its fiscal regime is strongly geared to the family and its working-time regime is unfavourable because of long working hours and the low incidence of part-time jobs (with long working hours). Policy on the combination of work and care is largely lacking; childcare and parental leave are only minimally facilitated. Ireland's strong trump card, however, is its spectacular economic growth:

> probably the least talked about aspect of the current strong growth in the Irish economy is the crucial role which women are playing. Almost all the employment growth which has taken place over recent years has been female ... Highest (and rising) rates of participation occur among mothers with younger children, reflecting a generational difference in the labour market behaviour of women. More younger women stay in the work force during child rearing and the rate at which this is happening is rising all the time (Barry, 1999, p. 8/11).

Germany has a fairly traditionally oriented employment regime, while its social policy focuses on the privatization of care time, at least in so far as the care of young children is concerned. As regards supply and demand, Germany is battling against a worrying economic situation and inability to create jobs. Moreover, Germany has two faces: the strongly egalitarian east and the far more traditional west. In this respect, the unification process appears western (i.e. traditional) in orientation: women's labour-market participation is declining, while the east's favourable regulations on the combination of work and care are gradually being superseded by less beneficial measures.

The employment regimes of Belgium and France are also fairly traditional in orientation, although their working-time regimes score rather more favourably than Germany's. In addition, Belgium and France

invest much more in childcare, resulting in a high labour-market participation of mothers with young children. It is striking that Belgium (like
Italy, Greece and Austria) scores a negative on the attitude factor. Nevertheless, Belgium scores favourably on equal opportunities when these
are defined in terms of an absence of gender gaps.

United Kingdom, Finland, Luxembourg, Austria and Portugal

This cluster of countries seems to be the most puzzling. The me-
dium/high score of the United Kingdom, for example, is rather remarkable, given its lack of a consistent care policy and its unfavourable working-time regime. The medium/high overall scores of Portugal and Austria also raise some doubts. The equality ideal has rather shallow roots in
Austria; and Portugal, despite its rather high overall performance, fails to
score a single "plus" with regard to the determining factors.

Further analysis of the radar charts in figures 2 and 4 above shows
that neither Austria nor the United Kingdom scores highly on equal opportunities when defined as an equal division of paid and unpaid work,
which seems consistent with their scores in table 6. However, if equal
opportunities refer to the position of women on the labour market, then
Austria's performance improves considerably, because of the favourable
unemployment situation of women. The United Kingdom, for its part,
scores particularly well on the employment indicator, and its score on
indicator 4 (share of women in higher positions) is also above average.
The medium/high overall performances of the United Kingdom and Austria
thus partly reflect the methodology employed, whereby a low unemployment rate generates an equally good score as a high employment
rate, or a non-existent wage gap between women and men.

Portugal stands out in many respects. Whereas the other southern
European countries feature the lowest scores, Portugal ranks "medium"
with regard to the equal distribution of paid and unpaid work and occupies the third highest position when equal opportunities refer to the position of women on the labour market. It scores especially well on the
employment indicators. Presumably, in this country, informal care services (domestic servants, grandparents and other relatives) are of particular importance.

SUMMARY AND CONCLUSIONS

What lessons can be distilled from the foregoing exercise? To start
with, it should be emphasized once more that equal opportunity is a complex issue whose many aspects are difficult to chart unequivocally. The
above overview shows that within Europe there are many different institutional and social arrangements, all of which affect the distribution of

work, income and care. Without insight into the socio-economic context, it is hard to identify general patterns. Still, a few conclusions are inescapable, with regard both to the methodology applied and to the empirical results obtained.

The success of any responsible benchmarking procedure depends entirely on the availability of comparable, harmonized data. Reliable data sources are scarce, especially in the fields of earnings, income and time use. Obviously, such statistical limitations influence the selection of performance indicators; it is indeed tempting to focus on the relatively well-charted area of paid work and/or unemployment, thereby implicitly narrowing the definition given to equal opportunities.

In the field of paid work itself, however, a number of developments have been hampering international comparative research. Until very recently, distinct boundaries could be drawn between paid and unpaid work, between occupational and non-occupational activity. But these distinctions appear to be fading under the influence of subsidized jobs, leave regulations and varied working-time patterns. The statistical processing of those developments has so far focused mainly on the part-time factor: by taking account of contractual working time, the employment levels of, say, mothers with young children can be recalculated in full-time equivalents. By contrast, the statistical processing of leave arrangements has received much less attention. Statistical data is still usually arranged around such apparently unequivocal categories as "active" and "non-active". People who find themselves in transition between "active" and "non-active" — because they are on (parental) leave — are not registered as such, which considerably complicates comparative research.

In promoting equal opportunities, guideline 20 of the European Council's 1999 Employment Guidelines states that the focus should be on "tackling gender gaps". This would appear a relatively useful approach for some indicators. Unpaid work, for example, is clearly a distributional issue, and its absolute level a matter of lesser importance. However, this is not always the case by any means. For example, unemployment also plays a significant role in absolute terms and cannot be considered solely in terms of male-female differentials. Moreover, if gender equality is defined as the absence of gender gaps, movements in time will be difficult to evaluate because the gap between, say, female and male unemployment can be reduced either through a rise in the employment rate of women or through a rise in the unemployment rate of men. In short, without information on backgrounds and context, the effectiveness of an equal opportunities policy cannot be measured by the extent to which it is able to reduce gender gaps.

A problematic aspect of the performance indicators is that some are more sensitive to economic conditions than others. The division of unpaid work, for example, appears fairly policy resistant, and can only be changed through the influence of gradual cultural processes. In contrast, the level of (youth) unemployment is far more sensitive to economic growth and/or social policy. If both dimensions are considered side by side, then an improvement in the structural indicator can be negated completely by a deterioration in the economic indicator, while there could — in a longer-term perspective — still be reason for cautious optimism. This difference in "economic sensitivity" highlights the need for a careful selection of indicators and an equally careful analysis of overall performance.

From the above research results, it appears that an equitable division of paid and unpaid work is still a long way off. On a scale of 0 to 1, all countries scored less than 0.5, which is a very low mark. Only the Scandinavian countries produce a *relatively* reasonable score in the range of 0.40 to 0.44. As expected, the greatest inequality is found in unpaid work. On this indicator — considered here in terms of unpaid time spent looking after children and other persons — the average score is around 0.25. This means that women spend about four times as much time as men on caring tasks. The division is somewhat more equitable only in Denmark and Sweden, with scores of 0.55 and 0.44 respectively. The division is most unequal in Greece and Portugal, with a score of 0.15 in both cases.

In terms of the position of women on the labour market, the differences between the countries under study here are much greater. In 1997 Luxembourg, Sweden, Portugal, Denmark and Austria had the highest overall performance, whereas Italy and Spain performed rather poorly.

Policy on equal opportunities is partly explicit and partly implicit. In many countries, the employment regime in particular still comprises a large number of measures which discourage a more equal division of work and care and/or facilitate (financially) an unequal division. This implicit gender order is an expression of certain cultural notions on the most desirable social division of labour, but it also implies a continued affirmation of those notions. More specifically, it appears that in most countries equal opportunities are shaped primarily by emphasis on equitable access to the labour market. Income policy, however, is much less individualized and remains focused on the household.

Based on the empirical research, it can be concluded that gender equality in work and income can only be achieved if there is complementary policy on (unpaid) care. As long as care responsibilities continue to be seen primarily as a private concern, the unequal division of unpaid work will translate into an unequal position of women on the labour market.

References

Barry, Ursula (in association with Rosemary Gibney). 1999. *Benchmarking gender equality in Ireland.* Dublin, Women's Education, Research and Resource Centre, University College Dublin/Brussels, European Commission Group of Experts "Gender and Employment", EC Equal opportunities Unit (DG V).

Bettio, Francesca; Prechal, Sacha. 1998. *Care in Europe: Joint report of the 'Gender and Employment' and the 'Gender and Law' Groups of Experts.* Equal opportunities for women and men and matters regarding families and children (DG-V/D/5). Brussels, European Commission.

Bruning, Gwennaële; Plantenga, Janneke. 1999. "Parental leave and equal opportunities. Experiences in eight European countries", in *Journal of European Social Policy* (London), Vol. 9, No. 3 (Aug.), pp. 195-209.

Deven, Fred; Inglis, S.; Moss, Peter; Petrie, P. 1997. *State of the art review on the reconciliation of work and family life for men and women and the quality of care services.* Brussels, EC Equal Opportunities Unit (DG V).

European Commission. 1999a. *Employment performance in the Member States: Employment rates report 1998.* Luxembourg, Office for Official Publications of the European Communities.

—. 1999b. *Employment Policies in the EU and in the Member States — Joint Report 1998.* Luxembourg, Office for Official Publications of the European Communities.

—. 1998a. *Monitoring the employment guidelines: Basic performance indicators — Report by the ELC expert group on employment indicators.* V/A/GDM D(98), Directorate-General for Employment, Industrial Relations and Social Affairs. Brussels, European Commission.

—. 1998b. *Employment in Europe 1998.* Luxembourg, Office for Official Publications of the European Communities.

—. 1998c. *Equal opportunities for women and men in Europe? Eurobarometer 44.3: Results of an opinion survey.* Luxembourg, Office for Official Publications of the European Communities.

European Council. 1999. "Council Resolution of 22 February 1999 on the 1999 Employment Guidelines", in *Official Journal of the European Communities* (Luxembourg), Vol. 42, No. C69, 12 Mar., pp. 2-8.

—. 1996. "Council Directive 96/34/EC of 3 June 1996 on the framework agreement on parental leave concluded by UNICE, CEEP and the ETUC", in *Official Journal of the European Communities* (Luxembourg), Vol. 39, No. L 145, pp. 4-9.

—. 1992. "Council Recommendation of 31 March 1992 on child care (92/241/EEC)", in *Official Journal of the European Communities* (Luxembourg), Vol. 35, No. L 123, pp. 16-18.

Eurostat. 1998. *Labour Force Survey: Results 1997.* Luxembourg, Office for Official Publications of the European Communities.

Grift, Yolanda. 1998. *Female labour supply: The influence of taxes and social premiums.* Unpublished Ph.D. thesis. Utrecht University.

Maier, Friederieke; Rapp, Zorica. 1999. *Benchmarking gender equality: Germany.* Berlin, European Commission Group of Experts "Gender and Employment", EC Equal opportunities Unit (DG V).

Meulders, Danièle. 1999. *Tax systems and households in the European Union.* Unpublished manuscript. Brussels, Département d'Économie Appliquée de l'Université Libre de Bruxelles.

—.; Hecq, Christian. 1999. *Benchmarking gender equality in Belgium*. Brussels, European Commission Group of Experts "Gender and Employment", EC Equal Opportunities Unit (DG V).

O'Donoghue, Cathal; Sutherland, Holly. 1998. *Accounting for the family: The treatment of marriage and children in European income tax systems*. Innocenti Occasional Papers, Economic and Social Policy Series, No. 65. Florence, UNICEF International Child Development Centre.

OECD. 1997. *The OECD Jobs Strategy — Making work pay: Taxation, benefits, employment and unemployment*. Paris.

—. 1994. *The OECD Jobs Study: Taxation, employment and unemployment*. Paris.

Pastner, Ulli. 1999. *Benchmarking gender equality — Austria*. Vienna, FORBA — Forschungs- und Beratungsstelle Arbeitswelt/Brussels, European Commission Group of Experts "Gender and Employment", EC Equal opportunities Unit (DG V).

Plantenga, Janneke; Hansen, Johan. 1999. *Benchmarking equal opportunities in the European Union. Synthesis report based on eight European countries*. Report for the Equal Opportunities Unit (DG V), Commission of the European Communities. Utrecht, Institute of Economics.

Plantenga, Janneke; Schippers, Joop; Siegers, Jacques. 1999. "Towards an equal division of paid and unpaid work: The case of the Netherlands", in *Journal of European Social Policy* (London), Vol. 9, No. 2 (May), pp. 99-110.

Roelofs, Ellie. 1995. "The European Equal Opportunities Policy", in Anneke van Doorne-Huiskes, Jacques van Hoof and Ellie Roelofs (eds.): *Women and the European labour markets*. London, Paul Chapman, pp. 122-142.

Rolstadås, Asbjørn (ed.). 1995. *Performance management: A business process benchmarking approach*. London, Chapman and Hall.

Rubery, Jill. 1999. *Gender mainstreaming in European employment policy*. Report by the European Commission's Group of Experts on Gender and Employment. Brussels, European Commission.

—; Fagan, Colette. 1995. "Wage determination and sex segregation in employment in the European Community", in *Social Europe* (Luxembourg), Supplement 4/94.

—; Smith, Mark; Fagan, Colette. 1998. "National working-time regimes and equal opportunities", in *Feminist Economics* (London), Vol. 4, No. 1, pp. 71-101.

—; —; —; Grimshaw, Damian. 1998. *Women and European employment*. London, Routledge.

Speckesser, Stefan; Schütz, Holger; Schmid, Günther. 1998. "Benchmarking labour markets and labour policies performance with reference to the European Employment Strategy", in Tronti, pp. 76-97.

Tronti, Leonello (ed.). 1998. *Benchmarking employment performance and labour market policies: Final report 1997*. Berlin, Institute for Applied Socio-Economics (IAS).

THE FAMILY, FLEXIBLE WORK
AND SOCIAL COHESION AT RISK

15

Martin CARNOY*

Radical changes in work have significant repercussions on the family and the community, the traditional social integrators and transmitters of values. Women's large-scale entry into the labour market also plays an important part. The increasingly knowledge-based and flexible labour market makes greater demands on families just as they are undergoing increased stress. They are called upon to provide continuing stability, to focus on early childhood development, to help children acquire the needed knowledge, and to bolster their members against unemployment and periods of retraining, while society is expected to provide childcare facilities and flexible education.

Analysing changes in working life at any time in history requires an understanding of women's and men's relationships to social institutions outside the workplace, particularly the family and the community. Today, this is even more true than in the past because of women's massive return to wage work at a time of profound change in the workplace, in families and in communities. This chapter focuses on the family in a globalizing economy, on what these changes may mean for the way in which women and men in postindustrial society confront the information age, and how social policy needs to change to be relevant in the new environment.

Originally published in *International Labour Review*, Vol. 138 (1999), No. 4.

* Professor of Education and Economics, Stanford University. This article draws on a forthcoming publication, *Sustaining the new economy: Work, family, and community in the information age* (Harvard University Press, Russel Sage and Editions Fayard).

FORCES FOR CHANGE IN THE FAMILY AND WORKPLACE

Globalization and the intensified economic competition it engenders are profoundly altering the way we live and relate to each other. For a start, work is undergoing such transformation that in future the notion of a "job" may change its meaning entirely. More intense competition on a worldwide scale makes firms acutely aware of costs and productivity. The solution many employers have reached is to reorganize work around decentralized management, customized products, and work differentiation, such that work tasks become individualized and workers differentiated. This makes it much easier to subcontract tasks, employ part-time workers and hire temporary labour for some specific tasks, while other "core" work is multi-tasked and carried out in teams. Workers are being defined less in terms of the particular long-term jobs they hold than in terms of the knowledge they have acquired through studying and working. The acquisition of a "knowledge portfolio" enables them to move between firms and even between types of work, as jobs are redefined and demand shifts.

The effect of individualization and differentiation is to separate more workers from the kind of permanent, full-time job in stable businesses that characterized post-Second World War development in Europe, Japan, the United States and other industrialized countries. An earlier factory revolution drove a wedge between workers and the products they made (in a Taylorist model); the new transformation is dissolving the identity that workers developed in relation to industrial institutions, especially the corporation and the trade union. Workers are being separated both from their traditional identities built up over more than a century and from the social networks that enabled them to find economic security. The job and everything organized around the job — the friends at work, the after-work meeting places, the trade union, even group transport — lose their social function. They are becoming as "permanently temporary" as the work itself.

The traditional social integrators, apart from the workplace and job-centred social networks, are the family and the community. In times of transition, whether from agricultural society to industrial, industrial to postindustrial, or (as now) local or national to global, families and communities are called upon to bear the greatest responsibility for preserving social cohesion. Families also transmit much of the skills and knowledge needed by children to succeed in the adult work world. So it is not surprising that, whenever these workplace transitions occur, families and the communities that form around work organizations are strained.

Families have changed profoundly over the past hundred years. Women have gradually rejected bearing the sole responsibility for social cohesion and for educating the next generation. They began in the late nineteenth century, by reducing family size through sexual abstinence.

Smaller families made social cohesion easier, gave more time for community-building, and allowed women to create a social life for themselves outside the family, even, and increasingly, at the workplace. But the last round of women's revolt, which started in the late 1960s in a number of countries, struck at the gender relations underlying both family and work. Women rejected the homemaker identity assigned them by industrial society. Masses of married women entered the labour market, first on a part-time and then on a full-time basis. Many of them ended heading families without men. All this happened both *before* and *independently* of globalization and the arrival of new information technology.

So, when workplace restructuring came along only a short decade later, employers were inevitably influenced by women's new willingness to work, and hired them in great numbers as a new source of relatively highly educated labour. In the meantime, the nuclear family with a full-time mother managing the home — the family that sustained and nurtured the Industrial Revolution — has been transformed. The new style of work organization that is successfully responding to the competitive pressures of a globalized economy has come to depend on the relatively cheap, highly productive and highly flexible labour increasingly supplied by these wives and mothers. And this has occurred just as there is the greatest need for a strong, cohesive family with time and energy to invest in the education and well-being of both adults and children during the difficult transition towards new forms of work and personal life.

Furthermore, communities that developed during the Industrial Revolution, such as the factory towns and the industrial cities with their ethnic and other highly organized suburban enclaves, have fragmented as a result of the post-industrial flight to new urban formations or "metapols" (Ascher, 1998). A wave of accelerated urban-suburban sprawl has largely destroyed the material base of neighbourhood sociability. Globalization produces work arrangements that are less secure and more geographically dispersed than did earlier styles of production organization. Families with two working adults are now the norm, and parents and children tend to build up networks within the various institutions where they spend their time, rather than by socializing in a common community of proximity. This renders these already semi-transitory communities even less relevant to integrating the disaggregated workers of the globalized age.

Unravelling the meaning of this combined process of family and work restructuring for the daily lives of the 800 million men and women in the postindustrial countries is not easy, for many changes are concurrent:

- The family is undergoing profound change. All over the world, women are demanding and winning new rights, such as equal access to wage work (and sometimes equal wages), which transforms traditional relations within the family. In all the developed countries, women are proving much less willing to devote their lives to raising children than they were just a generation ago. Of course, family changes do vary greatly among the industrialized countries. Southern Europe and Japan have much lower divorce rates and lower women's labour force participation rates than northern Europe, the United States, Canada, Australia and New Zealand. In southern Europe and Japan, fewer married women with children work, and traditional family structures are more persistent. Are these differences lasting or temporary cultural differences? Is a relentless process of change in gender relations now under way, whatever its current differences, that will reach into all developed societies and transform the family?

- Labour markets are also being transformed, though these changes also vary from one country to another, seemingly in relation to change (or lack of it) in the family. Are changes in the family being spread and hastened by the new transformation of the workplace? Are current attempts by business to make labour markets more flexible linked to, even dependent on, the existence of different and much more "flexible" families?

- The transformation of labour markets places great demands on families. To do well in flexible labour markets, workers need to have extensive information networks. Workers with more and better education enjoy greater access to information, have larger networks and more choices, and can more easily adjust to change. Labour markets favour highly educated parents and encourage their children's education. The networks needed for parents to be effective in flexible labour markets require more sophisticated decision-making and organization than in the past. Families lacking the capacity to make informed decisions or the resources to act on them are still forced to be flexible but are much less sustainable. Some countries have publicly subsidized systems of support for working parents that make it easier simultaneously to work and to rear a healthy family. Other countries rely heavily on the rapidly changing private family to rear children, with all the strain that entails as working hours remain long. Does the family need new forms of support? Can workplaces take on new functions to support the family? Without new arrangements to help families acquire the necessary skills, can families be successful in the new environment?

With the sea change under way in work and the family, postindustrial society faces a dilemma. Today's workplace demands well-informed, highly organized, stable families that can support all their members as they try to operate in a flexible work environment. But the new work environment is marked by greater job instability, causing family members to change their work situations more often, and new jobs may well entail having to acquire new skills, hence more education. Since there is no end to this trend in sight, the existing pressures on adults to acquire more education for their own work will be compounded in the case of their children. Thus, family involvement in children's education is both more important and more complicated than in the past.

All this places an enormous strain on the family. Anticipating these stresses, many young people hesitate to form a family, and ties formed tend to be more unstable. This results in a serious social contradiction: the new workplace requires even greater investment in knowledge than in the past and families are crucial to such knowledge formation, for adults as well as children. But the new workplace destabilizes the child-centred nuclear family, degrading the very institution crucial to further economic development.

One solution to this dilemma might be to maintain more traditional, industrial era labour markets, in which men earn a family wage, and labour markets are relatively rigid — organized to protect the employed. But the evidence from countries such as Spain and Italy, where formal labour markets are still quite rigid, suggests that this solution does not work well. Not only is market rigidity difficult to maintain in the face of global competition; it is organized around male workers and takes little account of the struggle women have waged for a new identity. And although labour market rigidity is only one of many reasons that unemployment is now high in continental Europe, it also has unintended and highly undesirable consequences: it contributes to higher youth unemployment and therefore delayed marriage and even lower fertility rates (see below). Rigidity also contributes to lower fertility rates because in rigid, male-run markets, maternity tends to increase working women's risk of permanent job loss. So though labour market rigidity may make life more peaceful at home by easing pressure on family time, in the context of women's redefined roles and global competition, it tends to reduce family formation and to increase tension as women are forced to maintain unsatisfactory, traditional roles.

Changes in the way women define their identity and the increased demands placed on the family by flexible production also may pose serious economic problems. As labour markets inevitably become more flexible, incorporating more married women into wage jobs and expecting men to be more flexible in their schedules and yet dedicated to their work, labour productivity and political stability will be conditioned by the manner in which private and family structures and government support for families adjust. Ironically, the societies with the least flexible labour markets today may be those best positioned to move to greater flexibility if they are able to maintain the private and public family support structures presently in place. And the societies with the most flexible markets today may prove the least well positioned to sustain flexibility unless they make drastic changes in family support systems.

In a flexible work system the family is at the hub of productive and reproductive activity. Because of the new demands placed on the traditional family by flexible labour markets, and because the traditional family as a social form is disappearing so quickly in developed countries, the family may have to be redefined, with the help of the community and the State, if it is to survive at all. But before addressing the kind of help that may be needed, a clearer picture is needed of how families are actually changing in the industrialized countries.

A STYLIZED HISTORY OF THE FAMILY

A helpful analysis of the family is provided by Young and Willmott (1973), who characterize its history as occurring in three stages:

Stage 1 was the "family as production unit",[1] with all members working in the home, on the farm or in small-scale home factory production, doing domestic work, child-rearing and market work all at the same place. Men and women were totally dependent on one another and the home was the centre of all activity, including income generation.

In stage 2, this home-centred family broke down, with disastrous consequences for women. Both men and women (as well as children) were employed outside the home, but if there were young children in the home, women could not work; and men controlled income. There was little incentive for men to limit the number of children because they could still hold back income, and children could go to work at a young age. Women suffered most, followed by children.

Towards the end of this stage there occurred an important, and little-discussed, phase in women's struggle to gain control over their bodies and the allocation of their time. At the end of the nineteenth century, middle-class women learnt to understand their fertility cycles and simply refused to have sexual relations during periods of greatest fertility. Though it spread slowly, this practice, together with new forms of contraception, child labour laws, and the introduction of compulsory schooling (which made it increasingly costly to have children), reduced family size even before the First World War. There was a trend towards smaller families, in emulation of the increasingly affluent middle class. Women's liberation movements at the end of the nineteenth century also succeeded in improving women's rights to leave abusive men.

Once families became smaller in the late-nineteenth and early-twentieth centuries, married women gradually started returning to work after the roughly 20 years it took to raise all their children up to age 14, when they would leave school and go to work. Although the percentage of married women active in the wage labour market was still small in the

1920s, it rose until the Great Depression of the 1930s. The other factor that changed the family was the development of household aids and appliances such as electric refrigerators, stoves, washing machines, and home tools that revolutionized housework and made it more interesting for men to come home and engage in house maintenance. Fewer children and higher wages made the home environment more pleasant. Families actually had disposable income to spend on goods beyond what they needed just to sustain themselves. The family increasingly became a centre of activity for men as well as women, with men and women forming a consumption partnership focused on the home and the family. Young and Willmott (1973) see the family as crucial to the expansion of the domestic economy in the industrial stage of development, and increased consumption of consumer durables as its main new economic function. So rather than just reproducing cheap labour for industrial expansion (stage 2) — mainly at the expense of women who were responsible for that reproduction while men led essentially separate lives — by stage 3, which developed after the Second World War, men and women became partners in consumption. Many thought that, once freed from the need to work collectively, the family unit would be able to focus on more spiritual, non-economic needs and concerns, and would become more of a democratic union of life companions (Calhoun (1919) cited in Ehrenreich (1983)). Stage 3 reached its highest point in the 1950s and 1960s, and provided the model for the "traditional family" still extolled by neo-conservatives in almost every industrialized country.

Yet Young and Willmott miss two important points about the stage 3 family. First, it was not only a consumption family but also an investment family, investing in its children so that they would be able to earn more than their parents and move up the consumption ladder. This investment role became increasingly important after the Second World War, spreading from upper-middle-class families through to working-class families. And although the original aim of introducing welfare state support for families in the 1930s was to maintain consumption, from the 1950s this aim became subordinate to the maintenance and enhancement of the family's investment role in providing potentially more productive labour for the increasingly flexible, competitive economy.

By the 1980s, with the emergence of flexible production and the increasing importance of education in determining access to high-paying jobs, the investment role of the family had become even more important. As both parents worked more even when the children were young, parents increasingly consumed all kinds of services previously available only to higher-income families; in the best of cases, such services had large investment components, enhancing the health and learning of children. In Europe and Japan, the State provides or subsidizes childcare, pre-schooling and, especially, health care precisely because of its concern about the family's investment role. Families themselves — particularly mothers — want more publicly provided services both because they need some freedom from child-rearing and because they believe that such collective environments enhance learning.

The second point that Young and Willmott could not foresee in the early 1970s was that, even as stage 3 reached its apex, the family was already undergoing transformation. The consumption partnership, formed in part because of smaller families and higher incomes, was already dissolving as they wrote. Women wanted broader options, including participation in the social world defined by work and greater decision-making power over the larger issues in family life, including the division of family labour. Women's rising access to remunerative work increased their chances of gaining some economic independence from men. As divorce rates rose, women were even more compelled to seek employment in order to protect themselves financially against potential family break-up and income loss.

THE TRANSFORMATION OF THE FAMILY

The continuous increase in the number of women entering the labour force in most industrialized countries and the formation of families with two wage-earners have had a tremendous impact on families. So have the increased ability and willingness of men and women to undo marriages (Cherlin, 1981). The family has lost the stability provided when one parent — usually the mother — centres her activities on the home, accepting a single source of income. Two separate individual projects and two separate working schedules make the compatibility of the individual work projects and the family project more difficult to sustain. Women's rising wage contribution to family income increases their bargaining power in the family, and undermines the structure of the traditional, patriarchal family.

It is no surprise, then, that the interaction of social forces producing these changes is having a measurable impact on the family in industrialized countries. Moreover, there are significant psychological and social effects beyond measure. There is a process of change moving across countries.

Data for the industrialized countries of OECD show three significant changes:

- The chances of a marriage dissolving are much greater in the 1990s than they were in the 1960s. (See figures 1a and 1b.) Admittedly, divorced people often remarry (and re-divorce). But the fact that marriage is more likely to be a temporary arrangement and that more marriages are recombinations of previously married people itself redefines the notion of the family. In the late 1960s, crude divorce rates (the number of divorces per hundred marriages) began rising

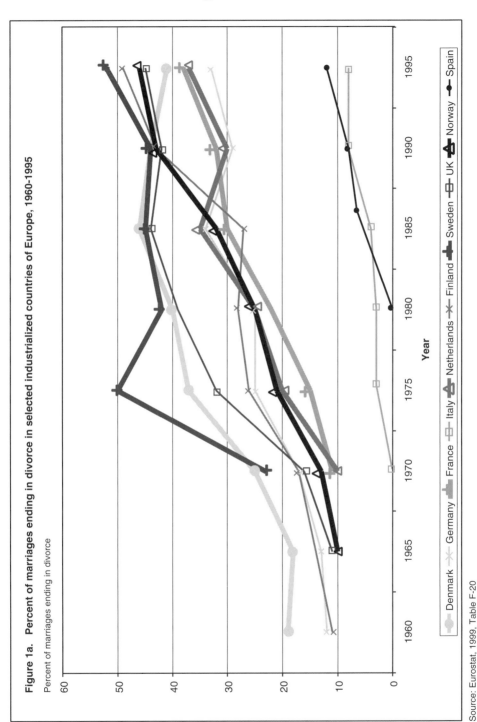

Figure 1a.   Percent of marriages ending in divorce in selected industrialized countries of Europe, 1960-1995

Percent of marriages ending in divorce

Source: Eurostat, 1999, Table F-20

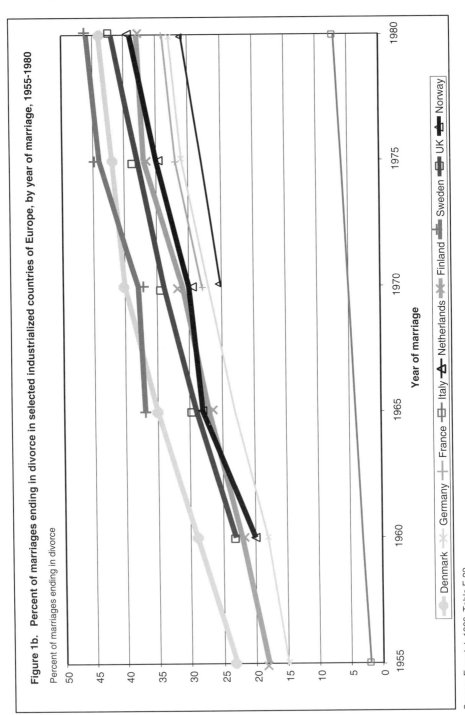

Figure 1b. Percent of marriages ending in divorce in selected industrialized countries of Europe, by year of marriage, 1955-1980

Percent of marriages ending in divorce

Year of marriage

Denmark   Germany   France   Italy   Netherlands   Finland   Sweden   UK   Norway

Source: Eurostat, 1999, Table F-22

314

Table 1. Fertility rates in selected industrialized countries, 1970-96 (children per woman 15-44 years of age)

Country	1970	1980	1990	1996
Denmark	2.0	1.6	1.7	1.8
France	2.5	2.0	1.8	1.7
Germany	2.0	1.6	1.5	1.3
Italy	2.4	1.6	1.3	1.2
Japan	...	1.8	1.5	1.4
Netherlands	2.6	1.6	1.6	1.5
Spain	2.9	2.2	1.3	1.2
Sweden	1.9	1.7	2.1	1.6
United Kingdom	2.4	1.9	1.8	1.7
United States	2.5	1.8	2.1	2.1

... Not available.

Source: Eurostat, 1997.

first in the United States, then in Scandinavia, the United Kingdom, and Germany, reaching the highest European levels in Denmark and Sweden. By the mid-1980s, more than one in every two marriages in the United States ended in divorce and, in Denmark and Sweden, almost one in every two. But rates in other countries, such as the United Kingdom, also rose very rapidly, reaching Scandinavian levels in 1985 from a much lower starting-point. Divorce rates in France and Germany rose to over 30 per cent of marriages. However this pattern is not universal. Despite the liberalization of divorce laws, divorce rates in countries such as Italy and Spain rose slowly and are still relatively low in the 1990s.

• The increased difficulty of making marriage work, the greater participation of women in working life, the apparently decreased willingness of men to enter into marriage (Ehrenreich, 1983), and now, in the 1990s, the greater insecurity surrounding work have all delayed the ages of marriage and child-rearing, increased partnerships without marriage, and greatly reduced women's fertility rates (see table 1). Birth rates have fallen below population reproduction levels in most of Europe as well as Japan. The higher first-marriage age in lower-income industrialized countries in 1960 was partly the result of the economic situation: married couples generally prefer to live apart from their parents, but affording a separate place to live is more difficult in lower-income countries, so couples wait longer to marry. But the recent rise in marriage age in most industrialized countries is more closely related to women's new role in the labour market and, in Europe, to the difficulty for young people to obtain any job at all. By the late 1970s, many more women were entering work careers that caused them to delay having children and to delay marriage. In the United States, the fastest-growing group among women consists of those who have their first child between the ages of 30 and 35. Most women still marry before age 25 and have their first child in their early twenties, but this group is declining proportionately, while the proportion of women bearing their first child after age 25 is growing.

- Fewer and later marriages and less child-rearing, plus more divorce, single parenting, and an aging population, have meant that by 1990 a smaller percentage of the population lived in a household consisting of a married couple or a nuclear family than did in 1960. Moreover, fewer and later first marriages and fewer children per family mean that men and women are far less occupied with child-rearing in the prime of their lives than in the past. Even if women do not go out to work while their children are growing up, the average time they now spend caring for young and pre-teen children is 14 years. For men, in turn, even when they are the sole source of family income and stay married for life, their families are less costly than in the past, and divert them less from other activities. Family life involving children is thus far less central to adults' lives today than it was 30 years ago. There may be as much thought and talk about the ideal of family life — husband, wife, and children living together, with the focus on child-rearing — as in the past, but the reality is quite different. Child-raising is being relegated to a secondary role in people's lives.

Just as interesting as these trends is the way in which they vary from one country to another. At one end of the spectrum evident in the major industrialized countries, Italian and Spanish families are much more likely to conform to the traditional pattern of a nuclear family, although they now include very few children. At the other end of the spectrum, American and Scandinavian families have experienced the greatest structural change, with high divorce rates and proportionately far fewer nuclear families. But birth rates in the 1980s and 1990s were much higher in the United States and Scandinavia than in Italy and Spain. The Swedish rate dropped in the mid-1990s but still remains above the low levels found in southern Europe. Other countries lie in between, with the United Kingdom nearer the United States and Scandinavian end of the spectrum, France, Germany, and particularly Japan nearer Italy and Spain. Though the traditional family is in decline in all these countries, significant differences remain, relating to culture, labour markets and public policies concerning family support. These differences also affect labour markets. The persistence of more traditional families in Spain and Italy, for instance, allows high rates of youth unemployment to be supported by families willing to keep their adult children at home. And, in turn, the persistence of traditional, relatively rigid labour markets supported by traditional family structures has unintended effects on the formation of future families.

There is also diversity within countries. For example, in the United States immigrants from Mexico and Asia tend to be more traditional: they have more children, lower divorce rates, and are more likely to live in extended families. In Europe, immigrants, mainly from North Africa, also live in more traditional family structures than do people of European origin.

Even so, younger women from immigrant groups or in the countries at the Italian and Spanish end of the spectrum react to family life in ways similar to non-immigrant women in the United States. They delay marriage, avoid having children, prefer to work rather than stay at home and, if they can get a job, arrange for day care (often with their parents) rather than taking care of their children themselves on a full-time basis. The sharp drop in fertility to extraordinarily low levels in Italy and Spain is another sign that traditional family life is changing radically there and that women's (and to some extent men's) conception of family life is being transformed everywhere in the developed world. This implies that many of the quantitative differences between industrialized countries may reflect the behaviour of older women who, unlike non-immigrant older women in the United States, tend not to divorce even when they are unhappily married. The differences may also reflect economic factors, such as the fact that, because of the difficulty of finding work, children in Europe live at home till a much later age than their counterparts in the United States. Nuclear families form a larger proportion of families in such situations partly because high youth unemployment prevents young people from moving out and living alone.

However, the greater fertility rates of less-educated, lower-income families affects societies, especially in the current global environment. It could mean that most children today are growing up in families that cannot prepare them adequately for the ever-higher educational requirements needed to succeed in labour markets. This is not to say that higher-educated men and women make better parents than those with less education. But being a parent in the global economy requires much more information than in the past, and the stakes in children's educational success are much higher. On average, less-educated parents are increasingly at a disadvantage in supplying what is required to prepare young children to do well at school.

Flexible workplaces and the new family

Far from losing its fundamental importance to work, the family will be even more crucial in this respect as the economy shifts to flexible, knowledge-based production. Not only is an ever-increasing proportion of jobs in the industrialized world organized around knowledge rather than around physical skills; today's younger workers are also likely to need to acquire new kinds of knowledge at various points in their careers as they move through different kinds of work.

In a flexible work system the family is at the hub of productive and reproductive activity. When it is potentially strong (with two highly educated adults at its core), it serves as a risk hedge against periods of unemployment and as a source of child development for its offspring, of investment capital for adults' and children's education and training, of networking for job search and upward mobility, and of personal security and growth. If linked into larger information and communication networks, it can also become a production unit.

Yet, low birth rates can threaten population reproduction and future economic growth. Even in more traditional societies, divorce rates will almost certainly increase and then stay high, perhaps at levels comparable to those of the United States and Scandinavia. Even with traditional forms of support, as men and women try both to rear children and to satisfy their own needs for status and social interaction as wage-earners in remunerated work, the increased stress on their families could have a serious negative effect on adult productivity and on children's well-being. The combined effect of flexible production with its demands for individualized, work-focused activities, of women's fight for greater equality in the family and in the labour market, and of the increased importance of the family as an investment unit is now shaping the next, emerging stage of family life. The family could and should be the social institution tempering the stress induced by the processes of disaggregation of labour and of individualization of social and economic life. But for the family to be able to play its fundamental role of sustaining work, it has to be redefined and strengthened under the new cultural and technological conditions now obtaining in industrialized countries.

Models for the new family?

The United States model is appealing to employers and to many politicians in Europe because its job creation potential and low rate of unemployment stand in stark contrast to Europe's frustrated struggle to create jobs and reduce unemployment. But flexible American-style markets have a down side that understandably reduces their appeal to the average European and Japanese: flexibility expands job growth, but in the United States' highly deregulated economy it is characterized by stagnant or falling wages for a significant percentage of workers. Most workers have to pay much more attention to keeping their jobs simply because of the threat of losing them. Flexibility also tends to increase the number of hours families work. In less skilled jobs, American-style flexible markets promote people to work more in order to earn more, rather than letting them earn more for the hours they do work. In highly skilled jobs, high pay is the norm but only for those who are willing to commit themselves to a supercharged work schedule, meeting crucial deadlines at all costs, and out-competing other workers in the do-or-die global economy. In some of these occupations, the financial incentives are great: workers who make the right moves may earn a great deal in a few years. So the long hours have a potentially high payoff. All this promotes higher profits, economic growth, and higher average family income, but at the cost of job security, more intensified family and work schedules, and increased individual stress and isolation.

Europeans and Japanese may admire the vitality of the current United States "job machine", but consider its system of work and family relations to be too costly in social terms. They read about high levels of open poverty in the United States, deteriorating living conditions, lack of childcare, stressful dual workdays, long commuting hours, downgraded schools, violence, and a significant percentage of the young male black and Latino populations in prison. Americans tend to live either in cities that are no longer very safe for children and adolescents, or in suburbs which hold risks too for young people, as evidenced by shocking and increasingly frequent killings in suburban schools. According to a national survey conducted in 1994, the decline in the quality of childcare in the United States had reached crisis proportions, and children's development was at risk (Government Accounting Office, 1994). In the United States, all political parties and leaders invoke a strengthened family as a solution to the nation's social ills. But its social legislation in support of the family lags behind that of all other industrialized countries. Not only do most children in the United States live in families broken by divorce (Chira, 1995); more than a third also live in or close to poverty. In some ethnic minorities the crisis of the family is very deep, playing a major role in perpetuating the underclass status of a significant segment of the minority population (Wilson, 1987). About half of all African-American children are conceived out of wedlock, and many do not know their fathers (Jaynes and Williams, 1990). Not only do less-educated mothers in the United States have more children than higher educated mothers (just as in other industrialized countries); they are also likely to raise their children in relatively worse economic conditions, with less access to child centres and early educational services than in most of the rest of the industrialized world.

Another issue for Europeans concerned about the American model of flexible work is that it puts an ever-increasing emphasis on work and earnings as the purpose of human existence. This is not a completely new phenomenon in the United States. Yet, with increased competition in the globalized economy and the rapidly rising capacity to operate in global time to enhance productivity, the ideal worker is one who never sleeps, never consumes, never has children, and never spends time

319

socializing outside the workplace. As Hochschild (1997) argues, it is in the employer's interest to make the workplace more socially congenial for workers because they will then be willing to spend more time there. However, it is also in the employer's interest to make workers believe that if they do not spend more time there, the employer will find someone else who will.

Of course, the socially congenial work organization is hardly alien to the Japanese or to many Europeans. Japanese workers are renowned for placing company loyalty above almost all else, and Japanese companies for demanding such loyalty in return for guaranteed employment. Indeed, many of the methods used by American and European companies to build company spirit and dedication were imported from Japan. Company loyalty means long hours of work in Japan. In 1979, the average employed Japanese worked about 200 hours more per year than the average United States worker; even today, after several years of recession, the Japanese employee works only slightly fewer hours than a United States worker — who works longer hours than anywhere else in the industrialized countries. But in Japan these long hours affect mostly male workers; married women with children are likely either not to work or to work part time. The relative intactness of traditional family relations in Japan still preserves male company loyalty and female family loyalty. Fewer Japanese families may have children today than a generation ago, but those who do still tend to divide their work and family responsibilities along traditional gender lines.

Europeans may not have Japanese-style company loyalty, but a high proportion of European men have similar work guarantees to those given the Japanese. Furthermore, Europeans work many fewer hours. Although OECD data on hours worked are not strictly comparable, they do show that employed French, German, Italian and British workers all worked far fewer hours than United States workers even in the mid-1980s before today's employment problems. A recent ILO publication confirms this (ILO, 1999).

So, despite their promise of more, badly needed employment, most Europeans and Japanese are not anxious to work in American-style flexible labour markets — even though to some extent they are already doing so. In most of Europe, this is not because of fear that more women will enter the labour market, or because relations between men and women will change. A high proportion of women are already in paid employment, and relations between the sexes have changed in most countries without the introduction of American-style flexibility in hiring and firing.[2] Nor is there serious resistance to the possible introduction of more part-time and temporary work. In the late 1970s, Scandinavian and several other countries, including the United Kingdom and Japan, displayed rates of part-time work that were as high or higher than those of the United States. Nor, in Japan, is it a problem of being wedded more to work: Japanese *men* are heavily committed to their jobs, yet seem to want to keep their wives at home. In Europe, however, increasing the number of hours required by full employment could pose serious political problems.

None of these reasons is grounds for major resistance to American-style flexible markets. The common ground is rather that the Europeans and Japanese see United States flexibility as a combined assault on their rising wage rates, on social incorporation through the social benefits of work, and on the relationship that they have established between family, work and leisure — a relationship that in Europe sets constraints on employers' ability to demand intensive, year-long work schedules, and that in Japan hinders married women from being drawn into full-time career work.

However, resistance to American-style flexibility does not mean that Japanese and European work organization continues unchanged. Nor does it mean that Japanese and European workers will be able to preserve existing work and family relations: they are already in flux to some extent. Nor does it mean that the present United States work system is socially desirable or even sustainable. That leaves open the end state of Europe, Japan and the United States in the new global economy.

SOME POLICY IMPLICATIONS

Arguably, a desirable end state would reflect a shift to a larger knowledge-intensive component in work generally. Industrialized countries are rapidly becoming knowledge societies in which communicative, co-operative and cognitive skills form the basis for the production of wealth rather than raw materials, human strength or machines. Because knowledge is now much more important in work, and also because women's identity is now more closely associated with income-earning capacity, family formation is increasingly determined by the pattern of knowledge acquisition (e.g. the length of professional development and career formation). Hence, the quality of family life will increasingly be gauged by the availability of learning opportunities for adults and by the capacity of the adults in the family to provide learning opportunities for their children. An intense emphasis on learning as a factor in life decisions has already emerged in the upper middle-income groups across the industrialized countries, where women are choosing to establish careers before having children. The availability in Europe and Japan of subsidized childcare centres for youngsters of all ages and the lack of such centres in the United States influence the sustainability of marriages and the number and timing of children, especially for professional couples. Such learning-driven behaviour as a dominant shaper of family formation, now limited to higher-educated young people, will influence the rest of the population, just as middle-class fertility reduction influenced the working class at the beginning of the twentieth century.

With knowledge and information potentially playing such important roles in flexible work, family formation and family relations, support systems consistent with improving both individual productivity and family life should increasingly be organized around enhancing access by both children and adults to high-quality learning opportunities. Households' integration into learning networks is the linchpin of a flexible, knowledge-based work system. Government family policies are fundamental to this integration, since the State is the only institution that has both the material resources to support the household's investments in its members and the political accountability to do so. Such policies need to enhance the family's capacity to invest in learning without interfering in the privacy of its decisions. The State can do this by helping families acquire education for their children even as parents are on flexible work schedules; giving parents new possibilities to take up further education and training themselves; guaranteeing family health care provision even when adult family members are unemployed or studying; providing widely available training to young people, prospective parents and parents on childcare and child development; using fiscal policies to reward families who invest in education; and strictly enforcing laws ensuring that parents, whether they are married, living together or divorced, contribute financially to the support of their children.

Knowledge acquisition depends heavily on early childhood development, and early childhood is generally lived out in families. Not only are most parents uneducated about child development but, in the free-market Anglo-American model, collective society pays little attention to the crucial early years of a child's development. Again, this is a remnant of pre-industrial and industrial society, when the knowledge children acquired at school was far less important to their subsequent work lives.

Those industrialized countries that have been especially conscious of the need to ensure children's welfare when both parents or a single parent work, or even to provide respite for women who do not work, organize all-day, high-quality subsidized day care. In Scandinavia and France, day care is the centrepiece of family policy. More recently, Japan has begun well-staffed day-care centres for working mothers (Kristof, 1995; Hewlett, 1991). In all these countries, state-run day care employs well-trained, certified teachers who are specialized in early childhood development.

In addition to supporting early childhood development, governments need to ensure that schools are also community learning centres, where parents can leave their children in a learning environment while they themselves are at work or studying and during that part of the school holidays when parents are not on leave. The community learning centres should also be places where parents and seniors can engage in forms of learning — some related to their children's education and some to adult activities, including community-run business courses for the self-employed. Existing local educational institutions — from primary and secondary schools to community colleges and universities — are the logical sites around which the State can build all-day, all-year, lifetime learning networks for households to link to, whether parents are employed, unemployed or self-employed. Yet, these institutions have to evolve to meet different needs in the various communities. In low-income communities, for example, demand both for full-day children's education and even for adult education may be far greater than in high-income communities. Government allocation of resources for education should seek to meet such needs as an integral part of policy on equal opportunities and social protection, particularly in light of the fact that less-educated families have more children but a lesser capacity for providing them with the information and networks they need to become productive in a flexible, knowledge-intensive economy.

Which model is more likely to be able to respond to this integrative challenge? The United States version has the distinct advantage of a highly flexible educational system that allows young people and adults to leave and re-enter college, change their main subject of study, and retrain for new careers at any age. In the United States, women especially have availed themselves of this flexibility to shape their re-entry into the labour force after rearing young children or divorcing. The greatest growth in college enrolment in the 1970s and 1980s occurred among women aged 30 or over returning to college to train for a different job. Flexibility also allows for modular supplements to basic public education, such as private after-school tutorial programmes.

But the United States model has major drawbacks in meeting knowledge needs for a flexible economy. Americans and their political leaders seem unwilling to confront the public crisis of the family and related child poverty. One way to deal with this crisis is to invest heavily in early, high-quality, publicly funded education for low-income children. Child development centres, so central to Europe's public approach to family poverty, are virtually non-existent in the United States. Beyond providing early childhood education, the schools of the future will probably have to serve as community knowledge centres open from dawn to late evening.

Europe and Japan have much more rigid educational systems than does the United States. Adult education is not readily available in France, Italy or Germany, and it is unusual for young people to leave the educational system and re-enter it later. It is also difficult for university students to change their main subject of study. Women seeking to redefine themselves are not well served by an educational system that is youth centred and highly linear. This makes education-based responses to the crisis in the traditional family more difficult to organize.

However, despite growing disillusion with the State on many levels, continental Europeans (and the educationally more flexible Scandinavians) are much more willing than Americans (or the British or Australians) to acknowledge the role of the public sector in equalizing opportunity and providing important services. Japan relies less on government agencies than on corporate organizations for lifelong support systems but, like the continental Europeans and Scandinavians, the Japanese have a relatively homogeneous society and a sense of collective responsibility.

Can this sense of collective responsibility and willingness to organize and spend substantial public funds on early childhood education be extended to developing lifelong, flexible knowledge provision systems in response to changing family needs? Or will citizens or political leaders extend their current advantage in flexible education by taking responsibility for high-quality, publicly funded early education and other forms of family education and network-support systems?

The collective and public approach to education will be a fundamental issue for the viability of these societies in the high-speed future ahead. Obviously, the capacity of an economic system to innovate and organize the production of goods and services is crucial in a competitive global system. But social cohesion is also crucial, and the family — the main institution for ensuring social cohesion — needs help in an age of flexible production and changed gender roles. The capacity and willingness of a society to provide this help, especially through support for learning and learning networks for families with a low capacity to provide them privately, will be major elements in sustaining innovation and work systems over the long haul.

Notes

[1] I characterize early family production as inseparable from reproduction, and Young and Willmott (1973) characterize the family as totally devoted to production. The two characterizations show the difficulty of separating production from reproduction in subsistence culture. But at some point, family subsistence production becomes a source of accumulation, with the product of family work much greater than what is needed just to meet the family's basic needs. This makes the family a production unit.

[2] In Japan, however, work for married women is more of an issue.

References

Ascher, François. 1998. *La République contre la ville*. Paris, L'Aube.

Cherlin, Andrew. 1981. *Marriage, divorce, remarriage*. Cambridge, MA, Harvard University Press.

Chira, Susan. 1995. "Struggling to find stability when divorce is a pattern", in *The New York Times* (New York, NY), 19 Mar. 1995, p. 1.

Calhoun, Arthur. 1919. *Social history of the American family*. Vol. 3: *Since the Civil War*. Cleveland, OH, Arthur Clarke Co., cited in Ehrenreich (1983), p. 4.

Ehrenreich, Barbara. 1983. *The hearts of men*. New York, NY, Anchor Press.

Eurostat. 1999. *Demographic statistics, 1998 edition*. Luxembourg, Office for official publications of the European Communities.

—. 1997. *Statistics in focus, population and social conditions, 1970-1990*. No. 10. Luxembourg, Office for official publications of the European Communities.

Government Accounting Office. 1994. *Child care: Promoting quality in family child care*. GAO/ HEHS-95-36. Washington, DC. Dec.

Hewlett, Sylvia Ann. 1991. *When the bough breaks*. New York, NY, Basic Books.

Hochschild, Arlie Russell. 1997. *The time bind: When work becomes home and home becomes work*. New York, NY, Henry Holt and Co.

ILO. 1999. *Key indicators of the labour market 1999*. Geneva.

Jaynes, Gerald; Williams, Robin (eds.). 1990. *A common destiny*. Washington, DC, National Academy of Sciences.

Kristof, Nicolas D. 1995. "Yokohama Journal; Japan invests in a growth stock: Good day care", in *The New York Times* (New York), 26 Jan.

Wilson, William Julius. 1987. *The truly disadvantaged: The inner city, the underclass, and public policy*. Chicago, IL, The University of Chicago Press.

Young, Michael; Willmott, Peter. 1973. *The symmetrical family*. London, Routledge and Kegan Paul.

ASSIGNING CARE: GENDER NORMS AND ECONOMIC OUTCOMES

16

M. V. Lee BADGETT* and Nancy FOLBRE**

In societies that link femaleness to familial altruism, women tend to be disproportionately represented in caring occupations. This reinforces occupational segregation, sex-based pay differentials and the very norms that dictate appropriate behaviour for women and men. Research on the interaction between marriage markets and labour markets shows another reason why such gender norms are resistant to change. The analysis of the relationship between caring labour, social norms and economic outcomes implies a need not only to reassign responsibilities for care, but specific measures to protect caring work, including strict quality standards on the provision of marketed care.

In many different cultures, being female is associated with care for others. Women are generally held to higher standards of family responsibility than men. A daughter who neglects her parents, a wife who leaves a husband, a mother who abandons a child — all are considered more culpable than a son, husband or father who does the same. Gender norms governing interpretation of appropriate behaviour for women and men are closely linked to socially constructed concepts of familial altruism and individual self-interest. Women who seem highly independent or ambitious, like men who seem highly dependent or family-oriented, are often considered sexually unattractive. In the sociological literature, the interpersonal enactment of culturally specified roles is sometimes termed "doing gender" (Berk, 1985; Brines, 1994).

Originally published in *International Labour Review*, Vol. 138 (1999), No. 3.

*Associate Professor of Economics, University of Massachusetts, Amherst.   ** Professor of Economics, University of Massachusetts, Amherst.

Doing gender typically involves assigning care. No matter who performs it, caring labour is expensive (England and Folbre, 1999). A parent who devotes time and energy to "family-specific" activities typically experiences a significant reduction in lifetime earnings (Joshi, 1990 and 1998; Waldfogel, 1997). The human capital that housewives and/or househusbands acquire is less transportable than that of a partner who specializes in market work, leaving them in a weaker bargaining position in the family and economically vulnerable to separation or divorce (Braunstein and Folbre, 1999; Weitzman, 1985). Furthermore, employees in caring occupations are typically paid less than others, even controlling for a large list of other personal and job characteristics (England, 1992; England et al., 1994). Women are disproportionately concentrated in these jobs.

This chapter offers an interdisciplinary analysis of the relationship between caring labour, social norms and economic outcomes, and explores some of the ways in which this relationship may be modified by the process of capitalist development. The first section reviews the feminist literature on caring labour, explaining its implications for both Marxist and neoclassical economic theories. The second section focuses on gender norms, arguing that an economic analysis of their consequences can shed some light on their remarkable durability. The final section presents a specific example of their resistance to change, describing research on the interaction between marriage markets and labour markets that helps explain why occupational segregation remains widespread.

CARING LABOUR

Scandinavian feminists were the first to develop and dwell on the concept of caring labour, emphasizing the ways in which it departs from more traditional economistic definitions of work (Waerness, 1987). The concept describes a type of work that requires personal attention, services that are normally provided on a face-to-face or first-name basis, often for people who cannot clearly express their own needs, such as young children, the sick or the elderly. But in addition to describing a type of work, caring labour describes an intrinsic motive for performing that work — a sense of emotional attachment and connection to the persons being cared for (Folbre, 1995). In this respect, it is closely related to another concept that has received more attention in the sociological literature — emotional labour (Hochschild, 1983). Abel and Nelson put it this way: "Caregiving is an activity encompassing both instrumental tasks and affective relations. Despite the classic Parsonian distinction between these two modes of behavior, caregivers are expected to provide love as well as labour, 'caring for' while 'caring about'"(1990, p. 4). Similarly, Sara Ruddick defines "maternal thinking" as a "unity of reflection, judgement, and emotion" (1983, p. 214).

The meaning of care

The meaning of care is often mediated by prepositions. To care for someone is different from "to care about"; "to care" is distinct from "take care" which in turn means less, somehow, than to "take care of". The *American Heritage Dictionary* gives two rather negative definitions of the noun care: (1) A burdened state of mind, as that arising from heavy responsibilities; worry. (2) Mental suffering; grief. As a verb, its first two meanings are positive: (1) To be concerned or interested. (2) To provide needed assistance or watchful supervision. The upshot may be that to be concerned or interested is to assume a burden.

But these meanings do not seem quite right. Feminist thinkers have begun to use the word care in a more specific way, to describe something more than a feeling — a responsibility. It is useful to make a distinction between "care services", a type of work, and "caring motives", which are intrinsic to the worker. Care services are services that involve personal contact between provider and recipient. In activities such as teaching, nursing and counselling, personal identity is important. The service provider generally learns the first name of the service recipient or client. However, the service provider does not necessarily have an emotional or social connection to the client and may work simply to be paid or to avoid being punished.

Many, though certainly not all, care services are motivated by motives more complex than pecuniary or instrumental concerns. They involve a sense of connection with the care recipient that may be based on affection, altruism or social norms of obligation and respect. In this case, the delivery of the service includes an extra component, a sense of "being cared for" that may augment and enhance the delivery of the service itself. This extra component is often present even in wage employment. Individuals often choose caring jobs because they are a means of expressing caring motives, as well as earning a living. Even if they were not initially motivated by care, workers often come to acquire affection and/or a sense of responsibility for those they care for.

In describing caring services, therefore, it is necessary to go beyond standard economic dimensions such as output or pay and attend to personal and emotional content. Whether or not someone providing caring services is partially motivated by intrinsic rather than extrinsic motives has extremely important implications for the quality of her/his work. Because the feminist analysis of care is an emerging discourse that remains somewhat underdeveloped as an economic theory, it is useful to highlight its differences from both Marxist and neoclassical economic approaches to the labour process.

Care and alienation

Scholars influenced by the Marxian tradition often squeeze caring labour into their own category of unalienated labour — production for use rather than for exchange. The implication is that caring labour flourishes in non-capitalist institutions such as the family and is necessarily attenuated by capitalist organization of work. Sue Himmelweit (1995) argues persuasively that when non-market activities are interpreted simply as a form of unpaid "work" — as, for instance, in efforts to place a market value on household production — their personal and emotional dimensions are obscured. Nel Noddings (1984) goes further, hinting that care is an activity that is intrinsically rewarding (as well as morally transcendent).

But many feminists shun overly sweet descriptions of caring labour, rejecting the implication that it is necessarily more enjoyable or fulfilling than other types of work. Indeed, much attention focuses on the contradictory dimensions of care as an activity that is frustrating as well as rewarding. Arlie Hochschild (1983) treats the demands of emotional labour as a dimension of new forms of exploitation unique to the emerging service sector.

Not just the Marxian tradition, but also the broader legacy of Weberian scholarship tends to locate caring labour in the family and the community, outside the modern sphere of the market. It follows that the expansion of market relations must undermine care, and that a return to more personal, family-based relations would restore it, an implication of much communitarian writing (Etzioni, 1988). Feminist scholars are suspicious of this implication for the obvious reason that personal relations have often been patriarchal relations. Movement away from capitalist relations of production is not necessarily movement towards less alienated or more fulfilling forms of care provision.

The line between caring and "un-caring" labour does not coincide with the line between non-market production and work for pay. Indeed, feminist scholarship emphasizes the remarkable similarity between women's responsibilities for care in the home and their responsibilities for care in paid jobs such as teaching and nursing. By emphasizing this similarity, the concept of caring labour focuses attention on the gendered character of social norms that shape the division of labour in both the family and the market. Women are expected, even required, to provide more care than men.

The new institutional economics, like most functionalist brands of sociology, interprets social norms as essentially benign devices that make it easier for societies to solve coordination problems (Schotter, 1981). Marxist theorists in both economics and sociology often interpret norms as tools of collective domination, but tend to focus on class rather than gender implications. None of these approaches tells much about how we might try to modify norms of care. Nor is it clear what overall level of care can be sustained in an economy that rewards the individual pursuit of self-interest far more generously than the provision of care for others. Marxist analyses of alienation and feminist analyses of care come from different directions, but they converge on a set of questions and concerns about the future quality of life in a capitalist marketplace in which paid care services are playing an increasingly important role.

Care and utility maximization

Neoclassical economic theory largely relies on a stylized model of rational economic man, pursuing his own self-interest. Altruism is acknowledged only within the family, where it is treated as a stylized assumption. The notion that a paid worker might "care for" the person receiving his or her services confounds the self-interest assumption. If individual X derives some utility from the welfare of individual Y, then utility-maximizing individuals must make intersubjective utility comparisons. She (and even he) must ask whether doing something that will inconvenience them will leave the person being cared for sufficiently better-off to compensate. Neoclassical theory stipulates that such intersubjective comparisons are impossible, leaving rational economic man in a something of a pickle.

The standard analysis of labour supply presumes that individuals compare the utility they gain from income with the disutility resulting from labour and stop working when these countervailing forces equalize at the margin. Caring labour implies that people get some utility from caring work itself, as well as from the improvement in the welfare of the person being cared for. It shifts attention to the parameters of utility function — attention which generally makes neoclassical economists squirm. The social construction of individual preferences suddenly becomes relevant.

Neoclassical theorists have traditionally avoided this issue by drawing a strict boundary between a world of altruism (the family) and a world of self-interest (the market). But the feminist analysis of caring labour asserts that family work may sometimes be coerced rather than altruistic, and that the choice of paid occupations may sometimes be motivated by altruistic concern for other people. This blurring of boundaries raises extremely uncomfortable questions: Why do some people — and also some distinctive groups of people — "care" more than others? Robert Frank (1998), among others, calls attention to the importance of both emotions and altruism but stops short of exploring the ways these may be related to the social construction of gender or the changing organization of family life.

It is difficult to name a precept more central to the neoclassical vision than its confidence in individual pursuit of self-interest. This confidence has historically been lodged in the presumption that the family, existing "outside" the economy, would provide the necessary levels of altruism and care. Needless to say, this presumption has been shaken by the destabilization of the patriarchal family and the movement of wives and mothers into paid employment. Once it becomes apparent that the family is susceptible to economic reorganization and change it can no longer be so easily excluded from the larger picture. Once it is included, it becomes apparent that the larger economy has never been entirely based on the individual pursuit of self-interest. It has always depended on some provision of care for others, especially dependants.

Dependants have been almost entirely omitted from mainstream economic (and political) theory. Rational economic man is a self-sufficient adult. We can trust his choices if we assume that he has decent preferences and rational capabilities. Consumer sovereignty implies that he knows what is best for him. But even if we accept this principle for adult men and women, it obviously does not apply to young children. Nor does it apply to many of the sick or the infirm elderly. Even if rational economic man could subsist entirely on his own during part of his life span, it seems unlikely that he could either reach adulthood or survive to old age without some distinctly altruistic assistance.

GENDER AND NORMS OF CARE

Whether approaching the concept of caring labour from the Marxist or the neoclassical economic direction the analytical path leads to pressing questions about the evolution of social norms. In recent years, economists have begun to pay more attention to this topic. However, they generally treat norms as solutions to coordination problems, rather than acknowledging the ways that they may reflect collective forms of social power (Schotter, 1981). But groups often seek to enforce norms and preferences they find beneficial. As Edna Ullmann-Margalit writes, a norm may

> be conceived of as a sophisticated tool of coercion, used by the favoured party in a status quo of inequality to promote its interest in the maintenance of this status quo. It will be considered sophisticated to the extent that the air of impersonality remains intact and successfully disguises what really underlies the partiality of norms, viz. an exercise of power (1977, p. 189).

Feminist theory emphasizes the coercive dimensions of social norms of masculinity and femininity, describing norms as important elements of gendered structures of constraint (Folbre, 1994).

Socially imposed altruism

Men as a group have much to gain by encouraging women's caring propensities. Of course, the opposite is also true: women have much to gain by enforcing norms, and preferences of caring in men. But our constructs of gendered behaviour emerged from societies in which men had far more cultural and economic power than women. The result can be described as "socially imposed altruism" or a gender-biased system of coercive socialization (Folbre and Weisskopf, 1998). Another apt phrase is "discriminatory obligation" (Ward, 1993, p. 103).

The social imposition comes about through the development of highly gendered norms of familial obligation. Regardless of the extent of innate differences between men and women, social norms create strong pressures for differentiation of roles by gender. Specifically, they assign women greater responsibility for the care of dependants, an assignment that almost literally requires altruism. Experimental studies suggest that while there are no significant overall differences in *levels* of altruism between men and women, the forms in which it is expressed are quite gendered (Kohn, 1990). Helping behaviours are highly context dependent. Men are more likely to help someone carry their laundry, women are more likely to help someone fold it. On a less banal level, men are far more likely to go to war and risk death and injury than women are. However, women are more likely to behave in helping and altruistic ways towards kin and community. Their altruism is more likely to find expression in caring labour.

A telling example is the United States General Social Survey, which includes components designed to measure adherence to traditional gender norms. Several of these components explicitly link care, altruism and femininity. Since 1972, for instance, respondents have been asked if they strongly agree, agree, disagree or strongly disagree with the following statement: "It is much better for everyone involved if the man is the achiever outside the home and the woman takes care of the home and family." Note that not only are women expected to do the housework — they are expected to "take care". In surveys administered in 1972-82, 65 per cent of all respondents either strongly agreed or agreed with this statement. By 1994, only 34 per cent did so (Cherlin, 1996). This substantial decline almost certainly reflects women's rapid entrance into paid employment and their enhanced cultural ability to contest traditional norms. Yet it is striking that — in a country often considered the most "modern" in the world — a third of respondents believe that women should specialize in family care.

Attitudinal surveys such as these are seldom conducted in developing countries, but in his classic study of differential mortality by gender among children Amartya Sen (1990) points out that women often lack a concept of themselves as individuals with interests separate from those

333

of their family members (see also Kabeer, 1994). Indeed, explicit policies of male domination may actually exert less force than cultural norms equating femininity with selflessness.

Feminist theorist Joan Tronto points out that robbing individuals of opportunities to effectively pursue their own self-interest may encourage them to live through others, using caring as a substitute for more selfish gratification (1987, pp. 647 and 650).

Maternal altruism often seems to be stronger than paternal altruism among a number of important dimensions. Mothers generally devote a significantly larger share of their income and earnings to family needs than fathers (Benería and Roldan, 1987; Chant and Campling, 1997). Income that is controlled by women is more likely to be spent on children's health and nutrition and less likely to be spent on, say, alcohol (Dwyer and Bruce, 1988; Hoddinott, Alderman and Haddad, 1998). In many countries, a large proportion of fathers provide little or no economic support for their children (Folbre, 1994).

Why do women tend to devote more time and effort to care than men do? Sociobiologists emphasize the greater biological investment in each child made by females (Daly and Wilson, 1983). But one can concede the importance of biology without dismissing the importance of culture. Even Edward O. Wilson, the most famous advocate of sociobiology, writes that divergence in male/female behaviour is "almost always widened in later psychological development by cultural sanctions and training" (1978, p.129). Gary Becker makes a similar point in his *Treatise on the family* (1991). Women are far more likely than men to care for the infirm elderly, as well as children — hardly a pattern that can be explained by the fact that female eggs are few in number compared to male sperm.

Most societies reinforce female altruism towards family and children far more strongly than male altruism. If women "naturally" choose to specialize in care, why do societies develop coercive rules and practices that make it difficult for them to do otherwise? The historical evolution of family structure and social policy in different countries strongly suggests that women's collective economic and political power affects their ability to persuade men — and society in general — to help bear the costs of caring for dependants (Folbre, 1994).

Cultural bargains

Caregivers are often held hostage by care itself. Most forms of bargaining are based on the threat to withhold something valuable. But caregivers, almost by definition, are motivated by intrinsic concerns that make it difficult for them to withhold their care. A mother (or father) cannot tell an infant to stop crying else it will no longer be loved. Nurses and teachers dislike going on strikes that hurt patients and students as much as, if not more than, employers. In the larger process of cultural bargaining, women may prefer a world in which they continue to provide a disproportionate share of care to a world in which no one provides any care at all.

Fundamentalist religions promote the gendered assignment of care responsibilities by threatening that if women don't provide care, no one will. Conservative Linda Weber puts it this way: "How can we possibly imitate the Creator in our relationship if we can't learn from our mothers to give of ourselves, to offer ourselves in love to another, and to control our fleshly impulses for the sake of another?" (Weber, 1994, p. 195). A speaker at a Moral Majority conference in the United States explains: "The less time women spend thinking about themselves, the happier they are ... Women are ordained by their nature to spend time meeting the needs of others" (quoted in Mednick, 1989). And it is argued that if women fail in their selflessness, boys will grow up to be aggressive and out-of-control, and men will revert to barbarism (Gilder, 1992).

Care is often scripted in ways that require docility. In June 1998, the convention of Southern Baptists, the largest Protestant denomination in the United States, declared that a wife should "submit herself graciously" to her husband's leadership (see Niebuhr, 1998). In Egypt, a 1985 Supreme Court decision struck down a law giving a woman the right to divorce her husband should he take a second wife. Sudan's military regime does not allow women to leave the country without permission from a father, husband or brother (Beyer, 1990). The policies implemented by the Taliban in Afghanistan represent a more extreme version of the same response — using explicit laws as well as social norms to ban female employment outside the home.

The resurgence of religious fundamentalism around the world testifies to anxiety about the destabilization of traditional patriarchal relationships that have ensured a relatively cheap supply of caring labour. Some of this anxiety reflects political interests based on nation, race, class and gender. But it also reflects a more generalized concern about the threat of what Benjamin Barber calls "McWorld" — a fast-care society in which individuals buy cheap, standardized, pre-packaged units of supervision, instruction and therapy. In a world of spot markets and instantaneous transactions, there is little room for the development of solidarity or affection. If more and more individuals opt for an individualistic strategy that emphasizes autonomy over commitment, the costs and risks of commitment will increase. The result can be a bit like an arms race, in which individual efforts to gain strategic superiority lead to a tremendous waste of social resources and, ultimately, a destructive war of all against all.

Conservatives often castigate feminists as proponents of western or liberal values of individualism (Fox-Genovese, 1991). This is inaccurate. Asserting that women should have exactly the same individual rights as men leaves open the questions of how individual rights should be defined, and how they should be balanced against social responsibilities. Women have always been especially aware of the tensions between care and individualism. A cultural bargain that simply allows women to act more like men, that redefines femininity in more masculine, self-interested terms, is less appealing than a bargain that redefines masculinity in more feminine, caring terms. Such a bargain, however, is particularly difficult to negotiate.

De-gendering care

Traditional social norms of masculinity are being questioned. Influential discussions of occupational segregation by gender conclude with the need to "challenge stereotypes" (Anker, 1998). This process, however, is a great deal more difficult than it sounds. Stereotypes are particularly resistant to change when they benefit those who have the economic and cultural power to defend them.

Many social scientists are optimistic about efforts to encourage male participation in care as a means of reducing gender inequality (Mahoney, 1995). Sociologist Scott Coltrane favours increasing men's involvement in family work (1998, p. B8). Male participation in childcare, insists sociologist David Popenoe, is good for men themselves, as well as for society (1996, p. 218). One study of single fathers (none of whom had actively chosen their role) found that having responsibility for childcare fostered nurturance and sympathy (Risman, 1987). Some cross-cultural anthropological research shows that children who are given responsibility for other children become more caring adults (Monroe, 1996, p. 176). Gay men have responded to the AIDS epidemic in personally and collectively caring ways.

A movement towards redefining masculinity is by no means limited to the United States and other developed countries. The Programme of Action of the United Nations 1994 International Conference on Population and Development states that:

> Special efforts should be made to emphasize men's shared responsibility and promote their active involvement in responsible parenthood, sexual and reproductive behaviour, including family planning; prenatal, maternal and child health; prevention of sexually transmitted diseases, including HIV; prevention of unwanted and high-risk pregnancies; shared control and contribution to family income, children's education, health and nutrition; and recognition and promotion of the equal value of children of both sexes. Male responsibilities in family life must be included in the education of children from the earliest ages (United Nations, 1995, p. 27, para. 4.27).

Such exhortations are noble and worthwhile. But it is important to examine the sources of resistance to change. Care is costly. Men are reluctant to assume responsibilities that will lower their market income, just as they are reluctant to enter caring occupations that pay less than most male jobs. In a global economy characterized by increased competition, the relative costs of care are probably increasing. There is another reason why traditional gender norms are resistant to change. They are reproduced by interaction between the job market and the marriage market.

REPRODUCING GENDER

Two of the most significant demographic trends of the twentieth century — fertility decline and increased female labour force participation — have had a destabilizing effect on traditional gender roles. A major counterforce, however, has been occupational segregation in the labour force, a pattern that reflects the traditional division of labour in the home. Even in a country like the United States where women acquire, on average, slightly more education than men, and legal sanctions prohibit gender discrimination, women continue to be highly segregated in female occupations. By one recent estimate, 53 per cent of men and women would need to change occupations to equalize the occupational distributions (Blau, 1998); occupational segregation accounts for as much as 40 per cent of the gap in earnings between men and women (Petersen and Morgan, 1995).

Occupational segregation and care

That women are for the most part concentrated in "feminine" jobs implies that their jobs tend to involve responsibilities for care. It is difficult to assess this relationship, because the conventional international standards for occupational categories emerged from a theoretical framework that distinguished the production of material goods (called "production") and the provision of less tangible services, and placed great emphasis on the educational credentials required for different jobs as well as authority roles within the hierarchical firm. However, some distinctly "caring occupations" are discernible.

Most conspicuous are nursing and teaching, two subcategories of "professional, technical and related" occupations that are poorly paid, especially relative to the education they require. In the United States, almost one-half of all women in professional and technical work were either nurses or teachers in 1991, and these two occupations help explain why women throughout the world are overrepresented in this occupational category (Anker, 1998, p. 163).

In the OECD countries, considerable attention is now focused on two relatively low-paid occupations — childcare workers and elder care workers — that are generally included in the larger category of "service workers". Growth in women's labour force participation has led to significant reductions in informal family care, leading to concerns about low pay, high turnover, and resulting low quality in the provision of social care (Christopherson, 1997).

But caring responsibilities are not limited to the most explicitly caring occupations. Ethnographic studies of work show that secretaries are expected to protect their bosses from stress and construct a supportive and reassuring environment (Alexander, 1987; Kanter, 1993). Waitresses are encouraged to be kind as well as personable (Spradly and Mann, 1975). Airline attendants are expected to be heroic in crises as well as cheerful in serving beverages (Hochschild, 1983). Paralegals are expected to mother the lawyers engaged in "Rambo" litigation (Pierce, 1995). Conventional categories cannot be used to tally up the exact percentage of jobs that fit the profile of caring labour.

In any case, the more important question is why women continue to enter these jobs, even in economic environments in which they seem to have some choice, and when the earnings advantages of going into male-dominated jobs are clear. One obvious explanation is that they are socialized as young children to specialize in traditionally female tasks (England, 1992; Jacobs, 1989). Still, one would expect such forms of socialization to be weakened, if not eroded, by a growing awareness of the economic penalty. Another possibility is that women may face a double bind: the gains from choosing a non-traditional occupation may be countervailed by losses in access to male income.

Gender norms and the marriage markets

Marriages tend to join individuals of similar class, race and educational attainment (South, 1991). On the one hand, men have an economic incentive to marry a high-earning wife who will contribute more to family income. On the other, they may worry about marrying a partner with increased bargaining power who will pressure them to take on more household responsibilities and threaten their masculinity (Mason and Lu, 1988; Goldscheider and Waite, 1991).

Anecdotal evidence has long suggested that certain career paths — those dominated by men — are clearly considered "unfeminine" either because they are predominantly held by men or because they also make it difficult for women to live up to norms of femininity in dress and behaviour. What is often overlooked is the economic impact of this normative influence. Conventional models of investment in human capital, including occupational choice, point to rates of return in the labour market as a primary influence (Mincer and Polachek, 1974). But occupational choice may have implications for the marriage market as well.

Whether and whom a woman marries has a significant impact on her economic position. Even in countries like the United States, where women's paid labour force participation is relatively high, women benefit greatly from the earnings of a spouse. In 1997, the median married couple family enjoyed US$51,591 in income. Assuming a married woman had access to half this amount, her income exceeded the median income of a family headed by a women with no spouse present by 23 per cent (United States Department of Commerce, 1998, table 6).

Women who choose non-traditional occupations may have a harder time finding and keeping a high-income husband. Consider the following experiment conducted by Austrian economist Doris Weichselbaumer in a free newspaper published in Massachusetts. She placed ads by two fictive single white females who differed significantly only in the gender conformity of their occupation (one described herself as a nurse, the other as an electrician). The ads read as follows:

> SWF, 31, good looking, slender nurse. Enjoys x-country skiing and films. Financially stable. Would like to meet a man for a lasting relationship.
> SWF, slim, attractive, electrician 30, financially stable, likes movies and rollerblading, seeks man for lasting relationship (Weichselbaumer, 1999).

The ads ran for five weeks. The nurse received 77 responses, the electrician 39. This result suggests a significant penalty for gender nonconformity.

Badgett and Folbre (1999) pursued this theme using factorial surveys designed to identify the importance of many different characteristics of a choice option. They tested the attractiveness of certain characteristics of different individuals by asking groups of students from three large lecture classes of the University of Massachusetts at Amherst (introductory courses in physics, sociology and economics) to rate ten short vignettes describing individuals. The respondent sample was chosen partly for convenience but also because individuals in college are typically actively engaged in the two relevant activities: preparation for particular occupations and search for romantic partners.

The vignettes were systematically varied to allow comparison of outcomes for gender-conforming and nonconforming individuals, controlling for status (which is correlated with earnings). The occupations were sorted into four categories: low status/high femininity (e.g. nurse), high status/high femininity (e.g. pediatrician), low status/low femininity (e.g. carpenter), and high status/low femininity (e.g. airline pilot). To give the occupations more interesting detail, as would be present in a personal ad, and to be clear about the level of education needed for certain occupations, a specific level of education was assigned to each occupation. The prediction was that, holding status and physical characteristics constant, the conformity between a vignette's sex and occupation would have a significant impact on the desirability rating. More specifically, men would rate the women in traditionally female occupations higher than those in traditionally male occupations. And if women did, in fact, consider the gender implications of their occupational aspirations and choices, then women would rate a gender-nonconforming woman as less attractive to men, as well. Similarly, male vignettes that described a man in a female-dominated field would be rated lower by both men and women.

The results generally confirmed the hypothesis that gender nonconformity — controlling for status and education — reduces ratings of likely responses to the personal ad, and therefore the pool of suitors. Individuals who hold traditional attitudes towards "appropriate" gender roles impose a higher penalty on nonconformity than others. The effects are particularly strong for women who enter traditionally masculine jobs that do not require educational credentials and do not offer relatively high status or prestige. A female orthopaedic surgeon, for instance, is penalized less than a female electrician.

Men as well as women in gender-atypical occupations are considered less attractive — but their earning power seems to matter more than their gender conformity. The main point of this comparison is that men who invest in market-specific human capital enjoy two positive pay offs — one in the labour market and one in the marriage market. Women also enjoy a positive payoff in the labour market (though it may be lowered by discrimination) but their payoff in the marriage market is much reduced if they enter what is considered an "unfeminine" occupation.

Less is known about how gender nonconformity might affect dating and marriage outcomes in developing countries, though research opportunities are ample. Marriage searches are often conducted by third parties, either parents or professional matchmakers, and some are conducted via the Web. The following ad, for instance, appeared on a Sri Lankan website in December 1998 (www.lanka.net/lakehouse): "Govi Buddhist parents seek professionally qualified teetotaller nonsmoker partner same caste below 43 for pretty well educated slim excellent charactered daughter 37, qualified computer field executive ... Reply with horoscope and details."

Educational credentials can serve as a substitute for a dowry for young women — especially if they provide access to the small number of lucrative occupations culturally coded as appropriate for women. Indeed, educational credentials that provide access to feminine professions or to relatively new jobs such as computer programming that have not yet been heavily "gendered" may be the only way that women can escape the cultural sanctions against entering traditionally masculine jobs. Women without access to higher education remain stuck behind a particularly high occupational barrier that is probably reinforced by threats of sexual harassment against women who try to "wear pants".

The interaction between marriage markets and job markets probably varies considerably between countries and over time. None the less, the basic dynamic described here has significant implications for the evolution of gender norms. The impact of childhood socialization is likely to diminish over time if conformity to traditional gender norms becomes increasingly costly for women. Stereotypes tend to weaken over time. If, however, women's decisions are informed by concerns about future family formation, their response to opportunities to enter better-paying non-traditional jobs may be slow. The benefits of earning a male salary may be diminished by a fear of reduced success in marriage — or simply by the more diffuse fear of being considered unattractive.

CONCLUSION

Social norms of masculinity and femininity can be and have been openly contested. At a key juncture in the struggle to end foot-binding in China in the early twentieth century, a group of men including the young Mao Tse-Tung publically vowed never to marry a woman whose feet had been bound. They sought to counteract the widespread fear among parents that their daughters would not be able to find a husband unless their feet were appropriately stunted and misshapen. The young men obviously did not seek to eliminate all differences between men and women, though they were accused of such. Rather, they challenged a social construction of femininity that they felt was not only distasteful but morally wrong.

The assumption that women have a greater responsibility than men to subordinate themselves to the needs of children and family is in some respects analogous to binding women's feet. It restricts their mobility, their independence and their productivity. Social norms that closely link being female to care of others have significant economic consequences that contribute to gender inequality within both the household and the labour market. As women enter paid employment, these gender norms are reproduced by occupational segregation and enforced by sanctions against women who are deemed unfeminine. Not surprisingly, women often mobilize collectively to challenge oppressive gender stereotypes, and as the example above indicates, they are sometimes joined by men.

Patriarchal power retains strong economic as well as cultural influence. But there is a more profound reason why women may choose to assume greater responsibilities for care even though they recognize its costs. Sometimes it seems that the only alternative to a world without patriarchy is a world without any care at all. Global capitalist development may help destabilize traditional forms of patriarchal power, but it also promotes an individualist war of all against all (Folbre and Weisskopf, 1998). Particularly in countries with high levels of income inequality and racial/ethnic conflict, economic development is associated with significant disruption of family ties, increases in the percentage of families maintained by women alone, and high levels of poverty among mothers and children (Folbre, 1994). Cheap market substitutes for family care are often designed simply to cut costs rather than to develop human capabilities.

We need to remind ourselves that there are alternatives between the devil and the deep blue sea. We can reassign responsibilities for care. We can forge a new social contract that shares responsibilities for care between men and women. We can develop new gender norms that balance strength with tenderness, autonomy with connectedness, money with love. We could even refuse to marry, partner with (or even date) individuals who specialize in one side of these dualisms at the expense of the other. But we will also have to address the basic dynamics of global capitalism. The only way to support and protect caring work is to reduce the pressures of paid employment on family life, to impose strict quality standards on the provision of market care, and to foster the development of new levels of skill and commitment among paid care workers. Rather than binding women's feet, we could bind capitalism to its domestic responsibilities and restrict it to its proper, limited sphere.

References

Abel, Emily K.; Nelson, Margaret K. 1990. "Circles of care: An introductory essay", in Emily K. Abel and Margaret K. Nelson (eds.): *Circles of care: Work and identity in women's lives.* New York, NY, State University of New York Press, pp. 4-34.

Alexander, J. Davidson. 1987. *Gendered job traits and women's occupations.* Unpublished Ph.D Dissertation. Amherst, MA, University of Massachusetts Department of Economics.

Anker, Richard. 1998. *Gender and jobs: Sex segregation of occupations in the world.* Geneva, ILO.

Badgett, M. V. Lee; Folbre, Nancy. 1999. *Job gendering: Occupational choice and the marriage market.* Unpublished manuscript. Amherst, MA, University of Massachusetts Department of Economics.

Becker, Gary. 1991. *A treatise on the family.* Enlarged edition. Cambridge, MA, Harvard University Press.

Benería, Lourdes; Roldan, Martha. 1987. *The crossroads of class and gender.* Chicago, IL, University of Chicago Press.

Berk, Sarah Fenstermaker. 1985. *The gender factory: The apportionment of work in American households.* New York, NY, Plenum.

Beyer, Lisa. 1990. "Life behind the veil", in *Time* (New York, NY), 8 Nov.

Blau, Francine D. 1998. "Trends in the well-being of American women 1970-1995", in *Journal of Economic Literature* (Nashville, TN), Vol. 36, No. 1 (Mar.), pp. 112-166.

Braunstein, Elissa; Folbre, Nancy. 1999. *To honor or obey: Efficiency, inequality, and patriarchal property rights.* Unpublished manuscript. Amherst, MA, University of Massachusetts Department of Economics.

Brines, Julie. 1994. "Economic dependence, gender, and the division of labor at home", in *American Journal of Sociology* (Chicago, IL), Vol. 100, No. 3 (Nov.), pp. 652-688.

Chant, Sylvia; Campling, Jo. 1997. *Women-headed households: Diversity and dynamics in the developing world.* New York, NY, St. Martin's.

Cherlin, Andrew. 1996. *Public and private families: An introduction.* New York, NY, McGraw-Hill.

Christopherson, Susan. 1997. *Childcare and elderly care: What occupational opportunities for women?* Labour Market and Social Policy Occasional Papers, No. 27. Paris, Organisation for Economic Co-operation and Development (OECD).

Coltrane, Scott. 1998. "Fathers' role at home is under negotiation", in *Chronicle of Higher Education* (Washington, DC), Vol. 45, No. 6 (2 Oct.), p. B8.

Daly, Martin; Wilson, Margo. 1983. *Sex, evolution, and behavior.* Second edition. Belmont, CA, Wadsworth.

Dwyer, Daisy; Bruce, Judith (eds.). 1988. *A home divided: Women and income in the third world.* Stanford, CA, Stanford University Press.

England, Paula. 1992. *Comparable worth: Theories and evidence.* New York, NY, Aldine de Gruyter.

—; Folbre, Nancy. 1999. "The cost of caring", in *Annals of the American Academy of Political and Social Science* (Philadelphia, PA), No. 561, Jan., pp. 39-51.

—; Herbert, Melissa S.; Kilbourne, Barbara Stanek; Reid, Lori L.; McCreary Megdal, Lori. 1994. "The gendered valuation of occupations and skills: Earnings in 1980 census occupations", in *Social Forces* (Chapel Hill, NC), Vol. 73, No. 1 (Sep.), pp. 65-100.

Etzioni, Amitai. 1988. *The moral dimension.* New York, NY, Free Press.

Folbre, Nancy. 1995. "Holding hands at midnight: The paradox of caring labor", in *Feminist Economics* (London), Vol. 1, No. 1 (Spring), pp. 73-92.

—. 1994. *Who pays for the kids? Gender and the structures of constraint.* New York, NY, Routledge.

—; Weisskopf, Thomas. 1998. "Did father know best? Families, markets and the supply of caring labor", in Avner Ben-Ner and Louis Putterman (eds.): *Economics, values and organization.* Cambridge, Cambridge University Press, pp. 171-205.

Fox-Genovese, Elizabeth. 1991. *Feminism without illusions: A critique of individualism.* Chapel Hill, NC, University of North Carolina Press.

Frank, Robert. 1998. *Passions within reason.* New York, NY, W. W. Norton.

Gilder, George. 1992. *Men and marriage.* New York, NY, Pelican.

Goldscheider, Frances; Waite, Linda. 1991. *New families, no families: The transformation of the American home.* Berkeley, CA, University of California Press.

Himmelweit, Susan. 1995. "The discovery of unpaid work: The social consequences of the expansion of work", in *Feminist Economics* (London), Vol. 1, No. 2 (Summer), pp. 1-19.

Hochschild, Arlie Russell. 1983. *The managed heart: Commercialization of human feeling.* Berkeley, CA, University of California Press.

Hoddinott, John; Alderman, Harold; Haddad, Lawrence (eds.). 1998. *Intrahousehold resource allocation in developing countries: Methods, models and policy.* Baltimore, MD, Johns Hopkins University Press.

Jacobs, Jerry. 1989. *Revolving doors: Sex segregation and women's careers.* Stanford, CA, Stanford University Press.

Joshi, Heather. 1998. "The opportunity costs of childbearing: More than mothers' business", in *Journal of Population Economics* (Berlin), Vol. 11, pp. 161-183.

—. 1990. "The cash opportunity cost of childbearing: An approach to estimation using British evidence", in *Population Studies* (London), Vol. 44, Mar., pp. 41-60.

Kabeer, Naila. 1994. *Reversed realities: Gender hierarchies in development thought*. New York, NY, W. W. Norton.

Kanter, Rosabeth Moss. 1993. *Men and women of the corporation*. New York, NY, Basic Books.

Kohn, Alfie. 1990. *The brighter side of human nature*. New York, NY, Basic Books.

Mahoney, Rhona. 1995. *Kidding ourselves: Breadwinning, babies, and bargaining power*. New York, NY, Basic Books.

Mason, Karen Oppenheim; Lu, Yu-Hsia. 1988. "Attitudes toward women's familial roles: Changes in the United States, 1977-1985", in *Gender and Society* (Newbury Park, CA), Vol. 2, No. 1 (Mar.), pp. 39-57.

Mednick, Martha. 1989. "On the politics of psychological constructs: Stop the bandwagon, I want to get off", in *American Psychologist* (Washington, DC), Vol. 44, No. 8 (Aug.), pp. 1118-1123.

Mincer, Jacob; Polachek, Solomon. 1974. "Family investments in human capital: Earnings of women", in *Journal of Political Economy* (Chicago, IL), Vol. 82, No. 2, Part 2 (Mar.-Apr.), pp. S76-S108.

Monroe, Kristen Renwick. 1996. *The heart of altruism: Perceptions of a common humanity*. Princeton, NJ, Princeton University Press.

Niebuhr, Gustav. 1998. "Wives should 'submit', Baptists say", in *International Herald Tribune* (Zurich), 11 June, p. 3.

Noddings, Nel. 1984. *Caring: A feminine approach to ethics and moral education*. Berkeley, CA, University of California Press.

Petersen, Trond; Morgan, Laurie A. 1995. "Separate and unequal: Occupation-establishment sex segregation and the gender wage gap", in *American Journal of Sociology* (Chicago, IL), Vol. 101, No. 2 (Sep.), pp. 329-365.

Pierce, Jennifer L. 1995. *Gender trials: Emotional lives in contemporary law firms*. Berkeley, CA, University of California Press.

Popenoe, David. 1996. *Life without father*. New York, NY, The Free Press.

Risman, Barbara J. 1987. "Intimate relationships from a microstructural perspective: Men who mother", in *Gender and Society* (Newbury Park, CA), Vol. 1, No. 1 (Mar.), pp. 6-32.

Ruddick, Sara. 1983. "Maternal thinking", in Joyce Trebilcot (ed.): *Mothering: Essays in feminist theory*. Totowa, NJ, Rowman and Allanheld, pp. 231-262.

Schotter, Andrew. 1981. *The economic theory of social institutions*. London, Cambridge University Press.

Sen, Amartya. 1990. "Gender and cooperative conflicts", in Irene Tinker (ed.): *Persistent inequalities: Women and world development*. New York, NY, Oxford University Press, pp. 123-149.

South, Scott J. 1991. "Sociodemographic differentials in mate selection preferences", in *Journal of Marriage and the Family* (Minneapolis, MN), Vol. 53, Nov., pp. 928-940.

Spradly, James P.; Mann, Brenda J. 1975. *Cocktail waitress: Women's work in a man's world*. New York, NY, McGraw-Hill.

Tronto, Joan. 1987. "Beyond gender difference to a theory of care", in *Signs: Journal of Women in Culture and Society* (Chicago, IL), Vol. 12, No. 4 (Summer), pp. 644-663.

Ullmann-Margalit, Edna. 1977. *The emergence of norms*. Oxford, Clarendon Press.

United Nations. 1995. *Report of the International Conference on Population and Development — Cairo, 5-13 September 1994*. Document A/CONF.171/13/Rev.1. New York, NY.

United States Department of Commerce. 1998. *Money income in the United States: 1997.* Current Population Reports, Consumer Income P60-200. Washington, DC, Department of Commerce.

Waerness, Kari. 1987. "On the rationality of caring", in A. S. Sassoon (ed.): *Women and the State*. London, Hutchinson, pp. 207-234.

Waldfogel, Jane. 1997. "The effect of children on women's wages", in *American Sociological Review* (Washington, DC), Vol. 62, No. 2 (Apr.), pp. 209-217.

Ward, Deborah. 1993. "The kin care trap: The unpaid labor of long term care", in *Socialist Review* (Oakland, CA), Vol. 23, No. 2 (Jan.-Mar.), pp. 83-106.

Weber, Linda. 1994. *Mom, you're incredible*. Colorado Springs, CO, Focus on the Family.

Weichselbaumer, Doris. 1999. *Sally and Peppermint Patty looking for a partner*. Unpublished manuscript. Linz (Austria), University of Linz Department of Economics.

Weitzman, Lenore. 1985. *The divorce revolution: The unexpected social and economic consequences for women and children in America*. New York, NY, The Free Press.

Wilson, Edward O. 1978. *On human nature*. Cambridge, MA, Harvard University Press.

PARENTAL LEAVE
Patrick BOLLÉ*

17

One of the new options available to many workers for managing the distribution of working time over a working life is parental leave. But if it is really to fulfil its intended role — to help both parents reconcile their work and family responsibilities — it needs to be clearly distinguished from maternity leave and offered on terms that do not drive women out of employment. After providing an international comparison of provisions for parental leave and data on its take-up, its implications for employment, demographic trends, the economy and gender equality are considered in turn.

After decades of unquestioning commitment to the industrialized society ideal of self-fulfilment through "typical", full-time paid employment, many workers — both men and women — now want a better balance between their work and other interests. Accordingly, the current debate about enhancing well-being — also increasingly seen as a measure of social progress — features many good ideas about redesigning jobs in recognition of the growing belief in life outside work. These include the shortening of working time and job-sharing,[1] the promotion of part-time work, home work,[2] teleworking, etc.[3] Yet, while such arrangements may offer hope, they are still by definition atypical and not always voluntary.[4]

"Jobs were designed for full-time working men with full-time wives at home. Although women are overtaking men in the workforce and technology has changed hugely, working patterns are little different."[5] After

---

Originally published as a "perspective" in *International Labour Review*, Vol. 136 (1997), No. 1.

* French-language editor of the *International Labour Review*.

declining steadily for over a century, the average number of hours worked per year has stabilized and even increased in some OECD countries since the 1980s.[6] In the United Kingdom, for example, between 1985 and 1993 working men lost a further 4 per cent of their free time and working women, a further 10 per cent.

For obvious reasons, the pressure of work on people's lives is felt particularly strongly by working parents. And it is not only women who feel torn between work and home: men also want to be more active fathers.[7] In the OECD countries, the increasing participation rates and labour market attachment of women, together with the growing number of dual-earner and single-parent households, have resulted in demands for more flexibility in working arrangements and increased pressures on parents combining work and family responsibilities. "Hence, issues such as child care and leave arrangements for parents have come to the forefront of policy debates." [8] But unlike the debate on work arrangements that would give workers more free time generally, initiatives to help workers cope with family responsibilities have produced tangible results in the form of institutionalized parental or family leave. Moreover, parental leave also offers the advantage of being a voluntary means of introducing flexibility into employment relationships, although its statutory availability depends very much on a country's prosperity and economic development, and also on the social role of women. Provision for parental leave is also ahead of arrangements for care of the elderly, though population aging is likely to increase the pressure to introduce equivalent schemes for this purpose in the future.

The first two countries to introduce parental leave were Hungary in 1967 and Sweden in 1974.[9] The list got steadily longer over subsequent years. And most recently, the November 1995 agreement on parental leave reached between the trade union and employers' organizations of the European Union (EU) bypassed the European Commission in initiating European legislation on the subject (see box 1).

While the primary reason for legislating parental leave is to enable workers to combine work and family responsibilities related to child rearing, it is evident from relevant labour legislation and from available data on the take-up of parental leave that many other factors also come into play: demographic patterns and family policy, the economic situation and employment policy, enterprise profitability, the extent of equality between men and women at work, as well as new attitudes towards the balance between work and leisure time. This partly explains why the regulatory framework within which workers may take parental leave varies so much from one country to another (see table 1).

Without going into the specific definitions of parental leave under national legislation, the following pages focus on countries where parental leave is expressly provided for. However, some countries' legislation provides for more "generic" leave entitlements within which workers

---

Box 1. The European Directive on Parental Leave

On 3 June 1996 the Council of Ministers of the European Union adopted the draft directive on parental leave which had been negotiated by the European employers' and workers' organizations in November 1995.[1] This was the first time that the social partners had successfully availed themselves of the negotiating procedure provided for in the Social Policy Agreement appended to the Treaty on European Union and thus bypassed the European Commission in initiating legislation. According to this procedure, a draft directive concerning a social policy matter on which agreement has previously been reached between the social partners at European Union level is placed directly before the Council of Ministers of the European Union for adoption. If adopted, the directive in question takes immediate effect in all the Member States without the Commission having to be informed formally. In the case in point, however, it was the Commission which had handed over the project to the social partners in the first place.

Beyond the fact that this event is a first in international labour law, the incorporation of the Directive's provisions into national legislation has a number of practical implications.[2] Admittedly, the Directive sets standards that are mostly lower than those already in force in Member States: the minimum period of leave is three months; both men and women are entitled; leave-takers are protected against dismissal and, at the end of their leave, must be reinstated in their original jobs or given equivalent posts with maintenance of their acquired rights. On these points the only countries which will have to change their law are Ireland, which only provides for an optional extended maternity leave, and Luxembourg, where "parental" leave is granted only to women.[3]

However, a fair number of Member States will have to take action on two important points in order to comply with the new Directive. First, it provides that the right to parental leave is an *individual* right, making both father and mother entitled to full parental leave. And second, under the Directive, the period during which the leave may be taken extends up to the child's eighth birthday.

---

[1] ETUC (European Trade Union Confederation), CEEP (European Centre for Public Enterprises) and UNICE (Union of Industrial and Employers' Confederations of Europe): *Framework Agreement on Parental Leave*, Brussels, 14 Dec. 1995.

[2] The Member States parties to the Social Policy Agreement have until 3 June 1998 to make legislative provision for measures at least as favourable as those set out in the agreed text. The United Kingdom, not being a party, is under no such obligation at present. However things could change in the coming months, following the recent announcement by the new Prime Minister, Tony Blair, of the United Kingdom's forthcoming accession to the Social Policy Agreement.

[3] The United Kingdom will also be in this category if it accedes to the Social Policy Agreement.

---

can take a "career break" (e.g. Belgium) or "family leave" (e.g. the United States) to spend time with their children if they so choose. These two countries, together with Iceland — which offers an extended "maternity leave" entitlement for either parent — are included in the table and subsequent discussion to illustrate situations where equivalent flexibility is available to workers under a different name. Of course the list of countries covered here is not exhaustive, but sufficient to give an idea of the general picture.

Table 1.   Terms on which parental leave may be taken, as at 1 April 1997

Country	Statutory right to parental leave	Length-of-service conditions	Duration	Period during which leave may be taken	Option of taking leave on a part-time basis	Option of breaking the leave up into periods	Allowance	Granted on individual or family basis
Australia	Yes	12 months of continuous service	Up to the child's first birthday	Up to the child's first birthday	Yes	No	No	Family
Austria*	Yes, except for provincial civil servants and agricultural workers	None	104 weeks	Up to the child's fourth birthday	Yes	No	Lump sum over two years	Family
Belarus	Yes	None	Up to the child's third birthday	Up to the child's third birthday	Yes	No	No	Family
Belgium*	Yes ("career break" subject to employer's agreement)	12 months of continuous service	260 weeks	Throughout career	Yes	Yes	Lump sum if employee	Individual
Bulgaria	Yes	(1) None	(1) Up to first child's second birthday; up to age of six months for each subsequent child	(1) Up to first child's second birthday; up to age of six months for each subsequent child			(1) Yes	(1) Family
			(2) Up to child's third birthday	(2) Up to child's third birthday			(2) No	(2) Family
Canada	Employees covered at federal level	Six months of continuous service	24 weeks	Up to child's first birthday	No	No	Earnings-related, for ten weeks	Family
Denmark*	Yes	(1) None	Ten weeks	Following maternity leave	No	No	100 per cent of unemployment benefit	Family
		(2) 120 hours over three months of continuous service	26 weeks	Up to child's ninth birthday	No	Yes	60 per cent of unemployment benefit	Individual
Finland*	Yes	None	(1) 26 weeks	(1) Following maternity leave	No	Yes	66 per cent of annual earnings	Family

Table 1. (cont.)

Country	Statutory right to parental leave	Length-of-service conditions	Duration	Period during which leave may be taken	Option of taking leave on a part-time basis	Option of breaking the leave up into periods	Allowance	Granted on individual or family basis
			(2) From the end of the first leave up to the child's third birthday	(2) From the end of the first leave up to the child's third birthday	Yes	Yes	Lump sum	Family
France*	Yes	12 months of continuous service	Up to the child's third birthday	Up to the child's third birthday	Yes	No	Lump sum as from second child	Family
Germany*	Yes	Four weeks with the same employer	Up to the child's third birthday	Up to the child's third birthday	Yes	Yes	Lump sum over two years	Family
Greece*	Yes, except for employees of enterprises with fewer than 100 employees	12 months of continuous service	13 weeks	Until the child is aged 2½	No	Yes	None	Individual
Hungary	Yes ("family leave")		Two years					Individual
Iceland	In private sector: leave merges with maternity leave		Six months				Yes	The month preceding and the month following the birth are taken by the mother; remaining four months may be shared
Israel	Yes	24 months	Proportionate to length of service, up to maximum of 12 months				None	Family

Table 1. (cont.)

Country	Statutory right to parental leave	Length-of-service conditions	Duration	Period during which leave may be taken	Option of taking leave on a part-time basis	Option of breaking the leave up into periods	Allowance	Granted on individual or family basis
Italy*	Except for farmers, the self-employed and domestic servants	None	26 weeks	Between the fourth and the tenth month following the birth	No	No	30 per cent of earnings	Family
Japan	Except for seasonal workers and workers employed by the day	None	Up to the child's first birthday	Up to the child's first birthday	No	No	25 per cent of earnings on condition of length of service	Family
Lithuania	Yes		Up to the child's third birthday	Up to the child's third birthday	Yes	Yes		Family
Netherlands*	Yes	12 months of continuous service	Three months	Up to the child's sixth birthday	Yes		None	Individual
New Zealand	Yes	Ten hours a week for at least 12 months of continuous service	Up to the child's first birthday	Up to the child's first birthday	No	No	None	Family
Norway	Yes	None	Up to the child's first birthday	Up to the child's first birthday	Yes	No	80 per cent of earnings for 52 weeks or 100 per cent for 42 weeks	Family
Poland	Yes	Six months	Three years	Up to the child's fourth birthday			Family allowance and health insurance	
Portugal	Yes	Six months	26 weeks	Following maternity leave	No	No	None	Family
Russian Federation	Yes		Up to the child's third birthday	Up to the child's third birthday	Yes		For the first 18 months	Family

Table 1. (cont.)

Country	Statutory right to parental leave	Length-of-service conditions	Duration	Period during which leave may be taken	Option of taking leave on a part-time basis	Option of breaking the leave up into periods	Allowance	Granted on individual or family basis
Slovenia	Yes		One year	105 days following the birth			100 per cent of previous earnings	Family
Spain*	Yes	None	Up to the child's first birthday	Up to the child's first birthday	No	No	None	Family
Sweden*	Yes	Six months	18 months	Up to the child's eighth birthday	Yes	Yes	75 per cent of earnings for 12 months, then a lump sum for three months	Family: one month must be taken by the father, one month by the mother
Ukraine	Yes		Up to the child's third birthday	Up to the child's third birthday	Yes		For the first 18 months	Family
United States	Except for armed forces personnel, for employees of enterprises with fewer than 50 on the payroll, and for strategic staff members	12 months of service and 1,250 hours with the same employer over the 12 months immediately preceding the leave	12 weeks	Before the child's first birthday	Yes	Yes	None	Individual

Countries providing for optional extended maternity leave or so-called "parental leave" open only to the mother: Afghanistan, Burkina Faso, Cuba, Egypt, Guinea, Republic of Korea, Iraq, Ireland,* Luxembourg,* Mongolia, Romania, Switzerland, Tunisia, Turkey, United Kingdom and Viet Nam.

* Country which should introduce changes in the law following adoption of the EU Directive (see box).

Sources: ILO: "Maternity and work", in *Conditions of work digest* (Geneva), 1994, Vol. 13; OECD: *Employment Outlook* (Paris), 1995, pp. 172-202: *European Industrial Relations Review*, (London), 1995, No. 262, pp. 14-23 ("Parental leave in Europe").

VARYING DEFINITIONS AND FORMS OF PARENTAL LEAVE

The ILO's Workers with Family Responsibilities Recommendation, 1981 (No. 165), which concerns equal opportunities and equal treatment for men and women workers, considers that "either parent should have the possibility, within a period immediately following maternity leave, of obtaining leave of absence (parental leave), without relinquishing employment and with rights resulting from employment being safeguarded" (para. 22.1).[10] According to this (international) definition, the distinctive features of parental leave are that it may be taken by either the mother or the father, that it is distinct from maternity leave, and that it does not entail loss of employment or of any associated rights.

Parental leave differs from *maternity leave* in that its concern is not the health of the mother but the care and upbringing of young children, making both the father and the mother eligible.[11] It also differs in this respect from *extended or optional maternity leave* (up to several months granted immediately after maternity leave, generally to enable the mother to breast-feed). It typically differs from *paternity leave* (a very short period immediately after birth) and from *family leave* (normally an annual entitlement of a few days not necessarily related to childcare) in that it lasts longer, from several weeks to several years. And, lastly, it differs from *sabbatical leave* and general-purpose *career breaks* in that it is intended only for workers with young children. In national practice, however, as will be seen below, these distinctions are not watertight. For example, there is an increasing tendency for the right to optional "maternity leave" to be granted to the father, thus changing it in effect into parental leave. In some countries (e.g. Belgium) parental leave does not exist as such, since there is provision for career breaks open to all subject to agreement of the employer. Finally, there is a widespread tendency for the leave rights associated with the birth of a child to be granted in cases of adoption.

As may be seen from the table, the form taken by parental leave varies from one country to another as to the categories of persons eligible, the length of service required for eligibility, the duration of leave and the period within which it may be taken, the ways in which parental leave may be shared or staggered over that period, or taken on a part-time basis, whether the leave is granted to the individual or to the family unit,[12] and the payment or not of a parental leave allowance. In countries where parental leave is not provided for by law it can be provided under collective agreements. In practice, the only unchanging aspects of parental leave are the guaranteed return to work at the end of the leave period, the fact that it may be taken either by the mother or by the father, and that its aim is the care of young children. However, there are also inter-country variations in the extent to which these three criteria are met. The return-to-work guarantee ranges from a guaranteed return to the same post with inclusion of the leave in the worker's length of service, to no more than a guaranteed return to whatever post is available in the enterprise. In some countries, a so-called parental leave entitlement is available only to women, while in others there is a tendency to grant fathers the right to optional "maternity leave". And in countries like Belgium, which allow agreed long-term leave, there may be no need for parental leave as such although the option to take it is clearly available to workers in the form of a general-purpose career break.

Generally speaking, there has been a lengthening of the period during which parental leave may be taken. When it was first introduced, parental leave was typically available for a brief period immediately after maternity leave; today the entitlement often extends until the child reaches the age of three and can start pre-school, or even up to the age when compulsory schooling starts. The new European Directive on the subject (see box 1) provides that parental leave be granted to parents "until a given age up to eight years to be defined by Member States and/or Social Partners". In France the Government has just announced it intends to extend the limit up to the child's sixteenth birthday.[13]

Such international diversity in parental leave is a reflection of the various concerns and aims of the legislator at the time the right to parental leave was introduced, for example, the achievement of greater equality between men and women, or the influence of concerns arising from the employment or demographic situation.

TAKE-UP RATES OF PARENTAL LEAVE

All the studies consulted mention the lack of data with which to make international comparisons and trace the development of parental leave over time. The problem is further compounded by the fact that the right to parental leave is often stipulated under one law and payment of an allowance under another, which means that two separate authorities may be involved. Moreover, a meaningful comparison has to take account of both the ratio of the number of beneficiaries to the number of persons eligible, and the ratio of the duration of leave actually taken to its theoretical maximum. Though the data are insufficient for a rigorous international comparison, the figures available for certain countries do make it possible to establish which factors help and which hinder the take-up of parental leave. The OECD study already mentioned refers to several of these.[14]

The highest take-up rates are found in Sweden, Norway, Finland, Denmark and the western part of Germany; they are much lower in the Netherlands and in France. The difference between the Nordic countries and the Netherlands or France can easily be explained by the payment in the first group of countries of an allowance which compensates in good

---

Box 2. The United States Family and Medical Leave Act, 1993

In the United States, the right to parental leave formerly depended on agreements made within the enterprise and on laws or regulations adopted by 34 of the federal States (plus Washington, DC, and Puerto Rico). The Family and Medical Leave Act passed in February 1993 established a federal right to 12 weeks of unpaid annual leave for family or medical reasons with a return-to-work guarantee, subject to length-of-service conditions and a minimum of 50 workers being employed at the workplace (a little over half the country's employed workforce was eligible in 1996). Such leave can be taken for medical reasons, for maternity/confinement, for the care of a sick member of the family, or for the care of a new-born (or newly adopted) child. In the latter case, amounting to parental leave, it can be taken on a part-time or staggered basis up to the child's first birthday. The concerns put forward by Congress in passing the new legislation (section 2(a)) suggest strong emphasis on provision for this particular form of leave because:

(1)　the number of single-parent households and two-parent households in which the single parent or both parents work is increasing significantly;

(2)　it is important for the development of children and the family unit that fathers and mothers be able to participate in early childrearing ...;

(3)　the lack of employment policies to accommodate working parents can force individuals to choose between job security and parenting;

[...]

(5)　due to the nature of the roles of men and women in our society, the primary responsibility for family caretaking often falls on women, and such responsibility affects the working lives of women more than it affects the working lives of men; and

(6)　employment standards that apply to one gender only have serious potential for encouraging employers to discriminate against employees and applicants for employment who are of that gender.

Source: *Labour Law Documents* (Geneva), 1993, No. 2, pp. 103-116 (1993-USA 1).

---

measure for the loss of wages. In Sweden, moreover, a fiscal policy which renders this leave more attractive than the associated wage loss also grants a more than proportionate tax deduction. In the Netherlands there is no allowance, and in France it is low and payable only after the birth of a second child. The situation in the Netherlands is further complicated by the fact that, until recently, parental leave could only be taken part time, regardless of the very high proportion of the female labour force already employed on a part-time basis.[15] The law there has only just been changed to allow parental leave to be taken on a full-time basis. In Germany and Austria take-up rates are high although the allowance is low. This may be due to the poor provision of other forms of childcare for young children (crèches or child-minders). Although the general tendency is for the law to provide for increasingly long parental leave, its actual take-up rate appears to remain low. The reasons are partly financial (households cannot continue to manage on a reduced income) and partly professional (parents prefer to take a shorter break for the sake of their careers).

In the United States, a study conducted three years after the entry into force of the Family and Medical Leave Act (see box 2 above) by the Commission on Family and Medical Leave [16] (set up to monitor the application of the legislation) found that parental leave accounted for about 13 per cent of all the forms of leave taken under the new Act. Leave taken for other reasons was distributed between: health of the eligible employee (60 per cent), health of a daughter or son (8 per cent), health of a spouse, parent or other relative (15.5. per cent), and maternity (4 per cent). Considering all these forms of leave, the Commission also found that:

– 66 per cent of workers were employed by companies meeting the criteria fixed by the Act, but only 55 per cent met the length-of-service requirements;

– over half the parents eligible for leave did not know they were, while 86 per cent of employers did;

– the chances of being granted parental leave increased with company size;

– 16.5 per cent of employees had taken one form of leave, while 3.5 per cent had given up the idea because of the loss of income it entailed;

– leave was taken for an average of ten days, but parental leave tended to be taken for longer;

– parental leave (13 per cent of the total) was more or less equally distributed between women (12.5 per cent) and men (14.5 per cent).

However, aspects of the take-up of parental leave such as distribution by sex or recourse to part-time leave should be examined in the light of links between conditions of entitlement to such leave and other factors, including demographic policy, employment policy, economic concerns, gender equality and time-sharing.

PARENTAL LEAVE AND DEMOGRAPHIC POLICY

In countries experiencing a falling birth rate, two opposing concerns come into conflict: one which encourages women to stay at home and bear children, the other which seeks to reconcile work and family life through an appropriate social policy. Already in the 1930s Sweden explicitly sought to reconcile work and family life.[17] It is therefore not surprising that Sweden was a pioneer as regards parental leave. In fact, the Nordic countries (Denmark, Finland, Iceland, Norway and Sweden), where provision is made for long parental leave with substantial allowances, have both a birth rate higher than average for western Europe (between 1.806 and 2.143 as against 1.5 for the rest of the continent) and significant female labour force participation rates.[18]

However, implementation of the right to parental leave varies according to how much importance is given to pro-natalist objectives and demographic policies. In France, for example, the rights to parental leave and to an allowance are governed by two distinct legal approaches. In principle, no allowance is attached to parental leave, which is a form of unpaid leave. But, when one of the parents stays at home, family policy provides for a "parental education allowance" as from the second child. Another allowance for the first child up to the age of three is payable to unemployed parents living alone, whether or not they worked before the child's birth. In effect, the first measure encourages women to return rapidly to work after the birth of their first child, by entrusting their child to a crèche or child-minder; it entitles beneficiaries to an allowance, a tax deduction, and to payment by the family allowance fund of any social charges associated with the childcare scheme. With the birth of a second child, however, it becomes more attractive — especially in the case of low-income households — for one of the parents to stop working and receive the parental education allowance, rather than see his or her wages much reduced by childcare costs for two children, notwithstanding the incentives mentioned above. Generally speaking, it is the mother who stops working, either because childcare is seen as being her role or because the household's income suffers less from the loss of her wages given women's typically lower pay. Thus, parental leave in France features in an overall policy package combining both pro-natalist incentives and removal — however temporary — of women from the labour market. Similarly, one of the effects of the allowance for single parents is to cut certain unskilled young women off from the labour market when they have a second, then a third child, once entitlement to the allowance paid for the second child stops. Such a policy thus seems to hesitate between concern with reconciling work and family life, on the one hand, and the temptation of paying mothers a "maternity wage" to stay at home, on the other.[19] This is why it is difficult to consider a country's parental leave provisions in isolation from its employment situation.

PARENTAL LEAVE AND EMPLOYMENT POLICY

Provision for leave, whether unpaid or paid through the social protection system, can include the aim of reducing the labour supply, either explicitly or implicitly. In some countries, decisions regarding the extension of maternity or parental leave also involve calculating the number of posts thus temporarily made available. In Belgium, for example, a career break is granted subject to agreement by the employer, and an allowance is payable under the law on unemployment insurance only if the employer hires an unemployed person to replace the worker on leave. In Denmark, parental leave and other forms of long-term leave were deliberately introduced as part of job rotation policy. In that country, the various entitlements are as follows:

- family parental leave (to be shared by the father and the mother) of ten weeks, to be taken at the end of maternity leave, with entitlement to an allowance equivalent to 100 per cent of the maximum unemployment benefit;

- individual parental leave (for which both parents are eligible) of 26 weeks which can be broken up and taken in stages up to the child's ninth birthday, with entitlement to an allowance equivalent to 80 per cent of the unemployment benefit; it can last up to one year, but this is discretionary, not a right;

- two other forms of leave, one for training and the other for sabbatical purposes, giving entitlement to an allowance of 100 per cent and 80 per cent of the unemployment benefit, respectively; both can last for up to one year; although they do not concern childcare in any way, they are part of the job rotation package.

These forms of leave, especially individual parental leave, have proved very popular in Denmark — indeed they have been victims of their own success. A study conducted by Kongshøj Madsen [20] of the first 18 months following their introduction (between the first quarter of 1994 and the third quarter of 1995) shows that, with 71,300 take-ups, these forms of leave proved more popular than any other employment policy measures — e.g. subsidized jobs (63,000) — and that the number of unemployed fell from 383,600 to 281,400 over that period. However, this policy package also had a perverse effect and triggered off labour shortages in certain occupations. The most famous case is that of the nurses and nursing assistants, whose fertility rate is above average: in 1994, out of a total of 49,000, 2,900 of them benefited from one of these forms of leave, of whom 2,300 took parental leave. Hospitals and health care establishments had to recruit replacement staff from neighbouring countries.[21] These forms of leave were also criticized by employers for the way they distorted the labour market and for their cost. In the event, the allowances payable under the parental and sabbatical leave schemes were reduced to 70 per cent, then to 60 per cent of unemployment benefit as from 1 April 1997. According to Madsen, "in a longer-term perspective the paid leave schemes merit serious consideration because they constitute a new approach to exploiting the potential offered by the underpinning reduction of the time spent at work— which has been noted in the Nordic countries during the entire postwar period." Thus, such forms of leave would follow on from the shorter working day or week, longer paid holidays, or the lowering of retirement age.

ECONOMIC ADVANTAGES AND DISADVANTAGES

Though the paucity of available data precludes a comprehensive evaluation, a number of case-studies do give some indication of the economics of parental leave. According to the OECD: "[t]here is currently little evidence to indicate that parental leave gives rise to serious personnel problems for employers." [22] If informed in advance that the leave will be taken, employers can make the necessary plans. There are three possible approaches: hiring a replacement, sharing the work of the absent colleague amongst his/her colleagues, and waiting for the employee's return to do the work. The first solution is sometimes imposed either by law or by collective agreement. Various factors influence choice: the size of the enterprise, the availability of employees capable of filling in for the leave-taker, recruitment costs, etc. For example, a low-skilled worker is more easily replaced than is a highly skilled worker, as the cost of recruiting and training a replacement is lower. A study conducted in France showed that, in the private sector, middle managers were less frequently replaced (42 per cent) than low-skilled workers (59 per cent), though the reverse was found to be the case in the public service, with 86 and 65 per cent, respectively. The same study showed that the longer the workers' length of service in the enterprise, the less frequently they were replaced. In Denmark, women are more frequently replaced (65 per cent) than men (54 per cent). The economic situation also has an impact on replacement rates: if it is bad, they fall.

Though parental leave can disrupt enterprise organization, especially in the case of small enterprises or when it involves highly qualified workers, the absence of formal arrangements for reconciling work and family life has also been found to entail heavy costs for employers. The United States Department of Labor cites surveys which show a link between factors such as absenteeism or unproductive time at work with the fact that workers have children.[23] One survey showed that about 57 per cent of women and 33 per cent of men spent unproductive time at work because of childcare concerns. The reasons given for absence or for unproductive time at work were: caring for a sick child, caring for a child when the usual provider was unavailable, medical appointments, teacher conferences, telephone calls home if the children were alone, and stress in general. These difficulties are exacerbated when parents' working time is very different from school hours. In conclusion, the Department of Labor stressed the need for high-quality, reliable childcare services and for greater flexibility in working time organization.

Another cost study was conducted in the United States on the basis of data supplied by a high technology corporation with a liberal parental leave policy.[24] Taking into consideration the various costs and advantages (productivity, training, work reorganization, etc.), as well as the full range of options open to the employer (replacement, temporary recruitment, reassignment of the work among the remaining employees, work at home, etc.), the authors concluded that it was much more cost-effective to evolve a well-planned parental leave policy than to lose the worker concerned and have to replace him/her permanently. The average cost of leave was 32 per cent of annual salary: it was 28 per cent for non-management and 39 per cent for management staff, whereas the cost of replacing an employee permanently ranged from 75 per cent of annual salary for the former to 150 per cent for the latter. The less skilled the worker, the lower the cost of leave; the better the leave times were planned, the easier it was to reassign the work among remaining employees. However, the cost was higher if the leave was taken for longer, if the leave-taker was a high-performing employee or member of a small team, if the leave-taker was replaced permanently, or if the supervisor had a negative attitude towards parental leave.

There is no doubt some link between findings such as these and the changes that occurred in United States legislation in 1993. Indeed, under the Family and Medical Leave Act (see box 2 above) employers are entitled to deny reinstatement to "highly compensated employees ... if ... such denial is necessary to prevent substantial and grievous economic injury to the operations of the employer". This provision would thus seem to be a disincentive for those employees whose parental leave, as shown above, costs employers most. However, the Commission on Family and Medical Leave, set up to monitor the application of the Act (i.e. all forms of leave covered), found that only 2.5 per cent of the employers surveyed in 1996 reported savings thanks to a slow-down in staff turnover and higher job commitment.[25] In general, the application of the Act was regarded as having no particular impact on the various indicators concerning company and employee performance (in 80 to 95 per cent of the companies surveyed). Reported positive effects outweighed reported negative effects on employee performance, especially as regards productivity (12.5 against 5 per cent); while reported negative effects outweighed reported positive effects on company performance. The small proportion of employers who stated they had made savings appears to contradict the findings of the 1992 study of parental leave (see note 24). However, that study also made it clear that for the leave to be cost-effective certain conditions regarding forward planning and implementation had to be met. Indeed, the short average duration of leave actually taken and the variety of reasons for its take-up show that in practice it serves more as leave for family and medical reasons (as its name implies) than as parental leave as such, which is intended to be taken for longer and in a less fragmented way.

PARENTAL LEAVE AND GENDER EQUALITY

One of the main features of parental leave is that it is available to both parents, either because the entitlement can be shared (family leave) or because each parent is individually entitled (individual leave). In practice, however, it is clear from the gender distribution of take-up in most countries for which data are available that parental leave is typically taken up by mothers, not fathers. The exception in this respect is the United States, where the remarkably balanced gender distribution (with slightly more men than women taking parental leave) is a particularly important aspect — maybe even the most crucial aspect — of the application of the country's recent legislation on this subject. According to the OECD,[26] under 5 per cent of eligible fathers take parental leave in Denmark, Finland, Germany and Norway. In Sweden, however, the proportion was 25 per cent in 1987 (up from 20 per cent in 1978), though Swedish fathers take such leave only for short periods and often on a part-time basis. In terms of the number of days of paid parental leave taken in Sweden, the proportion taken by men falls to 7 per cent in 1988 (4 per cent in 1978). Elsewhere this proportion is around 1 per cent.

Parental leave is intended to help women enter the labour market, in so far as it enables them not to have to choose between a career and caring for their children. In principle, it provides them with three options: that of taking a career break to look after their children, with a guaranteed return to work; that of pursuing their careers while the father takes a career break with the same guarantee; and that of sharing the career break with the father. But as the above figures suggest, men show little enthusiasm for parental leave. This leaves the first of the three options, whose success in practice can be judged from the rate of women's return to work once their leave entitlement is used up.

A study conducted for the Commission of the European Communities on the characteristics of women's working lives in the 12-nation European Union produced a number of interesting findings in this respect.[27] First it showed an inverse relationship between female labour force participation and women's career continuity. In countries where the participation rate is high (over 90 per cent), the percentage of women who take a career break is under 60 per cent (Denmark, Germany, United Kingdom). Conversely, when female labour force participation is low (between 60 and 70 per cent), the percentage of women who continue their careers without a break is higher, between 70 and 80 per cent (Greece, Italy and Spain). In these three countries, women consider that family concerns are less disruptive to careers than do their counterparts in northern Europe. The authors of the study established a typology which "reflects the availability of child care for children of pre-school age, as well as national attitudes and policies with regard to the education of very young children, the role of the mother and the independence of women". According to this, in southern Europe (Greece, Italy, Portugal, Spain) working women do not seem to find family life incompatible with working, whereas in northern Europe (Germany, Ireland, Luxembourg, Netherlands, United Kingdom) conditions do not seem favourable to women wishing to combine work and a rewarding family life. An intermediate group of countries (Belgium, Denmark, France) provides a range of measures for reconciling work and family life, e.g. long-term, paid parental leave and widely available subsidized childcare facilities.

The above-mentioned OECD study (see note 8) contains further information on the effects of parental leave in this context. In Finland, Sweden and the Netherlands, most people who take parental leave subsequently return to work, generally for their former employer. They return to work less frequently in Germany and Austria (about half and one third, respectively). In Germany, however, the proportion of single mothers returning to work after parental leave is much higher, at about 80 per cent after the first child, and 65 per cent after the second. These differences are probably due to the short duration of the leave entitlement (which is not linked in any way to the age when children start school) and to poor childcare services for young children. Unless women simply cannot afford to do so (as in the case of single mothers), they choose to look after their children and not to return to work. Measures to extend the leave entitlement up to the age when children start school and to provide an adequate allowance would undoubtedly improve the rate of return to work. However, there is often an early return to work through fear of loss of employment for economic reasons or of deterioration of skills. France and Spain, where parental leave may be taken for a long period, have therefore legislated a right to training after parental leave. There is also a correlation between the rate of return to work and the skill level and appeal of the worker's job.

"Sweden is currently the only case where ... long-term impacts can be observed and studies exist. All conclude that there have been significant positive effects of combined parental leave <u>and</u> working-time arrangements on the career patterns of Swedish women".[28] These positive effects are an increase in the full-time participation rate before the birth of the first child and a steady reduction in the number of women staying at home after the first child is born; in short, an improvement in women's career continuity. However, one should guard against generalization as there is certainly a link between these outcomes and the sophistication of Swedish legislation in this respect. In other circumstances, several factors can come into play to turn parental leave into a trap locking women, or at least some of them, out of the labour market. One such factor is the low take-up rate among fathers. This is certainly linked to prejudice, but equally certainly to the gender pay gap. The fact that women are typically paid lower wages than are men acts as an incentive for mothers to take parental leave, since this will have a lesser effect on the couple's income. Another source of inequality is reflected in the fact that women with fewer skills or less interesting jobs are those that tend to return to work later or not to return at all. The lack of alternative forms of child care or their high cost tends to reinforce the exclusion of such women from the labour market. Thus, the positive effects of parental leave on equality between men and women are in fact dependent on other factors such as income inequality, initial position on the labour market, the availability of childcare facilities, and the amount of the allowance payable during parental leave.

THE OUTLOOK

Several general tendencies emerge clearly today. In particular,

- the right to parental leave is being recognized in a growing number of countries, either as such or as a modified form of the right to extended maternity leave, which is now being extended further and opened up to fathers or even other household members (e.g. grandparents);

- parental leave entitlements are becoming longer;

- the period during which the leave may be taken is also being extended, up to the age at which children may or must start school, i.e. either the age of pre-school entry (three years) or the age of compulsory schooling (six to eight years);

- the ways in which the leave may be taken are becoming more flexible and diverse: it can be taken part time, staggered over time, or in the form of work at home;

- parental leave is increasingly granted on an individual basis as opposed to a family basis;

- parental leave arrangements may have a positive effect on the birth rate, on employment and on gender equality, provided that certain conditions are met, notably if an allowance adequately compensates for lost income and if other forms of childcare are available to facilitate a return to work.

This last point calls for two further comments. First, for parental leave to be fully effective — i.e. to allow *both parents* to combine work and family responsibilities — it must be made attractive to both. In other words, it should be available on an individual basis and the allowance paid must be adequate to compensate for income lost. However, adequate income replacement imposes a considerable cost burden on the state or social protection budget. In 1993, for example, its cost amounted to 1.1 per cent of GDP in Finland, 1.07 per cent in Sweden, 0.75 per cent in Norway and 0.51 per cent in Denmark.[29] Some countries, like Denmark, have in fact recently reduced their parental leave allowance. Current budget constraints and the questioning of the Welfare State are indeed likely to cast a shadow over the future of parental leave by inducing reductions in allowances (where available) or only minimal provision under new legislation. This involves a risk of effective parental leave becoming available only to management-level employees and otherwise acting as a trap locking the least-skilled women workers out of the labour market.

Second, since the effectiveness of parental leave also depends on take-up rates and the conditions governing return to work, the increasingly precarious nature of employment must be seen as a threat. Fewer and fewer workers are likely to meet the length-of-service requirements to qualify for parental leave and, especially, for the associated allowance when two separate administrations are involved. Besides, a return to work is of course conditional upon employment being permanent. Workers on precarious contracts will be reluctant to take parental leave for fear of losing their jobs while they are away.

Last, there remains the question of whether parental leave can be seen as part of a trend towards redistribution of time between work and private life. Indeed, it supplements — and sometimes overlaps with — other forms of extended leave or career breaks, such as sabbatical leave, training leave, or various time-saving schemes.[30] In the event, the question as posed by Kongshøj Madsen [31] is whether such leave arrangements foreshadow the way in which working time will be further reduced in the future — provided of course that its reduction continues or rather resumes, since it seems to have come to a halt with the slow-down in productivity gains in the OECD countries. Such forms of leave can also serve as a means of redistributing or rotating jobs, in countries where they are perceived as a way of fighting mass unemployment.

Notes

[1] See "Working time and employment: New arrangements", in *International Labour Review* (Geneva), Vol. 134 (1995), No. 2, pp. 259-272.

[2] See ILO: *Home work*, Geneva, 1994, reviewed in *International Labour Review* (Geneva), Vol. 134 (1995), No. 2, pp. 286-288.

[3] For an optimistic outlook see, for example, Alan Reynolds: "Workforce 2005: The future of jobs in the United States and Europe", in OECD: *OECD societies in transition: The future of work and leisure*, Paris, 1994, pp. 47-80 (especially pp. 74-75).

[4] See "Labour markets and employment practices in the age of flexibility: A case study of Silicon Valley", by Martin Carnoy, Manuel Castells and Chris Benner; and "Atypical employment in the European Union", by Andries De Grip, Jeroen Hoevenberg and Ed Willems, both published in *International Labour Review*, Vol. 136 (1997), No. 1.

[5] Mary Ann Sieghart: "Go home, your job is wrecking you", in *The Times* (London), 29 Sep. 1995.

[6] ILO: *World Employment 1996/97: National policies in a global context*, Geneva, 1996, pp. 16-19 and figure 2.1.

[7] Moreover, parents' interest in spending more time with their young children is likely to grow in the light of research findings suggesting that intensive exposure to language spoken by a dedicated person in the first year of life may have a critical impact on a child's brain development and future skills. See, for example, Sandra Blakeslee: "Making baby smart: Words are the way", in *International Herald Tribune* (Zurich), 18 April 1997, p. 1.

[8] OECD: "Long-term leave for parents in OECD countries", in *Employment Outlook* (Paris), July 1995, p. 171.

[9] ILO: *Social security and social protection: Equality of treatment between men and women*, Tripartite Meeting of Experts on Social Security and Social Protection: Equality of Treatment between Men and Women, Geneva, 1994, p. 21.

[10] ILO: *Workers with family responsibilities*, International Labour Conference, 80th Session, Geneva, 1993. This document summarizes national policies on the question of parental leave. Convention No. 156 and Recommendation No. 165 are reproduced in an annex.

[11] "If one wants to achieve genuine equality between men and women and avert the negative effects of overprotection of women workers, it will be important to distinguish the physiological demands that pregnancy and confinement impose on women from the bringing up of children and the care they need, since these responsibilities can be shared by men and women" (Chantal Paoli: "Women workers and maternity: Some examples from western Europe", in *International Labour Review* (Geneva), Vol. 121 (1982), No. 2, p. 14). The 1999 and 2000 Sessions of the International Labour Conference will have on their agenda the revision of Convention No. 103 and Recommendation No. 95 concerning maternity protection. For a description of the full range of national provision and practice (with commentary) as regards the various forms of leave associated with maternity, see ILO: "Maternity and Work", in *Conditions of Work Digest* (Geneva), 1994, Vol. 13.

[12] Parental leave is said to be family parental leave if it is available to either of the parents to the exclusion of the other, and the leave entitlement may be transferred from one to the other in full or in part; it is said to be individual when both parents may take it together in full or in part.

[13] *Le Monde* (Paris), 19 March 1997.

[14] OECD: op. cit. (note 8), chapter 5.

[15] See Andries de Grip, Jeroen Hoevenberg and Ed Willems, op. cit.

[16] *A workable balance: Report to Congress on Family and Medical Leave Policies*, Washington, DC, The Women's Bureau, US Department of Labor, 1996.

[17] See Alva Myrdal: "A programme for family security in Sweden", in *International Labour Review* (Geneva), Vol. 39 (1939), No. 6 (June). An abridged version of this article was published in *International Labour Review* (Geneva), Vol. 135 (1996), No. 3-4, pp. 347-357.

[18] Åke Nilsson: "Nordic women have both children and job", in *Nordic Labour Journal* (Copenhagen), 1996, No. 2, pp. 12-13.

[19] Alain Norvez: *La politique familiale française depuis 1980: entre la conciliation des tâches familiales et professionnelles des mères et la tentation du salaire maternel*, paper presented to the European Forum: "The cost of being a mother, the cost of being a father", European University Institute, Florence, 1995.

[20] Kongshøj Madsen: "Popular acceptance for Danish leave-scheme — but do they work?", in *Nordic Labour Journal* (Copenhagen), 1996, No. 1, pp. 16-20.

[21] *Le Monde* (Paris), 14 August 1995.

[22] OECD: op. cit. (note 8), p. 172.

[23] United States Department of Labor, Office of the Secretary, Women's Bureau: *Employers and child care: Benefiting work and family*, Washington, DC, 1990, pp. 7-11.

[24] Rebecca Marra and Judith Lindner: "The true cost of parental leave: The Parental Leave Cost Model", in Dana E. Friedman, Ellen Galinsky and Veronica Plowden (eds.): *Parental leave and productivity: Current research*, New York, Families and Work Institute, 1992, pp. 55-78.

[25] See note 16.

[26] OECD: op. cit. (note 8).

[27] Marianne Kempeneers and Eva Lelièvre: "Employment and family within the Twelve", in *Eurobarometer* (Brussels), 1991, No. 34 (special issue), p. 134 et seq.

[28] OECD: op. cit. (note 8), p. 189.

[29] OECD: op. cit. (note 8), p. 192, table 5.6.

[30] See "Working time and employment: New arrangements", in *International Labour Review* (Geneva), Vol. 134 (1995), No. 2, p. 263, table 2.

[31] Kongshøj Madsen: op. cit. (note 20).

LABOUR, GENDER AND THE ECONOMIC/SOCIAL DIVIDE

18

Julie A. NELSON*

The conceptual framework and methodology that hold sway in the social sciences are closely linked to the topics they study. The effects are not always benign. For example, focusing on autonomous individuals leaves out a range of relationships — cooperative and coercive — that influence economic outcomes. The devaluation of "soft", "feminine" concerns has impoverished economics, as it has other disciplines. The hazards that arise when economic policies are derived from analyses that exclude the social are highlighted, and then some indications of how economics could be enriched by including issues like the security of workers and the care of children are given.

Are there separate economic and social spheres? Is the economy comprised of distinct activities, and run according to rules different from those governing society, itself a distinct entity? Certainly, discussion in political, popular and academic arenas often proceeds as if this were the case, especially in an ideological climate that puts great emphasis on market solutions to most problems. And the resulting partitioning of areas of human constitution and activity has important implications as to how they are studied and considered, and for policies that flow from them. The issues that end up on the non-market, "social" side of the divide tend to be considered less central or important than those on the market, "economic" side. Such a divide — to the extent that it exists — is particularly problematic for labour, which is present in both spheres.

Originally published in *International Labour Review*, Vol. 137 (1998), No. 1.

* Department of Economics and Graduate School of International Economics and Finance, Brandeis University, Waltham, MA.

One speaks of taxation, the national debt, inflation, banking system stability, maintenance of communications infrastructure, the encouragement of enterprise and the financing of national defence as hard-core economic issues. Attention to these issues is assumed to be of primary importance, for without a healthy economy any other goals will suffer. Attempts to argue that economic progress is a prerequisite for social progress are still current — evidence to the contrary notwithstanding. Issues of health care, education, worker safety, childcare, youth unemployment, and poverty are considered to be softer and social — to be addressed, if at all, after the core economic issues have been addressed. In budget discussions, this means that programmes to address problems in these areas tend to be considered secondary — luxuries — and are therefore often postponed and first to be eliminated or scaled back in any time of budget tightening, except when social unrest threatens the economic sphere itself. Bailing out insolvent banks is economics; helping insolvent families is merely social. The availability of labour to employers as a commodity, a factor input, is economic; the welfare of the labourers as living, breathing human beings is of a lesser order. Surely something important is lost when this separation is pursued unchecked.

This dichotomy is also highly evident in the academic field, though it was not always thus. To illustrate: An introductory textbook on economics typically includes core chapters on supply and demand, competition, monopoly and macroeconomic models, while issues like poverty, inequality and discrimination may be recommended only as possible topics for further study (see, for example, Baumol and Blinder, 1994). Before the turn towards "professionalization" of the social sciences, distinctions between social and economic questions were much less clear (see Furner, 1975; Rothman, 1985). As economics developed, professionals selected certain areas for study — most notably markets and, to a more limited extent, government behaviour as related to markets. Social work, social reform and sociology split off. The last was considered by some to be made up of "leftovers: marriage, the family, poverty, crime, education, religion, and sex" (Furner, 1975, p. 298).

Why has such a division emerged? One explanation may be that it reflects a simplified but logical division of issues and tasks, effected in the interest of specialization. An examination of the implicit value judgements, however, and the problems caused by this split, cast some doubt on this explanation.

This chapter will first review several examples of how the social/economic dualism has influenced discourse in various arenas, and discuss the problems it causes. Following this, an explanation for the strength of this dualistic thinking will be advanced, drawing particularly on feminist scholarship on language and the social sciences. The last section suggests an alternative way of analysing economic and social behaviour, centring around the notion of "provisioning".

PITFALLS OF A DUALISTIC APPROACH

The idea that economics is about "economic structures" or "economic laws" uncontaminated by the social sphere, combined with the common assumption that "economic" is more important than "social", implies certain values and epistemological premises. Since most serious considerations of ethics take human misery to be a problem, and human welfare (with some variety of definition) to be the object of "good" economic, social and political organization, the neglect of human welfare in a purely economic approach might therefore seem surprising. Yet economic analysis and economic policies can expend much energy not tied to a meaningful, democratic goal. The implications are twofold: first, human welfare then does not get priority and, second, actual human behaviour is not taken into account in the analysis. Thus there are problems both in terms of ethical judgement (objectives) and in ways of proceeding (taking account of human beings).

Various sorts of bad policies can result from excluding social questions from economics. Most obviously, for those concerned with human welfare, welfare enhancing programmes can be grossly underfunded relative to the requirements of an ethical engagement. In addition, policies are often designed as though only the economics of the situation mattered. There may be little or no apparent recognition that the expertise of demographers, anthropologists, sociologists, political scientists, etc., might be useful in promoting "economic" development. For example, a catalogue could be made of reports of how IMF stabilization policies have run amok due to unanticipated social dislocation and political upheaval. There is, of course, a more cynical interpretation possible: the neglect of human welfare in general may simply reflect an implicit institutional bias towards enhancing the financial power of an elite.

The view that economic behaviour and social behaviour operate at different levels can lead to impoverished economic analysis. The notion that workers are paid their marginal product in competitive labour market equilibrium, for example — a central teaching of mainstream (neoclassical) economic models — leads to great difficulty in dealing with issues of discrimination and unemployment which then get explained only in terms of market rigidities. For example, economist Solomon Polachek (1995) assumes that societal discrimination affects the division of work within families, and thus women's investment in education. "Societal discrimination" is not, however, in his view, linked in any way to the behaviour of firms, presumably since they are, instead, in the economic realm.[1] He thus sees only the tiniest of roles for anti-discrimination policy. Of course many economists, including some of the most eminent, have been promoting a coherent view. Nobel laureate economist Robert Solow, in a 1990 book entitled *The labor market as a social institution*, takes a step towards breaking down the economic/social divide (Solow,

1990). He argues that workers' social behaviour — in particular, their habit of comparing their situation to that of those around them — leads to perceptions about fairness being a significant factor in actual wage setting. Models which neglect this will simply not be adequate, especially in explaining the persistence of unemployment.

Sociologists are not immune to supporting the divide from their own side of the line. This defence may stem from a desire to protect social values from "commodification". For example, sociologists Bruce G. Carruthers and Wendy Nelson Espeland (forthcoming) reiterate a distinction between personal and altruistic gift exchange in the social realm, and impersonal and self-interested commodity exchange in the economic realm (see also Nelson, forthcoming). The limitations of this way of thinking have been explored by a number of social scientists who do not see the economy as independent of social relations as this position suggests (e.g. Zelizer, 1994; Carrier, 1997).

Economist James Duesenberry once joked, "Economics is all about how people make choices. Sociology is all about why they don't have any choices to make" (1960, p. 233). While economics may indeed overemphasize individual agency, choice and markets, a choice perspective may be a necessary counterpoint where social-level and deterministic analysis has been given too strong a role. Similarly, the economist's emphasis on abstraction, logic and precision can help avoid getting bogged down in detail or being illogical or vague. However, academic economics has been considered a "social science", with the emphasis on the "science" rather than the "social". The economy is often envisioned more like a machine — it is no coincidence that the core models of mainstream economics are based on 19th century physics — than as a study of embodied, emotional, developing and changing people in interaction with each other and with their natural environment.

STRENGTHS AND WEAKNESSES OF THE NEOCLASSICAL MODEL

The neoclassical economic model is populated by autonomous, rational, self-interested agents, whose preferences are set in advance; who make choices that maximize their well being, and whose main form of interaction is through exchanges on impersonal markets. Neoclassical economics is primarily concerned with efficiency and the workings of markets; in that context, issues of fairness and the functioning of other institutions are of marginal interest at best. Most introductory textbooks carefully distinguish between the work of economists in "contributing the best theoretical and factual knowledge" and decisions involving "ethical opinions", which are considered beyond the realm of social science practice (Baumol and Blinder, 1994, p. 17). In the core model, labour is only considered insofar as it is necessary for the worker to earn a wage in order to buy consumption goods and to induce him or her to exert the necessary effort in production. Economists who have gone well beyond that view, and incorporate issues of fairness and welfare, often wear additional hats, e.g. as moral philosophers. Amartya Sen is a prominent one who comes to mind (see, for example, Sen, 1987).

The study of this world of rational choice behaviour typically revolves around mathematical models, in which the various preferences and interactions are expressed in terms of variables and logical expressions or functions. Often the research stops there, showing how a particular set of assumptions can logically lead to a particular outcome. Being logically coherent, this approach is obviously rigorous in its own way. And by relying on relatively few foundational assumptions (e.g. rationality, self-interest) it can often claim to be very general. While economists do not deny that these fundamental assumptions abstract from reality — in fact, some abstraction is essential — the problem arises when all other approaches are denigrated as being less rigorous.

Yet an exclusive focus on the individuality, autonomy and agency of the economic actor ignores the social and physical nature and familial upbringing and responsibilities of actual human beings, as it does the possibility of relationships of control and coercion. Methodological emphasis on the formal, the precise and the abstract tends to circumvent real world phenomena relevant to the question purportedly being examined. In the process of applying logical and analytical thinking to real problems, mathematical formulas are used as metaphors, a translation that necessarily involves some use of less precisely defined verbal analysis — sometimes referred to as the "intuition" behind a model. As McCloskey (1985) has pointed out, by not being conscious of the use of both mathematical and verbal language, economists often use the latter very badly, and fail to see the narrowness and irrelevance of much of the former. The risk, both here and more generally, is that the practitioners of a discipline that claims to be entirely "positive" (value-free), rather than "normative" (value-laden), may remain ignorant about the values implicit in their own fundamental assumptions. And any scientific approach that fails to recognize its own biases when determining what is an interesting research question, and what is not, or what is a legitimate research methodology, and what is not, can be very risky indeed.[2]

Labour questions

Neoclassical economic agents supply labour to the market because they want money to buy consumer goods. Labour time does not count directly in the agent's utility function. It only appears as a necessary path to consumption goods, and as a residual — that which is left over after leisure time is enjoyed. In other words, in such models labour is not seen as adding well-being — much less social identity, individual pride in accomplishment, or meaning to life. Nor does a harmful or demeaning job subtract well-being; the model is typically neutral, indifferent. Only when one moves out of the core model into more specialized labour models is it admitted that people may care about the characteristics of their work. The theory of "compensating wage differentials" states that, all else being equal, people will be willing to accept lower wages in jobs that have characteristics they enjoy; conversely, they will demand higher wages for jobs with disagreeable characteristics. Even here, however, the analysis can be extremely reductionistic. Indeed, the underlying assumption is that working life qualities can be measured in terms of the extra wages forgone or demanded, i.e. that qualities are commensurable with money income, through the utility function that ranks all outcomes on a single scale. Given additional assumptions of perfect information and complete markets, the work-choice outcomes can even be shown to be socially efficient.

For example, the ideas that some working conditions are outright inhumane and should be banned, or that the social structure of work is important in human actualization and deserves careful analysis, or that the condition of being unemployed means more than just a loss of wage (see Sen, 1997), will not fit naturally into neoclassical analysis, and therefore will be vulnerable to distortions induced by the analytical process itself. In the extreme, the question of how to identify and ban totally inhumane practices may thus be analytically rationalized into a question of measuring the degree of disutility caused by a practice, by looking at wage differentials across jobs. In other words: "how much additional wage do workers demand in order to be subject to this practice?" Following this reasoning, the tendency might then be to see the fact that some people do, in fact, endure these practices as an optimizing outcome — i.e. these workers must, prima facie, prefer these jobs, for some reason, to others that are available. The fact that there may not be any other jobs available or that workers take the jobs in ignorance of their dangers, while violating the assumptions of perfect markets and perfect information, may in practice be downplayed. As for the possibility that people may be forced into certain jobs by extreme poverty, this falls outside standard analysis since economic agents are theoretically assumed to have only "wants", not "needs".

In other cases, the application of standard theories may be more helpful. If it can be shown that workers are in fact reasonably affluent (well-paid), are well informed about hazards, and have alternatives to working at a hazardous job that could afford them a decent standard of living, then the economist's perspective that they have "chosen" the hazards is not so far-fetched. In this sort of case, a well-intentioned non-economist's claim that, for example, "No cost should be spared in making workplaces as safe as possible!" can be shown to be poorly thought out. For, in fact, hazards are only one of many things about which a worker is concerned, and most human beings will, at some point, be willing to take on some statistical risk of harm in exchange for other things they value — higher wages and comfort on the job being a couple of the most commonly relevant in this case. The raising of safety to an absolute is in its own way a reductionistic proposition. The economist's notion of "opportunity cost" is a helpful one in this and many other discussions. For example, the cost of increasing safety standards can be measured not only in terms of monetary expenditures needed to implement a change, but also in terms of the most favoured alternative uses of resources that must be forgone in order to implement those standards: Do I want increased safety at my job if it means having a lower salary? Do we want more social expenditures on safety equipment if it means less expenditure on immunizations? The application of economic analysis to the perspective of choice can sometimes be elucidating, even critical to sound decisions.

While a naive belief in the allocative efficiency of markets can be irritating, the notion that markets can be efficiency-enhancing can be useful. The belief on the part of some non-neoclassical analysts that private ownership and private trading are always bad is no less an obsession than the neoclassical's fascination with market efficiency.

Some amount of mathematical and formal analysis can also be elucidating. For example, on the matter of measuring income or wage inequality, there are numerous proposed statistical formulae such as those underlying the Lorenz curve, the Gini coefficient, the Atkinson index, the percentage of the population in poverty, etc., which can, in some contexts, yield ambiguous or conflicting rankings of the degrees of inequality in two distributions. Some formal analysis which reveals some of the value judgements implicit in such measures (e.g. Sen, 1976; Atkinson, 1987) makes possible an informed use of the measures. Sometimes an analysis of the "little picture" is exactly what is required — as long as "little" does not degenerate into "trivial."

It has been said that there are three kinds of theory in economics: theory about the world, theory about theory, and theory about maths. It is the distorted proportioning of the prestige and volume of work among these categories — the most prestige and volume in academic economics now tending to fall towards the latter categories — as well as along theoretical vs. more empirical and applied lines, that is the problem, not theorizing *per se*.

Social justice

Discussions of justice can also occupy a severely circumscribed area within a strictly market-focused study of the economy. Even compared to discussions in a liberal strain of philosophy, the concept of the economic agent looks narrow indeed (Nelson, 1993b). While philosophical definitions of rationality may include a general "reasonableness", the economic definition is limited to completeness and transitivity of preference orderings. While philosophers may talk about diverse legitimate interests, and even about needs, neoclassical economic theory holds that all of an agent's interests are commensurable and only preferences matter. Indeed, the core theory generally assumes that the outcome of utility maximization is not comparable between agents, so that no judgements of comparative well-being (even in the very limited context of preference satisfaction) can be made. As a result, the only normative judgement that can be made is that efficient outcomes are better than inefficient outcomes — a point with which few would disagree in the abstract. While the subfield of social welfare theory eases the assumption of interpersonal incomparability (in specific and highly formal ways), the resulting choice theory characterizations of utilitarian and "Rawlsian" social welfare functions are barely recognizable to philosophers and of limited use for policy analysis. Other notions of justice, such as those coming from communitarian or "neo-Aristotelian" philosophers (e.g. Nussbaum, 1993), are generally disregarded by mainstream economists, even among those focusing on theories of justice (e.g. Hausman and McPherson, 1993).

In practice, of course, to enter into policy discussions, economists are forced to depart to some extent from these strict assumptions. For example, in welfare economics and in applied cost-benefit analysis the criterion of Pareto improvement (whereby at least one person is made better off without making someone else worse off) is weakened to that of *potential* Pareto improvement, i.e. could the suggested change lead to a Pareto improvement *if* it were accompanied by transfers of income to compensate the losers?[3] Of course the question of whether such compensating transfers would *actually* take place is rarely, if ever, pursued.

AN EXPLANATION FROM FEMINIST SCHOLARSHIP

Why has there been this tendency to divide the world so harshly, with "hard" economic/public/legal structures on one side and "soft" human needs, emotions and relationships on the other? Feminist scholarship, drawing on an analysis of language, suggests that it has roots both in cultural sexism and in the habits of human cognition. It is rooted in gendered associations of "hardness" with masculinity and superiority, and "softness" with femininity and inferiority, along with a sort of cognitive laziness that finds such dualistic constructions a tempting habit of thought (see Nelson, 1992 and 1996).

The analysis of links between modern Western social beliefs about gender and about types of knowledge was the accomplishment of works by feminist scholars starting in the 1980s, such as physicist Evelyn Fox Keller (1985) and philosopher Sandra Harding, who argues that

> Mind vs. nature and the body, reason vs. emotion and social commitment, subject vs. object and objectivity vs. subjectivity, the abstract and the general vs. the concrete and particular — in each case we are told that the former must dominate the latter lest human life be overwhelmed by irrational and alien forces, forces symbolized in science as the feminine. All these dichotomies play important roles in the intellectual structures of science, and all appear to be associated both historically and in contemporary psyches with distinctively masculine sexual and gender identity projects (1986, p. 25).

Such associations were sometimes explicit in the language used by the early scientists to define their endeavour. In the early 1660s, Henry Oldenburg, the first secretary of the Royal Society of London for Improving Natural Knowledge, stated that the intent of the Royal Society was to "raise a masculine Philosophy . . . whereby the Mind of Man may be ennobled with the knowledge of Solid Truths" (quoted in Keller, 1985, p. 52). That is, scientific knowledge in general has been socially constructed to conform to a particular image of masculinity.[4]

"The essence of metaphor is understanding and experiencing one kind of thing in terms of another," as George Lakoff and Mark Johnson say in their work, *Metaphors we live by* (1980, p. 5). According to them and numerous other researchers in the areas of cognition, philosophy, rhetoric and linguistics, metaphor is not merely a fancy addition to language, but is instead the fundamental way in which we understand our world and communicate that understanding from one person to another. Lakoff and Johnson give many examples of how language reflects metaphorical elaborations of more abstract concepts on the foundation of basic physical experiences, including that of "up/down."

Gender and value tend to be linked, both cognitively and metaphorically. Indeed, the power of the idea that masculine science is "good" rests on a general cultural association of masculinity with superiority and femininity with inferiority or, in other words, a mental linking of value (superior/inferior) and gender (masculine/feminine) dualisms:

economic/social
independent/related
rational/emotional
self-interested/other-interested
self-sufficient/needy
commodity/gift
efficiency/equity
mechanical/organic
hard/soft
rigorous/intuitive
abstract/concrete

To highlight further the gendered nature of the split, one should consider that areas traditionally of greater concern to women, such as marriage and families, end up on the "social" side. Public/private and firm/family could be added to the list, especially since in most countries there are still aspects of intra-family abuse for which there is no legal redress.

In Western culture, the figure given above cannot be taken as representing symmetry in value. Rather, the dualisms are hierarchical in nature. Overcoming too-easy dualisms and masculine biases, however, is not just a matter of turning the tables and, say, putting feminine-associated issues on top. That would just replace one set of biases with another, whatever the discipline (economics, medicine, law and so on). Consider, instead, the different interpretations that can be made, and the different vision of a more adequate understanding of human behaviour that can be discovered if one thinks of gender and value not as marking out the same space but as operating in distinct dimensions. Then one can see both valuable and harmful aspects to qualities culturally associated with masculinity and with femininity.[5]

	Positive		
Masculine	Masculine, Positive	Feminine, Positive	Feminine
	Masculine, Negative	Feminine, Negative	
	Negative		

Consider, for example, the idea that a "hard" discipline of economics is clearly preferable to a "soft" economics. This judgement relies on an association of hardness with valuable, masculine-associated strength, and softness with inferior, feminine-associated weakness. However, hardness may also mean rigidity, just as softness may also imply flexibility.

M+	F+
strong-hard	flexible-soft
M–	F–
rigid-hard	weak-soft

A pursuit of masculine hardness that spurns all association with femininity (and hence with flexibility) can lead to rigidity, just as surely as a pursuit of feminine softness (without corresponding strength) leads to weakness. There is no benefit to specialization on the side of one sex to the exclusion of the other: neither rigidity nor weakness — the two extremes of hardness and softness — are desirable. Together, in fact, they define brittleness. There is benefit, however, from exploiting the positive complementarity. Strength tempered with flexibility yields a balanced and resilient discipline.

Consider the dominant idea that people, when acting in their role as "economic agents", can be considered as radically separated from their embodied and "social" dimensions — from their human needs and familial and community ties. In such a case, one carries out the suggestion of Thomas Hobbes who wrote: "Let us consider men . . . as if but even now sprung out of the earth, and suddenly, like mushrooms, come to full maturity, without all kind of engagement to each other" (quoted in Benhabib, 1987). For there to be an "economic agent" who is not a social creature, he must spring up fully formed, with preferences fully developed, and be fully active and self-contained. The economic agent can have no childhood or old age, since these would imply dependence, nor can the agent have responsibility for anyone, since that would also imply a social tie.

But humans do not simply spring out of the earth. Humans are born of women, nurtured and cared for as dependent children and when aged or ill, socialized into family and community groups, and perpetually dependent on nourishment and a home to sustain life. These aspects of human life, whose neglect is often justified by the argument that they are unimportant, or intellectually uninteresting, are, not just coincidentally, the areas of life thought of as "women's work". The economic/social divide draws a firm line between the activities and choice of the presumedly autonomous adult, on the one hand, and the way in which that person is formed, is affected by need or illness, and acts on the basis of a group identity or an adopted social role, on the other.

What is needed, to replace these extreme conceptions of the person without sacrificing logical inquiry, is a conception of *human* identity that can encompass both autonomy and dependence, individuation and relation, reason and emotion, as they are manifested in individuals of either sex and worked out in complex social organizations. Such an identity could be described in a diagram such as:

M+	F+
individuated	connected
M–	F–
isolated	engulfed

The M–, isolated, mythical person is the Hobbesian agent, unaffected by community, emotion or bodily needs — what we might call a "separative self" (England, 1993) — and the image of the agent of economic analysis. The F–, engulfed, mythical person could be thought of as, for example, the wife in the old "husband as head" models of families, or the socially determined entity with "no choices to make" in the above quote by Duesenberry about sociology (1960, p. 233). Rather than flop back and forth between extreme alternatives, this diagram suggests that a model of people as persons-in-relation, both to each other and to nature, would be a more adequate starting point.

Note that this feminist analysis, while related to issues of women and culture, is related in a rather subtle and complex way. It does not argue for a "feminine" academic discipline or society in which the masculine-sided biases are replaced by their feminine contrasts, nor for a "female" discipline or society, in which women take leadership and do economics or politics differently from men. The argument is that gender is a strong cognitive construct — for both men and women — and that breaking the sexist association between gender and value is the first step towards a more cogent view of human behaviour and welfare, to be practised by both men and women. (Breaking the social expectations of "masculine" behaviour for men and "feminine" behaviour for women would be the second step in battling sexism.) While the entrance of women into the discipline of economics has, for example, facilitated the feminist critique therein, it is not because women "bring something different" with them when they enter the field. Rather, it is primarily because the social presence of women makes the metaphorically gendered nature of the economics atmosphere more noticeable.

Some may still object that there really is a set of "economic laws out there", and that the notion of centring policy and study on a more human basis can therefore be dismissed. To these persons, one may put the following questions: "How do you know? Are you perhaps confident in this largely because your own social network supports this belief?" While there are certainly some mathematical functions and some behaviour regularities which may be useful to know, the concentration on seeing a complex world in terms of particular formulas and laws certainly reflects a particular cognitive bias.

A NEW DEFINITION: PROVISIONING

If one allows that humans acting in economic ways do so with a full complement of complex emotions, physical needs, familial and cultural influences, social relationships and political interests, then economics has been brought within the realm of an expanded notion of society. To the extent that this concept of economic functioning retains any notion of mechanical or a-human economic forces, the latter can only be seen as embedded in, and propelled by, human societies and institutions. Social needs are not the frosting on the cake, as suggested by some, but rather the *raison d'être* of economic processes. How can it be otherwise?

One can anthropomorphize, as in talk of a healthy economy, but without healthy *people* what could this possibly mean?

But what is meant here by "economic" ways? Is there still a way to talk about what a group called "economists" or "economic policy analysts" might do? Of course there is.

Currently, a broad definition of the core topic of economics to which most economists might agree is that of markets. Economics is often defined as the study of processes by which things — goods, services, financial assets — are exchanged. By this definition, however, most of the traditional non-market activities of women — care of the home, children, sick and elderly relatives, and so on — have been considered "non-economic", and therefore inappropriate subjects for economic research. Families, in fact, often seem to disappear entirely from the economists' world. Consider this textbook discussion: "The unit of analysis in economics is the individual . . . [although] individuals group together to form collective organizations such as corporations, labor unions, and governments" (Gwartney, Stroup and Clark, 1985, p. 3).[6] The economic/social divide could be easily re-established, if this definition were retained. And note that drawing the distinction about what is and what is not economic and at the household door leads increasingly to odd dead ends and bifurcations in analysis. Why should childcare, elder care, and care of the sick be economic when provided by markets (or sometimes government), but unworthy of study by economists when done in private homes? Is it really just the exchange of money that society values?

Rather than using marketization as the criterion for demarcating economics (or using the rational choice model, another popular alternative) a broader definition of economics as concerned with "provisioning" could delineate its subject matter without using such biased assumptions about what is and what is not important (Nelson, 1993b and 1993c). Adam Smith, for example, defined economics as being not simply about choice and exchange but also about the production and distribution of all of the "necessaries and conveniences of life", placing emphasis on the things that human beings need to survive and flourish (quoted in Heilbroner, 1986, p. 159). These things may include activities, such as meaningful work, as well as goods and services such as food and health care. While some goods and services may be freely selected by adult individuals acting in markets, many are provided to individuals by their parents during childhood or by other family members. They can also be provided as gifts or through community or governmental programmes. The distribution of many "necessaries and conveniences" is also strongly influenced by tradition and by coercion.

Such a definition of economics as concerned with the realm of "provisioning" breaks down the usual distinctions between the so-called "economic" (primarily market-oriented) activities and policies, on the one hand, and familial or social activities and policies, on the other. The

381

absence of entries for household production in the National Income and Product Accounts is one obvious example. Another would be the question of attention to investment in children, or the question of who bears the costs of such investment (Folbre, 1994). Programmes to improve child nutrition or pre-school and primary education, for example, are usually thought of as social programmes, rather than as economic programmes designed to advance investment in human capital. Programmes to increase the quality of paid childcare arrangements are often thought of as consumption goods for parents, rather than as investments in children and in necessary infrastructure for parental participation in the life of the community (and particularly, given stereotyped patterns of work distribution within families, that of mothers).

In the "provisioning" view suggested here, topics like health care, education, worker safety, childcare, youth unemployment and poverty are central, rather than tangential, and the worker is seen as a living, breathing, feeling and contributing member of a system that is both economic and social (or economic *within* being social). Such a view cannot in itself fully counter an excessive emphasis on market solutions to the range of economic and social problems, but it can help to make economics better prepared to confront those problems and contribute to more relevant policy prescriptions.

Notes

[1] This has been referred to as the theory of the "virgin birth" of firms (Nelson, 1995).

[2] For a discussion of similar issues in the social sciences generally and in legal studies, see Supiot, 1996.

[3] There is a substantial, though dated literature on compensation tests, starting with Nicholas Kaldor. Tibor Scitovsky was also a prominent contributor to this literature, though he may now be known more for his pieces critical of reductionistic psychology (e.g. Scitovsky, 1992).

[4] For a discussion of the issues this raises, particularly in the medical field, see Tavris, 1992.

[5] The analysis which follows draws heavily on Nelson, 1993 and 1996.

[6] I thank Marianne Ferber for pointing out this reference.

References

Atkinson, A. B. 1987. "On the measurement of poverty", in *Econometrica* (Evanston, IL), Vol. 55, pp. 749-764.

Baumol, William J.; Blinder, Alan S. 1994. *Economics: Principles and policy*. Sixth edition. New York, NY, Harcourt Brace & Company.

Benhabib, Seyla. 1987. "The generalized and the concrete other: The Kohlberg-Gilligan controversy and moral theory", in Diana Meyers and Eva Feder Kittay (eds.): *Women and Moral Theory*. Totowa, NJ, Rowman and Littlefield, pp. 154-177.

Carrier, James G. (ed.). 1997. *Meanings of the market: The free market in Western culture.* Oxford, Berg.

Carruthers, Bruce G.; Espeland, Wendy Nelson. Forthcoming. "Money, meaning and morality", in *American Behavioral Scientist* (Thousand Oaks, CA).

Duesenberry, James S. 1960. "Comments", in National Bureau of Economic Research (ed.): *Demographic and Economic Change in Developed Countries.* Cambridge, MA, NBER, pp. 231-234.

England, Paula. 1993. "The separative self: Androcentric bias in neoclassical assumptions", in Marianne A. Ferber and Julie A. Nelson (eds.): *Beyond economic man.* Chicago, IL, University of Chicago Press, pp. 37-53.

Folbre, Nancy. 1994. *Who pays for the kids? Gender and the structures of constraints.* New York, NY, Routledge.

Furner, Mary O. 1975. *Advocacy and objectivity: A crisis in the professionalization of American social science, 1865-1905.* Lexington, KY, University Press of Kentucky.

Gwartney, James D.; Stroup, Richard; Clark, J. R. 1985. *Essentials of economics.* New York, NY, Academic Press.

Harding, Sandra. 1986. *The science question in feminism.* Ithaca, NY, Cornell University Press.

Hausman, Daniel M.; McPherson, Michael S. 1993. "Taking ethics seriously: Economics and contemporary moral philosophy", in *Journal of Economic Literature* (Nashville, TN), Vol. 31, No. 2, pp. 671-731.

Heilbroner, Robert L. (ed.). 1986. *The essential Adam Smith.* New York, NY, W. W. Norton & Company.

Keller, Evelyn Fox. 1985. *Reflection on gender and science.* New Haven, CT, Yale University Press.

Lakoff, George; Johnson, Mark. 1980. *Metaphors we live by.* Chicago, IL, University of Chicago Press.

McCloskey, Deirdre. N. 1985. *The rhetoric of economics.* Madison, WI, University of Wisconsin Press.

Nelson, Julie A. Forthcoming. "One sphere or two? Comments on 'Changing forms of payment'", in *American Behavioral Scientist* (Thousand Oaks, CA).

—. 1996. *Feminism, objectivity, and economics.* London, Routledge.

—. 1995. "Economic theory and feminist theory: Comments on chapters by Polachek, Ott and Levin", in Edith Kuiper and Jolande Sap (eds.): *Out of the margin: Feminist perspectives on economics.* London, Routledge, pp. 120-125.

—. 1993a. "Household equivalence scales: Theory vs. policy?", in *Journal of Labor Economics* (Chicago, IL), Vol. 11, No. 3 (July), pp. 471-493.

—. 1993b. "A feminist perspective on economic justice". Paper presented at the Conference of the International Association for Feminist Economics, Washington, DC. July.

—. 1993c. "The study of choice or the study of provisioning? Gender and the definition of economics", in Marianne A. Ferber and Julie A. Nelson (eds.): *Beyond economic man.* Chicago, IL, University of Chicago Press, pp. 23-36.

—. 1992. "Gender, metaphor, and the definition of economics", in *Economics and Philosophy* (Cambridge), Vol. 8, No. 1, Spring, pp. 103-25.

Nussbaum, Martha C. 1993. "Non-relative virtues: An Aristotelian approach", in Martha C. Nussbaum and Amartya Sen (eds.): *The quality of life.* Oxford, Clarendon Press.

Polachek, Solomon W. 1995. "Human capital and the gender earnings gap: A response to feminist critiques", in Edith Kuiper and Jolande Sap (eds.): *Out of the margin: Feminist perspectives on economics.* London, Routledge, pp. 61-79.

Women, gender and work

Rothman, Gerald C. 1985. *Philanthropists, therapists, and activists: A century of ideological conflict in social work*. Cambridge, MA, Schenkman Publishing Company.

Scitovsky, Tibor. 1992. *The joyless economy: The psychology of human satisfaction*. Oxford, Oxford University Press.

Sen, Amartya. 1997. "Inequality, unemployment, and contemporary Europe", in *International Labour Review* (Geneva), Vol. 136, No. 2, pp. 155-172.

—. 1987. *On ethics and economics*. Oxford, Blackwell.

—. 1976. "Poverty: An ordinal approach to measurement", in *Econometrica* (Evanston, IL), Vol. 44, No. 2, pp. 219-231.

Solow, Robert M. 1990. *The labor market as a social institution*. Cambridge, MA, Blackwell.

Supiot, Alain. 1996. "Perspectives on work: Introduction", in *International Labour Review* (Geneva), Vol. 135, No. 6, pp. 603-614.

Tavris, Carol. 1992. *The mismeasure of woman: Why women are not the better sex, the inferior sex, or the opposite sex*. New York, NY, Simon and Schuster.

Zelizer, Viviana A. 1994. *The social meaning of money*. New York, NY, Basic Books.

WOMEN, MEN AND MANAGEMENT STYLES

Marie-Thérèse CLAES*

19

*The aim is to disentangle the terminological complexities be-
hind opposed concepts such as sex and gender, masculine and
feminine, biological and socially constructed attributes. The
result shows that stereotypes are often less clear-cut than they
seem and that erstwhile weaknesses can come to be viewed as
valuable skills, formerly perceived strengths as inflexible and
one-dimensional. As management culture starts to appreciate
and incorporate gender differences it is coming to see the value
of a mixture of so-called feminine and masculine characteristics in the panoply of management skills needed in the highly
competitive global market-place.*

Although only 3 to 6 per cent of top managerial positions are held
by women, employers have come to realize that they neglect managerial
talent in nearly half their workforce if they do not appoint women to such
positions. However, it is true that managerial work is undergoing rapid
change and as Kanter has pointed out: "Change-adept organizations cul-
tivate the imagination to innovate, the professionalism to perform, and
the openness to collaborate" (Kanter, 1997, p. 7). Women are said to
possess "feminine" qualities such as relationship building and teamwork
that are valued in a more collaborative and creative management environment. This chapter will examine the implications of the use of the
word "feminine" in psychological, social and cultural contexts. It will
consider the application of the concepts of gender difference in language
use, in theories of leadership and in communication styles.

Originally published in *International Labour Review*, Vol. 138 (1999), No. 4.

* Professor, ICHEC Business School, Brussels, and University of Louvain-la-Neuve,
Belgium; President, International Network for Women in Management.

GENDER AS A SOCIAL CONSTRUCT

Man, woman, male, female, masculine, feminine are used in the discussion of sex and gender issues in biology, anthropology, social science, psychology, cross-cultural studies and even management theories. The concepts of sex and gender are often used interchangeably in written material and in conversation, as are the adjectives male and masculine, female and feminine. In order to know what is being discussed, therefore, these terms need to be defined more clearly.

Biology divides species according to sex: male or female, and these sex categories are mostly taken for granted. The biological dichotomy lends its structure to one of the current frameworks of gender studies, the "sex role theory". According to this, being a man or a woman means enacting a general role as a function of one's sex. But this theory also uses the words masculine and feminine, asserting that the feminine character in particular is produced by socialization into the female role. According to this approach, women acquire a great deal of sex role learning early in their lives, and this can lead to an attitude of mind that creates difficulties later, during their working lives (Lipsey et al., 1990). It is a form of "culture trap".

Most sex role theory is constructed not on field observation but on analysis of standard cases. Role theory is often seen by psychologists as amounting to a form of social determinism whereby individuals are trapped into stereotypes, which people then choose to maintain as customs.

Psychological traits of masculinity or femininity were measured a quarter century ago on "gender scales" in the Bem Sex Role Inventory (Bem, 1974). On the masculine side of the scale were the characteristics of dominion, ambition, cynicism and rebelliousness, while on the feminine side were consideration, tact, dependence, emotion. Typical masculine activities included repairing electrical appliances, for example, whereas typical feminine activities included paying attention to physical appearance. Such results did not dispel the frequent confusion between "sex difference" and "masculinity, femininity", although some items reflected an intuitive notion of what "masculinity" and "femininity" mean (Constantinople, 1973). For, as will be seen in the section on concepts of gender and culture below, the masculinity-femininity spectrum is a dimension of societal culture quite independent of sex. Accordingly, femininity and masculinity as attributes of women and men need not be treated as polar opposites. Rather they may be treated on separate scales, and the same person may get high scores on both.

Women and men have also been tested on their respective verbal ability, anxiety and extroversion. Popular perceptions suggest that "women have greater verbal ability" and that "men are more aggressive". In fact, studies have revealed few clear-cut generalized differences. Indeed, the striking conclusion is that the main finding, from about 80 years of research, is a massive psychological *similarity* between women and men in the populations studied by psychologists (Connell, 1987).

Gender is a social construct. Whereas sex is the term used to indicate biological difference, gender is the term used to indicate psychological, social and cultural difference. This is a practice-based theory according to which sexuality is socially constructed, as are the differences (other than biological) between men and women. Goffman (1977, p. 305) speaks of a "genderism" as "a sex-class linked individual behavioral practice" — a practice linked to gender as class. Gender identity thus emerges from rearing patterns, and is not determined by the hormones. Gender is determined by social practice, and its patterns are specifically social. Social structure is not preordained but is historically composed, thus femininity and masculinity should be seen as historically mutable. According to Harding (1986), the concept of gender applies at different levels. It is: (1) a dimension of personal identity, a psychic process of experiencing self; (2) an element in social order, the foundation of social institutions such as kinship, sexuality, the distribution of work, politics, culture; and (3) a cultural symbol which can be variously interpreted, the basis for normative dichotomies.

The femininity and masculinity dimension has also been applied in intercultural studies. As shown below, differentiation between groups implies that within so-called intercultural groupings — according to country, ethnicity, religion or language — new intracultural distinctions should be made according to gender, as well as generation and social class. Gender is generally considered as representing a cultural category (Cox, 1993), as normative and value differences between women and men are perceived as significant (Hennig and Jardim, 1976; Gilligan, 1982; and Helgesen, 1990).

Gender and language

One of the areas to which gender has been widely applied is language. Gender, language and the relation between them are all social constructs or practices, under constant development by a group of individuals united in a common activity, e.g. a family, a sports team, colleagues, etc. (Eckert and McConnel-Ginet, 1992).

Until the 1970s, linguists' descriptions of sex differences in speech were based on intuitive observation rather than on scientific research. In sociolinguistics, the interaction between linguistic variation and sex has been examined, though the linguistic variation found between men and women may be a function of gender, and only indirectly a function of sex (Eckert, 1989).

In practice, male speech and conversation strategies are usually taken as the norm, so that female speech has been assessed in relation to male speech. Female speech is said to be less rational and to display greater sensitivity, to use fewer abstract words, a smaller vocabulary and a simpler structure. Women are said to use more adjectives, modal verbs, interjections, tag questions, etc. Female language has been defined as polite and insecure, male language as assertive and direct. The conversational styles of women have been described as cooperative, those of men as competitive. However, evidence to this effect is not fully convincing — sex differences in language use have sometimes been demonstrated, sometimes not. Moreover, differences have also been found according to the status and age of the speaker relative to the status of the person spoken to (Verbiest, 1990; Brouwer, 1982, 1991).

There are currently two approaches to gender differences in conversation styles: one stresses the dominance factor, the other, the cultural factor. The former, represented by Cameron (1985, 1995), West and Zimmerman (1983) and Zimmerman and West (1975), focuses on the unequal distribution of power in society: men have more social power, which enables them to define and control situations. As male norms are dominant in social interaction, when the interaction takes place between men and women, observable influences emerge. The approach based on cultural factors, represented by Maltz and Borker (1982) and Tannen (1990, 1994), stresses socialization: men and women learn different communication strategies and develop distinct conversational styles because they belong to different subcultures.

Broadly speaking, men and women inhabit different worlds, which gives rise to sex-differentiated meanings attached to words. According to Spender (1980), language is literally "man-made" because the meanings of words were determined by men who established themselves as the central and positive norm: feminine forms in any language are often pejorative and reflect the inferior position of women in society and in the family. It may be that women face barriers in the use of language at both the deep (semantic) level and the surface (register) level. In other words, there may be an additional process, an extra stage in which women must engage: they have to translate their meaning into words that have been established by the male-defined register. As reality is constructed and sustained primarily through language, those who control language are thus also able to control reality. This male control of meaning extends to the register of public discourse, a medium in which men are generally more at ease than women. There is a distinction between female speech and male speech which is related to differences in explicitness and implicitness, or directness and indirectness as observed in cross-cultural studies and to politeness and face-saving strategies as they are described in pragmatics — the application or use of an existing syntactic and semantic structure (Brown and Levinson, 1987). If female language can be described as displaying insecurity this may be because such insecurity is a face-saving strategy on the part of women.

However, what was initially seen by Lakoff (1975) as powerless and weak in female language can be redefined as being a valuable interactional skill. Indeed, what linguistics considers to be "women's talk" could be described as "feminine". In women's culture, people are requested to perform tasks, not commanded; hedges and disclaimers are frequent; directness is considered rude; and conflict and aggressive behaviour are avoided. An indirect use is made of language, with rising intonations, in order to avoid offending and to preserve good relations at all costs. This pattern can also be seen in the light of the accommodation theory developed by Giles and Coupland (1991), who state that conversational partners adapt to one another by showing converging conversational styles. This makes interaction easier because it reduces felt differences between conversational partners.

However, generalizing about language use on the basis of socio-cultural constructs such as gender or ethnicity is also problematic: it perpetuates a stereotype that is based on the assumption of group homogeneity (Davis, 1996). The context and institutionalization of language involve not only pragmatics but also their historical evolution. Indeed, Segal (1987) remarks that an overemphasis on language marginalizes the grass-roots concerns of the feminist movement. For example, most major publishers now have a feminist, women's studies or women writers' list — one of the most successful areas in contemporary book publishing. According to Connell, "To some extent the exclusion of women is replaced by marginalization, through such devices as a separate publishing list, or media trivialization. The main narrative of the public world — wars, rockets, governments falling, profits rising — carries on as before" (1987, p. 248). Gender concerns should extend beyond crude categorical assumptions about power and the relations between person and group, and should encompass institutions, economics, politics and the media.

Gender and culture

Social and cultural studies categorize people by country, region, ethnicity, religion or language but also by gender, generation and social class. Within each category, however, cultural differences may be found and Hofstede (1980, 1991) identified four dimensions to these:

- individualism/collectivism (loose or tight group bonds);
- "power distance" (unequal power);
- femininity/masculinity (emphasis on relationships and caring vs. money, progress, success); and
- "uncertainty avoidance" (the degree to which individuals feel threatened by unknown or uncertain situations).

Hofstede describes the masculine and feminine poles as follows:

Masculine pole	Feminine pole
Fighting: "May the best man win"	Negotiation and compromise
Rewards to the strong	Solidarity with the weak
Economic growth	Protection of the environment
Arms spending	Aid to poor countries

Source: Hofstede, 1991.

A closer look at "feminine" as opposed to "masculine" values shows expected feminine and masculine behaviour. Of course, no culture is either wholly feminine or wholly masculine: there are many gradations, and a culture may be more or less feminine in one respect and more or less masculine in another.

Masculine pole	Feminine pole
Success, progress, money	Relationships, caring
Facts	Feelings
Living to work	Working to live
Decisiveness, assertiveness	Intuition and consensus
Competition	Equality
Confrontation	Compromise, negotiation

Source: Hofstede, 1991.

What people look for from their work also varies, according to their values:

Masculine pole	Feminine pole
Good income	Good relations with boss
Recognition	Collaboration
Promotion	Pleasant environment
Challenge	Security

Source: Hofstede, 1991.

Thus, looked at from a cross-cultural perspective, "appropriate" managerial skills appear to be "masculine" skills. They highlight the dominant, assertive, decisive aspects of behaviour and downplay the team and supportive behaviours which are more readily identified with women. But this traditional view is now giving way to a more nuanced approach (see below).

Box 1. Implications of cultural differences in management

	Collectivist	Individualist
Communication		
Circulation	Top-down	Bottom-up/top-down
Mode	Direct	Indirect
Interpersonal relations	Hierarchical	Egalitarian
Separation of work and social life	Integrated	Separate
Leadership		
Style	Autocratic	Participative
Decision-making	Centralized	Decentralized
Perception of role of superior	Expert	Animator
Negotiation		
	Autocratic	Consultative
	Win/lose	Win/win
Organization and control		
Responsibility	Dependence	Independence
Structure	Collective	Individualistic
Organizational mode	Simultaneous	Sequential
Formalization	Implicit	Explicit
Recruitment, selection, promotion	Belonging to socio-cultural environment	By achievement, results
Promotion	Seniority	Competence, results
Planning, evaluation, innovation	Harmony	Control
	Past	Future
Leadership	External control	Initiative
Conflict resolution	Avoidance	Confrontation
Training	Theoretical	Experience

Source: Adapted from Gauthey and Xardel (1990), p. 50.

The cultural differences described above imply different management styles, as expressed in communication, leadership, negotiation, organization and control. The differences are summarized in box 1. Although the focus here is on differences between collectivist and individualist cultures, it is clear that some management styles can be characterized as "feminine" or "masculine", though they are seldom unequivocally one or the other. Moreover, in some countries, cultural norms may display more "feminine" characteristics than in others. International management has now come to understand and accept differences in national management styles. The result has been a reappraisal and upgrading of feminine styles relative to the dominant "American management style", which is mostly masculine. Team behaviour is seen as increasingly important to successful management. Barham, Fraser and Heath (1988) portray the manager of the future as concerned less with giving instructions and controlling subordinates and more with maintaining a network of relationships within the organization and with those outside, e.g. customers. The criterion used to assess managers may indeed discriminate against women, but it may also have been formulated according to a model of management now no longer appropriate for the work of managers as a whole (Hirsh and Jackson, 1989).

WOMEN IN MANAGEMENT

Although still considered an untapped resource, women are now said to be welcome in management because of the values they bring. In more "feminine" cultures, values traditionally considered feminine, such as intuition, communication and social aptitude, already naturally form part of management style and of life in general.

Nevertheless, though increasing, the number of women managers remains small. Women are under-represented in highly-paid occupations; proportionately fewer women than men attain higher-paid jobs in the occupations in which both are represented; and it takes them longer to do so (Lipsey et al., 1990). Where women are present in management, they are usually in middle management. They seem unable to shatter "the glass ceiling" blocking access to top management. One of the reasons for this may be women's so-called lack of ambition. Gail Rebuck, chief executive of the Random House publishing group, feels that women's frequent failure to reach the top is largely due to lack of confidence and aspirations. Moreover, women usually pay a higher personal price for top positions than men do: "While men and women managers often share common stressors, females in managerial positions are often faced with additional pressures, both from work and from the home/social environment, not experienced by male managers ..." (Davidson and Cooper, 1992, p. 38).

In March 1995, the Federal Glass Ceiling Commission in the United States released a report which stated that women have made little progress in winning the power posts of corporate America. It reported that women make up a mere 5 per cent of senior managers — vice-president or higher — in Fortune 1000 companies. Furthermore, it concluded grimly that "At the highest levels of business, there is indeed a barrier only rarely penetrated by women or persons of color". However, *Newsweek* (1995) stated there are "holes in the glass ceiling theory", because women thrive in the rest of the economy, citing as evidence the fact that Fortune 1000 companies employ about 20 per cent of the nation's female workers and that even in the Fortune 1000 companies the 5 per cent of women senior managers represented progress from the proportion of 1.5 per cent in the mid-1980s. ILO (1997), on the other hand, concluded that, almost universally, women have failed to reach leading positions in major corporations and private sector organizations, irrespective of their abilities.

One of the reasons often given for the relative absence of women from top management positions is the way women act and react in organizations, in leadership posts, in negotiations, etc. Kanter (1977) summarized the barriers preventing women's access to the top as follows:

- Women do not behave in an authoritarian way: tasks become requests, women do not use imperatives.

- Women behave in a rather unaggressive way: they avoid conflicts.

- Women feel responsible: they frequently say "sorry ..." .

- Women are available: their door is always open.

- Women get personally involved: relationships are important.

- Women seek approval: they use indirect formulations, particular intonations in their speech.

- Women want to be "nice", and fear abuse of power: they are smiling, indirect, hesitant.

- Women attribute their success to others.

Lipsey et al. (1990) also consider sex role socialization to be a major cause of women's low representation in top management:

> The causes of gender differences in labor-market attachment have attracted attention from both social psychologists and from economists. There is ample evidence that *sex role socialization* is an important factor. To the extent that women and men are socialized to accept the view that women should be the primary caretakers of young children, some social scientists argue that differences in labor-force attachment arise from a form of indirect discrimination (p. 394).

This culture trap operates at different levels: the locus of control, low expectations, fear of success, assertion, the desire for power and the dependent role.

Locus of control. There is a strong tendency for women to be externalizers (to feel that events affecting them are the result of luck or chance), whereas men are more likely to be internalizers (to feel that events are the result of their own actions). This implies that women acquiesce more readily than men. But there are other possibilities: men may not be discouraged so quickly as women because as children they received more stimulation in their environment (from their parents, for example) than girls did. However, it is not always easy to distinguish cause and effect.

Low expectations. When performing a stereotypically male job, women may feel that their abilities are unequal to the requirements of the tasks involved.

Fear of success. In order to behave in a socially approved manner, women are said to avoid success or "the appearance of success".

Assertion and desire for power. Women are often socialized not to be assertive or aggressive or not to seek control and power.

The dependent role. Women are said to be more easily swayed and more reliant on others. The caring nature commonly attributed to women was said by Gilligan (1982) to be a result of psychological evolution whereby girls, seeing themselves as a continuation of their mothers, fear independence and so try to maintain the dependent relationship with their mothers. Boys, on the other hand, have to force a clear break with their mothers in order to prove their own separate identity, and as a result develop a fear of emotions. Society's constant emphasis on women's dependence, other-directness, self-sacrifice and nurturing, caring role contributes to women's ambivalence about their own worth (Finn, Hickley and O'Doherty, 1969).

However, Davidson and Cooper (1992) interviewed a sample of women managers and found a more nuanced pattern. For example, a majority of women in the sample were internalizers, in common with many male managers. Women who were firmly established in managerial careers often appeared both ambitious and career-oriented. In some studies they were found to be more ambitious than men and to be motivated more by intrinsic factors (such as personal growth) than by extrinsic factors (such as salary and status). The majority of women managers had learned not to fear success: they had gained in confidence and experience. Yet, assertive, power-seeking behaviour also presents women with a dilemma: the qualities perceived as displaying leadership in a man are often judged to be traits of hostility and aggression in a woman (Dipboye, 1978).

Too often, a woman is in a no-win situation. In order to be viewed as competent, she has to project certain masculine characteristics; but if she does, she is seen as non-conformist, and consequently as unpredictable and unsuitable for promotion. The solution women managers often find to this dilemma is to behave entirely like their male counterparts. Some women managers are proud to achieve this, while others strongly disapprove.

These findings confirm the theory of gender as a social construct. That which in one society is considered as a weakness in women, in another society is found to be a generally accepted cultural factor and a necessary element in cross-cultural communication. Behavioural differences between men and women are, then, simply differences between cultural groups, and should be studied as such. Indeed, given the present tendency toward less hierarchical organizations, with a stress on training, teamwork, the sharing of power and information, and networking, the talents of women in these fields may well turn to their advantage.

Leadership styles

For more than a decade now, new values, sometimes called feminine values, have appeared in business. These values contrast with the competitive and authoritarian approach usually associated with traditional masculine management as they are based on consensual relations and inspire a different management approach to communication, leadership, negotiation, organization and control. Increasingly, this rebalancing of values is seen as key to business success.

At the end of the twentieth century, the workplace is radically different. Flexibility and innovation characterize global economic conditions and fast-changing technology. Cameron (1995) calls this the "shift in the culture of Anglo-American capitalism" (p. 199) away from traditional (aggressive, competitive, individualistic) interactional norms and towards a new management style stressing flexibility, teamwork and collaborative problem-solving. According to Connell, "commercial capitalism calls on a calculative masculinity and the class struggles of industrialization call on a combative one. Their combination, competitiveness, is institutionalized in 'business' and becomes a central theme in the new form of hegemonic masculinity" (1987, p. 156).

There seems to be a true structural change under way here. The business world is questioning the structure it copied from the military hierarchy at the end of the Second World War. The masculine culture of large corporations cannot easily adapt to a context of uncertainty and constant evolution. The team and supportive behaviours more readily identified with women are perceived as increasingly important for management (Hirsh and Jackson, 1989) and women's interactive style is often better suited to dealing with problems.

In the 1970s, women managers were supposed to act and talk like men, if they wanted to reach the top. Harragan (1977), characterizing business as a "no-woman's-land", urged women to recognize that the modern corporation was modelled on military structures and functioned according to the precepts of male team sports. This implied that, in order to master corporate culture, women had both to indoctrinate themselves with the military mindset and to study the underlying dynamic of confrontational games such as football. Hennig and Jardim (1976) also urged women to study football in order to master the male concept of "personal strategy": winning, achieving a goal or reaching an objective.

Grant (1988) studied what women can offer to organizations and identified the psychological qualities that are relevant to organizations and are commonly found in women. His findings support those of other studies that stress women's more cooperative behaviour (important for relational consultation and democratic decision-making) and their need for a sense of belonging rather than self-enhancement; their ability to express their vulnerability and their emotions; and their perception of

---

Box 2. Sex differences in managerial styles

Male managers	Female managers
The executives worked at an unrelenting pace, and took no breaks in activity during the day.	They worked at a steady pace, but with small breaks scheduled throughout the day.
They described their days as characterized by interruption, discontinuity and fragmentation.	They did not view unscheduled tasks and encounters as interruptions.
They spared little time for activities not directly related to their work.	They made time for activities not directly related to their work.
They exhibited a preference for live encounters.	They preferred live encounters but scheduled time to attend to mail.
They maintained a complex network of relationships with people outside their organizations.	They maintained a complex network of relationships with people outside their organizations.
Immersed in the day-to-day need to keep the company going, they lacked time for reflection.	They focused on the ecology of leadership.
They identified with their jobs.	They saw their own identities as complex and multifaceted.
They had difficulty sharing information.	They scheduled time for sharing information.

Source: Helgesen, 1990.

---

power less as domination or ability to control, than as a liberating force in the community.

The feminine style of management has been called "social-expressive", with personal attention given to subordinates and a good working environment; by contrast, the masculine management style has been described as instrumental and instruction-giving. However, these qualities are not necessarily reflected in the way women managers actually manage. An attempt to examine their managerial behaviour was made by Helgesen (1990), who repeated Minzberg's diary study, only this time with women. Minzberg (1973) analysed the diaries of managers, all of them male: he described what managers actually did, discerning several patterns. In 1990, Helgesen conducted the same research with women managers. The differences that appeared are shown in box 2.

Rather than a comparison between male and female managers, this could be seen more as a comparison of management cultures that changed over time. In the 1960s, great value was placed on narrow expertise, on the mastery of prescribed skills and on conformity to the corporate norm. There was no need to integrate workplace and private-sphere responsibilities. In today's organizations, hierarchies tend to give way to less formal structures. The economy is more diverse, the focus is on innovation and fast information exchange, value is placed on breadth of vision and on the ability to think creatively. Top-down authoritarianism has yielded to a networking style, in which everyone is a resource (Naisbitt and Aburdene, 1986).

Helgesen (1995) considered that feminine principles (such as caring, intuitive decision-making, non-hierarchical attitudes, integration of work and life, social responsibility) reflected basic cultural assumptions about differences in the ways that men and women think and act. She added, however, that belief in these notions was intuitive rather than articulated, that it was backed up with anecdotes instead of argument.

Women managers surveyed in the United Kingdom reported that the characteristics their organizations valued most highly in a manager were competitiveness, cooperation and decisiveness, and those they least valued were emotionalism, manipulativeness and forcefulness (Traves, Brockbank and Tomlinson, 1997). These obviously cut across styles that are identified as typically masculine or feminine.

One can perhaps detect a shift in values towards the "feminization" of management style, but one can also speak of a shift away from individualism and from explicitness. This resembles a shift from a left-brain conception of organizational structure (with analysis, logic and rationality predominating) towards a right-brain conception (with intuition, emotion, synthesis predominating). One anthropologist has described women as "high context integrating, feeling, intelligent" (Hall, 1996). But it seems that, in practice, management styles are evolving towards valuing a mixture of the so-called masculine and feminine characteristics.

Flexibility and teamwork are among the feminine characteristics; and team behaviour is seen as increasingly important for management. Drucker (1994) pointed out that, in "knowledge work" (adding value to information), teams rather than the individual become the work unit. The idea of "group intelligence" has been explored (Williams and Sternberg, 1988), and according to Goleman, "the single most important element in group intelligence ... is not the average IQ in the academic sense, but rather in terms of emotional intelligence" (1996, p. 160). This emotional intelligence, or empathy, seems to result from the socialization of girls and much less from that of boys, with the result that "hundreds of studies have found ... that on average women are more empathic than men" (ibid., p. 132; see also Goleman (1998)). In their approach to work women have been found to be more relationship-oriented than men, more often defining themselves in terms of their relationships and connections to others (Belenky et al., 1986).

In their meta-analyses, Eagly and Johnson (1990) suggest that men demonstrate a more autocratic leadership style and women a more democratic leadership style, and a more interpersonally-oriented style: helpful, friendly, available, explaining procedures, tending to the morale and welfare of others. According to Kabacoff (1998), these assessment and laboratory studies may not be applicable to organizational settings, and moreover the role of women in management positions may have changed since.

Kabacoff's extensive study of gender differences in leadership styles records gender differences which were both self-described and observed (Kabacoff, 1998). Kabacoff found that women tend to be rated higher on empathy (demonstrating an active concern for people and their needs, forming close supportive relationships with others), and communication (stating clear expectations for others, clearly expressing thoughts and ideas, maintaining a flow of communication) than men. Women are also rated higher on people skills (sensitivity to others, likeableness, ability to listen and to develop effective relationships with peers and with those to whom they report). However, they are not seen as more outgoing (acting in an extroverted, friendly, informal fashion), or more cooperative in their leadership styles. Contrary to expectations, women tend to score higher on a leadership scale measuring an orientation towards production (strong pursuit of achievement, holding high expectations for self and others) and the attainment of results. Men tend to score higher on scales assessing an orientation towards strategic planning and organizational vision. Women tend to be rated higher on people-oriented leadership skills, men on business-oriented leadership skills. Overall, bosses see men and women as equally effective, while peer and direct assessment rate women slightly higher than men.

Women are rated higher on excitement (they are energetic and enthusiastic), communication (they keep people informed), feedback (they let others know how they have performed) and production (they set high standards). Men are rated higher on tradition (they build on knowledge gained through experience), innovation (they are open to new ideas and willing to take risks), strategy (they focus on the big picture), restraint (they control emotional expression, remain calm), delegation (they share objectives and accountability), cooperation (they are good team players) and persuasiveness (they sell ideas and win people over).

One can conclude with Eisler that in the movement toward more "feminine" or nurturing management styles, men's socialization into the "masculine" traits of domination, conquest and control is dysfunctional for the new styles of leadership, but that "other qualities also considered masculine, such as decisiveness, assertiveness, and risk-taking, have been, and will continue to be, highly functional, particularly for the effective exercise of leadership" (Eisler, 1997, p. 107).

Communication styles

A different management style implies changes in language and behaviour in business communication. Since women are concerned not just with content but also with relationships, their aims when communicating are different, as are the modes and strategies they adopt. There seems now to be a need in organizations to create a favourable context for the coexistence of the male and the female model, in order to make the most of their synergy.

Grice (1975) geared his "Rules of conversation" to the transmission of information:

- do not give more or less information than necessary;
- do not say anything you do not believe;
- link your contribution to the previous contribution;
- formulate your views as clearly as possible.

But communication is more than just a matter of passing on information. Relations should also be — and stay — good; communication involves seeking and working together at a productive relationship. Rules of conversation should include the principle of collaboration.

From the cross-cultural perspective, men and women inhabit substantially different worlds, and so their conversation styles are different: Tannen (1990) called female talk "rapport talk" (relationships are important), and male talk "report talk" (facts are important). This difference could be compared to that between the Latin and the Anglo-Saxon cultures (Gauthey et al., 1988): the Latin culture tends towards deductive reasoning (concepts first), implicit communication and the importance of emotional relations in work, whereas the Anglo-Saxon culture tends towards inductive reasoning (facts first), an explicit communication style and a separation of work and personal relationships.

Differences in strategy can be related to differences in group behaviour, described by Fischer and Gleijm (1992) as the "pecking order" for men and the "crab basket" for women. In the pecking order, where hierarchy rules, it is important that rank order is clear to everyone present. Only once agreement has been reached on this, can attention be given to content. In the crab basket, by contrast, the group is important, so everyone is involved. Women expect to have their turn and to see a fair outcome, whereas men compete for the floor in order to establish a winner. Men will thus interrupt women (and other men) in discussion, but women will tend to fall silent after such an interruption.

The concept of leadership is also linked to public discourse. Men talk more often in meetings, and are more likely to determine the topics of conversation. If women in authority speak in ways expected of women, they are seen as inadequate leaders. If they speak in ways expected of leaders, they are seen as inadequate women. Fairclough argues that "power in discourse is to do with powerful participants controlling and constraining the contributions of non-powerful participants" (1989, p. 46).

Though there is little evidence for these assumed characteristics of women's speech, with the shift to new "softer" management styles, it is often said that male managers must learn feminine styles of behaviour and speech. One wonders what will happen to traditional styles of communication that express dominance, such as the "tough" stances so admired in business, or the use of "aggressive marketing" as a term of approval (Connell, 1987).

CONCLUDING REMARKS

At a time when the ability to manage change is becoming so important, communication plays a major role. Yet a significant source of dissatisfaction in organizations today is the poor structures and networks for mediating and diffusing knowledge, values and experience within the organizational environment. The assumption by large numbers of women of leadership positions is an essential element in the shift from the traditional, hierarchical organization to one based on partnership and teamwork. This implies organizations need to create a favourable climate allowing the masculine and feminine models to co-exist and operate in synergy. Given the proper encouragement, women managers could apply their natural talents for empathy and relationship-building. For, it has been proved, women possess qualities which could contribute significantly to improved communication, cooperation, team spirit and commitment within organizations — qualities which today are essential for achieving excellence and maintaining the necessary networks of contacts and relationships.

Given that the leadership skills of the future appear to be developing into a combination of masculine and feminine traits involving strategic thinking and communication skills, both women and men have something to learn and to gain from working together (Powell, 1988). The final result of this evolution in required leadership skills should contribute to making organizations more competitive and more successful. Considering the trend towards flatter organizations with the emphasis on training, teamwork, networking and the sharing of power and information, women's aptitudes in these fields should work to their advantage. This is especially true if the emerging working environments allow for diversity. For "appropriate" managerial skills now tend to take into account cultural awareness, that is, the awareness and tolerance of differences. Openness and acceptance of cultural differences will lead to synergy, enabling change and promoting excellence in business and communication.

References

Barham, K.; Fraser, J.; Heath, L. 1988. *Management for the future*. Foundation for Management Education/Ashridge Management College.

Belenky, M. F.; Clinchy, B. M.; Goldberger, N. R.; Tarule, J. M. 1986. *Women's way of knowing*. New York, Basic Books.

Bem, S. L. 1974. "The measurement of psychological androgyny", in *Journal of Consulting and Clinical Psychology* (Washington, DC), Vol. 42, No. 2, pp. 155-162.

Brouwer, Dédé. 1991. *Vrouwentaal. Feiten en verzinsels*. Bloemendaal, Aramith.

—. 1982. "The influence of the addressee's sex on politeness in language use", in *Linguistics* (Berlin), Vol. No. 20-11/12, pp. 679-711.

Brown, P. M; Levinson, S. C. 1987. *Politeness: Some universals in language use*. Cambridge, Cambridge University Press.

Cameron, Deborah. 1995. *Verbal hygiene*. London, Routledge and Kegan Paul.

—. 1985. *Feminism and linguistic theory*. Houndsmill, MacMillan Press.

Connell, Robert W. 1987. *Gender and power*. Cambridge, Polity Press.

Constantinople, A. 1973. "Masculinity-femininity: An exception to a famous dictum?", in *Psychological Bulletin* (Washington, DC), Vol. 80, No. 5, pp. 389-407.

Cox, Taylor, Jr. 1993. *Cultural diversity in organizations*. San Francisco, CA, Berrett-Koehler.

Davidson, Marilyn J.; Cooper, Cary L. 1992. *Shattering the glass ceiling: The woman manager*. London, Chapman.

Davis, Hayley. 1996. "Theorizing women's and men's language", in *Language and Communication* (Oxford), Vol. 61, No. 1, pp. 71-79.

Dipboye, R. L. 1978. "Women as managers", in Bette Ann Stead (ed.): *Women in management*. Englewood Cliffs, NJ, Prentice-Hall, pp. 2-10.

Drucker, Peter. 1994. "The age of social transformation", in *The Atlantic Monthly* (Boston, MA), Vol. 274, No. 5 (Nov.), pp. 53-80.

Eagly, A.; Johnson, B. 1990. "Gender and leadership style: A meta-analysis", in *Psychological Bulletin* (Washington, DC), No. 108, pp. 233-256.

Eckert, P. 1989. "The whole woman: Sex and gender differences in variation", in *Language Variation and Change* (Cambridge), Vol. 1, No. 3, pp. 245-267.

—; McConnel-Ginet, S. 1992. "Think practically and look locally: Language and gender as community-based practice", in *Annual Review of Anthropology* (Palo Alto, CA), Vol. 21, pp. 461-490.

Eisler, Riane. 1997. "The hidden subtext for sustainable change", in Willis Harman and Maya Porter (eds.): *The new business of business: Sharing responsibility for a positive global future*. San Francisco, CA, Berrett-Koeler/World Business Academy.

Fairclough, N. 1989. *Language and power*. London, Longman.

Finn, F.; Hickley, N.; O'Doherty, E. F. 1969. "The psychological profiles of male and female patients with CHD", in *Irish Journal of Medical Sciences* (Dublin), 7th series, Vol. 1-2, pp. 339-41.

Fischer, Mary L.; Gleijm, Hans. 1992. "The gender gap in management: A challenging affair", in *Industrial and Commercial Training* (Bradford, UK), Vol. 24, No. 4, pp. 5-11.

Gauthey, Franck; Xardel, Dominique. 1990. *Le management interculturel*. Collection Que Sais-Je? Paris, Presses universitaires de France.

—; Ratiu, Indrei; Rodgers, Irene; Xardel, Dominique. 1988. *Leaders sans frontières: le défi des différences*. Paris, McGraw Hill.

Giles, H.; Coupland, N. 1991. "Accommodating language", in H. Giles and N. Coupland (eds.): *Language, context and consequences*. Buckingham, Open University Press, pp. 60-84.

Gilligan, Caroll. 1982. *In a different voice: Psychological theory and women's development*. Cambridge, MA, Harvard University Press.

Goffman, Irving. 1977. "The arrangement between sexes", in *Theory and Society* (Dordrecht), Vol. 4, No. 3, pp. 301-331.

Goleman, Daniel. 1998. *Working with emotional intelligence*. New York, Bantam Books.

—. 1996. *Emotional intelligence*. London, Bloomsbury.

Grant, J. 1988. "Women as managers: What they can offer to organizations", in *Organizational Dynamics* (New York), Vol. 16, No. 3, pp. 56-63.

Grice, H. P. 1975. "Logic and conversation", in P. Cole and J. P. Morgan (eds.)*: Syntax and semantics*. Vol. 3: *Speech acts.* New York, Academic Press.

Hall, Edward T. 1996. Oral presentation at the 22nd Linguistic Agency, University of Duisburg (LAUD) Symposium on "Intercultural Communication", held at Duisburg.

Harding, S. 1986. *The science question in feminism*. Ithaca, NY, Cornell University Press.

Harragan, Betty L. 1977. *Games mother never taught you*. New York, Warner Books.

Helgesen, Sally. 1995. *The web of inclusion*. New York, Doubleday.

—. 1990. *The female advantage: Women's ways of leadership*. New York, Doubleday.

Hennig, Margaret; Jardim, Anne. 1976. *The managerial woman*. New York, Anchor/Doubleday.

Hirsh, Wendy; Jackson, Charles. 1989. *Women into management: Issues influencing the entry of women into managerial jobs*. Institute of Manpower Studies Paper No. 158. Brighton, Institute of Manpower Studies, University of Sussex.

Hofstede, Geert. 1991. *Cultures and organizations: Software of the mind*. London, McGraw-Hill.

—. 1980. *Culture's consequences: International differences in work-related values*. London, Sage.

ILO. 1997. *Breaking through the glass ceiling: Women in management*. Report for discussion at the Tripartite Meeting on "Breaking through the Glass Ceiling: Women in Management". Sectoral Activities Programme. Geneva.

Kabacoff, Robert I. 1998. *Gender differences in organizational leadership: A large sample study*. Paper presented at the Annual American Psychological Association Convention, held in San Francisco.

Kanter, Rosabeth Moss. 1997. *On the frontiers of management*. Boston, MA, Harvard Business School Press.

—. 1977. *Men and women of the corporation*. New York, Basic Books.

Lakoff, Robin. 1975. *Language and woman's place*. New York, Harper & Row.

Lipsey, Richard G.; Steiner, Peter O.; Purvis, Douglas D.; Courant, Paul N. 1990. *Economics*. New York, Harper & Row.

Maltz, Daniel; Borker, Ruth A. 1982. "A cultural approach to male-female miscommunication", in John J. Gumperz (ed.): *Language and social identity*. Studies in Interactional Sociolinguistics No. 2. Cambridge, Cambridge University Press.

Minzberg, Henry. 1973. *The nature of managerial work*. New York, Harper & Row.

Naisbitt, John; Aburdene, Patricia. 1986. *Reinventing the corporation*. New York, Warner Books.

Newsweek. 1995. "Holes in the glass ceiling theory", 27 Mar., pp. 26-27.

Powell, Gary N. 1988. *Women and men in management*. Newbury Park, Sage Publications.

Segal, Lynne. 1987. *Is the future female?* London, Virago.

Spender, Dale. 1980. *Man-made language*. London, Routledge and Kegan Paul.

Tannen, Deborah. 1994. *Talking from 9 to 5*. New York, William Morrow and Co.

—. 1990. *You just don't understand: Women and men in conversation*. London, Virago.

Traves, Joanne; Brockbank, Anne; Tomlinson, Frances. 1997. "Careers of women managers in the retail industry", in *The Service Industries Journal* (London), Vol. 17, No 1 (Jan.), pp. 133-154.

Verbiest, Agnes. 1990. *Het gewicht van de directrice: taal over, tegen, door vrouwen.* Amsterdam, Contact.

West, Candace; Zimmerman, Don H. 1983. "Small insults: A study of interruptions in cross-sex conversations between unacquainted persons", in B. Thorne, C. Kramarae and N. Henley (eds): *Language, gender and society.* Rowley, MA, Newbury House, pp. 103-124.

Williams, Wendy; Sternberg, Robert. 1988. "Why some groups are better than others", in *Intelligence* (Norwood, NJ), Vol. 12, No. 4, pp. 351-377.

Zimmerman, Don H.; West, Candace. 1975. "Sex roles, interruptions and silences in conversation", in B. Thorne and N. Henley (eds): *Language and sex: Difference and dominance.* Rowley, MA, Newbury House, pp. 105-129.

EQUAL TREATMENT, SOCIAL PROTECTION AND INCOME SECURITY FOR WOMEN

20

Linda LUCKHAUS*

The financial dependency of women and their disproportionate share of unpaid work infect social protection systems, rendering them discriminatory. Thus they are less successful in providing income security to women than to men. Despite a commitment to equality, European Court of Justice case law reveals a mixed result. The gender basis of social protection systems and the effects of women's more fragile employment histories are not being effectively countered by that attempt to enforce legal equality. Discriminatory practices are identified in line with several definitions of equality and then options for making progress are examined, including individualization and caregiving credit.

Ensuring income security is a major function of social protection.[1] Arguably, that is its defining task. However, the ability of social protection to provide an adequate and reliable source of income for women is problematic — partly because of the other functions that, historically, social protection has been required to perform. These include the promotion of specific forms of financial dependency which are rooted in and characteristic of gender and employment relations in the wider society.[2] These relations of dependency provide a fragile source of income for women; this fragility is then imported into the social protection systems giving them effect. The insistence on sex- and gender-based equality[3] in the field of social protection can minimize or even eliminate this fragility, depending on how the notion of equality is defined and its purpose construed, and there are many ways of doing this. Which of these definitions

Originally published in *International Labour Review*, Vol. 139 (2000), No. 2.

* Senior Lecturer in Law, University of Warwick. The research on which this chapter is based was funded partly by the British Academy, under its Research Leave Scheme, and by the Robert Schuman Centre for Advanced Studies of the European University Institute, Florence.

dominates legal and political discourse at any one time depends on prevailing views of the proper role of social protection and the appropriateness of the pattern of income provision and dependency to which this role relates. It also crucially depends on the changing nature of cultural and economic practices which ultimately set new limits in this sphere.

This chapter first explores the links between income security, sources of income support, and definitions of sex and gender equality in social protection. The focus is social protection as provided in developed countries, particularly those of western Europe; reference is made to developing and transition economies where possible. Next, the chapter identifies the different types of discrimination still to be found in social protection systems, applying the definitions of equality developed in the preceding section. Discriminatory practices are selected for examination from among recent developments in those systems for what they show of shifts towards greater or lesser discrimination. Finally, the chapter examines the relationship between equal treatment, social protection and income security, concluding with some normative thoughts on which of the various definitions of equal treatment is to be preferred, and with some ideas on how sex and gender equality may be secured in social protection.

INCOME SECURITY AND SOCIAL PROTECTION

In everyday terms, the two important aspects to income security are: the amount and adequacy of income; and the regular flow of income. In other words, income security means that there should be a constant flow of income adequate to live on. Probing further, it is clear that both adequacy and reliability are contingent on the source of the income, that there is more than one possible source, and that one source may be more effective than another. In developed, western economies, there are three main sources: sexual relationships between cohabiting married or non-married partners of the opposite sex; social protection systems; and employment and self-employment.[4] Income derived from employment may take the form of pay or benefits. Benefits derived from the employment relationship may be regarded both as deferred pay and as a form of social protection.

However, these main income sources are not immutable; nor is the pattern of use made of them by individuals and groups. As the economic activity of married women in most west European states has increased in recent years, so has their reliance on paid employment as an income source. There is, however, one fairly constant feature in the pattern of use. People caring at home for children, the elderly or persons with disabilities (i.e. not as part of a commercial arrangement) are precluded from engaging in paid employment during that period and thus from access to income from this source. Such people, therefore, must look either to their partner or to social protection for material support so long as they are engaged in this activity. However, they are not free to choose in this. Social protection systems are generally structured in such a way as to ensure that a partner is the first port of call in these situations. There is, for example, no social insurance benefit to cover the risk involved in giving up paid employment to care for children, the elderly, people with disabilities, etc.[5] Someone engaged in informal unpaid caring work of this kind is assumed to have a partner who is a paid worker (a "breadwinner") and, therefore, able to provide for them. Only if the breadwinner partner is not engaged in paid work (because of unemployment, sickness, old age, etc.) can an unpaid worker have recourse to social protection. However, being regarded as a dependant, the unpaid worker tends not to receive the money directly, and payment is made to their breadwinner partner on their behalf.

The gender-based nature of social protection systems has been much discussed[6] but bears repeating here because of its relevance to the adequacy and reliability of income sources and hence to *people's* income security. (The switch of focus to the income security of *people* rather than *women* is deliberate.) The gender-based nature of social protection systems and the income insecurity to which this gives rise are rooted in the designation of the unpaid care worker as a dependant of the paid worker-provider. Unpaid caring work, not the sex of the unpaid worker, is the clue to understanding why social protection systems prove a fragile source of income for women.

The lack of income security of unpaid workers in social protection systems arises in two related sets of circumstance. First, because the partner concerned may be engaged in low-paid, erratic employment, he/she may not pass on income he/she may have, or may do so only on terms which are unacceptable for sexual, emotional or physical reasons. Moreover, income flow from a partner may be terminated at any time by separation, divorce or death. Second, the lack of income security for unpaid workers arises because their other source of income (social protection) imports — through the gender-based structure outlined above — most if not all of the insecurities associated with the financial relationship between an unpaid worker and their "breadwinner" partner. The United Kingdom's cohabitation rule which provides for withdrawal of benefit from widows and single parents immediately they form a new sexual relationship, irrespective of their financial or other circumstances,[7] is perhaps the clearest example of the fragility of the support offered to unpaid workers by the social protection system.

Another aspect to the relation between income security and social protection and how this produces insecurity for women concerns paid employment. Even in the present state of fluctuating labour markets, this income source can produce adequate and reliable incomes for some categories of workers. There are many, however, for whom periods out of employment and periods in employment in part-time or low-paid work with little prospect of enhancement are the norm. For these workers — men or women — paid employment offers neither an adequate nor a reliable income source. More to the point, for present purposes, social protection systems tend to reproduce these insecurities rather than remove them.

This is because entitlement is conditional, in respect of occupational benefits, on employment with a specific employer and, in respect of many social insurance benefits, on having been in paid work (in order to be able to pay contributions). For both occupational benefits and social insurance, entitlement may be further restricted because it is conditional on beneficiaries being in paid work for a certain number of hours or earning a certain amount per week. Even where the existence of a low-earnings threshold does not in effect exclude low-paid workers from access to schemes, if the method of calculating benefits is geared closely to earnings their benefit payments will be low. People who move in and out of employment will have difficulty satisfying the lengthy contribution periods required to qualify for benefits such as pensions. Intermittent employment involving periods of low pay or no pay can also affect the amount of retirement pension awarded, depending on the calculation formula used. Finally, movement in and out of work for different employers makes it difficult for workers to build up entitlement to occupational benefits, particularly pensions.

This income insecurity in social protection systems is rooted in unpaid work and in either non-employment or employment in forms of work which are not full time, relatively highly paid and continuous over a working life. It follows that these systems tend to provide an unreliable and inadequate source of income for persons in such situations. Moreover, and this is where women are re-introduced into the analysis, groups with these unpaid work and precarious labour market characteristics are largely — though not entirely — made up of women. For women continue to undertake most unpaid caring work, whilst entering the labour force in increasing numbers. They also continue — more than do men — to move in and out of employment and to dominate part-time,[8] low-paid jobs in many economies,[9] being obliged in many instances to seek these precarious and peripheral forms of employment because of the demands of their unpaid caring work.[10] This link between unpaid work activity and participation in precarious forms of employment is crucial to explaining why social protection systems fail to provide women with an adequate and reliable source of income.

The next part of the chapter analyses the relationship between equal treatment and social protection by looking at the various ways in which equal treatment for men and women in social protection has been defined. One important question underpinning the analysis is whether women's income insecurity in social protection systems is considered relevant to the definition of equal treatment — whether poverty is regarded as an equality issue.

EQUAL TREATMENT AND SOCIAL PROTECTION

There are at least five variants of the meaning of equal treatment in social protection. The legal version is that constructed through the practice of legislators and the courts. The other four have been developed by interest groups, policy-makers and academics, with a view to influencing government policy. The first of the political notions seeks to end the disadvantages suffered by women in social protection systems through non-coverage of their unpaid work. The second specifically aims for the financial independence of women. The third regards full social protection rights for women as a means of encouraging their labour market participation, while the fourth seeks to remove those aspects of social protection perceived as acting as a disincentive to women's paid work.

The legal formulation of equal treatment

Many international and national legal instruments espousing the cause of equality could provide the basis for a discussion of the legal notion of equal treatment. However, relatively few of these human rights instruments make specific reference to sex or gender on the one hand and to social protection on the other.[11] Equality instruments adopted by European Union (EU) institutions are rare examples of the latter[12] and form the basis of the legal notion of equal treatment discussed here.[13]

EU equality law defines the principle of equal treatment in terms of a prohibition on discrimination; more specifically, a prohibition on discrimination on grounds of sex and marital status. This ban extends to both indirect and direct forms of discrimination. An example of direct discrimination, once common in northern European systems but now largely abolished, is the granting of unemployment benefit to married women at a rate lower than that applied to men and single women (explicitly on grounds of sex and marital status). An example of indirect discrimination is a rule limiting access to benefits to those earning above a certain threshold or working more than a specified number of hours a week. In this case, the same rule is applied to all workers, but it has a differential effect, depending on people's earnings and weekly hours: the effect is adverse on those with earnings or hours below the threshold (i.e. low-paid or part-time workers) since they will be barred from access to benefit. Where a rule of this kind adversely affects more women than men (or men than women), it is said to constitute indirect discrimination on grounds of sex, unless the rule or threshold can be justified on "objective" grounds, i.e. on grounds other than sex.

The basic idea underlying this somewhat technical concept of discrimination is that people in the same situation should be treated in the same way,[14] and people in different situations should be treated differently. The ban on direct discrimination meets the first requirement, to treat like as like. Married women should accordingly be treated the same as men and single women, i.e. granted the same, not a lower, rate of unemployment benefit. The ban on indirect discrimination meets the second requirement, to treat unlike as unlike. Accordingly, the same earnings rule should not be applied both to the low-paid and the highly-paid, since the two groups of workers are not in the same situation.

The treat-like-as-like approach to equality is both elastic and flexible, one reason being the absence from EU equality legislation of specific criteria for determining what constitutes the same and what constitutes different situations. Are persons engaged in paid work in the same situation as those in unpaid work? Are people with high and low earnings in different situations? Although the EU legislation gives some guidelines,[15] the answers to these crucial questions have largely been left to the European Court of Justice to determine in the cases brought before it and to EU Member States when implementing the EU legislation at the national level.

Another reason for this flexibility is the narrow interpretation given by the European Court of Justice and others of what is intended by equal treatment in the social protection field.[16] According to this narrow interpretation, equal treatment has two aims. The first is to ensure that social protection rules treat people as individuals and do not make assumptions about their characteristics on the basis of their membership of a particular group.[17] This provided the justification for abolishing the different, and adverse, treatment of married women in social protection schemes, since the adverse treatment involved the assumption that as a group married women did not engage in paid work and were financially supported by their husbands — an assumption that proved to be incorrect in many cases, given married women's increasing labour market activity.[18] A second aim is to ensure that the law relating to social protection accurately reflects socio-economic reality. This argument was also used to justify abolition of the adverse treatment of married women on the basis that the rationale for the treatment (married women's non-participation in the labour market) was an increasingly outmoded assumption no longer in accord with economic reality (see Hoskyns and Luckhaus, 1989).

Seeking to promote the integrity of the individual and to safeguard the integrity of the law are not unimportant aims, but they do not relate specifically to social protection, nor do they seek to alter the pattern of existing financial and social relationships (unlike some of the political notions of equal treatment). Furthermore, they are largely procedural in nature. As a result, when major substantive questions have arisen, e.g.

whether equality must be implemented so as to avoid increasing poverty or whether Member States may be required to alter their social policy in order to achieve equality, they have been determined by the European Court of Justice in a negative way.

A narrow interpretation of the purposes of equal treatment in the social protection field was not inevitable. It was open to the European Court of Justice to adopt a more expansive interpretation, using some of the political notions as a guide. And in a different political and economic climate, it might well have done so.[19]

Political notions of equal treatment

In their current forms, the political formulations of equal treatment emerged in political debates at European and national level from the late 1960s onwards. The first of these notions, calling for an end to the financial disadvantages suffered by women in social protection systems, arose out of the detailed and rigorous analyses of these systems carried out by policy-makers, women's groups and academics. This analysis linked women's disadvantaged position in social protection systems to their unpaid work and to their (often connected) participation in the sort of part-time, low-paid, intermittent employment poorly covered by social protection systems. For this reason, the demand for equal treatment was specifically framed in terms of equality for *women*. The idea that men would need to invoke the equality principle was not conceivable within that analytical framework. The focus on women's disadvantaged position within social protection also implied a close link between this notion of equality and the avoidance of poverty. This link in turn presupposed that the disadvantages would be removed and equality secured by "levelling up" women's position so that they would enjoy the same degree of income security within social protection systems as men do. Of all the variants of equality discussed here, this formulation gives the greatest priority to securing income security for women.

The second political formulation of equal treatment, the claim for women's financial independence, is again specific to women but the emphasis is on ending the institutionalization of female unpaid workers' financial dependence on their male breadwinner partners. Calling as it does on women to end their financial dependence on men by securing their financial independence through employment, this claim concerns more than social protection alone. This broader claim also incorporates a narrower one (specific to social protection), namely, that the rules and concepts determining entitlement within these systems should be restructured around an individualized model of entitlement rather than the relationship between breadwinner/paid worker and dependant/unpaid worker. In short, this notion of equal treatment seeks to remove the concept of dependency between partners from social protection systems.

The third and fourth political formulations of equal treatment both give priority to promoting women's paid employment and both regard social protection systems as playing an instrumental role in this respect, but the mechanism is different in each case. The third version sees the guarantee to women of full rights to social protection as a way of encouraging them to participate in the labour market in order to secure these rights. Here, social protection is seen as a financial incentive to paid work. This notion has its origin in the late 1960s and early 1970s when there was concern in the EU about labour shortages and their effect on national economies. Interestingly, a variant of this argument focusing on part-time work has recently surfaced in Spain where there is concern in some quarters about both the relative absence of part-time forms of employment and women's low labour market participation. The argument is being made that full social protection rights should be extended to part-time work in order to encourage non-employed women to take up part-time work; see *European Industrial Relations Review* (1999).

The fourth political formulation of equal treatment concerns the ways in which social protection systems operate so as to discourage women from taking or remaining in paid employment. Social protection is therefore seen as a disincentive rather than an incentive to women's labour market participation. Concern about the disincentive effects of social protection emerged, in the United Kingdom at least, in the late 1970s and 1980s and initially focused on men rather than women. It coincided with a macroeconomic concern to lower wages and social charges in order to improve competitiveness and reduce unemployment. In the 1990s, as preoccupation with work incentives grew in the United Kingdom, attention turned to women whose partners were unemployed and claiming social assistance; it was said that women in such situations left the labour market or remained non-employed because it was not financially worth holding on to what could only be — if the argument is to ring true — low-paid employment. One report typifying this preoccupation with the perceived disincentive effect of social protection systems on women's employment explicitly linked it to the issue of women's independent income (see Duncan, Giles and Webb, 1994).

This seemingly innocuous link needs to be examined closely. Though such a task is beyond the scope of this chapter, two points may be made. One is to note statisticians' growing preoccupation with increasing numbers of households composed of jobless persons of working age in the United Kingdom[20] and many industrialized countries.[21] At one level, the preoccupation arises from concern for the material welfare of people in these households (OECD, 1998a, p. 1); at another, it reflects a desire to identify "labour market slack" (OECD, 1998a, p. 1) and to have data offering some support for the otherwise speculative proposition that social protection systems discourage the female partners of men in receipt of benefits from getting (low-paid) jobs.[22] The second point is that "women's independent income" is likely to be very different from that intended in the claim for financial independence. Since the preoccupation with disincentives coincides with a concern to reduce wages and social charges (and hence with removing people from receipt of benefit), the reference to "independence" in this context probably has more to do with non-reliance on social protection as an income source than with non-reliance on a partner (as is the case with the claim for financial independence). Moreover, given the relatively low rates of benefit (at least in the United Kingdom), the logic of the disincentives argument strongly suggests that this independent income will almost certainly be derived from forms of part-time, low-paid and intermittent employment which provide little, if any, income security for women.

IMPLICATIONS FOR EQUAL TREATMENT OF RECENT DEVELOPMENTS IN SOCIAL PROTECTION

The various formulations of equal treatment described above provide the criteria for assessing whether, and to what extent, existing social protection systems may be said to be discriminatory. The first part of the assessment deals with aspects of systems reflecting the concept of dependency and the breadwinner/dependant model of entitlement. The second deals with provisions within these systems that privilege full-time, relatively well-paid, continuous employment patterns and disadvantage more precarious forms of employment and unpaid work. Reference is also made in this part to provisions within a social protection system which may operate to mitigate the adverse effects of the bias elsewhere in the system against precarious employment and unpaid work. The third part deals with two sets of social protection rules — relating to pension age and life expectancy — which raise sex and gender issues.

Social protection and the concept of dependency

This section examines three sets of social protection provisions, all linked through the concept of financial dependency between adult partners (hereafter referred to simply as "dependency"). They are widow's (and survivor's) benefits, social assistance schemes and the rules providing for pension sharing on divorce. *Widow's benefits* are structured around dependency because they link benefit entitlement to contributions by the deceased spouse, because they insure against the loss of a breadwinner-provider, and because they may be withdrawn (as in the United Kingdom) if the recipient enters a new sexual relationship. *Survivor's benefits* are here taken to be benefits granted on the death of a spouse, i.e. to widowers as well as widows. They are based on the same principles as widow's benefit but are not sex-specific. The second set of social protection provisions, *social assistance schemes*, are structured around dependency in so far as entitlement is determined according to the resources and needs of a unit comprising a man and a woman in a sexual relationship. The third set of provisions enabling *pension sharing on divorce* presuppose dependency between the two members of a formerly married couple. They also presuppose that the acquisition of pension rights is uneven between spouses and that the lesser or non-existent rights of the wife will be lost if the marriage is terminated by divorce prior to the retirement or death of the husband.

Widow's and survivor's benefits

Widow's benefits are a long-standing feature of social insurance schemes and of occupational schemes. Two recent developments have been the introduction of survivor's benefits in both statutory and occupational schemes and the conversion of some statutory schemes from entitlement based only on contributions to entitlement based on means testing or a mix of means testing and contributions. The introduction of statutory survivor's benefit is well advanced, at least in the EU. Periodic payments of this kind now exist in all EU Member States except Denmark. In 1992, Denmark abolished the statutory periodic payment to widows and replaced it with the more limited provision of a lump-sum payment to both widows and widowers on the death of their spouse. The United Kingdom is the last EU Member State to remove the special treatment accorded to widows in statutory schemes and is doing so by extending provision — including periodic payments — to male survivors on the same terms as those applicable to female survivors. The 1999 legislation abolishing widow's benefit and inserting the new system of bereavement benefits is due to come into force in April 2001. As regards occupational schemes in the EU, there is some evidence pointing to extension of widow's benefit to widowers, in the process of reform rendered necessary by a European Court of Justice ruling on the discriminatory nature of occupational widow's benefit in 1993.[23]

The second development concerning statutory survivor's benefit involves its conversion to a means-tested benefit. Governments in France, Italy, Sweden and the Netherlands have all introduced an element of means testing into their schemes (United Kingdom, 1998a, chapter 3, para. 7). The United Kingdom's 1999 reforms adopted a similar approach. In brief, the widow's pension payable on a periodic basis to women aged 45 and over for as long as they remain widows or do not cohabit has been replaced by a bereavement allowance available to both male and female surviving spouses aged 45 and over. However, this allowance is restricted to 12 months' duration. Thereafter, widows and widowers will be able to claim means-tested income support but will only gain entitlement to this benefit if, and so long as, they can demonstrate insufficient income, availability for work and the other conditions applicable to this benefit. In the long term, these new rules are expected to lead to a significant reduction in the level of provision for older widows (United Kingdom, 1998a, chapter 3, para. 5).[24]

An assessment of the equal treatment implications of widow's benefit and the recent developments in their regard is appropriate here. In principle, widow's benefit offends the legal notion of equal treatment since it directly discriminates against men. The restriction of this benefit to female survivors in occupational schemes was held unlawful by the European Court of Justice in 1993, as already noted. This benefit continues to be lawful in EU statutory social protection schemes by virtue of the exemption of the broader category of survivor's benefit under EU equality law.[25] Survivor's benefits under occupational schemes are non-discriminatory since they treat both male and female survivors the same, as dependants. Statutory survivor's benefits also satisfy this non-discrimination principle (subject to the terms being identical for men and women, which is not always the case), but their discriminatory status is not a live issue since, as already noted, they are exempted from application of equal treatment principle by EU equality law.[26] The fact that the means testing of survivor's benefit can result in reduced social protection for some widows raises in stark form the question of whether, according to EU law, equality between men and women can be implemented by reducing provision for some or all groups: in short, whether equality can be implemented in a way which may result in poverty for some or all of those concerned.

The levelling down of provision in the process of implementing equality is a common strategy in both statutory and occupational schemes. In the 1970s and 1980s, in the first cases to come before it in which this point was raised directly or indirectly, the European Court of Justice either proceeded on the assumption that the result of a successful discrimination claim would lead to extension of provision to the disadvantaged group[27] or simply avoided the issue.[28] It then developed a neat formulation of the equal treatment principle, the consequence of which was automatic extension of the privileged treatment to the disadvantaged group.[29] However, when pressed to rule on whether Member State legislatures could implement equality by reducing provision, it responded positively, expanding on the idea, developed elsewhere in its case law, that the practical implementation of equal treatment was a matter of social policy over which Member States continued to retain considerable discretion and control.[30]

To summarize the legal situation, widow's benefits are discriminatory whereas survivor's benefits are not, although statutory widow's benefit is exempted under Directive 79/7 from application of the equal treatment principle. In addition, EU Member State implementation of equal treatment involving a reduction in provision for some or all groups previously entitled to benefit is permissible under EU law. As to the political notions of equal treatment, widow's benefit goes some way to meeting the call for an end to the disadvantages women suffer in social protection systems through non-coverage of their unpaid work activity, although it does so by focusing on sex and marital status rather than on engagement in unpaid caring work (or indeed on participation in the peripheral sections of the labour market). The extension of widow's benefit to male survivors is not compatible with this notion of equal treatment, nor is the levelling down of provision which has tended to accompany that process. The existence of widow's benefit runs directly counter to the ideal of ending dependency in social protection systems, a situation exacerbated by the extension of this status to men in the form of survivor's (widower's) benefit. Finally, the application of means testing to survivor's benefit may raise the prospect of increasing disincentives to work for women, contrary to the notion that equal treatment requires their reduction.[31]

Social assistance

The application of means testing to survivor's benefit is indicative of another development in social protection with implications for equal treatment, namely the expansion of social assistance. A study of the 24 OECD countries showed that social assistance is becoming more important in nearly all the countries, in terms both of expenditure and claimant numbers (Eardley et al., 1996, p. 178). The osmotic spread of means testing to nearly all forms of social protection including in many non-OECD countries is illustrated by its application to contribution-based family allowances in Italy,[32] the introduction in the United Kingdom in the early 1990s of a means-tested in-work benefit for persons with disabilities,[33] and the announcement in Bangladesh in 1998 that a means-tested pension of 100 takas (about 2 US dollars) per month was to be awarded to some 90 people in each of the country's 4,479 districts. State social assistance programmes for the elderly are also run in other parts of Asia, notably India; see ILO/EASMAT (1997), p. 24. A feature common to these programmes, to all the schemes operated in OECD countries and, most likely, to social assistance everywhere, is the testing of means on the basis of a unit larger than the individual seeking entitlement to the benefit. In some instances, the unit may be very large and embrace distant as well as near relatives. In the majority of OECD countries, the unit is restricted to a claimant and his/her spouse (Eardley et al. 1996, p. 65) and, in some cases, to a claimant and the (hetero)sexual partner with whom he/she is held to be cohabiting.

Potentially, the implications for equal treatment of this spread of social assistance and the linking of entitlement to these benefits to the resources of both partners are quite far-reaching. The root of the problem with means testing based on a couple's resources is that where women's earnings are considerably lower than men's, as is customarily the case, more women than men fail to establish entitlement to means-tested benefits because their partner's earnings bring the couple's combined resources above the minimum income allowed. Moreover, where a male partner succeeds in establishing entitlement (aided by the low or non-existent earnings of his partner), the element of the benefit intended to meet his partner's needs is paid to him and not to his female partner.

As to the discriminatory status of the dependency notion in social assistance, a number of cases have come before the European Court of Justice seeking to establish that taking into account a partner's income in means-tested schemes constitutes indirect discrimination against women. Acknowledging its adverse effect on women's entitlement, the Court none the less ruled that the practice was not discriminatory because it could be objectively justified on the grounds that provision of a minimum income was an integral part of Member States' social policy and that Member States had a "reasonable margin of discretion" in determining the nature of social protection measures and the actual means by which they were to be implemented.[34] As with its application in relation to levelling down by Member States, this formula nicely illustrates how easily the abstract form of the "treat-like-as-like" approach to equality can be moulded into the proposition now clearly established in this area of EU law that poverty and material well-being are irrelevant to the concept of equality, as interpreted by the Court.

As to compatibility with the political notions of equal treatment, social assistance schemes themselves can be a welcome lifeline for a woman who is not entitled to other forms of social protection because of her unpaid work activity. These schemes do not actually conflict with the call for an end to the disadvantages women encounter in these other spheres of social protection as a result of their unpaid work. However, the treatment of a woman's partner's (usually higher) income as hers tends to displace if not destroy the potential of these schemes to alleviate her income insecurity. At the same time, the income assessment rules bring the schemes into conflict with the equal treatment ideal of ending disadvantages for women arising from their unpaid work activity. In addition, the payment of money to a man to meet his partner's needs runs counter to the principle of equality which regards the financial independence of a woman from her partner as paramount. Finally, means-tested schemes are a prime target for advocates of the notion that equal treatment requires an end to the disincentives to work embedded in social protection schemes. This argument goes as follows: the tendency for a woman's earnings to be low (or non-existent) permitting her (unemployed, disabled, older) partner to qualify for means-tested benefits results in a disincentive to work for women in (low-)paid employment, because the couple is generally not much better off if the woman does so.[35]

Pension sharing on divorce

A third development in social protection serving to extend further and consolidate the principle of dependency in social protection systems

417

is the practice of dividing the pension rights of spouses on divorce. In principle, pension sharing (or pension splitting, as it is sometimes known) is applicable to all types of pension schemes and has a fairly long history in statutory schemes. It was introduced in Germany in 1977 (Solcher, 1978, p. 308) and in Canada in the following year.[36] It has attracted attention recently in relation to occupational schemes. Pension sharing in occupational schemes was introduced in Ireland in 1996. It was proposed in the United Kingdom in 1997 and in South Africa in 1998. In the United Kingdom, the proposal became law in 1999 when legislation was passed providing for the transfer of pension rights from one spouse to another on divorce. The legislation supplements existing arrangements which can be made by British courts, but which fall short of outright transfer of rights; the main beneficiaries of the 1999 legislation are expected to be women (United Kingdom, 1999). In South Africa, the Law Commission's 1998 consultation paper (South African Law Commission, 1998) suggested pension sharing might be extended to all spouses, including those entering marriage under customary law. Its recommendation following consultation, however, is to restrict pension sharing to marriages recognized as such by existing law (South African Law Commission, 1999). In the United States, a variant of pension sharing (called earnings sharing) is being actively promoted by the Cato Organization as part of a plan to abolish the United States social security system and replace it with a fully funded, defined contribution system financed solely by the individuals receiving the benefit (Shirley and Spiegler, 1998; see also Olsen, 1999).

If pension sharing on divorce is available to men and women on the same terms, it seems to be compatible with the legal notion of equal treatment.[37] Since the aim of pension sharing is to secure a fair division of the wealth acquired during a marriage on the ground that both spouses have contributed to that acquisition through the sharing of paid and unpaid work, pension sharing also seems to conform with the call for an end to disadvantages in social protection systems arising from the non-coverage of unpaid work. Pension sharing is sometimes misguidedly regarded as a means of individualizing benefit rights (establishing the financial independence of one partner from the other). But pension sharing proceeds on the basis of one spouse being financially dependent on the other and so extends and reinforces the principle of financial dependency throughout social protection systems.

In summary, then, financial dependency between partners provides the analytical link between the social protection developments described so far in this chapter. The striking feature about these developments is the extent to which this form of financial dependency is spreading in both statutory and occupational schemes. Recent attempts at EU level to achieve recognition of homosexual (cohabiting) relationships as equivalent to heterosexual (cohabiting) ones in order thereby to secure for the dependent homosexual partner the financial advantages awarded to the dependent partner in a heterosexual relationship indicate a readiness on some people's part to consider further expansion of this form of dependency in the social protection schemes of the future.[38]

Social protection regulations and different forms of employment

The rules governing the transmission of income security from the labour market to the social protection system are examined in this section, as are rules within the social protection system capable of countering the adverse effects of these labour market rules to some extent.

The labour market rules are: obligation to be in paid work, satisfaction of an earnings or hours threshold, entitlement linked to payment of contributions over a lengthy period, benefit amounts linked to earnings in work and lengthy contribution periods. These rules feature in some statutory and occupational schemes but not in others.[39] The earnings and hours thresholds and the lengthy contribution conditions in statutory schemes are discussed here,[40] partly because of recent or proposed changes and partly because their potentially discriminatory status has been the subject of legal challenge.

An earnings or hours threshold is a fairly common feature of social protection systems. A comparison by the OECD of provision in 21 OECD countries published in 1998 showed that the systems in all but five of those countries — Greece, Hungary, New Zealand, Norway and Spain — operated either an hours or an earnings threshold or a combination of both.[41] Recent developments in relation to these thresholds were mixed. Some involved a reduction in the hours or earnings threshold and thus raised the possibility for part-time or low-paid workers of gaining access to the systems. Thus, in 1994, the threshold applicable to the social protection system in Japan was reduced from 30 to 20 hours a week and in Canada earnings and hours thresholds previously applying to unemployment benefit were abolished from 1997 (OECD, 1998a, p. 172).

In Germany, in 1997 too, the first step was taken to reduce the hours and earnings thresholds governing access to the pension, health and unemployment insurance schemes. This involved reducing the 18-hour threshold, below which people could not gain access to the unemployment insurance scheme. Thenceforth, people could participate in all three schemes — pension, health and unemployment — if they worked 15 or more hours a week or earned more than the minimum earnings threshold. This threshold is fixed at a low level (630 DM per month in 2000) so, in practice, it is this earnings threshold rather than the hours threshold which determines who can participate in the insurance schemes. In April 1999 further changes to the German pension insurance scheme were introduced related to this minimum earnings threshold. The changes are complex but the most important element, for our purposes, is the partial removal of the minimum earnings (630 DM) threshold in relation to pension insurance. Henceforth, employers are obliged to pay contributions of 12 per cent on earnings below this level, while employees (earning between 300 and 630 DM per month) may make voluntary contributions of 7.5 per cent. Employees who do not make the voluntary contributions acquire less than the full range of pension rights. The idea behind these changes was to help low-paid female employees improve their social protection in old age.[42]

Other developments concerning thresholds have been less favourable to low-paid workers.[43] Thus, in Finland in 1996 an income threshold was introduced into the sickness insurance scheme for the first time.[44] In the United Kingdom, the lower earnings limit is gradually being raised to bring it into line with the tax threshold,[45] the possible consequence being an expansion of the 2.6 million people presently excluded from statutory social protection by that threshold.[46]

Rules linking pension entitlement to a specified number of years of contribution have also undergone change, often as part of a general package of government reforms designed to reduce social protection costs (and budget deficits). In general, changes are likely to restrict access to pensions for people with a pattern of intermittent employment. Thus, in Sweden the contribution period required to achieve full pension entitlement was raised from 30 years to total lifetime contributions; while, in Italy, the ability of private-sector workers to obtain a full pension after 35 years of contribution and public-sector workers after 20 years has been removed and replaced by a condition requiring lifetime contributions (Pierson, 1999, p. 25). Changes to pension earnings formulas in these two countries may also result in reduced pensions for this group.[47] In France, Portugal, Austria and Finland, the number of years of earnings on which the pension is based has been increased (Commission of the European Communities, 1998b, p. 24). In the United States, there is concern that a proposal to raise the number of years of covered earnings from 35 to 38 in order to gain full entitlement to a pension will have a disproportionate effect on women, the estimate being that fewer than 30 per cent of women retiring in 2020 will have the required 38 years (compared with nearly 60 per cent of men) (Shirley and Spiegler, 1998). In Spain, however, there has been a slight improvement in the number of years part-time workers are required to contribute in order to gain full entitlement to a pension. An agreement between the Spanish Government and Spanish trade unions signed in October 1998 resulted in a change in the method of calculating the contribution years of part-time workers, giving them entitlement to a pension after 21 years rather than 30. Full-time workers continue to gain entitlement after 15 years. As already noted, one aim of this reform is to encourage women to take up part-time work (*European Industrial Relations Review*, 1999, pp. 30-31).

The question needing to be addressed is whether these labour market rules are compatible with the legal and political notions of equal treatment outlined earlier. As regards the legal construction of equality, it is possible that these rules are incompatible with the requirement of equal treatment if a case can be made that they are indirectly discriminatory and that they are not objectively justifiable. Since the low-paid, part-time, intermittently employed workers adversely affected by the rules tend to include more women than men (because of their unpaid work activity), a discriminatory claim may have some chance of success, particularly since the European Court of Justice generally seems prepared to regard part-time (low-paid) workers as being in a different situation from full-time (higher-paid) workers and has not always demanded that detailed statistical evidence needed to establish differential effect be produced in support of the claim. However, the availability of the defence of objective justification gives the Court at EU level and national levels considerable flexibility if it wishes to reject the claim. The discriminatory status of these labour market rules, therefore, remains unknown until a claim is made and the Court gives its ruling. In the meantime, though the rules may be regarded as potentially discriminatory they are none the less lawful.

There is some certainty with respect to the rules excluding part-time and low-paid workers from access to social protection schemes. Here, as with widow's benefit, the legality of the rules differs as between statutory and occupational schemes. In occupational schemes, the European Court of Justice took the view that an hours threshold excluding part-time workers from access to a pension is indirectly discriminatory and cannot be objectively justified.[48] In two cases concerning the mix of hours and earnings thresholds existing, prior to 1997, in the German unemployment, invalidity and old-age insurance schemes, the Court held that their discriminatory effect was objectively justified. The justification accepted by the Court was that employers should be relieved of the liability of paying contributions on this form of employment (employment of fewer than 18 and 15 hours a week, in which earnings fell below the minimum specified), so that they would be encouraged to create the type of part-time, low-paid jobs covered by these thresholds.[49] It may be noted that the Court is here accepting that equality is not only restricted to those engaged in paid (as opposed to unpaid) work, but also to those engaged in the type of employment — full-time, higher-paid — already privileged within social protection schemes.[50]

So far as the four political notions of equal treatment are concerned, two call for particular comment in the context of these social protection rules privileging full-time, higher-paid continuous employment. Since these rules are a major cause of the income insecurity suffered by women in social protection systems — women's unpaid work being a reason for their non-employment or engagement outside this privileged realm — they are in direct conflict with the notion of equal treatment which calls for an end to the structural features of social protection systems which disadvantage unpaid work activity. To a lesser extent, these structural features are incompatible with the idea that full social protection rights should be accorded to women to encourage them to take up paid employment, since in this way they will gain access to those rights. It could be argued, for example, that knowledge of the lengthy period of contribution and relatively high earnings needed to qualify for a pension, combined with a realization that caring activity will prevent those requirements being met, may prevent the promise of such a pension acting as an incentive to women to enter the labour market.

Attention will now briefly be given to another set of rules some of which, despite the austerity currently ruling European statutory social protection systems, are being preserved and, it seems, slightly enhanced. These rules operate so as to enhance coverage for people engaged in unpaid work either by specific reference to that activity or by breaking the link between social insurance and participation in paid work. The first type targets unpaid caring work either by transforming the work into a form of (non-market remunerated) paid work (as the United Kingdom's invalid care allowance and Finland's home childcare allowance effectively do), or by ensuring that periods of unpaid work do not jeopardize entitlement to social insurance benefits by crediting the individuals' accounts with contributions for the relevant periods of care activity. The latter, termed caring credits, are effective in a number of European states in enhancing pension entitlement for carers.[51] Contribution credits were introduced into the (AVS) pension scheme in Switzerland in 1995 along with pension splitting (as it was then called) for married and divorced couples (Bonoli, 1997, pp. 119-122). The United Kingdom and Ireland have implemented a variant of the caring credit in their home responsibilities protection, a measure whereby years of low or no earnings may be disregarded in the computation of pension amount. In 1996, Ireland increased the number of years for which such protection could be available by increasing the age of qualifying children from 6 to 12 (Commission of the European Communities, 1997, p. 50).

It should also be noted that a form of crediting for carers operates in relation to occupational pension schemes where employers continue to make contributions on behalf of employees on maternity (or parental) leave. The extent of this practice by employers is unknown. However, it is a requirement of EU law that contractual rights (including acquisition of pension rights) be maintained during the 14 weeks (normally paid) maternity leave mandatory in the EU.[52] A recent decision of the European Court of Justice paves the way for an expansion of caring credits in occupational systems. The Court ruled that it was unlawful for employers not to continue contributing to their pension fund on behalf of employees on *unpaid* maternity leave, where the pension funds are financed by employers' contributions alone.[53]

Examples of the second type of rule, which breaks the link between social protection entitlement and participation in employment, are non-contributory, residence-based benefits and provisions permitting voluntary contributions. In 1997, Italy combined both the voluntary contribution principle and the targeting of unpaid work by establishing a new fund for homemakers (*casalinghe*), which provides insurance against occupational accidents and old age and which is entirely voluntary.

As to the discriminatory status of these compensatory provisions, it is clear that when they are available to both men and women they are not in conflict with the legal notion of equal treatment — at least as far as the prohibition on direct discrimination is concerned. In practice, their effect may be to advantage more women than men. Even if an argument could be made out that this adversely affects more men than women, rendering the provisions indirectly discriminatory, the Court would almost certainly be encouraged to hold the provisions to be objectively justified. The legal position is different where the compensatory provisions single out women for special treatment by excluding men. The European Court of Justice, again, would almost certainly hold sex-specific provisions of this kind to be in conflict with the ban on direct discrimination,[54] but the point is not likely to arise in relation to statutory schemes because such provisions are exempted from application of the equal treatment principle by EU law itself (Art. 7(1)(b) of Directive 79/7).

The two political notions of equal treatment relevant here, again, are the calls for an end to the disadvantages in social protection schemes arising from peripheral paid work and unpaid work activity and for measures to encourage women to enter the labour market. Provisions targeting unpaid work as part of social protection schemes based on employment (as opposed to residence) — such as caring credits — are particularly apt to satisfy these two notions of equal treatment and hence to produce gender equality. They also sit happily with notions of financial independence of one partner from the other and do not appear to operate as a disincentive to women to take employment. A qualification must be entered here, however, for it is not clear that the level of benefit resulting from provisions such as caring credits and residence-based entitlement will be such as to produce an adequate income for beneficiaries, while voluntary contributions are extremely problematic for those who by virtue of their unpaid work have no source of income other than through their partner.

To summarize, then, social protection rules which penalize unpaid work activity look set to stay, although some minor improvements have been made. These rules — in statutory but not occupational schemes — appear to be compatible with the legal notion of equality but are in conflict with the political ideals of removing disadvantages in social protection schemes arising from non-coverage of unpaid work and of using the offer of full social protection rights to encourage women into the labour market. Compensatory measures, especially those targeting caring, appear to be holding their ground well. Unusually, the compensatory measures appear to conform comfortably with both legal and political notions of equality, except where the measures are available to women only.

Social protection, pension age and life expectancy

The two aspects of social protection discussed here have a demographic link. The first concerns the setting of different pension ages for men and women. The second concerns assumptions about individual life expectancy based on statistical averages and the use of such factors to justify different benefit rates for men and women.

Where there is a difference between men's and women's pension ages, that of men has traditionally been set, seemingly without exception, at the higher level. Thus, in 1995, 15 OECD countries applied the same pension age for men and women and eight applied different pension ages. The situation in 1961 was roughly the same. In 1995, all but two of the 15 countries (France and New Zealand) operated equal pension ages of 65 or above. Of the EU states operating differential pension ages, six have implemented or propose implementing reform involving raising women's pension age to that of men. These six states are: Austria, Belgium, Germany, Greece, Portugal and the United Kingdom (Commission of the European Communities, 1998b, p. 24). In the case of the United Kingdom and Austria, the equalization process is to be phased in over a long period. Outside the EU, Australia, Hungary and Japan are said to be equalizing by raising women's pension age to that of men (OECD, 1998b, p. 53). Switzerland raised women's pension age from 62 to 64 in 1995 (men's pension age remained 65). Raising the pension age for women therefore seems to be becoming the norm in statutory schemes, a pattern which may be reproduced in occupational schemes, at least in the United Kingdom (Luckhaus and Moffat, 1996, pp. 72-78). It should be noted, however, that the reforms in individual countries can be complex in detail, as governments and employers attempt to combine equalization with the introduction of various forms of "flexible" retirement provision and with transitional measures intended to soften the financial blow for those who would otherwise suffer a concomitant reduction in entitlement. This is part of a wider scenario in which European governments are moving towards raising pension age and extending working life as ways of coping with rising pension costs and increased longevity.

As regards the compatibility of different pension ages with the legal notion of equality, such a difference is precluded, in principle at least, by the ban on direct forms of discrimination. For this reason, the different pension ages in occupational pension schemes were held to be unlawful by the European Court of Justice as from 17 May 1990.[55] However, differential pension ages in statutory schemes continue to be lawful by virtue of the provision exempting them under EU law (Art. 7(1)(a) of Directive 79/7). In relation to these statutory schemes, the Court has held further that once Member States take action to equalize pension ages (even though unequal ages are exempted) they cannot retain or introduce measures relevant to that scheme which treat men and women differently. In particular, they cannot retain a sex-specific provision, which involves calculating the amount of pension on a more generous basis for women than for men, as the Belgian Government attempted to do when it equalized pension ages at 60 in 1990.[56] In this respect, the Court was unimpressed with the argument that the more generous method of calculating pension amounts for women was a justifiable means of compensating the women for the disadvantages they encountered in the social insurance system because of their unpaid work activity.

In addition, the Court has held that it is permissible for employers to implement equality in occupational schemes by raising women's pension age to men's, even though this may worsen the women's financial position,[57] and that it is impermissible for employers and pension funds to introduce transitional measures to protect the women who suffer loss of rights because of the decision to implement equality by raising their pension age rather than reducing men's.[58] This nicely illustrates, once again, the point that the legal version of equality is not geared in any way to the social protection function of providing income security and avoiding poverty. So far as the political notions of equal treatment are concerned, the most significant one in the pension age context is the call for an end to the disadvantages for women arising from social protection's non-coverage of unpaid work. On one view, women's lower pension age is fully compatible with this notion of equal treatment, because it can be regarded as a way of compensating women for their past years of unpaid care work and of offsetting some of the disadvantages arising within the social protection system as a result of that activity. Thus the original lower pension age for women was justified in the German Constitutional Court[59] as a means of compensating women for their "double burden" and for the difficulties they encountered in fulfilling the insurance contribution period needed to obtain a pension. By the same token, equalizing pension ages by raising that applicable to women deprives them of this "reward".

It can be argued more pertinently that raising the pension age for women can bring both advantages and disadvantages in financial terms. For women in full-time, higher-paid, highly skilled jobs, the prospect of being able to work longer is likely both to be welcome as an end in itself and to facilitate acquisition of pension rights and, ultimately, higher pension benefits. For women in more precarious forms of employment, however, a higher pension age is likely to mean an exacerbation of the income insecurity they already encounter in employment — and indeed, in the social protection system, through its incorporation of the insecurities attached to precarious forms of employment.

The other demographic aspect concerns the different benefit rules applied on the basis of an assessment of the differential risk to which men and women are said to be exposed. The attribute currently receiving the greatest attention is women's propensity to live longer than men. The result of this differential risk assessment is that the same pension cover may cost more for women than for men, or women may receive a lower benefit for the same level of contributions. For technical reasons, some intermediary pension benefits may be larger for women than for men. At the end of the day, however, women's level of pension tends to be lower than men's once actuarial factors linked to differences in longevity are taken into account.[60] The alternative is for pension schemes to ignore these statistical averages and to calculate pension amounts on a "unisex" basis. Men and women in the same situation would then receive the same pension.

A full picture of the extent to which sex-based actuarial factors are used in various types of schemes is not yet available. However, some information is available on pensions and it is clear that occupational rather than statutory schemes are the ones affected. A survey of occupational schemes carried out in the United Kingdom in 1991 showed that sex-specific factors were used in various ways by many of the schemes, although a considerable number of them adopted a unisex approach.[61] In Denmark, in 1996 just under one half of 1.3 million employees were in defined contribution schemes using actuarial factors based on sex. The remainder of the employees were in unisex schemes (Commission of the European Communities, 1997, p. 53). The unisex approach is believed to be widely adopted in insurance and pension schemes in the United States; see, for example, Equal Opportunities Commission (1998), p. 29. When proposals for the new Hungarian mandatory social security system and associated private pension scheme were being discussed in that country, the possibility of incorporating sex-based actuarial factors into the private pension scheme was discussed and rejected. The scheme enacted in 1997 thus requires that when calculating benefits in the private scheme, the mortality rate of both men and women shall be determined according to a *unified* mortality table.[62]

The issue of sex-based actuarial factors gives rise to tricky conceptual and practical problems in the light of the practices adopted by many insurance companies and pension funds and the political weight these interests can bring to bear on EU institutions. Asked to rule on the issue, the European Court of Justice concluded that actuarial factors based on different assumptions about men's and women's longevity do not generally fall within the scope of EU equality law.[63] The Advocate General, advising the European Court of Justice prior to its decision, came to a contrary view. Discrimination exists for him when men and women are treated not as individuals but as a *group*, and unequal treatment for *individual* men and women arises as a result. Thus the treatment of individual women on the basis of assumptions about their life expectancy derived from statistics concerning women as a group was a clear case of direct discrimination. The Advocate General's reasoning here nicely evokes the integrity of the individual and the undesirability of stereotypes which underpin the notion of equality as usually (but not ultimately in this case) applied by the Court.

In so far as sex-based actuarial factors do not, at present, contravene the legal notion of equality as it relates to social protection, the same would seem to apply as regards compatibility of these factors with the political notions of equality. Clearly, however, if women have to pay more to acquire the same pension benefits as men, this is going to compound the disadvantages they already suffer within the social protection system on account of their peripheral labour market activity and engagement in unpaid work.

CONCLUSION

Women's dependency on men during periods of unpaid work activity and their peripheral connection with the labour market give rise to income insecurities which then tend to be incorporated into and reproduced by social protection systems. The extension of this dependency, the increase in social protection's bias towards already privileged forms of employment signalled by lengthening minimum contribution periods (an increase mitigated only slightly by a relaxation in some earnings and hours thresholds and some extension of caring credits), and the failure to resolve the pension age and longevity issues in a way likely to increase rather than diminish women's access to social protection in old age reinforce the tendency of social protection systems to reproduce wider income inequalities affecting women.

What then of equal treatment? Can its implementation eliminate or alleviate the generally insecure nature of social protection as an income source for women? Certainly, one can conclude that the legal notion of equality is exceedingly ill equipped in this respect. It has had some financially beneficial effects: enabling women to obtain the same rate of unemployment benefit as men is one example; enabling them to gain access to benefits from which they were previously excluded on sex and marital grounds is another. But these effects are fortuitous in that they depend on the vagaries of interpretation and on the willingness of Member States to implement equality by extending provision rather than by reducing or eliminating it.[64] To be an effective mechanism to combat the income insecurity encountered by women in social protection systems, the legal notion of equality must address the problem of poverty and be concerned with unpaid and peripheral workers as well as those employed in full-time, higher-paid, continuous forms of work. Instead, as it has developed at EU and Member State levels, equal treatment has been fairly effective in its limited aims of preventing the stereotyping of individuals (especially married women), and of helping ensure that social protection law bears some relation to social and economic practices, in particular the increasing participation of married women in the labour market. Its failure to address wider substantive issues, such as poverty and unpaid work, however, ensures that it is also fairly effective at maintaining the status quo.

Four political notions of equal treatment were addressed in the context of income security for women. Two concern financial incentives and disincentives to women working. The equal treatment ideal of using social protection as a financial incentive to women to work is conducive to improving women's position within social protection since the logic of the incentives argument points to an extension and expansion of social protection for women. The re-emergence in Spain of this notion of equal treatment dating from the 1960s-70s — adapted to the modern world of part-time work — is interesting. The more recent interpretation of equal treatment as supporting the removal of financial *dis*incentives to women working appears principally concerned to delimit women's reliance on social protection systems, particularly the means-tested ones, and to urge them into the labour market irrespective of the type of work available to them there. This is the risk — one also carrying with it the risk of perpetuating the pattern of income insecurity presently the lot of many women inside and outside the social protection system.

The financial disincentives variant of equal treatment may well be the dominant political form it assumes in the future. In the mean time, the two notions struggling for hegemony outside the legal sphere are that of remedying women's disadvantage in social protection arising from their unpaid work and that of financial independence of one partner from the other. The first, especially, has women's financial insecurity as a central concern. The second has the removal of dependency on a partner as its central concern partly because this often proves a fragile source of income but also because of the risk, inherent in all forms of dependency, of one partner in the relationship being subjected to the arbitrary will of the other.[65] If social protection provisions can be taken to be a measure of the strength of popular and official support for these principles, the continuing spread of dependency-related provisions like survivor's benefit and the comparatively healthy state of measures such as caring credits, designed to end the disadvantages encountered by women because of their unpaid work, suggest that there is slightly more support for ending those disadvantages than for ensuring financial independence for women. However, a realistic rather than an optimistic appraisal of the situation suggests that neither principle has sufficient official support and popular acceptance to overturn the status quo.

The stalemate in the practical sphere is replicated in debates in the theoretical sphere. Proponents of one principle appear to have concluded that advancement of their principle necessarily involves erosion of the other. For example, it is argued that financial independence for women requires the individualization of entitlement. This in turn means abolishing dependency-related provisions, such as survivor's benefit and pension sharing, which currently operate so as to offset some of the financial disadvantages women suffer because of the poor or non-existent coverage of unpaid work in social protection systems. Within this framework, women's financial independence — their autonomy from men — is pitted against their continuing income insecurity — their poverty. The result is theoretical stalemate. There are, however, a number of ways out of this impasse. One is to challenge the assumption that dependency-related provisions are effective in offsetting the poverty which women would otherwise suffer because of social protection's poor coverage of unpaid work. The references in this article to the ways in which and reasons for which a sexual relationship is a fragile source of income for unpaid workers are intended to do precisely this.

Another way is to acknowledge, first, that dependency-related provisions are not the only way of offsetting the disadvantages encountered by women in the social protection system arising from their unpaid work and, second, that they may not be the most effective and efficient way of doing so. Arguably, caring credits, caring allowances and other measures targeted on the unpaid work activity of the non-employed and of those engaged in peripheral forms of employment provide a more effective and efficient way of tackling these disadvantages. As demonstrated, though still in embryonic form, measures of this kind are already a feature of some social protection systems. They may easily be combined with individualization of entitlement. Moreover, so long as they are available to both men and women, they can lay claim to being compatible with all the notions of equal treatment discussed in this paper. There is therefore a way out of the theoretical stalemate between women's financial independence and their poverty — if the political will to jettison dependency is there.

Individualization coupled with caring credits and other measures targeted on unpaid work within social protection systems provide a starting point for advancing the position of women currently caught in the web of income insecurities caused, ultimately, by their unpaid work. But it is limited and does not profess to provide a solution to the income insecurities experienced by groups such as the non-employed, part-time workers and the low-paid, which are not linked to unpaid work activity. Solutions to these problems are to be found elsewhere and little is to be gained from rejecting individualization, caring credits and other such measures on the grounds that they create inequities between different groups of paid and unpaid workers, all of whom risk sharing the same impoverished state.

Even for unpaid workers, individualization and measures such as caring credits (all of which can be implemented in an incremental, low-cost, way) need to be part of a wider strategy developed in response to the question of how best to provide for caring needs. A strategy focused on producing flexible working hours (without diminution of employ-ment conditions and social protection), on developing and expanding the range of different kinds of caring services of a formal and informal kind, and on providing a similarly wide-ranging and innovative system of financial payments for men and women carers both inside and outside the social protection system may go some way towards providing a satis-factory answer.[66] Only then will it be possible to say that sex and gender equality in the social protection field has been achieved.

Notes

[1] Here defined as social insurance, social assistance and private schemes, the premia for which are not wholly market determined.

[2] Social protection systems may also reinforce non-financial aspects of gender and em-ployment relations by, for example, facilitating the recruitment, retention and disciplining of labour. Additional functions of social protection include: encouraging social cohesion and stabil-ity and the avoidance of public disorder; promoting growth of capital markets and financial services; facilitating economic growth (through expansion of demand or, alternatively, by en-couraging saving).

[3] The term "gender" is seldom, if ever, used in national and international instruments prescribing equality, equal treatment or non-discrimination between men and women. The term normally used in this legal context is "sex" and this applies especially to instruments adopted by the European Community (hereinafter the EU) which are the main legal focus of this chapter. Claims to equality under the relevant EU legislation must be made in terms of sex rather than gender and this, rather than any insistence on "biological differences" accounts for use of the term alongside gender which, for all other purposes in this chapter, is the more appropriate term.

[4] A developing country and transition economy perspective would require the list to incor-porate wider "family" relationships, national and international aid organizations, and employment relationships in the informal economy.

[5] Although there are care allowances, short-term maternity and parental leave which enable paid and unpaid leave to be taken for care purposes.

[6] In relation to northern European and north American schemes, but not in relation to southern European schemes. For a contribution filling the latter gap, see Addis (1999).

[7] These circumstances include participation in the New Deal for Single Parents training scheme, a place on which, in practice if not in accordance with regulations, is immediately lost (along with benefit) if a single parent is held to be cohabiting.

[8] In the EU, 83 per cent of part-time workers are women (Commission of the European Communities, 1998a, p. 15).

[9] In 15 countries in the early 1990s, the proportion of women in low-paid employment was consistently higher than the proportion of men and in some countries considerably so. For

example, Japan 37.2 per cent women, 5.9 per cent men; the United Kingdom 31.2 per cent women, 12.8 per cent men; Switzerland 30.4 per cent women, 6.8 per cent men; and Germany 25.4 per cent women, 7.6 per cent men (OECD, 1996, table 3.2, p. 72).

[10] On the economic inactivity and part-time work rates of women and men with children under 17 years, see Commission of the European Communities (1998a), pp. 4-5.

[11] The International Covenant on Economic, Social and Cultural Rights, and the European Social Charter are partial exceptions here. The International Convention on the Elimination of all Discrimination against Women is another partial exception since it specifically mentions discrimination against women. Other more general human rights instruments are the Charter of the United Nations, the Universal Declaration of Human Rights and the International Covenant on Civil and Political Rights. To complete the picture, regional-based instruments such as the African Charter on Human and Peoples' Rights and employment-based instruments such as ILO Convention No. 156 on the reconciliation of employment and family responsibilities should also be mentioned.

[12] Council Directive 79/7/EEC on equal treatment for men and women in statutory social security schemes (hereinafter referred to as Directive 79/7); Council Directive 86/378/EEC as amended by Council Directive 96/97/EEC on equal treatment of men and women in occupational social security schemes. Despite the existence of the latter Directive, following the *Barber* case (*Barber v Guardian Royal Exchange Assurance Group* (Case C-262/88) [1990] ECR I-1889), Art. 119 of the EC Treaty (now renumbered Art. 141 by the Treaty of Amsterdam) prescribing equal pay for men and women is the principal provision governing occupational benefits, including occupational pensions.

[13] It should be noted that this EU-derived legal formulation does not necessarily accord with interpretations under other international and constitutional instruments.

[14] "...women are entitled to be treated in the same manner, and to have the same rules applied to them, as men who are in the same situation..." *Borrie Clarke v Chief Adjudication Officer* (Case 384/85) [1987] ECR 2865.

[15] Directive 79/7 applies to the "working population", thereby seeming to exclude unpaid workers and the non-employed from the scope of the equal treatment principle embodied in it. It applies to statutory schemes covering specified risks — such as unemployment, old age, sickness — traditionally associated with paid employment; caring is not included. These provisions covering the personal and material scope of Directive 79/7 would seem to imply limitation of the Directive and the equal treatment principle to paid work.

[16] The EU equality instruments do not assist a great deal. Directive 79/7 merely states the purpose of the Directive to be "the progressive implementation of equal treatment between men and women in matters of social security".

[17] See, for example, the Advocate General's opinion in *Coloroll Pension Trustees Limited v Russell and Others* (Case C-200/91) [1994] ECR I-4389.

[18] See, for example, the Advocate General's opinion in *Caisse d'assurances sociales pour travailleurs indépendants 'Integrity' v Nadine Rouvroy* (Case C-373/89) [1990] ECR I-4243.

[19] In its 1986 judgment in *Drake v Chief Adjudication Officer* ((Case 150/85) [1986] ECR 1995), the European Court of Justice by some clever reasoning managed to bring a benefit for caring within the material scope of Directive 79/7, so enabling the exclusion of married women from that benefit to be held unlawful; see Luckhaus (1986).

[20] In spring 1999, some 17.2 per cent (3.2m) of all working-age households had nobody in work (Cooper-Green, 2000, p. 28).

[21] See OECD (1998a), p. 21. It should be noted that much of the increase is attributable to a growth in households consisting of a single jobless adult, but statistics also show the share of households consisting of two or more jobless adults to be either static or increasing slightly in some countries. The report also makes specific mention of the particular situation of women in the latter type of household.

[22] The OECD report on employment illustrates how this can be achieved indirectly, by explaining the preponderance of what it calls "work-poor" households in terms of "the disincentive effects arising from the interactions of the tax and benefit systems"; see OECD (1998a), p. 21.

[23] *Ten Oever v Stichting Bedrijfspensioenfonds voor het Glassenwassers-en Schoonmaak-bedrijf* (Case C-109/91) [1993] ECR I-4879. The French AGIRC and ARRCO occupational schemes introduced survivor's benefits in 1994 and 1996 respectively. For trends in occupational schemes in the United Kingdom, see Luckhaus and Moffat (1996), pp. 78-79.

[24] Men and women aged 55 or over when the legislation comes into force and who are widowed in the subsequent five years will be able to claim income support when their bereavement allowance expires without being available for work. They will also receive an additional amount of income support bringing that payment up to the level of the bereavement allowance. This transitional provision will ensure that widows do not lose out financially with the introduction of the bereavement allowance, but this protection is not afforded to those under 55 when the legislation comes into force and who are subsequently widowed.

[25] Art. 3(2) of Directive 79/7. The United Kingdom's decision to reform widow's benefit was prompted in part by legal proceedings begun in 1997 in *Willis v UK* (application No. 36042/97 to the European Commission on Human Rights). The absence of widower's benefit was challenged as contrary to the ban on sex discrimination in the European Convention on Human Rights, there being no exemption of survivor's benefit in this instrument, as there is in Directive 79/7.

[26] Art. 3(2) of Directive 79/7. All exemptions under Directive 79/7 are due to be abolished as a result of the "progressive implementation of the principle of equal treatment". A proposal for a draft directive aimed at completing equal treatment in statutory schemes was introduced in 1987 (COM(87) 494). This proposal suggested exemptions should be abolished by individualizing entitlement in preference to extending dependency-related provisions to men. The proposal was amended heavily in negotiations, and was finally shelved.

[27] In the 1970s' cases on equal pay under Art. 119 of the EC Treaty (renumbered Art. 141 by the Treaty of Amsterdam). The idea that women would take an equal pay claim to secure reduction of men's pay to theirs did not appear to be within the contemplation of the European Court of Justice nor, arguably, of anyone else.

[28] *Teuling v Bedrijfsvereniging voor de Chemische Industrie* (Case 30/85) [1987] ECR 2497.

[29] Women were to have the same rules applied to them as men in the same situation since, where the Directive has not been implemented, those rules remain the only valid point of reference: see *Borrie Clarke v Chief Adjudication Officer* (Case 384/85) [1987] ECR 2865.

[30] *Queen v Secretary of State for Health ex parte Richardson* (Case C-137/94) [1995] ECR I-3407 in respect of statutory schemes and *Smith and Others v Avdel Systems Limited* (Case C-408/92) [1994] ECR I-4435 in respect of occupational schemes.

[31] This point is discussed later in relation to social assistance schemes. It has also been suggested that widow's benefit itself provides a disincentive to work since it enables a woman not to have to take paid work if her husband dies.

[32] First introduced in 1934, the *assegni familiari* have had an uneven history, but since 1994 have been favourably regarded and expanded in scope by successive Italian administrations; see Addis (1999).

[33] Called disability working allowance and now replaced by a very similarly structured benefit called a disability tax credit.

[34] *Commission v Belgium* (Case C-229/89) [1991] ECR I-2205; *Moelenbroek v Bestuur van de Sociale Verzekeringsbank* (Case C-226/91) [1992] ECR I-5943. These rulings have the

effect of taking poverty-related benefits outside the scope of Directive 79/7 and the equal treatment principle, a point specifically decided by the Court in relation to the United Kingdom's income support in *Jackson and Cresswell v Chief Adjudication Officer* (Case C-63-64/91)[1992] ECR I-4737.

[35] This is because, in their turn, the women's earnings are deducted from the benefit that would otherwise have been awarded. Whether or not people make employment decisions exclusively on monetary terms is a moot point, not least because women might decide to take employment in order to gain direct access to the money. If one accepts the logic of the disincentives argument, it can only operate in relation to work which is low paid. Women (or men) motivated solely by money are not going to give up the financial rewards of highly paid work for the relatively low levels of income granted to their partners under social assistance schemes.

[36] O'Neil and Ciffin, 1978, pp. 64-77. For details of pension sharing in some EU Member State schemes, see Luckhaus (1994), pp. 147-161. Under the US social security system, a divorced woman is entitled to benefits equal to 50 per cent of her former spouse's benefits provided the marriage lasted ten years; see Shirley and Spiegler (1998).

[37] Although it will undoubtedly benefit more women than men and, by the same token, adversely affect more men than women, it would presumably be held to be objectively justifiable.

[38] In the United Kingdom case of *Grant v South-West Trains Ltd* (Case C-249/96) [1998] 1 CMLR 993, the applicant employee challenged the failure by her employer to grant her female partner travel concessions granted to married or cohabiting heterosexual partners of employees, as a violation of the equal pay principle under Art. 119 of the EC Treaty (renumbered Art. 141 by the Treaty of Amsterdam). The European Court of Justice ruled against this being an instance of sex discrimination but pointed favourably to the new Art. 13 of the EC Treaty (as renumbered by the Treaty of Amsterdam) enabling the EU Council to adopt measures to eliminate discrimination on the grounds of sexual orientation. The implications of (ultimately) requiring the same treatment of homosexual and heterosexual couples in relation to dependency in social protection systems could be far reaching. It seems Belgium already takes into account the income of a homosexual partner for the purposes of assessing entitlement to means-tested supplements: see Royal Decree of 4 August 1996 (Commission of the European Communities, 1997, p. 47). This extension of dependency leads to savings in expenditure on social protection and a loss to the individual who might be deprived of benefit because their partner's earnings are taken into account in assessing that individual's entitlement and to the couple (the couple rate being less than two individual rates). Extending survivor's benefits to homosexual partners and permitting pension sharing on "divorce" (to name just two of the possibilities) would, however, increase expenditure in occupational as well as statutory schemes, a reason perhaps why there may be some reluctance to extend dependency in this sphere.

[39] See Luckhaus and Ward (1997), pp. 237-253, for a detailed analysis of rules in statutory and occupational schemes and of how they interact with different forms of employment in EU Member States.

[40] Discussion of their incidence in occupational schemes is hampered by lack of data. Some information concerning hours thresholds in the United Kingdom is to be found in Luckhaus and Moffat (1996), pp. 81-85. Cases concerning hours thresholds in Germany and the Netherlands continue to be referred to the European Court of Justice, which suggests that such thresholds still operate in occupational schemes in those countries.

[41] OECD, 1998a, pp. 170-172. The report referred to the three benefits — public health, old age and unemployment — said to be the most likely to operate thresholds.

[42] In addition the reform was aimed at avoiding the creation of jobs with pay set at just below the minimum earnings threshold (Germany, 1999). This was thought to have been encouraged by the absence of a requirement on employers and employees to pay contributions on employment below the minimum earnings threshold, a 20-per-cent tax being levied on employers

in respect of this employment instead. The 20-per-cent tax has been abolished now that employers are obliged to pay contributions on employment below the 630 DM threshold.

[43] It should be noted that social protection was excluded from the scope of EU legislation (Directive 97/81) providing for an end to discrimination against part-time workers.

[44] Kuhnle, 1999, p. 17. In 1994, 8.7 per cent of women, compared with 3.3 per cent of men were in low-paid employment in Finland (OECD, 1996, table 3.2, p. 72). This difference between men and women might not be sufficient to establish disproportionate adverse effect for the purposes of an indirect discrimination claim under EU law.

[45] The two-fold aim being (according to the new Labour Government's 1998 Green Paper on welfare): "to increase the incentives for employers to take on staff and to make work pay for all employees" (United Kingdom, 1998b, para. 31, p. 30). The first step in this process was the raising of the limit for payment of employers' contributions to the tax threshold, with effect from April 1999. The second step is the raising of employees' contributions over two stages, so that by April 2001 the level of earnings at which contributions must be paid will be fully aligned with the tax threshold.

[46] Of the 2.6 million, 2 million are women and 0.6 million are men; 70 per cent of the men are under 25 (McKnight, Elias and Wilson, 1998, p. vi). It should be noted that the United Kingdom Government has taken steps to try to prevent an increase in the numbers already excluded by the lower earnings limit by providing that people earning above this limit but below the new (tax) threshold will continue to qualify for contributory benefits by assuming "notional payments".

[47] In Sweden, prior to reform the amount of pension was calculated on earnings in the best 15 years and after reform on average earnings over the entire working life. The "best" earnings formula enables years of no or low-paid work to be excluded from the pension calculation and in this way to benefit intermittent and low-paid workers. Italy has modified its pension formula from last five and last one year (private and public sector workers, respectively) to an average of the entire working life. Other European states using the final salary or best earnings formula are also moving in this direction.

[48] *Vroege v NCIV Instituut voor Volkshuisvesting BV and Pensioensfonds NCIV* (Case C-57/93) [1994] ECR I-4541.

[49] The assumption being that employers are less likely to create jobs of this kind if they have to pay contributions in respect of them: *Nolte v Landesversicherungsanstalt Hannover* (Case C-317/93) [1995] ECR I-4625; *Megner v Innungskrankenkasse Rheinhessen-Pfalz* (Case C-444/93) [1995] ECR I-4740.

[50] The discriminatory status of the United Kingdom's low earnings threshold was challenged indirectly and unsuccessfully in legal proceedings before the Employment Appeal Tribunal in *Banks v Tesco Stores Ltd and Secretary of State for Social Security*, Judgment 15 Sept. 1999.

[51] Credits are also granted with the benefits for caring, such as the German long-term care insurance and the United Kingdom's invalid care allowance. For further details of these credits in the EU, see Luckhaus and Ward (1997), pp. 249-250.

[52] Directive 92/85 on the safety and health of pregnant or breastfeeding workers.

[53] *Boyle v Equal Opportunities Commission* (Case C-411/96) [1998] All E.R. (EC) 879. The particular point was decided by the European Court of Justice under Council Directive 92/85/EEC concerning the safety and health of pregnant workers, rather than under EU legislation making specific reference to equality.

[54] See, for example, the European Court's ruling in *Van Cant v Rijksdienst voor Pensionen* (Case C-154/92) [1993] I-3811 (footnote 56 below). The construction of equality by Constitutional Courts in this context is also of interest. The Austrian Constitutional Court has declared illegal legislation restricting to women the entitlement to an allowance for part-time working up to

the time a child reaches 18 months (*Equality Quarterly News*, 1998, p. 28). But see the German Federal Constitutional Court's decision (footnote 59 below) which viewed provisions exclusively for women as justified by past unpaid work activity and hence non-discriminatory.

[55] The date of the European Court of Justice's judgment in *Barber v Guardian Royal Exchange Assurance Group* (Case C-262/88) [1990] ECR I-1889, when it was finally and conclusively settled that occupational pensions constituted pay under Art. 119 of the EC Treaty (renumbered Art. 141 by the Treaty of Amsterdam), and that different pension ages breached the equality principle in that article.

[56] *Van Cant v Rijksdienst voor Pensionen* (Case C-154/92) [1993] I-3811. The Belgian Government has since reinstated the previous pension age of 65 for men and provided for the increase in women's pension age from 60 to 65 to be phased in over a 13-year period. The flexible retirement provisions have been retained and women's pensions are still calculated on a more generous basis than men's. The Court has held in *De Vriendt and Others v Rijksdienst voor Pensioenen and Others* (C-377/96 to C-384/96) [1998] ECR I-2105 that the retention of different methods of calculating the amount of pension is permissible under Directive 79/7 while different pension ages for men and women are maintained.

[57] *Smith and Others v Avdel Systems Limited* (Case C-408/92) [1994] ECR I-4435.

[58] *Van den Akker and Others v Stichting Shell Pensioenfonds* (Case C-28/93) [1994] ECR I-4527.

[59] Ruling of the Federal Constitutional Court of 28 Jan. 1987 concerning Article 3(2) GG and s.25(3) Employees' Insurance Act and s.1248(3) Reich Insurance Act.

[60] In a defined contribution scheme, contributions produce a lump sum on retirement which is then used to buy an annuity, the arrangement underpinning subsequent periodic pension payments made until death. The same lump sum will buy a higher pension for a man than for a woman because in her case the lump sum has to be spread over a longer period. The intermediary benefit which has to be larger is the transfer value. This is the amount paid by one scheme to another when a person changes employment and pension schemes. It is based on the expected cost of buying a deferred annuity equal to the pension to be paid. So the transfer value for a woman, taking the same benefits, will be larger at the same age than for a man. See Ward (1994), pp. 108-109.

[61] Confederation of British Industry and William M. Mercer Fraser Ltd., 1991, p. 14. See also Luckhaus and Moffat (1996), pp. 80-81.

[62] Act LXXXII of 1997 on Private Pension and on Private Pension Funds, Article 31(2). Unofficial translation of the legislation.

[63] More precisely Art. 119 of the EC Treaty (renumbered Art. 141 by the Treaty of Amsterdam). The Court held, in relation to defined benefit schemes, that these matters were part of the funding arrangements not the employer's promise to pay a pension, the latter being a matter of pay under Art. 119, the former not: *Neath v Hugh Steeper Ltd* (Case C-152/91) [1993] ECR I-6935, *Moroni v Firma Collo GmbH* (Case C-110/91) [1993] ECR I-6591. The legality of using sex-based factors in defined benefit schemes only is reaffirmed by Art. 6 of Council Directive 86/378/EEC as amended by Council Directive 96/97/EEC.

[64] Experience in the United Kingdom (in relation to invalid care allowance and the European Court's judgment in *Drake v Chief Adjudication Officer* ((Case 150/85) [1986] ECR 1995) suggests that popular mobilization in support of an extension of benefit is essential in order to prevent a successful equal treatment claim leading to a reduction in provision.

[65] For a discussion of the controversial propositions made here, see Luckhaus (1994), pp. 147-161.

[66] The European Commission, away from the distraction of mainstreaming, is developing an interesting multidimensional approach of this kind; see Commission of the European Communities (1998a).

References

Addis, E. 1999. "Gender in the reform of the Italian welfare state", in *South European Society and Politics* (London), Vol. 4, No. 2 (Autumn), pp. 122-149.

Bonoli, G. 1997. "Switzerland: Institutions, reforms and the politics of consensual retrenchment", in Clasen, pp. 107-129.

CBI (Confederation of British Industry) and William M. Mercer Fraser Ltd. 1991. *Pensions post-Barber: Equalising occupational pension schemes.* London , Oct.

Clasen, J. (ed.). 1997. *Social insurance in Europe.* Bristol, The Polity Press.

Commission of the European Communities. 1998a. *Reconciliation between work and family life in Europe.* CE-V/2-98-008-EN-C. Brussels.

—. 1998b. *Social protection in Europe 1997.* DGV/E.2 (Apr. 1998). Luxembourg, Apr.

—. 1997. *Monitoring implementation and application of Community equality law 1996.* CE-V/2-98-007-EN-C. Brussels, July.

Cooper-Green, Emma-Jane. 2000. "Labour Force Survey household data: Spring 1999 analyses", in *Labour Market Trends* (London), Vol. 108, No. 1 (Jan.), pp. 25-34.

Duncan, Alan; Giles, C.; Webb, S. 1994. *Social security reform and women's independent incomes.* Equal Opportunities Research Discussion Series No. 6. Manchester, Equal Opportunities Commission.

Eardley, Tony; Bradshaw, Jonathan; Ditch, John; Gough, Ian; Whiteford, Peter. 1996. *Social assistance in OECD countries.* Vol. 1: *Synthesis report.* Research Report No. 46. Department of Social Security. London, HMSO.

Equal Opportunities Commission. 1998. *Equality in the 21st century: A new sex equality law.* Manchester.

Equality Quarterly News (Brussels). 1998. "Constitutional Court has withdrawn part-time allowances for self-employed mothers", in Spring issue, p. 28. Since the beginning of 1999, available in electronic form only, on http://europe.eu.int/comm/dg05/equ_opp/index_en.htm [visited 12 Apr. 2000].

European Industrial Relations Review (London). 1999. "Part-time work agreement signed", in Issue 300, Jan., pp. 30-31.

Germany, Government of. 1999. "Gesetzentwurf zur Neuregelung der geringfügigen Beschäftigung eingebracht". Press release on website http://www.bma.de/de/asp/aktuell/presse.asp?id+968 [visited 7 Apr. 2000]. Ministry of Labour and Social Affairs. Bonn, 22 Jan.

Hoskyns, C.; Luckhaus, Linda. 1989. "The European Community Directive on Equal Treatment in Social Security", in *Policy and Politics* (London), Vol. 17, No. 4, pp. 321-335.

ILO/EASMAT. 1997. *Ageing in Asia: The growing need for social protection.* Bangkok.

Kuhnle, S. 1999. *The Scandinavian model: Trends and perspectives.* European Forum Seminar Paper WS/23. Florence, European University Institute.

Luckhaus, Linda. 1994. "Individualisation of social security benefits", in McCrudden (1994), pp. 147-161.

—. 1986. "Payment for caring: A European solution?", in *Public Law* (London), Winter, pp. 526-537.

—; Moffat, G. 1996. *Serving the market and people's needs? The impact of European Union law on pensions in the UK.* York, York Publishing.

—; Ward, Sue. 1997. "Equal pension rights for men and women: A realistic perspective", in *Journal of European Social Policy* (Bath, UK), Vol. 7, No. 3 (Aug.), pp. 237-253.

McCrudden, C. (ed.). 1994. *Equality of treatment between men and women in social security.* London, Butterworths.

McKnight, A.; Elias, P.; Wilson, R. 1998. *Low pay and the National Insurance System: A statistical picture.* Equal Opportunities Research Discussion Series. Manchester, Equal Opportunities Commission.

OECD. 1998a. *Employment Outlook.* Paris, June.

—. 1998b. *Maintaining prosperity in an ageing society.* Paris.

—. 1996. *Employment Outlook.* Paris, July.

Olsen, Darcy Ann. 1999. "Social security and women", testimony of Darcy Ann Olsen, Entitlements Policy Analyst, Cato Institute, before United States House of Representatives Committee on the Budget. 4 May 1999. http://socialsecurity.org/dailys/05-04-99.html [visited 31 Mar. 2000].

O'Neil, Maureen; Ciffin, Shirley. 1978. "Social security and divorce in Canada", in *Social security provisions in case of divorce.* Studies and Research No. 11. Geneva, International Social Security Association, pp. 64-77.

Pierson, P. 1999. *The comparative political economy of pension reform.* European Forum Seminar Paper. Florence, European University Institute, 24 Feb.

Shirley, Ekaterina; Spiegler, Peter. 1998. *The benefits of social security privatization for women.* SSP No. 12. The Cato Project on Social Security Privatization. 20 July. http://socialsecurity.org/pubs/ssps/ssp12es.html [visited 21 Dec. 1999].

Solcher, Hans. 1978. "Sharing of pension rights in the event of divorce under German law", in *International Social Security Review* (Geneva), Vol. 31, No. 3, pp. 308-317.

South African Law Commission. 1999. *Sharing of pension benefits: Report.* Project 112. http://www.law.wits.ac.za/salc/salc.html [visited 7 Apr. 2000]. Pretoria, June.

—. 1998. *Sharing of pension benefits.* Discussion Paper 77. Project 112. http://www.law.wits.ac.za/salc/salc.html [visited 7 Apr. 2000]. Pretoria.

United Kingdom, Government of the. 1999. "Government announces consultation on draft pension sharing regulations". Press Release 99/316. Department of Social Security. London, 15 Nov.

—. 1998a. *A new contract for welfare support in bereavement.* Department of Social Security. Command No. 4104. London, HMSO.

—. 1998b. *A new contract for welfare.* Green Paper. Command No. 3805. London, HMSO, Mar.

Ward, Sue. 1994. "Equality of treatment between women and men in occupational social security", in McCrudden (1994), pp. 99-113.

PART V

THE ROLE OF LAW:
WHERE HAVE WE GOTTEN?

AFFIRMATIVE ACTION IN EMPLOYMENT: RECENT COURT APPROACHES TO A DIFFICULT CONCEPT

21

Jane HODGES AEBERHARD*

Ever since its introduction, affirmative action to combat discrimination based on race or sex has attracted controversy over its validity, allegedly unfair, perverse or stigmatizing effects, and over whether the available evidence is conclusive. Major decisions taken in the late 1990s in the United States, South Africa and by the European Court of Justice are examined — decisions in which the courts, faced with similar factual situations, reached different conclusions. Explanations for these differences are suggested and a case made for more rigorous reasoning by lower jurisdictions and new international standards that might enable courts to reach just and realistic decisions.

Affirmative action is an extension of the notion of equality of opportunity and non-discrimination. It aims to overcome the effects of past discrimination by enabling the person or group discriminated against either to compete on level terms with the favoured group or, more controversially, to achieve equality outright ("equal results"). Special measures with this aim, whether they are called affirmative action, positive action, employment equity, workplace diversity, maximalization or inclusion,[1] are not a new idea: they were first introduced in the United States[2] in the 1930s to make up for past unfair labour practices against union organizers and members and later used to assist war veterans' reinsertion in the labour market. Other groups, too, have long benefited from special programmes in employment linked to their special needs, such as persons with disabilities.[3] The use of this form of labour market intervention, however, aroused controversy from the moment it was applied to two particular areas of discrimination, namely race and sex.

Originally published in *International Labour Review*, Vol. 138 (1999), No. 3.

* Senior Specialist in International Labour Standards and Labour Law, ILO Southern African Multidisciplinary Advisory Team, Harare, Zimbabwe.

Critics of affirmative action — leaving aside those who play the semantic game of calling it a form of "reverse" or "negative" discrimination — claim that the concept has several fatal flaws and that it should be removed from the toolbox of possible instruments for use in adjusting imbalances in the labour market. It is variously argued that non-discrimination is such an absolute concept that it can brook no exemption; that such measures start out as temporary and narrowly tailored to the goal to be achieved but end up permanent and broad; that within the favoured group the benefits of the measure go disproportionately to those already at the top of the group in employment status; that in any case there is very little in the way of data on the real successes or achievements of affirmative action; that such measures create distortions and inefficiencies in labour markets; that the measures are usually poorly planned and permit cheating on the results; and — in relation to race-based programmes in particular — that colour-conscious policies are polarizing and fuel resentment and violence.[4] There are also politically motivated critics who claim that affirmative action implies equal results, which make it anathema in certain laissez-faire cultures.

Those in favour of affirmative action argue back that labour market policies should be realistic and admit that since society is not colour-blind or non-sexist some proactive policies are essential; that, while the planning might not always be perfect, any measure is better than inaction; that data gathering is improving and that cheating, in any system, can be controlled by better monitoring and stronger penalties; that such programmes have in fact provided too little rather than too much assistance; and that, apart from the societal advantage of better utilization of the full workforce, there are proven economic advantages.[5]

Behind this debate lies a subtler contradiction. Affirmative action allows disadvantaged groups the chance to get experience and prove themselves, but at the same time it perpetuates the perception that they intrinsically lack the characteristics for success in employment and will always need special assistance.

Despite this four-decade-old controversy, governments continue to legislate for affirmative action in employment to favour designated groups (most commonly those described as suffering the effects of past discrimination on the basis of their race, colour, sex or disability). Witness the adoption by South Africa and Namibia, near the end of 1998, of legislation requiring employment equity through means including affirmative action (the Employment Equity Act, No. 55 of 1998 in South Africa and the Affirmative Action (Employment) Act, No. 29 of 1998 in Namibia).[6] In some countries the concept is well accepted in the fight against sex discrimination, but women are not the only beneficiaries: Norway's Ordinance No. 622 on the special treatment of men, adopted on 17 July 1998, provides for action to favour men in occupations where they are under-represented — such as education and childcare — through training and job opportunities, together with procedural rules for enforcement. There are over 20 countries that have specific laws mandating affirmative action for employment on the basis of race, sex or disability, and many others that permit it. Yet court challenges to the measures have been restricted to a small number of jurisdictions. To see how they have grappled with this difficult concept is the aim of this chapter.

The late 1990s saw several major court decisions on the subject of affirmative action, variously reflecting hostility, lukewarm acceptance and full endorsement. They were handed down in different jurisdictions across the world, and at different levels, but all throw light on the academic and public debate on the usefulness of special measures to overcome past (and continuing) discrimination. This chapter selects decisions from three different jurisdictions — the United States, South Africa and the European Court of Justice — as being those which received the most attention at the time of their delivery, both from the media and from academe. Some details are added from Commonwealth jurisdictions to show that, even in the face of great public controversy, courts have supported the concept as an acceptable tool in the struggle to eliminate discrimination in employment.

This chapter highlights how the courts, faced with similar factual situations, arrived at different results on different occasions. Reasons for such variations are suggested, and the point is made that more rigorous reasoning at the level of lower jurisdictions and, generally, a better use of international standards might assist the courts in arriving at just and realistic decisions. The question is put whether the time has not now come for the adoption of an international instrument on affirmative action.

SELECTED COURT DECISIONS CONCERNING AFFIRMATIVE ACTION/DISCRIMINATION ON THE BASIS OF RACE OR SEX

United States

It is not surprising that the United States provides the most examples of judicial examination of affirmative action schemes, since it is there that the legislation permitting such measures has existed longest. The Civil Rights Act 1964, enacted in response to the civil rights movement of the early 1960s, outlaws, in its Title VII, discrimination on the basis of race and sex; but it lies in the shadow of the Fourteenth Amendment to the Federal Constitution, which gives every citizen equal protection before the law and thus imposes severe limits on any legislative scheme that may attempt to remedy the effects of past discrimination.

In the late 1970s special schemes based on race were largely upheld (Jones, 1981), but a wave of cases in the 1980s involving race or sex discrimination in the public and private sectors gave rise to conflicting results. There were many close decisions and strongly argued dissents. The judges did not agree on a common "test" or set of principles by which to assess the acceptability of such schemes. Sometimes the supremacy of the Constitution was the key; sometimes social norms or compelling state interest overrode the strictly juridical approach. The lack of agreement was most noticeable in the Supreme Court, where a number of conservative appointees led by Justice, later Chief Justice, Rehnquist, refused to uphold any affirmative action programmes, using the argument that they were invalid under the Constitution and the wording of the Civil Rights Act. There were, however, certain recurring clues to the standards that the Supreme Court would later apply: it would look favourably on affirmative action if there was strong evidence that discrimination had in fact occurred; if preferential treatment was clearly the only means of eradicating the lingering effects of that discrimination; and if the measure under scrutiny had been worded narrowly enough not to run counter to the principal statute, the Civil Rights Act. Ten years later, however, in the mid-1990s, when United States courts again considered the permissibility of various affirmative action schemes, they withdrew the approval that this type of measure seemed to have earned, given the passage of time and the continuing labour market distortions based on past discrimination.

Two early successes for proponents of affirmative action concerned special admission programmes to university. These are relevant to the theme of this chapter, in that the definition of employment in Convention No. 111 specifically includes access to vocational training. The first was the case of *DeFunis v Odegaard*,[7] in which a White[8] applicant to the University of Washington Law School alleged discrimination on the basis of his race. The Supreme Court held that the equal protection clause of the Federal Constitution did not make all racial classifications illegal. The next affirmative action programme to be tested in the Supreme Court was *University of California Regents v Bakke*.[9] Mr. Bakke, a White male, was denied admission to the medical school of the University of California at Davis for two consecutive years because of a special admissions programme. The programme provided that only disadvantaged members of certain minority races could be considered for 16 of the 100 places in each year's intake, leaving members of any race free to compete for the other 84 places. The complainant argued that he would have been offered a place if not for the special reservation of places based on the criterion of race. At the level of the state court, the judges struck down the special admissions programme as contravening the Civil Rights Act, the State Constitution and the Equal Protection Clause of the Federal Constitution. At the level of the Federal Supreme Court, the judges were split: although the minority warned that the use of race as the criterion for selection was inherently suspect, a 5:4 majority none the less accepted that racial classifications could be used to achieve important state policy objectives, such as remedying past social discrimination, as long as they were substantially related to the achievement of those objectives. Accepting that minorities were substantially and chronically under-represented in medical schools owing to past racial discrimination, the judges upheld the University's affirmative action measure to redress the situation.

The following year the majority of the Supreme Court followed this opinion in *Steelworkers v Weber*.[10] The United Steelworkers and a company had entered into a collective bargaining agreement that included an affirmative action programme designed to eliminate racial imbalances in the company's almost exclusively White craft workforce. In one plant the craft workforce was less than 2 per cent Black, even though the local labour force was 39 per cent Black. One aspect of the scheme was a training programme to which entry was based on seniority, except that at least 50 per cent of the new trainees were to be Blacks until the percentage of Black craft workers rose to approximate the percentage of Blacks in the local labour force. During the first year of the training course, most of the Black trainees had less seniority than several of the White applicants whose requests for training were refused, Mr. Weber being one of the latter. The majority of the Supreme Court held that such measures did not contravene Title VII of the Civil Rights Act because that Act did not condemn all private, voluntary, race-conscious affirmative action programmes. Nor did it require them to be imposed. The Court held that, to be valid, affirmative action plans should be designed to eliminate conspicuous racial discrimination, should not lead to White workers losing their jobs or being barred from advancement and should be temporary. Such measures were, after all, intended not to maintain racial imbalances but rather to eliminate them. Focusing on the use of the words "to require"[11] in Title VII of the Civil Rights Act, the Court ruled that the Act's prohibition of racial preferences as a remedy for past discrimination did not extend to voluntary plans. However, there could not be an unlimited use of preferences in voluntary plans, which were permissible only when they were designed to break down old patterns of racial segregation and hierarchy, open up employment opportunities that had been closed to Blacks and, crucially, did not "unnecessarily trammel the rights of white employees", although this phrase was not clarified. Two of the judges, however, argued that affirmative action programmes were ruled out altogether by the plain language of the Civil Rights Act and its spirit and legislative history.

In *Firefighters v Stotts*[12] the Supreme Court was faced with a Federal District Court order disallowing the proposed layoff and demotion of junior Black employees according to an established, strict-seniority layoff procedure. The proposals would have largely undone the progress made by a hiring and promotion plan that had been agreed upon in a consent decree settling a lawsuit brought by minorities and a Black person alleging racial imbalances in the workforce. The Supreme Court held that the lower court had erred because its injunction was neither an enforcement of nor a valid modification to the original consent decree, and no evidenciary hearing had been conducted. The majority decision recalled that Title VII prohibits courts from requiring racial preference as a remedy for past discrimination unless the preference benefits only the actual victims of that discrimination; but this interpretation was strongly attacked by the minority dissenting judges.

The uncertainty induced by these decisions — including doubts over the degree to which federal courts are limited in the kind of relief they can order to remedy past discrimination — was partly cleared up by a series of Supreme Court decisions in the mid-1980s.

In *Local No. 93, International Association of Firefighters v City of Cleveland*,[13] the Supreme Court upheld (5:4) a consent decree by a Federal District Court requiring that a specified number of promotions (half of the scheduled promotions to lieutenant and 10 of the promotions to captain and battalion chief) be given to firefighters from racial minorities for four years. The fact that there was clear evidence of past racial discrimination in the promotion of firefighters was the key to this support for the special measure, even though it used the sensitive criterion of race. The dissenting judges again argued that the application of the law ought to be colour-blind. Likewise, in *Sheet Metal Workers v EEOC* [Equal Employment Opportunity Commission][14] the Supreme Court upheld an affirmative action programme, imposed by a Federal District Court to increase the non-White membership of a union, because a pattern of manifest discrimination by the union had been proved. The case thus clarified that affirmative action was a permissible remedy for a class of individuals, even if there was no proof that every one of the individuals had actually suffered under the discrimination involved. In this way the "egregious" test was born, allowing class-based relief where an employer or labour union had engaged in persistent or egregious discrimination. The judgement of the majority referred repeatedly to the evidence proving the Union's blatant discrimination. Would this mean, in future cases, that only particularly repugnant situations would justify a court upholding affirmative action measures? Again, three judges dissented on the same grounds as in the *Local No. 93* case.

The dissenters just won the day in a third case heard by the Supreme Court in 1986, *Wygant v Jackson Board of Education*.[15] In that case, a Board of Education and a teachers' union in Michigan had added to their collective bargaining agreement an affirmative action provision giving special treatment to teachers from minority groups during layoffs: dismissals could not exceed the percentage they represented in the teaching workforce. As a result, some White teachers, including Ms. Wygant, were laid off, while minority teachers with less seniority were retained. In a 5:4 decision, the Court held that the layoffs violated the Equal Protection

Clause of the Constitution. Yet the following year a sex-based affirmative action programme was upheld in *Johnson v Transportation Agency*.[16] The Transportation Agency of a Californian County had adopted an affirmative action plan for the promotion of female employees in jobs where women had been traditionally under-represented. The plan clearly stated that its objective was to achieve a statistically measurable yearly improvement in the hiring, training and promotion of women and minorities. Alongside the short-term goals, the plan provided for annual evaluation and adjustment, so that it could be used as a realistic guide for actual employment decisions. When, in filling one vacancy for promotion, the director of the agency did not follow the interviewing panel's recommendation of Mr. Johnson but chose the third-ranked female applicant, taking account of the affirmative action policy, as well as the candidates' qualifications, test scores, expertise and backgrounds, Mr. Johnson challenged his non-promotion. The choice was found, however, to be consistent with the prohibition of discrimination in employment imposed under Title VII of the Civil Rights Act on the grounds, inter alia, that consideration of the applicant's sex was justified by the existence of a manifest imbalance reflected in the under-representation of women in traditionally segregated job categories. The Court held that an employer, when seeking to justify the adoption of an affirmative action plan, did not need to show evidence of its own prior discriminatory practices, or even of an arguable violation on its part, but need only point to a conspicuous imbalance in the job categories. The Court also used the test introduced in *Weber* that the agency's plan did not unnecessarily trammel the rights of male employees or create an absolute bar to their advancement. Again, there was a forceful dissent, on the grounds that the Civil Rights Act was being misused to protect discrimination instead of eliminating it. The Supreme Court has not decided any gender case relating to the public sector.

Reasoning on which decisions were based

Analysis of these 1980s decisions shows that, while the Supreme Court handed down conflicting decisions, it was starting to build a matrix of reasoning that overrode the plain language of the Civil Rights Act. First, it rejected the argument that affirmative action should benefit only the actual victims of discriminatory behaviour when it accepted that a plan need not be linked to the employer's own practices but could be justified by traditional imbalances in the workforce. Second, the basis on which an affirmative action plan had been adopted appeared to be crucial to its success. In *Wygant* there had been a voluntary agreement with a union to quell racial tension. In *Local No. 93* there had been a consent decree whereby a court had approved a settlement reached by the parties to a lawsuit. This was different from the *Stotts* situation, where a court had attempted to add to the original consent decree without the employer's specific agreement to the injunction against out-of-seniority layoffs. In *Sheet Metal Workers* there was a court order following a trial. In *Johnson* there had been the agency's clear policy decision, tempered by several checks and balances like the monitoring and annual change to the plan. Another emerging factor was the type of measure involved: in *Wygant* the fact that layoffs from existing jobs were at issue weighed heavily in the Court's disapproval of the measure, but in *Local No. 93* the preferential hiring and training goals were upheld, given that the burden to be borne by non-preferred groups was diffused among society generally. Denial of future employment opportunity was seen to be less intrusive than loss of a current job, although this raises the question whether affirmative action will be judged permissible by the courts during periods of economic growth when employers are hiring and promoting but not during hard times when layoffs are common. Lastly, the amount of evidence proving the existence of discrimination entered into the matrix of factors considered by the Court.

The trend of court support for affirmative action was reversed in the mid-1990s under the new conservative majority of the nine-member Supreme Court, including Black Justice Clarence Thomas, who had been nominated by President Bush in 1991. Its reasoning appeared to favour a return to reading the Constitution as protecting the individual rather than groups and to diluting the role of government in addressing racial discrimination. The use of the specific criterion of race, barred to the government by history and by statute, was now anathema to the Court. Its attack on affirmative action led President Clinton to order a thorough review of government affirmative action programmes in February 1995[17] and caused the Attorney-General to issue policy guidelines to all federal agencies using affirmative action measures.[18]

In *Adarand Constructors Inc. v Peña*,[19] a case concerning affirmative action aimed at improving racial balance in the domain of public procurement, the Court (again by a close 5:4 majority) applied a strict judicial scrutiny test to affirmative action programmes adopted by the federal government. It followed the 1989 decision in *Richmond v J. A. Croson Co.*,[20] which had struck down race-conscious affirmative action at the level of local and state governments using a strict judicial scrutiny test of whether the measure in question met an overriding government concern. The test involved past discrimination being identified by a properly authorized government body, and past societal practice generally. The City of Richmond's plans to overcome race discrimination did not meet this test and they were declared unconstitutional. The programme under examination in *Adarand*, the Small Business Administration, provided a financial bonus to contractors on federal highway projects in Colorado who subcontracted to firms owned by socially and economically disadvantaged individuals. The decision clarified that the Fourteenth Amendment afforded individuals, not groups, the right to demand equal protection before the law and that this was a fundamental principle of conventional jurisprudence. However, although the Court sent the case back to a lower court with directions to apply strict scrutiny to the contract requirements in order to assess whether they were sufficiently narrowly tailored to meet the stated aim of a compelling government interest, seven out of the nine members of the Court specifically reaffirmed, as a matter of principle, the legitimacy of results-oriented preferential treatment of disadvantaged persons, subject always to the strict scrutiny requirements.

In *Hopwood v State of Texas*,[21] the Fifth Circuit Court of Appeals struck down affirmative action for non-Whites which had been implemented under the University of Texas Law School's preferential admissions programme set up in 1992. The reasoning followed the strict legal construction put on the Civil Rights Act, that race could not be used as a criterion in admitting students. Leave to appeal to the Supreme Court against this decision was refused.

In *The Coalition for Economic Equity and Others v Pete Wilson and Others*,[22] the Ninth Circuit Court of Appeals was called on to decide whether a provision of the Californian Constitution prohibiting race and gender preferences violated the Equal Protection Clause of the Federal Constitution and the Civil Rights Act. On 5 November 1996 54 per cent of Californian voters had adopted Proposition 209, which aimed at eliminating public race- and gender-based programmes in areas of public employment, contracting and education. Outraged by this result, groups representing the interests of racial minorities and women won a temporary restraining order and a preliminary injunction to stall implementation of the Proposition. They won at the District Court level, but the decision was overturned by the Court of Appeals, which appeared to be at pains both to protect the divide between the legislature and the judiciary and, as a federal tribunal construing a state law that had not yet been challenged at the highest level within the state apparatus, not to upset the federal/state power balance.

The decision merits attention for its insistence that discrimination on the grounds of race and gender requires "a compelling governmental interest, an extraordinary justification" (para. 10). It does not analyse the concept of affirmative action but devotes most of its reasoning to issues of legal construction and the hierarchy of laws, thus following the approach of strict judicial scrutiny endorsed in *Adarand*. It concludes that a ban on race and gender classifications does not, as a matter of law and logic, violate the Fourteenth Amendment to the Constitution from the point of view of either the constitutionality test or the "political structure" test, which asks whether a given measure removes to a remote level of government the right to fight certain issues (paras. 11-12). In response to legal and procedural arguments, the decision states that Title VII of the Civil Rights Act does not pre-empt — override or automatically invalidate — Proposition 209, since section 1104 of the Act permits general pre-emption only if a specific inconsistency is apparent. When it does address the substance of the case, the court reverts to the criterion of individual suffering under the discriminatory practice concerned, arguing that the Fourteenth Amendment guarantees equal protection to individuals and not to groups. As the decision does not throw light on the "egregious" test nor on the weight to be given to the type of measures covered, it remains doubtful whether future cases will follow its approach.

European Court of Justice

Another challenge to affirmative action received much publicity in the early 1990s, when the European Court of Justice (ECJ) delivered its decision in *Kalanke v City of Bremen*.[23] This was the first case in which the ECJ was asked to consider whether a legal rule laying down affirmative action for women was compatible with the Equal Treatment Directive,[24] Article 2(4) of which reads: "This Directive shall be without prejudice to measures to promote equal opportunity for men and women, in particular by removing existing inequalities which affect women's opportunities in the areas referred to in Article 1(1)" [employment, including promotion, vocational training and working conditions]. In this case, Bremen's public sector Equal Employment Law, section 4(2), provided that for both recruitment and promotion in sectors where women were under-represented — that is, if they did not constitute 50 per cent of the personnel in each of the various grades of the category concerned — a woman having the same qualifications as a male applicant must be given preference over him. When it was decided to appoint a female candidate to be section manager in the City's Park Department on the grounds that there were fewer women section managers than men, Mr. Kalanke appealed against his loss. He argued that he was better qualified and that, even if he and the female chosen had been equally qualified, the preferential treatment given to her amounted to discrimination against him because of his sex. Had it not been for section 4(2) of the law, he would have been promoted on social grounds because he had to maintain three dependants (a wife and two children), whereas the female candidate had no such obligations. Mr. Kalanke lost his case at both the local and regional Labour Court levels, and the Federal Labour Court asked for a ruling from the ECJ on whether the national law was consistent with the Equal Treatment Directive. The ECJ struck down the national law, saying that any automatic preference for equally qualified women had to be considered an infringement of the Directive:

> A national rule that, where men and women who are candidates for the same promotion are equally qualified, women are automatically to be given priority in sectors where they are under-represented involves discrimination on grounds of sex [para. 16] ... National rules which guarantee women absolute and uncon-

ditional priority for appointment or promotion go beyond promoting equal opportunities and overstep the limits of the exception in Article 2(4) of the Directive [para. 22].

By referring explicitly to automatic preference, the ECJ restricted the scope of its judgement to unconditional preferential treatment, without introducing other tests, such as individual hardship or trammelling the rights of other groups. In considering the scope of Article 2(4) of the Directive, the ECJ noted that the provision was designed to allow measures which, although discriminatory in appearance, were in fact intended to eliminate or reduce instances of existing inequality: for example, it was acceptable to give women a specific advantage in the sphere of employment, including promotion, with a view to improving their ability to compete in the labour market and pursue a career on an equal footing with men. At the same time, a derogation from an individual right laid down in the Directive had to be interpreted strictly. However, although the Court appeared to attempt to examine the overall aim of the affirmative action measure — as the United States Supreme Court had tried in the 1980s — the wording used was peculiarly opaque and the fact that it was placed at the end of the judgement implies, moreover, that it was an adjunct to the main line of reasoning:

> Furthermore, in so far as it seeks to achieve equal representation of men and women in all grades and levels within a department, such a system substitutes for equality of opportunity as envisaged in Article 2(4) the result which is only to be arrived at by providing such equality of opportunity [para. 23].

The ECJ appeared to be saying that, even if the goal of the measure were to be a factor in evaluating affirmative action, the method chosen in the Bremen statute went beyond ensuring equality in access to career paths and promotions because it aimed at ensuring a particular result; as Faundez (1994) puts it, this is the dilemma between ensuring equality of opportunity and equality of result.

The ECJ decision gave rise to a great deal of controversy throughout Europe, where European Community (EC) member States had been active in adopting and implementing affirmative action programmes in favour of women in the belief that this was not only legally permissible because of Article 2(4) of the Directive, but politically, socially and economically advisable. Academics and equality practitioners criticized the decision as interpreting the Directive over-narrowly. Some commentators (for example, Schiek, 1996) argued that section 4(2) of the Bremen law simply served to exclude selection criteria (such as being the "breadwinner" or having longer service, which worked in the German civil service to the advantage of men) which would have amounted to indirect discrimination against female candidates. Others tried to put the outcome down to the wording of the affirmative action measure, which lacked the flexibility to look at other criteria such as the individual hardship suffered by those not covered by the measure. The Commission of the EC drew together all these currents of thought in the communication it decided to present to the European Parliament and the Council of Ministers containing its interpretation of the *Kalanke* judgement.[25] The Commission concluded that the ECJ had condemned only the automatic character of the Bremen measure, whereby women were given an absolute and unconditional right to appointment or promotion. The Commission thus took the position that the only type of quota system which was unlawful was one which was completely rigid and did not leave any possibility of taking account of individual circumstances. EC member States were therefore free to have recourse to all other forms of affirmative action, including flexible quotas.

On 11 November 1997 the ECJ delivered its second decision on affirmative action in *Marschall v Northrhine-Westphalia*.[26] Mr. Marschall, a teacher, had applied for a higher position along with a woman candidate; since the two were equally qualified and fewer women than men were employed in the relevant pay and career bracket, the woman had to be appointed by virtue of the 5 February 1995 amendment to the Law on Civil Servants in that *Land*. The provision in question reads: "Where, in the sector of the authority responsible for promotion, there are fewer women than men in the particular higher grade post in the career bracket, women are to be given priority for promotion in the event of equal suitability, competence and professional performance, unless reasons specific to an individual [male] candidate tilt the balance in his favour." The Administrative Court to which Mr. Marschall appealed had doubts, in view of *Kalanke*, as to whether the *Land* law was compatible with the Equal Treatment Directive and referred the question to the ECJ. The Court's decision was eagerly awaited, since, by contrast with *Kalanke*, the national law in question included a proviso, or saving clause, under which reasons specific to the other (male) candidates could predominate.

The ECJ held that the rule was not precluded by Article 2(1) and (4) of the Directive, provided that, in each individual case, the rule gave male candidates who were as qualified as the female candidates a guarantee that the candidatures would be the subject of an objective assessment taking account of all criteria specific to the candidates and would override the priority accorded to females candidates where one or more of those criteria — if not discriminatory against the female candidate — tilted the balance in favour of the male candidate. According to the judgement:

> In providing [the saving clause], the legislature deliberately chose, according to the *Land*, a legally imprecise expression in order to ensure sufficient flexibility and, in particular, to allow the administration latitude to take into account any reasons which may be specific to individual candidates. Consequently, notwithstanding the rule of priority, the administration can always give preference to a male candidate on the basis of promotion criteria, traditional or otherwise [para. 5].

The ECJ outlined the rationale for permitting special measures under Article 2(4) of the Directive, accepting, however, *Kalanke*'s approach that, since Article 2(4) constitutes a derogation from an individual right laid down by the Directive, a national measure specifically aimed at favouring female candidates cannot guarantee absolute and unconditional priority for women in granting promotion without going beyond the limits of the exemption laid down in that Article. The inclusion of a saving clause did not necessarily ensure that the limits would be respected; saving clauses must ensure an objective assessment of all criteria specific to the individual candidates, at the same time without discriminating against the female candidates. The judgement gave no insight into how the other criteria could be tested as not being discriminatory against women, although it stated:

> it appears that, even where male and female candidates are equally qualified, male candidates tend to be promoted in preference to female candidates particularly because of prejudices and stereotypes concerning the role and capacities of women in working life and the fear, for example, that women will interrupt their careers more frequently, that owing to household and family duties they will be less flexible in their working hours, or that they will be absent from work more frequently because of pregnancy, childbirth and breastfeeding [para. 29].

This may mean that, in evaluating factors pertaining to individual male candidates, items that might tilt the balance in their favour, such as longer service, will not be acceptable, since competing women may have had career interruptions or breaks in service due to family responsibilities.

Analysis of these ECJ decisions shows that the warmth with which affirmative action for women had been greeted in the 1970s and 1980s in Europe cooled when laws gave automatic preference to female candidates for promotion. But the most recent judgement in the matter demonstrates that the problem can be resolved by including a saving clause in the affirmative action provision. The fact that the Court requires the insertion of these saving clauses to ensure that no new discriminatory element creeps in re-establishes the strong European support for permitting proactive measures in the struggle to eliminate discrimination in employment. Further confirmation of this appears in Article 141 of the new Amsterdam Treaty (former Article 119 of the Treaty of Rome), paragraph 4 of which states:

> With a view to ensuring full equality in practice between men and women in working life, the principle of equal treatment shall not prevent any Member State from maintaining or adopting measures providing for specific advantages in order to make it easier for the under-represented sex to pursue a vocational activity or to prevent or compensate for disadvantages in professional careers.

South Africa

Two recent cases in South African lower courts demonstrate that, even in an environment where affirmative action to overcome past discrimination is openly accepted as being the most appropriate method to achieve equality, there can still be misconceptions about it as a form of discrimination.

The Constitution to end the former apartheid dispensation (Act No. 108 of 1996) makes it clear that race and sex discrimination must be eliminated.[27] The interim Constitution of 1994 had given special emphasis to affirmative action in the public service when it proclaimed, in section 212:

> (2) Such public service shall ... (b) promote an efficient public administration broadly representative of the South African community ... (4) In the making of any appointment or the filling of any post in the public service, the qualifications, level of training, merit, efficiency and suitability of the persons who qualify for the appointment, promotion or transfer concerned, and such conditions as may be determined or prescribed by or under any law, shall be taken into account ... (5) Sub-section (4) shall not preclude measures to promote the objectives set out in sub-section (2).

The Public Service Act's provision on the filling of vacant posts reflected the political decision to make the former bastion of the White labour force "broadly representative of the South African community".[28]

The creation of a representative civil service through affirmative action was thus an immediate constitutional objective; yet, in *Public Servants Association of SA and Others v Minister of Justice and Others* (1997),[29] the Minister of Justice's appointment of women to 30 vacant posts in his Ministry, on the basis that they came from under-represented groups, was struck down by the High Court (Transvaal Provincial Division).

When 16 White males working in the Ministry applied for the posts and were not interviewed, then saw the posts filled by women, they alleged unfair discrimination against them because of their race and sex. They and their staff association requested the High Court to issue, inter alia, (1) an interdict to stay the appointments as being illegal under the Public Service Act and the terms of an agreement negotiated within the Public Service Bargaining Council, and (2) a declaration to set aside the appointments made to the vacant posts because they took into account the race, colour or gender of the applicants. Swart J., in an extraordinarily frustrating judgement, repeated the constitutional and statutory requirements of a representative public service and the various staff codes and agreements, attempting to reconcile the new approach with previous civil service practice, but devoted much of his reasoning to an intricate examination of the personal attributes of the 16 White male applicants and a summary examination of the attributes of those who won the vacancies. In assessing why the 16 should have been given the posts on merit and in evaluating their qualifications as superior to those of the female candidates ("the ladies" is the term used, p. 253), the judge listed their school achievements, giving details of their sporting prowess at rugby and cricket and using phraseology such as "outstanding sportsman". He praised some of them as having served previously in the South African Police Force or intelligence forces or as deacons and elders of the Church, apparently unaware of the lack of sensitivity in using the apparatus of the former apartheid era as the benchmark for holding posts under the new regime. Likewise, there appeared to be no consciousness of attributes that are inherent to legal positions in government service, such as university qualifications, although he gave weight to length of service, without evaluating why these candidates had not moved up in the civil service hierarchy but had been upwards of 15 years in the same posts. In discussing length of service, he noted that some of the women appointed had qualified as lawyers only about five years earlier and, if appointed, would "jump several officers on the merit list" (p. 253). He gave weight to the fact that similar information on the outstanding qualities of the women appointed had not been presented by counsel for the respondent so as to justify their appointment on grounds other than affirmative action.

Swart J. barely disguised his contempt for the concept of special measures, stating "I think these excerpts from the staff codes amply illustrate that up to this stage, despite the provisions of the Constitution calling for representativity, affirmative action had not raised its head and inter alia promotion[s] ... were filled strictly in accordance with an extensive and detailed merit system in which race and gender could not be taken into account" (p. 259).

When the judge examined the law and codes regulating promotions in the public service, he wrote at length about the procedures that were discussed with a view to accommodating the new race and gender representativeness requirements. There was no doubt that the Public Service Act had been an important element in the Ministry's rationalization and affirmative action plans. Yet the judge concluded that "suitability" as a criterion for public service appointment and promotion — which historically took no account of race and gender — could not be replaced to take account of race and gender under the new dispensation. Five tests were used to show that the non-appointment of the White males did not fit with the interim Constitution's proscription of racial and sexual discrimination, nor had it been proven that the appointments were of the kind permitted under the Constitution's special measures exception.[30] The tests, according to Swart J., were: (a) the measure must be designed (not a random action); (b) it must be designed to achieve something (a causal connection between the measure and the aim); (c) the objectives of the measure must be adequate protection (not out of proportion) to overcome previous disadvantage; (d) the adequate protection must be in order to give the disadvantaged person or group their full and equal enjoyment of all rights and freedoms (not without limits, but with due regard to the rights of others and the interests of the community); and (e) the measure must fit with the constitutional requirement of an efficient public administration broadly representative of the South African community (representativeness cannot override efficiency). He concluded that the earmarking of the 30 posts did not fit into any overall plan or policy; it did not meet the representativeness requirement; it went far beyond what might have been an adequate response because it affected high-level posts rather than entry-level posts; it disregarded the rights of others by ignoring the "outstanding qualifications" of the White males; and, lastly, it did not respect the efficiency requirement, since the women promoted were unimpressive when compared to the White men.

Critics of affirmative action in South Africa applauded this decision, but within months the Industrial Court handed down a far more positive evaluation of affirmative action, this time in the private sector.

In *George v Liberty Life Association of Africa Ltd* (1996),[31] President Landman undertook the first full examination of the concept itself, using the newly adopted sources such as the 1996 Constitution and the 1995 Labour Relations Act, as well as seeking inspiration from the ILO Discrimination (Employment and Occupation) Convention, 1958 (No. 111). In that case, Mr. George, a White employee of the firm, had applied for a higher post in the company advertised on an internal notice board as "corporate only", which meant that it was open exclusively to internal candidates in accordance with the policy outlined in the firm's Staff Handbook. Although during interviews and talks with personnel staff he was informed that he was a suitable candidate, a Coloured affirmative action candidate from outside the company was given the job. It transpired that the post had also been advertised externally. The applicant argued that the appointment of the outsider constituted an unfair labour practice because race was the deciding factor and that the appointment was invalid because the employer had failed to comply with its own policy of giving preference to internal candidates. In giving primacy to section 8(3)(a) of the interim Constitution, the President of the Court defined affirmative action not as the value or norm — the attainment of equality and non-discrimination — but as the method, strategy or procedure by which equal employment opportunities would be achieved. The Court took care to clarify that, in accordance with South African judicial policy of not intervening in areas of managerial prerogative, it would not comment on the merits of the candidates but would restrict itself to examining the appointment in the context of respect for the law, both substantive (the balance of competing values and the role of affirmative action in achieving them) and procedural. This is a marked turn away from the approach of the Transvaal High Court.

The Industrial Court found that the candidate appointed was historically disadvantaged educationally and that, from this angle, his appointment could not be said to amount to an unfair labour practice in the contemporary circumstances of the South African workplace. However, with regard to the procedure followed by the firm in making the appointment, the Court held that, upon a proper interpretation of the company's job posting and placement policy, Mr. George ought to have been given preferential consideration over any external candidate. It was on this count that the Court found the appointment to constitute an unfair labour practice and allowed the applicant's claim for costs. Leaving aside the actual decision, the establishment of reasoned support for affirmative action in this decision is to be applauded. Given that these cases were heard at different levels, it remains to be seen which jurisdiction's approach will be followed in other challenges to affirmative action in South Africa.

Other jurisdictions

Australia

Also in the mid-1980s, special measures appearing in Australian legislation were put to the test. In *Gerhardy v Brown*,[32] section 8 of the Commonwealth Racial Discrimination Act 1975, which provides that special measures on the basis of race are not discrimination, was used to uphold a state law denying certain rights to non-members of an indigenous Aboriginal tribe. Under the Pitjantjatjara Land Rights Act of South Australia 1975, a large area of north-west South Australia was vested in the Pitjantjatjara people, who had unrestricted access to the land, while non-Pitjantjatjaras had to have special permission. Brown went on to the land without permission and, when charged with an offence, argued that the South Australian statute was inconsistent with the Racial Discrimination Act and consequently invalid. The High Court held that the South Australian Act was a special measure for the purposes of section 8 of the federal Act and not inconsistent with it. Consequently, non-Pitjantjatjaras could be excluded from the land.

In the area of sex discrimination, too, the Australian jurisdictions have based moves to achieve equality and overturn past discrimination on the statutory support for special measures. Section 33 of the federal Sex Discrimination Act 1984 provides that it is not unlawful to perform an action to ensure that persons of a particular sex or marital status or pregnant women have equal opportunities with others. In that connection, the Industrial Relations Commission[33] approved a rule, in a proposed amalgamation of three unions into one, whereby the post of branch vice-president for each branch of the union was reserved for a woman, voted in by women members. The Commission held that the provision was a special measure designed to assist the achievement of factual equality and thus permissible under section 33. The following year, another specialized tribunal examined allegations that the arrangements by which the federal and Australian Capital Territory (ACT) governments jointly funded the ACT Women's Health Service discriminated against men because it was available only to women. In *Proudfoot v ACT Board of Health and Others* (1992),[34] the Human Rights and Equal Opportunity Commission held that the governments had concluded, after extensive consultation, that special measures of the kind taken were required for the promotion of women's health. In the Commission's opinion, such a conclusion was not unreasonable. Consequently these measures came within the terms of section 33 of the Sex Discrimination Act. Although not a case in the field of employment law, it is cited here because of the interesting approach towards the role of the deciding body. It stands in sharp contrast to the complex arguments put forward by the United States Supreme Court in the 1980s when attempting to justify its upholding of certain affirmative action programmes despite the wording of the federal laws. The American judges seemed to be grappling with tests of the necessity and appropriateness of a given programme or measure, whereas the President of the Australian Commission stated:

> Ultimately, it is not for the Commission to actually determine whether the challenged initiatives are in fact necessary or even wholly suitable for achieving the purposes of promoting equal opportunities as between women and men in the field of health care. All that s[ection] 33 requires is that those who undertake the measures must do so with that purpose in view and that it be reasonable for them to conclude that the measures would further the purpose.

India

In 1992 the Supreme Court of another Commonwealth country likewise upheld affirmative action measures, even though there were major public protests surrounding them. The Constitution of India permits the State to make provision for posts to be reserved for any backward class of citizens not represented adequately in state services and to promote with special care the educational and economic interests of the weaker sections of the population, in particular the scheduled tribes and scheduled castes.[35] After four decades of implementing a reservation policy, the representation in the civil service of these latter two groups was still considered inadequate. In 1979, a special body, known as the Mandal Commission after its President, was set up to determine how to improve conditions for the socially and educationally disadvantaged classes. In its report to parliament, the Commission recommended that 27 per cent of the posts in undertakings and educational establishments of the central and state governments be reserved for the Hindu, as well as the non-Hindu, disadvantaged classes. On 31 August 1990 the central Government issued a memorandum reflecting the 27 per cent reservation, which was amended by a further memorandum reserving 10 per cent of civil service posts for other "backward sections" not covered by other reservation schemes, that is for poor upper-class people. The memorandum was challenged in the case of *Indira Sawhney and Others v Union of India and Others* (1992).[36] The Supreme Court declared that the 27 per cent reservation was valid as a means of overcoming past and continuing discrimination on the basis of social origin and ruled that it should be implemented except in respect of socially advanced persons (the so-called "creamy layer" of society). Following the Court's validation of the measure, an expert committee was established to specify the scope of the creamy layer exclusion and on the basis of its recommendations the central government issued a Notification in September 1993 announcing a 27 per cent reservation for the 1,200 Other Backward Classes in central government posts.

THE UNITED NATIONS AND ILO POSITION

The ideological roots of affirmative action are international, appearing in the various United Nations declarations and treaties, in ILO instruments and in the jurisprudence of the ILO supervisory bodies. It is the notion of equality permeating United Nations instruments from the Charter onwards that forms the bedrock on which affirmative action was built.

The Universal Declaration of Human Rights, whose fiftieth anniversary has just been celebrated, contains the classic statement that: "All human beings are born free and equal in dignity and rights. They are endowed with reason and conscience and should act towards one another in a spirit of brotherhood" (Art. 1).[37] The International Convention on the Elimination of All Forms of Racial Discrimination[38] stressed the importance of proactive measures against racism and provided the basis for future tests as to the acceptability of such measures by including the notions of necessity, the holistic approach, proportionality to the aim to be achieved, and temporal limits. Its Article 2(2) states that:

> States Parties shall, when the circumstances so warrant, take, in the social, economic, cultural and other fields, special and concrete measures to ensure the adequate development and protection of certain racial groups or individuals belonging to them, for the purpose of guaranteeing them the full and equal enjoyment of human rights and fundamental freedoms. These measures shall in no case entail as a consequence the maintenance of unequal or separate rights for different racial groups after the objectives for which they were taken have been achieved.

The International Covenants on Civil and Political Rights, and on Economic, Social and Cultural Rights likewise required States Parties to adopt and implement policies to eliminate discrimination on a number of grounds.[39] In the struggle for women's equality, the Convention on the Elimination of All Forms of Discrimination against Women[40] adopted the

459

corollary of the simple ban on discrimination, namely an obligation to take specific action to overcome the results of past and present discrimination. Its Article 4(1) reads:

> Adoption by States Parties of temporary special measures aimed at accelerating *de facto* equality between men and women shall not be considered discrimination as defined in the present Convention, but shall in no way entail as a consequence the maintenance of unequal or separate standards; these measures shall be discontinued when the objectives of equality of opportunity and treatment have been achieved.

The ILO, being the oldest specialized agency of the United Nations system, had already adopted texts on eliminating discrimination in the areas under its mandate — employment — some years earlier. The 1958 Session of the International Labour Conference adopted the Discrimination (Employment and Occupation) Convention (No. 111), with the accompanying Recommendation No. 111.[41] It requires ratifying States to adopt and implement, with the cooperation of the social partners (and, as the Recommendation points out, appropriate national machineries), a national policy to eliminate discrimination in employment. The Convention defines employment broadly, to cover not only access to jobs and terms and conditions of employment but also access to training; and indeed the supervisory bodies have included access to schools and tertiary education as well as vocational training institutions in their scrutiny.

The key provision for the employment equity debate is Article 5(2):

> Any Member may, after consultation with representative employers' and workers' organizations, where such exist, determine that other special measures designed to meet the particular requirements of persons who, for reasons such as sex, age, disablement, family responsibilities or social or cultural status, are generally recognized to require special protection or assistance, shall not be deemed to be discrimination.

The last phrase of that Article makes it clear that the principal international instrument on equality in employment gives rise to no semantic or ideological confusion, or juggling with the concept of equality. Affirmative action is not discrimination under Convention No. 111. Despite that clear position, there has still been ideological opposition to the concept, over and above the complaints about the difficulty of applying it in practice and the media reactions referred to above. As Faundez (1994) puts it, "Critics of affirmative action, on their part, generally argue that these measures violate the principle that individuals competing for goods ought to be treated as equals" (p. 1).

The ILO supervisory bodies,[42] when verifying whether ratifying States have adopted "special measures", have welcomed affirmative action and employment equity measures, without differentiating between the terms.[43] The supervisory bodies consider them part of national policy to overcome past or present workplace discrimination. They have stated, in line with what is in the text itself, that such measures are not, for the purposes of the Convention, discrimination; therefore the ILO does not use phrases like "reverse discrimination", since the instrument itself makes it clear that proactive steps, preferences and "favouritism", as some critics call it, have to be accepted as legitimate tools in the fight against employment discrimination. This logic flows from the realization that the statutory proscription of discrimination is not enough to make it disappear in practice.

The Committees have not had to assess the United States' and South Africa's varied court approaches to affirmative action, as the former has not ratified Convention No. 111[44] and the latter ratified on 5 March 1997, with the first report on its application due for examination only in 1999. However, as Germany has ratified the Convention, the CEACR had to examine how far the sex equality rules adopted by the City of Bremen, struck down by the European Court of Justice in *Kalanke*, were compatible with Article 5. The CEACR avoided any statement indicating criticism of the automatic preference for women where candidates of different sexes shortlisted for promotion were equally qualified, in sectors where women were under-represented. Instead, it noted that this development would affect Germany's application of Convention No. 111 and asked the Government to inform it of the practical impact of the ECJ decision. This information was provided by the Government in its next report (see ILO (1998a, p. 337)). In the case of the Indian Supreme Court ruling upholding affirmative action on the basis of caste, the CEACR welcomed the measure and asked to be kept informed of the results it achieved in relation to workforce participation and working conditions. The Australian cases were not brought to the CEACR's attention when reports on the Convention were submitted.

The ILO supervisory bodies, in their most recent General and Special Surveys on aspects of discrimination in employment (ILO, 1996 and 1998b), have not delved into an analysis of affirmative action from the point of view of the notions of equality of opportunity and equality of result. They have not felt it part of their remit to attempt to take sides in the debate of whether special measures should be aimed only at giving all groups a level playing field on which to compete, thereafter leaving the outcome up to merit, or whether they should actually ensure an equal outcome. Commentators on the different systems in place throughout the world, such as Castle (1995), Edwards (1995), Faundez (1994), Hofmeyr (1993), Innes, Kentridge and Perold (1993), Loenan and Veldman (1996), O'Neill and Handley (1994) and Solomos (1989), have written much on the advantages or disadvantages of each approach. Others, like Bacchi (1994) generally and Scutt (1990, pp. 120-123) on the merit principle, argue that the judging of contested concepts should itself be revisited. Management guides on affirmative action also warn of the risk of subjectivity in a blind reliance on "merit" without carefully defining what it means in each enterprise context (see CCH (1990), para. 106). From the international perspective, however, the ILO text (Art. 2) requires a ratifying State "to declare and pursue a national policy designed to promote, by methods appropriate to national conditions and practice, equality of opportunity and treatment ... with a view to eliminating any discrimination" in respect of employment and occupation. The aim is to end discrimination, but the way of doing so is left to each country's discretion.

The CEACR has, however, stated its position on some aspects of both the concept and the way it is applied. For example, it considers that such measures should be designed to restore a balance, and therefore be proportional to the nature and scope of protection needed by the target group (ILO, 1996, paras. 134ff). Once adopted, the special measures should be re-examined periodically, in order to ascertain whether they are still needed and still effective. That is as far as the CEACR has gone in assisting the institutions charged with overseeing the legality of affirmative action — the courts — to work within a framework of clearly stated international rules or guidelines on the subject.

The ILO membership, in adopting the Organization's programme and budget, has given support to a number of research projects which throw light on different countries' conceptual and pragmatic approach to affirmative action. The publications of Chari (1994), Davis (1993), Ghee (1995), ILO-CEET (1997), Lim (1994), O'Regan and Thompson (1993), Ronalds (1998), Serna Calvo (1996) and Ventura (1995) all explain, in varying degrees of detail, how affirmative action was introduced and how it works today in countries throughout the world — in Africa, Asia, Europe, North America, South America. The Office has also in recent years prepared a number of training manuals and tools relating to affirmative action in employment, such as ILO (1995 and 1997) and Lim (1996).

CONCLUSIONS

Why is it that, as the widely different decisions in affirmative action cases described above show, judges have not been able to agree on some common standards for assessing such schemes? It seemed in the late 1980s that the United States Supreme Court was slowly moving towards a set of principles: that a measure should be proportional to its goal; that affirmative action should benefit only the actual victims of discriminatory behaviour (an argument at one stage rejected, then accepted again); that measures should be tempered by the inclusion of checks and balances, like monitoring and annual changes; and that the type of measure involved was crucial to its acceptability (layoffs from existing jobs being viewed less favourably than preferential hiring and training goals), as was the method by which it was adopted. A decade later, however, the decisions returned to a narrow, strictly juridical reading of the Federal Constitution and the Civil Rights Act to strike down affirmative action. Even in Europe, where strong political and social support for the promotion of women's equality exists, the ECJ came to different conclusions when examining laws attempting to change the profile of the male-dominated public service labour force. The most recent case, together with the political commitment to affirmative action now repeated in Article 141 of the Amsterdam Treaty, shows that the concept has returned to its former popularity with policy-makers. But again, why should affirmative action be struck down in a country like South Africa, where the conditions for such measures exist *par excellence*?

Could it be that, as noted earlier, the very concept of fighting an evil using methods linked to that evil is still too hard to swallow? Or does the answer lie in the nature of judicial training and procedures generally, with their emphasis on the strict legal reading of texts (as with Judge Rehnquist's dissenting opinions in the United States Supreme Court in the 1980s), or judges' loathing of entering into political issues (as in the Californian case), or their characteristic slowness in accepting changes in social norms (as in the South African High Court case)? Much could be said, also, about the composition of courts, and the need for greater gender and race sensitivity on the bench.[45] Or could it be that the proponents of affirmative action, the practitioners arguing cases and the courts themselves are unaware of the legal concepts that could come to their aid in deciding such matters? As pointed out above, the international law on the subject, in both United Nations and ILO texts, is clear; but bodies such as the supervisory organs of the ILO, whose task it is to evaluate such schemes in the context of international texts on equality, have been timid in coming forward with strong guidance, even if, when given the chance to do so in reports on ratified Conventions, they have commented favourably when examining measures for achieving equal employment opportunities.

Perhaps the available information is not widely applied because it is not widely disseminated. The ILO's structures, particularly its multidisciplinary teams throughout the world, are charged with spreading international developments in relation to employment, but perhaps more programmes could be embarked on with a view to highlighting affirmative action, its strengths and weaknesses, so that a wider public could assess the position.

Yet again, there might be a need for further international action of a normative character. Is the time not ripe for an international labour Convention (and/or Recommendation) on the subject? The ILO, with its tripartite membership and thorough standard-setting procedures (involving representatives of governments, labour and management throughout the preparations, debate and, ultimately, voting on texts by the full membership at the International Labour Conference), provides a solid institutional framework within which such a possibility could be discussed. The procedure for having items considered to be ripe for an international labour standard placed on the agenda of the International Labour Conference has developed in recent years: the Governing Body chooses from a portfolio of possible topics the subject to be worked on for a first debate at the Conference two years later.[46]

This chapter's analysis of the court decisions of the late 1990s demonstrates that some tighter tests, or norms, are needed for clarity at the national level, for the benefit of not only the victims — or alleged victims — of discriminatory practices, but also the policy-makers who are responsible for eliminating discrimination in employment. As a minimum, an international labour standard could: (1) define the concept, highlighting the temporary nature of such measures, (2) clarify once and for all that affirmative action is not "reverse" discrimination, (3) outline the limits of its aims, (4) give examples of methods proportional to those aims, (5) provide guidance on the relative claims of individual and group damage, (6) clarify the balance to be reached in respecting/diminishing other groups' rights and (7) take a stand on the egregious nature of the discrimination to be overcome.

Such a text would allow courts throughout the world, whether their countries had ratified it or not, to find inspiration in their judgements on factual situations. From what appears above, they certainly need a helping hand. But, even without an international labour standard on the subject, affirmative action in its many forms is here to stay and courts will have to come to grips with the concept sooner rather than later.

Notes

[1] To clarify the use of different terms, it should be noted that the ILO Convention principally concerned — the Discrimination (Employment and Occupation) Convention, 1958 (No. 111) — uses the wording current at the time of its adoption: "special measures". The term "affirmative action" is used in the United States and the recent Namibian legislation, for example. Another term is "employment equity", used in the recent South African legislation and coined by Judge Rosalie Abella, who headed the Canadian Royal Commission into Equality in Employment (1984). The term "positive action" is generally used in Europe, possibly as a translation back from the French "action positive". Other countries, perhaps disillusioned with the negative fallout attaching to the words "affirmative action", prefer "promoting or managing diversity", which, implying as it does a societal change where differences will be valued, sounds less aggressive. It appeals to managers in that it assumes that the diversity of the real world will inevitably reach the enterprise workforce, where one can learn to "manage" it in the interests of the enterprise. See also Agocs and Burr (1996).

[2] The term first appeared in the 1935 National Labor Relations Act (the Wagner Act), 29 U.S.C. in section 160(c). It subsequently appeared in the 1961 Executive Order 10925 requiring all government contractors to take affirmative action to ensure that employees were employed without regard to race, colour or national origin; in the 1965 Executive Order 11246, which repeated the language of the earlier order; and in the 1966 creation of the Office of Federal Contract Compliance Programs to enforce the Orders. In 1967 the Orders were amended by

Executive Order 11375 to include discrimination based on sex and Congress expressed its approval by the adoption of the 1972 amendments to Title VII of the Civil Rights Act 1964, section 717. Other affirmative action requirements appear in the Rehabilitation Act 1973, the United States Code and the Americans with Disabilities Act 1990.

[3] For example, see Hodges-Aeberhard and Raskin (1997). Also see ILO (1998b, paras. 186-191), for a discussion of permissible "special positive measures" under the ILO's Vocational Rehabilitation and Employment (Disabled Persons) Convention, 1983 (No. 159), and Recommendation No. 168.

[4] For example, see various articles in *The Economist* (London), 4 March 1995, p. 16; 11 March 1995, p. 57; 15 April 1995, pp. 11-12 and 19-20; 17 June 1995, pp. 50 and 73-74; 13 January 1996, p. 34; 22 November 1997, p. 82; in *Business Day* (Johannesburg), 29 September 1998, p. 3; and in *Sunday Times* (London), 1 November 1998, p. 25.

[5] Literature is remarkably scarce on this clearly crucial aspect of affirmative action; but see, for example, Black (1996), Joseph and Coleman (1997), and University of Cape Town Graduate School of Business (1997).

[6] The full text of these Acts is available in the ILO's national labour law database (NATLEX) on the Internet at <http://natlex.ilo.org>.

[7] 416 US 312 (1974).

[8] "White" and "Black" are capitalized and used throughout this chapter for consistency, while recognizing that designations differ between southern Africa, Europe and the United States.

[9] 438 US 265 (1978).

[10] 443 US 193 (1979).

[11] Section 708 of Title VII of the Act reads: "Nothing in this title shall be deemed to exempt or relieve any person from any liability, duty, penalty, or punishment provided by any present or future law of any State or political subdivision of a State, other than any such law which purports to require or permit the doing of any act which would be an unlawful employment practice under this title."

[12] 467 US 561 (1984).

[13] 478 US 501 (1986).

[14] 478 US 421 (1986).

[15] 476 US 267 (1986).

[16] 480 US 616 (1987).

[17] See, for example, *Washington Post* (Washington, DC), 10 April 1995, A1 and A9, and 1 June 1995, A7; *The Economist* (London), 17 June 1995; and *New York Times* (New York, NY), 8 December 1995, A24.

[18] See *Washington Post* (Washington, DC), 23 June 1995, A.

[19] 115 S. Ct. 2097 (1995).

[20] 488 US 469 (1989).

[21] Docket No. 94-50569 (1996).

[22] Docket No. 97-15030 (1997).

[23] Case C-450/93: Eckhard Kalanke v Freie Hansestadt Bremen, delivered 17 October 1995, reported 1995 IRLR 660.

[24] Council Directive 76/207/EEC of 9 February 1976, in *Official Journal of the Communities* (Brussels), 1976, No. L. 39/40.

[25] COM(96)88 final, catalogue no. CB-10-96-159-EN-C, Office for the Official Publications of the European Communities, L-2985, Luxembourg.

[26] Case C-409/95 (reference for a preliminary ruling from the Verwaltungsgericht Gelsenkirchen): Helmut Marschall v Land Nordrhein-Westfalen, in *Official Journal of the Communities* (Brussels), C7 of 10 January, 1998, p. 4.

[27] Section 9 reads: "... (2) Equality includes the full and equal enjoyment of all rights and freedoms. To promote the achievement of equality, legislative and other measures designed to protect or advance persons, or categories of persons, disadvantaged by unfair discrimination may be taken. (3) The State may not unfairly discriminate directly or indirectly against anyone on one or more grounds, including race, gender, sex, pregnancy, marital status, ethnic or social origin, colour, sexual orientation, age, disability, religion, conscience, belief, culture, language and birth. (4) ... National legislation must be enacted to prevent or prohibit unfair discrimination [by individuals]."

[28] Act No. 103 of 1994, section 3(5)(a)(vii) reads: "The [Public Service] Commission may, in accordance with section 212(5) of the Constitution and notwithstanding the provisions of section 11, give directions regarding measures to promote the objectives set out in sub-section 212(2) of the Constitution."

[29] Reported in *Industrial Law Journal* (Kenwyn, SA), Vol. 18, Part 2, 1997, pp. 241-322.

[30] Section 8(3)(a), the precursor to section 9 of the 1996 Constitution quoted in footnote 27 above, reads: "This section shall not preclude measures designed to achieve the adequate protection and advancement of persons or groups or categories of persons disadvantaged by unfair discrimination, in order to enable their full and equal enjoyment of all rights and freedoms ..."

[31] Reported in *Industrial Law Journal* (Kenwyn, SA), Vol. 17, 1996, pp. 57ff.

[32] *David Alan Gerhardy v Robert John Brown* (1985) 159 CLR 70.

[33] Industrial Relations Commission Decision 93/1991; 93 IRCommA.

[34] HREOCA 6 (17 March 1992).

[35] For an analysis of the 1960s and 1970s court challenges to India's constitutionally entrenched affirmative action, which turned on the definition of caste and class in the Constitution, see Faundez (1994), pp. 22-25.

[36] Writ petition (Civil) No. 930 of 1990, Ministry of Welfare, India.

[37] The full text of the Universal Declaration is included in a special issue of the *International Labour Review* on "labour rights, human rights" (Vol. 137 (1998), No. 2).

[38] General Assembly resolution 2106 A (XX) of 21 December 1965.

[39] General Assembly resolution 2200 A (XXI) of 16 December 1966, Articles 2(1) and 3, and Article 2(2), 3 and 7(c), respectively.

[40] General Assembly resolution 34/180 of 18 December 1979.

[41] As of 31 March 1999, it has received 132 ratifications, making it one of the most widely ratified of the ILO's labour standards.

[42] Principally the Committee of Experts on the Application of Conventions and Recommendations (CEACR) and the Conference Committee on the Application of Standards.

[43] See, for example, ILO (1996, paragraphs 183-185).

[44] But Congress is to consider ratification in the near future: see Governing Body document GB.274/LILS/5 (March 1999), paragraph 54.

[45] The ILO has addressed the need for continuing professional development for labour courts by publishing Hodges-Aeberhard (1997) and by organizing seminars for labour courts and tribunals on equality issues, such as those held in Harare for southern African labour courts and in Port-of-Spain for the Caribbean courts.

[46] See, for example, Governing Body document GB.274/3 entitled "Date, place and agenda of the 89th Session (2001) of the Conference", adopted at the Governing Body's March 1999 Session.

References

Agocs, C.; Burr, C. 1996. "Employment equity, affirmative action and managing diversity: Assessing the differences", in *International Journal of Manpower* (Bradford), Vol. 17, Nos. 4-5, pp. 30-45.

Bacchi, Carol Lee. 1994. *The politics of affirmative action: "Women", equality and category politics*. London, Sage.

Black, P. A. 1996. "Affirmative action in South Africa: Rational discrimination according to Akerlof", in *South African Journal of Economics* (Pretoria), Vol. 64, No. 1, pp. 74-82.

Castle, Jane. 1995. "Affirmative action in three developing countries: Lessons from Zimbabwe, Namibia and Malaysia", in *South African Journal of Labour Relations* (Pretoria), Vol. 19, No. 1 (Autumn), pp. 6-33.

CCH. 1990. *Implementing affirmative action for women*. Personnel Management in Practice Series. Sydney.

Chari, Unity A. 1994. *Positive action measures to promote the equality of women in employment in Zimbabwe*. Interdepartmental Project on Equality for Women in Employment, Working Paper No. 16. Geneva, ILO.

Davis, Fania E. 1993. *Affirmative action in the United States and its application to women in employment*. Interdepartmental Project on Equality for Women in Employment, Working Paper No. 15. Geneva, ILO.

Edwards, John. 1995. *When race counts: The morality of racial preference in Britain and America*. London, Routledge.

Faundez, Julio. 1994. *Affirmative action: International perspectives*. Geneva, ILO.

Ghee, Lim Teck. 1995. *Social and economic integration of different ethnic groups in South-east Asia, with special reference to Malaysia: A review of the literature and empirical material*. International Institute for Labour Studies, Labour Institutions and Development Programme Discussion Paper No. 82. Geneva, ILO.

Hodges-Aeberhard, Jane. 1997. *An outline of recent developments concerning equality issues in employment for labour court judges and assessors*. Geneva, ILO.

—; Raskin, Carl (eds.). 1997. *Affirmative action in the employment of ethnic minorities and persons with disabilities*. Geneva, ILO.

Hofmeyr, K. B. 1993. "Affirmative action in South African companies: Lessons from experience", in *South African Journal of Labour Relations* (Pretoria), Vol. 17, No. 2 (June), pp. 36-51.

ILO. 1998a. *Report of the Committee of Experts on the Application of Conventions and Recommendations*. General report and observations concerning particular countries. Report III (Part 1A), International Labour Conference, 86th Session, 1998. Geneva.

—. 1998b. *Vocational rehabilitation and employment of disabled persons*. General survey on the reports on the Vocational Rehabilitation and Employment (Disabled Persons) Convention (No. 159) and Recommendation (No. 168), 1983. Report III (Part 1B), International Labour Conference, 86th Session, 1998. Geneva.

—. 1997. *Breaking through the glass ceiling: Women in management*. Report for discussion at the Tripartite Meeting on Breaking through the Glass Ceiling: Women in Management. Sectoral Activities Programme. Geneva.

—. 1996. *Equality in employment and occupation*. Special survey on equality in employment and occupation in respect of Convention No. 111. Report III (Part 4B), International Labour Conference, 83rd Session, 1996. Geneva.

—. 1995. *Gender issues in the world of work: Briefing kit*. Geneva.

ILO-CEET. 1997. *Ethnic minorities in Central and Eastern Europe: Guidelines and rec-ommendations promoting their employment.* ILO Central and Eastern European Team/ ILO Equality and Human Rights Coordination Branch, Working Paper No. 19. Geneva.

Innes, D.; Kentridge, M.; Perold, H. (eds.). 1993. *Reversing discrimination: Affirmative action in the workplace.* London, Oxford University Press.

Jones, James E. 1981. "'Reverse discrimination' in employment: Judicial treatment of affirmative action programmes in the United States", in *International Labour Review* (Geneva), Vol. 120, No. 4 (July-Aug.).

Joseph, Alma M.; Coleman, Henry A. 1997. "Affirmative action and economics: A framework for analysis", in *Public Productivity and Management Review* (San Francisco), Vol. 20, No. 3 (Mar.), pp. 258-271.

Lim, Lin Lean. 1996. *More and better jobs for women: An action guide.* Geneva, ILO.

—. 1994. *Female employment: The window of opportunity for poverty alleviation in Bangladesh.* Bangkok, ILO East Asia Multidisciplinary Advisory Team (EASMAT).

Loenen, Titia; Veldman, Albertine. 1996. "Preferential treatment in the labour market after *Kalanke*: Some comparative perspectives", in *International Journal of Comparative Labour Law and Industrial Relations* (The Hague), Vol. 12, No. 1 (Spring), pp. 43-53.

O'Neill, Nick; Handley, Robin. 1994. *Retreat from injustice: Human rights in Australian law.* Leichhardt, N.S.W., Federation Press.

O'Regan, Catherine; Thompson, Clive. 1993. *Collective bargaining and the promotion of equality: The case of South Africa.* Interdepartmental Project on Equality for Women in Employment, Working Paper No. 8. Geneva, ILO.

Ronalds, Chris. 1998. *Discrimination: Law and practice.* Leichhardt, N.S.W., Federation Press.

Schiek, Dagmar. 1996. "Positive action in Community law: Case C-450/93, Kalanke v Freie Hansestadt Bremen", in *Industrial Law Journal* (Oxford), Vol. 25, No. 3 (Sep.), pp. 239-246.

Scutt, Jocelynne A. 1990. *Women and the law.* Sydney, The Law Book Company Ltd.

Serna Calvo, María del Mar. 1996. *Legislation on women's employment in Latin America: A comparative study.* Labour Law and Labour Relations Programme, Occasional Paper No. 11. Geneva, ILO.

Solomos, John. 1989. "Equal opportunities policies and racial inequality: The role of public policy", in *Public Administration* (Oxford), Vol. 67, No. 1 (Spring), pp. 79-93.

University of Cape Town Graduate School of Business. 1997. *Breakwater Monitor: Comparative developments in affirmative action.* Annual report. Cape Town. Mar.

Ventura, Caterina. 1995. *From outlawing discrimination to promoting equality: Canada's experience with anti-discrimination legislation.* ILO Employment Department, International Migration Paper No. 6. Geneva, ILO.

SUPRANATIONAL ACTION AGAINST SEX DISCRIMINATION: EQUAL PAY AND EQUAL TREATMENT IN THE EUROPEAN UNION

22

Ingeborg HEIDE*

European law has contributed substantially to the promotion of equality between men and women throughout the Union. Its unique supranational character has led to revisions of domestic law in all Member States. Starting with a presentation of the historical development of European institutions and legislation, the author goes on to show how this ongoing process is furthered by the ground-breaking judgements of the European Court of Justice. The importance and scope of this case law are illustrated by a wide selection of non-discrimination rulings on pay, pensions, part-time work, pregnancy and maternity, night work and eligibility for particular occupations.

The vision of a united Europe took its initial shape more than four decades ago, with the Treaty of Rome. Many of the original expectations of greater prosperity, social justice and lasting peace, as expressed in that Treaty, have materialized. This was possible because, from the start, the Community was designed not as a static concept but as a dynamic one, open to changes through amendments to the Treaty of Rome — its primary source of law — and through secondary legislation. Developed in this context, European equality law has had a strong impact on the national legal systems of Member States. Indeed, it shares the unique supranational character of all European law. All workers in all Member States, including the French overseas departments, the Azores, Madeira, Gibraltar and the Canary Islands, can rely on it. European equality law is also applicable to employment outside the Union if both parties to the employment relationship reside in the Union and the discriminatory act took place in the Union. Its scope may be further broadened as prospective

Originally published in *International Labour Review*, Vol. 138 (1999), No. 4.

* Bureau for Gender Equality, ILO, Geneva; seconded from the German Federal Ministry of Labour.

new members of the Union — Bulgaria, Cyprus, the Czech Republic, Estonia, Hungary, Latvia, Lithuania, Malta, Poland, Romania, Slovakia and Slovenia — transpose into their systems the *acquis communautaire*, i.e. the body of common rights and obligations that apply to all Member States.

Yet neither the general public nor even legal specialists are widely familiar with European equality law. Lack of awareness of its concepts and scope has been identified as a major reason for the relative scarcity of equality litigation.[1] Individual employees display very little knowledge of the rights it affords them, especially in respect of the less transparent forms of inequality, like indirect discrimination. But developments in the past few years testify to an enhanced conviction that "Europe matters". The number of equality cases referred to the European Court of Justice (ECJ) for preliminary rulings has been rising consistently. These proceedings are a test of the interpretation of European law in individual cases pending before the national courts. Judges, lawyers and other experts have obviously become more conscious that European law might count in such cases, although the extent to which this is reflected in actual practice varies between the Member States.[2] In 1999, as many as 23 preliminary rulings were pending, with Germany and the United Kingdom in the lead, accounting for 11 and six cases respectively.[3]

This chapter aims to show how European law has helped to promote equality between women and men. It opens with an outline of the development and operation of the relevant European instruments, to set equality law in its broader, historical context of European social policy, legislation, application and law enforcement. A selection of the ECJ's case law is then presented, with a focus on equal pay and equal treatment at the workplace.[4] European equality law being such a vast legal field, other important areas are left aside, either because they deserve separate treatment or because they are covered by recent instruments which have not yet entered into force or not gained sufficient practical relevance. Thus, parental leave and part-time work, aiming at gender equality in a broader sense, will be addressed only briefly. Legislation and case law on occupational and statutory social security systems are touched upon only in the context of equal pay.[5] And maternity protection is discussed only in connection with legislative procedures and direct discrimination.

FROM ROME TO AMSTERDAM: FROM ECONOMIC TO SOCIAL EUROPE

In a strict legal sense, the European Union is the body established by the Treaty on European Union. It is a body without precedent in history whose status is still not clearly and fully defined. Though not a state in itself, it is a *supranational* body "founded on the principles of liberty, democracy, respect for human rights and fundamental freedoms, and the rule of law, principles which are common to the Member States" (Article 6(1) EU).[6] It is vested with its own sovereignty, legislative powers, jurisdiction and law-enforcement mechanisms. In many areas, however, its action remains subject to the agreement of the Member States. Its institutions consist of the following: a Commission, which proposes and monitors European law; a Council, with legislative powers, composed of national ministers; a European Parliament;[7] a Court of Justice; and a Court of Auditors. Central to the Union's operation is the Treaty establishing the European Community, which governs its legislative and law-enforcement functions.

Legislative background and framework

The Treaty of Rome,[8] which established the European Economic Community, focused on the creation of the single market and related social issues. Because not all parties agreed on a stronger commitment to a *social* Europe, "only" the European *Economic* Community was established initially. The Treaty's chapter on social policy thus represented a compromise between the main opponents on this question, Germany and France, the latter being in favour of an enhanced social commitment.[9] However, Article 117 EEC Treaty (now Article 136 EC) made it clear that social progress was primarily expected to be a side effect of economic growth. Any related legislation was to take place under other, specific provisions of the Treaty, e.g. that on the free movement of workers.[10] Legislation on further social matters was envisaged only as a third and last resort.[11] The conflict of opinions over social policy lingered and has dominated all negotiations on amendments to the Treaty and on legislation, including in the field of equality. As a result, the authority of the European Community over social matters has remained limited, with all legal acts requiring competence based upon an article of the Treaty and observance of the principle of subsidiarity as laid down in Article 3b EC Treaty (now Article 5 EC). Yet, despite the general reluctance to pursue common social policies, a crucial provision on equal pay for equal work was incorporated into the original Treaty itself: Article 119 EEC Treaty (now Article 141 EC).

Though part of the Treaty's social chapter, this provision was not included with a view to promoting social justice. Rather, the reason was that some of the founding Members had already ratified the ILO's Equal Remuneration Convention, 1951 (No. 100),[12] which calls for "equal remuneration for work of equal value" (Article 2). Of these, France, in particular, feared a competitive disadvantage for its industries and insisted on the inclusion of such a clause.[13] In its later rulings, however, the European Court of Justice (ECJ) attached great importance to this provision, highlighting its social objectives despite this history.[14]

During its first three decades, the Community thus concentrated on the creation of its internal market, with social policy generally relegated to a minor role. Important legislation on equal pay and equal treatment in employment, as well as in state and occupational social security schemes, was none the less adopted in the 1970s and 1980s. And as market liberalization made progress, the conviction gained ground that the legislative process should be facilitated and the influence of the European Parliament strengthened. In response to the changing economic, political and social environment, the Treaty was amended three times to facilitate, deepen and widen Community policies.[15] This process was first launched in a field which is closely linked with production costs: safety and health at the workplace. The Single European Act (SEA) of 1987[16] introduced the possibility of adopting minimum standards to improve the working environment by majority vote in the Council — whereas unanimity was formerly required in all social matters — and in cooperation with Parliament.[17] This paved the way for the adoption of Directive 92/85/EEC on maternity protection.

In December 1989, all Member States except the United Kingdom made a policy statement in the Community Charter of the Fundamental Social Rights of Workers, emphasizing that the single market must benefit workers as well as employers. Though not legally binding, the Charter represented a political commitment to further codification on a number of issues including equality between women and men and family responsibilities. This was followed up by the Social Policy Agreement (SPA) annexed to the 1992 Treaty of Maastricht,[18] which significantly amended the Treaty of Rome and renamed it "Treaty establishing the European Community" (EC Treaty). In particular, the EC Treaty introduced a new legislative mechanism of *co-decision*[19] that strengthened the Parliament's influence on legislation, though this did not yet apply to social policy. The SPA, however, extended the scope of qualified majority voting beyond occupational health and safety to include hitherto contentious policy issues such as equality between men and women regarding labour market opportunities and working conditions. Legislation on social security and social protection, though, remained subject to unanimity in the Council, acting in consultation with Parliament. Social dialogue was strengthened through a unique procedure involving the social partners in the legislative process.[20] Under Article 6 of the SPA, Member States were allowed to maintain or adopt "measures providing for specific advantages in order to make it easier for women to pursue a vocational activity or to prevent or compensate for disadvantages in their professional careers". This, however, did not prevent the European Court of Justice from setting strict limits to affirmative action in the important *Kalanke* case (see below).

With the entry into force of the Treaty of Amsterdam[21] in May 1999, these provisions were written into the revised Chapter on Social Provi-

---

Box 1. Equality legislation in the European (Economic) Community

Council Directive of 10 February 1975 on the approximation of the laws of the Member States relating to the application of the principle of equal pay for men and women (**75/117/EEC**) — OJ L 45, 19.2.1975

Council Directive of 9 February 1976 on the implementation of the principle of equal treatment for men and women as regards access to employment, vocational training and promotion, and working conditions (**76/207/EEC**) — OJ L 39, 14.2.1976

Council Directive of 19 December 1978 on the progressive implementation of the principle of equal treatment for men and women in matters of social security (**79/7/EEC**) — OJ L 6, 10.1.1979

Council Directive of 24 July 1986 on the implementation of the principle of equal treatment for men and women in occupational social security schemes (**86/378/EEC**) — OJ L 225, 12.8.1986 — amended by the Directive of 20 December 1996 (**96/97/EC**) — OJ L 46, 17.2.1997

Council Directive of 11 December 1986 on the application of the principle of equal treatment between men and women engaged in an activity, including agriculture, in a self-employed capacity, and on the protection of self-employed women during pregnancy and motherhood (**86/613/EEC**) — OJ L 359, 19.12.1986

Council Directive of 19 October 1992 on the introduction of measures to encourage improvements in the safety and health at work of pregnant workers and workers who have recently given birth or are breastfeeding (tenth individual Directive within the meaning of Article 16(1) of Directive 81/391/EEC) (**92/85/EEC**) — OJ L 348, 28.11.1992

Council Directive of 3 June 1996 on the framework agreement on parental leave concluded by UNICE, CEEP and the ETUC (**96/34/EC**) — OJ L 145, 19.6.1996 — and Council Directive of 15 December 1997 amending and extending, to the United Kingdom of Great Britain and Northern Ireland, Directive 96/34/EC on the framework agreement on parental leave concluded by UNICE, CEEP and the ETUC (**97/75/EC**) — OJ L 10, 16.1.1998

Council Directive of 15 December 1997 on the burden of proof in cases of discrimination based on sex (**97/80/EC**) — OJ L 14, 20.1.1998

Council Directive of 15 December 1997 concerning the Framework Agreement on part-time work concluded by UNICE, CEEP and the ETUC (**97/81/EC**) — OJ L 14, 20.1.1998.

---

sions of the Treaty establishing the European Community.[22] Positive discrimination in working life is now recognized — though its limits are still to be tested — in the fourth paragraph of Article 141 EC. Its third paragraph provides the Community with its own legal basis for adopting "measures to ensure the application of the principle of equal opportunities and equal treatment of men and women in matters of employment and occupation, including the principle of equal pay for equal work or work of equal value", by majority vote of the Council acting in co-decision with Parliament. Article 13 EC, as amended, sets out a procedure for adopting measures against discrimination in areas other than employment, including legislation to combat discrimination linked with sexual orientation. A more solid, more extensive and more democratic legal basis for action has thus been established.

Application and enforcement of European equality law

How European legislation is applied depends on its form and content. Ratification is required for the basic Treaties of Rome, Maastricht and Amsterdam,[23] but not for legislation made thereunder — i.e. regulations and directives. While regulations are directly applicable, without requiring any further action at the national level, directives are binding on all Member States only with respect to their objectives (see Article 249 EC/ex Article 189 EEC Treaty). Thus each individual state may, in principle, freely decide on how to apply a directive; and states obviously have an interest in using their own administrative structures and keeping the monitoring in their own hands. All legal instruments in the field of equality between women and men have been adopted in the form of directives.

All equality directives impose on the Member States the duty to ensure that any statutory, regulatory or contractual provisions at variance with equality principles be removed, that an effective judicial system be in place, that workers be informed of their rights, and that they not be victimized for upholding their rights. Accordingly, laws and regulations must be scrutinized, amended and/or enacted to comply with the aims of each directive. This legislative process involves government, parliament, heads of state and often also the social partners and other civil-society organizations, which is why all directives determine a time frame for their implementation and a further period for submission of national reports thereon. These periods vary: for the Equal Pay Directive (75/117/EEC), the period for compliance was one year[24] with a further two years for the submission of national reports; the Equal Treatment Directive (76/207/EEC) allowed 30 months, plus two additional years for reporting, and the Directive on Equal Treatment in Statutory Social Security (79/7/EEC), six years and one additional year, respectively. If a state fails to transpose a directive into its national law in time, individual claimants cannot avail themselves of its provisions directly, though the state at fault is then liable for compensation. In *Francovich and Bonifaci v Italian Republic*, the Court made the following ruling:

> 1. The provisions of Council Directive 80/987/EEC of 20 October 1980 on the approximation of the laws of the Member States relating to the protection of employees in the event of the insolvency of their employers, which defines employees' rights, must be interpreted as meaning that interested parties may not assert those rights against the State in proceedings before the national courts in the absence of implementing measures adopted within the prescribed period.
>
> 2. A Member State is obliged to make good the damage suffered by individuals as a result of the failure to implement Directive 80/987/EEC (Cases C-6/90 and C-9/90, ECR 1991, p. I-5357).[25]

In its later judgements on *Dillenkofer and Others v Federal Republic of Germany*,[26] the Court confirmed state liability for failure to implement a directive under three conditions: (a) the result prescribed by the directive must entail the grant of rights to individuals; (b) the content of those rights must be identifiable on the basis of the provisions of the directive; and (c) there must be a causal link between the breach of the obligation resting on the State and the damage sustained by the injured parties.

In *Grimaldi v Fonds des Maladies Professionnelles*, the Court ruled that even recommendations of the Commission must be taken into account for the interpretation of Community law:

> In the light of the fifth paragraph of Article 189 of the EEC Treaty, the Commission Recommendation of 23 July 1962 concerning the adoption of the European Schedule of industrial diseases and Commission Recommendation 66/462 of 20 July 1966 on the conditions for granting compensation to persons suffering from occupational diseases cannot in themselves confer rights on individuals upon which the latter may rely before national courts. However, national courts are bound to take those recommendations into consideration in order to decide disputes submitted to them, in particular where they are capable of casting light on the interpretation of other provisions of national or Community law (Case C-322/88, ECR 1989, p. 4407).

This view may have motivated the judges of the High Court of Catalonia to set a precedent by referring to the Commission's *Code of practice to combat sexual harassment*. They held that "repeated jokes of bad taste with sexual connotations", as interpreted by the Commission as sexual harassment, constituted grave misconduct on the part of the worker which justified his dismissal.[27] This case law may likewise become relevant for other "soft law", such as the Commission's *Code of conduct concerning the implementation of equal pay for women and men for work of equal value*.

Under Article 6 of the Equal Treatment Directive — and similar provisions in the other directives — all Member States are required to "introduce into their national legal systems such measures as are necessary to enable all persons who consider themselves wronged by failure to apply to them the principle of equal treatment ... to pursue their claims by judicial process after possible recourse to other competent authorities". The meaning of this Article was at issue in *Johnston v Chief Constable of the Royal Ulster Constabulary*.[28] This case dealt with a national-law provision invoked by the defendant to substantiate an exception from the general prohibition of discrimination which was not reviewable by any court or other independent body. In its ruling, the ECJ stressed that access to justice was a principle common to the constitutional traditions of the Member States, which were also addressed in Articles 6 and 13 of the European Convention for the Protection of Human Rights and Fundamental Freedoms of 1951, so that all persons who felt discriminated against must be able to obtain judicial recourse and effective remedy in a court or tribunal.

Only employees of Community institutions can involve the ECJ *directly* for discrimination in their employment relationship.[29] Normally, individual litigation takes place in the national judicial systems, under national rules and procedures. But the national courts are bound to observe European law and to interpret national law accordingly. The *preliminary rulings* of the ECJ are meant to ensure that Community law is interpreted consistently throughout the Union.

> The Court of Justice shall have jurisdiction to give preliminary rulings concerning:
>
> (a) the interpretation of this Treaty;
>
> (b) the validity and interpretation of acts of the institutions of the Community ... Where such a question is raised before any court or tribunal of a Member State, that court or tribunal may, if it considers that a decision on the question is necessary to enable it to give judgment, request the Court of Justice to give a ruling thereon.
>
> Where any such question is raised in a case pending before a court or tribunal of a Member State against whose decisions there is no judicial remedy under national law, that court or tribunal shall bring the matter before the Court of Justice (Article 234 EC/ ex Article 177 EC Treaty).

National courts thus have the option or, in the last instance, the obligation to refer to the European Court of Justice (ECJ), whenever European law might be relevant to a particular case. Non-observance of this duty constitutes a breach of Community law which may lead to *infringement* proceedings against the state concerned. The questions referred to the Court, as well as its responses, usually take the form of an abstract "dialogue between judges". The Court's interpretation of Community law must then be applied to the case in point by the national court when it takes its final decision.

Besides its legislative and executive functions, the European Commission also plays an important part in supervising the implementation of Community law on the basis of national reports, petitions or other information. The Commission may bring a case of non-compliance before the ECJ where a state fails to comply, within a prescribed period, with a *reasoned opinion* delivered by the Commission after the state concerned has been given the opportunity to submit its observations.[30] Such proceedings can also be initiated by other Member States.[31]

If the Court finds that a state has failed to fulfil an obligation, the state in question is required to take the necessary measures to comply with the judgement. The Commission can again institute infringement proceedings if it considers the measures taken as insufficient, and request that the Court impose a lump sum or penalty payment. It did so this year in the case of France, for non-implementation of an earlier judgement on the ban of nightwork by women.[32] The Court has dealt with infringement cases against Belgium,[33] Denmark,[34] Germany,[35] Greece,[36] France,[37] Italy,[38] Luxembourg[39] and the United Kingdom.[40] Only recently, the Commission initiated a number of proceedings for failure to transpose Directives 92/85/EC, 96/34/EC and 96/97/EC.[41]

Primarily aimed at bringing national law into line with Community law, infringement proceedings account for a relatively small share of the Court's equality case law, compared to more than 100 preliminary rulings. Indeed, most problems are corrected and settled during the pre-judicial phase.[42] Yet infringement cases, though not significant in numbers, are of great political importance. The mere possibility of action against a Member State, combined with the threat of compensation and penalties, have certainly promoted observance of Community law and pushed equality issues higher on the national agendas.

THE EUROPEAN COURT OF JUSTICE'S RULINGS ON EQUAL PAY

ECJ rulings share the supranational character of European legislation. They are directly binding and must be applied throughout the European Union. Some 120 Court rulings have dealt with equality matters. Although the nature of case law implies that there is no systematic and continuous development, the Court has generated remarkable principles of interpretation which will be presented in the following sections.

Equal pay for men and women — a fundamental workers' right

1. Each Member State shall ensure that the principle of equal pay for male and female workers for equal work or work of equal value is applied.

2. For the purpose of this Article, "pay" means the ordinary basic or minimum wage or salary and any other consideration, whether in cash or in kind, which the worker receives directly or indirectly, in respect of his employment, from his employer.

Equal pay without discrimination based on sex means:

(a) that pay for the same work at piece rates shall be calculated on the basis of the same unit of measurement;

(b) that pay for work at time rates shall be the same for the same job.

3. The Council, acting in accordance with the procedure referred to in Article 251, and after consulting the Economic and Social Committee, shall adopt measures to ensure the application of the principle of equal opportunities and equal treatment of men and women in matters of employment and occupation, including the principle of equal pay for equal work or work of equal value.

4. With a view to ensuring full equality in practice between men and women in working life, the principle of equal treatment shall not prevent any Member State from maintaining or adopting measures providing for specific advantages in order to make it easier for the underrepresented sex to pursue a vocational activity or to prevent or compensate for disadvantages in professional careers. (Article 141 EC/ex Article 119 EC Treaty).

The original version of Article 119 EC Treaty covered only the right to equal pay for *equal work*. But Article 1 of the Equal Pay Directive (75/117/EEC) subsequently broadened this concept to include equal pay *for work to which equal value is attributed*. The Treaty of Amsterdam finally amended the wording of Article 119 EC Treaty accordingly (now Article 141 EC, as reproduced above). This broader approach may require the introduction of a suitable job classification scheme to enable individuals to obtain recognition of equivalence. Yet in an infringement case (61/81) against the United Kingdom, where the introduction of a job classification system was left to the employer's discretion,[43] the Court regarded national legislation as being at all events contrary to European law if it failed to provide for an appropriate authority before which workers could claim that their work had the same value as other work in the event of disagreement.

Roughly one-third of ECJ equality cases have dealt with pay equality under Article 119 of the Treaty (now Article 141 EC) and Directive 75/117/EEC. As early as 1976, the Court's ruling on the *Defrenne II* case paved the way for dynamic evolution. Ms. Defrenne worked as a stewardess for the Belgian airline Sabena from 1951 to 1968. While she was so employed, female stewardesses received a lower salary than did male cabin stewards. In 1968, her contract was terminated under a clause which provided that women should cease to be members of the air crew on reaching the age of 40. Ms. Defrenne first sued the Belgian State for "equal pay", on grounds of discrimination under the applicable statutory retirement pension scheme.[44] She later challenged Sabena on the pay differential during her employment,[45] and then claimed compensation for loss of earnings after her dismissal.[46] All three cases were referred to the ECJ for interpretation.

The Court dealt with the question of the retirement pension in *Defrenne I*, concluding that Article 119 of the Treaty was not applicable to payments under state pension schemes (Directive 79/7/EEC, which covers such schemes, was not yet adopted). Ms. Defrenne's compensation claim for sex discrimination linked with her dismissal (*Defrenne III*) was also rejected: Article 119 of the Treaty does not cover elements other than pay, and Directive 76/207/EEC (on equal treatment) did not yet exist in 1968. Her second claim, concerning the pay differential during her employment (*Defrenne II*), was successful.

In this case of paramount importance, the parties had agreed that the work of an air hostess was identical to that of a cabin steward so that pay discrimination was no longer disputed. The main legal problem was that she had been employed from 1951 to 1968, before Directive 75/117/EEC was adopted, and that Belgian legislation guaranteeing equal pay did not yet exist.

The specific issues to be resolved included the following: Could Article 119 of the Treaty serve directly as a legal basis for pay claims? Could it be invoked by individuals not only against the State but also — in connection with collective agreements and contracts — between individuals? Did it matter that the European Commission had not pursued further the application of the principle of equal pay enshrined in the Treaty? What were the criteria to be applied in determining "equal" pay if the relevant conditions were null and void because of their discriminatory nature? Could a pay claim be made for a past period and, if so, for which period? Would all workers in a similar situation be entitled to retroactive payments? This last question in particular raised serious concern, and the Member States pleaded for retroactive validity to be restricted to pending cases at the most.

The Court stated that, because of its distinct and fundamental character, Article 119 of the Treaty had *direct vertical and horizontal effects*. In other words, it could be invoked for claims against private employers before the national courts as well as against the State "in particular in the case of those forms of discrimination which have their origin in legislative provisions or collective labour agreements, as well as where men and women receive unequal pay for equal work which is carried out in the same establishment or service, whether private or public". From the Member States' commitment to improve living and working conditions under Article 117 EEC Treaty (now Article 136 EC), the Court reasoned that the persons discriminated against should receive higher pay aligned on that of the reference group (i.e. no "levelling down"). The right to equal pay was granted from 1 January 1962 in the founding countries and from the time of accession to the Community in other countries. Due to overriding considerations of legal certainty, however, the ruling's retroactive effects were limited to persons who had already taken steps to safeguard their rights. Others are entitled to retroactive payments from 8 April 1976, i.e. the date of the *Defrenne II* judgement. A similar limitation was later introduced into the case law on occupational pension schemes by the 1990 judgement on the *Barber* case.[47]

In all its subsequent judgements concerning equal pay, the Court has made reference to the *Defrenne II* case and based its arguments exclusively or primarily on Article 119 of the Treaty, notwithstanding the more detailed provisions of Directive 75/117/EEC. In the recent past, this Directive has been mentioned as well, but merely as implementing Article 119 and therefore sharing its direct effect. The Court has thus avoided comment on the fact that, in principle, directives do not have direct effect in national law. For this reason also, the scope of Article 119 has been interpreted extensively.

The wide scope of the right to equal pay

Article 141 EC (ex Article 119 EEC/EC Treaty) guarantees equal pay for *work of equal value* and applies not only to ordinary wages or salary *per se*, but also to "any other consideration, whether in cash or in kind, which the worker receives, directly or indirectly, in respect of his [or her] employment from his [or her] employer" — in line with the definition of remuneration in ILO Convention No. 100 (1951). The principle of equality is constructively applicable to: contributions to an occupational pension scheme paid by an employer;[48] payments from such schemes after retirement;[49] temporary payments effected by an employer after cessation of work, such as severance grants;[50] and maintenance of salary in the event of sickness.[51] Any fringe benefits provided by an employer to former employees — even without legal obligation — are covered as well. In the recent judgement on *The Queen v Secretary of State for Employment, ex parte Seymour-Smith and Perez*,[52] payments made to compensate for unfair dismissal were also regarded as pay. The Court's wide approach is illustrated by the following examples.

Ms. Garland[53] sued her former employer, British Rail, because although it granted reduced train fares equally to its former male *and* female employees, this benefit extended only to the relatives of male retirees — not to those of the female pensioners. The Court argued that additional benefits that are paid voluntarily after termination of employment fell within the scope of Article 119 of the Treaty, rendering *any* differentiation on grounds of sex illegal.

Similar travel concessions — this time demanded for a homosexual partner — were the subject of a recent ruling on *Grant v South-West Trains Ltd.*[54] According to the employer's staff regulations, concessionary tickets were granted to an employee's married partner or to a partner of the opposite sex with whom a "meaningful relationship" existed. Ms. Grant claimed the benefit for a female cohabitee, which the employer rejected. In the Court's view, the denial of the benefit was based on sexual orientation, not sex. Discrimination on the basis of sexual orientation was not seen as covered by current European law, though it was highlighted in the judgement that legislation to eliminate discrimination on that basis could be adopted under Article 13 EC once the Treaty of Amsterdam had entered into force. This provides that "the Council, acting unanimously on a proposal from the Commission and after consulting the European Parliament, may take appropriate action to combat discrimination based on sex, racial or ethnic origin, religion or belief, disability, age or sexual orientation".

Although *Ms. Murphy*[55] and her 28 female colleagues performed work that required undisputedly *higher* skills than did their male colleagues' work, they were paid *less*. Their claim for the *same* pay was rejected because, in the opinion of the equality officer responsible, the right to equal pay could only be invoked for work of the same value, not for work of superior value. The ECJ, to which the case was referred, pointed out that Article 119 EC Treaty *a fortiori* precluded rejection of the equal pay claim but did not entitle the workers to *higher* pay.

In *Macarthys Ltd v Smith*,[56] the Court had to deal with the case of a female employee who was paid UK£10 less per week than her male predecessor, whose post she had taken over after an interval of four months. Here also, the principle of equal pay was applied because it is not confined to situations in which men and women perform equal work *at the same time.*

A similar situation came up more recently in *Levez v T. H. Jennings (Harlow Pools) Ltd.*[57] In 1991, Ms. Levez had replaced a male employee with an income of UK£11,400 per year; but her remuneration was only UK£10,000. She had been misinformed by the employer as to the salary paid to her predecessor. Furthermore, a national restriction limited the award of pay arrears to two years prior to the commencement of proceedings. Since the application of this provision would have limited her pay claim, the Employment Appeal Tribunal referred the matter for interpretation to the ECJ, which stated that under such circumstances the time limit could not be applied.

Pay issues were also raised recently in the context of pregnancy, maternity and parental leave. *Pedersen and Others v Fællesforeningen for Danmarks Brugsforeninger and Others*[58] was a case brought by several women employees who had suffered pregnancy-related complications *prior* to the three-month period preceding their expected date of confinement. Danish legislation provided that pregnant women who, due to their pregnancy, were unfit for work before that period, were not entitled to full pay, whereas employees unfit to work because of illness were entitled to full pay. The Court regarded as discriminatory this detriment resulting from a "pathological condition connected with her pregnancy". Two further cases concerned the denial of a Christmas bonus to mothers on reduced working time or parental leave following maternity.[59] Here the Court ruled that a Christmas bonus paid voluntarily or by contractual agreement was to be regarded as "pay" and that the exclusion of part-time workers constituted "indirect discrimination" if a large majority of the workers adversely affected were women. The exclusion of mothers on parental leave was held to constitute indirect discrimination only if the bonus was a reward for past service, as opposed to an incentive for the future — an issue to be determined by the national courts.

Part-time work, occupational pensions and the concept of indirect pay discrimination

In recognizing that certain forms of unfavourable treatment can amount to indirect sex discrimination, the Court has considerably improved the protection afforded to part-time workers. In Europe, part-time workers are far more likely to be women than men. In 1998 women's share of part-time employment ranged from 63 per cent in Finland to 97 per cent in Sweden.[60] The case law of the ECJ has helped to draw greater attention to the fair interests of this particular group of workers. Indeed, improving the situation of part-time workers may also contribute to a better sharing of paid and unpaid work.

Indirect sex discrimination occurs where laws or agreements that appear to be gender-neutral and egalitarian actually have different effects on men and women, with statistical evidence showing that, say, many more female than male workers are excluded from certain payments, positions or benefits. Any rule or practice causing such effects is unlawful unless it can be justified on grounds unconnected with sex discrimination. Following a number of ECJ rulings, indirect discrimination is now defined in Article 2 (2) of Directive 97/80/EC which will come into force on 1 January 2001 (see Box 2 below).[61]

The Court's jurisprudence on pay in the context of part-time work and indirect discrimination started with the case of *Jenkins v Kingsgate Ltd.*[62] Kingsgate, a clothing company, paid hourly rates to part-timers that were 10 per cent lower than those paid to full-timers; all part-time workers were women. Ms. Jenkins, who worked 75 per cent of the normal working time, brought an equal pay claim by comparing her hourly income with that of a full-time male employee. Even the employer agreed that the work they performed was identical. Considering her case to be one of indirect pay discrimination, the Court stated that: "A difference in pay between full-time workers and part-time workers does not amount to discrimination prohibited by Article 119 of the Treaty unless it is in reality merely *an indirect way of reducing the pay of part-time workers* on the ground that the group of workers is composed exclusively or predominantly of women". It made it clear, however, that such intent ought to be assumed because the same employer had previously paid all its female workers less.

The notion of indirect discrimination was further developed in *Bilka Kaufhaus v Weber von Hartz*. Bilka belonged to a group of department stores which employed several thousand workers who normally joined the company's occupational pension scheme. Part-time workers, however, were contractually excluded from the scheme unless they had worked full time for at least 15 years. Ms. Weber von Hartz, who had worked for Bilka for 15 years — including four years part time — was denied an occupational pension. She sued the employer for indirect pay discrimination, arguing that almost all part-time workers were female. The Court regarded the benefits of the pension scheme as linked to employment and, therefore, "pay". Accordingly, it ruled that:

1. Article 119 of the EEC Treaty is infringed by a department store company which excludes part-time employees from its occupational pension scheme, where that exclusion affects a far greater number of women than men, unless the undertaking shows that the exclusion is based on objectively justified factors unrelated to any discrimination on grounds of sex.

2. Under Article 119 a department store company may justify the adoption of a pay policy excluding part-time workers, irrespective of their sex, from its occupational pensions scheme on the ground that it seeks to employ as few part-time workers as possible where it is found that the means chosen for achieving that objective correspond to a real need on the part of the undertaking, are appropriate with a view to achieving the objective in question and are necessary to that end.

3. Article 119 does not have the effect of requiring an employer to organise its occupational pension scheme in such a manner as to take into account the particular difficulties faced by persons with family responsibilities in meeting the conditions for entitlement to such a pension (Case 170/84, ECR 1986, p. 1607).

It was thus explicitly acknowledged that no intention of discrimination was required to regard a certain policy as illegal under European law. The following guidelines were used to tackle the problem of indirect discrimination: it is up to the claimant to show that a certain policy has negative effects on considerably more members of one sex than the other; the employer may justify its policy by *objective reasons* which appropriately respond to a *specific need* of the company, with respect not only to the *goals* pursued but also to the *commensurate means* employed; it is then up to the national court to determine whether the policy in question amounts to sex discrimination. Bilka was unable to justify its policy and had to change it.

The requirement of a strict test for objective justification based on necessity and proportionality was later extended to the negative effects of national legislation. Challenged in *Rinner-Kühn v FWW Spezial-Gebäudereinigung GmbH & Co. KG* was the legality of Germany's law on the continued payment of wages during illness, which obliged employers to pay sick leave for up to six weeks, but excluded part-time workers working less than ten hours per week or 45 hours per month. The large majority of the part-timers adversely affected were women. Ms. Rinner-Kühn, who normally worked ten hours per week, claimed pay for eight hours during which she was unable to work because she was sick. The Court held the statutory provision on the basis of which her claim was rejected to be contrary to Community law unless the German State could show that it was *justified by purely objective considerations*:

> Article 119 of the EEC Treaty must be interpreted as precluding national legislation which permits employers to exclude employees whose normal working hours do not exceed 10 hours a week or 45 hours a month from the continued

payment of wages in the event of illness, if that measure affects a far greater number of women than men, unless the Member State shows that the legislation concerned is justified by objective factors unrelated to any discrimination on grounds of sex (Case 171/88, ECR 1989, p. 2743).

The national labour court which then resumed its consideration of the case did not accept the Government's argument, so the law had to be amended.

In *Kowalska v Freie und Hansestadt Hamburg*,[63] the question was whether a collective agreement may allow employers to exclude part-time workers from a temporary benefit payable to full-timers on termination of their employment. In *Nimz v Freie und Hansestadt Hamburg*,[64] the collective agreement contained a provision whereby part-timers took much longer to qualify for promotion to a higher salary range. Again, the disfavoured groups were predominantly women. The Court was unimpressed by the autonomy of the social partners. It pointed out that Article 119 of the Treaty was sufficiently clear and precise to be relied upon before a national court in order to set aside a discriminatory provision in a collective agreement.

A recent preliminary ruling dealt with an incremental credit determined on the basis of actual time worked in job-sharing situations. In *Hill and Stapleton v The Revenue Commissioners and Department of Finance*,[65] two women participating in a job-sharing scheme challenged a rule whereby two years' job-sharing service counted as one year's full-time service, thus leading to slower progression on the pay scale. With women accounting for 98 per cent of all job-sharing contracts, the Court again concluded that such a rule was contrary to the principle of equal pay unless it could be justified by objective factors alone. In its reasoning, the Court stressed that about 83 per cent of the job-sharers used this option to better combine work and family responsibilities, and that Community policy in this area was to encourage such schemes and to protect women in the same way as men.

While some cases on occupational pensions have clearly served women's financial interests, this has not always been so. The *Barber* and so-called *post-Barber* cases,[66] dealing with the legality of different pensionable ages for women and men, have led to the loss of women's privileged position in this respect. The background to these cases was that, although Member States were allowed to determine different pensionable ages for women and men under state social security schemes,[67] a significant number of occupational pension schemes had taken up the same differentiation for employer-financed pensions as well.

Mr. Barber filed a lawsuit because he felt discriminated against due to the different minimum pensionable ages set for female and male workers. Under the applicable occupational pension scheme of the Guardian Royal Exchange Assurance Group, women were normally entitled to old-age pensions from the age of 57, and men from the age of 62. Former employees who were unemployed received benefits under the scheme from the age of 50 (women) or 55 (men). For a state pension, the pensionable ages were 60 for women and 65 for men. The occupational pension scheme was organized as a contracted-out scheme which replaced the state pension scheme and was primarily based on contributions from the employer.

Dismissed for organizational reasons at the age of 52, Mr. Barber claimed the occupational pension which his female colleagues in the same situation were entitled to receive. The case was referred to the ECJ, which held that occupational pension schemes resulting in higher accumulated benefits for female than for male pensioners were inconsistent with the right to equal pay. For reasons of legal certainty — as in *Defrenne II* — retroactive claims were limited to persons who had already taken steps to defend their rights before a court or tribunal. Other disadvantaged persons are entitled to retroactive claims from 17 May 1990, the date of the Barber judgement.

As a result of this ruling, a large number of occupational pension schemes had to be changed to incorporate the principle of equal pay, often with the involvement of the social partners. As long as there were no contractual agreements or provisions in place allowing the use of other criteria and until the new schemes were put in place, the hitherto disadvantaged group of men was entitled to the better treatment so far accorded to women (i.e. "levelling up").

The Court's ruling provoked intense discussion because the schemes had to be reorganized in a period of economic restraint, on the basis of cost-neutral calculations, which led to an unfavourable revision of pension rights for women workers. Nevertheless, the ruling was in line with the Court's logic of promoting *absolute equality* between women and men. It also makes sense from the point of view of equal labour market opportunities, which are certainly promoted through the equalization of non-wage labour costs.

Several "post-Barber" judgements have since dealt with more specific situations. Of particular relevance among these were two cases dealing, inter alia, with a Protocol annexed to the Maastricht Treaty which was meant to limit the effects of the Barber and post-Barber case law, namely:

> For the purposes of Article 119 of this Treaty, benefits under occupational social security schemes shall not be considered as remuneration if and in so far as they are attributable to periods of employment prior to 17 May 1990, except in the case of workers or those claiming under them who have before that date initiated legal proceedings or introduced an equivalent claim under the applicable national law *(Protocol concerning Article 119 of the Treaty establishing the European Community)*.

An ancillary question the Court had to answer was whether the limitation of effects in time — consequent upon the Barber judgement and this Protocol — also applied to workers unlawfully excluded from the benefits of an occupational pension scheme. This was the case in *Dietz v Stichting Thuiszorg Rotterdam*[68] and in *Magorrian and Cunningham v East-ern Health and Social Services Board and Department of Health and Social Services*[69] — two cases in which the claimants were part-timers. Following its judgement on the Bilka case, the Court stated that in a case of indirect sex discrimination — which is up to the national court to determine — benefits from occupational pension schemes must be taken into account as from 8 April 1976 (the date of the judgement on *Defrenne II*), not from the date of the Barber judgement or any later date. A number of cases raising similar problems are still pending.[70]

The burden of proof and "work of equal value"

When a person files a legal complaint, it is in principle up to her or him to prove the facts of the alleged claim. The *burden of proof* is a procedural rule dealing with situations where, in the presentation of a case, an assertion is not clearly provable. The ECJ has developed a set-tled case law on the burden of proof in a number of important rulings on equal pay. The new directive on the burden of proof in sex discrimina-tion cases (97/80/EC), due to come into force on 1 January 2001, ex-tends the new rules on the burden of proof to situations covered by Arti-cle 119 EC Treaty (Article 141 EC) and by Directives 75/117/EEC, 76/207/EEC, 92/85/EEC and 96/34/EC (see Box 2).

In *Handels-ogKontorfunktionærernes Forbund i Danmark v Dansk Arbejdgiverforening (acting on behalf of Danfoss)*,[71] there was statistical evidence that women working for that company averaged considerably lower earnings than men, though the reasons for the pay gap were un-clear. It was ruled that where a system lacks transparency and a *prima facie* case of pay discrimination is made, the burden of proof shifts to the employer who can rebut the evidence by showing that the pay system is entirely gender-neutral.

Enderby v Frenchay Area Health Authority[72] dealt with the pay sys-tem of the British public health service in which (mainly male) pharma-cists received higher pay than speech therapists (who were mainly fe-male) by virtue of two separately negotiated collective agreements. The Court ruled that their common employer had to abide by the principle of equal pay irrespective of the validity of the underlying bargaining pro-cesses. It also spelled out criteria for the possible justification of specific additional payments, such as seniority, special demand, flexibility, mo-bility, etc.

In May 1999, the Court delivered a ruling on psychotherapists with different training and qualifications employed by the same institution. In *Angestelltenbetriebsrat der Wiener Gebietskrankenkasse v Wiener Gebiets-krankenkasse*,[73] it held that the employer is not obliged to pay the same

---

Box 2. Excerpt from the Directive on the burden of proof in sex discrimination cases (97/80/EC)

Article 1

Aim

The aim of this Directive shall be to ensure that the measures taken by the Member States to implement the principle of equal treatment are made more effective, in order to enable all persons who consider themselves wronged because the principle of equal treatment has not been applied to them to have their rights asserted by judicial process after possible recourse to other competent bodies.

Article 2

Definitions

1. For the purposes of this Directive, the principle of equal treatment shall mean that there shall be no discrimination whatsoever based on sex, either directly or indirectly.

2. For purposes of the principle of equal treatment referred to in paragraph 1, indirect discrimination shall exist where an apparently neutral provision, criterion or practice disadvantages a substantially higher proportion of the members of one sex unless that provision, criterion or practice is appropriate and necessary and can be justified by objective factors unrelated to sex.

Article 3

Scope

1. This Directive shall apply to:

(a) the situations covered by Article 119 of the Treaty and by Directives 75/117/EEC, 76/207/EEC and, insofar as discrimination based on sex is concerned, 92/85/EEC and 96/34/EC; ...

Article 4

Burden of proof

1. Member States shall take such measures as are necessary, in accordance with their national judicial systems, to ensure that, when persons who consider themselves wronged because the principle of equal treatment has not been applied to them establish, before a court or other competent authority, facts from which it may be presumed that there has been direct or indirect discrimination, it shall be for the respondent to prove that there has been no breach of the principle of equal treatment. ...

---

salaries to persons who perform seemingly identical tasks but who draw upon knowledge and skills acquired in different disciplines and who do not have the same qualifications to perform other tasks that may be assigned to them. Further interpretation of "work of equal value" can be expected in the pending *Svenaeus* case,[74] where the question asked is whether the same value can be assigned to the work of a midwife and that of a clinical technician.

DISCRIMINATION BASED ON SEX UNDER THE EQUAL TREATMENT DIRECTIVE

The principle of equal treatment, as laid down in Article 2(1) of the Equal Treatment Directive (76/207/EEC), requires that there be "no discrimination on the grounds of sex either directly or indirectly by reference in particular to marital or family status". About one-third of the ECJ's rulings on equality matters have dealt primarily or solely with the interpretation of this Directive. Some of the rulings have had little practical relevance, but are nevertheless noteworthy because they reflect the Court's perception of sexual self-determination.

In *P. v S. and Cornwall County Council*,[75] the dismissal of a transsexual was questioned. This dismissal was regarded as "based on sex" and therefore contradictory to Article 5(1) of Directive 76/207/EEC. Another reference for preliminary ruling concerned the legality of a national policy of discharging from the armed forces any person of homosexual orientation.[76] This would have been an opportunity to clarify whether sexual orientation can, in terms of equal treatment, be seen differently from what the Court decided in the above-mentioned *Grant* case, but the case was withdrawn.

Most of the equal treatment cases have improved the situation of a large majority of working women by defining discrimination in the context of pregnancy, affirmative action, part-time work, night work, and work with weapons, as well as the consequences of violations of the right to equal treatment.

Direct discrimination associated with pregnancy and maternity

It is settled ECJ case law that the dismissal of a female worker on account of pregnancy constitutes direct discrimination on grounds of sex.[77] This held even for the dismissal of a pregnant women who had originally been employed, under a contract of unlimited duration, to replace an employee on maternity leave.[78]

Since the Court's ruling on *Dekker v VJV-Centrum Plus*,[79] it is also established that an employer who refuses to engage a woman because she is pregnant commits an act of direct discrimination. In this case, the job was given to another woman, so the question that came up was whether one could speak of sex discrimination if the successful applicant was also a woman. The Court answered with a resounding "yes": since the basis for rejection of the job application was a criterion which could only affect women, direct discrimination was clearly present without any need for comparison.

The pending *Silke* case[80] is about whether an employer may refuse an applicant for a permanent post which she is qualified to hold, because she is pregnant and cannot *from the outset and for the duration of her pregnancy* do the specific work required because of a prohibition under maternity law.

The Court's position on the consequences of pregnancy-related sick leave has been inconsistent. In the case of *Ms. Hertz*,[81] it argued that the Directive did not envisage "illness attributable to pregnancy" and therefore did not preclude dismissal on grounds of absences due to such illness. This interpretation was confirmed in the case of *Ms. Larsson*,[82] but was later reversed in *Brown v Rentokil Ltd*.[83] It is now established that even if a contractual agreement permits dismissal after a certain period of absence, absence in connection with pregnancy does not count:

> Articles 2(1) and 5(1) of Council Directive 76/207/EEC of 9 February 1996, on the implementation of the principle of equal treatment for men and women as regards access to employment, vocational training and promotion, and working conditions, preclude dismissal of a female worker at any time during her pregnancy for absences due to incapacity for work caused by illness resulting from that pregnancy. The fact that a female worker has been dismissed during her pregnancy on the basis of a contractual term providing that the employer may dismiss employees of either sex after a stipulated number of weeks of continuous absence does not affect the answer given (Case C-394/96, ECR 1998, p. I-4185).

In 1998 the Court ruled upon the important issue of performance assessment in the context of motherhood: *Ms. Thibault*[84] had been employed by *CNAVTS* since 1973; during her pregnancy in spring 1983, she was absent for a few weeks on account of sickness; and from June to November, she took paid maternity leave for 16 weeks, followed by maternity leave on half pay for a further six weeks (such maternity leave being provided for under the applicable collective agreement). Her employer subsequently refused to carry out an assessment of her performance for that year, because she did not meet the relevant contractual condition of at least six months' presence at work.

The Court, requested to comment on the legitimacy of the employer's refusal, stressed the importance of regular performance assessment for career development. Denial of the performance assessment would therefore discriminate against the claimant merely because she had been pregnant and made use of the maternity leave to which she was entitled:

> Articles 2(3) and 5(1) of Council Directive 76/207/EEC of 9 February 1976 on the implementation of the principle of equal treatment for men and women as regards access to employment, vocational training and promotion, and working conditions preclude national rules which deprive a women of the right to an assessment of her performance and, consequently, to the possibility of qualifying for promotion because she was absent from the undertaking on account of maternity leave (Case C-136/95, ECR 1998, p. I-2011).

Unequal treatment of part-time workers[85]

The Equal Treatment Directive generally has no direct effect under national law, but it can be invoked against the State if the employer is a public body or institution.[86] As shown above, the Court has usually interpreted the right to equal pay extensively, thus leaving relatively few cases to equal treatment. A considerable number of judgements have therefore dealt with unequal treatment of part-time public servants. These cases are highly relevant in practice because a large majority of part-time workers in public services are female.

In *Gerster v Freistaat Bayern*[87] the issue was a provision requiring that, in calculating length of service, periods of employment be reckoned less favourably for part-timers. *Kording v Senator für Finanzen Bremen*[88] centred on the application of the national Tax Consultancy Act, which required a minimum of 15 years' professional experience in a revenue office to qualify for admission to the profession of tax consultant without an examination. For part-time employees, this provision was interpreted to mean that the minimum period should be prolonged depending on actual time worked. In both cases, the underlying rationale for these practices was an alleged special link between length of service and acquisition of a certain level of knowledge or experience. The Court saw this as too general an assumption, which could not be justified by entirely gender-neutral criteria. In both cases, more than 90 per cent of those adversely affected were women.

Affirmative action in favour of women — discrimination against men?

Two highly disputed rulings have been delivered on the legality of affirmative-action policies. Both cases dealt with national provisions on recruitment and promotion in the public sector which gave preference to women under certain conditions.

The first ruling was on the case of *Kalanke v Freie Hansestadt Bremen*.[89] Mr. Kalanke had applied for a higher post, but the public authority concerned gave priority to a woman, citing legislation of the *Land* of Bremen which aimed at increasing the proportion of female employees, especially in higher positions. This law stipulated that in recruitment or promotion procedures, where a female has the same qualification as a male candidate, the woman should be given preference *generally and automatically*, as long as women are under-represented at that level. Having failed to be promoted on account of this law, Mr. Kalanke challenged its validity before the national court, claiming to have been discriminated against. The provision at issue was found to be compatible with German law, but the question of its conformity with Directive 76/207/EEC was referred to the ECJ. The Court held that the provision contained *direct* discrimination against men which was not justified by the nature of the job or the context in which it was carried out, as provided for under Article 2(2) of the Directive:

> Article 2(1) and (4) of Council Directive 76/207/EEC of 9 February 1976 on the implementation of the principle of equal treatment for men and women as regards access to employment, vocational training and promotion, and working conditions precludes national rules such as those in the present case which, where candidates of different sexes shortlisted for promotion are equally qualified, automatically give priority to women in sectors where they are underrepresented, under-representation being deemed to exist when women do not make up at least half of the staff in the individual pay brackets in the relevant personnel group or in the function levels provided for in the organisation chart (Case C-450/93, ECJ 1995, p. I-3051).

The Court argued that Article 2(4), which provides that the Directive "shall be without prejudice to measures to promote equal opportunity for men and women, in particular by removing existing inequalities which affect women's opportunities", was a *derogation* from the individual right to equality set out in the first paragraph of the same Article. Whereas the principle of equality required extensive interpretation, exceptions from this principle were to be interpreted strictly. In the Court's view, paragraph 4 was specifically and exclusively designed to authorize measures which, although discriminatory in appearance, were in fact intended to eliminate or reduce instances of inequality which may exist in the reality of social life. National rules which guarantee absolute and unconditional priority under the conditions mentioned went beyond promoting equal opportunities and overstepped the limits of possible exceptions to the principle of equality.

In 1997 the ECJ delivered its second judgement on quota policies in the case of *Marschall v Land Nordrhein-Westfalen*.[90] Mr. Marschall challenged a similar rule of the Land's Civil Servants Act, with the difference that reasons specific to an individual (male) candidate could "tilt the balance in his favour". This time the Court ruled that a national law which gives priority to equally qualified women does not conflict with Community law as long as women are under-represented in the given area of work and the male competitor is not excluded from the outset.

In its reasoning, it stressed that certain deep-rooted prejudices and stereotypes as to the roles and capacities of women in working life still persist. If national legislation gives priority to women for a transitional period with the aim of restoring the balance, such legislation does not contradict Directive 76/207/EEC provided that an objective assessment of each individual candidate in question is assured. Now most of the affirmative action policies in force throughout Europe must be considered compatible with European law.[91]

Two preliminary rulings on affirmative action were still pending at the time of writing. In the *Anderson* case,[92] the Court was requested to rule on its precise limits. For example, does conformity with the Directive require that candidates' qualifications be entirely equal? Or are quota policies permissible even when the female candidate's qualifications are judged lower than those of her male counterpart, but still considered sufficient for the post? The second case — that of *Badeck and Others v Hessischer Minis-terpräsident*[93] — deals with targets in a women's advancement plan for posts in the academic field.

Exclusion from certain types of work: Armed service and night work

Protection of women might have negative repercussions on their participation and opportunities in the labour market. The exclusion of women from certain types of work is an important and topical issue, because perceptions of women's presence in formerly "male" occupations are undergoing societal changes.

The case of *Johnston v Chief Constable of the Royal Ulster Constabulary (RUC)* dealt with a woman whose contract of employment was not renewed after the RUC introduced the carrying of firearms in the police service. The ECJ was called upon to rule, inter alia, on the scope of Article 2(3) of Directive 76/207/EEC, which allows certain measures to protect women. The Court emphasized that this provision, as an exception from the principle of equality, had to be interpreted strictly so that the general exclusion of women was unjustified: "The differences in treatment of men and women that Article 2(3) of Directive No 76/207 allows out of a concern to protect women do not include risks and danger, such as those to which any armed police officer is exposed in the performance of his duties in a given situation, that do not specifically affect women as such" (Case 222/84, ECR 1986, p. 1651).

Political issues of major relevance are currently pending before the Court. The question in both of the following cases is whether defence is a sector within the exclusive competence of the Member States or whether it is also subject to the principle of equality and, if so, to what extent. In other words: Is it the sovereign prerogative of the national state to allow only males to join the armed forces?

Ms. Kreil[94] claims eligibility for work as a technician in the armed forces of Germany. But according to Germany's Armed Forces Act, women who enlist as volunteers may be appointed only to duties in the medical and military-music services and are excluded in any event from armed service. The Advocate General's opinion on the case suggests that this general exclusion be declared incompatible with the Equal Treatment Directive. *Ms. Sirdar*[95] claims access to service as a cook in the Royal Marines of the United Kingdom. She had been employed as a cook in the British Army since 1983 and was assigned to the Royal Artillery in 1990. After receiving notice of redundancy in 1994, she submitted a request to be transferred to the position of cook in the Royal Marines. But this request was rejected on the grounds that this corps did not admit female employees.

On the latter case, the Advocate General recently stressed that requirements imposed in the interest of national defence must be seen in the light of *proportionality*. The arguments of governments, according to which defence should remain within the exclusive competence of the Member States, were unfounded, and Community law therefore applies. He stressed that the nature of military activities was not sufficient in itself to permit such an exemption. In its ruling of 26 October 1999,[96] the Court confirmed that the principle of equal treatment generally applied to the armed forces as well, though the exclusion of women from the Royal Marines was accepted because that particular corps differed fundamentally in organization from other units of the British armed forces.

The issue of night work, first raised in the case of *Mr. Stoeckel*,[97] implies a conflict between the international labour standards of the ILO and supranational European law. The question in the case in point was whether a national provision banning women from night work — in accordance with the ILO's Night Work (Women) Convention (Revised), 1948 (No. 89) — was in compliance with European equality law.

Mr. Stoeckel had been sentenced by a French court because he had employed women for night work in breach of Article L 213-1 of the French Labour Code. But the ECJ held that the general ban on night work for women was discriminatory, and that the principle of equal treatment required that women, except during pregnancy and maternity, should also have the option of working at night. However, it avoided comment on the relationship between international and supranational European law, although the statutory provision at issue had been adopted to comply with the ILO Convention prohibiting women from night work, which France had ratified:

> Article 5 of Directive 76/207/EEC on the implementation of the principle of equal treatment for men and women as regards access to employment, vocational training and promotion, and working conditions is sufficiently precise to impose on the Member States the obligation not to lay down by legislation the principle that night work by women is prohibited, even if that obligation is subject to exceptions, where night work for men is not prohibited (Case C-345/89, ECR 1991, p. I-4047).

France maintained Article L 213-1 of its Labour Code unchanged, which led to infringement.[98] Indeed, following the French Government's denunciation of ILO Convention No. 89, the French legislation was undisputably incompatible with European law. Although France had declared it did not apply the contentious provision because it was null and void, in its judgement of 1997 the Court ruled that France had failed to fulfil its obligations under Article 5(1) of Directive 76/207. It commented that while the article was in existence, individuals were unsure of their legal situation and exposed to unwarranted criminal proceedings. Incompatibility of national legislation with Community law could be finally remedied *only by binding national provisions having the same legal force as those which had to be amended.* A similar case was successfully brought against Italy.[99]

Still, neither France nor Italy has amended its legislation; and infringement proceedings have now been instituted under Article 228 EC (ex Article 171 EC Treaty),[100] which may lead to sanctions. The European Commission recently asked the ECJ to impose a daily fine of 142,425 Euros on France for non-implementation of its earlier judgement.[101]

The *effet utile:* Enforcement through effective remedies and sanctions

If the right to equal pay has been violated, the claimant is entitled to retroactive pay; but what is the redress for violations of the right to equal treatment? The Court has developed a convincing body of case law whereby, in dealing with the implementation of directives, national states are, in principle, free to choose the form of sanctions. Remedies and sanctions must, however, be effective both in protecting against discrimination and in compensating for the harm or loss suffered as a consequence of a breach of law; this principle is called the *"effet utile".*

The first cases on the *effet utile* were *Von Colson and Kammann v Land Nordrhein-Westfalen*[102] and *Harz v Deutsche Tradax GmbH.*[103] The female claimants had applied for jobs and were obviously rejected because of their sex. Their claim was to be appointed to the respective posts or to receive adequate compensation. German law provided compensation only for mailing or other minor expenditure incurred in connection with applying for the job. The Court held that it was up to national law to determine whether redress was provided by appointment to the job or by compensation, but if *compensation* is chosen, it must be an effective deterrent and adequate to make good the damage suffered:

> Although Directive 76/207/EEC, for the purpose of imposing a sanction for the breach of the prohibition of discrimination, leaves Member States free to choose between the different solutions suitable for achieving its objective, it nevertheless requires that if a Member State chooses to penalise breaches of that prohibition by the award of compensation, then in order to ensure that it is effective and that it has a deterrent effect, that compensation must in any event be adequate in relation to the damage sustained and must therefore amount to more than purely nominal compensation such as, for example, the reimbursement only of the expenses incurred in connection with the application. It is for the national court to interpret and apply the legislation adopted for the implementation of the Directive in conformity with the requirements of Community law, in so far as it is given discretion to do so under national law (Case 14/83, ECR 1984, p. 1891).

A subsequent amendment to Germany's Civil Code set a ceiling of three months' pay on individual awards of compensation and an aggregate limit of six months' pay where compensation was claimed by several parties; it furthermore required an individual fault on the part of the employer. *Mr. Draehmpaehl*,[104] whose application had been turned down for a post advertised only for female assistants, challenged its legality. The Court rejected the requirement of a *fault* on the part of the employer. In cases where the claimant would have obtained the vacant position, the ceiling of three months' pay was interpreted as incompatible with the Directive. The ceiling for the aggregate amount of compensation was regarded as illegal unless comparable ceilings existed in other provisions of domestic law:

> Directive 76/207/EEC precludes provisions of domestic law which, unlike other provisions of domestic civil and labour law, impose a ceiling of six months' salary on the aggregate amount of compensation which, where several applicants claim compensation, may be claimed by applicants who have been discriminated against on grounds of their sex in the making of an appointment (Case C-180/95, ECR 1997, p. I-2195).

CONCLUDING REMARKS

As this chapter has shown, European legislation and case law have given new momentum to legal equality between women and men by contributing substantially to respect for the principle of equal pay for work of equal value and to the elimination of discrimination — both direct and indirect — in regard to eligibility for particular occupations, part-time work, night work, pensions, pregnancy and maternity. Their unique supranational character has led to the revision of domestic law in all Member States, thus stimulating a new way of thinking. The European Court of Justice has not confined its interpretations to the principle of "judicial self-restraint" and has thereby rendered European equality law more effective in testing national rules and practice. Workers who have had the courage to challenge unfavourable decisions, as well as judges, lawyers and other experts — who have become increasingly aware of supranational instruments and willing to use them — have contributed to this development. The challenge is ultimately to utilize these instruments to achieve full equality at the workplace in practice.

Notes

[1] See Judith Blom, Barry Fitzpatrick, Jeanne Gregory, Robert Knegt and Ursula O'Hare: *The utilisation of sex equality litigation procedures in the Member States of the European Community: A comparative study*, V/782/96-EN, Brussels, European Commission, 1995; on national litigation procedures, see also Barry Fitzpatrick, Jeanne Gregory and Erika Szyszczak: *Sex equality litigation in the Member States of the European Community: A comparative study*, V/407/94-EN, Brussels, European Commission, 1993.

[2] For a comparative overview of equality cases from the different Member States, see European Commission: *Equal opportunities for women and men in the European Union – Annual Report 1996*, CE 98-96-566-EN-C, Luxembourg, Office for Official Publications of the European Communities, 1997, p. 109.

[3] See *Equality Quarterly News* (http://europe.eu.int/comm/dg05/equ_opp/index_en.htm), No. 1/99, Winter 1999.

[4] The judgements of the European Court of Justice have often provoked fierce debates, with a correspondingly vast number of publications. In view of the large quantity of secondary literature published in all Member States, the citations in this chapter are mostly restricted to original or comparative sources and easily accessible publications from European Union institutions. The most comprehensive list of publications is probably the *Legal bibliography of European integration*, Luxembourg, Office for Official Publications of the European Communities (since 1981); for an excellent selection of publications in the social and equality fields, see Hans von der Groeben, Jochen Thiesing and Claus-Dieter Ehlermann (eds.): *Kommentar zum EU-/ EG-Vertrag*, Baden-Baden, Fünfte neubear beitete Auflag, 1999, pp. 3/903-3/915 and pp. 3/ 1192-3/1198. See also *Women's rights and the Maastricht Treaty on European Union* and *Women's rights and the Treaty of Amsterdam*, Working Papers of the European Parliament, Women's Rights Series, No. 10/94 and No. 5/98, respectively, and, more generally, http:// europe.eu.int/comm/dg05. The ECJ cases discussed in this chapter are indexed and summarized in European Commission: *Handbook on equal treatment for women and men in the European Union*, Second edition, Luxembourg, Office for Official Publications of the European Communities, 1999. Additional information on the ECJ is available at http://curia.eu.int/en.

[5] See, for instance, Karl-Jürgen Bieback: *Indirect sex discrimination within the meaning of Directive (CE) 79/7 in the social security law of the EC Member States*, V/1333/96-EN, Brussels, European Commission, 1996.

[6] In the absence of a uniform system of citation, the system followed here is that set out by the European Court of Justice (ECJ) in ECJ Press Release No 57/99 of 30 July 1999 (http:// curia.eu.int/en/cp/index.htm). Accordingly, reference to articles as they stood before 1 May 1999 (when the Treaty of Amsterdam entered into force) is made by "EU Treaty", "EEC Treaty" or "EC Treaty", whereas "EC" or "EU" denotes articles as they stand since that date. One of the amendments introduced by the Treaty of Amsterdam was to renumber the articles, titles and sections of the Treaty on European Union and the Treaty establishing the European Community. Treaty articles cited in the following pages are numbered according to the new consolidated version of the Treaty of Amsterdam, unless reference is made to an earlier version. The equivalences between the two numbering systems are given in most cases. References to "the Treaty" should be understood to mean the founding Treaty of Rome as amended at the relevant time.

[7] Because of its basically passive role, the European Parliament cannot be regarded as a true legitimating body for the European Union; its position was further strengthened through the Treaty of Amsterdam, but it still has no power to initiate legislation.

[8] The Treaty establishing the European Economic Community was concluded by Belgium, Germany, France, Italy, Luxembourg and the Netherlands on 25 March 1957; it entered into force on 1 January 1958. The Community was later enlarged with the accession of Denmark, the United Kingdom and Ireland (1973), Greece (1981), Spain and Portugal (1986), Austria, Finland and Sweden (1995).

[9] On the history of the social chapter, see Hans von der Groeben, Jochen Thiesing and Claus-Dieter Ehlermann (eds.), op. cit. (note 4), p. 3/926-3/986.

[10] See Article 39 EC (ex Article 48 EEC Treaty).

[11] See Article 117 (2) EEC Treaty.

[12] Belgium had ratified this Convention on 23 May 1952, France on 10 March 1953, and Germany and Italy on 8 June 1956.

[13] See Hans von der Groeben, Jochen Thiesing and Claus-Dieter Ehlermann (eds.), op. cit. (note 4), pp. 3/1207 et seq.

[14] Since its famous *Defrenne II* ruling on Case 43/75, ECR 1976, p. 455 (see below).

[15] For further information see Emil J. Kirchner: "The social framework of the European Union", in *European Union Encyclopaedia and Directory 1996*, Second edition, London, Europa, 1996, pp. 140-144.

[16] Concluded on 17 February 1986, in force since 1 July 1987, OJ L/169, 29.6.1987.

[17] Under this procedure, the European Parliament is consulted twice and can reconsider decisions after the Council of Ministers has reached a "common position". See Article 118a EEC Treaty (now Article 138 EC) and Article 189c EEC Treaty (now Article 252 EC).

[18] Treaty on European Union, signed in Maastricht on 7 February 1992, in force since 1 November 1993. Because the United Kingdom was not a party to the SPA, the Agreement was mostly regarded as an instrument of international, not supranational, character.

[19] See Article 189b EC Treaty (now Article 251 EC): this procedure enables the EP and the Council to make laws jointly in specific policy areas; the EP can, by absolute majority, eliminate proposals in these areas.

[20] This procedure considerably speeded up the adoption of directives on parental leave (96/34/EC) and on part-time work (97/81/EC). On these instruments in international perspective, see, respectively, "Parental leave", in *International Labour Review* (Geneva), Vol. 136 (1997), No. 1, pp. 109-128; and "Part-time work: Solution or trap?", in *International Labour Review* (Geneva), Vol. 136 (1997), No. 4, pp. 558-579.

[21] Treaty of Amsterdam amending the Treaty on European Union, the Treaties establishing the European Communities and Certain Related Acts, signed at Amsterdam, 2 October 1997, in force since 1 May 1999, OJ 97/C 340/01.

[22] Articles 136 et seq. EC; for further information see Berndt Schulte: "Juridical instruments of the European Union and the European Communities", in Wolfgang Beck, Laurent van der Maesen and Alan Walker (eds.): *The social quality of Europe*, The Hague, Kluwer Law International, 1997, pp. 45-67; and Suzanne Berthet: *L'Union Européenne et l'Organisation internationale du Travail*, Lyon, Université Jean Moulin/Lyon III, 1997.

[23] Sometimes referred to as the "Founding Treaties", these instruments are of *inter*national, not *supra*national, character.

[24] When this directive was adopted, the transition period for Article 119 EEC Treaty on equal pay (now Article 141 EC) had come to an end more than 13 years earlier; the reluctance of the Commission to enforce its implementation in the meantime gave rise to very critical comments by the ECJ in the case *Defrenne v Société Anonyme Belge de Navigation Aérienne Sabena (Defrenne II)*, ECR 1976, p. 455.

[25] See also Cases C-46/93 and C-48/93, *Brasserie du Pêcheur*, ECR 1996, p. I-1029.

[26] Joined Cases C-178/94, C-179/94, C-188/94, C-189/94 and C-190/94, ECR 1996, p. 4845.

[27] See *Equality Quarterly News* (http://europe.eu.int/comm/dg05/equ_opp/index_en.htm), No. 1/99, Winter 1999, p. 35.

[28] Case 222/84, ECR 1986, p. 1651.

[29] See Article 236 EC (ex Article 179 EC Treaty); Article 230 EC (ex Article 173 EC Treaty), paragraph 4, allows direct litigation under certain conditions, but it does not apply to directives, which are addressed to the Member States.

[30] See Article 226 EC (ex Article 169 EEC/EC Treaty).

[31] See Article 227 EC (ex Article 170 EEC/EC Treaty).

[32] See Article 228 EC (ex Article 171 EEC/EC Treaty) and http://europe.eu.int/comm/dg05/equ_opp/news/infring_en.htm.

[33] Case C-229/89, *Commission of the European Communities v Kingdom of Belgium,* ECR 1991, p. I-2205, on Directive 79/7/EEC; Case C-173/91, ECR 1993, p. I-673, on Directive 76/207/EEC and 119 EEC Treaty (now Article 141 EC).

[34] Case 143/83, *Commission of the European Communities v Kingdom of Denmark,* ECR 1985, 427, on the transposition of Directive 75/117/EEC.

[35] Case 248/83, *Commission of the European Communities v Federal Republic of Germany,* ECR 1985, p. 1459, on transposition of Directive 75/117/EEC.

[36] Case C-187/98, *Commission of the European Communities v Hellenic Republic,* OJ/C 258/18, on Directives 75/117/EEC and 79/7/EEC (pending at time of writing).

[37] Case 312/86, *Commission of the European Communities v French Republic,* ECR 1988, p. 6315, on transposition of Directive 76/207/EEC; Case 318/86, ECR 1988, p. 3559, on access to posts in public service under the same Directive; Case C-197/96, ECR 1997, p. I-1489, on prohibition of night work under the same Directive; Case C-354/98, OJ 98/C 340/24, on Directive 96/97/EC, judgement of 8 July 1999 (nyr) (see http://curia.eu.int/en).

[38] Case 163/82, *Commission of the European Communities v Italian Republic,* ECR 1983, p. 3273, on transposition of Directive 76/207/EEC; Case C-207/96, ECR 1997, p. I-6869, on prohibition of night work under the same Directive.

[39] Case 58/81, *Commission of the European Communities v Grand Duchy of Luxembourg,* ECR 1982, p. 2175, on Directive 75/117/EEC (transposition); Case C-438/98, OJ 98/C 20/28, on transposition of Directive 96/97/EC (pending at time of writing).

[40] Case 61/81, *Commission of the European Communities v United Kingdom of Great Britain and Northern Ireland,* ECR 1982, p. 2601, on transposition of Directive 75/117/EEC; Case 165/82, ECR 1983, p. 3431, on transposition of Directive 76/207/EEC.

[41] For details see *Equality Quarterly News* (http://europe.eu.int/comm/dg05/equ_opp/index_en.htm), No. 1/99, p. 9.

[42] See *Equality Quarterly News,* No 4/98 (CE-V/2-98-019-EN-C), p. 20 et seq.

[43] See note 40 above.

[44] Case 80/70, *Defrenne v Belgian State (Defrenne I),* ECR 1971, p. 445.

[45] Case 43/75, *Defrenne v Société Anonyme Belge de Navigation Aérienne Sabena (Defrenne II),* ECR 1976, p. 455.

[46] Case 149/77, *Defrenne v Société Anonyme Belge de Navigation Aérienne Sabena (Defrenne III),* ECR 1978, p. 1365.

[47] See note 66 below. For an overview of this and related cases, see also "Occupational pension schemes: Towards perfect equality?", in *International Labour Review* (Geneva), Vol. 132 (1993), No. 4, pp. 440-450.

[48] Case 69/80, *Worringham and Humphreys v Lloyds Bank Limited,* ECR 1981, p. 767.

[49] Case 170/84, *Bilka-Kaufhaus GmbH v Weber von Hartz,* ECR 1986, p. 1607; see also note 66 below.

[50] Case C-33/89, *Kowalska v Freie und Hansestadt Hamburg,* ECR 1990, p. I-2591.

[51] Case 171/88, *Rinner-Kühn v FWW Spezial-Gebäudereinigung GmbH & Co. KG,* ECR 1989, p. 2743.

[52] Case C-167/97, judgement of 9 February 1999 (nyr), in *Equality Quarterly News* (http://europe.eu.int/comm/dg05/equ_opp/index_en.htm), No. 2/99.

[53] Case 12/81, *Garland v British Rail Engineering Limited,* ECR 1982, p. 359.

[54] Case C-249/96, ECR 1998, p. I-621.

[55] Case 157/86, *Murphy and Others v An Bord Telecom Eireann*, ECR 1988, p. 673.

[56] Case 129/79, ECR 1980, p. 1275.

[57] Case C-326/96, judgement of 1 December 1998 (nyr), see ECJ Press Release No. 73/98 (http://curia.eu.int/en).

[58] Case C-66/96, judgement of 19 November 1998, (nyr), see ECJ Press Release No. 70/98 (http://curia.eu.int/en).

[59] Cases C-281/97, *Krüger v Kreiskrankenhaus Ebersberg*, judgement of 9 September 1999 (nyr), in ECJ Press Release No. 60/99; and C-333/97, *Lewen v Denda* (nyr), in ECJ Press Release No. 82/99; on the legality of section 23a(3) of the Austrian Employee Act, see Case C-249/97, *Gruber v Silhouette International Schmied GmbH & Co. KG*, judgement of 14 September 1999 (nyr), in ECJ Press Release No. 62/99; (see http://curia.eu.int/en).

[60] See OECD: *OECD Employment Outlook — June 1999*, Paris, OECD, 1999, p. 240, table E; and, more generally, http://europa/eu.int/en/comm/eurostat.

[61] In those areas covered by ECJ case law on equal pay, this definition applies already.

[62] Case 96/80, ECR 1981, p. 911. In view of the fact that Ms. Jenkins was able to substantiate her claim with concrete evidence of the income of a man who performed the same work, this could be regarded as a case of *direct* discrimination as well.

[63] Case C-33/89, ECR 1990, p. I-2591.

[64] Case C-184/89, ECR 1991, p. I-297.

[65] ECR 1998, p. I-3739; see also Case C-360/90, *Arbeiterwohlfahrt der Stadt Berlin eV v Bötel*, ECR 1992, p. I-3589; Case C-297/93, *Grau-Hupka v Stadtgemeinde Bremen,* ECR 1994, p. I-5535; Joined Cases C-399/92, C-409/92, C-34/93, C-50/93 and C-78/93, *Stadt Lengerich and Others v Helmig and Others,* ECR 1994, I-5727; Case C-457/93, *Kuratorium für Dialyse und Nierentransplantation eV v Lewark*, ECR 1996, p. I-243 (on part-time employees in the public service).

[66] Case 262/88, *Barber v Guardian Royal Exchange Assurance Group,* ECR 1990, p. I-1889; other important cases in this context are C-110/91, *Moroni v Collo GmbH*, ECR 1993, p. I-6591; C-152/91, *Neath v Steeper Ltd,* ECR 1993, p. I-6935; C-200/91, *Coloroll Pension Trustees Limited v Russell and Others,* ECR 1994, p. I-4389; C-408/92, *Smith and Others v Avdel Systems Ltd,* ECR 1994, p. I-4435; C-147/95, *Dimossia Epicheirissi Ilektrismou (DEI) v Evrenopoulos,* ECR 1997, p. I-2057.

[67] See Article 7, paragraph 1(a) of Directive 79/7/EEC.

[68] Case C-435/93, ECR 1996, p. I-5223.

[69] Case C-246/96, ECR 1997, p. I-7153.

[70] See *Equality Quarterly News* (http://europe.eu.int/comm/dg05/equ_opp/index_en.htm), No. 2/99, on Case C-50/96 *(Schröder)*; on Case C-78/98 *(Preston and Others v Wolverhampton and Others)*, see the Advocate General's recently delivered opinion in ECJ Press release No. 64/99 (http://curia.eu.int/en/cp/cp9964en.htm).

[71] Case 109/88, ECR 1989, p. 3199.

[72] Case C-127/92, ECR 1993, p. I-5535; see also Case C-400/93, *Specialarbejderforbundet i Danmark v Dansk Industri, formerly Industriens Arbeijdgivere, acting for Royal Copenhagen A/S,* ECR 1995, p. I-1275.

[73] Case C-309/97 (nyr), ruling of 11 May 1999; see ECJ Press Release No. 29/99 (http://curia.eu.int/en).

[74] Case C-236/98, *Jämställdhetsombudsmannen Lena Svenaeus,* OJ 98/C 278/32 (pending at time of writing).

[75] Case C-13/94, ECR 1996, p. I-2143.

[76] Case C-168/97, *The Queen v the Secretary of State for Defence, ex parte: Perkins* (withdrawn), OJ 97/C 199/22; since the scope of sex equality is wider under Directive 76/207/ EEC than it is in the context of equal pay, a more generous interpretation than in the *Grant* Case (see note 54 above) would have been possible.

[77] See Case 179/88, *Handels- og Kontorfunktionærernes Forbund i Danmark v Dansk Arbejdsgiverforening (Hertz v Aldi)*, ECR 1990, p. I-3979; C-421/92, *Habermann-Beltermann v Arbeiterwohlfahrt, Bezirksverband Ndb./Opf.e.V.*, ECR 1994, p. I-1657.

[78] Case C-32/93, *Webb v EMO Air Cargo (UK) Ltd,* ECR 1994, p. I-3567.

[79] Case 177/88, ECR 1990, p. I-3941.

[80] Case C-207/98, OJ 98/C 234/21 (pending at time of writing).

[81] Case 179/88 (see note 77 above).

[82] Case C-400/95, *Handels- og Kontorfunktionærernes Forbund i Danmark (acting on behalf of Larsson) v Dansk Handel & Service, acting on behalf of Føtex Supermarked A/S,* ECR 1997, p. I-2757.

[83] Case C-394/96, ECR 1998, p. I-4185; on payment of wages during pregnancy-related illness, see note 58 above.

[84] Case C-136/95, *Caisse nationale d'assurance vieillesse des travailleurs salariés (CNAVTS) v Thibault,* ECR 1998, p. I-2011.

[85] For recent data on women in part-time employment, including the public sector, see OECD: *The future of female-dominated occupations,* Paris, OECD, 1998, p. 24 et seq. and 96 et seq.; see also Jill Rubery and Colette Fagan (in association with Claire Faichnie, Damian Grimshaw and Mark Smith): *Equal opportunities and employment in the European Union*, Vienna, Federal Ministry of Labour, Health and Social Affairs, 1998, Chapter 2.

[86] See Case 152/84, *Marshall v Southampton and South-West Hampshire Area Health Authority (Teaching),* ECR 1986, p. 723; this case did not involve a part-time worker, but a woman who had been dismissed only because she had reached the pensionable age which was interpreted as discriminatory under Directive 76/207/EEC; see also case C-188/89, *Foster and Others v British Gas,* ECR 1990, p. I-3313.

[87] Case C-1/95, ECR 1997, p. I-5253.

[88] Case C-100/95, ECR 1997, p. I-5289.

[89] Case C-450/93, *Kalanke v Freie Hansestadt Bremen,* ECR 1995, p. I-3051.

[90] Case C-409/95, *Marschall v Land Nordrhein-Westfalen,* ECR 1997, p. I-6363.

[91] See *Communication from the Commission to the European Parliament and the Council on the interpretation of the judgement of the Court of Justice on 17 October 1995 in Case C-450/ 93, Kalanke v Freie Hansestadt Bremen,* 27.3.1996, COM(96)88 final; see also European Commission Press Release: *Statement by Commissioner Flynn on the Marschall Case,* 11 November 1997 (http://europe.eu.int).

[92] Case C-407/98, *Abrahamsson and Anderson v Fogelqvist,* OJ 99/C 1/10 (pending at time of writing); on the basis of the argument in the *Marschall* case, such a provision is hardly acceptable.

[93] Case C-158/97, *Badeck and Others v Hessischer Ministerpräsident and Landesanwalt beim Staatsgerichtshof des Landes Hessen,* OJ 97/C 199/20 (pending at time of writing).

[94] On Case C-285/98, *Kreil v Federal Republic of Germany,* see ECJ Press Release No. 84/ 99 (http://curia.eu.int).

[95] On Case C-273/97, *Sirdar v The Army Board and Secretary of State for Defence,* judgement of 26 October 1999 (nyr), see ECJ Press Release No. 83/99 (http://curia.eu.int).

[96] See note 95.

[97] Case C-345/89, *Ministère Public v Stoeckel,* ECR 1991, p. I-4047.

[98] Case C-197/96, *Commission of the European Communities v French Republic,* ECR 1997, p. I-1489.

[99] Case C-207/96, *Commission of the European Communities v Italian Republic,* ECR 1997, p. I-6869.

[100] See *Equality Quarterly News* (http://europe.eu.int/comm/dg05/equ_opp/index_en.htm), No. 2/99.

[101] See note 32 above.

[102] Case 14/83, ECR 1984, p. 1891.

[103] Case 79/83, ECR 1984, p. 1921.

[104] Case C-180/95, *Draehmpaehl v Urania Immobilienservice OHG,* ECR 1997, p. I-2195.

SEXUAL HARASSMENT IN EMPLOYMENT: RECENT JUDICIAL AND ARBITRAL TRENDS

23

Jane HODGES AEBERHARD*

The aim here is to evaluate the application in employment of recent legislation on sexual harassment by examining judicial and arbitral decisions since 1990 in north America, Europe, the far East and Africa. National legislation and relevant international instruments are outlined, and then key cases also brought under labour law, laws on non-discrimination, equality of opportunity, human rights, health and safety, civil and criminal law are reviewed. Trends emerge in the perception of sexual harassment as employment discrimination; the importance of the legal framework used and the composition of the hearing body; individual or employer liability; remedies and sanctions.

The decision in the spring of 1996 by the Equal Employment Opportunity Commission (EEOC) of the United States to file suit against Mitsubishi Motor Manufacturing of America for "continued physical and verbal abuse against women" at its car assembly plant in Normal, Illinois, has given rise to a wave of media attention. Press coverage of the case, to be heard by a United States district court as one of the EEOC's largest sexual harassment suits, stressed not only the gross offence (the sex parties allegedly occurring at the factory), but also the reaction of the factory's management to the filing of the suit (calling a staff meeting to encourage workers to deny the allegations; alleged seeking out of private records, including gynaecological and divorce records, of the 28 women who have also filed suit against the company). This has led to speculation over the amount of damages that might be awarded if the company is found guilty of sexual harassment in employment.[1]

Originally published in *International Labour Review*, Vol. 135 (1996), No. 5.

* Equality and Human Rights Coordination Branch, International Labour Office.

Recent intense debate over the outcome of sexual harassment claims, such as the foregoing, has prompted this chapter. Over the last ten years a broad literature — of an academic, legal and sociological nature — has become available on sexual harassment.[2] Most commentators on this subject start by tracing the emergence of the concept through development of the civil rights legislation in the United States in the 1970s. Most then mention the adoption, on 27 November 1991, of the European Commission's Recommendation on the protection of the dignity of women and men at work and associated Code of Practice on measures to combat sexual harassment,[3] and go on to analyse national legislation concerning sexual harassment in employment. It is pointed out that sexual harassment can be dealt with either through equal employment opportunities and human rights legislation, labour legislation, civil remedies such as torts and negligence and, in at least one country, criminal law. Some commentators add the jurisdiction of health and safety legislation as another area where sexual harassment can be attacked (see, for example, Escudero, 1993, and Serna Calvo, 1994, on the situation in Spain; Halfkenny, 1996, on that in South Africa; Pose, 1995, on Brazil; and Schucher, 1995, on Canada).[4] Yet others look at it from the point of view of a claim for workers' compensation, and examine the difficulties of double recovery in compensating sexual harassment victims (see Vance, 1993, and Lewis, Goodson and Culverhouse, 1993-94, considering the situation in the United States). All appear to seek a clear definition of sexual harassment which would allow actions in the greatest number of alleged cases.

The definition most regularly cited is that of the European Commission's 1991 Recommendation mentioned above, namely:

> Article 1. It is recommended that the Member States take action to promote awareness that conduct of a sexual nature and other conduct based on sex affecting the dignity of women and men at work, including conduct of superiors and colleagues, is unacceptable, if:
>
> (a) such conduct is unwelcome, unreasonable and offensive to the recipient;
>
> (b) a person's rejection of, or submission to, such conduct on the part of the employers or workers (including superiors or colleagues) is used explicitly or implicitly as a basis for a decision which affects that person's access to vocational training, access to employment, continued employment, promotion, salary or any other employment decisions; and/or
>
> (c) such conduct creates an intimidating, hostile or humiliating working environment for the recipient.

This definition is repeated in the European Commission's recommendation on the protection of the dignity of women and men at work.

In the Code of Practice itself, the definition is given as follows (section 2):

Sexual harassment means unwanted conduct of a sexual nature, or other conduct based on sex affecting the dignity of men and women at work. This can include unwelcome physical, verbal or non-verbal conduct. Thus, a range of behaviour may be considered to constitute sexual harassment. It is unacceptable if such conduct is unwanted, unreasonable and offensive to the recipient; a person's rejection of, or submission to, such conduct on the part of the employers or workers (including superiors or colleagues) is used explicitly or implicitly as a basis for a decision which affects that person's access to vocational training or employment, continued employment, promotion, salary or any other employment decisions; and/or such conduct creates an intimidating, hostile or humiliating working environment for the recipient (op. cit., supra note 3, p. 4).

Most commentators attempt to reflect key court cases that have contributed to definitions and to sanctions and remedies for the distinct legal wrong of sexual harassment in the workplace. This chapter seeks, at one level, to help readers assess which countries and which jurisdictions in those countries are advancing the law (for better or for worse) through legal interpretation of statutes relating to sexual harassment in employment. At another level, it aims to demonstrate that sexual harassment in employment now attracts the full attention of the law. The focus is on decisions taken since 1990 in the United States and Canada; in France, Ireland, Spain and the United Kingdom; in Japan, Australia and New Zealand; and in South Africa and Côte d'Ivoire.

NATIONAL AND INTERNATIONAL LEGAL BACKGROUND

Before turning to a description of specific recent cases and arbitral awards, it is important to set the legislative framework in which cases are filed and decisions taken. In *Conditions of Work Digest: Combating sexual harassment at work* (ILO, 1992), the ILO published comprehensive comparative data on 23 industrialized countries. Husbands (1992) and Halfkenny (1995) analysed yet further countries, this time touching on certain developing countries' treatment of sexual harassment in the workplace. In the last few years there has been a major increase in legislative attention to the question, with several countries adopting — particularly in 1995 — specific legislation declaring sexual harassment to be a prohibited activity, or general legislation covering sexual discrimination under which protection from sexual harassment can be provided.

- In Argentina, the Presidential Decree of 18 November 1993 penalizes sexual harassment in the public service.

- In Chile, a Bill on sexual harassment (No. 77-332 of 29 May 1995) is still awaiting enactment.

–   In Costa Rica, Act No. 7476 of 3 February 1995 on sexual harass-
    ment in employment and education has proved to be a milestone in
    the outlawing of sexual harassment in the workplace.

–   In the Philippines, the Anti-Sexual Harassment Act No. 7877 of
    8 February 1995, represents a similar breakthrough; it followed
    on earlier administrative attention to the matter evidenced by the
    Department of Labor and Employment Administrative Order
    No. 80/1991 "Policy against sexual harassment" amended by Ad-
    ministrative Order No. 68/1992, which both suffered from enforce-
    ment weaknesses as the policy did not contain penalties for viol-
    ations.

–   In New Zealand, a 1993 amendment (in force in 1994) to the Hu-
    man Rights Act, 1993, specifically covers sexual harassment.

–   In South Africa, Government Notice 804 of July 1996 entitled "Green
    Paper on Employment Equity" proposes to ban sexual harassment
    on the job (section 4.1.1).[5]

The many European countries to have taken specific action in this
field include:

–   Austria, where the Equality of Treatment Act, 1979 (which did not
    explicitly cover sexual harassment) was amended by Act No. 833/
    1992, in force on 1 January 1993, to include sexual harassment by
    an employer or a third party within the concept of prohibited sexual
    discrimination for which damages can be claimed. Still in Austria,
    Federal Act, No. 100/1993 of 13 February 1993 concerning the fed-
    eral public service equates sexual harassment with prohibited sexual
    discrimination.

–   Belgium, also, where the Royal Order of 18 September 1992 con-
    cerning protection of workers against sexual harassment in
    workplaces is complemented by the Royal Order of 9 March 1995
    concerning federal ministries; both texts specifically prohibit such
    behaviour.

–   Finland, where Act No. 206 of 17 February 1995 amends the Equal-
    ity Act, 1986.

–   Germany where the Second Act on Equality for Men and Women of
    24 June 1994, in section 10, comprises several Acts including the
    Employee Protection Act to safeguard the dignity of women and
    men by protecting against sexual harassment.

–   Ireland, where the Employment Equality Bill No. 38 of 1996 con-
    tains a comprehensive ban on sexual harassment.

–   Italy, where a Senate Labour Commission Bill to combat sexual har-
    assment in the workplace is currently under discussion.

–   Malta, where amendments to the employment legislation were to be tabled in Cabinet in 1995; they were to include protection of the dignity of all employees against unacceptable behaviour, including sexual harassment.

–   Switzerland, where the Federal Act on Equality between Women and Men, dated 24 March 1995 and in force on 1 July 1996, deems sexual harassment to be a case of prohibited sexual discrimination.

–   The United Kingdom, where the Sexual Discrimination and Employment Protection (Remedies) Regulations of 22 November 1993 removed the previous £1,000 ceiling on damages to be paid to victims of sexual discrimination, so as to bring the situation in the United Kingdom into compliance with the decision of the European Court of Justice in *Marshall v. Southampton and South-West Hampshire Area Health Authority.*[6]

The most important development in Europe concerns the passage in France of legislation on abuse of authority and sexual matters in employment relations (Act No. 92-1179 of 2 November 1992 amending the Labour Code and the Code of Criminal Procedure), implemented by Circular No. 93-88 of 1 December 1993 to apply the Act in the public service; the new law specifically refers to sexual harassment in the workplace as a penal offence punishable under s. 152-1-1 of the Labour Code with one year's imprisonment and fines of up to 25,000 French francs. The same harassment can carry sanctions under the Penal Code of a maximum of two years' imprisonment and a fine of up to 100,000 French francs. This cumulative guilt of an employer (or its representative) is commented on by Roy-Loustaunau (1993, 1995). As Earle and Madek (1993) and Mas (1996) point out, there has as yet been no resort to these new penal provisions.

Despite this plethora of new laws on sexual harassment, it is courts' interpretation of these statutes which can give reality to the concept of sexual harassment as a prohibited practice in employment. So how have the courts in these various jurisdictions reacted to the new laws? To date research has uncovered decisions in very few cases — but this is not surprising given that many of the above-mentioned Acts were adopted only in 1995 and that other new legislation was to come into force in the same year. There have, however, been several major cases in jurisdictions mentioned in ILO (1992). A key year was 1993, when both the Supreme Court of the United States and certain lower-level jurisdictions in European countries (including France and the United Kingdom) as well as in Japan arrived at significant decisions on various aspects of sexual harassment.

At first view, these decisions appear to echo well-established concepts of sexual harassment in the various jurisdictions. In the United States, sexual harassment has recently again been confirmed as sexual discrimination in employment. In France, sexual harassment continues to be treated as an abuse of authority or power and compensated as such. In Spain, it is perceived more as a violation of the right to health and safety at work under the Worker's Statute, 1980, and of the General Ordinance of Safety and Health at Work, 1971. The few, but telling, cases dealt with by the Japanese jurisdictions have judged harshly harassment of young female workers by male supervisors in situations of quid pro quo harassment.

At the same time, several decisions have confirmed those of lower-level jurisdictions which held that there was no sexual harassment either on the basis of the facts presented to them or on the basis of those facts in the context of the current legislation. For example, in France the Versailles Court of Appeal [7] confirmed the decision of a labour court of 23 October 1991 that passionate poems and love-letters containing no indecent or obscene terms did not constitute a sufficient factual basis for harassment to be established and that therefore the non-renewal of the recipient's contract was equivalent to the resignation of the employee and did not amount to unjustified or constructive dismissal. Likewise in Chile, the Supreme Court of the Province of Santa Fe [8] confirmed the finding of the Court of First Instance that, despite the testimony of several women concerning the lascivious behaviour of a judge, there was no proof of sexual harassment, and that the testimony was all based on hearsay. The judge, who had been suspended during the appeal, was consequently allowed to resume his position. Yet again, a labour tribunal of Abidjan, Côte d'Ivoire,[9] granted the claim of a victim of harassment that his dismissal was unfair and ordered the employer to pay 2 million CFA francs in damages plus termination indemnities, concluding that the employer's reason for dismissal (40 minutes absence from post) was merely a pretext and that the real reason for dismissal was the victim's membership of a committee recently formed in the undertaking to complain about homosexual abuse by one of the managers there. But, on appeal the decision was reversed, the finding being that the reason for dismissal had in fact been the 40 minutes' absence from post (even though the appeal court acknowledged that the absence was linked to the employee's membership of the anti-harassment committee).[10]

And yet, in Belgium, in a 1991 decision turning again on whether the facts could be seen as a sexual harassment case, the Labour Appeal Court of Liège confirmed a labour court's decision holding to be unfair the dismissal of a woman worker who had claimed that the real reason for the termination of her contract was her written complaint about the sexual harassment she alleged she had been suffering at the hands of the manager. The Court held that, as the employer did not bring evidence to refute her claim or supply any real reason for the dismissal, the woman deserved redress.[11]

Another initial comment of a general nature is the fact that few court decisions in the jurisdictions researched make any reference to international standards which might be of relevance in deciding sexual harassment cases. While there has been a tendency in the last decade to use international law, in particular ILO standards, in national case-law (Bronstein and Thomas, 1995), the same trend is not discernible in the area under discussion here. Commentators generally point out that the law is not always clear in the domestic jurisdictions they write on (Rubenstein, 1994; Roszkowski and Wayland, 1993; Johnson, 1994), but do not call for the United Nations and regional bodies that might pay attention to sexual harassment in their standard-setting agendas to do so. Thus the absence of international standards specifically on this subject could be one reason for the lack of reliance on international standards in domestic decisions concerning sexual harassment.

But an end to the dearth of international attention to the matter is in sight. Whether this is because more women are visibly active in public life and in the labour market generally, because of women's non-governmental organizations' active presence in the various international forums, because of the thaw in the Cold War during which attention had been concentrated on other aspects of human rights, or because of the growing impact of pre-existing instruments concerning women's rights, who can tell? These factors are often cited (e.g. MacKinnon, 1979) to explain the increased attention to sexual harassment in employment at the domestic level, but they appear to be equally valid at the international level.

While the Universal Declaration of Human Rights adopted on 10 December 1948 set out the general ban on discrimination of any kind, including on the basis of sex (article 2), and the two international Covenants adopted on 16 December 1966 likewise prohibited discrimination on that basis in general terms,[12] it was not until the adoption by the General Assembly of the United Nations on 18 December 1979 of the Convention on the Elimination of All Forms of Discrimination against Women that the broad definition of discrimination specifically against women gained international acceptance.[13]

Article 11.1 of the Convention requires ratifying States to "take all appropriate measures to eliminate discrimination against women in the field of employment". It was against this general background that the Committee on the Elimination of Discrimination against Women (CEDAW), set up under the Convention, adopted in January 1992 General Recommendation No. 19 on violence against women.[14] While general recommendations of this sort are not binding on ratifying States, it is worth citing the clarification of sexual harassment given by CEDAW in order to show how useful it is for national courts faced with claims where the domestic laws might not be clear. This states the following.

> (Para.) 17. Equality in employment can be seriously impaired when women are subjected to gender-specific violence, such as sexual harassment in the workplace.

(Para.) 18. Sexual harassment includes such unwelcome sexually determined behaviour as physical contact and advances, sexually coloured remarks, showing pornography and sexual demands, whether by words or actions. Such conduct can be humiliating and may constitute a health and safety problem; it is discriminatory when the woman has reasonable grounds to believe that her objection would disadvantage her in connection with her employment, including recruiting or promotion, or when it creates a hostile working environment.

...

(Para.) 24. In light of these comments, the Committee on the Elimination of Discrimination against Women recommends that

...

(j) States parties should include in their reports information on sexual harassment, and on measures to protect women from sexual harassment ... in the workplace;

...

(t) States parties should take all legal and other measures that are necessary to provide effective protection of women against gender-based violence, including, inter alia:

(i) Effective legal measures, including penal sanctions, civil remedies and compensatory provisions to protect women against all kinds of violence, including ... sexual harassment in the workplace;

(ii) Preventive measures, including public information and education programmes to change attitudes concerning the roles and status of men and women; [15]

There could be no clearer statement on the matter. However, a perusal of the States' reports submitted to CEDAW under the Convention over the last five years reveals that very few governments do in fact include information about sexual harassment either in general or in employment.[16] Likewise, the experts sitting on CEDAW make few comments concerning sexual harassment in general or in the workplace.

In addition to the United Nations treaty bodies' treatment of sexual harassment, its functional commissions, notably the Commission on Human Rights, have dealt with the question – albeit in an oblique way. At its Fiftieth Session, the Commission adopted a resolution [17] in which it decided to appoint, for a three-year period, a Special Rapporteur on violence against women, including its causes and consequences. In her preliminary report to the Commission on Human Rights, the Special Rapporteur on violence against women gave particular prominence to the problem of sexual harassment of women by placing it in a separate section.[18] Her second report concentrated on domestic violence against women and therefore sexual harassment in employment was referred to more in the context of violence against domestic workers.[19]

Amongst the specialized agencies of the United Nations system, the International Labour Organization has been in the vanguard in addressing discrimination against working women, particularly through the adoption of the Discrimination (Employment and Occupation) Convention, 1958 (No. 111).[20] In examining States' reports on Convention No. 111 over the years, the ILO Committee of Experts on the Application of Conventions and Recommendations has often noted with interest the advances made in the elimination of sexual harassment in employment. In its 1988 *General Survey* on the Convention,[21] the Committee of Experts lists a number of examples of sexual harassment in employment. These include insults, remarks, jokes, insinuations and inappropriate comments on a person's dress, physique, age, family situation, and a condescending or paternalistic attitude undermining dignity, unwelcome invitations or requests that are implicit or explicit whether or not accompanied by threats, lascivious looks or other gestures associated with sexuality, unnecessary physical contact such as touching, caresses, pinching or assault. The Committee of Experts stressed that in order to be qualified as sexual harassment, an act of this type must also be justly perceived as a condition of employment or a precondition for employment; or influence decisions taken in this field or prejudice occupational performance; or humiliate, insult or intimidate the person suffering from such acts. In short, the Committee of Experts postulated that any act, the unwanted nature of which could not be mistaken by its author, shall be deemed sexual harassment. In its recent *Special Survey* on the Convention,[22] the Committee of Experts also provides examples of what constitutes sexual harassment in employment, stressing that it is the unwelcome nature of such behaviour and the direct or indirect impact it has on the working relationship that makes it an element of prohibited sexual discrimination under Article 1 of the Convention.

The ILO also has the distinction of being the only international body to have adopted an instrument containing protection against sexual harassment. The Indigenous and Tribal Peoples Convention, 1989 (No. 169), states that governments shall do everything possible to prevent any discrimination between workers belonging to the peoples concerned and other workers, in particular through measures which would ensure that workers belonging to these peoples enjoy equal opportunities and equal treatment in employment for men and women, and protection from sexual harassment (Article 20(3)(d)).[23]

The ILO's attention to the issue is also evident in a number of non-binding instruments: the 1985 International Labour Conference resolution on equal opportunity and equal treatment for men and women in employment;[24] the conclusions of the 1989 ILO Meeting of Experts on Special Protective Measures for Women and Equality of Opportunity and Treatment, categorizing the personal security of workers (notably sexual harassment and violence arising from work) as a safety and health problem; the conclusions of the 1992 Tripartite Symposium on Equality of Opportunity and Treatment for Men and Women in Employment in Industrialized Countries, referring specifically to sexual harassment;[25] as well as the 1991 International Labour Conference resolution concerning ILO action for women workers, requesting the International Labour Office to develop guidelines, training and information materials on issues of specific and major importance to women workers, such as sexual harassment in the workplace.[26] Internally, the International Labour Office worked in the 1980s on a draft guide of practice for equal opportunity and treatment in employment which, in its section entitled "Terms and conditions of employment", recommended policies and action so as to protect employees against harassment or pressure on the basis of their particular group or sex in any term or condition of employment. While not published for general distribution, promotional documents of this kind should, in the opinion of the ILO Committee of Experts on the Application of Conventions and Recommendations, be developed by the secretariat.[27] It is also interesting to note that the Director-General of the International Labour Office distributed to each member of staff Circular No. 6/543 of 2 November 1995 entitled "Sexual harassment policy and procedures". However, this has not served as the basis for a published decision of internal disciplinary bodies, in that the Administrative Tribunal has not had to rule on any ILO cases turning on this circular, or been involved in any of the domestic cases researched for this chapter.

Other international agencies have also addressed the problem, notably the International Monetary Fund, the World Bank, and UNESCO.[28]

Will greater impetus be given to the use of these various international standards on the subject in the wake of the United Nations Fourth World Conference on Women held in Beijing in September 1995? After all, the Conference's Platform for Action calls on governments, trade unions, employers, community and youth organizations, as well as non-governmental organizations, to eliminate sexual harassment.[29]

RECENT KEY CASES IN VARIOUS JURISDICTIONS

Northern America

In the United States, sexual harassment is not defined in federal law but is recognized as a form of discrimination based on sex under Title VII of the Civil Rights Act, 1964.[30] Judicial decisions on the subject appear to move forward in time-periods of a decade: in the mid-1970s there were the first reported cases of attempts to use Title VII protection against repeated verbal and physical advances on the part of supervisors against female employees (*Barnes v Train*, *Corne and De Vane v Bausch & Lomb, Inc.* and *Barnes v Castle*).[31] While the lower courts were conservative, the appeal jurisdictions were prepared to find in favour of harassment victims on condition that they could prove they suffered repercussions in their employment. In *Corne and De Vane v Bausch and Lomb,*

Inc. the Arizona District Court refused to hold the employer liable because the harassing supervisor's conduct served no policy of the employer and in no way benefited the employer; it viewed the behaviour as a "personal proclivity, peculiarity or mannerism". Two years later in *Barnes v Costle*, the District of Columbia Circuit Court of Appeal, however, held that dismissal of a female employee for refusing sexual advances did amount to sexual discrimination because it adversely affected a job condition. Introducing the famous "but for her womanhood" test (but for the female employee's sex her participation in sexual activities would never have been solicited), the Court of Appeal ushered in recognition of sexual harassment as sexual discrimination, but still required actual employment repercussions before coming to a finding of unlawful discrimination. The same court advanced the law again in 1981 by holding in *Bundy v Jackson* [32] that sexual harassment can be actionable without proof of loss of any tangible job benefits.

The first breakthrough case at the level of the Supreme Court came a decade after the first attempts to use Title VII. In *Meritor Savings Bank, FSB v Vinson* [33] the Supreme Court unanimously recognized two types of sexual harassment in employment: "quid pro quo" sexual harassment (literally "this for that", i.e. job-related sexual blackmail) where there is a demand by a hierarchical superior directed to a subordinate that the subordinate grant the supervisor sexual favours in order to keep or obtain certain job benefits (this type of harassment involves abuse of authority); and a broader type of sexual harassment involving unwelcome sexual advances or other verbal or physical conduct of a sexual nature which have the purpose or effect of unreasonably interfering with an individual's work performance or creating an intimidating, hostile, abusive, offensive or poisoned working environment (commonly termed "hostile working environment" sexual harassment). The second, broader type of sexual harassment does not require the complainant to show a tangible economic loss in terms of losing a promotion, etc., because of refusal to accede to sexual advances. But on the same occasion the Supreme Court commented that sexual harassment must be sufficiently severe or pervasive as to alter the conditions of the victim's employment.

In 1991, in *Ellison v Brady*,[34] the decision of the Court of Appeal of San Francisco made some progress on sexual harassment by granting the appeal of a woman who had filed suit because she had not been consulted on the internal sanction taken against her harasser by the employer company, when that sanction had included temporary transfer away from the joint place of work with a warning to the harasser not to engage in any sexual harassment of the victim on pain of dismissal, and then his return to the same joint place of work. This case introduced the concept of the "reasonable woman's" appreciation of the behaviour involved, a concept that has been widely discussed in the United States in academic writings on sexual harassment in employment. Again in the early 1990s, an advance was made on a different aspect of sexual harassment, namely the importance of public policy against sexual harassment. In *Strochmann Bakeries Inc. v Teamsters Local 776* [35] the Court of Appeal of California was faced with the difficult task of reviewing an arbitration decision to reinstate a harasser who had claimed that procedural weaknesses leading up to his dismissal were contrary to negotiated procedural protections. The Court decided to move away from the traditional respect accorded by courts to the negotiated terms of agreements, given the weight of the public policy against sexual harassment in employment, and found that despite the procedural weaknesses the dismissal had been justified.

Seven years on from the key Supreme Court case of *Meritor*, in 1993 another unanimous decision of that Court advanced the law yet again: in *Harris v Forklift Systems Inc.*,[36] the judges held that the victim need not prove tangible psychological breakdown in justifying a claim of hostile environment sexual harassment. This decision also heralded a return to the reasonable person test in deciding whether behaviour was unwanted. Yet the decision has been criticized by commentators. Robinson, Fink and Allen (1994) claimed it does not go far enough in defining what conduct could satisfy the "severity or pervasiveness" criterion enunciated in *Meritor*. Estes and Futch (1994) argued it does not give enough guidance on whether conduct is to be judged in relation to a reasonable person or a reasonable woman (the latter apparently being preferred by federal courts). Halfkenny (1995) would have liked more clarity on the question of just how much misconduct qualifies as "creating a hostile sexual harassment environment". Campanella (1994) lauded the decision and saw it as a model for other jurisdictions where the recognition of sexual harassment as a distinct cause for suit is just emerging. Also in 1993, the Supreme Court of New York, in *Starishevsky v Hofstra University*,[37] examined the elimination of sexual harassment at work in the context of a claim for prohibitive action under legislation concerning education. It held on the facts that the internal procedures were tainted by procedural defects and improprieties so that the dismissal of the harasser member of the academic staff was invalid. It tempered the trend towards severe sanctioning of harassers who abuse their positions of power, by explaining that the "at will" doctrine (concerning employers' right to hire and fire) does not give an employer an unencumbered right to terminate the employment relationship of an employee. Hamilton and Veglahn summed up the decision thus: "The court clearly indicates that due process rights must be observed. An employer cannot resort to employment-at-will status to circumvent the mandated sexual harassment procedures" (1994, p. 591). In 1994 in another case involving a university, the United States Court of Appeals demonstrated a tougher approach towards harassers. In *Karibian v Columbia University*,[38] the female plaintiff had lost at the district court level on counts of both theories of sexual harassment, namely quid pro quo and hostile work environment. In finding in favour of the university, that court held that it could not be liable under the quid pro quo theory because the person had failed to prove any actual economic loss resulting from the harassment by her supervisor; likewise the court rejected the hostile work environment theory because the university did not have notice of the sexual harassment and had in any case provided a reasonable avenue for complaints against harassment. On reversing that decision, the Court of Appeals held, first, that the female employee should not have been required to present evidence of actual, rather than threatened, economic loss in order to win a valid claim of quid pro quo sexual harassment; and that imposing actual economic loss in cases where the employee submits to the supervisor's unwelcome sexual overtures places an undue emphasis on the victim's response, whereas the focus should be on the prohibited conduct. Secondly, it held that the lower court had failed to apply the proper legal standard to determine an employer's liability for the hostile work environment created by a supervisor. It made it clear that it is fair to hold the employer responsible because the supervisor is acting within at least the apparent scope of authority entrusted to him/her by the employer. Some commentators refer to this decision as proof of the need for employers' comprehensive educational employee workshops on how to avoid sexual harassment (Brown and Codey, 1994).

At this juncture it is worth mentioning the restrictive approach of several district courts towards sexual harassment in employment, even though these are not key cases. For example, in *Sexton v AT&T* [39] a district court rejected the plaintiff's claims that she had been denied a promotion because she did not accede to her supervisor's advances and that she had suffered a hostile work environment, arguing on the first ground that she had not asserted that the harasser, whether directly, indirectly or remotely, had suggested his conduct was more than inappropriate advances by a person with whom she had apparently become comfortable in a one-to-one situation. The court opined that the plaintiff fared no better under a hostile environment analysis because, for a hostile environment to be created, the misconduct had to be sufficiently severe or pervasive to alter the conditions of the alleged victim's employment and to create an abusive work environment. In the case at hand, the harasser's condescending remarks, impatient attitude and teasing about her other relationships, while showing a lack of professionalism, did not amount to evidence that his treatment was so pervasive and debilitating that it became "hostile". The court added that its decision did not rest solely on the insufficient facts of sexual harassment or the lack of job-related detriment, but also took into account the fact that, once notified of the allegations, AT&T had taken the appropriate corrective action.

Also in the United States, certain recent cases have shown a trend towards extremely heavy damages in sexual harassment cases, as well as moves by different jurisdictions to insist on guilty parties adopting and implementing a sexual harassment policy so as to avoid recurrence of such incidents. In *Robinson v Jacksonville Shipyards, Inc.*,[40] the female plaintiff won a hostile work environment claim with legal costs and injunctive relief, but no monetary award. The court decided that Jacksonville Shipyards were to take such steps as were within their power to control the work environment on ships, including consultations with shipowners about the removal or covering-up of pictures posted on board and the storage of crew belongings during repair visits; Jacksonville Shipyards were enjoined not only to put an end to the hostile environment which had given rise to the sexual harassment, but also to remedy it by implementing forthwith the sexual harassment policy which the court annexed in total to its judgement. The well-publicized case of *Weeks v Baker & McKenzie*,[41] was decided by a jury – jury trials being permissible under Title VII claims following the 1991 amendment to the 1964 Civil Rights Act, which also introduced monetary damages of between US$50,000 to US$300,000 (depending on the size of the enterprise involved). In this case, the jury awarded punitive damages against the legal firm of 7.1 million US dollars, believed to be the largest such award ever. Although the male partner harasser in the case has since left the company, the decision is on appeal.

In Canada, although the labour legislation at both federal[42] and provincial levels clearly covers sexual harassment in employment as a distinct actionable wrong, recent cases have shown victims using human rights legislation successfully. The leading case of *Janzen v Platy Enterprises Ltd.*[43] clarified that sexual harassment was a form of sexual discrimination banned by the human rights statutes in all jurisdictions in Canada. The case in question was an appeal under the Human Rights Act of Manitoba. It followed a trend in the use of human rights legislation which began in the early 1980s with the case of *Bell and Korczak v Alders and Flaming Steer Steakhouse*.[44] French-speaking jurisdictions in Canada have adopted the same approach: in *Commission des droits de la personnes de Québec c. Marotte*,[45] the Human Rights Commission of Quebec awarded damages to a female victim under the relevant provincial human rights statute, but pointed out that damages would have been higher if the plaintiff had produced expert evidence of the psychological damage she had suffered as a result of the offensive behaviour.

The search for arbitral decisions advancing sexual harassment law in recent years has uncovered a richer seam in Canada than in other jurisdictions. Aggarwal provides an interesting breakdown of arbitration of sexual harassment cases between 1990 and 1993 (1994, pp. 74-76). He estimates there were 34 arbitration cases, of which 14 were reported in *Labour Arbitration Cases* (Aurora, Ontario) and 20 went unreported. Only two cases were brought on behalf of the alleged victims of sexual harassment, in both of which the grievances were denied. As noted in general comments above, the decisions seemed to turn on the question of whether the facts of the case met the requirements of the legal definition and thus whether the behaviour constituted sexual harassment. For example, in *Quality Inn v UFCW, Local 175* [46] the arbitrator, even after finding in favour of one complaint against the supervisor's misconduct, declined to hold that the behaviour constituted sexual harassment amounting to sexual discrimination. Although the harasser's behaviour included, for example, the statements that the woman had been sleeping with more than one guest at the hotel and that she "thinks she can open her legs and make a living that way" as well as references to his own sexual experiences, the decision stated "it is surely not discrimination on the basis of sex if the propositions are distributed indiscriminately among employees of both sexes".[47] Aggarwal suggests that courts examining these facts in a human rights context would not have arrived at the same conclusion. However, in 1991 in *Chaw v Levac Supply Ltd.*,[48] an Ontario Board of Inquiry took a broader view of what constitutes sexual harassment. It held that negative and demeaning comments of a sexual nature, together with the comment that women should be at home looking after their children, formed a pattern of conduct which amounted to sexual harassment.

On the question of arbitral decisions based on the provisions of collective bargaining agreements, it is worth pointing out that, in Canada, advances have been made concerning both procedural and substantive aspects of sexual harassment claims: many require that the burden of proof that there was no sexual harassment shall be on the alleged harasser once the complainant has made a case.[49] It will be interesting to see how arbitration based on such agreements decides sexual harassment claims.

What happens in the Canadian jurisdiction if a complainant files both a human rights claim and a civil suit at the same time on the basis of the same alleged sexual harassment? Aggarwal attempts to answer that question (1994, pp. 82-83). While pointing out that, as a general rule, two types of proceedings cannot go forward at the same time, he quotes *Meiklem v Bot Quebec Ltée* [50] as demonstrating that the civil suit had to be rejected if the complainant had filed a related human rights cause, because the Human Rights Commission and the court might make different findings of the facts or give different damage assessments for similar compensation, and because the plaintiff could get double recovery. He also points out that in recent cases (for example, *Lehman v Davies*) [51] the courts have allowed civil suits to proceed on an undertaking by the complainant to postpone the human rights claim pending the resolution of the civil suit. Regarding procedural questions in arbitration cases in Canada, adjudicators appear to take lack of due process extremely seriously and, accordingly, punish employers who do not permit defendants in sexual harassment cases to have access to the full facts so as to prepare their defence properly. For example, in *School District No. 22 v Chilliwack*

Teachers' Association [52] the arbitrator, in exonerating the griever from the allegation of sexual harassment, stated that the management had failed to investigate properly the complaint made by a student; the investigator had had no training or experience in such matters and the complainant had made no written statement and had never attended a meeting on the matter. The griever had been given no information about the alleged incident or the identity of the complainant and the investigator had only very briefly interviewed the complainant and briefly questioned the griever. In *Hughes v City of Etobicoke*,[53] an Ontario court awarded 180,000 Canadian dollars to the alleged harasser in damages for wrongful dismissal — even where the employer had accepted the truthfulness of the allegations of sexual harassment — because a thorough and proper investigation had not been held. Indeed, the court stated that it had serious doubts as to the credibility of at least one of the complainants whom it believed to feel animosity towards the alleged harasser. In *MacLean v Canada (Treasury Board)* [54] the alleged harasser had not been provided with a written copy of the specific allegations made against him and in fact had only been able to obtain a copy by using the access to information process. The adjudicator therefore found in his favour, on the grounds of the basic principle of justice that one has the right to be informed of the specific charges made against one.

Europe

One of the trends in French judicial decisions has already been referred to in relation to the strict examination of the facts and their characterization as unwanted harassment by the labour court. A similar decision was taken in 1991 in *Manpower France c. Defadat*,[55] where a lower court stated that it was difficult to determine the threshold beyond which jokes and bad-taste rowdiness become sexual harassment. The Court of Appeal approach appears to have been confirmed two years later in the EuroDisney case [56] where it upheld the company's decision to dismiss a homosexual harasser because of his sexual innuendos and comments which were contrary to decency. Research has been unable to identify any cases as yet brought under the new penal provisions introduced in 1992.

The tendency in compensation cases in France has been for payment of damages, sometimes aggravated and punitive, with interest rather than reinstatement, for example in the cases of *Société bourguignonne de supermarchés c. Pascal* and *SA Rockwell International c. Loiseau*.[57] The latter was an interesting case in that heavy damages were awarded against an employer not for failing to sanction the harasser and to improve the situation whereby an abuse of power had occurred, but because the employer had moved to dismiss the harasser without providing him with sufficient reasons to allow him to prepare a defence. In 1990 a case also before the Court of Appeal of Nancy — *Risse c. Chardin* [58] — held that the complacency of the victim (which could be interpreted as being due to a number of factors including fear of making a fuss by complaining of the harassment) should not be counted when assessing evidence that the behaviour complained of amounted to abuse of authority in the terms of prohibited sexual harassment.

No key cases have been identified in Ireland, but it is interesting to note that the labour courts have been noticeably progressive in their decisions. For example, in the case "A company and a worker" (names supplied to the court) [59] it was held that a sexual relationship between consenting adults does not imply that the consent is unlimited as regards either the time-scale or acts which may take place between the parties subsequently. The woman therefore won her claim under section 3(4) of the Irish Employment Equality Act, 1977. However, when deciding the sum of its compensation award, the Labour Court took into account her "imprudence" in leaving herself at risk by not seeking outside help before bringing the case to court.

A spate of sexual harassment cases in Spain in the 1990s present two marked characteristics: the labour courts have consistently found in the victim's favour on the facts, using both the provisions of the Workers' Statute, 1980 (ss. 4(2)(e), 54 and 55), and the Act on Labour Law Procedure, 1995 (ss. 180 and 181); and the appeal courts have preferred to overturn these findings or lessen the compensation granted. For example, Barcelona Labour Court No. 21, in a 1991 judgement, used sections 4(2)(e) and 50 of the Workers' Statute, 1980, as the basis for finding in favour of a woman subjected to sexual harassment in the workplace, in a factual situation where the manager of the enterprise was regularly spying on the women employees through peepholes hidden in the wall between the men's and women's toilets. [60] In two separate cases in 1995 (both heard by female judges), the Madrid labour courts declared null and void the dismissals of female employees where the employer companies involved had not proved that dismissal was for a reason other than that claimed by the women, namely sexual harassment at the hands of supervisors. In both cases immediate reinstatement, with full repayment of salaries and allowances from the date of the unjustified dismissals, was ordered. [61] A case [62] before a Cádiz Labour Court rejected the claim of a dismissed harasser — who protested that the reasons for his dismissal had not been clear in the dismissal notice — since he obviously knew that his behaviour amounted to sexual harassment of his female subordinates. As mentioned above, however, several commentators and the ruling in at least one case equate sexual harassment with a violation by the employer of safety and health obligations. The decision of the Superior Court of Justice of Castille [63] reaffirmed that the incapacity suffered by a female worker because of sexual aggression by a co-worker in the workplace had to be seen as temporary incapacity to work arising from a work accident, and not as a common sickness for which incapacity benefits could be claimed under the Workers' Statute.

As regards striking recent decisions by appeal courts on sanctions and remedies, that of 23 August 1994 is perhaps the one most criticized by commentators.[64] The Galicia Appeal Court decided — even in a case where the initial finding of sexual harassment was reaffirmed — to reduce from 1,500,000 to 500,000 pesetas the amount of compensation awarded to the female victim of verbal sexual baiting, on the ground that the burden of proof was not on the individual worker, but was rather the responsibility of the undertaking. In that case the female worker had claimed compensation from one of her superiors and from the enterprise on the ground of the sexual harassment she had suffered with resulting temporary incapacity to work through depression. The labour court had sentenced the two defendants to the above-mentioned heavy damages for violation of the victim's fundamental rights, but she appealed for a punitive ruling, with the aim of letting society know that the law punishes this type of behaviour. The Galicia Appeal Court rejected her appeal for exemplary punitive damages, arguing that she herself had admitted satisfaction with the initial compensation order, and partly rejected the counter appeal of the undertaking that its employee alone was to blame according to the law of vicarious liability established under the Civil Code (section 1093.4). Three other decisions [65] by the Galicia Appeal Court in 1995: (1) reduced an "absolutely disproportionate" 7 million pesetas award for moral damages to 600,000 pesetas and cancelled the 1 million pesetas physical damages award; (2) reduced a 1 million pesetas award to 150,000 pesetas when a female kitchen helper who had won her claim for sexual harassment appealed for an increase in damages of 10 million pesetas; and (3) overturned a 775,000 pesetas award — even where some of the company manager's behaviour was affirmed as sexual aggression — on the ground that the harassment did not produce the mental upset and disturbance alleged, since the female victim had remained on friendly terms with him. This latter case went to appeal.

In the United Kingdom, many commentators have described the use of the Sex Discrimination Act, 1975, and section 55(2)(c) of the Employment Protection (Consolidation) Act, 1978, in pursuing sexual harassment claims. Suffice it here to recall that *Porcelli v Strathclyde Regional Council* [66] was the first victory in a sexual harassment case. The Scottish Court of Session (Court of Appeal) found in favour of a female laboratory technician, after she had undergone three different hearings. The initial industrial tribunal had concluded that, although there had been a degree of sexual harassment, the male co-workers would have treated a man they disliked just as unpleasantly as they had treated the female complainant. The Employment Appeals Tribunal had decided that the aspects of the men's conduct (jokes, innuendos, remarks and gestures of a sexual nature) which had sexual overtones "could have no relevance in their conduct towards a man" and found that she had suffered job-related detriment by being forced to seek a transfer from the school at which she worked, but also that just experiencing a hostile environment may well be enough to succeed in a sexual harassment case. Finally, on appeal, the Court of Session made it clear that the issue was the nature of the treatment, and not the motive of the harassers. If the behaviour included elements of a sexual character which would not be used against a person of the same sex as the accused (in this case a man), then a case was made out.

As regards advances in judicial interpretations of sexual harassment at work, 1990 appears to have been a breakthrough year. In *Bracebridge Engineering Ltd. v Darby* [67] the Employment Appeals Tribunal dismissed the appeal by the enterprise against an industrial tribunal decision which had found in favour of the woman subjected to offensive behaviour on the grounds of both constructive dismissal and sexual discrimination. It held that a single incident, if sufficiently serious, is enough under the Sex Discrimination Act, 1975, and in the course of employment to constitute a violation. In *James v Eastleigh Borough Council* [68] the House of Lords established another general principle for United Kingdom law relating to sexual harassment, namely that a discriminatory motive or intention is not necessary for finding unlawful discrimination. In short, the argument often put forward by harassers that "I did not mean any harm" could be rebuked by reference to the impact that the behaviour had on the victim. This parallels the approach taken by the United States courts, described above, in using the "impact on the victim" test, rather than the *mens rea* (intent) of the accused harasser. However, the Employment Appeals Tribunal did not move sexual harassment law forward in 1994 in the case of *Steward v Cleveland Guest (Engineering) Ltd.*[69] It upheld an industrial tribunal ruling that pictures of women in sexual contexts did not amount to less favourable treatment of women because of their sex, arguing that sensitive men would also have been offended, thus following the trend set by other Employment Appeals Tribunals not to interfere with an industrial tribunal finding unless it is irrational, offends reason or is certainly wrong.

Cases throwing light on the courts' approach to employer liability predate the period researched for this chapter, but a brief description is merited since it shows the advances made in this area. Section 41(1) of the Sex Discrimination Act, 1975, makes it clear that the employer's mere ignorance of the occurrence of sexual harassment is not sufficient to escape the vicarious liability test (*Aldred v Nacanco*) [70] where the Court of Appeal decided that the employer is responsible for acts actually authorized by him and also for the way the employee performs those acts. However, in *Balgobin and others v London Borough of Tower Hamlets* [71] the Employment Appeals Tribunal allowed a Sex Discrimination Act section 41(3) defence, where an employer could prove that he took such steps as were reasonably practicable to prevent his employee from acting in violation of the Sex Discrimination Act, 1975.

The United Kingdom courts' approach to sanctions and remedies, typified in *Alexander v The Home Office* [72] in which the Court of Appeal set non-pecuniary damages where the employer was shown to have acted in a "high-handed, malicious, insulting or oppressive manner", was followed in two interesting industrial tribunal cases in 1993. In *Pedelty v Rotherham Metropolitan Borough Council* the Industrial Tribunal decided that the female victim's co-workers had made her "feel like a leper" for having brought the sexual harassment claim under examination and equated this with unlawful victimization under section 4 of the Sex Discrimination Act, 1975; in *Knox v Lurgan Community Workshop and McConville*, the Belfast Industrial Tribunal awarded aggravated damages under section 66(4) of the Sex Discrimination Act, 1975, in a sexual harassment case where a 16-year-old girl had been forced to recount in an open tribunal the behaviour she had suffered and was cross-examined on her evidence. [73]

Asia and Pacific

Although the landmark case on sexual harassment in Japan was lodged in 1989, just before the time-period researched for this article, the well-publicized decision by the Fukuoka District Civil Court of 16 April 1992 merits attention here as it appears to be the only major decision in recent years. The female plaintiff, using article 14 of the Japanese Constitution which prohibits discrimination on the basis of sex, and article 13 which guarantees the pursuit of happiness in respect, as well as basic labour rights, was able to prove her claim that her employer (a publishing company) and one of its executives had created a hostile work environment based on sexually offensive behaviour (spreading of slanderous rumours about her in the office). The Court ordered the company and the harasser to pay a total of 1.65 million yen in compensation (the woman had sought 3.6 million yen in damages). The judge appeared to accept that both types of sexual harassment (quid pro quo and hostile environment) had been involved when he ruled that the forced resignation of the plaintiff by tarnishing her reputation as a female worker and aggravating her working conditions in the office had been the result of the harasser's remarks. It should be noted the judge avoided using the words "sexual harassment" (*seku hara*, as it is now known in Japanese). It is also worth noting that the Court blamed not only the supervising editor who circulated the false stories, but also the publishing company concerned whose only corrective action had been to attempt to restore company harmony by pressurizing the victim to resign. Newspaper reports tell of a case lodged in 1991 in Kumamoto District Court by a young woman alleging sexual harassment by her supervisors. [74] According to another press source, in 1995 an Osaka court ordered a company president to pay 1.5 million yen in damages to a 19-year-old female employee whom he had pestered for sexual favours. This is the first time a Japanese woman won a suit for sexual harassment that did not involve touching or defamation.[75]

The Industrial Relations Court of Australia, in *Andrew and Another v Linfox Transport (Aust.) Pty. Ltd.*[76] (judgement delivered on 4 December 1995) held that the dismissal of a delivery driver for an act of sexual harassment was harsh and unjust, and thus contrary to the Industrial Relations Act, 1988, since the employee had not been provided with any education on sexual harassment. Other reasons for this decision were the lengthy unblemished employment record of the driver and the failure of the employer to follow an agreed disputes procedure. This is an example similar to the above-mentioned cases in the United States and Canada, where respect for due process overrides punishment of a harasser. Interestingly, the employee's trade union, in a meeting with the employer over the incident, had threatened industrial action if the harasser was dismissed. Moreover, it emerged in the trial that the employer's staff handbook for employees did state that sexual harassment was unlawful and would not be tolerated, but the Court evidently gave weight to the employer's admission that its sexual harassment policy was new and that the company's education programme on the subject had not yet reached the provincial city where the harasser was based. In a decision delivered on 19 January 1996, the Queensland Anti-Discrimination Tribunal in *Hambleton v Gabriel the Professional Pty Ltd. and Another*[77] found the company vicariously liable for the offensive words and actions of its employee, the harasser of a female job applicant, and found the employee guilty under the Queensland Anti-Discrimination Act, 1991, since the facts (his luring the applicant to an apartment for an interview; his ascertaining that she was anxious to re-enter the workforce) showed that a reasonable person could have anticipated that the other person would be offended, humiliated or intimidated by the conduct. Despite this, the Tribunal refused to include a component for economic loss in its award of damages, referring to the victim's confused presentation of her case on this issue; the award against both the company and the employee amounted to a mere 3,000 Australian dollars for hurt and humiliation. In a judgement delivered on 20 February 1996, *Drew and Others v The Delegate of the Anti-Discrimination Commission and Another*,[78] the Supreme Court of the Northern Territory overturned certain procedural decisions taken by the Anti-Discrimination Commissioner in a sexual harassment complaint lodged by a female employee against her employer, a bookshop company, and two of the company directors. This is another example of higher courts giving precedence to procedural fairness where a piece of legislation (in this case, the Northern Territory Anti-Discrimination Act, 1992) lays down rules concerning the handling of complaints.

In Australia, the annual reports of the Human Rights and Equal Opportunity Commission (HREOC) contain case studies relevant to the mandate of that Commission, including sexual harassment cases. In every year in the period under review, its reports have included a number of such case studies. For example, the 1989-90 annual report describes the case of a woman employed as a secretary who alleged sexual harassment by her supervisor, including an uninvited visit to her home and an occasion of sexual intercourse against her will. The woman was frequently threatened with the loss of her job if she refused the supervisor's advances or told anyone of his behaviour. On returning from vacation and after refusing the continued advances of her supervisor, the woman was denied work. Following her complaint to the employing company's board of administration, the supervisor resigned his position and the woman was provided with employment. However, the woman claimed that on her return to work she suffered victimization by her replacement supervisor, and that this eventually resulted in her dismissal. While the respondent company denied that the woman had been dismissed in an act of victimization, she was paid 17,500 Australian dollars in damages by way of compensation.[79] Likewise, the 1990-91 annual report tells of the complaint of a woman employed by a statutory authority as a word-processing operator: she had been dismissed from her position for poor work performance but alleged that the real reason was her rejection of the sexual advances of the head of her section. The authority carried out an internal investigation and concluded that there was no evidence of sexual harassment, although it did find that the dismissal may have been unfair as the appropriate counselling procedures had not been followed. The authority agreed to pay the complainant the equivalent of four weeks' pay in settlement of the complaint.[80]

Annual reports of state-level human rights and equality offices also regularly summarize sexual harassment complaints. For example, a company sought the assistance of the Human Rights Office in resolving allegations of sexual harassment made by a female employee against a co-worker, a man with whom she was required to a work in a situation where no one else was present. In conciliation the defendant did not acknowledge that the events had occurred, yet at the same time maintained that there would be no cause for concern in the future; the complainant was satisfied with this response, as was the company, and the company made it clear to the alleged harasser employee that if other allegations were made in the future more serious action would be taken.[81] While it is interesting to note that the various jurisdictions are reporting on their conciliation actions, it should also be pointed out that most of these procedures are bound by the Privacy Act, 1988, and cannot provide feedback to the employer about individual complaints unless these go to a hearing. Moreover, the HREOC has stated that even if it could provide feedback, successfully conciliated complaints rarely result in clear admissions of guilt

by respondents; typical outcomes include rather apologies "without prejudice", undertakings to change or reinforce sexual harassment policies,
and financial settlements.[82]

In Australia, recent amendments to the Industrial Relations Act,
1988,[83] notably to section 93 thereof, provide that "in the performance
of its functions, the [Industrial Relations] Commission shall take account
of the principles embodied in the ... Sex Discrimination Act, 1984 ...
relating to discrimination in relation to employment". Likewise, its section 111A provides that "if an award is referred to the Industrial Relations Commission under section 50A of the Sex Discrimination Act, 1984,
the Commission must convene a hearing to review the award. In a review
under this section: (a) the parties to the proceedings in which the award
was made are parties to the proceedings on the review, and are entitled to
notice of the hearing; and (b) the Sex Discrimination Commissioner is a
party to the proceedings." [84] It will be interesting to see whether the Industrial Relations Commission will be called upon to convene hearings
concerning alleged violations of the Sex Discrimination Act, and whether
such procedures will cover sexual harassment claims.

In New Zealand, not only does the anti-discrimination law form a
basis for sexual harassment suits, but also the Employment Contracts
Act, No. 22 of 7 May 1991. The ILO describes the personal grievance
framework for dealing with such complaints contained in section 27(1)(d)
of that statute as "among the most extensive of any legislation reviewed",
with provisions setting out "all relevant matters including the definition,
legal protection afforded, employer liability, remedies, and personal grievance procedures" (1992, p. 56). New Zealand is thus the only country to
have introduced specific detailed procedures under its labour law for
handling claims of sexual harassment. Section 39(1) of the Act makes it
clear that the personal grievance procedure is an alternative, not an additional, means to make a complaint under the Human Rights Commission
Act, No. 49 of 21 November 1977. Some of the cases in the early 1990s
focused on procedural issues concerning the processing of sexual harassment claims under the previous legislation. A recent case also examined an aspect of procedure related to sexual harassment cases, where
confidentiality is often vital to both the alleged victim and the alleged
harasser. In *M. v Independent Newspapers Ltd. and Wellington Newspapers Ltd.*,[85] a male university lecturer accused of harassing a female student (who was later employed as a tutor) denied the allegations but, after
an internal meeting, signed certain undertakings; she later made a formal
complaint which led, after mediation, to the signing of another agreement resolving the matter; the alleged victim then initiated personal grievance proceedings as she was having problems renewing her contract as
tutor but, when the problems were solved, decided not to pursue the
grievance. When approached by a journalist over the matter of the complaint against him, the lecturer applied for and won a permanent injunc-

tion against both newspapers, since the contents of the informal agreement ending the matter were confidential and thus subject to protection in equity. Another recent case under the new legislation throws light on the courts' assessment of what, on the basis of the facts, constitutes sexual harassment. In *Fulton v Chiat Day Mojo Ltd.*,[86] the applicant in the personal grievance procedure who, when hired, had been warned of the off-beat workplace sense of humour, was tricked into repeating obscene puns over the company paging system. The offending staff were spoken to and she received an assurance that the incident would not be repeated. Shortly thereafter her work performance was criticized, to which she responded by referring to the sexual harassment to which she had been subjected, but was told she was overreacting to a joke. When it was suggested that she might want to reconsider continuing with the job, she felt forced to resign and did so the following day. In finding that she had been unjustifiably constructively dismissed, the Employment Court awarded her 3,000 NZ dollars plus costs, but rejected her sexual harassment claim on the grounds that, although the offending words fell within the definition given in the Employment Contracts Act, 1991, the employer had taken all practicable steps to prevent a recurrence of the incident and had warned her that she ought to accept such behaviour if she wanted to fit in.

Africa

For French-speaking Africa, apart from the *Koffi* decision in Côte d'Ivoire already referred to (supra notes 9 and 10), no key cases — indeed no cases at all — concerning sexual harassment have been identified.

In English-speaking Africa, however, a number of cases have been decided in South Africa. The four cases on the subject brought before industrial courts have relied on the unfair labour practice provision of the Labour Relations Act, 1956 (recently replaced by the Labour Relations Act, 1995). The leading case of *J v M Ltd.*,[87] although slightly prior to the time-period covered in this article, merits discussion as it clearly confirmed certain trends in this area of the law. In that case, an Industrial Court found that dismissal of a harasser for sexual harassment in employment was fair because the man in question knew that his behaviour was unacceptable, had received several warnings from his general manager and yet had continued to harass. It defined sexual harassment broadly as covering both the narrower quid pro quo and the hostile environment types. While placing a duty on the employing firm to ensure that its employees are not subjected to such treatment, the Court left to management the task of setting the standard of conduct for employees. Halfkenny (1995) points out that since management is usually male, the standard of conduct thus set might not reflect the interests of female employees. A recent arbitration decision — *Pick'n Pay Stores Ltd. and an individual*[88]

— attempted to give a detailed definition of sexual harassment in employment. However, Campanella (1994) considered this avoided the question (put in argument), that *mens rea* (intent) was an essential element of sexual harassment, and therefore also avoided the question of whether there should be no liability without fault. The arbitrator in that case used both the subjective (victim's viewpoint) and objective (alleged harasser's viewpoint) tests to determine whether the conduct was unwanted. Under both measures, he found that there had been sexual harassment. And yet the arbitration found that dismissal was too harsh a sanction against a harasser, and ordered the company to reinstate him and to issue an internal circular to all employees outlining its future policy on sexual harassment in the workplace. In *Lynne Martin-Hancock v Computer Horizons*,[89] an Industrial Tribunal examined an unfair labour practice claim from a woman, in which the company had dismissed her following a disciplinary inquiry's conclusion that her false accusations of sexual harassment against one of its managers were creating an atmosphere of dissension detrimental to the company's business interests. Concentrating on the procedural and substantive fairness of the internal inquiry leading to the dismissal, the Tribunal held that she had been unfairly dismissed and left the relief to the parties to resolve.

CONCLUDING REMARKS

Despite the dearth of recent, high-level (High Court, Supreme Court, Constitutional Court) decisions in the field of sexual harassment in employment, the cases described do suggest either confirmation of existing trends in various jurisdictions or significant advances in sexual harassment law through the courts and arbitral decisions. It will be interesting to see whether, in ten years' time, such trends have stopped, continued, or advanced in certain major areas, particularly on questions concerning choice of forum, employer liability and sanctions and remedies.

What do the various decisions show about advances in the law concerning sexual harassment in employment? First, that many jurisdictions are adopting the approach taken by the United States courts, namely that sexual harassment should be clearly identified as a form of sexual discrimination and, as such, a barrier to women's integration in the labour market. In that sense, in the United States decisions have exerted a strong influence on those in other jurisdictions. However, national law approaches remain remarkably different: France's recourse to penal sanctions, Spain's use of health and safety legislation, and the ongoing debate in South Africa about the need to prove fault for tort liability show that different legal systems are prepared to experiment with different legal standards in the attempt to establish the unacceptability of certain behaviour.

A second conclusion is that, depending on the type of legal framework used, victims of harassment may obtain widely different results. Employment opportunity laws may be advantageous to complainants because special procedures for judicial action are usually in place and specialized bodies having expertise in discrimination based on sex are better able to judge both the facts presented to them and the law in reaching their findings. In countries where sexual harassment is considered to be a labour law matter, the impact of the law may be confined to instances of quid pro quo harassment, thus imposing on the complainant the requirement to prove some actual — or, in more recent cases, threatened — employment disadvantage based on the behaviour. Some European labour law provisions on constructive or unfair dismissal are used to protect against sexual harassment. The use of criminal law in this context can be problematic because of the strictness of the burden of proof and because in most systems espousing the presumption of innocence this rests squarely on the shoulders of the party making the allegation.[90]

Another aspect of the choice of jurisdiction concerns the composition of the body which will hear the case. Many academics comment on the stereotypes applied to cases of sexual harassment by male judges in court systems throughout the world (Bronstein and Thomas, 1995; Chotalia, 1994-95; Conti, 1995; Earle and Madek, 1993; Flynn, 1996; Job, 1993; MacKinnon, 1979). Evidence supporting some of their criticisms may be found in decisions reached as recently as in the 1980s: in the United States case of *Rabidue v. Osceola Refinery Co.*[91] an apparently sex-biased assessment of the testimony of the parties resulted in a sexist application of the law; the fact that the majority judgement referred to the female victim as "troublesome" has been much criticized by academics and commentators. Likewise, in *Peake v. Automotive Products Ltd.*[92] a judge revealed his own perceptions of the role of the United Kingdom equality legislation in disclaiming a complaint brought by a male applicant alleging discrimination in the employer's practice of allowing female employees to leave work a few minutes early so as to avoid the crush at the end of the shift. In that case, Lord Denning states: "Although the 1975 Act [Sex Discrimination Act, 1975] applies equally to men as to women, ...[i]t is not discrimination for 'mankind to treat womankind' with the courtesy and chivalry which we have been taught to believe is the right conduct in our society." One Swiss study (Ducret and Fehlmann, 1993) notes that female victims of sexual harassment find it difficult, psychologically, to lodge complaints, probably because such harassment is not recognized as a social phenomenon. Similar criticisms have been made of arbitration systems, which are created by the dominant sex. Is arbitration, which depends on male-dominated lists of arbitrators, institutionally and structurally sexist? Some commentators argue that the arbiters' neutrality is often more an assumption than a fact. A second criticism of arbitration in this context is that it aims at the peaceful settlement of labour relations questions, rather than the promotion of equality in employment. However, some of the decisions described here have shown that, where sexual harassment is recognized to be a primary public policy issue, judicial and arbitral decisions will be overturned in favour of supporting the alleged victim's claim. When it comes to the difficult question of the overturning by appeal jurisdictions of industrial tribunal findings — which are sacred in several jurisdictions — most appeal jurisdictions appear willing to put remedying a sexual harassment wrong first.

Another element in the choice of forum concerns straightforward procedural matters. First, as regards lodging a complaint, this must usually be done within a certain time-frame. In the United Kingdom, for example, the legislation imposes a three-month time-limit from the date of the alleged incident or behaviour for cases to be taken to industrial tribunals. As regards the length of proceedings, some forums are better than others. The United Kingdom Equal Opportunities Commission cases take an average of two years before reaching the Employment Appeals Tribunal. In Canada, human rights commissions are notoriously slow in handling all cases before them, not just sexual harassment cases. In the United States, claims under Title VII of the Civil Rights Act, 1964, are subject to a statute of limitations of 180 days for filing before the EEOC; that is why Vance (1993) argues that tort actions might be swifter, as they can be filed directly without the need to exhaust administrative remedies as claimants under Title VII have to do. Another procedural aspect is what constitutes admissible evidence in cases to prove the claim: in France, criminal proceedings accept proof such as tape recordings, which may not easily be admitted in other legal systems. The court's approach to open hearings or closed hearings has already been commented on above. Most equal opportunities statutes set out procedures along the following lines: the person files a written complaint; there is investigation by officers of the specialized body; if the case has merit, the officers conciliate between the parties; if that fails, there is referral to a board of the specialized body or to another body such as the courts. Because of the relative simplicity and swiftness of such procedures equal employment avenues find favour with some writers (for example, Thomas and Taylor, 1994). Where labour laws are used, it is often pointed out that the labour inspection services (which are the first to become involved in hearing complaints or detecting violations of a sexual nature in employment) lack the necessary technical capacity to examine impartially and with expertise sexual harassment cases (see, for example, Serna Calvo, 1994). And again, litigation in all jurisdictions is generally costly and time-consuming and the outcomes uncertain. Some commentators claim that case-law has been slow in advancing protection against sexual harassment at the workplace (Van Tol, 1991). Others consider that the legal impetus provided by United States Supreme Court decisions has obliged a great many companies to devise and implement strategies to deal with sexual harassment (Fenley, 1988). Lindemann and Kadue (1992) argue that perhaps the most worrisome aspect of using legislation as the primary tool for eliminating sexual harassment in employment is that it could stunt the progress of women in their long struggle to gain workplace equality because, in an effort to avoid spurious charges, male employees would minimize any contact with female employees. What is clear is that a balance is needed so that sexual harassment law and jurisprudence do not drive a wedge between the sexes at the workplace, but are used to ensure respect for human dignity and to create working environments that are propitious for business.

The question of liability is the third major tendency and point of argument in much of the sexual harassment jurisprudence examined for this chapter. If employer liability is established, the complainant may have a better chance of recovering monetary damages. The employer may have a stronger incentive to implement an active no-harassment enterprise policy in that case. If, on the other hand, the liability of the individual harasser is established, this may be perceived as a personal victory for the complainant, which would send a powerful message to potential harassers that they would be personally responsible for any damages awarded were a case to be made out against them; they would therefore be more careful in their behaviour. If the liability of both the harasser and the employer can be established, the advantages of both these situations would be combined. Liability varies according to the type of laws involved: it differs under employment opportunity laws, labour laws, criminal laws, and has been the subject of a rich academic literature in the context of tort law. As the cases described show, under human rights and general sex discrimination laws, the employer would be liable for damage to the victim if the law prohibits sexual discrimination "by the employer", and the harasser would be liable if the law prohibits sexual discrimination "by any person". However, in the latter case, the principle of vicarious liability has often meant that the employer is found liable in any case, regardless of whether the harassment was committed by supervisors, co-workers or non-employees. In some countries the laws are scrupulous on this: section 41(1) of the United Kingdom Sex Discrimination Act, 1975, states that prohibited sexual harassment can be at the hands of an employer or any person under his/her control and, as pointed out above, case-law has held that mere ignorance of the fact that certain behaviour was going on in the workplace was not sufficient to escape the vicarious liability test. Under Spanish labour law, the employer has almost always been found responsible, because the legislative provisions in question are drafted in terms of the employer's responsibility to the employees. In tort, persons are responsible for their own actions but vicarious liability has been successfully argued to extend responsibility to the employer as well as to the harasser in such cases. Though in criminal law the harasser alone is liable, there is the added disadvantage that criminal proceedings are usually long, involve cross-examination of all parties involved, and are instigated by a police force which may not be trained in sensitive handling of such cases. As shown in some of the Canadian cases, certain provincial jurisdictions permit the alleged victim either to sue the harasser directly or to complain to one of the human rights commissions which can pursue the action on behalf of the complainant.

Liability can also depend on the type of harassment. The United States cases show that while employer liability is often found in cases of quid pro quo harassment, this is not necessarily so in cases of hostile environment harassment.

In his article on the merits and demerits of dispute resolution processes in Canada, Aggarwal (1994) compares the outcome of sexual harassment cases brought under the statutory route with that reached under arbitration. The advantages in the former are that the commissions of human rights prepare the case, represent the victim, bear the entire costs and give him or her moral support, whereas in arbitration cases where the claim has become a union case, the union provides moral and financial support and bears the legal and other associated costs, and a range of remedies can be included in collective agreements that may not be available through the statutory route. The disadvantages of both human rights investigations and tribunal proceedings are that they can take considerable time and are public, with the possibly embarrassing and offensive exposure to public scrutiny of the complainant's personal life; the disadvantages of arbitration hearings are that they may also be public, and may not always get enthusiastic support from the person's union (especially from male-dominated unions), or in cases where both the alleged harasser and the alleged victim are members of the same union.

Lastly, the question of remedies and sanctions is one of the most striking common threads in these recent cases, throughout the world. At the internal procedures level, the most common form of sanction is disciplinary action by the employer in the form of reprimand, transfer, salary and/or grade reduction, delay in promotion, withdrawal of annual salary increments (particularly in the public service), demotion, suspension or even actual dismissal. In Canada, collective bargaining agreements often authorize an arbitration board to impose a financial penalty against a harasser; [93] agreements in Denmark, Italy, the Netherlands and the United Kingdom are also starting to look at enforcement provisions where they touch on sexual harassment in employment in general terms. Serna Calvo (1994) notes that though a few collective agreements in Spain ban sexual harassment, they often fail to include a definition of such behaviour and do not address the question of enforcement and penalties. In the United States, the use of workers' compensation provisions leaves the employee without a remedy because most victims have negligible or no medical expenses and no loss of wages, particularly in hostile working environment claims, whereas the workers' compensation legislation remedy is linked directly to loss of earnings and medical benefits. Vance (1993) points out another shortcoming to the use of the United States civil rights legislation, since the 1991 amendments which introduced financial awards for victims of job discrimination under Title VII included a cap on those damages of between 50,000 and 300,000 US dollars. Courts, on the other hand, often use the principle of proportionality in assessing damages, as was clear in the 1995 Spanish Appeal Court's decisions. Courts can order reinstatement with or without back pay and benefits, and can also issue injunctions and other writs to enjoin the employer to cease the behaviour complained of, such measures often being paired with an order to carry out certain acts to repair the damage caused. This can take the form of training, and/or adoption and implementation of a specific policy on sexual harassment; or general sensitization of the workforce, as was shown in the US 1991 *Robinson v Jacksonville Shipyards, Inc.* case. In the United Kingdom, section 65(1)(c) of the Sex Discrimination Act, 1975, also envisages the transfer of the harasser. But by far the most common forms of remedy are damages and financial awards which can be either for actual pecuniary loss or as compensation for moral harm.[94] This ability to recover immaterial damages is important, for otherwise the victim may have no financial recovery as no tangible pecuniary job benefit was affected; however, as noted in some of the cases described, proof of tangible loss or detriment in the job is no longer required in most English-speaking jurisdictions. There is an interesting development regarding the award of compensatory moral damages in the United States: on 22 May 1996 the House of Representatives approved the Small Business Job Protection Act, one provision of which would amend the Internal Revenue Code so as to allow taxation of emotional distress damages recovered by victims of sexual harassment or other forms of employment discrimination or wrongful employment conduct. Under the present law, any damages (with the exception of some punitive damages) received on account of personal injury or sickness are not taxed under the Internal Revenue Code.[95] Whether this development was initiated following the huge awards won and reported above in recent United States cases, or whether it is part of a general move towards tighter tax provisions, is for the reader to judge.

Manifestly, it is important to have clear knowledge of what to expect when bringing a sexual harassment complaint, whatever the type of law or forum for complaint involved, and whatever the type of remedy and sanction requested. A recent article reflects just how important those choices can be.[96] In 1996, the United States Peace Corps agreed to pay 250,000 US dollars to settle a sexual harassment lawsuit, in what is described as perhaps the largest payment ever by the United States Government to a man who accused his female boss of making sexual advances.

The settlement was described by the male victim's lawyer as an acknowledgement of the important policy issue that sexual harassment applies to both sexes and as proof that the Government acknowledges that the harm done whether to a man or a woman in a sex power play is totally unacceptable. The Government, however, admitted no wrongdoing by the female supervisor of the Peace Corps managers and the victim agreed to retire and drop the lawsuit.

Will future sexual harassment victims in that jurisdiction prefer to settle out of court, so as to avoid tax on possible compensatory damages, or so as to avoid procedural problems and caps on damages? Will future victims using the French criminal proceedings see harassers imprisoned and hefty pay-outs by guilty employers? Will the Spanish lower courts continue to rule against guilty individuals and employers knowing that their decisions are overturned on appeal even when the factual findings of illegal sexual harassment are confirmed? In future, court and arbitral decisions may well provide answers to these questions.

Notes

[1] See, for example, *The Economist* (London), 13 Apr. 1996; *Financial Times* (London), 13 May 1996; *International Herald Tribune* (Zurich), 19 Apr. 1996; *Le Figaro* (Paris), 9 Aug. 1996.

[2] See, for example, Collier (1995), Collins (1992), Hauck and Pearce (1992), Martell and Sullivan (1994), Monat and Gómez (1986) and Rubenstein (1993).

[3] *Official Journal of the European Communities* (Brussels), Vol. 35, No. L.49, 24 Feb. 1992, annex, pp. 3-5.

[4] The American Psychiatric Association recognized sexual harassment as a "severe stresser" in its *Diagnostic and statistical manual of mental disorders*, 3rd edn., Vol. II, Chicago, 1987.

[5] Some commentators argue that the South African Interim Constitution (Act No. 200 of 1993) already contains a basis for suit in its guarantee of fair labour practices and prohibition of discrimination based on, inter alia, sex, as does the requirement of the Occupational Health and Safety Act (No. 85 of 1993) that employers take such steps as may be reasonably practicable to mitigate or eliminate any hazard or potential hazard to the safety or health of employees (section 8(2)(b)).

[6] *Equal Opportunities Review* (London), No. 51, Sep.-Oct. 1993, pp. 51-55.

[7] *Mlle. X c. Sté. Y, Onzième Chambre social de la Cour d'appel de Versailles*, Paris, 30 June 1993.

[8] Reported in *Mujer/Fempress* (Santiago de Chile), No. 143, Sep. 1993.

[9] Tribunal du travail d'Abidjan, *Kouame Koffi c. La librairie de France*, Arrêt No. 1119, 8 May 1991.

[10] Cour d'appel d'Abidjan, *Kouame Koffi c. La librairie de France*, Arrêt No. 643, 22 May 1992.

[11] Cour d'appel de Liège: *Chambre de droit social*, decision dated 16 Jan. 1991.

[12] International Covenant on Economic, Social and Cultural Rights (which entered into force on 3 January 1976), articles 2.2 and 3; International Covenant on Civil and Political Rights (which entered into force on 23 March 1976), articles 2.1, 3 and 26.

[13] Article 1 of the Convention states: "For the purposes of the present Convention, the term 'discrimination against women' shall mean any distinction, exclusion or restriction made on the basis of sex which has the effect or purpose of impairing or nullifying the recognition, enjoyment or exercise by women, irrespective of their marital status, on a basis of equality of men and women, of human rights and fundamental freedoms in the political, economic, social, cultural, civil or any other field." As at 30 June 1996, the Convention had received 153 ratifications.

[14] See United Nations: *Report of the Committee on the Elimination of Discrimination against Women: Eleventh Session*, General Assembly, Official Records, Forty-seventh Session, Supplement No. 38, A/47/38, New York, 1992, pp. 1-6.

[15] ibid., pp. 3-6.

[16] Examples of the type of references made, usually by the Government representative who introduces the State's report to CEDAW on the day allotted to examination of that report, are as follows: on Canada, see United Nations: *Report of the Committee on the Elimination of Discrimination against Women: Ninth Session*, General Assembly, Official Records, Forty-fifth Session, Supplement No. 38, A/45/38, New York, 1990, para. 413; on Australia, Colombia, Madagascar, New Zealand and the Federal Republic of Yugoslavia (Serbia and Montenegro), see United Nations: *Report of the Committee on the Elimination of Discrimination against Women: Thirteenth Session*, General Assembly, Official Records, Forty-ninth Session, Supplement No. 38, A/49/38, New York, 1994, paras. 371, 465, 213, 612 and 768, respectively.

[17] Resolution 1994/45 of 4 March 1994 entitled "Question of integrating the rights of women into the human rights mechanisms of the United Nations and the elimination of violence against women". See United Nations: *Report of the Commission on Human Rights on its Fiftieth Session, 31 Jan.-11 Mar. 1994*, E/CN.4/1994/132, Official Records of the Economic and Social Council, 1994, Supplement No. 4, E/1994/24, New York, 1994, pp. 140-145.

[18] See United Nations: *Preliminary report of the Special Rapporteur on violence against women to the Commission on Human Rights*, Commission on Human Rights, E/CN.4/1995/42, 22 Nov. 1994, Geneva, 1994, paras. 190-204. The Special Rapporteur included some examples of legislative and judicial action concerning sexual harassment in general, but also specifically in employment, and outlined other strategies, particularly on the part of women's non-governmental organizations, in combating sexual harassment.

[19] United Nations: *Report of the Special Rapporteur on violence against women, its causes and consequences, Ms. Radhika Coomaraswamy, submitted in accordance with Commission on Human Rights resolution 1995/85*, Commission on Human Rights, E/CN.4/1996/53, 5 Feb. 1996, Geneva, 1996, paras. 77-85.

[20] As at 30 June 1996, Convention No. 111 had been ratified by 120 member States. Article 1 gives a broad definition of the term "discrimination" to cover any distinction, exclusion or preference made on the basis of, inter alia, sex, which has the effect of nullifying or impairing equality of opportunity or treatment in employment or occupation.

[21] ILO: *Equality in employment and occupation*, General Survey by the Committee of Experts on the Application of Conventions and Recommendations, International Labour Conference, 75th Session, 1988, Report III (Part 4B), Geneva, 1988, paras. 45 and 46.

[22] ILO: *Equality in employment and occupation*, Special Survey by the Committee of Experts on the Application of Conventions and Recommendations, International Labour Conference, 83rd Session, 1996, Report III (Part 4B), Geneva, 1996, paras. 39 and 40.

[23] As at October 1996 there were ten ratifications of this Convention, but the first reports received by the International Labour Office and examined by the Committee of Experts on the Application of Conventions and Recommendations have not reported any judicial or arbitral decisions giving effect to that Article.

[24] ILO: *Official Bulletin* (Geneva), Vol. LXVIII, Series A, No. 2, 1985, pp. 85-95. Section 6 states: "Sexual harassment at the workplace is detrimental to employees' working conditions and to employment and promotion prospects. Policies for the advancement of equality should therefore include measures to combat and prevent sexual harassment."

[25] ILO: *Conclusions and Recommendations: Tripartite Symposium on Equality of Opportunity and Treatment for Men and Women in Employment in Industrialized Countries: Report*, SEEIC/1990/2, Geneva, 1990, paras. 24 and 25.

[26] ILO: *Official Bulletin* (Geneva), Vol. LXXIV, Series A, No. 2, 1991, pp. 81-83. Examples are: Husbands (1992), ILO (1994), O'Regan and Thompson (1993), Solano and Badilla (1993), Thomas and Taylor (1994), ILO (1996).

[27] ILO: op. cit., supra note 22, para. 307.

[28] See ILO (1992) for the internal policy of the International Monetary Fund (p. 200) and of the World Bank (p. 201); and UNESCO: Draft Recommendation concerning the Status of Higher Education Teaching Personnel in which para. 49 clarifies that dismissal of such staff should only be for just and sufficient cause related to professional conduct, including sexual or other assaults on students, colleagues or other members of the community, sexual blackmail and demanding sexual favours from subordinate employees or colleagues in return for continuing employment.

[29] See United Nations: *Report of the Fourth World Conference on Women (Beijing, 4-15 September 1995)*, A/CONF.177/20, 17 Oct. 1995, New York, 1995, para. 126(a).

[30] While it is clear that in the United States the distinct tort of sexual harassment does not exist, some commentators have stressed that victims can invoke various torts such as negligent hiring, negligent retention, intentional affliction of emotional distress, assault, battery, invasion of privacy (Vance, 1993). In all these cases, however, there is the problem of the employer defence that the harasser acted outside the scope of the employment relationship. Vance (1993) also argues that fraud could cover sexual harassment, in cases where the employer misrepresents the workplace environment to a prospective employee.

[31] Respectively, 13 Fair Employment Practice Case (BNA) 123 D.C.C. of 9 Aug. 1974; 390 F. Supp. 161 (D. Arizona, 1975); and 561 F.2nd 983 (D.C.C. 1977).

[32] 641 F.2nd 942 (D.C.C. 1981).

[33] 477 US 57 (1986).

[34] 9th C-A, 23 Jan. 1991.

[35] 969 F.2nd 1442 (CA-3, 1992).

[36] 114 S.CT.367 (1993).

[37] S.CT. NY, Index No. 15554/93.

[38] 14 F.3rd 733 (2nd Circuit, New York, 1994).

[39] No. 90C 4792 of 6 Feb. 1992; reported in 58 FEP cases 1171.

[40] 760 F. Supp. 1486 (M.D. Fla. 1991).

[41] Supreme Court of California, 1 Sep. 1994.

[42] The Canadian Federal Labour Code, Division XV.1 of Part III, makes it clear that the employee has the right to employment free of sexual harassment, and requires the employer to take action to prevent it.

[43] (1989) 1 SCR 1252.

[44] (Ontario 1980) 1 CHRR D/155.

[45] (1993) R.J.Q. 203.

[46] (1990) 14 L.A.C. (4th) 414 (Ontario).

[47] ibid., at p. 436.

[48] (1991) 14 C.H.R.D/36.

[49] For example, Saskatchewan Association of Human Rights and CUPE Local 3012.

[50] (1992) 41 C.C.E.L.51 (Ontario General Division).

[51] (1993) 1 C.C.E.L.(2d) 15.

[52] (1990) 16 L.A.C. (4th) 1994 (British Columbia).

[53] (1991) 92 C.L.L.C.14 (Ontario General Division).

[54] (7 May 1993) PSSRB file No. 166-2-22580.

[55] RJS, 1992, p. 78, n. 100.

[56] *Chambre sociale de la Cour d'appel de Paris*, 8 Oct. 1993.

[57] Reported, respectively, in *Chambre jurisprudentielle BS le Febvre, 1992/6*, Dijon, 1 Mar. 1990, p. 287; and Nancy, 23 Nov. 1992.

[58] *Chambre sociale de la Cour d'appel de Nancy*, 28 Mar. 1990.

[59] Labour Court 29 June 1990, Case No. EED 901.

[60] Decision 824/91, Barcelona, 1 Oct. 1991 (*María Jesús Guerrero Sotillo* frente a la *Fundición Silio Marín SA*). Workers' Statute, Act No. 8 of 10 Mar. 1980, as amended by Act No. 3 of 3 Mar. 1989. Section 4(2)(e) states: "As a party to an employment relationship a worker shall have the right ... to respect for his privacy and proper consideration for his dignity, including protection against offensive behaviour, verbal or physical, of a sexual nature." Section 50 states under "Termination at the workers' request":

"Subsection 1. The following shall afford valid reasons for a worker to request the termitionstions of his contract:

(a)   substantial alterations to his conditions of employment which adversely *affect his vocational training or personal dignity*;

(b)   failure to pay the agreed wage or repeated delay in paying it;

(c)   any other serious failure on the part of the employer to discharge his contractual obligations, except in cases of *force majeure*.

Subsection 2. In such cases the worker shall be entitled to the compensation specified for unlawful dismissal." (Emphasis added.)

[61] Respectively, Decision 65/95, Madrid, 22 Feb. 1995 (*Concepción Canet Ríos* frente a la *Compañía Nacional de Seguros y Reaseguros SA*), and Decision 291/95, Madrid, 30 May 1995 (*María Victoria Manzano García* frente a la *Empresa Tome SA*).

[62] Decision 74/95, Cádiz, 15 Mar. 1995 (*Fernando Z.G.* frente a la *Empresa H. SA*).

[63] Reported in *La Mancha*, 16 Nov. 1989.

[64] Appeal No. 3141/94, Sala de lo Social del Tribunal Superior de Justicia de Galicia, 23 Aug. 1994. (*Daniela Vázquez Martínez Herizalde* and counter appeal by *Emilio Toledo Rigote* and *Weldingtec SA*.)

[65] Respectively, Appeal No. 4522/94, 20 Jan. 1995 (*Alejandra Alvárez Baldomero*); No. 4354/95, 17 Feb. 1995 (*Ana Isabel Durán Vicente*) and counter appeal (*Moises Piñeiro Fontenla*); and No. 320/95, 9 Feb. 1995 (*Tiendas Galicia SL* and *Salvador Beloso Arenosa*).

[66] [1985] ICR 177 EAT, affirmed in 1986 [ICR 564] Scottish Court of Session.

[67] [1990] IRLR 3.

[68] [1990] IRLR 288.

[69] [1994] IRLR 440.

[70] [1987] IRLR 292.

[71] [1987] IRLR 401.

[72] [1988] IRLR 190.

[73] Respectively, I.T. case No. 62051/93 of 21 Sep. 1993 and I.T. case No. 452/93 of 7 Sep. 1993.

[74] "Accused accept harassment finding", in *The Japan Times* (Tokyo), 2 May 1992; "Kumamoto city assembly woman collapses while fighting sexual harassment suit", in *Asahi Evening News* (Tokyo), 19 June 1992.

[75] "Feminism reaches Japan", in *The Economist* (London), 1 June 1996, p. 90.

[76] Reported in *Australian and New Zealand Equal Opportunity Law and Practice* (North Ryde, Sydney), 92-807, pp. 78,966-78,968.

[77] Reported in *Australian and New Zealand Equal Opportunity Law and Practice* (North Ryde, Sydney), 92-791, pp. 78,834-78,836.

[78] Reported in *Australian and New Zealand Equal Opportunity Law and Practice* (North Ryde, Sydney), 92-823, pp. 79,058-79,072.

[79] Human Rights and Equal Opportunity Commission: *Annual Report, 1989-90.* Canberra, Australian Government Publishing Service, 1990, pp. 84-85.

[80] Human Rights and Equal Opportunity Commission: *Annual Report, 1990-91.* Canberra, Australian Government Publishing Service, 1991, pp. 85-86.

[81] *ACT Human Rights Office Annual Report, 1992-93*, Canberra, ACT Government Printer, 1993, p. 17.

[82] *Sex Discrimination Act, 1984: A review of CES Services and Programs*, Sydney, Human Rights and Equal Opportunity Commission, Apr. 1995, p. 34.

[83] No. 86 of 1988, commencing on 1 Mar. 1989, as amended by Act No. 132 of 1992, commencing 26 Nov. 1992.

[84] Amendments to the principal Act by Act No. 179 of 1992, commencing 13 Jan. 1993.

[85] [1992] 1 ERNZ, dated 20 Dec. 1991.

[86] [1992] 1 ERNZ, dated 2 Apr. 1992.

[87] (1989) 10 I.L.J.755 (IC).

[88] *Independent Mediation Services South Africa (IMSSA) Arbitration Digest* (Johannesburg), Vol. 3, Part 1, Aug.-Nov. 1993, p. 136.

[89] Case No. 11/2/14268 (Oct. 1994).

[90] The European Community attempted to address this question in its proposal for a Council Directive on the "burden of proof in the area of equal pay and equal treatment for women and men" (COM.(88)269, final in *Official Journal of the European Communities* (Brussels), C.176, S.7, Vol. 31, 5 July 1988). In sex discrimination cases in general, this would lighten procedures for alleged victims by requiring the complainant simply to produce a plausible case or prima facie evidence of discrimination, upon which the burden of proof shifts to the defendant involved. France, Germany, Italy and Switzerland have already opted for similar systems as regards burden of proof. The question is discussed in the 1996 *Special Survey* of the ILO Committee of Experts on the Application of Conventions and Recommendations mentioned earlier (paras. 230 and 298). That Committee considers that there is a great advantage in shifting the burden of proof from the complainant once a prima facie case has been made, since the substantial difficulty of proving discriminatory practices (which often occur with no witness and involve one person's word against another's) makes it extremely difficult for victims to win a case, especially when they accuse their superiors in the hierarchy.

[91] 805 F.2nd 611(6th Circuit 1986).

[92] [1978] 1 All ER 106.

[93] For example, Fraser Valley Regional Library and CUPE Local 1698; Municipality of Terrace (BC) and CUPE Local 2012.

[94] In the United Kingdom, section 66(4) of the Sex Discrimination Act, 1975, covers injury to feelings.

[95] "A new tax on the victims of employment discrimination" at National Employment Lawyers' Association (NELA) Internet resource centre website, http://www.nela.org/nela/emotdmgs.html.

[96] "A man wins a harassment suit", in *International Herald Tribune* (Zurich), 2 Aug. 1996.

References

Aggarwal, Arjun P. 1994. "Dispute resolution processes for sexual harassment complaints", in *Canadian Labour and Employment Law Journal* (Scarborough, Ontario), Vol. 3, No. 1 (Dec.), pp. 61-93.

Bronstein, Arturo; Thomas, Constance (eds.). 1995. *European labour courts: International and European labour standards in labour court decisions, and jurisprudence on sex discrimination.* Labour-Management Relations Series, No. 82. Geneva, ILO.

Brown, Steven D.; Codey, H. Carey. 1994. "Employee training may be the key to prevention of sexual harassment", in *Labor Law Journal* (Chicago, IL), Vol. 45, No. 11 (Nov.), pp. 726-727.

Campanella, J. 1994. "Sexual harassment as misconduct: Is there strict liability for the harassers?", in *Industrial Law Journal* (Kenwyn, South Africa), Vol. 15, No. 3, pp. 491-500.

Chotalia, Shirish P. 1994-95. "Sexual harassment laws in Canada: It's all a question of power", in *Journal of Individual Employment Rights* (Amityville, NY), Vol. 3, No. 2, pp. 155-165.

Collier, R. 1995. *Combating sexual harassment in the workplace.* Buckingham, Open University Press.

Collins, Helen. 1992. *The Equal Opportunities Handbook: A guide to law and best practice in Europe.* Oxford, Blackwell.

Conti, Augusto. 1995. "El acoso sexual en el lugar de trabajo", in *Actualidad laboral* (Bogotá), No. 67 (Jan.-Feb.), pp. 15-25.

Ducret, Véronique; Fehlmann, Chloé. 1993. *Harcèlement sexuel: la réalité cachée des femmes au travail.* Bern, Bureau fédéral de l'égalité entre hommes et femmes, OCFIM.

Earle, Beverly H.; Madek, Gerald A. 1993. "An international perspective on sexual harassment law", in *Law and Inequality* (Minneapolis, MN), Vol. 12, No. 1 (Dec.), pp. 43-91.

Escudero, Ricardo. 1993. "El acoso sexual en el trabajo", in *Relaciones laborales* (Madrid), Vol. 9, No. 24 (23 Dec.), pp. 28-39.

Estes, R. Wayne; Futch, Jennifer L. 1994. "Psychological injury not essential for sexual harassment claim", in *Labor Law Journal* (Chicago, IL), Vol. 45, No. 3 (Mar.), pp. 182-186.

Fenley, Tony. 1988. "Dealing with sexual harassment: American experience", in *Equal Opportunity International* (Hull), Vol. 7, No. 3, pp. 3-5.

Flynn, Leo. 1996. "Interpretation and disputed accounts in sexual harassment cases: *Steward v Cleveland Guest (Engineering) Ltd.*", in *Feminist Legal Studies* (Liverpool), Vol. 4, No. 1, pp. 109-122.

Halfkenny, Polly. 1996. "Legal and workplace solutions to sexual harassment in South Africa (Part 2): The South African experience", in *Industrial Law Journal* (Kenwyn, South Africa), Vol. 17, Part 2, pp. 213-231.

——. 1995. "Legal and workplace solutions to sexual harassment in South Africa (Part 1): Lessons from other countries", in *Industrial Law Journal* (Kenwyn, South Africa), Vol. 16, Part 1, pp. 1-14.

Hamilton, Arthur J.; Veglahn, Peter A. 1994. "Sexual harassment and employment-at-will: The intersection of two policies", in *Labor Law Journal* (Chicago, IL), Vol. 45, No. 9 (Sep.), pp. 586-591.

Hauck, V. E.; Pearce, T. G. 1992. "Sexual harassment and arbitration", in *Labor Law Journal* (Chicago, IL), Vol. 43, No. 1 (Jan.), pp. 33-39.

Husbands, Robert. 1992. "Sexual harassment law in employment: An international perspective", in *International Labour Review* (Geneva), Vol. 131, No. 6, pp. 535-559.

ILO. 1996. *As one employer to another ... What's all this about equality? Guidelines for employers on equality at work.* Geneva.

——. 1994. *Tripartite Regional Seminar on Combating Sexual Harassment at Work, Manila, 22-26 November 1993: Proceedings.* Interdepartmental Project on Equality for Women in Employment. Geneva.

——. 1992. *Conditions of Work Digest: Combating sexual harassment at work.* Vol. 11, No. 1. Geneva.

Job, Mary Hannorah. 1993. "Sexual harassment – The reasonable woman standard", in *Labor and Employment Law* (Lansing, MI), Feb., pp. 150-155.

Johnson, Holly. 1994. "Work-related sexual harassment", in *Perspectives on Labour and Income* (Ottawa), Vol. 6, No. 4 (Winter), pp. 9-12.

Lewis, Christine W.; Goodson, Jane R.; Culverhouse, Renee D. 1993-94. "Trends in compensating sexual harassment victims: The threat of double recovery", in *Journal of Individual Employment Rights* (Amityville, NY), Vol. 2, No. 2, pp. 123-132.

Lindemann, Barbara; Kadue, David D. 1992. *Sexual harassment in employment law.* Washington, DC, Bureau of National Affairs.

MacKinnon, Catharine A. 1979. *Sexual harassment of working women.* New Haven, Yale University Press.

Martell, K.; Sullivan, G. 1994. "Sexual harassment: The continuing workplace crisis", in *Labor Law Journal* (Chicago, IL), Vol. 45, No. 4 (Apr.), pp. 195-207.

Mas, Isabelle. 1996. "Les juges ne badinent plus avec le harcèlement sexuel", in *L'Expansion* (Paris), No. 518 (8-21 Feb.), pp. 92-93.

Monat, J. S.; Gómez, A. 1986. "Decisional standards used by arbitrators in sexual harassment cases", in *Labor Law Journal* (Chicago, IL), Vol. 37, No. 10 (Oct.), pp. 712-718.

O'Regan, Catherine; Thompson, Clive. 1993. *Collective bargaining and the promotion of equality: The case of South Africa.* Interdepartmental Project on Equality for Women in Employment, Working Paper No. 8. Geneva, ILO.

Pose, Carlos. 1995. "El acoso sexual en las relaciones laborales", in *Derecho del trabajo* (Buenos Aires), Vol. 55, No. 3 (Mar.), pp. 371-374.

Robinson, Robert K.; Fink, Ross L.; Allen, Billie Morgan. 1994. "Unresolved issues in hostile environment claims of sexual harassment", in *Labor Law Journal* (Chicago, IL), Vol. 45, No. 2 (Feb.), pp. 110-114.

Roszkowski, Christie L.; Wayland, Robert F. 1993. "Arbitration review: Is the public policy against sexual harassment sufficient cause for vacating an arbitration award?", in *Labor Law Journal* (Chicago, IL), Vol. 44, No. 11 (Nov.), pp. 707-716.

Roy-Loustaunau, Claude. 1995. "Le droit du harcèlement sexuel: un puzzle législatif et des choix novateurs", in *Droit social* (Paris), No. 6 (June), pp. 545-550.

——. 1993. "Le harcèlement sexuel 'à la française'", in *Semaine juridique* (Paris), Vol. 1, section 237, No. 15, pp. 187-200.

Rubenstein, Michael. 1994. "Pin-ups and sexual harassment", in *Equal Opportunities Review* (London), No. 57 (Sep.-Oct.), pp. 24-26.

——. 1993. *Discrimination: A guide to the relevant case law on race and sex discrimination and equal pay*. Sixth edition, Industrial Relations Service. London, Eclipse.

Schucher, Karen. 1995. "Achieving a workplace free of sexual harassment: The employer's obligations", in *Canadian Labour and Employment Law Journal* (Scarborough, Ontario), Vol. 3, No. 2, pp. 171-200.

Serna Calvo, María del Mar. 1994. "Acoso sexual en las relaciones laborales", in *Revista de Relasur* (Santiago de Chile), No. 2, pp. 33-48.

Solano, Marta Eugenia; Badilla, Ana Elena. 1993. *El acoso sexual en el empleo: ¿Qué se ha hecho hasta ahora en Costa Rica?* Interdepartmental Project on Equality for Women in Employment, Working Paper No. 9. Geneva, ILO.

Thomas, Constance; Taylor, Rachel. 1994. *Enforcement of equality provisions for women workers*. Interdepartmental Project on Equality for Women in Employment, Working Paper No. 20. Geneva, ILO.

Van Tol, Joan E. 1991. "Eros gone awry: Liability under Title VII for workplace sexual favoritism", in *Industrial Relations Law Journal* (Berkeley, CA), Vol. 13, No. 1, pp. 153-182.

Vance, Ruth C. 1993. "Workers' compensation and sexual harassment in the workplace: A remedy for employees or a shield for employers?", in *Hofstra Labor Law Journal* (Hempstead, NY), Vol. 11, No. 1 (Fall), pp. 141-201.

NOTES ON CONTRIBUTORS

Richard Anker is a senior economist in the International Labour Office. He chairs an Advisory Group on Statistics which is developing recommendations for an ILO strategy on statistics, and he has recently designed a conceptual framework for the measurement of child labour. He has written numerous articles and books on labour, economic, population, gender and statistical issues. The books include: *Gender and jobs*; *Gender equality and occupational segregation in Nordic labour markets*; *Sex inequalities in urban employment in the Third World*; *Women in the labour force*. He holds a Ph.D. in Economics from the University of Michigan.

M. V. Lee Badgett is an assistant professor of economics at the University of Massachusetts at Amherst. She also directs the Institute for Gay and Lesbian Strategic Studies, a national think tank. Her research focuses primarily on race, gender, and sexual orientation in labour markets, and her policy research interests include affirmative action, nondiscrimination laws, and marriage policy in the United States.

Carolyn Shaw Bell is Katharine Coman Professor of Economics Emeritus of Wellesley College. She served as the first chair of the Committee on the Status of Women in the Economics Profession (American Economic Association). She has published in the *American Economic Review*, *Quarterly Journal of Economics*, *Eastern Economic Review*, *Social Science Quarterly*, *Monthly Labor Review*, *Journal of Business*, *Harvard Business Review* and other "learned journals"; she has also written regularly for noneconomists in newspapers and journals, and has appeared in broadcast media and public hearings. She holds a Ph.D. in Economics from the University of London.

Lourdes Benería, an economist, is Professor of City and Regional Planning and Women's Studies and Director of the Gender and Global Change Program at Cornell University. She has also taught at Rutgers University and at several other universities in the United States, Canada, Spain and Latin America. Her work in academia has often been combined with work at United Nations and other international agencies, including the ILO. She is the author or editor of several books and a variety of articles on issues related to gender and development, women's paid and unpaid work, structural adjustment and globalization.

Patrick Bollé is a French-language editor of the *International Labour Review* and also contributes to the ILO's *World of Work* magazine. He formerly worked as an assistant to Members of Parliament in France and as a scientific and labour columnist. He holds diplomas in economics, sociology and demography.

Martin Carnoy, a labour economist, is Professor of Education and of Economics at Stanford University. He has published widely on many aspects of social policy (especially on education, technology, and race), and has consulted for the ILO, the World Bank and many other organizations. Most recently he has written *Sustaining the new economy: Work, family, and community in the information age* (Harvard University Press and Russell Sage). He holds a Ph.D. in Economics from the University of Chicago and a BS from the California Institute of Technology.

Marie-Thérèse Claes is Professor of Business Communication, Intercultural Communication and Intercultural Management at ICHEC Brussels Business School and at the Catholic University of Louvain; and president of the Society for Intercultural Education, Training and Research (SIETAR Europa) and of European Women Management Development (EWMD). She has contributed to research and publications on multicultural, diversity and gender issues. She holds a Ph.D. in Linguistics and a Master's degree in Management.

Sara Elder is an economist with the ILO project, Key Indicators of the Labour Market (KILM). She has served as an economist trainee with the United States Bureau of Labor Statistics, Division of Foreign Labor Statistics, and has held various other research positions within the private sector. She holds a B.Sc. in International Economics and a M.Sc. in Economic History.

Nancy Folbre, Professor of Economics at the University of Massachusetts at Amherst, has explored the interface between feminist theory and political economy in a variety of different ways. In addition to numerous articles published in academic journals, she is the author of *Who pays for the kids?: Gender and the structures of constraint* and *The invisible heart: Economics and family values*. She is an associate editor of the journal *Feminist Economics*.

Johan Hansen is a Ph.D. candidate at the Department of Sociology and Interuniversity Centre for Social Science Theory and Methodology (ICS), Utrecht University. His current research is a comparative study concerning the influence of organizational characteristics on careers of men and women. Other research topics are flexible working time patterns and the gender segregation within organizations.

Ingeborg Heide is a lawyer in the ILO's Department for Government and Labour Law and Administration. Formerly a senior civil servant in the German government involved with the relationship of European standards to national and international law, she was seconded to the European Commission and now to the ILO. She has worked on various aspects of social and labour policies and recently revised and updated the ILO publication, *ABC of women workers' rights and gender equality* (Geneva, 2000).

Jane Hodges Aeberhard is a labour lawyer with the ILO who has worked on international and human rights law issues. Specializing in freedom of association and equality of opportunity and treatment, she recently served in Africa. She has written articles and books for the ILO on affirmative action, HIV/AIDS and employment, and labour courts' treatment of gender equality, inter alia. She holds BA and LL.B. degrees, Australian National University; and is a notary and solicitor.

Lawrence Jeffrey Johnson is responsible for the development of the ILO project, Key Indicators of the Labour Market (KILM), prior to which he was with the ILO Bureau of Statistics and earlier worked at the United States Bureau of Labor Statistics. He holds a BA in Economics and Business Administration and an MA in Labour Economics.

Martha Fetherolf Loutfi is Editor-in-Chief, *International Labour Review*. Former positions include Senior Economist, Employment and Development Department, ILO; Senior Economist, Independent Commission on International Development Issues (Brandt Commission); and Assistant/Associate Professor of Economics, McGill University. She has published books and articles on employment, women, energy, environment, capital flows, and foreign aid. She holds a Ph.D. in Economics, University of California at Berkeley; and a BA (Economics), Wellesley College.

Linda Luckhaus is Senior Lecturer in Law at the University of Warwick, UK. She has written extensively on UK and European social protection systems, particularly in relation to gender and equality issues. Her more recent research is focused on pension systems operating worldwide and the reforms currently taking place in this sphere. She teaches a postgraduate course on pensions at the University of Warwick and is currently co-authoring a book on European law and pensions.

Adriana Mata Greenwood is a member of the ILO's Bureau of Statistics. She has written on labour statistics issues, mainly in the areas of working time and underemployment, and provides technical assistance on the design of labour force surveys and national occupational classifications. She holds a graduate degree in statistics from the University of Costa Rica.

Dominique Méda is a philosopher. She attended the Ecole Normale Supérieure (Paris) and the Ecole Nationale d'Administration (Paris), holds an *agrégation* in philosophy and is a specialist in social policy. She is the author of *Le travail: une valeur en voie de disparition* (Champs-Flammarion, 1998); *Qu'est-ce que la richesse?* (Champs-Flammarion, 2000); and of a number of articles on women and work, the most recent of which, "Les femmes peuvent-elles changer la place du travail dans la vie?", was published in *Droit Social* in May 2000.

Helinä Melkas is an independent researcher and editor working on gender equality and child labour issues, inter alia. She has previously worked for the Unit for International Affairs of the Finnish Ministry of Labour and for the ILO's Labour Market Policies Branch, as well as for other United Nations and international organizations. She has written several articles and papers on labour and development issues. She holds a Licenciate in political science.

Julie A. Nelson is a Visiting Associate Professor of Economics at the University of Massachusetts, Boston. An economist by training, her research interests include exploration of the relation of feminism to economic methodology, as well as the empirical analysis of household demand behaviour. Her research has been published in journals such as *Econometrica*, the *Journal of Political Economy*, and the *Journal of Economic Perspectives*, and she is the author of *Feminism, objectivity, and economics* (Routledge, 1996).

Martha Nussbaum is Ernst Freund Distinguished Service Professor of Law and Ethics at the University of Chicago, where she is appointed in Philosophy, Law, and Gender Studies. Her books include *Sex and social justice* (1999) and *Women and human development: The capabilities approach* (2000). She has been a Research Advisor to the World Institute for Development Economics Research of the United Nations University and a Consultant for the United Nations Development Programme in New Delhi.

Janneke Plantenga is a lecturer at the Institute of Economics of the University of Utrecht. She has written widely on the redistribution of unpaid work, changing working time patterns and European social policy. Together with Geske Dijkstra she edited *Gender and economics: A Euro-*

pean perspective (1997). She is the Netherlands member of the European Union-network of experts on employment and equality between women and men. She has a Ph.D. in Economics from the University of Groningen.

Derek Robinson is lecturing economics at Magdalen College, Oxford, and advising the ILO on wage policy. He was Senior Research Officer at Oxford University Institute of Economics and Statistics and Fellow of Magdalen College. A labour economist, he has worked mainly on wage analysis and wage policies, including two years as Interregional Adviser on wage policies at the ILO. He was Senior Economic Adviser to the Department of Employment and Productivity in the United Kingdom and Deputy Chairman of the Pay Board. He has been a consultant to the ILO, OECD and OAS on numerous occasions, working in many countries.

Amartya Sen is Master of Trinity College, Cambridge, and Lamont University Professor Emeritus of Harvard University. He is a past President of the Econometric Society, the Indian Economic Association, the American Economic Association and the International Economic Association. He is also honorary President of Oxfam. His books include *Choice of techniques*, *Collective choice and social welfare*, *On economic inequality*, *Poverty and famines*, *Employment, technology and development* and *Development as freedom*, among others. He received the Nobel Prize in Economics in 1998.

Linda Wirth is currently responsible for gender in the ILO's Social Dialogue Sector. Previously she has worked in the Office for Women Workers' Questions, the Conditions of Work Branch (on maternity protection, sexual harassment and working time) and in the Sectoral Activities Department (responsible for the financial professional services and the media and entertainment sectors). She is the author of an ILO report, *Breaking through the glass ceiling: Women in management*, of which an updated version will be published in 2001.

ANNOTATED LIST OF CHAPTERS: FRENCH

1. Femmes, genre et travail – vue d'ensemble
    Martha Fetherolf LOUTFI

    Le siècle qui s'achève aura été marqué par l'arrivée massive des femmes sur le marché du travail et par le passage de nombreuses économies de l'ère essentiellement agricole à celle de l'industrie, puis à celle de la prédominance des services. Mais le fait le plus important sans doute est la spectaculaire évolution de la situation des femmes, même si de graves abus subsistent encore. Ce changement a ouvert un vaste débat sur les rôles respectifs des hommes et des femmes, mais aussi une réflexion sur les valeurs humaines essentielles, y compris la place du travail dans la vie. C'est en rapprochant les résultats des travaux des philosophes, des économistes, des sociologues, des juristes et des statisticiens que nous appréhenderons au mieux l'évolution des choses et que nous saurons comment faire de l'égalité une réalité – et ce, dans l'intérêt de tous.

2. Une mise en perspective de la valeur travail
    Dominique MÉDA

    La conception du travail et la place primordiale qu'il a prise dans les sociétés occidentales sont des constructions de l'histoire plus qu'une expression de l'essence de l'homme. Charger le seul travail – serait-ce sous l'appellation ambiguë d'activité – de créer et maintenir le lien social, c'est se soumettre au type de lien social, fondé sur l'échange marchand, que promeut l'économie. C'est également reléguer au second plan la question qui doit d'abord occuper le philosophe comme le citoyen, celle de la bonne société, c'est-à-dire des finalités de la vie en société, de la nature de la richesse sociale et de la répartition des biens premiers (dont le travail) la plus susceptible de promouvoir la cohésion sociale.

3. Travail et droits   Amartya SEN

L'auteur analyse ici quatre aspects de l'action engagée pour assurer un «travail décent» dans le contexte de la mondialisation. Le premier objectif est d'intégrer les divers problèmes dans une évaluation d'ensemble au lieu de se focaliser sur les problèmes de certains groupes de travailleurs. Viser à l'universalité c'est s'atteler à des questions complexes – il existe de réels conflits d'intérêts – mais qu'il est possible de résoudre en adoptant une vision d'ensemble. La deuxième idée directrice est celle de la reconnaissance de droits généraux qui transcendent l'ordre juridique. La troisième caractéristique de l'action engagée consiste à situer le travail dans une large perspective économique, politique et sociale qui englobe les valeurs démocratiques. La quatrième caractéristique de l'approche proposée est l'exigence d'un dépassement des limites des relations «internationales» en adoptant une approche véritablement mondiale.

4. Femmes et égalité: l'approche fondée sur les capacités
                                              Martha NUSSBAUM

M. Nussbaum part de la notion de dignité humaine, qui implique celle d'égalité de valeur, pour se livrer à une application transculturelle de l'approche fondée sur les capacités à la question de l'égalité. Dans sa formulation de l'objectif recherché, cette approche transcende les critères de satisfaction des préférences ou d'allocation des ressources. L'auteur insiste sur ce que les êtres humains sont pleinement capables d'être et de faire, et propose une liste des capacités humaines fonctionnelles susceptibles d'orienter la réflexion politique. Chacun des éléments de cette liste permet de définir la qualité de la vie, la capacité d'exercer sa raison pratique et l'affiliation sociale, en somme ils aident à définir ce qui est véritablement humain.

5. Statistiques du travail: rendre également compte de la situation des femmes et des hommes
                                        Adriana MATA GREENWOOD

La production de statistiques du travail procède inévitablement d'une simplification de la réalité qui met en lumière certains phénomènes et en ignore d'autres, en fonction des priorités et des objectifs fixés, eux-mêmes conditionnés par les méthodes disponibles de collecte des données. L'auteur présente les grandes lignes que devraient suivre les statistiques du travail pour rendre pleinement compte, et dans toute leur diversité, des situations respectives des hommes et des femmes sur le marché du travail. Elle identifie les sujets qui doivent être couverts, le niveau de détail à atteindre pour mettre en évidence les disparités significatives; elle explique également comment le choix des méthodes de mesure et la façon de présenter les données peuvent influer sur le résultat.

6. Le travail non rémunéré: le débat n'est pas clos
Lourdes BENERÍA

Le débat sur la mesure du travail non rémunéré – donc sur la sous-estimation du travail des femmes dans les statistiques sur la main-d'œuvre et les comptes nationaux – ne date pas d'hier. L'auteur présente brièvement les grandes questions théoriques et pratiques débattues au cours des vingt dernières années. Elle fait le point sur les progrès réalisés en matière conceptuelle, théorique et méthodologique, de même qu'elle signale les problèmes nouveaux. Elle répond également à trois formes de critiques récurrentes selon lesquelles: cet effort de mesure n'a guère d'utilité pratique, le travail non rémunéré est qualitativement différent du travail marchand et ne doit pas être traité de la même manière, cette mesure conduit à une impasse théorique.

7. Données relatives à la race, à l'ethnie et au sexe: mises en garde à l'intention de l'usager   Carolyn Shaw BELL

La terminologie couramment utilisée pour indiquer les catégories de données relatives à la race, à l'ethnie et au sexe est, très souvent, plus chargée de sens qu'il n'y paraît. Compte tenu des changements inévitables dans les définitions et les variables socio-démographiques, il est essentiel de lire attentivement les notes de bas de pages rédigées en petits caractères ainsi que les annexes dont s'assortit toute série de données sérieuses. Faute de quoi on risque de tomber dans le piège de données apparemment objectives, mais qui sont en fait confuses voire erronées. Ce n'est qu'en tenant dûment compte des explications fournies à l'appui des données utilisées que les spécialistes des sciences sociales pourront procéder à des analyses pertinentes et que les responsables de l'élaboration des politiques pourront concevoir des programmes susceptibles de réussir.

8. Ségrégation professionnelle hommes-femmes: les théories en présence   Richard ANKER

La ségrégation professionnelle selon le sexe est un phénomène général, source d'inefficacité économique et de rigidités sur le marché du travail, qui provoque un gaspillage de ressources humaines, entrave les évolutions, pénalise les femmes et perpétue les inégalités entre les sexes. L'auteur présente les grandes explications de son existence et de sa permanence: théorie néoclassique du capital humain, théories institutionnelle et de la segmentation du marché du travail, et théories socioculturelles. Il se penche également sur les liens complexes de ce phénomène avec l'écart des rémunérations entre hommes et femmes. Si toutes les explications se révèlent pertinentes, les plus convaincantes sont celles qui se fondent sur les théories socioculturelles car elles mettent en évidence la très large similitude de capacités et d'inclinations individuelles chez les hommes et les femmes.

9. Les rémunérations comparées des hommes et des femmes au niveau des professions   Derek ROBINSON

La condition d'homme ou de femme détermine-t-elle des disparités de rémunération? Pour répondre à cette question, il faut pouvoir mesurer précisément les différences de rémunération en y déterminant la part de facteurs tels que la formation, l'expérience ou la profession. L'auteur propose une analyse originale des différences de rémunération entre les hommes et les femmes dans une série de professions, dans plusieurs pays pour lesquels il disposait des données appropriées, tirées de l'Enquête d'octobre sur les salaires de 1996 réalisée par le BIT. Ces résultats chiffrés portent sur deux grands groupes de professions dans le secteur médical d'une part, ainsi que dans la fonction publique, la banque et les assurances d'autre part. D. Robinson relève en outre certaines tendances observées au niveau national ou international. Il présente également les grands résultats de la recherche sur les disparités de rémunération entre les hommes et les femmes ainsi que les problèmes méthodologiques qui se posent, assortis de conseils sur les pièges à éviter.

10. Ségrégation professionnelle hommes-femmes dans les pays nordiques: une étude empirique
Helinä MELKAS et Richard ANKER

Les pays nordiques sont notoirement connus pour la vigueur de leur engagement politique en faveur de l'égalité entre les sexes. La réalité est plus complexe. A partir de données portant sur 200 professions, collectées entre 1970 et 1990, les auteurs constatent qu'un tiers de l'ensemble des travailleurs de Finlande, de Norvège et de Suède devraient changer de métier pour que soit supprimée toute ségrégation professionnelle entre les hommes et les femmes; cette proportion est nettement plus élevée que dans d'autres pays de l'OCDE.

Travaillant souvent dans des professions à prédominance féminine, ou à temps partiel, les femmes sont sous-représentées aux grades élevés et gagnent moins que les hommes. Cette ségrégation chronique ne va pas seulement à l'encontre de l'égalité entre les sexes mais aussi de l'efficacité de l'ensemble de l'économie.

11. **Le travail à temps partiel: liberté ou piège?   Patrick BOLLÉ**

Le travail à temps partiel peut faciliter l'entrée dans la vie active, ou la sortie de celle-ci; il permet de concilier vie professionnelle et exercice des responsabilités familiales, sociales ou civiques. Mais il peut aussi être un piège, surtout pour les femmes, en les rejetant aux marges du marché du travail. Cette «perspective» présente les problèmes associés au travail à temps partiel: définition, mesure et comparaison internationale; protection des travailleurs; évolution quantitative, notamment en fonction du taux d'activité des femmes; dangers de promouvoir excessivement cette forme d'emploi pour lutter contre le chômage.

12. **Postes de direction: les femmes vont-elles briser le «plafond de verre»?   Linda WIRTH**

Dans bien des pays, les femmes ont fait une énorme percée dans les professions intellectuelles et les fonctions de direction. Les données réunies sur la question montrent l'importance du rôle joué par l'instruction et la formation et la diversification croissante des carrières embrassées par les femmes. Toutefois, les travaux de recherche mettent en évidence la solidité du plafond de verre qui empêche les femmes d'accéder aux plus hautes responsabilités. Dans la plupart des pays, les femmes sont rarement plus de 20 pour cent à occuper des emplois de direction, alors qu'elles constituent plus de 40 pour cent de la population active mondiale. Plus on s'approche du sommet, plus la disparité entre les sexes est criante. Il est proposé d'élaborer des stratégies et des méthodes de gestion des ressources humaines qui permettent aux femmes de construire leurs carrières et de gravir plus rapidement les échelons pour accéder aux postes de haut niveau.

13. **Indicateurs du marché du travail: la situation comparée des hommes et des femmes**
Sara ELDER et Lawrence Jeffrey JOHNSON

Les auteurs font le point sur la situation comparée des hommes et des femmes dans le monde, révélée par les indicateurs clés du marché du travail (ICMT), instruments mis au point par le BIT pour rendre compte des nouvelles tendances de l'emploi. Les critères qui ont présidé à l'élaboration de ces indicateurs ont été l'intérêt conceptuel, la disponibilité des données et la comparabilité entre pays et régions. Compilées à partir de divers recueils statistiques existants, les données montrent que, partout dans le monde, la situation des femmes sur le marché du travail est nettement différente de celle des hommes: elles travaillent dans des secteurs différents, la durée de leur travail – rémunéré – est moindre, leurs taux de scolarisation et d'alphabétisation sont plus bas, elles font moins souvent partie des travailleurs indépendants et sont davantage exposées au risque d'être au chômage, en situation de sous-emploi ou exclues de la population active.

14. Analyse comparative de l'égalité des chances dans l'Union européenne　　Janneke PLANTENGA et Johan HANSEN

Une évaluation significative du degré d'égalité des chances nécessite une méthodologie novatrice. Les auteurs ont, pour ce faire, sélectionné des indicateurs des chances relatives des hommes et des femmes: différences dans l'emploi, les salaires et la répartition du travail non rémunéré; ils ont également retenu des indicateurs de la situation des femmes sur le marché du travail dans l'absolu. Ils ont ensuite procédé à une estimation empirique de ces indicateurs dans le cas de quinze Etats membres de l'Union européenne, obtenant ainsi des résultats extrêmement révélateurs. Pour finir, ils ont identifié les principaux facteurs déterminants de l'égalité des chances – notamment le taux de croissance économique, les régimes fiscaux, les régimes du temps de travail, les services de garde d'enfants et les systèmes de congé parental. Vus sous cet éclairage, les résultats obtenus par les pays considérés sont riches d'enseignements pour l'élaboration de politiques appropriées.

15. Famille et travail flexible: quels risques pour la cohésion sociale?　　Martin CARNOY

Les bouleversements qui se sont produits dans le monde du travail ont des répercussions notables sur la famille et la communauté qui sont, pour la société traditionnelle, les vecteurs de l'intégration et de la transmission des valeurs. L'arrivée massive des femmes sur le marché du travail joue également un rôle important. Pour M. Carnoy, le marché du travail flexible, qui fait de plus en plus appel aux connaissances, exige toujours plus de la famille alors même que celle-ci est soumise à des tensions de plus en plus aiguës. La famille doit être une source de stabilité permanente, assurer le développement des jeunes enfants, les aider plus tard à acquérir les connaissances nécessaires et apporter son soutien à ceux de ses membres qui sont frappés par le chômage ou qui traversent une période de reconversion. Pour sa part, la société se doit d'assurer les services de garde d'enfants et un système d'éducation flexible.

16. Responsabilités familiales et sociales: les normes du comportement masculin et féminin et leurs incidences économiques   M. V. Lee BADGETT et Nancy FOLBRE

Dans les sociétés qui établissent un lien entre la féminité et l'altruisme familial, les femmes sont largement surreprésentées dans les professions sociales et sanitaires. Ce phénomène accentue la ségrégation professionnelle, les inégalités de rémunération et les normes mêmes qui imposent un comportement convenu aux femmes et aux hommes. Les auteurs ont dirigé leur recherche sur les interactions entre les marchés du mariage et du travail, découvrant ainsi une autre raison pour laquelle ces normes résistent à toute évolution. Leur analyse des relations entre le travail dans ce secteur, les normes sociales et leurs incidences économiques les conduit à plaider non seulement pour une redistribution des responsabilités familiales et sociales mais également pour que des mesures de protection soient prises dans ce secteur d'activité, notamment l'imposition de normes strictes de qualité dans la prestation marchande de soins.

17. Congé parental   Patrick BOLLÉ

Le congé parental se développe et s'allonge; il apparaît comme l'une des nouvelles façons de répartir le temps de travail tout au long de la vie professionnelle. Mais, pour qu'il joue son véritable rôle, permettre aux *deux parents* de concilier vie familiale et professionnelle, il doit être bien différencié du congé de maternité et conçu en sorte de ne pas pousser les femmes hors de l'emploi. Cette perspective propose une comparaison internationale des modalités et de l'utilisation du congé parental, considéré ensuite sous divers angles: emploi, démographie, économie, égalité entre les sexes.

18. Travail, sexospécificité et dichotomie entre le social et l'économique   Julie NELSON

Dans les sciences sociales, cadre conceptuel et méthodologie en vigueur sont étroitement dépendants du sujet à l'étude. Les conséquences de ce phénomène ne sont pas minces. Par exemple, se fonder sur l'étude d'individus autonomes écarte de l'analyse toutes sortes de relations – de coopération ou de coercition – qui jouent sur les faits économiques. J. Nelson avance que la dévalorisation des préoccupations «féminines», «douces», appauvrit la pensée économique comme celle d'autres disciplines. Elle souligne les risques que comportent les politiques économiques dictées par une analyse qui évacue le social, et fournit certaines indications sur la méthode que devraient suivre les économistes pour que leur discipline s'enrichisse en prenant mieux en compte la participation des femmes, par exemple dans leur contribution à l'économie des ménages.

19. Femmes, hommes et styles de direction
Marie-Thérèse CLAES

L'auteur commence par une mise en ordre terminologique relative à certains couples de concepts tels que le sexe et le genre, le masculin et le féminin, et autres attributs d'ordre biologique et social. Ce faisant, elle montre que les stéréotypes ne se rangent pas aussi clairement que l'on pourrait le croire de part et d'autre d'une ligne de démarcation, que les faiblesses d'hier peuvent se révéler être des compétences précieuses, que ce que l'on tenait pour un point fort relève du manque de souplesse et de l'étroitesse de vue. La culture de l'entreprise commence à apprécier et à intégrer les différences entre les hommes et les femmes, et donc à reconnaître le grand intérêt de l'association des caractéristiques dites féminines et masculines au rang des compétences que la compétition acharnée sur le marché mondial exige dans les fonctions de direction.

20. Egalité de traitement, protection sociale et garantie de ressources pour les femmes
Linda LUCKHAUS

La dépendance financière des femmes et la place disproportionnée qu'elles occupent dans l'emploi non rémunéré entachent les systèmes de protection sociale qui comportent des dispositions discriminatoires à leur égard. Ces systèmes sont moins favorables aux femmes qu'aux hommes en matière de sécurité du revenu. Bien que la Cour européenne de Justice soit attachée au principe de l'égalité de traitement, sa jurisprudence révèle des résultats mitigés. En dépit des mesures prises en vue d'instaurer l'égalité juridique, les systèmes de protection sociale continuent de répondre à des critères fondés sur le sexe et les femmes demeurent plus vulnérables que les hommes dans le domaine de l'emploi. Les pratiques discriminatoires sont identifiées en même temps que sont évoquées plusieurs définitions de l'égalité. Des solutions sont envisagées en vue d'améliorer la situation, en particulier les prestations individualisées et les crédits pour responsabilités familiales et sociales.

21. L'action positive dans l'emploi: la jurisprudence récente face
    à une notion complexe   Jane HODGES AEBERHARD

    Dès qu'elle est apparue, l'action positive contre la discrimination
    fondée sur la race ou le sexe a vu sa légitimité contestée à cause de
    ses effets supposés inéquitables, pervers ou stigmatisants, de même
    qu'a été contestée la démonstration de son efficacité. L'auteur fait le
    point des grandes décisions de justice prises à la fin des années qua-
    tre-vingt-dix aux Etats-Unis, en Afrique du Sud et par la Cour de
    justice des Communautés européennes, constatant que, face à des
    situations de faits similaires, les tribunaux sont arrivés à des conclu-
    sions différentes. Elle propose des explications de ce phénomène et
    considère que les tribunaux parviendraient à des décisions plus jus-
    tes et plus réalistes si les juridictions de première instance faisaient
    preuve de plus de rigueur et si de nouvelles normes internationales
    étaient édictées.

22. La lutte contre la discrimination selon le sexe au niveau su-
    pranational: l'égalité de rémunération et de traitement dans
    l'Union européenne   Ingeborg HEIDE

    Le droit européen a contribué dans une très large mesure à la
    promotion de l'égalité entre les hommes et les femmes dans tous les
    pays de l'Union. Son caractère supranational unique a conduit tous
    les Etats membres à revoir leur législation nationale. Après avoir pro-
    cédé à un exposé approfondi de l'évolution historique des institu-
    tions et de la législation européenne, Ingeborg Heide montre com-
    ment, par les principes souvent novateurs qu'ils ont établis, les
    arrêts de la Cour européenne de Justice ont fait avancer la question.
    L'importance et l'ampleur de la jurisprudence sont illustrées par un
    vaste choix de décisions allant à l'encontre de toute discrimination
    dans des domaines aussi divers que la rémunération, les pensions, le
    travail à temps partiel, la grossesse et la maternité, le travail de nuit
    et le droit de postuler à certains emplois particuliers.

23. Le harcèlement sexuel sur les lieux de travail: jurisprudence
    récente   Jane HODGES AEBERHARD

    L'auteur dresse le bilan de l'entrée en vigueur des lois sur le harcè-
    lement sexuel au travail. A cet effet, elle se livre à un examen de la
    jurisprudence intervenue depuis 1990 en Amérique du Nord, en
    Europe, en Afrique et dans la région Asie-Pacifique. Après avoir fait
    le point sur l'état du droit national et international, elle passe en
    revue un certain nombre d'affaires déterminantes jugées par les tri-
    bunaux en vertu du droit du travail, des lois contre la discrimination,

des textes relatifs à l'égalité des chances, aux droits de l'homme ou à la santé et à la sécurité des travailleurs ainsi que du droit civil ou pénal. Elle relève les tendances qui s'amorcent: définition du harcè-lement sexuel comme une discrimination dans l'emploi; importance du cadre juridique de référence ainsi que de la composition de l'ins-tance saisie; responsabilités respectives de la personne fautive et de l'employeur; niveau des réparations et sanctions.

ANNOTATED LIST OF CHAPTERS: SPANISH

1. Mujeres, género y trabajo — Panorama general
    Martha Fetherolf LOUTFI

    Son numerosísimas las mujeres que se han incorporado al tra-
    bajo remunerado desde 1900. Durante este siglo, muchos países han
    pasado de una economía agrícola a otra de signo industrial y, de
    ésta, a la dominada por los servicios; pero lo más notable es que la
    condición de la mujer ha dado un vuelco, aunque siga sufriendo
    abusos manifiestos. Ello ha propulsado un vasto debate sobre las
    funciones que incumben al hombre y a la mujer, y una reflexión
    profunda sobre los valores humanos esenciales, entre ellos el de la
    misión del trabajo en la vida. Esta recopilación de análisis elabora-
    dos por filósofos, economistas, sociólogos, juristas y estadísticos
    tiene el propósito de esclarecer el proceso en marcha y los pasos
    necesarios para llevar a la práctica la igualdad, que beneficiará a
    todos.

2. El valor trabajo visto en perspectiva   Dominique MÉDA

    La concepción actual del trabajo y el lugar primordial que ocu-
    pa en las sociedades occidentales no son consustanciales a la huma-
    nidad, sino que se han construido a lo largo de los siglos. Pretender
    que el trabajo – aunque se le llame vagamente «actividad» – es la
    única vía para establecer y mantener los lazos sociales equivale a
    someterse al vínculo social de tipo mercantil promovido por la eco-
    nomía. Significa también relegar los asuntos esenciales que deben
    plantearse tanto el filósofo como el ciudadano: ¿Cuál es la mejor
    sociedad? ¿Cuáles deben ser sus fines? ¿En qué consiste la riqueza
    de un país? ¿Cómo han de repartirse los bienes principales (incluido
    el trabajo) para consolidar la cohesión social?

3. Trabajo y derechos   Amartya SEN

En este artículo se examinan las cuatro características del concepto de «trabajo decente» que son esenciales para la consecución de este objetivo de la OIT en el marco de la mundialización. En primer lugar, se parte de un planteamiento integral, que no se limita a una o varias categorías de trabajadores; aun cuando choca contra ciertos conflictos de intereses muy palpables, el propio enfoque integral hace posible vencer los escollos en aras de la universalidad. La segunda característica es el pensamiento basado en los derechos: los derechos fundamentales son válidos de por sí, es decir, antes incluso de que logren reconocimiento jurídico. La tercera consiste en situar al trabajo en un contexto económico, político y social general que promocione los valores democráticos. La cuarta y última estriba en sustituir la perspectiva internacional por un planteamiento de carácter mundial, universal.

4. Mujeres e igualdad según la tesis de las capacidades
Martha NUSSBAUM

El concepto de dignidad humana, que engloba la idea de igualdad de valía del hombre y la mujer, es el punto de partida de la tesis de las capacidades. Se trata de un planteamiento intercultural que está destinado a promover la igualdad entre los seres humanos y que trasciende los criterios clásicos basados en la satisfacción de las necesidades y en la asignación de los recursos. El objetivo es que las personas sean capaces de ejercer las funciones humanas y estén debidamente habilitadas para ello. La autora traza una lista de las capacidades humanas esenciales que influyen en la calidad de vida, entre ellas, dos que condicionan al resto porque sirven para distinguir el comportamiento verdaderamente humano: la razón práctica y la capacidad de entablar relaciones fructíferas con los demás. El propósito de esta lista de capacidades es que sirva de orientación para diseñar los planes políticos en pos de la igualdad.

5. Incorporación de las cuestiones de género a las estadísticas laborales   Adriana MATA GREENWOOD

En el proceso de recopilación de estadísticas se produce inevitablemente una simplificación de la realidad, pues se destacan algunos temas y se pasan por alto otros según los objetivos y prioridades que se hayan fijado y los métodos de recogida de datos que se apliquen. La autora presenta las innovaciones más urgentes que conviene hacer para que las estadísticas del trabajo reflejen con exactitud todas las diversas situaciones que viven los hombres y las mujeres en el mundo laboral. Enumera los temas que deben ser cubiertos y el grado de detalle necesario para que las estadísticas revelen las diferencias por sexo. Explica también que el método de medición y la manera de presentar los datos recogidos pueden modificar el resultado final.

6. El debate inconcluso sobre el trabajo no remunerado
Lourdes BENERÍA

Hace ya muchos años que se prolonga el debate sobre si debe contabilizarse el trabajo no remunerado y sobre el problema subyacente de la infravaloración del trabajo femenino en las estadísticas laborales y en las cuentas nacionales. He aquí un resumen de las principales cuestiones teóricas y prácticas que se plantean y de las novedades acaecidas durante los últimos años. La articulista rebate las tres críticas principales aducidas por quienes se oponen a la contabilización del trabajo productivo gratuito: que la medición no tiene resultados prácticos; que es muy diferente del trabajo dentro del mercado económico, por lo cual no debe tratarse de la misma manera, y que es un esfuerzo desencaminado desde el punto de vista teórico.

7. Deficiencias de las estadísticas sobre raza, origen étnico y sexo
Carolyn Shaw BELL

Muchos vocablos comunes referentes a las categorías de recolección de datos estadísticos, tales como la raza, el origen étnico y el sexo, encierran significados y connotaciones ambiguos; además, cambian con el tiempo las definiciones y las variables sociales y demográficas. Por todo ello, es indispensable estudiar con sumo cuidado la letra pequeña, las notas y los anexos de las series de datos, aunque éstos sean exactos. De no hacerse así, cifras que parecen objetivas se convierten en ambiguas o engañosas. Los especialistas en ciencias sociales y los gobernantes han de tratar los datos con cautela si quieren hacer estudios solventes y trazar planes políticos acertados.

8. La segregación profesional entre hombres y mujeres. Repaso de las teorías
Richard ANKER

La segregación profesional entre los sexos, que persiste por doquier, produce una notable rigidez en el mercado de trabajo y muchas secuelas: ineficiencia económica, desperdicio de recursos humanos e inmovilismo, amén de una desigualdad permanente y otros perjuicios para la mujer. El autor pasa revista a las principales teorías al respecto: la neoclásica del capital humano, la de la división del mercado de trabajo y la teoría feminista. También estudia en ese contexto las desigualdades salariales entre hombres y mujeres. Aunque las tres teorías mencionadas aportan explicaciones válidas, considera que la más completa es la tercera, pues la condición socioeconómica femenina es una causa decisiva de la segregación profesional en un mundo en que muchas mujeres tienen calificaciones y preferencias semejantes a las de muchos hombres.

9. Diferencias de remuneración entre los sexos según la profesión
Derek ROBINSON

¿La desigualdad entre los sexos ocasiona diferencias de remuneración? Para responder a esta pregunta es preciso medir exactamente el efecto sobre las remuneraciones de factores tales como la formación, la experiencia y la profesión. El autor presenta un análisis original del desnivel de ganancias que existe entre hombres y mujeres, con los datos sobre distintos países publicados en la Encuesta de Octubre de la OIT (edición de 1996). Explora concretamente varias profesiones de la sanidad y de la administración pública, la banca y los seguros. Su investigación revela algunas tendencias nacionales, así como diferencias entre los países considerados. Expone, además, determinados problemas de método, con consejos para evitar errores en los estudios al respecto.

10. La segregación profesional entre hombres y mujeres. Investigación empírica sobre los países nórdicos
Helinä MELKAS y Richard ANKER

Los países nórdicos tienen fama de ser firmes defensores de la igualdad entre los sexos, pero la realidad no es tan perfecta. En el artículo se analizan datos pormenorizados sobre 187 ocupaciones no agrícolas, según los cuales una tercera parte de los trabajadores de Finlandia, Noruega y Suecia tendrían que cambiar de profesión para acabar con el problema de la segregación. Las cifras son mucho más altas que en otros países de la OCDE. La mayoría de las mujeres trabajan en ocupaciones de predominio femenino o a tiempo parcial; ganan menos que los hombres y no suelen llegar a los puestos directivos. Es una segregación crónica contraria a la igualdad entre los sexos y al buen funcionamiento del conjunto de la economía.

11. El trabajo a tiempo parcial, ¿libertad o trampa?

Patrick BOLLÉ

El trabajo a tiempo parcial puede servir tanto para incorporarse a la vida profesional como para preparar el retiro. Ayuda a compaginar el trabajo con la familia y con las actividades cívicas y recreativas, pero puede ser una trampa, sobre todo si relega a las mujeres a los peores puestos del mercado laboral. La exposición versa sobre lo esencial de este régimen de trabajo: la definición; los problemas de medición y de comparación internacional; la protección a los trabajadores; la evolución de las cifras (efecto en el índice de actividad femenino, etc.); y el peligro de fomentar excesivamente el trabajo a tiempo parcial para luchar contra el desempleo.

12. Las mujeres en puestos de dirección: ¿Más cerca de romper las barreras invisibles?

Linda WIRTH

La mujer ha logrado un progreso enorme en muchos países al conseguir ocupar una proporción cada vez mayor de los puestos profesionales y directivos. Dos factores decisivos han sido la extensión de la enseñanza y la incorporación de la mujer a nuevas profesiones. Ahora bien, los estudios empíricos demuestran que la barrera invisible es muy difícil de cruzar: el número de mujeres que desempeñan puestos directivos rara vez excede del 20 por ciento en la mayoría de los países, a pesar de que constituyen más del 40 por ciento de la fuerza de trabajo mundial. Y en los puestos más altos es donde la desigualdad con los hombres es más notoria. Para ayudar a las mujeres a conquistar los puestos superiores, pueden trazarse estrategias de carrera y promoverse medidas de sostén en el ámbito de la empresa.

13. Los indicadores laborales por sexo revelan la situación de la mujer

Sara ELDER y Lawrence Jeffrey JOHNSON

Este artículo expone las diferencias de género que ponen de manifiesto los indicadores del mercado laboral ideados y recopilados por la OIT con el fin de estudiar la evolución del empleo a escala mundial. Estos indicadores fueron seleccionados conforme a los criterios de pertinencia conceptual y de disponibilidad de datos comparables sobre países y regiones en las diversas compilaciones internacionales existentes. Las cifras obtenidas indican que, en todo el mundo, la experiencia profesional de las mujeres difiere sustancialmente de la de los hombres: trabajan en sectores diferentes y durante menos horas; obtienen menos ingresos y tienen índices más bajos de escolarización y alfabetización; además, registran porcentajes inferiores de trabajo independiente y más elevados de desempleo, subempleo e inactividad laboral.

14. Balance de la igualdad de oportunidades en la Unión Europea
Janneke PLANTENGA y Johan HANSEN

Para valorar acertadamente la implantación real de la igualdad de oportunidades es necesaria una metodología innovadora. Los autores presentan una serie de indicadores destinados a medir la disparidad de oportunidades que tienen los hombres y las mujeres (la desigualdad de género) en materia de empleo, retribuciones, repartición del trabajo no remunerado y situación en el mercado laboral. Los datos de los quince Estados miembros de la Unión Europea arrojan resultados sumamente esclarecedores. Para cerrar el círculo se exponen los principales determinantes de la igualdad de oportunidades: la tasa de crecimiento económico, los regímenes fiscal y de tiempo de trabajo, los servicios de guardería y las disposiciones sobre permisos parentales. Las cifras país por país aportan lecciones interesantísimas para la labor programática y normativa.

15. La familia, el trabajo flexible y los riesgos que corre la cohesión social
Martin CARNOY

Los cambios radicales que atraviesa el trabajo tienen grandes repercusiones en la familia y en la comunidad, dos instituciones que desempeñan tradicionalmente el cometido doble de transmisión de valores e integración social. Otro factor decisivo es la incorporación de numerosísimas mujeres al mercado de trabajo. A juicio del autor, el trabajo – cada día más basado en el conocimiento y más flexible – está redoblando las exigencias que impone a la familia, ya de por sí sometida a apremios cada vez mayores: debe permanecer estable, atender a la crianza de los hijos, ayudarles a adquirir el saber necesario y amparar a todos sus componentes en los períodos de desempleo y de readiestramiento profesional. Es de esperar que la sociedad respalde a la familia brindándole guarderías suficientes y una instrucción flexible.

16. ¿Quién cuida de los demás? Normas sociosexuales y consecuencias económicas
M. V. Lee BADGETT y Nancy FOLBRE

En las sociedades donde se considera que la condición femenina lleva aparejado el altruismo para con la familia, suele haber un número desproporcionado de mujeres que se dedican al trabajo asistencial. De este modo se refuerzan la segregación profesional, la desigualdad salarial entre los sexos y las propias normas de conducta tradicionales de hombres y de mujeres. Las autoras estudian la influencia recíproca entre el mercado de trabajo y el mercado matrimonial, así como los nexos que unen trabajo asistencial, normas sociales y ganancias económicas, en los cuales anidan las razones de que las normas sociosexuales sean tan difíciles de cambiar. Además de redistribuir las tareas familiares del cuidado de los demás, propugnan que se adopten medidas concretas para proteger el trabajo asistencial remunerado, entre ellas la fijación de normas estrictas de calidad.

17. La licencia para el cuidado de los hijos   Patrick BOLLÉ

El llamado permiso parental se propaga y se alarga. Es acaso una manera innovadora de redistribuir el tiempo dedicado al trabajo y a las demás actividades humanas a lo largo de la vida. Para que cumpla su cometido primordial, es decir, permitir al padre y a la madre conciliar su trabajo y su vida familiar, debe distinguirse bien de la licencia por maternidad y ha de proyectarse con precaución, para que no induzca a las mujeres a abandonar indefinidamente el trabajo. Se presenta una comparación de las normas de permiso por hijos vigentes en una treintena de países, estudiadas desde varios ángulos: empleo, economía, demografía e igualdad entre los sexos.

18. Trabajo, sexo y división entre lo económico y lo social
Julie A. NELSON

El marco conceptual y la metodología que imperan en las ciencias sociales están estrechamente vinculados a sus objetos de estudio, con efectos no siempre beneficiosos. Por ejemplo, centrar la atención en el individuo autónomo significa pasar por alto toda una gama de relaciones – sea cooperativas, sea coercitivas – que influyen en los resultados económicos. Nelson argumenta que la infravaloración de las ocupaciones «femeninas» o «blandas» ha empobrecido el pensamiento económico y el de otras disciplinas. Pone de relieve los peligros que surgen cuando las políticas económicas se asientan sobre análisis que omiten lo social, y ofrece algunas indicaciones de cómo podría enriquecerse la ciencia económica dando mayor cabida a aportaciones de las mujeres tales como el aprovisionamiento del hogar.

19. Mujeres, hombres y estilos de dirección   Marie-Thérèse CLAES

La autora de este artículo se esfuerza en desenmarañar los significados de nociones encontradas como sexo y género, masculino y femenino, caracteres biológicos y atributos de origen social. Es consciente de que los estereotipos son, a menudo, menos tajantes de lo que parecen; que antiguas flaquezas pueden llegar a ser consideradas aptitudes valiosas y que atributos antes ensalzados pasan a tacharse de inflexibles y unidimensionales. Conforme los directivos empresariales empiezan a apreciar y asimilar las diferencias entre los sexos, comprenden que es ventajoso promover una síntesis idónea de rasgos masculinos y femeninos (o así llamados) dentro de la panoplia de aptitudes administrativas y de mando necesarias para afrontar la aguda competencia que impone el mercado mundial.

20. Igualdad de trato, protección social y seguridad de ingresos de las mujeres   Linda LUCKHAUS

La situación de la mujer, que suele depender económicamente del hombre y realizar una parte desmesurada del trabajo no remunerado, tiene efectos perversos en los sistemas de protección social, pues resultan ser discriminatorios al garantizar menos seguridad de ingresos a la mujer que al hombre. Ahora se proclama el objetivo general de promover la igualdad, pese a lo cual la jurisprudencia del Tribunal de Justicia Europeo demuestra que hay muchas lagunas. La igualdad jurídica no es todavía un contrapeso eficaz frente a las divisiones por sexo que persisten en los sistemas de protección social y a las desventajas que acarrea a muchas mujeres una carrera profesional corta o endeble. La autora expone las definiciones de la igualdad y las prácticas discriminatorias más comunes. Estudia las medidas que pueden allanar el camino hacia la equiparación real, entre ellas la personalización de los derechos y las bonificaciones y subsidios por dedicarse a cuidar de otras personas.

21. La acción positiva en el empleo, un concepto espinoso para los tribunales   Jane HODGES AEBERHARD

Las medidas afirmativas destinadas a luchar contra la discriminación basada en la raza y el sexo han sido polémicas desde el principio: se ha discutido su validez, se les han achacado consecuencias injustas, perversas y estigmatizadoras, y se ha alegado que se apoyaban en razones y pruebas rebatibles. La autora pasa revista a toda una serie de sentencias significativas dictadas por tribunales de los Estados Unidos y Sudáfrica y por el Tribunal de Justicia de las Comunidades Europeas, y comprueba que dictaron fallos divergentes en casos muy semejantes. Tras estudiar los motivos de estas discrepancias, aboga por que las jurisdicciones inferiores examinen con más rigor los casos y por que se fijen nuevas normas internacionales que capaciten a los tribunales para dictar sentencias más justas y realistas.

22. Medidas supranacionales contra la discriminación sexual. Igualdad salarial y de trato en la Unión Europea
Ingeborg HEIDE

La legislación europea ha contribuido sobremanera a fomentar la igualdad entre hombres y mujeres en toda la Unión. Su singular carácter supranacional ha provocado revisiones de la legislación interna de todos los Estados miembros. Tras un resumen esclarecedor de la evolución histórica de las instituciones y las normas jurídicas europeas, Heide expone los progresos conseguidos gracias a las sentencias innovadoras dictadas por el Tribunal de Justicia. La importancia y el alcance de esta jurisprudencia quedan ilustrados en una extensa muestra de fallos contrarios a la discriminación, que abarcan varios terrenos: salarios, pensiones de jubilación, trabajo a tiempo parcial, embarazo y maternidad, trabajo nocturno y acceso a algunas profesiones.

23. Jurisprudencia reciente sobre el acoso sexual en el trabajo
Jane HODGES AEBERHARD

Este artículo pasa revista a la aplicación en el trabajo de la legislación reciente sobre el acoso sexual, examinando los fallos judiciales y arbitrales más significativos dictados desde 1990 en América del Norte y en varios países de Europa, Extremo Oriente y África. Tras exponer a grandes líneas la legislación interna y las normas internacionales pertinentes, su autora analiza el estado de la jurisprudencia. Los tribunales aplican legislaciones muy diversas: la legislación laboral; las leyes contra la discriminación y en favor de la igualdad de oportunidades y los derechos humanos; las normas de seguridad y salud en el trabajo, así como el derecho civil y el penal. De los casos estudiados se desprenden varias tendencias y asuntos de interés, entre ellos la calificación del acoso sexual como discriminación laboral; la importancia del marco jurídico aplicado y de la composición del órgano al que se recurre; la responsabilidad respectiva de la persona culpable y del empleador; la cuantía del resarcimiento y la mayor o menor severidad de las sanciones.

DATE DUE